A WAY OF LOOKING AT THINGS

BY ERIK H. ERIKSON

Childhood and Society (1950, 1963, 1985)

Young Man Luther (1958)

Identity and the Life Cycle (1959, 1980)

Insight and Responsibility (1964)

Identity: Youth and Crisis (1968)

Gandhi's Truth (1969)

Dimensions of a New Identity (1974)

Life History and the Historical Moment (1975)

Toys and Reasons (1977)

The Life Cycle Completed (1982)

Vital Involvement in Old Age (1986) (*with Joan M. Erikson and Helen Q. Kivnick*)

EDITED BY ERIK H. ERIKSON

Adulthood (1978)

A WAY OF LOOKING AT THINGS

SELECTED PAPERS

FROM 1930 to 1980

ERIK H. ERIKSON

EDITED BY STEPHEN SCHLEIN, Ph.D.

W · W · NORTON & COMPANY *New York London*

Copyright © 1987 by Erik H. Erikson
Published simultaneously in Canada by Penguin Books Canada Ltd.,
2801 John Street, Markham, Ontario L3R 1B4.
Printed in the United States of America.
The text of this book is composed in Sabon, with display type set in
Garamond. Composition by PennSet, Inc.
Manufacturing by The Haddon Craftsmen, Inc.
Book design by Margaret Wagner.

First Edition

Library of Congress Cataloging-in-Publication Data

Erikson, Erik H. (Erik Homburger), 1902–
A way of looking at things.

"Bibliography, the complete writings of Erik H.
Erikson (1930–1985)": p.
  1. Psychoanalysis.   2. Imagination in children.
I. Schlein, Stephen P.   II. Title.
BF173.D654   1987   150.19′5   86–8493
ISBN 0-393-02267-6
W. W. Norton & Company, Inc., 500 Fifth Avenue,
New York, N. Y. 10110
W. W. Norton & Company Ltd., 37 Great Russell Street,
London WC1B 3NU

1 2 3 4 5 6 7 8 9 0

Permissions

We are grateful to *The Bulletin of the Anna Freud Centre* (originally entitled *The Bulletin of the Hampstead Clinic*) for permission to include "Dorothy Burlingham's School in Vienna" and "Anna Freud—Reflections"; "Psychoanalysis and the Future of Education" and "Configurations in Play—Clinical Notes" are reprinted by permission of *Psychoanalytic Quarterly*; "The Human Life Cycle" and "Psychosocial Identity" are reprinted by permission of the publisher from the *International Encyclopedia of the Social Sciences*, David L. Sills, editor, Volume 9, pp. 286–92 and Volume 7, pp. 61–65, respectively. Copyright © 1968 by Crowell Collier and Macmillan, Inc.; "Sex Differences in the Play Configurations of American Pre-Adolescents" is reprinted by permission from the *American Journal of Orthopsychiatry*. Copyright 1951 by the American Orthopsychiatric Association, Inc.; "Sex Differences in the Play Configurations of American Pre-Adolescents" is reprinted by permission from the *American Journal of Orthopsychiatry*. Copyright 1951 by the American Orthopsychiatric Association, Inc.; "Words at Delos" and "Thoughts on the City for Human Development" are reprinted by permission from *Ekistics*, 32, 191 (October 1971): 259–60, and *Ekistics*, 35, 209 (April 1973): 216–19, respectively. Copyright Ekistics, Athens, Greece; "Memorandum for the Conference on the Draft" is reprinted by permission of the publisher from *The Draft: Facts and Alternatives*, Sol B. Tax, editor (Chicago: University of Chicago Press, 1968), pp. 280–83; "Confirmation of the Delinquent" is reprinted by permission of *Chicago Review*, © 1957 by *Chicago Review*. All rights reserved. This article first appeared in the Winter 1957 issue of Chicago Review; "Childhood and Tradition in Two American Indian Tribes" is reprinted by permission of the publisher from *The Psychoanalytic Study of the Child*, 1 (New York: International Universities Press, 1945): 319–50; "The Dream Specimen on Psychoanalysis" is reprinted by permission of the publisher from the *Journal of the American Psychoanalytic Association*, 2: 5–56, 1954, International Universities Press; "Words for Paul Tillich" is reprinted by permission of *Harvard Divinity Bulletin*, 30, 2 (January 1966): 13–15; "Peter Blos: Reminiscences" is reprinted by permission of the Jewish Board of Guardians from *Psychosocial Process*, III, 2: 4–7, Fall 1974; "On Protest and Affirmation" is reprinted by permission of *Harvard Medical Alumni Bulletin*; "Plans for the Returning Veteran with Symptoms of Instability" is reprinted by permission of the publishers from *Community Planning for Peacetime Living*, L. Wirth, editor (Stanford, CA: Stanford University Press, 1945), pp. 116–21; "Ruth Benedict: A Memorial" is reprinted by permission of Wenner-Gren Foundation from *Ruth Fulton Benedict: A Memorial*, A. L. Kroeber, editor (New York: Viking Fund, Inc. 1949), pp. 14–17; "Observations on the Yurok: Childhood and World Image" is reprinted by permission of the publisher from the monograph of the same title, University of California Publications in American Archaeology and Ethnology, 35: 257–301, 1943; "Statement to the Committee on Privilege and Tenure of the University of California Concerning the California Loyalty Oath" is reprinted by permission of the William Alanson White Psychiatric Foundation from *Psychiatry: Journal for the Study of Interpersonal Processes*, 14: 243–245, 1951; "The Power of the Newborn" is reprinted Courtesy *Mademoiselle*. Copyright © 1953 by Street & Smith Publications, Inc. Courtesy Mademoiselle. Copyright © 1981 (renewed) by The Condé Nast Publications, Inc.; "Late Adolescence" is published by permission of The World Federation for Mental Health, Inc.; "Problems of Infancy and Early Childhood" is published by permission of the publisher from *Cyclopedia of Medicine* (Philadelphia: Davis & Co., 1940), pp. 714–30; "Environment and Virtues" is reprinted by permission of the publisher from *Arts of the Environment*, G. Kepes, editor (New York: George Braziller, Inc., 1972), pp. 60–77. Copyright George Braziller, Inc.; "A Memorandum on Identity and Negro Youth" is reprinted by permission of the Society for the Psychological Study of Social Issues from *The Journal of Social Issues*, XX, 4:29–42, 1964; "The Ontogeny of Ritualization in Man" is reprinted by permission of the Royal Society of London from *Philosophical Transactions of the Royal Society of London*, 1966; the drawings in the chapter "Configurations in Play—Clinical Notes" are from "Sex Differences in Play Construction of Twelve-Year-Old Children" and are reprinted by permission of the publisher from *Discussions on Child Development*, J. M. Tanner and B. Inhelder, editors (London: Tavistock Publications Ltd).

Dear Steve,

A number of the items selected for this summary volume claims to be written "with Joan Erikson". The fact is that in this whole collection there does not seem to be one bit of good writing that was not shared by her in thought as well as in formulation. Our over-all "Way of Looking at Things", therefore would have been unthinkable without her.

Thank you, Steve.

Erik H Erikson

Contents

List of Illustrations   xv
Acknowledgments   xvii
Editor's Preface   xix

I. PSYCHOANALYSIS AND ENLIGHTENMENT
    Dorothy Burlingham's School in Vienna (1980)
    WITH JOAN M. ERIKSON   3
    Psychoanalysis and the Future of Education (1930)   14
    Children's Picture Books (1931) TRANSLATED BY
    JOACHIM NEUGROSCHEL   31
    The Fate of the Drives in School Compositions (1931)
    TRANSLATED BY INGE SCHNEIER HOFFMAN   39
    Anna Freud—Reflections (1983)   70

II. CONFIGURATIONS IN PLAY AND DREAMS
     Configurations in Play—Clinical Notes (1937)   77
     *Studies in the Interpretation of Play: Clinical Observation of
     Play Disruption in the Young Children (1940)*   139

The Dream Specimen of Psychoanalysis (1954)   237

Sex Differences in the Play Configurations of American Preadolescents (1955)   280

Play and Actuality (1972)   311

III.   WAR MEMORANDA

On Nazi Mentality (1940)   341

A Memorandum Concerning the Interrogation of German Prisoners of War (1943)   346

Comments on Hitler's Speech of September 30, 1942 (1942)   351

Comments on Anti-Nazi Propaganda (1945)   362

A Memorandum to the Joint Committee on Post War Planning (1945)   366

IV.   CROSS-CULTURAL OBSERVATIONS: THE COMMUNAL ENVIRONMENT

Observations on the Yurok: Childhood and World Image (1943)   377

Childhood and Tradition in Two American Indian Tribes (1945)   446

Psychoanalysis and Ongoing History: Problems of Identity, Hatred and Nonviolence (1965)   481

Remarks on the "Wider Identity" (1966)   497

Environment and Virtues (1972)   503

Thoughts on the City for Human Development (1973)   522

Reflections on Activity, Recovery and Growth (1976)   531

V.   THOUGHTS ON THE LIFE CYCLE

Problems of Infancy and Early Childhood (1940)   547

The Power of the Newborn (1953)
WITH JOAN M. ERIKSON   569

The Ontogeny of Ritualization in Man (1966)   575

The Human Life Cycle (1968)   595

VI. REFLECTIONS ON IDENTITY, YOUTH, AND
YOUNG ADULTHOOD

*Plans for the Returning Veteran with Symptoms of
Instability (1945)* 613

*Statement to the Committee on Privilege and Tenure of the
University of California Concerning the California Loyalty
Oath (1951)* 618

The Confirmation of the Delinquent (1957)
WITH KAI T. ERIKSON 621

Late Adolescence (1959) 631

A Memorandum on Identity and Negro Youth (1964) 644

On the Potential of Women (1965) 660

Memorandum for the Conference on the Draft (1968) 670

Psychosocial Identity (1968) 675

*On Student Unrest: Remarks on Receiving the Foneme
Prize (1969)* 685

On Protest and Affirmation (1972) 699

VII. PORTRAIT SKETCHES

Peter Blos: Reminiscences (1974) 709

For Joseph Wheelwright—My Jungian Friend (1982) 713

Ruth Benedict: A Memorial (1949) 716

*For Larry Frank's Anniversary—the Couple Who Came
to Dinner (1965)* WITH JOAN M. ERIKSON 724

Words for Paul Tillich (1966) 726

For Marian C. Putnam (1971) WITH JOAN M. ERIKSON 729

Mary Sarvis—a Few Words of Testimony (1972) 731

Robert P. Knight: By Way of a Memoir (1972) 733

VIII. CONFIGURATIONS OF HUMAN POTENTIAL

Acceptance of the National Book Award for Gandhi's
Truth *(1970)* 741

Words at Delos (1971) 743

Landing on the Moon (1969) 745

Bibliography: *The Complete Writings of Erik H. Erikson (1930–1985)*   749

Index   757

Illustrations

Dorothy Burlingham   2

Kai   6

Jon   7

Mikey   8

Tinky   9

Bob   10

Marie (an older sketch from the Black Forest)   11

A Yurok Fisherman   376

Joseph Wheelwright   714

Ruth Benedict   718

Karla Homburger   719

Maria Martinez   720

Alexander Meiklejohn   721

Acknowledgments

Selecting and organizing these papers would not have been possible without the genuine interest, gentle support, and collaborative effort of Erik Erikson. His warmth, spirited nature, and thoughtfulness provided a consistent and sustaining presence for me that helped this experience hold together. I am grateful to him for affording me the privilege of serving as editor of this collection of his selected papers. This book is an expression of my deep respect and affection for him, and it is my hope that it honors him and that it is befitting his innovative contributions to the fields of psychoanalysis and human development. And to Joan Erikson, the real editor of the writings of Erik H. Erikson, I am thankful for her knowledge, decisiveness, and encouragement.

It was very meaningful to have had the support of George Brockway, editor and former chairman of W. W. Norton, whose expertise and guidance were essential at the outset of the project. I would also like to pay tribute to Linda Healey, editor at W. W. Norton, for her critical and thoughtful assistance and for the energy and skill she provided in order to steer this project toward its completion. Her participation has been invaluable. In addition, Katie Nelson at W. W. Norton has played an essential part in this process.

The following friends and colleagues have provided guidance and support along the way: Leston Havens, Mitchell Lasker, Richard

Melito and Peter Williams; Mairi Staples for her superior typing skills; and Inge Schneier Hoffmann and Joachim Neugroschel, who translated the two papers from 1931 by Erikson that were originally published in German. This book would not be complete without their efforts. Certain libraries have assisted in the important task of locating these papers: the Austen Riggs Center Library (Stockbridge, Massachusetts), the Countway Library of the Harvard Medical School (Boston, Massachusetts), and the Library of Congress (Washington, D.C.). My appreciation is also extended to all the publishers, editors, and organizations that granted permission to reproduce Erikson's published writings. My deep appreciation to authors Robert Coles and Paul Roazen for their authoritative biographies of Erikson. These books often served as personal guides to which I referred for particular insights or factual data.

I owe a very special debt to the Austen Riggs Center where I was fortunate to have completed a postdoctoral fellowship in clinical psychology and where I drew a great deal of knowledge and inspiration from my teachers. It was there that I had the opportunity of first meeting Erik Erikson, in 1971.

My father, Irving Schlein, an artist in his own right, has in less tangible ways given me the necessary strength and persistence. His active participation and precise editorial commentary will never be forgotten.

I would like to pay tribute to my wife, Toby, and express my deepest appreciation for her prolonged dedication, patience, and sensitivity. She reviewed every word I wrote and provided essential editorial skills and critical reading.

Lexington, Massachusetts   *S T E P H E N   S C H L E I N*
February 1985

Editor's Preface

The idea of publishing a collection of Erik Erikson's papers emerged one day while I was preparing a review of his writings on infancy and children's play for a presentation to the Psychology Department at the Children's Hospital in Boston. While I knew that many of his better-known journal articles had appeared in revised form in a number of his books, I began to realize that there was a significant number of important papers that had not been reprinted and had remained isolated as obscure journal articles unknown to most professionals in the field. I wrote to Erikson, who had been one of my teachers at the Austen Riggs Center (Stockbridge, Massachusetts), to tell him of my discovery and to suggest collecting these papers into one volume. Both Erikson and his editor at W. W. Norton, George Brockway, agreed that a volume of previously uncollected papers ranging from Erikson's earliest writings of the 1930s and 1940s to his most recent papers of the 1970s and 1980s would be a worthwhile contribution.

The challenge I then faced was to locate all the papers. Many of them appeared in journals no longer easily accessible and available only from large medical school libraries; other papers, published in obscure periodicals, were obtainable only through a major library search. Others came from the private collections at the Austen Riggs Center and the Library of Congress; a series of unpublished papers was obtained directly from Erikson; finally, two of the earliest papers were translated from German for the express purpose of this volume.

The result is a volume of forty-seven papers, reflecting fifty years of Erikson's work, from 1930 to 1980. Twelve of the papers appear here in print for the first time. Also included are thirteen drawings by Erikson depicting various individuals—ranging from children at the Vienna school in the 1930s to friends in later life.

It is worth noting that a number of the papers in this volume represent Erikson's earliest writings, based on direct clinical observations of children and American Indians. These particular articles were the original documents, containing his early formulations, which were later to become the core of *Childhood and Society*, his best-known and most widely read publication.

No previously published journal article which later appeared in its entirety in one of Erikson's books appears in this collection.* If, however, a journal article was substantially reworked or shortened in one of his books, it is presented in this volume in its complete original form. An important example of this is "The Dream Specimen of Psychoanalysis" (1954). While it is summarized in *Identity: Youth and Crisis*, a major portion of this contribution is unavailable to the reader who does not have access to the original journal article.

A complete bibliography of Erikson's writing appears at the end of this volume in an effort to provide a clear picture of what he has written and when and where it was published. The reader will note that four papers in this collection were written with Erikson's wife, Joan, and one with the collaboration of his son, Kai. In addition, one of the few exceptions to the fifty-year time span represented is a 1983 paper about Anna Freud. Erikson said that he was pleased that someone who had so much to do with his early professional development had been given "a special place in the book."

None of the papers in this volume has been altered in any significant way from its original state. This fits the spirit of the preface of *Identity: Youth and Crisis*, where Erikson says, "I have left to each 'period piece' its emphasis of tone and to the whole the character of a record." However, it was necessary, on occasion, to deal with the inevitability of repetitiousness, unavoidable in the natural overlapping of these articles, by editing particular papers. All such changes receive exact notation. Nevertheless, I hope the reader will be patient with a certain degree of repetitiousness, as Erikson reworks and

---

* Examples are: (1) "Observations on Sioux Education," first published in 1939 and later appearing in *Childhood and Society*; (2) "The Nature of Clinical Evidence," first published in 1958 and later appearing in *Insight and Responsibility*; and (3) "The Problem of Ego Identity," first published in 1956 and later appearing in *Identity: Youth and Crisis*.

rethinks his ideas under new circumstances and new surroundings, over the fifty-year period represented.

When I considered the overall plan for the book, it seemed that a thematic presentation of the articles, rather than simply a chronological one, was the most effective and convincing way to highlight the magnitude of Erikson's contributions. In fact, the articles seemed to fall naturally into a series of thematic-chapter headings, covering a wide spectrum of topics and providing some unity and coherence to a half century of writing. It is hoped that this style of organization gives the reader a richer appreciation of the substance of the papers. Erikson has added new words and phrases to our language that signify new ways to appreciate the meaning and complexity of human behavior. The thematic-chapter headings used emphasize some of these contributions. At times, deciding in which chapter a paper should be placed was difficult. In those cases, when an article covers a range of thematic areas—e.g., a paper about aspects of the life cycle with a cross-cultural, environmental focus—it has been placed where it seems to make the most sense to the overall organization of the book.

The five contributions appearing in the first chapter, "Psychoanalysis and Enlightenment," take the reader back in time to Vienna, where Erikson lived from 1927 to 1933, and provide a sense of his first encounters with the field of psychoanalysis and a glimpse of some of his early visions. Three papers represent his earliest publications, from 1930 and 1931. The two remaining articles are more recent, from 1980 and 1983. The papers deal with Erikson's beginnings in the field as a Montessori-trained teacher in the Vienna school and as a student in training in psychoanalysis.

During the summer of 1927 Erik Homburger Erikson, a young artist living alternately in his hometown of Karlsruhe, Germany, and in Florence, Italy, unsure of his professional direction, was encouraged by his childhood friend Peter Blos to come to Vienna to draw portraits of Dorothy Burlingham's children. This led to Erikson's joining the teaching staff at an experimental school established by Anna Freud and Dorothy Burlingham and directed by Blos. Erikson was unaware at the time that this was to become one of the most fateful moments in his life. For he was to meet the circle around Sigmund Freud and was eventually to be invited to become a candidate for psychoanalytic training at the Vienna Psychoanalytic Institute. His "training analyst" was to be Anna Freud.

The paper that opens this first chapter, "Dorothy Burlingham's School in Vienna" (1980), was written at Anna Freud's request for the *Bulletin of the Hampstead Clinic*, on the occasion of Dorothy Burlingham's death. It is coauthored with Joan Erikson, who also taught at the Vienna School. The Eriksons explain how the school was "dreamed up" by Dorothy Burlingham, Eva Rosenfeld, and Anna Freud in the late 1920s for children of different nationalities whose parents were undergoing analysis and who themselves were undergoing child analysis. During that period there was a growing interest in developing new pedagogic ways in the field of education based on the impact of psychoanalysis. This was the spirit with which the school was created, and it became for the Eriksons an innovative experience. The atmosphere emphasized the vital components of engagement, adventure, and involvement for children, emerging from the "free spirit" of the experimental project method. It was during this experience in Vienna that Erikson witnessed the period of ascendance of ego psychology with its emphasis on the importance of the ego's relation to the social-cultural environment.

The second paper in this chapter, "Psychoanalysis and the Future of Education," emerged from these philosophical beginnings and expresses the hope that society can achieve a utopian upbringing of children through psychological enlightenment. Erikson presented the paper to the Vienna Psychoanalytic Society in 1930, while he was still in psychoanalytic training. It is worth noting that Erikson studied clinical psychoanalysis with such prominent figures as August Aichhorn, Edward Bibring, Helene Deutsche, Paul Federn, Heinz Hartmann, and Ernst Kris as well as with Anna Freud.

This paper and the two others from the early 1930s were originally published in German in a Viennese journal, *Zeitschrift für psychoanalytische Pädagogik*, devoted to furthering the relationship between psychoanalysis and education. The editorial staff consisted of individuals such as August Aichhorn, Paul Federn, and Anna Freud. The journal, which began in 1926, continued until 1938, when Austria was invaded. It was around that time that the *Psychoanalytic Study of the Child* first appeared in the United States with a continued dedication to the development of psychoanalysis and its application to the field of education. In 1935, when Erikson was in America, "Psychoanalysis and the Future of Education" was translated into English and was published in the *Psychoanalytic Quarterly*. As Erikson's first published paper, both in German and in English, it truly deserves a special place of its own in this volume.

Two papers from 1931, "Children's Picture Books" and "The Fate of the Drives in School Compositions," appear in English for the first time in this collection. Reflecting the mood of the Vienna circle and the influence of Anna Freud especially, Erikson continued to discuss the mysteries of childhood. While describing how children project their inner worlds into their written compositions and drawings, he resisted the temptation of the time to see only the subjective or emotional side of the child's artistic efforts. In Robert Coles's biography of Erikson, he says, "The reader is made to realize that children draw and write about things that have both an objective and a subjective meaning".*

The last paper in this chapter was written in 1983 as a personal tribute to Anna Freud following her death. In response to an invitation to contribute to a special issue of the *Bulletin of the Hampstead Clinic*, Erikson was asked to comment about her position in history. While the article highlighted many areas of her professional and personal life, its unique contribution is its focus on how Anna Freud's life history "touched" Erik Erikson's. Thus the paper adds a vital component to this first chapter on Erikson's years in Vienna. Anna Freud shared a waiting room with her father at Berggasse 19, the building where the Freud family lived and where they worked at psychoanalysis. It is here that Erikson began his training analysis with Anna Freud in 1927. In his autobiographical notes he refers to this period as a "truly astounding adoption by the Freudian circle." He remembers the atmosphere in Vienna as "one of intense mutual loyalty and a deep devotion to a truly liberating idea."† In reviewing the format for this volume, he said that to have papers about Anna Freud and Dorothy Burlingham in the introductory chapter conveyed for him "a poetic sense."

One of the other unique sections of the book is Chapter III, "War Memoranda." During World War II the Institute of Intercultural Studies, a national wartime body, was formed to study German psychological warfare. Erik Erikson served as a consultant to one of its committees, the Committee for National Morale. He prepared position papers that focused on national character studies of Germany. The committee was formed to supply information and advisory services to various policy-making agencies. It brought together experts from many fields, including psychology and the social sciences. Some

---

* Robert Coles, *Erik H. Erikson: The Growth of His Work* (Boston: Little, Brown, 1970), 30.
† Erik Erikson, Autobiographic Notes on the Identity Crisis. "*Daedalus* (Fall 1970), 744; ibid., p. 735.

of the other renowned participants were Gordon Allport, Gregory Bateson, Edwin Boring, Kurt Lewin, Margaret Mead, Gardner Murphy, and Henry A. Murray.

Erikson's contributions to the Committee for National Morale have been on file at the Library of Congress as part of the collected papers of Margaret Mead. Five of these papers appear here in print for the first time. Erikson has referred to these unpublished papers as "war memoranda" and noted that "they had to be tentative since they dealt with history that was very much still in progress." The papers represent his first psychohistorical writings and present a microscopic analysis of a particular moment in world history. This period in Erikson's life was an important part of his early experiences in the United States, as a German immigrant, writing about a war that pitted his two countries against each other. He said that "the goal was to say what would be useful to America and not to be vengeful." Robert Coles remarks on these papers in his biography of Erikson: "As one goes through those old unpublished manuscripts, the clinical investigator who wrote them seems familiarly like the one who went to study the Sioux and the Yurok: appreciative as well as analytic, an observer of action as well as one who listens to free associations, the relaxed (and at times vastly amused) participant, who only later mulls things over and makes recommendations."*

In my communication with Erikson he suggested that I consider a title for the book beyond the more formal heading of "Selected Papers." Freud predicted in the exploration of the psychology of the ego that "it will be difficult to avoid what is already familiar and that it is more a question of new ways of looking at things and new groupings of the facts than of making new discoveries."† In keeping with Freud's distinction, one recognizes how Erikson adopted a view of his own contribution in 1950, in the closing chapter of *Childhood and Society*, where he said, "I have nothing to offer except a way of looking at things."** In an effort to find one overall theme that orchestrated this collection of papers, I realized that an unusual unity of theme and purpose was perceptible in the evolution of Erikson's psychosocial, ego-psychological formulations, as portrayed by the title *A Way of Looking at Things*.

Erikson entered psychoanalysis from the field of art, where he had been a children's portrait painter. It appears that he brought with

---

* Coles, op. cit., 99.

† Sigmund Freud, *New Introductory Lectures on Psychoanalysis*, tr. J. H. Sprott (New York: W. W. Norton, 1933, 86.

** Erikson, *Childhood and Society* (New York: W. W. Norton, 1950), 359.

him a configurational perspective which helped explain how things "hang together" and "hold together." As he built a bridge between art and psychoanalysis, he developed a configurational view of children's play which was influenced by Freud's emphasis on the vital importance of dreams. This contextual affinity considered how visual configurations precede words and formulations and observed that children's play, dreams, and free associations are visual data, originating from a series of images, only later put into words. Yet, as Erikson expanded his notion of a psychosocial theory of human existence, it emerged as a critical departure from Freud's psychosexual model of man. This perspective was an alternative to a focus on causality and the traumatological model and to the energy-libido theory of psychoanalysis. Erikson avoided seeing everything as a symbol for "something else" and believed that the human mind was more than drives and instincts. He emphasized a homeostatic quality of the organism rather than psychopathology. The configurational view studied the interaction and convergence of multiple processes and recurrent patterns. This was highlighted in *Childhood and Society* when Erikson said, "In recent years we have come to the conclusion that a neurosis is psycho-*and* somatic, psycho-*and* social, and *inter*personal,"* three aspects of human experience organized by a process of ego synthesis. It is here that his multidimensional perspective demonstrates the integration and convergence of various processes—biological, psychological, social, cultural, communal, and historical. These processes are seen as aspects of one process—i.e., human life and human existence.

Erikson's contextual way of looking at the world refers to his perspective of human growth and development. This configurational approach expresses his commitment to the strength of the human ego, to the conception that adult maturity is not the end of psychological growth, and to comprehension of the coherence of a person's unique qualities. His vision of the organic unity of the human life cycle utilizes a life-history perspective, in contrast with a case-history model, focusing not on interpretation but on the search for continuity in a given life—the life of a real human being. Erikson looks for the hopeful and active part of the person and for how human experience and human potential are organized in the communal environment, within a radius of significant social encounters. These themes run throughout the articles and papers in this volume as the reader finds Erikson painting contexts and backgrounds.

* Ibid., 23.

At Erik Erikson's eightieth birthday celebration in 1982, Daniel Schwartz, medical director of the Austen Riggs Center, presented a personal tribute and said, "Erikson began as a young artist. He became a psychoanalyst who helped all of us to see more clearly. In studies of dreams, of children's play, in the explication of the regularities in our sense of psychological space as influenced by our bodies and our cultures, he has helped us define crucial configurations."

I.
PSYCHOANALYSIS
AND
ENLIGHTENMENT

Dorothy Burlingham

Dorothy Burlingham's School in Vienna (1980)

WITH JOAN M. ERIKSON

Anna Freud has asked me to tell you about Dorothy Burlingham's small school in the Wattmanngasse in suburban Vienna. I, in turn, have asked Joan Erikson, who was also part of the staff for a while, to join me in writing this account of how some of us remember this innovative experience.

We believe that to begin with, Dorothy Burlingham as well as Eva Rosenfeld and Anna Freud dreamed the whole idea up together. Dorothy's four children were then being tutored by Peter Blos, a remarkably craftsmanlike young teacher with clear concepts about how children learn. But tutoring is, of course, individual and isolated learning, and the children lacked the interplay and companionship with other children which a group setting affords.

So a school was formed of children who were spending some time in Vienna—children of different nationalities whose parents were undergoing analysis or who were perhaps in analysis themselves. It was never a very large group, rarely more than twenty children. All the parents, however, were intensely interested in new pedagogic ways and the impact of psychoanalytic understanding on education in the modern world.

This little school, then, was quite a private educational undertak-

First published in the *Bulletin of the Hampstead Clinic* 3,2 (1980), 91–94.

ing. The classes met at first in the home of Walti and Eva Rosenfeld
and later in a small building constructed for the purpose in the Rosenfelds' garden. For Eva, this role of hostess of the school (at the
beginning, daily lunch was served in her home) was most meaningful
in that period following the death of her teenage daughter.

One might assume that such a school would be quite obviously
psychoanalytically oriented. In a sense this was, of course, so—but
never to the casual observer or in any overly intellectual or modish
sense. Dorothy was implementing the best possible school situation
which could be devised so it would be congenial to the special needs
of English-speaking children living in Vienna and yet also conducive
to an atmosphere hospitable to a psychoanalytic orientation. Anna
Freud, of course, was discreetly omnipresent in the whole improvisation.

Peter Blos, who became the director of this enterprise, had learned
about and become impressed by the kind of curriculum then known
as the Project Method which had revolutionized various school systems (first, we think, in Winnetka, Illinois) in America. This educational approach was in accord with John Dewey's theory that
children learn only where their interest is fully engaged and centered.
They are then amazingly capable of drawing all the facets of learning
the mandatory "three R's" into the focus of a given project and of
mastering otherwise dreary-to-learn skills.

So we taught by the Project Method. The whole school would for
a time become, for example, the world of the Eskimos. All subjects
were then related to Eskimo life—geography, history, science, math,
and, of course, reading and writing. This called for an ingenious
combination of playful new experience, careful experiment, and free
discussion, while it conveyed a sense of contextuality for all the details
learned.

A Christmas Journal carefully designed by the children in 1929 (a
copy of which was sent to us by one of the children, Professor Peter
Heller of Buffalo) is introduced with an overall statement of the
teachers:

Since the beginning of this school year our work has been newly divided.
The basic subjects (math, geography, Latin, languages) are taught every
morning in the first two hours. The rest of the time is dedicated to "free
work" and English. Every two weeks the teachers outline in big strokes
a new theme for the "free work" which is then elaborated by the students
with the help of books, pictures, and models. At the end of the second
week every student reports on his work, be its emphasis geography,

history, nature study, or physics, the most important aspect of which is noted down in a summary way by all students.

This statement is followed by an unbelievable list of themes worked on during the three concluding months of that year by students aged 11 through 14. In one of the individual essays there is a remark which throws some light on the functioning of one of us as a teacher-artist: "To illustrate the lessons Herr Erik drew so many posters that by the end of the year they covered all of the walls." We may add that the journal contains a number of the children's woodcuts (Herr Erik's specialty) which markedly illustrate their "themes."

Since "doing," itself, is a vital component of the Project Method and the skills of the different aged children had to be carefully brought into play, the little school was a veritable beehive. The children loved it, and they and the teachers learned a good deal. There were also trips into town to see whatever was to be seen of things related to the project, and art and music had an important place in it all. The Christmas Journal also notes that from time to time August Aichhorn would come for some free discussion with the children. In our memory, we experienced that rare joy which is evoked where a setting permits us to respond to the growth potentials of young people as they reveal and develop our own potentials.

Let us now share with you two more personal memories of the school experience which attest to the free spirit which prevailed in the setting. After our marriage we lived on the Kueniglberg, above the school. When our son Kai was born (after some time out for Joan) we daily carried him between us in a laundry basket to the tiny schoolyard or the Rosenfelds' back porch. It became routine that the children would tell us during class when he was crying ("Kai weint"), and in the intermission some watched him being nursed. It was enriching for us all to share this experience.

And there was a memorable old English Christmas—Yule log, carols, acrobats, dancers, and a boar's head and mistletoe—at the Burlinghams' house, and "the Professor" appearing to watch it.

In what respect, then, was this a "psychoanalytic school"? One was aware of some of the children's near-daily appointments. Not infrequently, one was told that this or that child was "having a difficult time," and some reasons for it were sometimes discussed in staff meetings. But otherwise, there was hardly any clinical talk, and certainly no individual interpretation. In this connection, however, it must be reported in this account that observations made at the school provided themes helpful in psychoanalytic training and suit-

Kai

Jon

Mikey

Tinky

Bob

*Marie (an older sketch
from the Black Forest)*

able for early psychoanalytic writings. They illustrate, we think, how psychoanalytic awareness can inform the staff and enrich such a school's work pedagogically. One of these papers is, in fact, based on a role which Dorothy Burlingham played in the school in her inimitable fashion. She would appear a few times a year to ask the children to freely answer a question in writing such as, "What would you like to be, if you could choose it?" or "How are you going to educate your children?" or "What would you do if you suddenly were alone in the world (that means without parents) and would have to help yourself?" One can learn much from the imaginative answers given to such questions. In regard to the last question, however, we felt that it was really not quite necessary for the children to respond as "psychoanalytically" as they did: twelve children described in detail the death of fifteen parents, three of whom were murdered, four died in accidents, and two in prisons. To paraphrase Nietzsche, the children had spent more time describing *from whom* they wanted to be free than *for what*. But maybe there was another factor at work: How could the children imagine so suddenly to be "alone in the world," without parents, *except* because of violent events? And, of course, there was very much else in these essays.

Another paper was based on some sessions Erik had during two successive years with a seven year old boy whose mother felt that he was asking her questions under a certain pressure: what did he "really" want to know? To give an illustration, the first questions in the second year were:

> "I don't know whether I should ask about people or the world."
> "What about rain?"
> "And what about the sun?"
> "How about ships—do they bump underneath?"
> "But you told me all that before and about trains and fire too."

All the questions were answered briefly and clearly, while no interpretations were given. But a careful comparison of the questions asked a year apart indicated the fate in the boy's mind both of the questions and of the answers and permitted some insight into the inner processes which determined that fate. At the same time, the whole procedure seemed to confirm Freud's conclusion that ". . . little Hans's case shows the importance of letting children express repeatedly, in conversation and in play, their questions about, and their conceptions of the world. The history of little Hans proves that more than half the battle is won when the child succeeds in expressing itself."*

This last paper (which, incidentally, was entitled, "Psychoanalysis and the Future of Education," indicating that young as we were, we expected our work to have a pretty decisive impact) also refers to a discussion with our twelve and thirteen year olds about rage and asocial behavior as well as about cultural uses of aggression such as the Eskimos' singing contests where the goal is for each contending group to outdo the other by making the most devastating fun of it and make everybody laugh. Here, the children made a strange confession:

One of them said, "In the other schools it was fun to pin a paper on the teacher's coat. Here there's no fun in it anymore." We were too nice!

In this memorable little school the children, no doubt, did learn many things. The teachers, however, observed unforgettably what Freud called the "strahlende Intelligenz" (the "radiant intelligence") displayed by children who for some moments are permitted (by themselves and by circumstances) to function freely.

* Sigmund Freud, "Analysis of a Phobia in a Five-Year-Old Boy" (1909). In *Collected Papers*, Sigmund Freud, ed. Joan Riviere (London: Hogarth Press and Institute of Psycho-Analysis). 1924–1950. Vol. III, 149.

Psychoanalysis and the Future of Education (1930)

Of all those who through their analytic training hope to be able to make some fundamental contribution to therapeutic or educational work, the teacher is the least able to foresee what he may achieve through analytical insight, which he gains from his own clinical analysis. The analytic situation does not offer him any direct suggestion as to how to face the specific situations he meets on returning to his work. An analyst is obliged for the most part to remain a silent observer while the teacher's work involves continuous talking—this fact alone roughly distinguishes the methods of analyst from that of teacher, representing the two extremes of all possible educational methods of approach. The clinical analyst maintains an attitude of impartiality throughout, thus making it possible for his patient's affects to reveal themselves according to their own laws and in the forms given to them by a pitilessly selective life; the passivity of the analyst is the necessary prerequisite for the proof of the scientific value, as well as for the therapeutic success, of the method. In the work of the teacher the relations are much more flexible. He not only has to deal with affects in his children, the ultimate forms of

Written under the name of Erik Homburger. Read before the Vienna Psychoanalytic Society in April 1930. First published in *Zeitschrift für psychoanalytische Pädagogik*, 4 (1930), 201–16. Reprinted in The *Psychoanalytic Quarterly*, 4 (1935), 50–68.

which are not yet fully determined (a feature also found in child analysis), but he also cannot avoid registering his own affective response. Although he is the object of transference, he cannot eliminate his own personality, but must play a very personal part in the child's life. It is the x in the teacher's personality which influences the y in the child's development. But, unlike child guidance workers, he accomplishes his educational purposes chiefly through the imponderables of his attitude in the pursuit of his work as teacher. There he finds the specific means for exerting his influence. His duty is to train, to present, to explain, and to enlighten. Therefore he should ask himself not where his work touches on the work of the analyst or the worker in child guidance, but where and how it in itself gives him the opportunity to make use of his new knowledge of human instincts.

Let us discuss enlightenment, taking the word first in the narrower sense of sexual enlightenment, and then let us inquire where and how this touches the problem of enlightenment as a whole. In the problem of sexual enlightenment, teaching and psychoanalysis can be seen to come to a fundamental convergence.

Some years ago, when I was engaged in teaching, the mother of a seven-year-old pupil of mine asked me to talk with him. She said that Richard revealed such a drive to ask questions about everything that she felt unable to satisfy his curiosity and she preferred to have a man answer his questions concerning sexual matters. I spent several afternoons with Richard. He asked questions and I answered; we talked about God and the universe, and where children come from. Every question was answered conscientiously. Richard was a very intelligent and receptive boy. One rule proved to be important— namely, never to give more information than was asked for. His questions ventured to the point of inquiring about the man's role in begetting children and there they stopped. He did learn, however, that the semen of the man enters the woman and that this makes it possible for her to bear a child.

One year later Richard again expressed a wish to ask questions. As soon as he began, however, I noticed a certain reserve. His questions were no longer eager and punctuated with large question marks; they rather took the form of statements—whispered, careful statements. I again answered him conscientiously but with enough reserve so as not to disturb the next question already formed in his mind. The continuous flow of his questions was not interrupted. I took notes during the interview, explaining that we would use them later to check up and make sure he had omitted nothing. The following are his questions, with tentative analytical interpretations. Let me state, however, that I interpreted nothing to the child. Throughout the interview I remained the teacher whose place it was to answer questions.

Richard's Questions

THE FIRST HOUR

"I don't know whether I should ask about people or the world?"

"What about rain?"

"And what about the sun?"

"How about ships—do they bump underneath?"

"But you told me all that before and about trains and fire too." PAUSE.

The little scientist would like to keep far away from the interesting and the dangerous world of people and remain with atmospheric phenomena. When, however, he does discuss men, he circumscribes a wide circle around the genitals. But increasing pressure from within leads him to associations which touch on an inner anxiety. At this point, as at the word "fire," he pauses. The reason will soon become clear.

"How long can a diver stay under water?"

"Must he always pump?"

"What does he do when he wants something?"

"Once someone made a man. Why did he spoil him again?"

"I heard that a house was burned and everybody who was in it."

"But—when a prison burns? Are there windows in prison?" PAUSE.

Again at the mention of "fire" comes a pause. In the depths, in prison, in a burning house—one cannot call, cannot breathe, one burns. A man was made and then destroyed again. We begin to see that these associations have something to do with a narrow room in which a man is made—revealing to the analytic eye an unconscious fantasy and anxiety about the womb and the child it contains.

"I've never seen a house burning."

"I've never seen a fire engine burning on a house—that must be fine but not nice."

The fantasy which was restrained before each time by silence now comes to the surface. It does so by means of a slip—the fire engine is burning instead of squirting water. The dangerous sensation of "burning" has replaced the pleasantly harmless and "manly" activity of the squirting fireman. The deeper meaning of this slip becomes clear later.

"After all I think I'd rather ask about people."

Apparently he does not know how much the inner voice has already asked about man. It would be interesting to know if and how the slip itself made this daring question possible.

"What about cars?"
"How can you talk?"
"How does hair grow?"

With the word "hair" he loses his wish to question further for the day. At this point I remember that already, the year before, a group of questions were always recurring which no answer satisfied—they dealt with "hair" and "blood." These probably were the expression of the deeper question whether the blood, which he had doubtless seen on the clothes of a woman as she undressed, signified the castration of the male organ or if the latter were only hidden by the hair.

These questions, according to their tone and content, form two special groups and may be classified as follows: (a) simple questions of interest, which seem to be only a kind of pretext, and the answer to which he already knew by heart; (b) the "hair and blood group," repeated from the first year, representing increasing anxiety. It is noteworthy that among all the new questions, which are obviously filled with dangerous matters of unconscious sexual meaning, there is not one direct sexual question.

THE SECOND HOUR

"Where does the air begin to get thinner?"
"What's around the sky?"
"What's a cloudburst?"

Now we have come back to earth, but along with a suggestion of something unpleasant—namely a cloudburst. Therefore, he pauses. Nevertheless, he makes a courageous decision.

"After all, I'd rather talk about people."[1]
"I know everything about the head."
"About the legs, too."
"Do I know everything about arms?"
"About elbows too?"

The wide circle around the genitals is worthy of note; but the boy's anxiety about them bursts through in the next question: "How do you snap back the elbow when it's come out of joint?" Does "coming out of joint" suggest erection? (Arms and legs are "members," called "*Glieder*" in German, while penis is also called a "member or "Glied.") In any case there is again a pause.

Then follows a still clearer anxiety about the penis. In the throat there is a tube for air and another for food. They must come out somehow below when you put your head down:

"And when food gets into the air tube?"
"Is it like that in a hen too?" (The association "hen" will be explained later.)
"In a snake too?"
"How does a snail push itself forward?"
"Where are there purple snails?"

The tubes that come out below, the snake, the snail that "pushes itself forward," the purple snail, all point clearly to the penis. The purple snail connects two ideas—snail and blood. Richard had heard the myth of the Greek shepherd who found his dog, bleeding, as he thought, at the mouth and then discovered that the animal had bitten a purple snail. Now, consequently, we approach the fear of "castration," which, being unconscious, threatens to overshadow everything:

"When you cut off your hand do you have to stop the blood with bandages?"
"When you're dead does the skin fall off? Do the bones go to pieces?"
"A celluloid factory can explode easily, can't it?"

The hour began with "cloudburst" and ended with "explosion."

THE THIRD HOUR
"How fast can a man run?"
"And an animal?" (Does he mean "run away"? It would seem so.)

"I'd like to know something about war. If Vienna hadn't stopped fighting would it have been all ruined?"

"Who started the fighting?"

"That was mean of England to help against Vienna."

Here it is necessary to consider what "fighting" and what "England" and "Vienna" mean. For some time Richard had shown occasional timidity on the street. Once, when questioned about his fear, he declared anxiously, "The dogs fight." A very enlightened little girl, hearing this remark, immediately explained, "They don't fight, they are marrying." Now people marry, too, and there are sufficient indications that physical conflict is involved. Many children overestimate these indications, especially in families where physical or psychic pain seems somehow to be connected with the events going on in the parental bedroom. Richard's mother, who seemed to be unhappy, had married in England, but shortly after the war had been compelled by various circumstances to leave his father and settle in Vienna. Richard explained this change by connecting the war, the fighting and his father, from whose aggression his mother had fled away to Vienna. The unconscious identification of the country in which one lives with the threatened or suffering mother, and the enemy with the brutal father against whom the boy, the young hero, has to defend her may be pointed out as a common one. It is important to see where Richard's fantasies are based on his special œdipus situation. "The sun and the moon," he once remarked, "can never be in the sky at the same time. They would eat each other up."

"How are the teeth made firm?"

"Why are lips so red?"

"Why is the head up straight?"

"When you bend it back it gets all red."

"Why do you bleed when you cut yourself?"

"The hair under the arm . . ."

References to blood and hair again terminate his desire to question further. The possible interpretations of this hour may, then, be summarized as follows: (1) pitying identification with the suffering mother; (2) the wish to be like her; but also (3) fear of this wish, because becoming a woman means castration. A further anxiety about becoming a woman, appearing in the next hour, demonstrates that we are on the right track.

THE FOURTH HOUR

"In your head there's an opening. Why doesn't everything run out?"
"Some people have something here" (goiter).
"Some people have a hunchback."
"If somebody hits somebody in the eye will he be blind right away?"
"Why are women so fat here?" (breast)
"And how is it when the woman has too much milk and the baby doesn't drink it all?"
"And when a woman has too little?"

Bursting skull, goiter, hunchback, the overfull breast, the dislodged eye; women grow fat, have children in their bodies and milk in their breasts. How do their bodies stand it? It is now possible to understand the strange intrusion of the "hen" in the second hour. It appeared in connection with the question as to what would happen if food should get into the wrong tube. [If we take] into account the familiar mechanism which disguises unconscious thought or fear by reversing the term used, as for example "below" to "above," "out" to "in," the question about the "hen" may mean: what would happen if that which should come out below (the egg from the hen, the child from the mother) tried to come out of another opening which was too small and burst?

At this point it is well to bear in mind Richard's actual difficulties at the time of this interview. He had attacks of *pavor nocturnus* in which he cried and asked if his bowel movement had been sufficient. When he was assured that this was the case he slept quietly. As this symptom disappeared he began to have difficulty with eating. His symptoms followed one another with a transposition similar to that of his questions, that is, from "below" to "above." Both were obviously aspects of the same anxiety: through which organ is the child begotten and through which is it born?

"Why do you see a strong man's muscles so plainly here?" (The veins of the arm.)
"What part of people do cannibals eat?"
"There were many in the war?"
"Once someone told me about cannibals and I always thought they ran around in the streets."
"When you stand for a long time your feet get all red."

These questions are followed by a clear symbolic description of the anxiety about the penis:

> "Is there a quite smooth ball here on your knee?" (i.e., gland)
> "When you stretch your mouth open why doesn't it tear here?" (in the corners)
> "But when you cut yourself somewhere on your skin, it could go on tearing couldn't it?"
> "There's a sort of bone around the eye?"
> "Why don't they put armor inside a soldier's uniform?"
> "Are there armored cars in Vienna?"
> "Around the neck there's a sort of skin collar?" (i.e., foreskin).

Again, in accordance with the displacement mechanism, the part most in danger is transferred above, but to a part of the body which also shares the danger of being cut off—namely, the neck.

THE FIFTH HOUR

As this was to be the last hour before the holidays, and as it was preferable not to let the boy leave without any enlightenment in the matter which was troubling him, I reminded him that he had asked no question about childbearing, which had interested him so greatly.

> "That's so."
> "Why is it [women's buttocks] so fat behind?"
> "What happens when the child stays in too long?"
> "How do you know when it's coming?"
> *"And when you marry then the semen comes from the woman into the man, doesn't it?"*

It is apparent that Richard, who had shown such intelligence in the understanding of all the enlightenment given him up to this point, had nevertheless been unable to maintain his sexual knowledge against the repressing forces. These had led him away from the masculine role and at the same time subjected him to intense anxiety concerning the factors likely to threaten him in the woman's role. The slip with which he first disclosed this change is noteworthy: the fire engine burns instead of squirting.

From this very limited insight into one child's mind which Richard's questions have provided, we may conclude that the formation of anxieties, fantasies, and unconscious and conscious theories continues regardless of sexual enlightenment. It is important to consider whether or not there is reason to believe that the infantile psyche (or, can we simply say the psyche?) always reacts in this manner.

At first the child had asked questions openly. His desire to question was very naturally so divided that his wish for general information appeared in the foreground, while behind it lay his easily accessible curiosity about sexual things. The further development of the œdipus complex brought about a repression of the now dangerous sexual questions. Questions are now set carefully, half dreamily and disinterestedly, and behind the words which would endeavor to hide the sexual content lurks a general permeation of sexual anxiety, born of the conviction that a catastrophe must take place. The grownups, of course, deny or conceal this, but there are too many indications of actual force in sexual life and too many catastrophic desires in one's own mind. Because of anxiety and one's own desire for aggression, all signs of aggression become overvalued. These signs are not lacking, since a sado-masochistic component is always evident in the tension of sexuality, even though in normal sexual life, in the general attitude of the adult, it may be balanced and imponderable. In any event the child in his preoccupation overvalues something real. Changing according to his stages of development, his affective relationship to the single components of sexuality is based on what he observes in the outer world, as well as upon the sensations of his own body.

For the adult these components have become imponderables, scarcely measurable in normal sex life, and only in the artificial situation of psychoanalysis is the old scheme of weights and measures temporarily reëstablished. In life, adult and child represent different stages of a development or, more accurately, are the result of different mathematical operations which are employing the same values; the sexual development of a child resembles a gradual addition while adult sexuality is the product of the same figures.

These oral, anal, phallic, sadistic imponderables, however, which the adult can no longer measure or name, are just those which are experienced in crude isolation by the child, one following the other inexorably. The child develops them, fights against them, tries to balance them, and this struggle is complicated by the fact that he is busily occupied with the pleasure zones of his age level (or of an earlier one from which he has only partly progressed), as well as that he experiences sensations which prevent him from grasping what the adult tells. In general, the sexual act as represented to the child is rationalized and made more or less gentle and noble according to the personal attitude of the individual adult. In any case sleeping restfully together is sure to be emphasized by the adult as the only pleasure involved, but it is just this feeling of protected rest from which the child is drawing away into the tumultuous fight for existence. Only yesterday he forsook his mother's arms and his possessive share of her body. Today he has a respite in which to accustom himself to his loss, but tomorrow, so he feels, something quite new and different and dangerous will present itself. Rest, however, is the reward for his successful battle. He, therefore, accepts sexual enlightenment exactly as he accepts general enlightenment in other fields—passing it off with an almost patronizing gesture and with the feeling (sometimes even conscious): "Maybe you're right, though you tell me enough lies. But I'm interested in something else, and that you apparently won't tell me about because you think I'm too stupid—or perhaps you can't tell me because you're too stupid yourself."

An example offered by one of Richard's classmates may be cited in this connection. He had upon occasion heard from me that children are nursed at their mother's breast, and very probably he had also had an opportunity to observe this. Nevertheless, he exclaimed one day in school: "You said that women have breasts to give milk, but that isn't so. What women have there is something to have fun with." What does the boy mean by "have fun with," the pleasant appearance or feeling of the breast or the enjoyable vague memory of nursing? In any case, he is not alone in this feeling. But when he asks about it no one appears to know anything, and his confusion and excitement are met with idealistic or scientific conceptions. Here, too, the interest of the child lies in a certain vividly felt emotional relationship, in response to which he is told something about sucking calves and lactating cows. But cow's teats resemble more nearly a multiple penis to the boyish mind, and the milking he observes very likely brings further confusion and new evaluations. In the face of such emotional relationships, education enforces repression and sets up in their place scientific law and order. We enforce with the patience of the drop that wears away the stone. But is there not ground for reflection when one reads what the laughing philosopher Zarathustra at the height of a gay science offers his fellow men as wisdom? *"Es gibt doch wenig Dinge, die so angenehm und nützlich zugleich sind, wie der Busen des Weibes."*[2] The philosopher, of course, can rediscover and express the obvious facts which the adult refuses the child.

On the basis of clinical experience, psychoanalysis has recommended sexual enlightenment as of very real assistance, but what the enlightenment presents remains a fairy tale for the affects of the child, just as the story of the stork remains a fairy tale for his intellect. Let us not forget that the stork story does offer the child something. Recently Zulliger [Hans Zulliger (1893–1965), a well-known Swiss analyst] interpreted it as follows: "The complete stork tale, as a more exact psychoanalytic examination is capable of showing, contains anal and genital birth theories (the chimney, the stove and the pond), the idea of the forceful and sadistic in connection with the acts of begetting and bearing (biting in the leg), castration idea (leg biting), the genital begetting idea (stork-bird as masculine symbol), etc."

Modern teachers forsake the symbol-filled darkness of ancient tales which combined so attractively the uncanny and the familiar, but in doing so they have no reason to be optimistic, for while replacing them with more logical interpretations expressing some facts more directly and clearly, they neglect to include even vaguely much that is more fundamentally important. Neither fairy tale nor sexual enlightenment saves the child from the necessity of a distrustful and derisive attitude toward adults, since in both cases he is left alone with his conflict.

Noteworthy in this connection is the section in The Analysis of a Phobia in a Five-Year-Old Boy where the child derides his father by means of remarks about the stork fairy tale.[3]* How dangerous must it then be when, instead of the fairy tale-telling adult or the adult who tries to carry out his theoretical duties, matters are taken in hand by the adult with pretensions of truthfulness or moral gravity.

That the adult who is questioned by a child is in the position to give interpretations seems to be only a first step forward. Above all, the adult must know that consistent and effective interpretation belongs in the realm of clinical analysis. Then, once he recognizes the twofold meaning of the child's questions, he is faced with two possibilities. He may either ignore the hidden meaning and consequently answer inadequately—perhaps even more dangerously and less adequately than the stork tale—or, disregarding the disguise of the question, he may interpret its hidden meaning, answering more than was intentionally asked. This may prove a shock for the child or, as is more probable, it will remain absolutely ineffective. And few things undermine the position of the adult more disastrously than serious but ineffective effort!

For the teacher there remains another individual problem. He must not only appreciate the sexual curiosity masquerading as desire for

---

* Sigmund Freud, "Analysis of a Phobia in a Five-Year-Old Boy" (1909), ed. Joan Reviere (London: Hogarth Press and Institute of Psycho-Analysis, 1924–50), Vol. III, 149.

knowledge, but he must make the greatest possible use of it. The child never learns more than he does at the time of disguised curiosity. At this time he learns with the coöperation of his affects, and now when he hopes finally to find out "the hidden secrets," the statement *"vita non schola discimus"* really holds good, for he is learning now for the sake of the life he dimly divines, and not for the sake of his lessons.

One might think that the teacher could make use of this situation to smuggle into his answer the sexual enlightenment that the child's questions have unconsciously requested. By general frankness he should be able to establish the certainty that there is nothing more secret about sex than about everything else. However, glimpses into the unconscious, such as described above, show that the sexual questions as they reach a complicated and dangerous point (a moment which enlightenment is supposed to guide) inhibit the desire for further questioning and the wish to learn. Softly the child speaks of the purple snail and fire engines, the food tube of the hen and the goiter that some women have. And still more softly come the inmost questions of the child which only barely make themselves heard to his inter-preter: "What about the desire and the fear of destroying, and the fear and desire of being destroyed?" With his most earnest questions, then, the child still remains alone.

Here, besides the limits established by mental and physical devel-opment, we meet an affect-barrier blocking openmindedness and readiness to learn. That which the affect has under its power is released only by means of stronger affective experience, and not by any intellectual interpretation alone. Here again the analytic situation in itself meets both requirements: it provides experience through interpretation and interpretation through experience. The teacher is only able to give a carefully selected picture of the world according to his best knowledge, and this is true also of sexual enlightenment.

However, since all early experiences disappear only to reappear later as a powerful stream, we must assume that both the infantile disappointments and the derision or surrender with which the child meets them play an important role in the unconscious life of adult human beings; that because of these childish doubts and despairs "healthy" humanity clings to its group neurosis—its conflict con-cerning knowledge and faith—just as the neurotic clings to his in-dividual symptoms. It is, therefore, not alone the attitude of the child toward the adult which is touched on by our question, but the attitude of humanity toward itself. The command which one received as a child is passed on to the coming generation, and it is the adult with the repressed doubts who unknowingly increases the confusion of unfruitful belief and knowledge in children who are desirous of learning. This is shown in a practical way by the method used by educators in selecting and arranging the material to be taught. Almost all courses of instruction, from the picture book to the study of history at the university, are as if designed to confuse man concerning his visual, perceptive, and other relationships to himself and his history. After prohibitions, doubt, revolt and surrender have helped to establish the basis of his intellectual life, it is difficult for him to direct his intelligence to the necessity of dealing with the dangers within himself; it is impossible for him to decide whether "to ask about the world or people." Deciding in favor of the first may often imply the unconscious prohibition of the second—an inhibition in thinking which will naturally also have its consequences for his conception of "the world."

A broader conception of enlightenment, the expansion of which will undoubtedly arise from psychoanalysis, is needed.

There is a footnote in Freud's Civilization and Its Discontents:

'Thus conscience does make cowards of us all. . . .' That the upbringing of young people at the present day conceals from them the part sexuality will play in their lives is not the only reproach we are obliged to bring against it. It offends too in not preparing them for the aggressions of which they are destined to become the objects. Sending the young out into life with such a false psychological orientation is as if one were to equip people going on a Polar expedition with summer clothing and maps of the Italian lakes. One can clearly see that ethical standards are being misused in a way. The strictness of these standards would not do much harm if education were to say: "This is how men ought to be in order to be happy and make others happy, but you have to reckon with their not being so." Instead of this the young are made to believe that everyone else conforms to the standard of ethics, i.e., that everyone else is good. And then on this is based the demand that the young shall be so too.[4]

About aggression as well as about sexuality the child hears at best a rationalization in the form of biological, historical, or religious purposefulness and is left alone with his own "purposeless" instinctive energies. He must feel himself alone, wicked in an apparently noble and purposeful world. He must repress the doubt born of firsthand evidence. How could we then believe that sexual enlightenment is sufficient, or, on the other hand, that all enlightenment is useless if sexual enlightenment is not sufficient? As a matter of fact the soul is a melting pot of inimical drives which urge the child from infant into adult life, forcing it through the vicious circle of guilt and expiation. The inwardly directed aggression (the most important psychic reality of civilization) is, according to Freud, best and first recognized in its sexual alloy—but not entirely to be understood in it.

Observing about ten of our twelve- and thirteen-year-old children outside of school and finding in their behavior some thought-pro-voking features, I determined to have a talk with them. Our discussion began with the explanation on the part of some of the children that much unsocial behavior lay in outbursts of rage—a rage (as they soon discovered) which was often unreasonable. Others soon became clear about the fact that this rage was inwardly directed and that it ex-cluded them from an unconcerned participation in the activities of the group. With this knowledge the analyzed and unanalyzed children then began to show an understanding which would have seemed impossible. As the opportunity arose in the discussion, I was able to give them examples from our history study which corresponded to the feelings we were speaking of. The children had learned facts about the Eskimos[5]—for example, that they have a so-called "singing con-test" instead of law court procedure, whereby the two opponents are forced to make fun of one another until the laughing observers declare one party or the other "knocked out." A little girl immediately had the correct idea: "They can do that," she declared, "because they haven't any nasty names. We would say 'pig' or 'idiot' right away and then everyone would be mad again."

Another example of applied history was offered by the story of Amundsen who, during the flight of the *Italia*, held himself strictly under Nobile's command in spite of an intense rage against the leader. In short, we discussed examples of rage, justified and unjustified, and examples of the social control of this emotion. With this ac-ceptance of rage as a general fact, that is, as something that is not merely the fault of the individual who carries it within him, a variety of thoughts began to stir in the children's minds. They spoke of aggression that is displayed and of aggression that is felt, of guilt and the desire for punishment, with an inner comprehension of which adults are hardly capable. They even discovered "civilization and its discontents" in our little progressive school. They admitted openly that their desire for punishment was not satisfied by us. One of them said, "In the other schools it was fun to pin a paper on the teacher's coat. Here there's no fun in it any more." Another declared, "We're like balls that are all ready to explode and suddenly are put into an air tight room."

Then we were able to discuss what one should do with this desire for punishment. The Puritans were mentioned—men who though expelled for their belief became the grimmest of religious tyrants as soon as they had the power to exercise tyranny. The older children discovered that their behavior towards the smaller ones represented a tendency to abreact their feelings regarding control by the teachers. This began to make it clear that valuing fairness so much more than mutual suppression, as we did, only one thing was possible—submission through understanding of the situation. Finally the children came to the conclusion that the only thing possible would be to speak often and penetratingly about the force which endangered this understanding from within until it lost its power.

Now, of course, all this is very easily said, but the reactions following such talks are not as easy to predict. This was demonstrated the next morning when, for the first time in two years, two of the older boys fought. I was reminded of Chancellor Snowden's remark at the London Conference: "Another such peace conference and we'll have war again." However, [because we knew] the neurotic condition of the two boys, it was possible to accept as a good omen the fact that they for once actually and spontaneously "went for each other."

In view of such experiences, one would think that modern education must often stand abashed before its own courage, the courage with which it hopes to lead young people, by means of good will, toward a new spirit and future peace. It is psychic reality which forces itself through, and this the more unexpectedly and unpleasantly the more it is denied. One can understand that many are panic-stricken and, as it were, throw to the winds the ideal of the primacy of intelligence.

Freud has written that an increasing sense of guilt must accompany the development of culture. It is certain that (wherever the temptation to forget what has already been learned is withstood) education will become increasingly understanding. However, experience and theory teach that the feeling of being loved and understood does not diminish the strength of the feelings of guilt but rather increases them, and this brings about an economic discrepancy similar to that discovered by Freud in sexual life when he found that the development of culture had brought with it a shift in the unconscious evaluation of sexuality which made worthless both of the conscious alternatives—asceticism or living out one's nature. The only remedy for this upset economy is to make unconscious material conscious, and to prevent the accumulation of unconscious material by continuous enlightenment. Apparently pedagogy now faces a similar problem in the question of aggression, guilt and desire for punishment, and perhaps here, too, steps taken toward suppression or liberation will not really touch the heart of the problem.

Perhaps a new education will have to arise which will provide enlightenment about the entire world of affects and not only about one special instinct which, in an otherwise entirely rationalized outlook of life, appears too obscure. This would imply a presentation of life in which the omnipresent instincts "without usefulness" (in reality the instinctive urge that opposes all "use") would no longer be denied. It is this denial which brings about the hopeless isolation of the world of children with their conflicts.

This isolation, it is true, is frequently overcome, but often only apparently. But the general fact, that the inner enemy is left concealed in darkness instead of having light focused upon him, gives him the power time and again to overthrow the sound will of the individual and the best-made plans of well-meaning leaders.

> Certainly men are like this, but have you asked yourself whether they need be so, whether their inmost nature necessitates it? Can an anthropologist give the cranial index of a people whose custom it is to deform their children's heads by bandaging them from their earliest years? Think of the distressing contrast between the radiant intelligence of a healthy child and the feeble mentality of the average adult.[6]

It is surely no coincidence that the desire for a science of education should appear on the scene at the moment when, in the form of psychoanalysis, the truth of the healing power of self-knowledge is again establishing itself in the world. And to this truth much has been added since the time of Socrates, namely, a method. If education earnestly seeks to rebuild on a new conscious basis of knowledge and intelligence, then it must demand radical progress to the point where clear vision results in human adjustment. Modern enlightenment can best achieve this through psychoanalysis.

Notes

[1] In the [*Zeitschrift für psychoanaly tische Pädagogik*] V. 7, Dr. Edith Buxbaum describes an experiment with a class of 10–11 year old girls of a public school in Vienna, to whom the liberty was given of asking any questions they wanted to. The girls as a group behaved almost exactly and literally like the questioning Richard. With the first questions they tried to cling to things which led far away, such as telephone, airplane, Zeppelin: "What is it like when you fly up into the sky, on and on, straight ahead?" Then came the opposite direction, "And if you bore down into the earth?," which led them to dangerous questions—"Why don't the stars fall down,?" to lightning on earthquake. The latter was explained by one girl as coming when "things which don't get along together bump underneath." One girl's question: "Why do you feel your heart beat?" was unanimously disapproved of by the class. And still they seemed to be waiting for something. When a birl asked: *"Wie berwegt sich der Mensch?"* ("How do men move?", half the class understood: *"Wie entsteht der Mensch?"* ("How are men made?")—and giggled. But finally they admitted just as Richard did: "After all, we would rather ask about people."

[2] "Indeed there are few things which are at the same time as pleasant and as useful as a woman's bosom."

[3] Though it seems rather hopeless to succeed in giving children the biological truth while they are concerned with the reality of affects, little Hans's case shows the importance of letting children express repeatedly, in conversation and play, their questions about, and their conceptions of, the world. The history of little Hans proves that more than half the battle is won when the child succeeds in expressing itself.

[4] Sigmund Freud, *Civilization and Its Discontents* (New York: Jonathon Cape and Harrison Smith, 1930), 123–24.

[5] Included under project work directed by Dr. Peter Blos.

[6] Sigmund Freud, *The Future of an Illusion*, tr. W. D. Robson-Scott, (London: Hogarth Press and Institute of Psycho-Analysis, 1928), 81–82.

Children's Picture Books (1931)

At our Montessori seminar we reviewed a number of highly diverse picture books. Our ultimate impression was that on the whole, they constitute a small, circumscribed world that reflects the big real world—with specific distortions. This I would like to document in psychological terms although the great variety of books may at first be confusing. We looked at the ominous *Struwelpeter* with its magical drawings, the pictures of toys in powerful colors, and some of those strange pages that delicately render a pale, sweet, mimosalike world.

Aside from all these, one bright genre of writing shone clear: the irresistible humor of *Max and Moritz* and *Adamson*. These books are not aimed directly at children; their mature humor addresses any receptive human being. We will discuss them later.

Let me first single out a critical word that I hear frequently. *Struwelpeter* is supposedly "sadistic." Yet this adjective must have a somewhat different meaning when applied to a different type of book. I am referring to a picture book that seeks to deplore animal torture by showing a tortured creature on every page. Obviously such de-

Paper given at the House of Children, Vienna, 1930. First published in *Zeitschrift für Psychoanalytische Pädagogik*, 5 (1931) 13–19 under the name of Erik Homburger. Translated from German especially for this volume by Joachim Neugroschel.

pictions tend to stir up cruel impulses rather than revulsion. *Struwelpeter*, in contrast, presents not only scenes in which a creature (a creature identifiable with the child reader) is tormented but also some in which a child is punished. We all expect that any reader will identify with the hero of a book. So we may conclude that the children reading this book feel punished when Struwelpeter is punished, and we know how lasting such an impact can be, and how unforgettable the perverse enjoyment. Even terrified children return to this book.

We recognize here two interpretations of the word "sadistic": not only "cruel to others" but also "cruel to oneself"—a far more dangerous interpretation, as we shall soon understand. For cruelty to others is checked by the strength of those other living creatures, who defend themselves. But what is it that curbs the paradoxical tendency to be cruel to oneself? I will say a few things about this later on, for it seems to me that if we condemn certain effects, we should try to recognize their root causes. Otherwise, they will return along unforeseen paths.

We ask ourselves: Why is it that adults draw cruel or childish pictures for children's books? And why do children feel joy and comfort at seeing themselves depicted as punished or excessively childish and saccharine? If we tell the artist that he doesn't know how a child sees the world, he will merely cite the appeal of his drawings and suggest that artists probably know more about children than we do. This seems to be true in some way, and we have to try to find the common ground that draws them together, the artist and the child.

I would like to digress for a moment and point to certain medieval paintings that are not difficult to find. In some depictions of the Mother of God or the Holy Family we see, among the mature, tender human faces, that the countenance of the little Savior or other children are strangely distorted: ill; somewhat embryolike; somewhat senile. One might initially believe that the Christ Child was meant to be depicted as an "old infant," mature at birth and childlike in death. Yet we cannot help feeling that here the adult artist, ascetically and mystically earnest about the true nature of childhood, has unconsciously shrunk back, refusing to recognize a child as he really is. The manner of distorting the child in order to contrast him with the Holy Mother is a special problem. What we are looking for in this phenomenon is one more symptom of a conclusion that forces itself upon us in picture books, too: that there is a general tendency to distort, to deny childhood.

In reality the very young infant certainly evinces nothing of this. He delights in himself and in the growing radius of his movements and impulses. His psyche seems to say, "This is good," to everything that he produces with his body and perceives with his senses. And he is used to having the big people (the powerful adults on whose love he depends) applaud his behavior—until he reaches an age at which he can be educated. Now, when he comes out with his most genuine and favorite behavior, adults more and more often state emphatically, "You mustn't do that. We won't love you when you're like that." Thus the child learns that certain action is not generally lovable. He has to find some way of maintaining his old self-love (which is necessary for human survival) while also keeping the love of adults, which he needs just as badly.

This solution operates (according to the research of psychoanalysis) as follows: The child condemns some of his impulses on his own; by some enigmatic mechanism, he internally develops an authority that appropriates and represents the prohibitions of adults. One part of his ego is transformed—psychoanalysis then calls it the superego—and repudiates the part that remains as it was originally. The positive aspect of this development is that the prohibiting part, too, belongs to the child's mind, representing the prohibition as his own desire, with which his self-love can side. But such disparate self-love survives at the price of one's inner unity.

The child likes himself now insofar as he, like the adult, has learned to watch over his thoughts and deeds. Thus he develops an often puzzling mechanism deciding what is "good, well behaved," and he enjoys picture books in which good children are rewarded and bad ones punished. And so it comes about that while he may very recently have hated much younger children, whom he saw as rivals, he now finds them "sweet, cute," at the urging of his inner authority, and enjoys sweet picture books that we would find silly and would rather keep away from him.

However, the adult who drew these pictures for him long ago went through the same transformation and experienced something highly important to boot: He then forgot what had happened. " 'I did this,' my memory says. 'I cannot possibly have done this,' my pride says, and remains adamant. Finally, the memory gives in" (Nietzsche). Thus, repressed childhood wishes are replaced by paradisiacal surrogate images or moralistic prejudices, as though one had been born a well-behaved creature. The adult (impelled by some urgent memory) feels the desire to draw a picture book for the child. He either establishes good and evil in his book or makes up a world of such doll-like infantility that it is without punishment only because it has no drives. Because of this connection, I can explain why I initially refused to be distracted by the difference between the punishing books and those books that use a delicate or schematic depiction to strip the world of flesh and blood. The former books show the world as threatening and advise caution; the latter advise capitulating immediately to the threat by behaving like a doll or a delicate mimosa, the kind of child so many adults like to see.

The advantages in the mechanism of conscience formation are obvious: The child catches up in a short time with thousands of years of upbringing. The natural creature of drives turns into a being with a twentieth-century conscience. The entire heritage ready for this development is now manifest. And the energy underlying the first instinctual expressions is now employed for purposes of general usefulness; it is integrated in mankind's efforts to endure its alienation from nature and to compensate for it. People accept this development without further ado, saying, "A normal child doesn't suffer all that much from this process."

I must therefore introduce the fact that the disadvantages of this process present us with our actual theme, leading us directly to an important pedagogical problem. For these disadvantages are great as they pile up with the growth of civilization. They threaten to turn into the mountain with which modern education, after a bold approach, finds itself unable to cope.

Let me repeat what we have said: A child can be educated because of a split in his mental makeup. Under the pressure of the alternative—forgoing love and protection—between remaining what *he* is or becoming like the adult in order to please *him*, the child undergoes a transformation in the psyche. An inner voice arises, taking over the prohibitions of the adult milieu and making sure that the child's instinctual energy is tamed and, whenever necessary, punished for unruliness. This authority, as we have said, censors all memories of the original and now-condemned world of the senses. The page of the psyche is blank again—not because nothing was written on it but because the censor has meticulously pasted over the primeval writing.

Now we have only to emphasize the distinct differences between the external prohibiting power and the internally established authority in order to recognize the danger of this inward shift. The internal authority becomes an absolute dictate and no longer a human being. A human being sees in another only what circumstances allow him to see: seldom his thoughts; never his unconscious feelings. But the conscience apprehends everything and finds even the most unconscious things punishable. A human being can be lenient when he sees that his prohibitions go too far or are made invalid by changed conditions. But the inner dictate is not the likeness of such a changeable person; it is *only* the reflection of his earlier, perhaps joyless and unperceptive admonition. (How many perceptive now-modern parents suddenly find themselves unable to cope with their overconscientious child, who is stuck in old ideals! They would gladly erase, modify, revoke, yet their earlier image in the child's mind is stronger than their living voice.) The overseverity with which this reflection in his psyche keeps the original part under constraint, this overseverity, that demands and prohibits, receives then additional support, which only an inner authority can accept. The cruel and deadly hatred that the small infant once aimed at the overpowerful adults is even internalized in the course of his capitulation, and since the child must despair of any resistance, his hatred is turned against his own flagging inner world. For no mobilized strength remains dormant: It rages inwardly as soon as the mind's eye perceives even an unconscious stirring of drive intensification. It harms us in a thousand possibilities of obvious or concealed self-punishment and self-degradation, illness and inhibition. And if it is not visible in flagrant symptoms, it is at least sensed in what Freud calls the "discontent of civilization," a malaise shared by us all.

In order to explain this dangerous self-directed sadism of the soul, I have introduced a small piece of psychoanalytical theory, to show in how many different connections such moralistic renderings as *Struwelpeter* can be called sadistic. For what is expresed as moralistic cruelty against others is merely a reflection of the effects of that internal sadistic impulse. As for the person who "moralizes" against others, we may assume that he presumably keeps his own instinctual impulses calm only by means of heavy fetters.*

Let us look back once more at the humorous picture books that we set aside before. What is the appealing ingredient in the depiction of human nastiness and human misfortune: humor. We can focus on

---

* I hardly need mention that as we review some picture books, we stumble upon numerous psychological essentials that I must leave aside here: the symbols in the depiction; the style of depictive manner itself, the fairy-tale element in picture books; and fairy tales in general.

a page in *Adamson*, the appeal of which to children is well known to you all. Adamson wants to smoke. But his better self, which (identifiable by its angel wings) stands behind him, takes the cigar from his mouth and throws it out the window. For a moment the Adamson self is stunned, but then it races downstairs and catches the cigar before it has reached the ground. Rebellion has acted faster than conscience and the force of gravity. Immoral? Yet the most conscientious person laughs.

"The wonderful thing [about humor] is obviously the victoriously defended invulnerability of the ego. The ego refuses to be offended and forced to suffer by any provocation in reality. It insists on not letting the traumas of the outer world get too close for comfort; indeed, it shows that they are merely an occasion for pleasure" (Freud).

Several external features of the Adamson figure show to what great extent it depicts the child in a human being, the infantile ego, which has to struggle with hindrances, prohibitions, and accidents. In the ratio of his head size to his torso Adamson is a childlike figure; he has a big hat, like a little child acting grownup; he is always alone; he has no manly adventures. And his adversaries, human beings ("the big man"), all are taller than he to the same degree that an adult is taller than a child.

How does humor speak through the depiction of this sly, struggling ego? It confronts the nasty superego with a kindly laugh, which says, "Just look, this is what the world is like, even though it appears dangerous. Child's play, just good enough to be joked about" (Freud).

We now can look through what is so liberating about these books: For an instant they relieve the ego of the pressure of the superego. Max and Moritz and Adamson are stupidly sly and cruel, as all of us feel we are at some point. But humor smiles at this, and we smile, too. We like ourselves a bit more and perform some tiny detail better than we would have managed without that bright moment.

On the other hand, there is probably nothing that forces us more to sin and do wrong than the constraint of an oversevere conscience. True, the development of the superego may be what shapes our civilization and its powerful characteristics, but the sense of guilt and the need for punishment can go beyond the usefulness of this process. They not only inhibit but can also hinder any improvement on, or restitution of, mistakes. And with the increase today of decent and peaceful ideals and of social awareness, mankind's heritage of guilt threatens to be renewed in every individual, for it more and more sharply contradicts the primal language of the drives, and with sternness of upbringing, it becomes more and more cruel to the ego. Therefore, human psyches increase both their tension and hypertension. We also notice that all the emancipations (whether sexual, political, or religious) toward which our era is striving fail sooner or later as they are overcome by the discontent in our civilization. They thus become retrogressive, simply repeating earlier patterns. Emancipators are apt to reckon without the superego.

Educators, however, insofar as they are willing to orient themselves psychologically, should certainly not proceed without counting on this factor. Here I call to attention an admirable element in Signora Montessori's work. We hear about it every day in the House of Children. The equipment surrounding us is arranged in a way that automatically and matter-of-factly points out the child's mistakes. The teacher is supposed quietly to leave the child who is as yet unable to perform his task alone and, if necessary, simply to supply an easier task. The process of educating the child is made "foolproof," as it were, by a sympathetic observance of this rule: The two superegos, the teacher's and the pupil's, are kept apart while the child's superego is still labile. A growing severity should preferably not adhere to his very first intellectual efforts. But the question of which strains on the superego formation we can spare the child without weakening the strength of his conscience—that is the problem of psychologically oriented pedagogy.

Montessori's solution is part of a system based on a rare combination of intuition and science. It is harder for *us* to draw individual practical conclusions from psychological research. Let us make sure that we are not again overzealous in allowing our lawmaking superego to assert itself. For example, should we simply suppress picture books and fairy tales* without further ado because we consider them dangerous? We can do so, but we should also know that an isolated action can be without significance. A child who is frightened by a picture book has already been disturbed and has merely been waiting for a chance to express it. But this opportunity he has everywhere in today's world, for anything to be found in fairy tales is also to be

---

* Since I have digressed to the parallel problem of fairy tales, I would like to reestablish the distance. The folk-fairy tale is related to the picture book by common use. But it is essentially remote from the picture book in terms of history and art. We must clearly distinguish the utterances of the modern person who deals with a child by the use of those fables that have trickled down through (and have virtually been filtered by) centuries and generations. Like humor, they appeal, with their reconciliatory strength, to all human beings, not just children, and they possess the magically solid form that has always been the higher condition for a comforting touch on the stern unconscious.

found in the air around us. The educator, however, has to know *what* is happening when the child is unable to tolerate some tendencies in certain books; he should investigate and become familiar with methods of recognizing the prevailing psychological symptoms. He may then refuse to offer books that are in any sense sadistic to an already frightened or easily frightened child. But that is an issue of pedagogic therapy rather than of pedagogy itself.

In order to get at purely pedagogical considerations, we still need one general reflection, with which I would like to conclude. The child pays less attention to the adult's actions than to the inner tension behind them. Whatever behavior we adopt toward the child, it has less influence than our real impulses—whether or not we have tried to suppress them. Children (like animals) can sniff the real essence through any surface: the cruel of kind, the strong or insecure tendency. If we wish to bring up a child harshly or kindly, suggestively or by merely observing, we must, above all, be able to do so inwardly. That is, it has to correspond to the relationship between our own ego and superego. This relationship is the crux of any effort to create a truly different environment for a child.

The Fate of the Drives
in School Compositions
(1931)

Foreword

The school essays of adolescents that are discussed here are from the collection of Mrs. Dorothy Burlingham, who founded a little school years ago in Vienna.[1] Several times a year she would ask the children to write freely about a given question. For instance: "What do you want to be when you grow up if you had a free choice?"; "How would you like to raise your children?"; or "What would you do if you were suddenly alone in the world (you perhaps had no parents) and had to take care of yourself from now on?" The question did not have to be answered too literally; Mrs. Burlingham (*die Schulmutter*) explained each time that a story (or fairy tale) was also welcome. Thus encouraged, the children let themselves go and followed their impulses and wishes beyond the confines of a usual school essay.

The answers to the third question, particularly, led us to search for the inner connections between the earlier and later writings of these children and to try to understand their meaning in a psychoan-

A longer version of this paper was first published in *Zeitschrift für psychoanalytische Pädagogik*, 5 (1931), 417–45 under the name of Erik Homburger. Translated from German especially for this volume by Inge Schneier Hoffmann.

alytic framework. For the third question, for example, a number of children allowed themselves a striking digression: They launched into such a detailed description of their fantasies of their parents' death that they lost sight of the point of the original question. Twelve children described the death of fifteen parents. Only six of these had died peaceful deaths, three had been murdered; four had died accidentally; two had ended in jail. Thus (as Nietzsche might say), maybe the children chose to write about what they wanted to be *free of* rather than what they wanted to be *free for*.

The question obviously arises: Have these children been influenced by psychoanalysis? As it happens, several had undergone a child analysis; others had little idea of psychoanalysis. On the other hand, only a psychoanalyst would notice a difference in the way in which these children handled their fantasies. What the analyst discovers, if he himself has analyzed one of these children, is quite interesting: The unconscious seems to express itself in a such a naïve manner as if it had never been touched by psychoanalysis; however, the symbols the children produce confirm the findings and therapeutic results of psychoanalysis. So we seem to find corroboration of Freud's afterthought, his remark made at the end of his first (indirect) child analysis (indirect, since the subject being analyzed was an adult recalling childhood)—namely, that the children forgot the analysis just as adults forget their dreams. One can analyze one's dream at night with the intention of using it consciously on awakening, but "in the morning, dream and analysis are forgotten."

I. The Bright-Eyed One

A girl of eleven laughs merrily when the theme is given, (question 3) as if to say, "Now I'll show you!" Then she writes:

> Once in spring, I got spring fever. All I wanted was to look out the school window to see whether the sky was still blue and whether the buds had already burst. I was so excited. After school I ran off and let my hair fly behind me. That was so beautifully cooling. At home I gulped my food quickly, pulled on my sandals, no socks at all, and ran out over a lovely green lawn. The bees buzzed, and the butterlies fluttered from one flower to another. I stormed all over the lawn and threw myself on the cool, moist grass. I rolled around and squinted into the sun and did not move for a long time, but I was baked like a pudding. As I lay there, a little rabbit hopped over and wiggled his snub nose. I stretched out my

hand and caressed him a bit. Suddenly I saw a horse running as wildly as I had done. So I jumped up and over to the horse and onto his back. And it stormed away. Throughout gallop and gallop, through racing and trot, I sat on the horse, but then I fell down and stretched my arms and legs in the burning spring sun. The bees hummed and buzzed, and the red sun shone through my lids . . . I awakened and looked around me.

Here she notices that she's gone a bit too far—for a little girl her age. And defiantly she adds in the margin, "That would be the way to get a bit toughened, just what my mother does not allow!" For, as she feels it, it is the prohibitions of Mother that are overridden in this flight into nature, simple commonplace prohibitions—One mustn't gulp down one's meal; one mustn't go without socks and roll in moist grass—but also a less clear and more dangerous taboo: against stroking a rabbit and dreaming of a masterful steed. Illicit in any case; the whole tone rings with the will toward unharnessed feelings and not the will to toughen up, as the girl tries to make the indulgent teacher (and reader) believe.

For the rest we shall note a detail. The first of the impetuously realized wishes is to let her hair fly loose. Now, on another occasion, the teacher heard that the child had had unusually beautiful hair that her mother had shortened. This loss is said to have made an inexplicably profound impression on the young girl; for a long time it was the focus of all resentment against her mother. Can it be accidental that the first event of this rebellion is to let the hair fly loose?

Another time she writes: "I would like to have as many children as possible. They shall not be so swaddled in diapers and covers when they are little. That's really too hot and sticky."

And then, with her mother in mind:

Before I have children, I would love to travel crazily: to Italy and Greece, to Egypt, Siberia, and Africa. I would also like to carve wood. I would like to grow very old, so as to see what happens afterward, and then, if I die, I'd like to be told afterward everything that I didn't know on earth. Then I'd like to return to earth every 1,000 years to visit everything new that has happened. I'd like to have a glass house.

So here is another wish, imagined, like the earlier ones, as limitless: *Looking!* But here, too, she becomes frightened: "I hope my husband will approve, if not, then woe is me!" For she thinks someone will always fill the role of the no-sayer.

Besides, she wishes to reproduce, not just to look; she wants to carve wood. In fact, the child is highly talented in drawing and painting. Her productions are round and cheerful, like her handwriting and her sentences.

The third time, we hear a little story in answer to the (same third) question of what she would do if she were suddenly on her own:

> The story is about a family that's very well off; they have two cars and riding horses at their disposal. They have a girl, about fourteen years old who was very vain about her long, curly hair. Then came bad luck: The father had an accident, became an invalid, was debt-ridden, drank, and ended in jail. The girl's first idea was to rush out to the edge of the city to pick many flowers and sell them. While her mother searched for work, she picked flowers, huge bunches, and tied them together with her gorgeous hair. Then she ran back, asking her way again and again, until she arrived exhausted at home. On the next day she tried unsuccessfully to sell the bouquets. Only one man came, asked for a few flowers, and gave two pennies. He told her she had splendid hair and could get a whole lot of money if she sold it. She thought, "That's a good idea," and ran across the street to the hairdresser and asked if he wanted her hair. "Oh, what lovely hair you have, but it is dirty. Let me wash it and then I'll buy it." She was given a very small sum, with which she ran to her mother, who was so happy and who found her daughter clever and kind.

So the theme of hair has reappeared, in a more weighty form. But we are left to deal with a puzzle: The girl who feels her mother has robbed her of her hair tells a story of a child who sacrifices her hair for her mother's sake.

A connection can be made between the first and third fantasy, albeit only thematic to begin with, but where does the second one fit? It contains the wish to look as well as the desire to create and reminds us that the girl has outstanding artistic gifts. Seeing the themes of "artist" and "hair" next to each other, however, immediately suggests a somewhat vulgar association. Many artists seem to value their hair and to set themselves clearly apart from other people by their haircuts. We might call it a cult of the self, a kind of narcissism, which they reveal in this way. Following this idea further, we note that it isn't necessarily the particular acts of personal vanity that document the narcissism of the artist; he has, after all, in his works a grander way of lifting the image of his being to the level of cultural refinement for all to share. And the very charm of a work of art and of the artist himself is undoubtedly attributable to that "self-sufficiency and inaccessability" that Freud saw as the attraction of the child, the animal, and the narcissistic woman, a parcel of sovereignty that does not tolerate any reduction. Still, we know from the lives of artists the setback, the kind of despair into which an artist is driven just when he has expressed his self-love most triumphantly, more triumphantly than his own culturally inhibited soul can bear, given its fear of its own hubris.[2]

In a long life an artist may experience this polar oscillation repeatedly and give form to this alternating despair and exuberance again and again. But confronted with a short life and a serene, luminous body of work like Raphael's or Mozart's, human opinion concludes that the dream of being the darling of beauty can't last long.

I find this theme in the first fantasies of the young girl, if, of course, on an infantile level: unlimited surrender to one's feelings and to nature as their soothing complement and then sudden fright. Her fright, however, springs not from the force of Providence, nor is it a pang of conscience that warns from within; no, it is Mother who prevents her from acting on her sensual desires. That Mother cut her hair was the most active example of how she opposes all cravings; it struck at the girl's strongest wish: to find herself beautiful and to allow others to admire her. If I were to follow our little girl and her problems along this path, which begins with her vehement and vulnerable self-love and then proceeds along many branching trails into the pathological and the musical domains, then I must admit that just this path of the gifted loses itself in dark paths as yet to be illuminated by psychological research, while narcissistic illness is being approached by psychoanalysis with better prospects in view.

About talent, psychoanalysis so far has had little to say. Still, we find some road signs among the works of I. Hermann. He writes in the *Zeitschrift für psychoanaytische Pädagogik* (this journal), vol. IV, 11–12: "If we direct our attention . . . to the complex of physical beauty and to what in my experience is the necessary spark of the talent for drawing, we find that in many cases the artist was indeed beautiful, especially in childhood. One outstanding painter (a patient) was so beautiful as a child that pregnant women would come to feast their eyes on him."

Did hair play an important role in the childhood of his patients? Hermann doesn't say. Therefore, I'll add the story of a little boy's fate which seems somewhat analogous to the little girl's. Unusually beautiful as a child, this boy noticed in particular that people admired his full head of hair. When his mother had it all cut off, he thought he had lost all his charm, and in fact, he did eventually because of all his grieving. Later he became gifted in drawing.

Absalom, the narcissist of the Bible, darling of his father yet rebel against him, would not let go of his hair. Only when it became too heavy to support did he have it cut and weighed to the applause of onlookers. Much admired, he sought posthumous fame through a memorial column for himself, a very unusual gesture among his people. In the end, however, his long hair became his doom (*Verhängnis!*); in a battle against his father he was hanged by his hair in the branches of a tree and was killed. The people celebrated the death of the insurgent whom they had previously encouraged with their applause, but David, his father, wailed his grief—until one of David's loyal followers spoke the bitter truth: "Were only Absalom alive and all the rest of us dead today, you would find it fitting." Thus is self-love punished, says the Bible, but see how ineradicable is the power of those beings who manage to carry the certainty of their childish self-love throughout adulthood. For people are constantly uncertain about whether they should be admiring or outraged (people admire what succeeds) when one among them reveals his impulsive drives for all to see, the very same impulses that had been buried within them early by taboos and feelings of guilt. The insurgent Absalom apparently had little sense of guilt. His upbringing had failed to fit him for a patriarchal society.

Also, for those who want to "elevate" the narcissism which, in any case, they cannot give up and even for those artistically gifted people who manage to raise their narcissism into the musical sphere where self-love clothed in beauty may silence the conscious judgement of others, it will still be an open question whether this self transcendence will entirely work for them or whether their efforts will yet be weighed down by strains of vanity—and illness.

Here a fundamental question arises, before which we must halt, but let us envisage it. Both the little girl and the little boy who are gifted in drawing have been subjected to a mother's interference with their sense of beauty. Can this experience be viewed as a positive factor in the development of their talent? Is it a loss by which artistic effort will be spurred—in compensation?

Here it is worth rereading a passage from Goethe's memoirs (cited by Hermann). He describes how painful Goethe's disfigurement by smallpox had been for him. "Particularly one of my lively aunts who used to adore me before could scarcely see me in later years without crying out: 'Horrors! (Pfui Tenfel!) Cousin, how ugly he has become!' Then she would tell me how she had previously found me adorable and what excitement she'd create when she'd carry me around to show off to others. . . ." One is tempted to see the mother behind the mocking, rejecting aunt in this example. As a matter of fact, Goethe, the great poet, was also a talented artist in drawing. Hermann speaks of his occasional "regression to artistic expression" when Goethe would turn to drawing at those times when a woman had disappointed him.

In fact, the children about whom I am writing are not yet "creative" but merely very talented at drawing. The alternative to our question is: Perhaps the experience of belittlement of their awareness of their own beauty does not contribute to the development of their talent but may yet limit it.

Hermann makes the interesting point that although Goethe provides the psychoanalytic researcher with material from his youth that might relate to his artistic talent, and although Leonardo, in turn, provides such material about his poetic and scientific gifts, both fail to throw light on their central achievement the radiance of which has enveloped mankind.

As to a straight *sense of guilt*, the scope and manifestation of which we might recognize in the stories of the little girl, Freud (in his *Civilization and Its Discontents*, [London, 1930]) recognizes two kinds. The first grows out of a "fear of parental authority," an authority that suddenly forbids tendencies which only a short while ago were displayed with the praise of the elders. This memory and occasional lapses create guilt in the form of a fear of losing protective love. But a greater guilt lies ahead for the little creature when acceding to the pressure at last, he has made the adult's demands his own and thus acquired a conscience of his own. Then, when the drives (*Triebe*) rebel nonetheless, the child's own judgment stands up against them, and one feels so incomprehensibly guilty; who will punish him now since the external authority doesn't even know about it or is no longer present? Subjected to this tension, man seeks punishment from fate; he needs the punishment of God and the world to satisfy his nagging conscience. He needs to humiliate himself, needs to make himself ill—or to remain "stupid."

The fear of authority, which is a simple form of guilt, is what we see in our little girl's first two fantasies. These say: "I want this and that, but Mother won't allow it." The need to be punished, which is connected with a more complicated form of guilt, is expressed in the last fantasy. By making this connection we can solve the puzzle of this curious story.

The little girl rebels no longer; she *sacrifices* what she loves most. The rigor of this renunciation clearly indicates the difference between the "fear of authority" and the "fear of one's own conscience." Would the mother ever have demanded the sacrifice of the hair had she suspected what this meant to the child? In reality—and from an aesthetic and practical point of view—she had merely sacrificed a few curls that to her seemed of no significance. Why, then, is the child's conscience—after all, a part of her very self—so much crueler afterward? It is because (according to Freud's view her conscience has inherited an idle aggression from another part of herself: hatred against the no-saying authority. This hatred is condemned to the unconscious, where it does battle and eventually submits to the ego ideal: the ego is now overwhelmed and used by the superego against itself. Now we understand why the fantasies of the little girl (which represent a more primitive period of her development) reveal her in the first story as a proud being.

Yet the puzzle of the sacrifice would still not be solved if we did not also discover the gratification hidden within it. Just as we could say about the artist that he withdraws behind his art even while offering an image of himself in his work, so does the little girl present herself to the eyes of her public through her hair, as if to say, "See, this is how beautiful I am." And an audience imagined by her will accept what the real people around her will no longer grant. The very words which have barely awakened feelings of triumph immediately dim it by devaluating the desires of the child, saying, "How beautiful is your hair! But it is dirty."

This theme of "sacrifice of hair" is of some historic significance, which urges us to heed the symbolism of the hair, for we know that the unconscious harbors the meaning of old customs and develops them. However, few symbols are so difficult to focus on, for its emphasis swings alternately toward raising the value of the woman and toward raising the value of the man. What applies equally to both appears to be this: gender value, beauty, and fecundity. Finally, the body itself announces its ripeness for procreation through the secondary sex characteristics of hair growth.

As a symbol of fecundity, hair seems to come closest also to expressing the value of the artistically creative person. Only when we approach the idea of maternity do the symbols become harder to grasp—an experience that the sciences of history share with those of the soul.

There actually were hair sacrifices in history. More recently it is the church that demands the offering of hair as a sign of final commitment. In Sparta girls' heads were shaved before their wedding night; experts consider this a remanant of the ancient Aphrodite cult. Sacrifice of one's hair seems to have been a redemption of the earlier obligation to satisfy the cult of prostitution for the temple.

Thus psychoanalysis has noted first that hair is a symbol for a payment to be made. In this interpretation sacrifice of hair may also signify the redemption from castration, or for women, at any rate, hair belongs to the realm of symbolic representations concerned with being a man or not being a man. I believe, however, that a continuing search along the scope of Freud's findings will do more justice to the wider meaning of such a symbol. Freud himself, when speaking of his new insights into the preoedipal phases of female sexuality, compares the astonishment which these ideas created with the alarmed surprise with which classical scholars greeted the discovery that before Greek culture there had been a Minoan-Cretan one.

II. The Adolescent

A wordless prelude illuminates the state of a fourteen-year-old as he is about to write his first "free school composition."

The other children had already gone to their rooms. But this boy was still standing, lost in dreams, in the schoolyard, ever again tossing his knife so hard against a wooden wall that it stuck there. He answered my call reluctantly. At his desk he grabbed the first sheet of paper and drew on it with hard strokes. Then he pushed the sheet carelessly aside. I looked at it; on it was an erect male organ which, because of its angularity, appeared like a curious symbol of aggression, probably made unrecognizable for the dreamy boy himself.

After the theme was given, he sat for a long time without doing anything and chewed on his pen. Suddenly he shot up, asked for permission to speak, and asked his teacher, "Can one say, 'Today Father is somewhat nervous'?" The teacher declared this grammatically correct. Thereupon inner excitement and external stimulus met on this bridge of words. The story:

It is evening. Father Alfred comes home and is as nervous as he usually never is. He has two children: one girl—eighteen—who also goes to work, and another girl, four.

At six the next morning the father and the [mother]³ older daughter get up and go to work. The father arrives at [school] the factory fifteen minutes late and has five percent of his salary deducted. The [child] little girl wakes up and realizes that her mother is not awakening her. So she gets up, dresses, eats a piece of bread, and goes to school. The [father] elderly man who comes every day suddenly hears someone scream in the apartment. He goes in and sees the [mother] the old woman lying on the⁴ covered with blood. Now she's no longer screaming—she is dead. The father is brought home from work. An investigation ensues. It turns out that the father (who as we know arrived at the factory late) returned home again and murdered the mother. Despite his denial he was "condemned to life imprisonment."

This part is stylistically simple reportage, and at the end the whole story is crossed out. Only a finale is kept, short and punitive as it is: "The only remaining relatives the children now had left were very stingy and said the children should feed themselves."

To get at some of the unconscious meaning in this story, we will concentrate on its most obvious feature: the deletions, first, of single words and, finally, of the whole text. The eliminated words are "mother," "school," "child," "father," and "mother." For a boy whose whole life is spent in school or around his closest relatives, these words are surely not irrelevant. Nor are they accidentally rejected. The eradication, at first, of single words proves that he attempted to avoid such in intrusion of the unconscious. It is probable, then, that each time he describes an imaginary family an association to his own family intervenes—and is suppressed. Thus the final crossing out of the whole story can be seen as the recognition (at some level) that the thoughts he had attempted to avoid had sneaked in after all and could be denied only along with the whole story.

In the family of our adolescent figure: the father, the mother, the older sister (with whom he shares part of the way to school), a younger brother, and he himself. The story, however, refers only to father, mother, older sister, and younger sister. The author is seemingly missing. Yet in all these stories it is easy to recognize the writer in the main character even when he appears in the third person. When the boy tells us by mistake that the father went to "school," he only confirms that he feels he is (also) the father in the story. When he mistakenly sends the "mother" (instead of the sister) along with the father on his way (to work), he has confused the constellation of a (family) pair because his feelings are unclear. Once he is that uncertain, he can no longer deny his younger brother's existence simply by replacing "mother" with the word "child." He replaces it with "little girl." Perhaps we go too far when we suspect that he almost had the "father" discover the murder—the very person who was supposed to have committed the crime. But that the word "mother" is unbearable and has to be replaced by the neutral "old woman" strengthens our assumption of a dangerous thought process involving the writer's next of kin. To summarize: The boy is, in this fantasy, the father and the murderer of the mother.

What "murderer" means in the language of his unconscious the boy has more clearly and naïvely expressed in a story he wrote two years earlier[5]:

> I often went on little digs—and once I found a stick which appeared very weird to me. There are so many different kinds of sticks, but this one in particular struck me very much. I went to my room, looked at it more closely, and saw nothing remarkable. In the evening my wife came home. "Well, did you find something again?" she asked me. I said, "No." Once in bed[6] she said, "How shall we live, then, if you don't find anything?" and she was in such a rage that she went to bed. While she was asleep, I sneaked around, took the stick which I had found, and beat her on her brain with it. She shook a little, and then it was over. The neighbors did notice something, though, and notified the police. The police came and asked me where my wife was. I said, "She's sleeping." But they didn't believe me, and I had to lead them to my bedroom. On the chair lay the stick. They asked me, "What's this stick?" "That's a stick which I found on one of my digs." They looked at my wife and said that she was well. They left again. I was happy. I realized that my stick had magic in it. So I have not murdered my wife after all. The two of us lived happily with our magic wand until we died.

Thus the wish, which seems more tolerable to his conscience disguised as murder, is to do something sexual to the woman. Together with the urges of his awakening potency, there exist fantasies of early childish-sadistic origin, when sexual union was suspected to be something destructive, an idea that was partly welcomed and partly repressed. These urges change the desire for possession into something furious, childishly raging, which is defensively projected onto the woman. It is she who went to bed in a rage; no wonder one gets so enraged oneself. Consequently what one then does seems neither free from being dreadful guilt nor close enough to what adults really seem to do to one another. And so it must be, not an act of destruction but magic—and even happiness—deserving a fairy-tale ending: "until they died."

We have not brought some analysis of one symptomatic act and two fantasies together into one formulation which the drawing illustrates unequivocally as genital-aggressive. But we must not generalize this too far for our real, live little boy. In truth I know hardly anyone who is more gentle and shy with little girls than he is and who, when he is in love with one, is so close to tears. This is no contradiction since every erotic wish for possession, as we have seen, arouses in him simultaneously some stormy aggression, which can find expression only in its antithesis: shyness and tears, the expression of inner-directed torment.

Till now we have described a well-known phenomenon of puberty. Many a reader may have found superfluous our projection of the origin of sadistic tendencies onto early childhood—that is, the genital phase of the child's sexual development. But when we examine our pupil's childhood records in the school files, we find it all points to a central phase of a still earlier period, when the mouth was the pleasure-giving and pleasure-denying organ. "After being weaned from the mother's breast, the boy had severe attacks of asthma. These dominated his life henceforth (until a few years ago)." Incidentally he is a bad student, lacking, above all, perseverance.

Several other children had similar records. When I compare their childhood accounts, I find that after weaning, they, too, developed pathological symptoms. One boy developed a glottal spasm at six months. These spasms recurred later as some fainting, followed by gentle weeping whenever a wish was denied. There was a third boy who was given the breast every two hours because he would scream excruciatingly for it. Then, in his greed, he would bite wildly. He developed the following symptom, which we found hard to explain: During his sleep he would bang his head so hard against the wall that he had to be moved into the inner rooms of the apartment on account of the neighbors.

All three boys had the following in common: Confronted with difficult tasks, they were quick to give up, but they also had sudden raging temper tantrums which rapidly changed into a mixture of pallor and breath holding.

Sudden violent irascibility usually betrays repressed unconscious aggression. Where more normal people would become very angry or deliberately vengeful, these suddenly enraged people mostly succeed only in hurting themselves. For they are afraid that their aggression, undeliberated and unrestrained as it is, is so excessive that it could really destroy their opponents. At the same time there is a reawakening of those infantile feelings of powerlessness that were engendered by their first objects—against whom this excessive rage was meant to be directed in the first place—and their wrath turned against themselves. It seems to me the origin of this mechanism is to be found in their reaction to their deprivations during the oral phase. Their particular oral aggressivity had to be turned back to help combat and dissipate oral symptoms or excitement, such as asthma or glottal spasm.

Reading and learning are like an oral taking in. As proof, look at language: It speaks of "devouring a book," of "spiritual nourishment," and of "drinking at the fount of wisdom." The mastery of material requires a measure of oral aggression; one has to "chew up" the material in order to "digest" it. Also, let's not forget the vanity and aggression that are required in order to compete against one's colleagues and get ahead in one's job.

III. The Gentle Girl

The fantasies of a girl who presents herself as gentle are contained in a story of this character trait:

FUTILE FRIENDSHIP (by Margaret, twelve years old)
Once upon a time there was a child named Margaret. One day her father, mother, and brother died. Margaret was very sad, but the mother had said to her, "Don't be sad, for things will be much better for me in heaven, and God willing, you will see me again in heaven." She paused and then continued: "Be really pious and put your trust in God, and someday you will have twice as much joy." The dying mother asked the family Castelneau to allow Margaret to come to them, for this is where she would find Yvette, whose friendship she sought. Never before had Margaret loved anyone heartily enough so that it could become a friendship. Margaret had already shed many tears. The Castelneaus were pleased to take her, and her mother died in peace. Happiness at the Castelneaus' did not last; the family was called back to its property in India. Parting was difficult. The train now began to move. She looked in the direction where it disappeared. She stood there a long time. Then, after crying, "Yvette," she fell into a deep faint. When she came to, she found herself in the Meyerheims' big room. She said not a word. Silently she looked in the direction of India. She moaned often. The expression of her face had changed. She looked sad; deep shadows of mourning moved across

her face. One detected a seriousness which had not been there before. She was silent; a silent submission was painted on her face. Sometimes one heard her sighing softly. "Yvette!" Finally she got up and went out into the garden. There she could air her pain undisturbed. There she sat, loudly sighing and moaning. Suddenly she fell silent and still, said, "Yvette," once more and sang a song to the setting sun. Then, more self-possessed and more calmly than before, she returned to the room.

The next day was Sunday. Quite early she rose and went to church, where she was again consoled, since the pastor spoke of the persecution of the Christians. On her way home she met a weeping boy, and she suspected that his mother was dying. The father (she learned in answer to her question) had left home in the morning "more silent than ever." She went home with the youth and spoke very reassuringly with him at the deathbed of his mother—until he quietly fell asleep at her bedside. She went away contented.

Subsequently she led a consistently sad life, in school—the only girl. The others were all coarse boys. One night, however, she could not sleep. She looked out; the moon shone pale on the plain. She went out, looked in the direction of India, and called very loudly, "Yvette. Yvette, if I cannot see you here on earth anymore, *oh, God, help children, with something like this*; take me up into your kingdom." Then she sank down, repeated, "Yvette," once more, and died.

When this child is asked to imagine herself alone in the world (this was the theme given), she avoids the practical side of her question and digs so deeply into its affective aspects that the death of a friend takes on overwhelming importance. Only the meeting with the forsaken lad and the description of the persecuted Christians could console her momentarily, and finally only death is an appropriate ending for the calamity. Among the welter of feelings, the "help" at the end sounds suddenly very immediate; one pricks up one's ears and only wonders all the more that such a capacity for pain was not at all stimulated by the death of the father, the mother, or the brother who all disappeared in one day, and their deaths were rapidly passed over with quickly consoled grief. Who might Yvette represent, that she merited the greater grief? But first let us hear once again about the death of a mother.

HOW A GIRL MEEKLY BORE HER MOTHER'S DEATH

Once upon a time there was a maiden named Yvette, she was a very meek girl, she lived in a tiny house, her father had been sent to Siberia. Yvette was very attached to him, but she submitted quietly to this fate. The mother lay sick in bed. Christmas neared. Christmas Eve was a glorious, moonlit night. Yvette walked for a long time in the snowy landscape until a voice called to her from heaven that after death things will be even better. Consoled, she walked through the front door, then listened at the door of the room; she heard not a sound, so Yvette quietly opened the door. She found her mother dying. It was completely still in the room, only from time to time some words were exchanged, no one understood them. Then Yvette laid her mother back into bed; her arms fell lifeless; she was dead. But on her face was a blessed glow. Yvette sank to her knees by her bed and let her head fall on the pillows and prayed. And so she fell into a deep, healthy sleep.

Now Yvette is the daughter whose mother dies. She, too, is consoled by the promise that life after death would be much more beautiful—the stars have told her so—and she confirms her faith in this promise by sleeping a deep, healthy sleep. But before that the two have "exchanged words which no one understood"—a sentence the interpretation of which remains open.

Nursing, the profession for which the child has revealed a clear inclination, will become the profession of the adult Margaret in her final story. Since nursing now becomes the key theme, let us turn to the guidelines which helped us to understand the "murder" described by the adolescent. With this approach, we can deduce an earlier and therefore unambiguous indication of what "nursing" means to the innermost self of this child. Two years before, she wrote the following story:

A maiden got lost in the woods and finally, by evening, sank down, exhausted. Sadly she said, "The brook"—she had to stop to get her breath—"the brook misled me." In the middle of the night a hissing awakened her, and not far from her she saw two stags and a snake; the stags fought each other, and the snake steadily bit one of the stags; the maiden fled up a tree; from there she watched the merciless battle, always thinking: "What is going to happen now?" The moon illuminated the landscape; only now she noticed that one of the stags lay sick next to the snake, who continued to bite him; the other stag kicked him; so then the maiden jumped from the tree, took the sick stag, nursed him till he was well; with his help she got home on his back, and her poor mother was happy.

We recognize in this dream image the rendition of the love act, accompanied by a child's question of such immediacy—she thought always: "What is going to happen now?"—gives it such immediacy that it makes us wonder whether an experience, whether a real observation could have been reproduced here. However it may be, the child's view of the grown-ups' love act is clear: She is sorry for the party who has been bitten by the snake; she nurses the female. This part of the story, which dominates the newer fantasies, was thus originally the ending of an older, previously buried, representation. It is a remnant, elaborated only later, which asserts itself obstinately.

Repeatedly used forms of fantasy owe their durability to two opposing forces: on the one hand, an unconscious wish that does not diminish in intensity, and, on the other, stubborn resistance to that wish. Since the little girl shows us again and again, through the fantasy of a nursing scene, that she is agitated by the "primal scene" and still in the grip of her reaction to it, the recollection of the primal scene is doubtless related to an always present instinctual desire, which the fantasies simultaneously ward off and fulfill. Moreover, according to Freud's observations about obsessive compulsive symptom formation (and the constantly repeated fantasies can be seen in this light), there is doubtless in the development of these defensive fantasies a tendency to move the hidden wish fulfillment gradually to the fore.

Now it becomes clear: The child perceived the love act as cruel, and she has not been able to overcome her ensuing fright. That she softens the fantasy into the story of her caring for the mother we may ascribe to the fact that she is a gentle and loving child.

But this is contradicted by what we find in the early-childhood school records of the girl. These describe her as a stubborn child who on occasion could be remarkably cruel. I don't feel I have the right to detail these traits. The intimate details are personal, but the most intimate ones are again typical. So it was an occasioanlly cruel child who considered the love act a cruel experience for the woman. We here first imagine the kind of relationship this girl had with her mother—one-half of her oedipal situation then. What we know of it leads us to suppose that she wanted to wish her mother away, wished her dead. This impulse, particularly strong in her case, had to be abandoned nevertheless—along with the other strivings of the oedipal phase. Its original vehemence corresponds to the immensity of the resistance that has been built up against the impulse: her pity. Mother is nursed in a thousand fantasies. That it ends in death suggests that the energy of the drive can be bent but not broken.

In the last story Margaret is the loving head nurse of an idyllic children's hospital. Deer and rabbits move among the garden beds where charming children await their recovery. But one little girl is more seriously ill. It is because of her that Head Nurse-Margaret stands so sadly at the window, looking out. "A dark cloud hangs over her brow. Then she turns and says sadly but firmly, 'Our Ellen will be blind, and perhaps God will take her up into heaven soon—but she was given a kind heart and a pure soul, and those she shall keep.' " On the eve of this day when Margaret's decision to go to the hungry of Russia ripens she sits with the dying Ellen. She points to heaven, where she will soon be happy. "As the sun set behind the mountains, Ellen said, 'Help the hungry children. My father beat me; but my heavenly father will be good.' Very softly she added something, but Margaret didn't understand it; then Ellen fell dead onto her cushion with a peaceful smile. Margaret continued to sit there until the stars appeared in the sky. Then she said, 'We have saved a soul,' and then went into the house." Now her soul has been saved. She pays for it with her sight and with her life. The chief (Margaret), the head nurse, praises such complete renunciation, for she—as her better self, as her caring self—knows that Ellen became guilty through her sight. Until now conscience has triumphed.

But there is something more. Once more we hear the plea to help the children. And we learn this time what they are suffering and dying of: Their father beats them. The father? What role did he play in these stories? In the first story he died unmourned. In the second he was sent to Siberia. The father of the little boy "left quietly," and that stag, which can be taken to be the masculine partner of the pair, disappeared when the girl turned toward the feminine one. Now we hear about a palpably present father—in contrast with the farthest-away heavenly one toward whom the father imago obviously is moving.

Freud has written an essay "A Child Is Beaten." He found this beating fantasy frequently in hysterics or in obsessive-compulsive patients, more frequently female, and he assumes its occurrence is probably more common among the healthy. He describes this notion as the last in a developing sequence of fantasies that he unrolls before us. The first notion, originating in early childhood, is called "The [my] father is beating the child whom I hate." This representation is clearly rivalrous. It is "not clearly sexual, not in itself sadistic, yet the stuff from which both will later come." But the second form of the fantasy is masochistic: "I'm being beaten by my father." This one is the most momentous of all and seldom becomes conscious. "In one of these cases the content [being beaten by the father] was allowed to venture again into consciousness as long as the [child's] identity was made unrecognizable by a thin disguise." But the third, conscious fantasy goes something like this: "Boys are being beaten [by their father or teacher]."

We could look for Margaret's fantasy behind her idea that she is "the only girl among a lot of bad boys." The second, masochistic fantasy we have heard in the scene of the dying Ellen. How did this previously sadistic child ever get that idea?

Freud thinks that before the appearance of the second fantasy, the oedipus complex must have passed and, with its repression, created guilt feelings: "It is the moment when sadism is transformed into masochism." All oedipal wishes now become their opposites or are directed against the self. If one wishes Mother ill, one nurses her. Instead of having something bad happen to her, something bad happens to the child or the child is beaten. Instead of the love one expects from Father, however, one is mistreated and consequently hates him instead of desiring him.

The father, the original sexual love object, will come back only if the girl has punished herself most cruelly: when she slides from her nursing role into her dying one. At that moment he appears as the agent of all that is bad in her, all that she has wished on her mother for his sake. But the unconscious has retained knowledge of the connection between mistreatment and lovemaking and demonstrates it in the way the language uses opposites to mean the same thing. By activating her earlier masochism, the girl may also wish for the love she earlier thought so cruel.

IV. The Inaccessible Boy

A boy with empty eyes and round face is the first to bring his completed composition to the teacher, and (in contrast with a certain shyness of the other children) he tells him, "Read it, read it right away!" Soon he returns. "Have you read it? Nice? This I would really like!" or "All this has really happened to me!" And with these words he lays his hand on the teacher's shoulder, needy of recognition, even love—a habit well known to the teacher from a hundred previous occasions when the boy usually prattles some confiding nonsense, without ever attempting to make serious contact. When the teacher attempts to encourage the boy to approach, he encounters his empty, uncomprehending eyes.

Once upon a time there was a boy who wanted very much to see the canal. So he sneaked aboard a ship, and as the ship left the harbor, he hid in a lifeboat, where he had a lot of food with him. When they reached the canal, he peered out through a little hole, and whom do you think he saw?

He saw his mother and his father on the deck of the ship, and so he watched who would get off at the next stop, but they did not.

But then he heard his father say that they wanted to get off at the next stop. So the boy followed them. He had a little money so he could stay overnight in the same hotel as his parents. On the next morning he was already downstairs eating when his parents came and saw him and asked where he had come from. He said that he had stolen his way here, and so they ate and went home after breakfast.

What, it seems, the boy "really wanted" was to meet his parents on a ship and to have breakfast with them and go home. Here is the real background: His father, divorced from his mother, lives in a colony abroad. It is this boy's unshakable dream to see his father again and to live with him in masculine friendship. This dream cannot be discouraged by his mother's assurance that the father doesn't want to see him or even through small hints from his father which prove that this is so. A man doesn't behave that way! He tries to demonstrate this to his teacher and to every man who appears in his circle by importuning him with confidences and fatiguing him with trivia. And he is always very touchy and angry when the inevitable rejection comes. It is as if he had a natural right to be loved without giving anything in exchange. How does he reach this conclusion?

HOW ONE SHOULD BRING UP A CHILD

Let's imagine that one is born, and it is a boy. First of all, you must not scare him and always tell him the truth.

When he is three or four years old, you shouldn't fondle the child all the time; for example, I will now tell you what happened to me when I was three or four or five years old. I can't remember the time anymore when my father was still living at home, but I learned that my father left me with my mother when I was three. When I was four, I was sent to a woman in the summer and my mother traveled to Europe. While I was there, she teased me and told me lies and wouldn't let me write to my mother anything of what was going wrong, and that's how it was. When I got up and dressed, I had to go to the pasture with the cows even though I had a red sweater on. I liked being in the pasture and I like cows and other animals, but there was a bull in the field and I knew that and I told the woman that there was a bull and she only laughed and I became furious and really couldn't write my mother, so I had a very bad time.

One day I was again outside with the cows, and the bull came and I became scared because he came toward me; in between there was a fat stone or boulder, I don't know the rest of it anymore. But one day I had to throw up, and my hair became wet and my whole bed, too, and in the morning I was bathed and then suddenly the woman took down the shaving strap and beat me like a dog. I've never forgotten that. And another day the boys took a folding chair and set it up in such a way that I had to fall down when I sat on it and I cut my left hand at the thumb; one can still see the scar today.

So I think you should be careful where you send your boy, and you should be certain that you know who these people are through other people's experience.

Most important of all, you should reflect a little before you do anything with your boys or your girls.

So our boy is in the position of creditor with adults rather than in the usual position of a debtor. His claim to love seems his right, justified by his fate. He has gotten too little love.

This certainty is more or less conscious in many young recalcitrant people who resist being educated. What they can actually reproach adults for is not so much lack of love as inconsistency in loving. They usually come from a family constellation where the world of the child is not illuminated equally by both parental stars. What love the child would get would vary with the moods of the single parent who has been robbed of his wedded partner and is needy of love himself or herself. The pressure to educate, to train the child would suddenly slacken and then again abruptly tighten. The boy describes it: "You shouldn't fondle the child all the time; for example I will now tell you what happened to me." And then he describes the harshness that struck him so cruelly after the pampering. After months of a dreamy, pastoral life when he was left to his play, he was chastised. If he thinks this was because he had a vomiting fit, he may permit us the supposition that he had wet his bed; we are familiar with this happening as a substitute for recently restrained masturbation. The punishment for this must have awakened a most horrifying earlier memory, which he doesn't tell us because he has repressed it and hidden it behind the episode he has just told. In his early childhood his mother, who had long vacillated, suddenly decided to call a doctor for help. The doctor used tying up and raw threats to cure him of his early habit of masturbating. The cut-up thumb is, of course, a reference to the doctor.

The scene with the bull also appears to have had a dramatic origin. This animal in the pasture brings to mind the steed in the field and the snake-stag in the woods; they are all father-animals. The choice of the bull seems to be determined here by the last impression the boy had of his father: It was an unexpected outburst of rage that put an end to family life.

We must remind ourselves once again how difficult it is for a child to feel the difference between an incomprehensible aggressive happening and the sexual act, which he perceives to be sadistic. And one must not forget that although the boy yearns to become a strong man like his father through the decisively masculine part of his being, he has kept more or less intact another fantasy, which also dates from a particular period of childhood, and that is to serve the father in a feminine way. He is also left with the fear that in his mother's place he is liable to be exposed to a similar paternal outburst of fury; he sees the bull charge toward him, and then he knows nothing more because within him has been built a wall that does not allow the knowledge of the fear engendered by the father, doctor, and teacher to penetrate. If they threaten, they are just lying, and "First of all, you must not scare him [a child] and always tell him the truth." He now tries to present himself to us as an unintimidated child. He looks glowingly at the teacher as long as work is a childlike game (and thus is a permissible substitute for his old dreamy "playing"). At the first serious word, however, he drops the visor.

One day a little glass tube broke in school. The teacher inquires half-absentmindedly who did it. He is accustomed to get an answer to such an inquiry. No one replies. So he is forced to ask more urgently. The children indicate with their gaze that it is our boy; he was the last to play with the little tube and water. We can now imagine what crime this signified for him, and we are not surprised (as the uninitiated must have been) that he denies, even though he knows that no one will be as angry at him for the deed as for the denial of it. Occasionally a sum of money is missing. Difficult not to suspect the boy since he has taken money on occasion in the past. "What for?" he was asked, and he replied that he was collecting money for the trip to see his father. We remember that in his reunion fantasy he says to the surprised parents that "he had stolen his way here."

So far there doesn't seem to be a *royal* road to the understanding of such "asocial" behavior. There are only smaller, more perilous tracks. A third composition prompted us to follow just one of these a little way.

MY ADVENTURES IN THE TENTH YEAR OF MY LIFE

Once I was in a church choir. I would always ride home in the car of a gentleman with another little boy who had brought me into the choir.

And I was paid fifty marks for travel expenses and fifty marks for singing. One evening the car broke down while we were just on our way. The man said that we should get out and he thought that a suburban train would come by, but it did not. So we waited a half hour.

Then we saw several boys, about thirteen years old; they looked through a shopwindow, and then they screamed quite suddenly, "Hands up!" and called over that we should give them our money. The little boy did that, but I thought it would be better to take all my money into my fist and that was the right thing; they didn't find it; only the boy had one mark taken.

We ran screaming into the shop and said that some boys had taken money away from us; then all the people ran out and looked around for them, and that was very strange, suddenly to see no one left in the store. But at any rate they caught the boys, and I came to the police station with my friend. They telephoned our mothers and two of them came home with us and we found it nice to sit between them in the train.

We came home and our mothers did not believe us, but when they heard that everything was true, they turned into the colors of a rainbow. We then had to appear three times in court. In the end I got five marks and the other boy also. That was a good store, I mean, business.

I'd like to point out three passages. First, the boy receives an unusually large amount of money for singing in the church choir. Anyone who has dealt with problem children is familiar, through the fantasies and tales of these "creditor" youths, with such exaggerations of gifts and earnings—that is, youths who are immoderate in their demands and in their taking. Furthermore, this boy stands there with the money in his clenched, raised fist and looks at the robbers. Can anyone doubt that he looks as if he were standing there denying that he had stolen the money? Here, too, we see clearly how he betrays himself, for what robber would allow his victim to hold up his hands high with fists closed? Finally, it is all over, the denial worked, and he even gets a little present, which is probably greater than the amount which he actually received for singing, while everything else, including the inquisition and the denial, has a dark background of failure. The tale of this small alleged gift is also typical of the stories of youths who steal; these youths justify their all-demanding behavior by insisting on their right to a reward.

Another youth with these typical traits, who, just like our youth, feels tenderness toward men and a hate-dread of the mother, had the same fateful experience in his earliest childhood. Our boy had his mother's milk for only a few days while the other had none at all. But nothing could have persuaded the other boy to admit this deprivation. In any case, he would have declared it trivial. In fact, he asserts stubbornly that he had been nursed for half a year, as if he knew what a traumatic effect the earliest denial must have had. His mother, however, tells of a touching symptom that sounds as unbelievable as our entire emphasis is on the importance of an experience: As a little child the boy grabbed after every woman's breast, and later he reached into their decolletage. He tells dark tales about big girls whom he loved as a little child ("she went into the woods with me, and there was a little house with two dwarfs inside"). These stories mask the earliest episodes of grabbing.

Such boys appropriate or comfort themselves with all manner of love bequests, of grants of money or playful things that serve as love substitutes. Yet withal they have a certain stubborn toughness, the degree of which provides a measure of the depth of their loss. What, in their unconscious, they fear to have lost is, first of all, the penis. They close themselves off from learning what other people learn because they would otherwise have to come face-to-face with proofs of possible castration. They flee into stupidity and unscrupulousness and even into something like a mental disturbance. They would rather appear mentally disturbed than face their feelings of guilt and its social consequences, for they do not believe in the bloodlessness of that general castration which we call education. Here one finds in all their starkness the first oral loss that kindled castration fears, or direct threats of castration, or the devaluation of protective love which can result from the atmosphere of broken homes.

The deepest (oral) layer can still be vaguely recognized in the compositions of our boy: how he betrays or betrayed its determining force through chattering and unctuous flattery, through lies and denial. Not only that, but bed-wetting, which brought about such dreadful damage, was transformed in his story into vomiting. In all these, and also where he fantasizes fulfillment, he fantasizes some oral gratification. And so the fairy tale of reunion ends with "they ate and went home."

V. The Sons

The last part of this review, rather than follow the stories of individual children, takes up a general theme—namely, the father image of boys—and shows how three boys treat it in their stories. The theme is, of course, of the greatest importance for the male teacher since he steps, somewhere, into the father's image—for better or for worse—

if he succeeds in establishing any contact at all. Where the aware teacher arouses hatred or love his responsibility really begins.

EXERCISE

A fourteen-year-old, of poor family, must now earn money for himself because his parents do not have money to further his continuing studies. He has to stop studying and find a job somewhere as a helper. He is reading the ads in the newspaper. He takes some stationery and writes. Now he awaits an answer. He gets none. He goes to the factory that placed the ad in the newspaper. No one could give him any information, and so, discontented, he went home. On his way he asked a newsboy if he might borrow the paper a moment, and he allowed him to do so. Upon looking through the ads, he found that a businessman could use a boy as helper. And so he decided to go there right away. When he arrived at the designated house and at the store, a salesman asked him what he needed. "I'd like to ask if I could get the job," asked the boy. "One moment," answered the salesman. After a few minutes the boss himself came and bargained for a long time about the salary. He wanted to begin his service the next day. But the boss treated him very badly and let him go after a few days. In the meantime, his mother had found him a job with a goldsmith. He went there and had to start work right away. He was always tired when he came home. He begged the goldsmith for one free day in order to be able to visit school on that day. He always had to give his parents his earnings. One day, when he came home, his mother lay dead in bed. His father had very little money. But he went to the pub often to forget his misfortune. The father's money shrank more and more. When he had no money left, he took his son's money. So their misery became worse and worse. In his drunken state the father prevailed on him to steal some jewelry from the goldsmith. At first he didn't want to do it, but when things got even worse for them, he stole. At first no one noticed it, but eventually he was discovered, and he was locked up. His father, too, soon had the same fate.

This is the story a fourteen-year-old wrote in answer to the question of what he would do without his parents. It is sparer in form than the answers of the other children. The icy breath of reality surprises the reader. It is a reality that he would normally have to face only in the courtroom or in a welfare agency. The reader thinks: What horror must a youth have experienced if his glance into the future plummets him into such depths? But the puzzle really begins with the fact that this story was written by a well-nourished son of the bourgeoisie, in a family with a certain flair for elegance.

When this youth entered the school, he was, to the teachers' surprise, unanimously rejected by the other children. "He is a bad, mean person," they said. The teachers, however, saw only a polite, some-what anxious, otherwise hard-to-understand youth. What the children had sensed immediately only becomes clear in the following passage taken from another essay: "When I was an even smaller boy, I always wanted to be a detective. But when I grew older, I changed my mind because I realized that I was much too fearful. The major reason was my mad passion for shooting [underlined three times]. If I could, I would buy a sample of every type of pistol and gun."

It's interesting how he won his comrades over. After several days of his shy stance he suddenly began to speak in the most sinister dialect and to play the idiot and the bum in the style of a common suburban clown. The children laughed and shook their heads. The more they laughed, the paler became the dispenser of all this levity, until the children, taken aback, were ashamed of themselves and let him off. Now he was accepted.

I tell this little story as an example of the stance this boy characteristically takes when he feels in danger: He sinks, so to speak, voluntarily to the depths. It so happens that he has a learning disability in the sense we discussed earlier; he is one of those irascible ones who are quick to fly into uncontrollable rages followed by rapid paralyses. I have described how these children shrink back from tasks because they get the feeling that they will destroy everything they take possession of. They feel a "mad passion" which they dare not or cannot act on but in the end can only turn against themselves. We may now interpret the fantasy of destitution as a retreat before the tasks of life.

Still, we haven't explained the most remarkable feature of the fantasy: its realism and its objectivity. Behind it must lie a real motive. One fact alone links the boy with the depths of social despair. His father is a physician in a reformatory for the young. He is a man who is passionately devoted to helping and donates his time from morning until night to the foster children.

Thus we can see the path the youth sees before him not only as an expression of self-denigration but also as the only way that will, according to his jealous experience, lead to the heart of his father.

A ten-year-old writes:

> Mr. Morningfield was in a very bad mood because he realized that his workers were demanding higher wages. While he was arguing with his wife, some street kids were fighting in the factory yard. They fought awhile until suddenly one of the boys picked something up and ran away.

The others ran after him. After a while one could see all those boys calmly sitting and smoking on the barrels of the Morningstar petroleum and gasoline storage houses. They thought that they were all grown up and that cigarette smoke was wonderful. Suddenly one heard steps in the factory yard. The boys quickly threw their cigarettes into the gas and petroleum barrels and ran away. After several minutes there was a dreadful crash; one saw a few walls fly into the air. Then it was over.

Some people came running. "What happened??" "The Morningstar factory has exploded into the air!" "Who has done it????????" A young worker stands there swaying back and forth, and he is as white as paper. "He did it," everyone thought. Several called loudly, "He's the one who did it!!!!!!" The young worker falls to the ground. "Here's proof that he did it!!!!" Several people go up to the worker. They say softly to him, "Hey you, Fritz. I wouldn't have thought it of you. Say, did you really do it?" They looked at the face of the worker. It was still as white as chalk. The two workers went away.

The door rang at the Morningstar home. "Mr. Morningstar, there's a worker outside, and he has something dreadfully important to tell you," says the maid. "I never receive anyone during the day. Send him away." But the worker at the door didn't go away. Mr. Morningstar got worried. But no, he thought. "My factory is safe, nothing can happen to it." Mr. Morningstar goes outside. "Get out of here," he screams at the worker. He opens the door; the worker goes out the door and throws a tenpenny piece toward Mr. Morningstar. "You should be grateful to me, Mr. Morningstar. You have less than I have. Your factory has exploded into the air." Mr. Morningstar faints. The worker runs down the stairs and laughs.

There's little one can add to this story except that the father of this boy is an industrialist, but not, as one can well imagine, of Mr. Morningstar's type. It is only in the different tellings of his fighting that the boy's settlement of accounts with his father can be recognized. He represents it in three persons: As a boy he explodes the factory into the air with his cigarette (attribute of his being already grown up) and disappears. As a worker he humiliates his father with the news; he proves to him that he is now superior. But as a younger worker, lying pale on the ground, he cannot free himself from the oppressive feeling of guilt.

The story of a third boy shall speak entirely for itself. He has been the oldest in that school and has puberty behind him. Although he is still as preoccupied with conflict (sometimes a hateful confrontation) as is his younger friend, he demonstrates through his powerful description that he has learned to see and choose people without a sense of guilt. His language thereby gains a certain tension of the kind we felt only with the little girl artist at the beginning of this study.

He will thus be the one to show us the difficult years of youth by giving them another form—one more ready to face life.

UNKNOWN

The old man sits in his living room, reads the paper and smokes a cigar. This man is over fifty years old and actually knows nothing—that is, although he knows a lot, has a huge library, and has read many books and newspapers and has had many conversations and debates, he was too lazy or too lacking in willpower; he didn't have enough energy to take advantage of all the opportunities that life offered him. Now he has been married for several years, has children, thinks, perhaps, that he is happy, has a fortune, a house, and other things. But if one were to ask him whether he was really happy, he would perhaps say yes, but behind that would still be another feeling, something dark, unpleasant, perhaps only a little, but in any case it would be there like a shadow, like something bleak, sad. And if one would ask him about honor and conscience, he wouldn't be able to say what this feeling is because he is too lacking in will and hasn't enough strength really to reflect about himself. . . . Well and good, this man is sitting in his living room; he is quite portly but not really fat. His face has tired, sagging features, and although he laughs sometimes, he really doesn't look in the least fresh or appealing. Now he is reading about politics. He's upset that the Social Democrats didn't get many votes or some other such irrelevance. But in reality this anger is not about this matter at all, but behind it is the anger about that "certain something," that dark shadow, that nagging, uncomfortable feeling. And so he throws his newspaper away and rings for the maid and scolds, lets himself be helped into his overcoat, and orders the chauffeur to take him to a restaurant. He goes to sit down at his table, orders a coffee and has some newspapers brought to him and reads (as if he would improve himself by doing so).

A young lad, poorly dressed, a tall, slender figure, enters the café. He looks a little emaciated, but behind that one can see him as he really is. One sees strength, power, self-confidence. He is tired; he lets himself fall into a chair; the chair creaks a little. The youth brushes his hair back, unaware, mechanically, with his left hand as is his wont. He pushes some used glasses and cups away from himself and leans both arms on the table, his head buried in his hands. The gentleman, the old man about whom we already know so much, looks around him uncomfortably when he sees the young man come in. He is thinking perhaps: "That's the life; that must be one of those . . ." He probably intended to say "bums," but probably he's really thinking: "One of those who will go far, who will make his way everywhere, who knows how to do everything." It makes him feel uncomfortable. Actually he would like to leave the place right away, would like to go away, but he stays nonetheless (because this shadow of his prevents him from doing what he would like to do). He looks at the youth indifferently with an arrogant, superior mien. The youth squints lazily at him and doesn't think anything in particular about him. What can one think about such a flaccid, unsympathetic older man, anyway?! The waiters know the older man very well: He gives them a good tip every time, he is a refined, distinguished man, and he comes very often. He is a source of income; they like him and are polite and helpful to him. But just as the older man expresses his distaste for the young lad, so, too, the waiters, knowing this young man is a bum, a criminal, an unworthy man, treat him accordingly. The lad orders a bowl of soup. The waiters look at him out of the corners of their eyes. Would he be able to pay? If not?! Well, he'll get it; we're not a soup kitchen! The waiter looks at the lad, and something in his gaze, something in the eyes of the young man, tells him that he will get his soup. He lies with one arm entirely on the table; with the other, he shovels in his soup slowly and greedily. He holds his spoon in his fist. "He has no manners," the old man thinks, and that's what all the waiters are thinking, standing at the buffet with their napkins under their arms and throwing glances at each other. "How this guy eats!" and of course, they hope that the old gentleman also sees it.

There is now no one in the restaurant beside the waiters, the lady who works at the buffet, and the old gentleman (and perhaps also a shabby dog of unknown breed, sleeping lazily behind the buffet). The lad has finished, pushes his plate away. He would like more, he is still hungry, but he has no more money or he can't spend what he has for more food because he needs it for other purposes. He waits. "Well, what's he waiting for anyway?" the waiters think, and gaze at each other knowingly. But not a one thinks of removing his dish or of bringing him a newspaper. They hope he will leave soon. Why, really? Now they know it! He is an unsympathetic, dirty bum, a weakling (yet every one of them would run away if he began to make use of his fists). They stand high above him. Naturally that's only logical. Much better clothing, good food, steady income, a good job. The youth rummages in his pocket. Coins jingle. He counts his money in small coins so that each clatters on the table in turn. He leaves no tip. The waiter is incensed, and the old gentleman makes a special effort to turn himself around with legs spread apart (because he is too fat and lazy even to turn his head). The young lad gets up, takes his cap, puts it on, and goes out. His broad shoulders swing a bit. When he has passed by the old gentleman, the latter looks after him disdainfully. He opens the door and disappears; the door clacks back and forth awhile. "Dumb guy," mutters the one waiter, and disgruntled, he goes to the door and closes it unwillingly. He would just love to call him back and scream at him, but he is really too afraid of the strong young man and so has to content himself just to grumble to himself.

It is becoming very still, even though it had already been still before. But now it's getting oppressively still. The old gentleman smiles compassionately and knowingly at the waiters, half gesturing in the direction where the young lad disappeared. Then he, too, leaves. What else can he do? Outside, his car is waiting and he's not even glad that he doesn't have to walk. But the feeling, this shadow within him, has become even stronger. He is actually jealous of this young boy; after all, he has to be disdainful: He is so far beneath him. Doesn't even have enough to buy a decent meal! Haha! So I *am* better off . . . and he buries himself again— in reality, without any interest—in the paper.

Once again we find the familiar elements of the conflict with the father: the wanting to be grown up, the hatred, and the guilt feelings. Like his younger comrades, he has the tendency to project the conflict onto the social sphere. Unlike his younger friends, he seizes hold of and shapes a story that expresses a strong will and a capacity to order his reality. He shows his ability to take on his future: here the past with feelings of guilt; there the future still untouched. In fact, in his life history as known to us, we can find no clue for the assumption that the old man of this story is intended to represent his real father. Infantile hatred is heightened, and out of it is created an exaggerated personage on whom all discontent can be projected. No doubt, the story has to deal with feelings, only recently overcome, about aging—whether in the sense of growing up or growing old— and has to deal with the life-and-death fears of the pubescent boy. The dangers of inner bankruptcy are taken in, penetrated, and finally rejected. In contrast, the young man is seen from the outside. He represents an ideal, evolving out of man's finest feelings, while skirting psychic disintegration around him. He is the only one who recognizes all that's become rotten around him. We are not told what's going on in the depths of the young person, but his portrait is rendered with bold, strong gestures, uninhibited and expansive.

The style of the boy's composition conveys two other thoughts to the reader: one, that the writer was brought up in a psychoanalytically enlightened environment, and the other, that he seems to promise that he'll not reduce things to simple intellectual dichotomies, to simple opposites. Rather, in small, particular strokes reality is so precisely conceived that one senses the boy's future power clearly.

Postscript

Those not familiar with psychoanalytic pedagogy are all too quick to suspect it of merely turning the inner process inside out and letting it go at that. So I'd like to point out that such compositions as are reviewed here were written at least a quarter of a year apart—and this not because there were any external constraints imposed by the school. Thus the psychoanalytically oriented observer must be intent on a spare and careful application of such methods, even if they are used for research purposes. I'm actually convinced that the success of their use is based on the kind of surprise such as is provided by the opportunity for the children to spend a few hours in contact with a person they can quickly and easily raise to a trustworthy ideal. Not every adult will succeed as well as Mrs. Burlingham in achieving such contact, and some, who think they have earned the children's confidence in their own strange ways will find the transference troubled by unconscious interferences. This will require skilled investigation.

When one succeeds in getting the children to speak freely, their compositions may be more naïve than the usual compositions, because in this way they will be forced to say more than they are aware they know and their stories will be more full of life. And whoever knows something about unconscious *Korrespondenz* between people will appreciate what it means to a teacher on occasion to take into himself a picture of the inner world of his children and to allow its imponderables to work themselves gradually out. If one wants to contemplate a wider influence, one might, of course, think of collecting such essays throughout the entire schooling of the children. They could also be used for diagnostic purposes and in the case of need to impart more fitting kinds of advice, since one more intimately works through the material produced in one's own circle. At this writing there are, of course, only few teachers who have the requisite psychoanalytic training.

Even eventual psychoanalytic treatment of some children will not make such compositions useless—either for the teacher or for the child. For such productions offer, in addition to material produced in a psychoanalysis, something else (perhaps akin to what poets do). Thus what they are trying to say merits being heard.

Notes

[1] The director was Peter Blos. Among the teachers were Joan Erikson and the writer.
[2] Greek. An arrogance which is too close to the pride of the gods and therefore punished by them.
[3] Words in brackets were crossed out in the original text.
[4] One word is missing.
[5] At that time this account was written for a teacher who was not psychoanalytically oriented and who allowed the children to write freely but, subsequently appalled, hid the results.
[6] Crossed out. Compare with the omitted words in the previous story.

Anna Freud—Reflections (1983)

In response to the invitation to contribute to this very special issue, I can only focus on a few well-known facts of Anna Freud's life in order to comment on her position in history. For while her death has evoked much individual mourning, we must all thank fate for letting us witness the uniqueness of her life and the dedication with which she rounded out and complemented the role ascribed to her by her life history—and by history.

Youngest daughter of a great father who came to need her in his most creative endeavors and then also in his most helpless states of physical suffering, responsive student of his newly created method of healing and of observing the dynamics of unconscious motivation, she proved prepared to complement his most complex conclusions by systematically demonstrating the early traces of human conflict in the most telling behavior of children.

But let me begin with an episodic item from the way in which Anna Freud's life history touched mine professionally. She conducted my training psychoanalysis in Berggasse 19. Therefore, to me, as to a now diminishing number of survivors of my kind, what comes to mind as I look back are the front door and stairway leading up

First published under "Personal Tributes" in the *Bulletin of the Hampstead Clinic,* 6 (1983), 51–54.

to the Freuds' apartment—and then the ever-welcoming Paula Fichtl responding to my ring and showing me to the waiting room shared by Sigmund and Anna Freud. On occasion, Freud's next patient or visitor might be waiting there, and I would see the old "Professor," with a formal bow, invite that person into his study, having briefly bowed to me as well. And then Anna Freud would open her door for me.

Readers acquainted with this setting will remember the atmosphere of utter privacy, on the one hand, and of a kind of historicity, on the other, both evoked by the closeness of these two studies and the closure of these doors. And here I mean the meditative style that marked the "fifty minutes" of almost daily psychoanalysis and the tangible historical meaning of the most minute dynamics observed right here where this unique method had been created.

Well, it is not necessary to underscore Anna Freud's overall calm and restrained therapeutic style. But there was also an occasional easy place for a tactful freedom from "technique." As an intimate illustration of this I recently, at the Erikson Institute in Chicago, used a story from my analysis which I would like to tell once more in this context. Anna Freud occasionallly attended to her handiwork in my psychoanalytic sessions, too. This for the most part seemed natural, although it could be rated as a somewhat chauvinistic prerogative of women analysts. I remember having referred to it once when I was speaking of Joan's and my newborn son. A number of sessions later Anna Freud, at the end of an hour, having said the usual goodbye with a firm handshake, smilingly handed me a small blue knitted sweater, saying, "This is for Kai."

This little story also leads me to a pervasive theme—namely, Anna Freud's role as a woman in those historical days. Here, let me return to the waiting room, as indeed I actually did on regular evenings during the concluding period of my analysis in order to attend the *"kinderseminar"* held there. This was characterized by a rare and on occasion even gay intimacy in the exchange of astonishing experiences with children while evoking at the same time a, shall we say, historical awe, often expressed in a most determined nodding of heads while considering conclusions never verbalized before. I happened to be one of the very few men in this seminar, and was sometimes astonished at the observations made by a (yes, overwhelming) majority of women analysts. And these observations naturally included the children's parents—a generational dimension missing from the oh-so-theoretical "adult" seminars.

If I seem to underscore Anna Freud's feminine generativity in her early decision to complement her father's creative intuition—as he no doubt wished her to do—I also mean to suggest that this life-historical complementarity was providential for their shared genius.

Now if I also seem to imply that only a woman could have carried through this historical assignment at that epoch in history, then—yes, I do. In principle, however, I by no means wish to dichotomize this matter: no doubt a man, and especially one of particular genius, has a complementary feminine as well as masculine intuition., This may have been, in fact, how Freud knew that he needed this daughter and understood what she was seeing—even though he is quoted as having joked afterwards that she was his only (= true) son. And as for her role in his life, there is, as mentioned, that other life-historical fact of Freud's fateful cancer, which called for Anna Freud's role as a nurse and no doubt at times as a very maternal daughter. We know today how aging and declining old people can be in need of younger caretakers and as patients can develop the corresponding parent transference to younger analysts.

At any rate, Anna Freud became her father's caretaker—even as she also represented him in person, for example at the Goethe Prize ceremony and the strenuous meetings of newly created national and international associations.

In matters theoretical and literary, of course, Anna Freud developed her own style, full of such terms as "technique" and "mechanisms" and "developmental lines," and yet opening to sensory awareness as well as to theoretical curiosity the many ways in which children seem to *experience* the developmental affairs of childhood often so vaguely and theoretically reconstructed from adult cases.

It is here that it became clear early, and against a persistent alternative view in some psychoanalytic institutes, that Anna Freud's work in no way represented a mere addition of another professional specialty that a psychoanalyst could choose to use or to ignore. For as Freud's conclusions regarding the origins of psychopathology of childhood had early suggested, some of the laws of unhindered growth thereby revealed themselves at the same time to the thoughtful imagination. How this trend eventually found mutual enrichment with other developmental schools such as Montessori and Piaget is well known. And here it was doubly helpful that Anna Freud's pre-psychoanalytic experience as an imaginative *volkssechul-Lehre* (a "people's-school teacher") helped to build a bridge to contemporary liberal and educational trends in Viennese eduction and re-education such as were represented by the powerful figures of Bernfeld and Aichhorn.

Emergent child analysis, then, was closely related to trends in the history of education. Nor did Anna Freud let it become a mere variation of private practice: from the very beginning it included the children of the poor, a fact that was not only an expression of social-mindedness but also opened up data beyond those provided in the analysis of child patients whose parents could afford to pay for treatment. This gave occasion for another favorite story of ours, namely, mother Freud's remark on seeing Paula take a plate with food into Anna Freud's study for a hungry little customer: *"Sie lässt sich's was kosten, die Kinderanalyse,"* meaning that Anna Freud spent quite a bit of money on child analysis—or, in shorter American, "A costly affair, child analysis!"

At the same time, of course, Anna Freud's concern with human development as a whole also enabled her to pay close attention to the ego and its central role, beyond its defensive inventiveness, of giving form and presence to each developmental step as it mediates between the id's physical nature and society's (then still called "the outer world's") institutional variations.

And here, finally, I must point to the gigantic historical paradox that eventually engulfed the Vienna scene—where psychoanalysis had come to represent an intellectual concentration on the inner dynamics of the human species as a whole while mannish political forces succeeded at the same time in imposing on the country a new type of political order dedicated to the murderous division of mankind into unreconcilable pseudo-species.

It made deep sense, then, that following her emigration and at the beginning of her work in England Anna Freud devoted her efforts to the emotional rehabilitation of German children saved from concentration camps and of bombed-out English children—concerns and services to be extended in the course of more peaceful times to the needs of various neighborhoods in London and to the training of professionals concerned with the practice and application of child analysis. In Maresfield Gardens Anna Freud has, it seems, re-established on a large scale the intimate sphere of shared privacy and of open historicity that had characterized life in the Berggasse.

I cannot emphasize all these themes of Care and Generativity, however, without mentioning what one must consider the necessary, "dystonic" counterpart of these adult strengths. We call it Rejectivity. This means here that any creative individual vitally preoccupied with universally important matters must at times firmly reject other theories and practices which seem to endanger his main objectives. In doing so, he arouses, of course, corresponding reactions in others.

But here again, what is decisive in the long run is the style in which such matters are spelled out at a given historical moment—and settled at another.

To end with a word on the impact of Anna Freud's contributions on corresponding work in the United States: When Joan Erikson and I had a chance to contribute to the Midcentury White House Conference (which carried with typical American optimism the motto "A Healthy Personality for Every Child"), we became most aware of the fact that, beyond their professional impact, Anna Freud's ideas (with the help of such messengers as Margaret Mead) had become a vital part of modern enlightenment.

We will need it in today's desperate search for the human potentials for peace.

II.
CONFIGURATIONS
IN PLAY
AND DREAMS

Configurations in Play
—Clinical Notes (1937)

Introduction

Listening to an adult's description of his life, we find that a clear vista into his past is limited by horizons: one is the onset of puberty, with its nebulous "screen memories;" another the onset of the so-called latency period through which, in retrospect, memories appear inaccurate and obscure, if at all. In our work with children we meet another horizon, the period of language development. "The material which the child furnishes us," says Anna Freud in her *Introduction to the Technic of Child Analysis*, "supplies us with many welcome confirmations of facts which up to the present moment we have only been able to maintain by reference to adult analysis. But . . . it does not lead us beyond the boundary where the child becomes capable of speech; in short, that time from whence on its thinking becomes analogous to ours."[1]

Associations, fantasies, dreams lead in the analysis of the adult mind to the land beyond the mountains; in child analysis these roads lose their reliability and have to be supplemented by others, especially the sequences which occur spontaneously in the child's play.

First published in the *Psychoanalytic Quarterly*, 6 (1937), 139–214 under the name of Erik Homburger.

It seems to me, however, that when substituting play for other associative material we are inclined to apply to its observation and interpretation methods which do not quite do justice to its nature. We tend to neglect the characteristic which most clearly differentiates play from the world of psychological data communicated to us by means of language, namely, the manifestation of an experience in actual space, in the dynamic relationship of shapes, sizes, distances—in what we may call *spatial configurations*.

In the following notes it is hoped to draw attention to this spatial aspect of play as the element which is of dominant importance in the specificity of *"Spiel-Arbeit."* These notes are based on observations made for the most part in the twilight of clinical experience, and must be supplemented by systematic work with normal or only slightly disturbed children. For although the adult who is not an artist must undergo the specific psychoanalytic procedure in order to reveal his unconscious in the play of ideas (a procedure which cannot easily be replaced for "scientific purposes" by less intimate and more systematic arrangements), the child in his play continuously and naturally "weaves fantasies around real objects.[2]"

I. "Houses"

An anxious and inhibited four-year-old boy, A, comes for observation. The worried mother has told us: (1) that he is afraid to climb stairs or to cross open spaces; (2) that as a baby he had eczema and that for eight months his arms were often tied in order to prevent his scratching; and (3) that until recently he continued to wet himself, with a climax at the time of a younger sister's arrival.

Let us see what he shows in the first minutes of play. Taking a toy house he places three bears close together in one corner. The father bear is lying in the bathtub, the mother bear is washing at the sink, while the baby bear is drinking water. The emphasis on water reminds us of the boy's urinary difficulty. It also must mean something that the family is placed so close together, for he then arranges a group of animals outside the house equally close to one another. "Can you build a cage around these animals?" he asks me. Provided with blocks, he builds the "cage" shown in Figure 1 *beside* them—a house-form which on a normative scale of infantile house-building would belong to a much younger age. At five one knows that a house is "around something"; but A has forgotten the animals. He seems to use the blocks in order to express the *feeling of being caged*; he

Figure 1

even places a small picture frame which he finds among the toys around the cage itself. Thus he is indicating in the *content* of his play what is libidinally the most important function of his body (urination) and in the *spatial arrangement* of the toys he expresses narrowness and the feeling of being caged, which we are inclined to trace to the early traumatic experience of being tied and to connect with his present fears of open spaces.

The boy then begins to ask persistently for many details about things in my room. When asked, "What is it you really want to know?," he quiets down quickly and in a dreamy way turns a shallow bowl upside down and puts many marbles into the cavity of its hollow base. This he repeats several times, then takes one toy car after the other, turns it upside down and examines it.

Here, finally, we have behavior which belongs to the "putting-into" and "taking-out" type of play. By his persistent questions, and his silent examination of the toy cars, he seems to express an intellectual problem: "What is the nature of the underside of things?" This question arises because of the real conflict with the objective world which began when his mother gave birth to his sister, and represents the material most accessible for future psychoanalytic interpretation.

Beneath this level we see that two aspects of his "physical" experiences are expressed in his play. The one indicating strong interest in a pregenital (urethral) function will, during treatment, offer material for interpretation and will at the same time necessitate retraining. The earlier experience, the feeling of being caged, seems to be connected deeply with the impression which a seemingly hostile world has made on this child when he was still so young that his only method of defense was a general withdrawal. This must have so influenced his whole mode of existence as to create severe resistances to the analytical or educational approach.

The crux of this resistance is shown in the fact that for an abnoramlly long time A wanted to walk only in a walker. To be tied, once distasteful, proved in this instance to be a protection. We may assume that it is this double aspect of physical restriction, what it once did to his ego and how his ego is now using it which A expressed in his very first play constructions when he was brought to me, because of his fear of openness and height.

In stating that A expressed some quality of his experience of body and environment in the form of a cage-house, we imply not only that alloplastic behavior may reproduce the pattern of a traumatic impression and an autoplastic change imposed by it, but also that in play a house-form in particular may represent the body as a whole. And indeed, we read of dreams that: "The only typical, that is to say, regularly occurring representation of the human form as a whole is that of a house, as was recognized by Scherner."[3] As is well known, the same representation of the body by the image of a house is found throughout the gamut of human imagination and expression, in poetic fantasy, in slang, wit and burlesque, and in primitive language.

It would not, therefore, be important to lay much stress on the fact that in play, as well, a house-form can mean the body were it not that it is simple to ask a child to build a house, which often reveals the child's specific conception of and feeling for his own body and certain other bodies. We seem to have here a direct approach through play to the traces of those early experiences which formed his body-ego.

This assumption led to interesting results when older children and even adults were given the task of constructing a house. Two extreme examples may suffice here.

A girl of twelve, B, had, at the age of five, developed a severe neurosis following the departure of her first nurse, who had been in the house from the time of the child's birth. The nurse had spoiled B; for example, by allowing her to suck her thumb behind her mother's back, and to eat freely between meals. During the mother's frequent absences, B and her nurse lived in a world of their own standards; the nurse shared the secret of the girl's first sex play with a little boy, while the girl was the first person to hear of it when the nurse became pregnant. B had just begun to puzzle about this fact when the parents discovered it and peremptorily discharged the nurse.

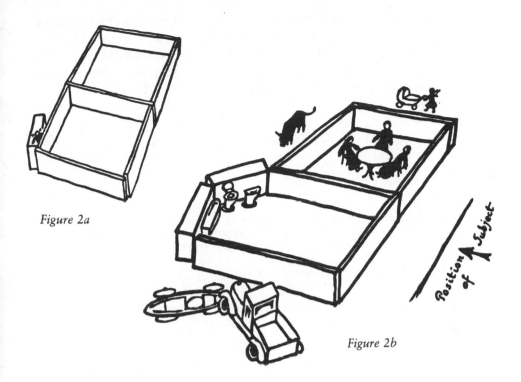

Figure 2a

Figure 2b

Knowing nothing of the shared secrets, they were unaware that in so doing they were suddenly depriving the girl of a queer and asocial intimacy for which she was unable to find a substitute, especially since the mother set out to break, in the shortest possible time, all of the bad habits left from the nurse's era. The result was a severe neurosis. When I saw the child for the time with no knowledge of the psychogenesis of her neurosis, I noted a protruding abdomen, and my first impression was, "She walks like a pregnant woman." The secrets she had shared with her nurse and their pathogenic importance became apparent only later, however, when she confided that sometimes she heard voices within herelf. One voice repeated: "Don't say anything, don't say anything," while others in a foreign language seemed to object to this command. She could save herself from the anxiety and the voices only by going into the kitchen and staying with the cook, obviously the person best fitted to represent the former nurse.

B first built a house without doors with a kind of annex containing a little girl doll (Figure 2a). Then she changed the house and built form 2b with many significant objects placed in and around it. In a vertical position we can see that the house-form could represent not only her own unusual posture but also the unconscious determinants for it, especially her identification with the pregnant nurse. The following superficial parallels (and I assume that deeper investigation of similar cases would reveal these as typical spatial elaborations of infantile body feelings) may be drawn:

CONSTRUCTION	HOUSE	BODY
1 A little girl with a baby carriage goes to the country (to the cow).	*Outside the House:* Where there is freedom.	*Head:* Where she thinks she would like to go away: to the nurse who gave her everything to eat.
2 A family around a table.	*In the Dining Room:* Where the child has conflicts with the parents about eating. Where she is present when the parents (immigrants) talk about her in a foreign language.	*Inside the Body:* Where one feels conflicts. Where she hears foreign voices quarrel.
3 A cow in the country.	*Outside the House.*	*In Front of the Chest:* Where women (nurses) have breasts which give milk.
4 Bathroom furniture behind thick protruding walls.	*In the Bathroom* (thick walls): Where the secret is (the closed doors); the forbidden (nakedness, masturbation); the dangers (threats concerning masturbation); the bloody things (menstruation); the dirty (toilet activities).	*In the Protruded Abdomen:* Where the secret is (the baby and it origin); that which is forbidden (the baby); the dangers (the growing baby); dirt (feces).
5 A red racer and a truck in collision.	*Outside the House:* Where the dangerous but fascinating life is, from which the parents try to protect the child. The accident.	*Under the Abdomen:* Where it seems a girl can lose something, since boys have something there and girls do not. Where people say girls will bleed. Where men do something to women. Where babies come out, hurt women and sometimes kill them (the nurse died shortly after childbirth).

The doorless house not only pictures the child's posture, and shows the unconscious idea of having incorporated the lost nurse, it seems also to indicate that part of her body which is firmly entrenched within the fortress of ego-feelings, as distinguished from what are only thoughts and fears concerning the body, felt as "outside": the expectation of breasts and the fear of menstruation, of which she had been warned.

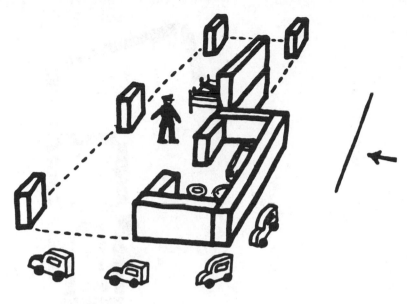

Figure 3

As a further example justifying our looking at the house from different positions and our assumption that the walls reveal something of the builder's body-ego, the following is of interest: A young schizophrenic man, C, a patient in the Worcester State Hospital, built the house shown in Figure 3.

He said it was a screen house all around, except for the back part. This patient complains of having no feeling in the front of his body. Ever since he was the "victim" of a spinal injection, he claimed that he suffered from a certain electric feeling drawing down from his spine to the rectum, and from difficulties in urination. He walked in a feminine manner with protruding buttocks. One may recognize this posture in the house-form. C strengthened that part of his house which corresponded to the spine of his body by placing two blocks on top of one another, and he furthermore placed walls around one room only (the bathroom) which in position corresponded to his buttocks. The cars are again put at the place corresponding to that of the urethro-genital region on the body and their arrangements suggested a symbolizing of the patient's urethral symptoms (he could urinate only "in bits").

In children without marked orality and adults without psychotic symptomatology, I have not found such detailed parallels between posture and house-forms as those of cases B and C. In laying out the play of their houses, they stood over it in such a way that the house,

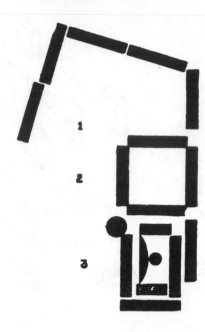

Figure 4

as compared with a body, was "dorsal recumbent," and therefore
might be said to represent more a baby's than an adult's body-ego.
By rotating the diagrams, we recognized in the same constructions
the subject's posture which could be interpreted as expressing an
identification with a mother image. It seems that the phenomenon
of most striking similarity between house-forms and posture is based
on the introjective and projective mechanisms of orality, which must
be assumed to be active in the establishment of the body-ego in earliest
childhood.

In attempting to find similar relationships between the growing
organism and the typical block-building of normal children, one will
have to be prepared for a much less striking and more sophisticated
spatial langauge in which more emphasis is laid on structural principles than on similarity of shape. Interestingly enough, from Ruth
Washburn's nonclinical material, only children with strongly emphasized orality produced parallels between body and house at all
similar to B's and C's constructions. The house-form shown in Figure
4 was built by D, who was a fat, egoistic boy of five, a heavy eater.
He explained that room 1 is the entrance, room 2 the living room.
About room 3 he said: "This is where the water goes through; it is
not going through now, though." He added, "There is a drawbridge;
when boats come, you pull it up." D's eagerness to "take in" and
his reluctance "to give away" are well illustrated by the large opening

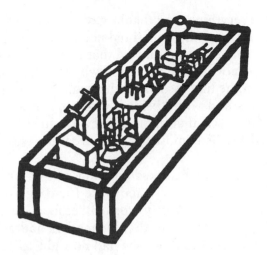

Figure 5

of the entrance and the complicated closing arrangements at the other end, where water and boats go through the house.

Returning to analytical material from children, we select a house-form of a boy of eight, E, which, in its primitiveness reminds us of A's construction. Upon my advice, E had been brought home from a special school where, diagnosed as defective, he had spent half his life. The problem was to find out whether with psychoanalytic help he could resume ordinary home and school life. When he came to his first hour, tense and hyperactive, he remained in my office just long enough to build a house with the blocks he found there (Figure 5). This house, primitive and without doors (like A's house), was filled chaotically with furniture. When, after a few minutes, he ran away shouting that he never would come back, he left behind him nothing but this doorless wall, dividing an outside from a chaotic inside.

I accepted this theme of a closed room and devoted the next few appointments to a short discussion of whether he had to stay and for how long, and whether or not the door of my room would remain open. On the second day he did not want to stay, although the door was not closed. He was immediately dismissed, sooner in fact than he really wanted to go. On the third day he stayed for a few minutes; on the fourth, he asked whether he could stay the whole hour; but when the door was closed, he was driven at once to manifestations of anxiety. He had to touch all the little buttons or protrusions in the room. I made the remark that it seemed as though he had to touch everything, and that he gave me somewhat the impression that for touching something (I did not know what) he expected to be put in jail. His blushing showed that he understood. Like most children who do not quite understand why they are detained with problem children, he had associated the sexual acts of some of them with his own sins and with "being a problem" in general. What he did not remember was that in his infancy, he, like A, had been tied when he rocked his bed (muscular masturbation with genital and anal elements).

The next day he asked questions, all of which began with, "Who has the power to . . ." and since I had heard from his mother that at home he was greatly worried because she wanted to get rid of a soiling cat, I told him that his mother had asked me about the cat and that I had told her she had no right to send the cat away. One should give cats and children a chance before one tries to get rid of them. He sat down and asked softly, "Why do I get so furious?"— and after a long silence, "Why do *boys* get so furious?" To every reader of Anna Freud's *Introduction to Child Analysis* it is obvious that this question shows a concern which is important for the therapeutic situation. While his defiant behavior at first had announced that he did not wish to be sent away or kept anywhere because of his violent aggression, his question showed insight, confidence, and a readiness for conversation. I asked him why he thought boys were "furious." "Maybe because they are hunters . . . ," he suggested.

Then we began to compare what boys wanted to be with what girls wanted to be, and to make out a written list containing on the one side the toys which boys liked: (streamline train, speedboat, gun, bow and arrow); and on the other those preferred by girls: (doll, doll's house, doll clothes, carriage, basket). The one group could be summed up under the symbol of an arrow and the other under that of a circle. I asked him whether this did not remind him of a certain detail in the difference between a boy's body and a girl's body. "That is why," he said thoughtfully, "I call my streamline train Johnny Jump-up.' " So we talked about the psychobiological implications of having a penis, the fear of the impulses connected with its possession and the fear of the possibility of not having one. He seemed somewhat relieved.

The next day the cat interfered again. Her regression as to toilet habits had, to say the least, been overdetermined: she was, as everybody at home now agreed, pregnant. But no one could tell just when the kittens would arrive. The questions *when* do the kittens *want* to come out and *when* will they be *allowed* to come out, became the

Figure 6

patient's main interest in life. Unfortunately, his unlucky father and his even more unlucky analyst happened to tell him different periods for the duration of a cat's pregnancy. He wondered seiously if God himself was sure when the kittens should come out.

One day, having left the office for a moment, I returned to find E all rolled up in the cover of the couch. He remained there half an hour. Finally, he crawled out and sat beside me. I began to talk about the kittens kept in the cat, children kept in special schools, babies tied in their beds and stillborn babies kept in glass jars. (I knew that not long ago he had seen such an exhibit, and that someone had jokingly told him it was actually a stillborn brother of his.) He probably could not remember, so I added that when he was a baby his father had tied him to his bed because he had rocked so loudly during the night. He blushed and when he got up from the sofa I noticed that he had tied his hands and feet before rolling himself up in the cover.

The toy which he subsequently chose for his first concetrated play in my office was a bowl (Figurc 6), a piccc of which was broken off. (It will be mentioned here in connection with several cases.) He turned it around to "shoot" marbles into it. For a while we competed at this game, until another cloud came up over the horizon.

As to Figure 5, one can see now how many different phenomena it "meant," all of them similar only in the possession of strong walls, no doors and chaos within—attributes at one and the same time of his tension of mind and body; his experience of being tied in bed; his concept of the female body as a claustrum; his experience and expectation of being kept at a place far from his family; and last, but not least, my office. In beginning our relationship with the "spatial" discussion of this last mentioned "cage" (office), we succeeded in lining up all his cage-conceptions before an interpretation which included them all was given. The play with the marbles, then, was the first free, though not yet quite uncompulsive, expression of that phallic tendency which, in its unsublimated form, had given him the impulse "to do something to women"—and the fear of "being put

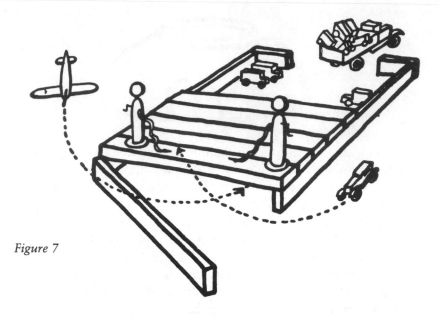

Figure 7

in jail." Soon afterwards his intrusive tendencies began to possess him entirely in the sublimated form of "scientific" curiosity. Appealing for comradely help from his father, and equipped with an extensible telescope, he entered Mother Nature's secluded areas and investigated birds' nests and other secrets.

In analyzing the full significance of a certain house-form in play, as in the evaluation of a well-known dream symbol, we need the aid of biographical material. On the other hand, the form of the house itself and the play activity provoked by it will sometimes tell at once where on the scale of object-relationships our small patient can be assumed to be; whether absorbed in narcissistic orality like B, C and D, or restricted by an early psychophysiological experience like A and E, or whether he has achieved a fearless, clear object-relationship, expressed in unrestricted functional play as in the case of F, which follows.

F, a boy of five, was not a patient—he was occasionally brought into the office to play for an hour (a pleasant procedure of regular, preventive observation). At the time of the visit to which I am referring, F talked at home in a rather unrepressed way about impulses towards his mother's body. She would, he hoped, let him put the next baby into her.

In my office he built a house (Figure 7), and played contentedly, without showing compulsion or anxiety, for a whole hour. Trucks drove into the backyard to unload dozens of little cars which were lined up. A little silver airplane and a red car were the favorites, and had individual rights: when the airplane majestically neared the house, the front door was opened to permit it to glide right in. The red car sometimes jumped on to the roof, to be fed by one of the two gasoline tanks stationed there. His remarks at home and his interest in his parents' bodies (so usual for this inquisitive age) justify the interpretation that F played with the house as his fantasies played around his mother's body. The little red car is fed by the two tanks just as F's sister drinks from the mother's breasts. The airplane enters the house from the front as his father's erect penis enters the mother's body. And his loading and unloading of trucks that like most children he has concluded that there are innumerable babies in the mother's body and that they are born through the rectum, the orifice through which the contents of his own body pass.

One was reminded of Santayana's recent description:

A boy at the age of five has a twentieth century mind; he wants something with springs and stops to be controlled by his little master-ego, so that the immense foreign force may seem all his own, and may carry him sky-high. For such a child, or such an adventurous mechanic, a mere shape or material fetish, like a doll, will never do; his pets and toys must be living things, obedient, responsive forces to be coaxed and led, and to offer a constant challenge to a constant victory. His instinct is masculine, perhaps a premonition of woman: yet he is not thinking of woman. Indeed, his women may refuse to satisfy his instinct for domination, because they share it; machines can be more exactly and more prodiciously obedient.[4]

II. Psychoanalysis Without Words

(ABSTRACT OF A CASE-HISTORY)

A little girl, G, two and one-half years old, had stopped looking and smiling at people and had ceased developing in her play. She had not learned to say a word or to communicate in any way with other children. Only occasionally, and then in connection with some tense, compulsively repeated play, did her pretty face lose its monotonous and melancholy expression. At such moments her excited sounds were strangely gutteral and were produced by noisy inhalations. No diagnosis meant much at this stage. The question was: Could one make contact with her at all? Could one reawaken her interest in this world?

Upon my first visit to her, one single fact induced me to make the trial. As she approached me slowly, coming down a stairway, she did not look at me directly but around me in concentric circles. She did not fail to see me, as had been supposed, but definitely avoided doing so.

My first subsequent observations revealed that her spells of excitement showed a mixture of pleasure and anxiety. I noticed this first during a spell which took place as she was banging a door, which in opening and closing touched a small chain that hung from an electric light. However, such "spells" could also occur when she was quiet. She would suddenly look out of the corners of her eyes at an extreme angle, focusing them far away, usually at the brightest point in the surroundings; then she would twist her hands almost convulsively and produce gutteral sounds, half like crying, half laughing.

She seemed never to have made any of the usual pre-language sounds; nor had she ever licked things as other children do, nor bitten anything. She would urinate only once in twelve or twenty-four hours, and often had bowel movements only once in forty-eight hours. Her room was overclean and her nurse seemed not without anxiety in regard to these matters.

When I heard this, and saw her exhibit the same excitement while simply throwing a ball again and again between a piano stool and a piano, I concluded that she had experienced training as a trauma, which in turn has been connected somehow with unknown traumata of her earlier life. I first tried to approach this symptom by suggestive play. Disregarding her, since she avoided looking at me, I threw stones into some old "potties" for almost an hour. When I then left, and observed her from a place where she could not see me, she played around these potties in concentric circles which grew narrower and narrower. Finally she dropped a stone in a potty, laughed heartily and loudly, and said clearly, "a-ba-ba-ba-ba." During the succeeding days her toilet habits changed completely, whether as a result of this simple suggestion I do not know, but an immediate relief of general tension was obvious.

We then tried by mild suggestion to influence her playing and her playful movements in space. Not only had she fortified her position against the outer world by not looking at people, not listening, not eating unfamiliar food, and by holding back urine and feces, but she behaved on the whole as if something actually inhibited the movements of her body in space. Her legs and arms were tense and stiff, so much so that a neurological disturbance was suspected and she was examined, with no findings to indicate disease. Even when ample space was at her disposal, she seemed to imagine limits and boundaries where she stopped suddenly, as if confronted with a fence or an abyss. It was an imaginary noise at a certain distance upon which she then focused her attention with an expression half anxious, half delighted. I was interested to see at what limit freer play and freer physical movement would be stopped by a real anxiety or end in the manifest excitement described above. If she threw things, I would try to induce her to throw them further; I would take her hand to run with her, to jump down or to climb steps—always somewhat more quickly or extensively than she would dare to do alone.

While I attempted to help her expand the limits of her expression, it became obvious that there was a correlation between the functions of focusing on objects, grasping objects, aiming at things, biting into things, forming sounds, having sufficiently large bowel movements, and touching her genitals. The manifestation of increasing aggressiveness in one of these functions was accompanied by similar improvements in the others; but when a certain limit was reached, anxiety inhibited all of them. A sudden large defecation on the porch was followed by severe constipation and regression in all functions, and a "talking" spell of four hours one night, in which she seemed to be able to talk all the languages of Babel, but unable to single out English from the confusion, had the same effect.

The first word she suddenly used—pronouncing it quite clearly— showed that it had been right to assume an early traumatic experience. While banging a door she looked far away into the sky and exclaimed (obviously imitating an anxious adult, quite in the fashion of a parrot), "Oh dear, oh dear, oh dear." On another occasion, she said clearly several times, "My goodness." A few days later I saw her pick out of a potty numerous stones and blocks which smelled of paint, and lick them. When I softly said, "Oh dear, oh dear," she vigorously threw the potty away, as if remembering a prohibition.

On the other hand, nothing could excite her more than having a bright, shining pinwheel moved quickly toward her face. I cannot report here all of the details of her play, which finally pointed to the following elements as possible aspects of a traumatic situation in her past: looking through bars (like those of a crib?); a light moving quickly toward her face; a light seen at a certain angle; a light seen far away; traumatic interference with licking and with play somehow connected with defecation. These corresponded to two of the definite fears she had occasionally manifested, i.e., of a light in the bathroom and of a traffic light blinking some hundred feet away from her window. She had also been terrified by the fringes of the covers on her parents' beds, a fear which seemed unconnected with this, until the chains of the lights which fascinated or frightened her proved to play an important role.

I then visited the hospital where she had been born. The most critical period of her short life had been its first few weeks, during which her mother had been too ill to nurse her for more than two days. The baby developed an almost fatal diarrhea. Not much was known about this period and her special nurse had left the country.

Another nurse, helping me to study the lights in the hospital, suddenly said, "And then we have another lamp which we only use with babies who have severe diarrhea." She demonstrated the following procedure with its clear parallels to the child's play behavior. The baby is laid on its side so that the lamp, which is put as near as possible to the baby's sore buttocks, can shine directly on them. The baby then must see the lamp from approximately the angle which this child's eyes always assume when she is preoccupied with her typical day-dream. The lamp has a holder which can be bent and the full light could then shine on the baby's face for a moment as the lamp is being adjusted. When this has been done, the lamp is covered so that it is, so to speak, in the bed. For the baby, then, the *light is where the pain is*.

The discovery of this traumatic event from the second week of her life helped us to meet a situation which arose when the child suddenly became frightened of a lamp in my office, stopped drinking milk at home and began, wherever she was, to play at being in bed. She would build a kind of cave out of the cover of my couch, crawl into it, and, terrified but fascinated, would look towards the dangerous light. We began to play with lights. Since at the time she liked all things which could be spun around quickly, I would put a light underneath the cover, presumably where the hospital lamp had been, and would spin it around. She began to love lights, and when she smiled for the first time at the light that she had been afraid of, she said, "ma-ma-ma-ma." At the same time her motor coordination improved so much that when the lamp above her bed had to be unscrewed because she played with it too much she could rock her bed across the room in the dark to pull another lamp chain.

At this point in the treatment the mother remembered another important part of the child's earliest history. In the third month of the child's life, when she had left the girl to take a trip, she had given instructions that an electric heater be turned on while diapers were being changed. After her return she was told that all through this month, dynamite had been used to blast rocks in the vicinity and had terrified the whole neighborhood. The baby, being upset already by the nervousness of the adults, had been further terrified when one day the electric heater suddenly exploded beside her. Here we have the connection between *the light where the pain is* and *the light where the noise is*. The flashing traffic light several hundred feet away, of which she consequently was afraid, apparently was a "condensation" of the exploding light near at hand and the terrifying noises at a distance.

After she had learned to play with lights without fear, we attempted to extend further the radius of her activities, and gave her hard toast in order to induce her to bite. She refused—and presently reacted with a show of fear on seeing a tassel hanging from the girdle of her mother's dress. At the same time, she began to bite into wooden objects. Having observed in her a similar fear of a lamp chain (usually, as I pointed out, the object of traumatic play) directly after she had first seen two little boys naked, I inquired whether, and how much, she could have seen of her father's and mother's bodies. Her fear spread to all objects which had tassels or fringes or were furry or hairy, when they were worn by a person. When offered her mother's belt to play with, she touched and finally took it between thumb and forefinger as if she were taking a living and detestable thing, and threw it away (with an expression much like that occasionally shown by women when they report a snake dream). When by playing with the fringe repeatedly, she had overcome her fear of it, she began staring down into the neck of her mother's nightgown, focusing her fascinated attention on her breasts. When we add to these observations the recollection of how she had formerly looked in a concentric circle around people, supposedly not seeing anybody at all, we may reconstruct one more of the traumatic impressions which were probably factors in arresting her development. We may assume that as a small child when seeing her parents undressing on a beach, she had experienced a biting impulse toward the mother's breasts and (a not uncommon displacement) the father's penis.[5] What this meant to her becomes clear when we remember the first two traumatic events we were able to uncover. The first had been the experience of intestinal and anal pain in association with light during the frustrated sucking period. The second was the experience of noise (the blasting) and exclaiming women ("Oh dear," "My goodness") in connection with the electric heater during the onset of the biting period. (Other material suggested that the nurse had exclaimed in a similar way when she once found the child playing with feces which she was about to put into her mouth.)

No doubt from the very outset this child had not been ready to master stimulations above a certain intensity. On the other hand, some meaning could be detected in her strange behavior and under the influence of our play and of simultaneous change of atmosphere in a now more enlightened environment, the child's vocalizations approached more nearly the babble of a normal child before it speaks. She began to play happily and untiringly with her parents and to enjoy the presence of other children. She had fewer fears, and she developed skills. This newly acquired relationshiip to the object world, though a precondition of any reorientation, was, of course, only a beginning.

III. Pregenitality and Play

A. CLINICAL OBSERVATIONS

1.

In her article *Ein Fall von Ebstörung*[6] [A Case of an Eating Disorder] Edith Sterba reports the case of a little girl who began to hold food in her mouth, after having been trained to release the feces which for an annoyingly long period she had preferred to retain in her rectum. This food she would turn around and around until it formed a ball, whereupon she would spit it out, thus using or rather misusing, the mouth to execute an act which had been inhibited at the anus.

A zone of the body with a specific muscular and nervous structure, the typical function of which is to accept, examine and prepare an incoming object for delivery to the inside of the body, is here used instead to hold for a while in a playful manner, and then return the object to the outside. This act resembles the anal act which it replaces only as a "gesture," but without any functional logic. Such as "unnatural" use of a substituted zone is one form of what is called *displacement*. In this case it implies a partial regression, since the mouth precedes the anus in the erogenous zones sequence, and offers the specific tactual pleasure sought after at an earlier period. It is hard to understand psycho-physiologically that a zone can replace another zone of different neurological quality and location, and serve dramatically to represent its function. Psychoanalysts have accepted

Figure 8

the interrelationship of these interchangeable zone-phenomena as being libido economical. Physiologists and psychologists in general are for the most part not even aware of the phenomena as a problem.

What interests us most in this connection is the relationship to play of such displacements from one organ to another. Most children, instead of displacing from one section of their own body to another, find objects in the toy world for their extrabodily displacements. If, in a moment of deep concentration in play, the dynamics of which are yet to be described, a child is not disturbed from within or without, he may use a cavity in a toy as a representative of a cavity in his own body, thus externalizing the entire dynamic relationship between the zone and its object.

Between displacements within the body (habits, symptoms) and the free external displacement in play, we find various arresting combinations. A little boy, H, two-and-one-half years of age, who struggled rather belatedly against enuresis, began to take to bed with him little boxes, which he held closed with both hands. When a box would open during the night, sometimes apparently with his unconscious help, he would cry out in his sleep, or awaken and call for someone to help him close the box. Then he would sleep peacefully, though not necessarily dry. But he continued to experiment. During the day he looked around for suitable boxes—obviously driven by an urge to materialize an image of "closedness." Finally he found what seemed to fit the image: it was a cardboard cylinder which had been the center of a roll of toilet paper, and two cardboard caps from milk bottles, which he put over the openings of the roll. (See Figure 8.) All through the night he would try to hold this arrangement firmly together with both hands—as an animistic guardian of the retentive mode. But no sooner had his training achieved a relative success in closing his body during sleep, then he began, *before* going to sleep, to throw all available objects out of the window. When this was made impossible, he stole into other rooms and spilled the contents of boxes and bottles on the floor.

Clearly, the first act, namely, holding a closed box as a necessary condition for sleep, resembles a compulsive act originating in the child's fear of being overpowered by his weakness to retain or his wish to expel. Emptying objects, on the other hand, or throwing them out of the window is "delinquent" and the result of the fear of being overpowered by the claims of *society to which he surrenders the zone but not the impulse*. The impulse begins an independent existence.

To prevent the little boy from throwing things out of the window, it was opened from the top. Thereupon he was found riding on it, leaning out into the night. I do not think he would have fallen out; he wanted only to show himself "master of openings," as compensation for the surrender of the free use of his excretory openings to society. When, in consequence, his mother kept his window closed until he was asleep, he insisted that the door should be ajar. At an earlier stage, the same boy, as he was learning to control his bowel movements, had gone through a short period of excessive running away. Thus not only sections of one's body and toys, but also the body as a whole in its spatial relationship to the whole room or to the whole house may serve the displaced impulse in various degrees of compulsive, naughty, or playful acts.

I may refer again to the wooden bowl which I mentioned on page 87 (see Figure 6). After a piece had been broken off, this bowl proved to be of manifold use to various children. They used it with deep concentration and with endless repetitions. As noted in page 79, A, curious and much restricted, turned it upside down to fill its hollow base and look at it; F, reassured about his phallic aggressiveness, used the opening, as thousands of boys at certain ages do, as a goal for his marbles; G, over-retentive, did not "retain" marbles in the bowl, but filled it again and again in order to spill them excitedly all over the floor. Similarly, a girl of three, who was fighting desperately against soiling herself, did not spill, but asked for the broken-off piece to close the bowl tightly, reminding us of the boy H with his animistic retention boxes. Thus we see the impulses appearing in play as the advance guard or rear guard of new sublimations.

It is conceivable that a form such as this bowl, as it is used by children of various age groups, could also prove of experimental value. We must keep in mind, however, that units of play behavior, like parts of dreams or single associations, seldom have independent meaning value. To know what a certain configuration in a child's

Figure 9

play means, we should know the contemporaneous changes in his growth, his habits, his character and his concepts of others.

2.

Let us look at an individual who showed pathological oscillation in the pregenital sphere, and let us place a specific bit of play in the center of our observational field.

At a certain period in his treatment, J, a boy of eight, untiringly repeated the following play: A caterpillar tractor slowly approached the rear end of a truck, the door of which had been opened. A dog had been placed on the tractor's chain wheels in such a way that he was hurled into the truck at the moment the tractor bumped into it. (Figure 9.)

Symptom. In a very specific way, J had failed to respond to toilet training. Dry and clean when he wished to be, he had nevertheless continued to express resistance against his mother by frequent soiling (as much as three times a day), an act which became a perverted expression of his highly ambivalent feelings about the other sex. In school, when angered by certain girls by whom he would feel seduced, he would take their berets to the toilet and defecate into them. His masturbatory habit consisted in rubbing the lower part of his abdomen, which caused genital excitement at first, but ended in defecation.

First treatment. The psychiatrist who first treated the boy was amazed to find that he offered "unconscious" material of a sexual and anal nature in a never ending stream. As the naïve preconception in some child guidance clinics would express it, the boy was a real "Freudian" patient. But the psychiatrist was well aware of the fact that the patient did not really respond to the explanations for which he seemed to ask. This was probably due to the fact that in being voluble he did not communicate with the therapeutic agency in order to get cured, but cleverly "backed out" by regressing to a new kind of oral perversion in "talking about dirty things."

Second treatment. When the boy's masturbation increased, it had been thought necessary to circumcise him, under the assumption that it was a slight phimosis which, though stimulating him genitally, did not allow him to have a full erection and led his excitement into anal-erotic channels. Simultaneously, he was subjected to an encephalogram. Following this, the boy had stopped soiling entirely; but he also underwent a complete character change. He talked little, looked pale, and his intelligence seemed to regress—symptoms which are apt to be overlooked for some time because of the specific improvement in regard to a socially more annoying symptom. In this case, the closing up was nothing but a further regression, an outwardly more convenient but in fact more dangerous retreat into orality (as was also shown by his excessive eating) and into a generalization of the retentive impulse. In consequence, his behavior soon gave rise to grave concern, and when he was first referred to me, I was doubtful as to the therapeutic reliability of his ego, which either seemed to be no longer or perhaps never to have been secure.

Psychoanalytic treatment. The first barrier which psychoanalysis was forced to attack was the castration fear, which, after the circumcision, had suppressed his soiling without ridding him of the impulse. Expecting new physical deprivations, the boy would appear equipped with two pairs of eyeglasses on his nose, three knives on a chain hanging out of his trousers, and a half dozen pencils sticking out of his vest pocket. Alternately he was a "bad guy" or a cross policeman. He would settle down to quiet play only for a few moments, during which he would choose little objects (houses, trees and people) no larger than two or three inches high, and make covers for them out of red Plasticine. Suddenly he would get very pale and ask for permission to go to the bathroom. When consequently the circumcision was talked over and reassurances given for the more important remainder of his genitals, his play and cooperation became more steady.

His first drawing pictured a woman with some forms enlarged so as to represent large buttocks. In violent streaks he covered her with brown paint. It was not, however, until his castration fear had been traced to earlier experiences that he began to look better and to play with real contentment.

J had witnessed an automobile accident in which the chief damage was a flat tire. In describing this and similar incidents to me he almost fainted, as he had also done merely while enlarging and protecting the little toys with covers of Plasticine. In view of his anxiety, I pressed this point. He felt equally sick when I asked him about certain sleeping arrangements. It appeared that he had seen (in crowded quarters) a man perform intercourse with a woman who sat on him, and he had observed that the man's penis looked shorter afterwards. His first impression had been that the woman, whose face seemed flushed, had defecated into the man's umbilicus and had done some harm to his genitals. On second thought, however, he associated what he had seen with his observations on dogs, concluding that the man had, as it were, eliminated a part of his penis into the woman's rectum out of which she later would deliver, i.e., again eliminate, the baby. His castration fear was traced to this experience, and the enlightenment given that semen and not a part of the penis remained in the woman.

First play. His first concenttrated skillful and sustained play was with the tractor and the truck. At that moment I made no interpretation of it to him, but to me it indicated that he wanted to make sure by experimenting with his toys that the pleasant idea of something being thrown into another body without hurting either the giver or the receiver was sensible and workable. At the same time, his eliminative as well as his intrusive impulses helped him in arranging the experiment. Finally he showed that his unresolved anal fixation (no doubt in cooperation with certain common "animalistic" tendencies and observations) did not allow him to conceive of intrusion in any other way than from behind. From his smearing of the woman's picture with brown paint to this game, he had advanced one step: it was not as before brown stuff or mud which was thrown into the truck, it was something living.

Technical consideration. Melanie Klein, in her arresting and disturbing book *The Psychoanalysis of Children* has given the signiticance of an independent, symbolical unit to the fact that in a child's play motor cars may represent human bodies doing something to one another. Whether or not this is unreservedly true in its exclusively sexual interpretation has become a matter of controversy. Probably the question cannot be given any stereotyped answer. Symbolism is dangerous because it distracts attention from the imponderables of interpretation. No doubt, any group of mechanical objects, such as radiators, elevators, toilet and water systems, motor cars, and so on, which are inanimate but make strange noises, have openings to incorporate, to retain, and to eliminate, and finally are able to move rapidly and recklessly, constitutes a world well suited to symbolize one of the early concepts which the child has of his body as he develops the agencies of self-observation and self-criticism. Encountering in himself a system of incalculable and truly "unspeakable" forces, the child seeks a counterpart for his inner experience in the unverbalized world of mechanisms and mute organisms. As projections of a being which is absorbed in the experiences of growth, differentiation, and objectivation, they are not as yet systematically described. Their psychological importance certainly goes beyond sexual symbolism in its narrower sense.

Likewise, play is much too basic a function in human and animal life to be regarded merely as an infantile substitute for the verbal manifestations of an adult. Therefore one cannot offer any stereotyped advice as to the form or time when interpretations of play are to be given to a child. This will depend entirely on the role of play at the specific age and in the specific stage of each child patient. In general, a child who is playing with concentration should be left undisturbed as long as his own anxiety allows him to develop his ideas—but no longer. On the other hand, some children, becoming aware of our interest in play, use this to lead us astray and away from quite conscious realities which should be verbalized. We are not in possession of a theory embracing the dynamics of play and verbalization for different ages in childhood. We do not want to make the child conscious of the fact that play as such means something, but only that his fears, his inability to play playfully, may mean something. In order to do this, it is almost never advisable to show to the child that any one element in his play "means" a certain factor in his life. It is enough after one has drawn one's own conclusions from the observation of play, to begin to talk with the child about the critical point in his life situation—in a language the sense of which is concrete to a child at a specific age. If one is on the right track, the child's behavior (through certain positive and negative attitudes not discussed here) will lead the way as far as it is safe. No stereotyped imagery should lure us beyond this point.

Return of the impulse. Outside the play hours, the eliminative impulse typically made its reappearance in J's life in macrocosmic[7] fashion and at the periphery of the life space: the whole house, the whole body, the whole world were used for the representation of an impulse which did not yet dare to return to its zone of origin. In his sleep, he would start to throw the belongings of other people, and only theirs, out of the window. Then, in the daytime, he threw stones into neighbors' houses and mud against passing cars. Soon he deposited feces, well wrapped, on the porch of a hated woman neighbor. When these acts were punished, he turned violently against himself. For days he would run away, coming back covered with dirt, oblivious of time and space. He still did not soil, but desperation and the need for elimination became so all powerful that he seemed to eliminate *himself* by wild walks without any goal, coming back so covered with mud that it was clear he must have undressed and rolled in it. Another time he rolled in poison ivy and became covered with the rash.

Resistance. When he noticed that, by a slowly narrowing network of interpretations, I wanted to put into words those of his impulses which he feared most, namely, elimination and intrusion in their relationship to his mother, he grew pale and resistive. The day I told him that I had the impression there was much to say about his training at home, he began a four-day period of fecal retention, stopped talking and playing, and stole excessively, hiding the objects. As all patients do, he felt rightly that verbalization means detachment and resignation: He did not dare to do the manifest, but he did not want to give up the latent.

Return of symptom. He did not live at home at this time. After many weeks, he received the first letter from his mother. Retiring to his room, he shrank physically and mentally, and soiled himself. For a while he did this regularly whenever his mother communicated with him.[8] It was then possible to interpret to him his ambivalent love for his mother, the problems of his bowel training, and his theories concerning his parents' bodies. It was here also that his first free flow of memories and associations appeared, allowing us to verbalize much that had been dangerous only because it had been amorphous. Interestingly enough, after the patient understood the whole significance of the eliminative problem in his life, the eliminative impulse, in returning to its zone did not flood, as it were, the other zones. Verbalization did not degenerate to "elimination of dirt" this time, as in the previous psychiatric treatment.

Sublimation. One day he suddenly expressed the wish to make a poem. If there ever was a child who, in his make-up and behavior, did not lead one to expect an aesthetic impulse, it was J.[9] Nevertheless, in a flood of words, produced during an excitement similar to that which had been noticeable when he had talked about dirt to the psychiatrist, he now began to dictate song after song about beautiful things. Then he proposed the idea, which he almost shrieked, of sending these poems to his mother. The act of producing and writing these poems, of putting them into envelopes and into the mailbox, fascinated him for weeks. He *gave* something to his mother and it was *beautiful*! The intense emotional interest in this new medium of expression and the general change in habits accompanying it indicate that by means of this act of sending something beautiful to his mother, part of that libido which had participated in the acts of retaining feces from women and eliminating dirt to punish them had achieved sublimation. The impulse had found a higher level of expression: the zone submitted to training.

3.

In part 1 page 94, I gave an example of what different children may do with one toy; in part 2, an example of the therapeutic significance of one play-event in a child's life. I would like to add a word about a child's behavior with different play-media:

A child playing by himself may find amusement in the play world of his own body—his fingers, his toes, his voice, constituting the periphery of a world which is self-sufficient in the mutual enchantment of its parts. Let us call this most primitive form of play *auto-cosmic*. Gradually objects which are close at hand are included, and their laws taken into account.

If, at another stage, the child weaves fantasies around the reality of objects, he may construct a small toy world which is dominated by the laws of his own growing body and mind. Thus, he makes blocks "grow" by placing them on top of one another; and, with obvious pleasurable excitement in repetition he knocks them down, thus externalizing the trauma of his own falls. Later the blocks may serve as the building stones for a miniature world in which an ever increasing number of bodily, mental and social experiences are externalized and dramatized. This manifestation we may call *micro-cosmic play*.

We can term *macrocosmic* that form of play in which the child moves as in a kind of trance among life-sized objects, pretending that they are whatever background he needs for his imagination. Thus he manifests his need for omnipotence in a material which all too often is rudely claimed by adults, because it has other, "grown-up" purposes.

These are a few of the more basic types of play which the child offers to us for comparison—each with its special kind of infantile fascination—developing one after the other as he grows and then shifting more or less freely from one to the other at certain stages.

Following an exceptional sequence of disappointments and frustrations, a girl of eight, K, a patient of Dr. Florence Clothier of Boston, made a veritable fortress of herself. Stubborn, stiff, uncommunicative, she would occasionally open all the orifices of her body, and annoy her environment by spitting, wetting, soiling, and passing flatus. One received the impression that these symptoms were not only animistic acts by which she eliminated hated intruders (her stepmother and her stepbrother) but also "shooting" with all available ammunition. While polymorphous in their zonal expression, these acts were clearly dominated by a combination of the eliminative and intrusive impulses. As the main object of the destructive part of this impulse, one could recognize the stepmother's body, in which the child suspected that more rival stepbrothers were growing. Naturally, this wild little girl was at the same time most anxious to find for herself a good mother's body in which to hide, to cry, and to sleep. Someone had told her that her own mother had died while giving birth to her; and one can imagine what conflicts arose when she first met the psychiatrist and saw that this potentially new and better mother was actually pregnant.

These biographic data are enough to explain the play which I am going to describe. Nevertheless, there is nothing essentially atypical in this play. This girl's constitution and experience simply made dominant the problem of intrusion which every child faces at least in one period of his life, namely, in the phallic period.

The phallic phase, last of the ambivalent stages, leads the child into a maze of "claustrum" fantasies, in which some children—for a longer or shorter time—get hopelessly lost.[10] They want to touch, enter and know the secrets of all interiors but are frightened of dark rooms and dreams of jails and tombs. As they flee the claustrum they would like to hide in mother's arms; fleeing their own disturbing impulses toward the mother's body they escape into willful acts of displaced violence, only to be restricted and "jailed" again. The mother's body, into which the baby wanted to retreat in order to find food, rest, sleep, and protection from the dangerous world, becomes in the phallic phase the dangerous world, the very object and symbol of aggressive conquest. Further obstructing this conquest are the father's rights (because of his strength) and the younger siblings' rights (because of their weakness); and thus the mother, a heaven and hell at the same time, becomes the center of a hopeless rivalry. Whether to go forward or backward, to be hero or baby—that is the question. It is in this phase that the boy, knowing there is no way back, sets his face towards the future (where all those ideals are waiting for him, which we symbolize by superhuman mother figures); while to the girl, her own body's claustrum offers a vague promise and new dangers.

In his play, the boy at this stage prefers games of war and crime, and expresses most emphatically the intrusive mode; the girl, by contrast, in caring for dolls, in building a small house with a toy baby or a toy animal in it or in other protective configurations expresses the procreative-protective tendency which will remain the point of reference for whatever course she may take in her future.

Dr. Clothier's patient, in her play during a period of transition from eliminative-intrusive to female tendencies, showed many distorted manifestations of these problems:

In *cutting* her own hair and eyelashes, and threatening to cut her eyes and teeth, she approzimated a return into the *autocosmic* sphere of play.

Microcosmic: (1) *Dramatic:* Five dolls, named after father, stepmother, stepbrother, sister and herself are approached from behind by a *snake* who *eats* everybody except herself and her pet animal.

(2) *Pictorial:* Drawings with long rows of houses which are being approached, entered, and left by a *stealing* cat: The house more and more assumed the appearance of the human body, with the two sides of the walk leading to it representing the legs between which the door was entered by the cat. The girl noticed this resemblance herself and made the giggling remark, "Do you think that a house can stand on the walk?"

Macrocosmic: (1) For several days she built "houses." The entrance had two round portal forms represented by a dish on each side. The patient began going in and out of the house on all fours, always entering the house backwards. When inside, she picked up one of the dishes and pretended to drink from it; then she curled up in a fetal position. Crawling backwards over and over again, she said to the psychiatrist, "You watch and tell me so I won't hit the back of the house." The psychiatrist told her when to stop, but each time she gave a vicious lunge backwards, *breaking* through the wall.

(2) Where her macrocosmic play expanded beyond the sphere of toys, i.e., became naughty, she climbed on tables, desks and shelves, *invaded* drawers, and *tore* papers. Often only bursting in and out of the room was an act big enough to express her intrusive rage.

(3) At a decisive point in her treatment, the girl was especially fascinated by a rubber syringe with which she *squirted water* everywhere. "Now I'm a wild Indian, so look out!" On a certain day, during a period of a general change in attitude, the girl squirted on the floor a big circle with one line representing a radius   ⊙   ; then she angrily made a puddle out of her design. The next day she repeated the same configuration, but added a small circle in the center of the big one: ◎   On the third day, she again drew a larger circle and, without the connecting radius, a smaller circle in the center, saying, "This is a baby circle."   ◎   This time she did not destroy the figure, but said giggling, "There are no cats here" (to enter the circle and steal the baby). The change of configurations

in this play from phallic (syringe) to female-protective is obvious. Moreover the little girl created a symbol and in doing so seemed to have a moment of clarity and pacification.

(4) Around the same time she dictated the following story to a teacher. She said she had heard it somewhere. We add it as an association which in a *narrative* and quite humorous form seemed to express symbolically an acceptance of the difference between boys and girls:

The Pumpkin and the Cat: The farmer put the pumpkin in the barn, and the cat came, and the cat said to the pumpkin, "Do you want to stay here? Let's go away." And the pumpkin rolled and tumbled, and the cat walked and walked, until it began to rain. The cat lifted up his wet paw. A woodcutter came by. The pumpkin said, "Mister, will you please cut my top off, and scrape all the seeds out, so the cat can come in?" The woodcutter cut off the top of the pumpkin and scraped all the seeds out.

They went on tumbling and rolling until morning. They started off again, tumbling and rolling. Then pretty soon it was night. And it began to rain harder, and the cat lifted up his wet paw, and the pumpkin said, "You'd better get inside." "Yes, but we haven't got any two windows and a nose and a mouth." The pumpkin said, "You get out and I'll go to the carpenter." He went to the carpenter and said, "Mr. Carpenter, will you please cut two windows and a nose and mouth?"

The cat came in the pumpkin and the pumpkin and the cat laughed. Then they rolled and tumbled, until they came to a little house. They heard a boy whistling and then a girl came out of the house and said, "What do you wish you had most for Halloween?" The boy said: "I wish I had a nice round pumpkin," and the girl said, "I wish I had a nice little black cat."

Up rolled the pumpkin to the little boy, and the girl said, "Look what the fairy brought us, and I think it's a cat inside!"

And off jumped the cover, and out jumped the little black cat, and right into the little girl's arms.

And they lighted the pumpkin, and put it on the table, and put the kitty next to it, until the mother came home.

B. ZONES, IMPULSES, MODES

It is not only in pathological cases that children's acts impress us as being unexpected and apparently incoherent. The observer of any child's life feels at moments that an essential factor is eluding him, as the loon in the lake eludes the hunter by sudden turns under the surface. Whether the child is playful, naughty or compulsive; whether his acts involve bodily functions or toys, person or abstracts, only analytic comparison reveals that what so suddenly appears in one category is essentially related to that which disappeared in another. Sometimes it is the mere replacement in time which makes the analyst become aware of the inner connection of two acts; sometimes it is a quality of an emotion or a tendency of a drive common to both. Often, however, (and this is especially true for the period of pregenitality on which we focus our attention here) the only observational link between two acts is what we wish to describe as the organmode.[11]

To clear the way for more systematic observations of the interrelationship between the intrabodily and extrabodily aspects of pregenitality, it seems best to reduce the displaced impulses to the simplest spatial terms, i.e., to signs which represent the dynamic principle of the body apertures in which the impulses are first centered. I propose that we accept the sign ⊍ as representing the incorporation of an object by means of *sucking*. ⊍ may represent the incorporation by means of *biting*; ◯ *the retaining of* or *closing up* against an object; ⊙ *expelling* and ⟨ *intruding*.

The organ-modes, then, are common spatial modalities peculiar to the appearance of pregenital impulses throughout their range of manifestation; whether gratification is experienced in the elimination of waste product by a body aperture, by the spilling of a bottle's content, by throwing objects out of a window, or pushing a person out of one's physical sphere, we recognize the mode of elimination as the common descriptive characterization of all these acts, and conclude that we are confronted with interchangeable manifestations of what was originally the impulse of elimination.

Surveying the field of these manifestations, one finds that what Freud has described as pregenitality is the development through a succession of narcissistic organ cathexes of impulses which represent all the possible relationships of a body and an object. Pregenitality not only teaches all the patterns of emotional relationship but also offers all the spatial modalities of experience. Led by pregenital impulses (or confused by them as the case may be) children experiment more or less playfully in space with all the possible relationships of one object to another one and of the body as a whole to space.

For didactic purposes, I have arranged the modes in a chart of pregenitality which (in formulation without words) indicates the network of original interrelationships of zones and impulses. This chart has been helpful in observation and teaching when used as a short-cut, leading to but by no means avoiding the knowledge of the other components of pregenitality.

Nobody who works in the field of human behavior can be unaware of the dangers of or blind to the necessity for such tentative systematization.

The chart is composed of single diagrams which represent the human organism in the successive stages of emphasis on certain erotogenic zones in pregenitality. I 1, for example, like all the other diagrams, consists of three concentric circles which represent three primitive aspects of the life of any organism: *a* the inner surface, *b* the outer surface, and *c* the sphere of outward behavior. The bodily impulses are represented in the diagram where certain organs connect the outer world with the inner surface of the body, respectively, 1 the oral-facial, 2 anal-urethral, and 3 genital-urethral zones.[12]

In each diagram one impulse is represented as being dominant by means of a heavier line; in I 1 it is the first ("sucking") mode in the oral system. Thus we indicate that we are concerned with that stage of development in which the libido is concentrated mainly in the oral system and serves normally to develop this impulse. Also the circle which represents the surface of the body is more heavily outlined, as is true for all corresponding circles in the diagrams which lie on the diagonal. This indicates that the principle of receptive incorporation legitimately dominates the whole "surface of the body" during the first oral stage. Skin and senses are ready to "drink in" all kinds of perceptual sensations as brought to them by the environment and to enjoy libidinally all kinds of touching, stroking, rocking sensations if they are only kept below the threshold at which motor response would be provoked. The heavy outlining of the outer circle indicates that at this stage social behavior also expresses expectant readiness to receive, as is obvious in the rhythm of waiting, crying, drinking, sleeping. Reactions to stimuli which require more than the holding on with mouth and hands to what has been offered by the environment remain diffuse and uncoordinated. All of this—degree of coordination, muscle and sense development, libido distribution and spontaneous behavior—will have to be represented in a final formulation of the first bodily manifestation of our impulse.

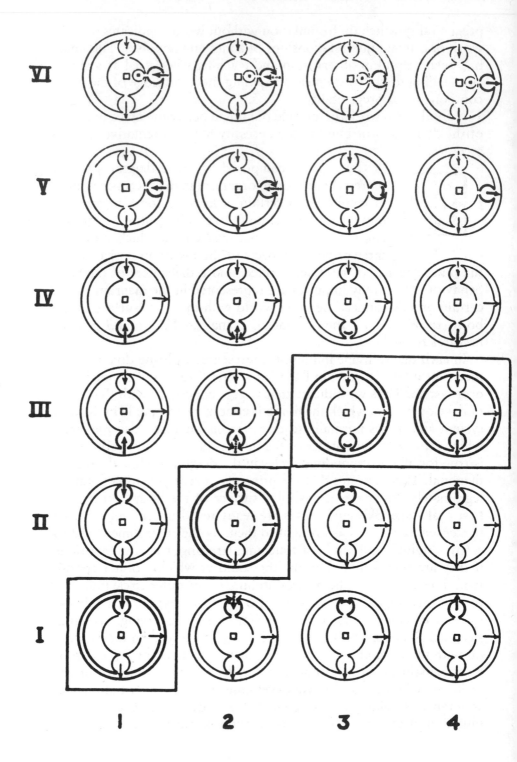

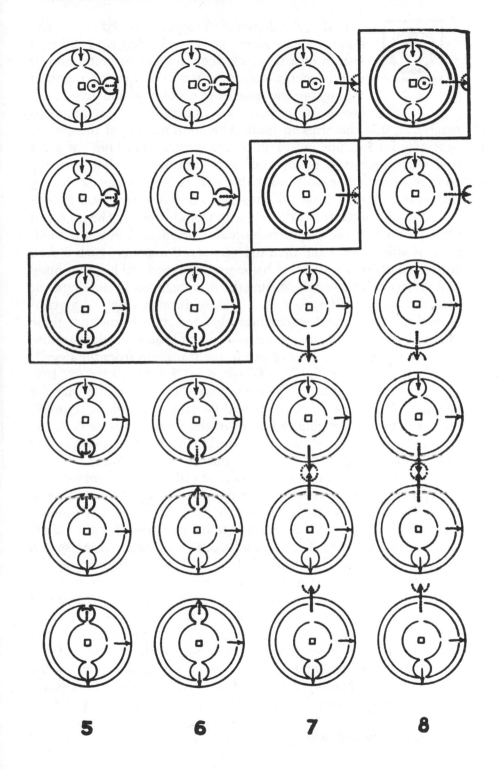

5   **6**   **7**   **8**

II 2

In II 2, the dominating impulse is ↻   The biting system (gums, jaws, neck, etc.) is in the possession of a relatively high amount of libido and of muscle energy which, at the same time, is manifest throughout the spheres of perception and action; the eyes learn to focus, the ears to locate, the hands to reach out, and the arms to hold. The coordination of the system necessary for reaching out to an object and the "plucking" of it for oral incorporation is established. Simultaneously, a change in the concept of the outer world probably occurs. This is represented by the dotted arrow, which indicates that the incoming object is conceived of in a somewhat different way from formerly. The object of libidinal interest and of psychobiological training is now the food. Later it will be feces and then the genitals. Presumably each is first conceived of by the infant as belonging inherently to his own body and subject to his own will, during the first stages of the development of each zone (I 1, III 3, 4, V 6). It is only through a sum of psychobiological and cultural experiences that the child learns that these objects belong to the environment—an expulsion from the paradise of omnipotence which takes place in the transition from the first (I, III, V) to the second (II, IV, VI) part of each stage. If we say psychobiological and cultural influences, we mean for orality that the changing conditions of the gums and the irresistible biting impulse, no less than the changing character of the food and of its delivery, participate in this expulsion into a world where "in the sweat of thy face thou shalt eat bread till thou return under the ground."

It is to be regretted that for the sake of orderly procedure we have to begin with the lower left corner of our chart which justly should be kept as vague as our knowledge of these stages of development is dark. But a principle of description to be used throughout the chart may be explained here: The normal succession of stages is represented in the diagrams on the diagonal. It is in these stages that impulse and zone find the full training of their function within the framework of growth and maturation. A deviation from the normal diagonal development can be horizontal, i.e., progressing to the impulse of the next stage before the whole organism has integrated the first stage; or, it can be vertical i.e., insisting on the impulse of the first stage when the organism as a whole would be ready for the training and integration of the dynamic principle of the next stage. Thus, a differentiation of zones and impulses is introduced which gives our chart its two dimensions: in the horizontal we have different impulses connected with one and the same zone; in the vertical we see one and the same impulse connected with different zones.

The stages, as well as their functional characteristics, are, of course, overlapping. The libido, during and after the stages of concentration shown in I 1, and II 2, becomes concentrated in the excretory system, can be pleasurably gratified by the retention and expulsion of the (now more solid) feces, while, or perhaps just because, the general impulses dominating the rapidly developing sensory and muscular behavior are retaining and expelling. Unlike the previous stages, when incorporation at any cost seemed the rule of behavior, now strong, sometimes "unreasonable," discrimination takes place: sensations are in rapid succession accepted, rejected; objects are clung to stubbornly or thrown away violently; or persons are obstinately demanded or pushed away angrily—tendencies which under the influence of educational factors easily develop into temporary or lasting extremes of self-insistent behavior, maintaining a narcissistic paradise of self-assertive discriminations. The sad truth to be learned in the anal stage and added to the experience of oral phase (which was: "You shall not find pleasure in incorporation except under certain conditions") is: "In your body, your self, your mind, your room, you shall find pleasure in retaining or expelling only under certain conditions."

Thus, the diagonal of the chart indicates and draws up for formulation some normal stages of development, in which certain zones are normally libidinized, certain impulses normally generalized. Where the outer circles are not heavily outlined (in the non-diagonal remainder of the chart) those configurations of impulses can be found which at the particular stage become dominant and generalized only when an abnormal situation arises; though as integrated part tendencies all the impulses are essential for all the zones of a living organism at all times. Wherever a specific case suggests it, the chart might be used to illustrate abnormal correlations by interchanging impulses and by outlining more heavily any untimely generalization of an impulse.

To use the example with which we started: Dr. Sterba's little patient having learned to exchange IV 5,[6] (anal retaining and releasing in accordance with the wishes of the environment) for III 3, 4 (insistence on her own jurisdiction in matters of elimination) managed to keep impulse 3 by partial regression to II 3 and 4 (oral retaining and expelling)—impulses which, of course, are normally developed during the oral phase (closing up against, spitting out of food) but become dominant later only through regression as in this case, or as a result of fixation and retardation—as for example in Case F, where a traumatic combination of constitutional and environmental circumstances had brought about a general "closing up" of body and mind.

In the case of J, we saw the pathological oscillation of the untrained impulses of an eight-year-old boy in the maze of channels which once and for all are established by the experiences of pregenitality: Trained to the toilet without, however, having allowed this training ever to dominate his psychobiological development and add to his character the traits which are the outcome of having passed through this stage (as would be indicated by IV 5 and IV 6), he used defecation as a means of expression of an asocial, omnipotent attitude (III 3–III 4). His fantasy of intruding by means of defecating into an object belonging to an ambivalently loved person would be represented by III 7. When talking about dirty things to the psychiatrist, he expanded impulse 4 over to the oral sphere (II 4) only to refuse all communication (II 3) as soon as the treatment appeared to him to be a punishment. We saw how under treatment the impulse of elimination returned to its original zone and was subliminated. Case K prepared us for a consideration of the phallic phase.

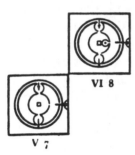

VI 8

V 7

The last two diagrams at the upper end of the diagonal are characterized by the dominance of the tendency to intrude. The general impulse to enter and to do something to another body or to another body's sphere of influence, although existing since earliest orality, is now emphasized and made into a social problem by the rapid development of sense-curiosity and motor-development and the phallic-clitoric erogeneity with its dangerous adherence to incestuous atavisms. Psychobiological emphasis and the forces of education work together at this stage to add another set of sad truths, again leaving it to the child's ego organization to make the best of it: "Not only the inner and outer surface of one's body and the zones connecting inside and outside are under foreign jurisdiction, but also those forces and organs which single out and seek fascinating objects in the environment in an ecstasy of action." "You may have the pleasure of touching and entering and finding out only under certain conditions."

VI   Girls, as we know, have a shorter or longer period of phallic tendencies (with clitoral erogeneity and the fantasy of having or achieving a penis) corresponding to the general development of the intrusive impulse. The question of when and in what way this phase is passed through and overcome, has

aroused much controversy in psychoanalysis. Here, too, direct observation of play might prove a *via regia*. It seems certain that the
penis-wish is absorbed more or less completely by the wish for a
baby. The girl, following her destiny, which is to libidinize, develop
and train a second organ system of incorporation with her procreative
organs as its center, can be said to undergo a partial regression to
the generalized sensitivity and receptive behavior first manifested
during the oral stages. Thus in the last line of the chart we tentatively
characterize female destiny by adding a procreative-protective impulse to the impulse of self-preservation "inside the body." Whenever
the chart is used for a female subject or patient, this impulse should
be outlined more heavily and generalized in order to give zones and
impulses, as well as the surface of the body and the motor sphere, a
new specifically female-procreative correlation.[13] It is this correlation
which differentiates the female tendency to incorporate from sexual
passivity in men.

The integration of all the vital impulses is essential and indispensible to physical, psychic and mental self-preservation and for social
and sexual intercourse. Whatever one does, it is essential that one
be able to accept, to keep, to digest and to eliminate; to give and to
receive; to take and to be taken in fair ratio. We find that the under-
or over-development of one impulse decisively changes the organization of all the others and creates a more or less pathological "type
of personality." There are "suckers," "biters," "retainers," "expellers," and "intruders" in all fields of human life. One could say that
without them there would not be so many various "fields" in life.
And there are types of personality which suffer from impotence in
one or more of these impulses. As the Arapesh says: "There are those
whose ears are open and whose throats are open; those whose ears
are open and whose throats are shut; those whose ears are shut and
whose throats are open; and those whose ears and throats are both
shut."[14]

The schematization of which we have been guilty might find an
excuse in the fact that its aim is to help organize not only very simple
infantile acts, but also the most primitive concepts the child has of
his own organism, and the theories and expectations he develops in
projecting his concepts onto others. Here, as we know, the origin of
some typical dreams and fears may be found, such as being swallowed
or robbed (by "suckers" and "biters"), being jailed and bound (by
"retainers"), driven away and banished (by "expellers"), stabbed and
raped (by "intruders").

This, then, is the system of zones and impulses which form the organic basis for the normal or irregular appearance of configurations such as those described in connection with G's, J's and K's auto-cosmic, microcosmic and macrocosmic behavior. The impulses are developed and, as it were, trained at their zones of origin during the (overlapping) stages of child development characterized by the general tendency to *incorporation* (oral-respiratory, nutritional, sensory-tactual), retentive-eliminative *discrimination* (muscular, anal-urethral), and *intrusion* (motor, phallic-urethral). In the course of phylogenetic and ontogenetic development the organ-modes are estranged (because overdue or precocious) from their original zones and can be observed as seeking new manifestations: the organism offers a limited range of safe displacements in habits and minor symptoms; reality allows for certain systems of projections; society accepts the expression through action of a number of character traits. The world of play affords opportunity to experiment with organ-modes in extra-bodily arrangements which are physiologically safe, socially permissible, physically workable and psychologically satisfying.

IV. Play Constructions of College Students*

Interest in the psychology of play ranges from the first playful movements of the baby to the various manifestations of the need for play in adults. Taking the most fascinating extremes of "play," that of the child on the one hand and the productions of the artist on the other, we find that in spite of the testimony of language popular opinion tends to evaluate them as antithetical phenomena, finding no "sense" in children's play, while looking at the artist's play as a phenomenon burdened—and in modern times, overburdened—with conscious problems and meanings.

When the writer undertook to participate in the studies of the Harvard Psychological Clinic on the development and character-formation of a group of average young college men his interest in the psychology of play led him to place these subjects in a play situation in order to observe what their late adolescent imaginations would do with it.

DESCRIPTION OF THE PROCEDURE
Each subject was brought into a room in which there was a table covered with small toys. He was told that the observer (who was

* Report on a procedure conducted as a part of the Studies in Personality at the Harvard Psychological Clinic (Dr. Henry A. Murray).

unknown to him) was interested in ideas for movie plays, and wished him to use these toys to contruct on a second table a *dramatic scene*. After answering a few typical questions (i.e., "Do I have to use all the toys?"), the observer left the room for fifteen minutes, but watched the behavior of the subject through a one-way mirror. In the following pages these first observations, made while the subject believed that he was unobserved, are referred to as the *Preparatory Period*. After fifteen minutes the observer reentered the room, wrote down the subject's explanations and sketched the scene (referred to as the *Dramatic Scene*).

Some of the toys were provided in large numbers, e.g., farmers, animals, furniture, automobiles, and blocks. To most of the subjects the principal toys suggested a family, consisting of father, mother, son, daughter, and a little girl. In addition, there was a maid and a policeman. It may be added that these toys were chosen without deliberate purpose according to what was available at the nearest toy store.

RESULTS

Five out of 22 subjects ignored the instructions and on the observer's return greeted him in a friendly way with some such remark as, "Everything quiet! Just a nice, harmonious, country scene!" Of the remaining seventeen subjects, only 4 constructed dramatic scenes which were not automobile accidents, while 13 subjects put in the center either an automobile accident or an arrangement which prevented one. Nine times in these scenes the little girl was the object of danger or the victim of an accident, other female toys twice. In other parts of these same scenes 7 female toys died, fainted, were kidnapped or were bitten by a dog. In all, 18 female toys (the little girl 10 times) and no male figures were in danger or perished, a theme which can be called the typical fantasy of the average member of the group. On the other hand, in the construction of the subject who could be classified as the most masculine and socially best adapted member, a dog was the victim of an accident. The red racer with its not specifically named driver came to grief in the constructions of the two subjects who respectively came nearest to manifest homosexuality and to manifest psychosis.

INTERPRETATION OF RESULTS

The examples to be given in this report will illustrate a few hypotheses which follow from the analysis of the results.

They suggest first that the five friendly subjects had not failed to

Figure 10

understand the instructions but that they could not construct a dramatic scene, because they had to suppress their first (most probably unconscious) response which corresponded to some traumatic childhood event (or to a screen memory which embraced a number of traumatic childhood experiences).

On the other hand, in most of the scenes which dared to be dramatic, traumatic childhood memories appeared either in the Preparation Time or in the Dramatic Scene—in the form of some characteristic symbolic fantasy, usually of an accident in which the little girl, rarely one of the other female figures, was the victim.

The constructed scenes will, of course, be the central object of our analytic efforts. We use as associative material whatever the subject said or did before or just after the construction of his scene, which seemed to be related in content or form specifically to what he did or said in other interviews and experiments.[15] This specificity was taken as the basis for interpretation only after it had been established in conference with other observers.[16]

I. M: Zeeno

1. *Preparatory Period.* The first toy that Zeeno touched was one of the twin beds. He set it at the extreme edge of the table beyond the edge of the sheet of paper. He did the same with the other twin bed on the opposite edge so that they were *as far away as possible from each other.* (Figure 10.) Next he placed a wall which separated a couch from the beds. Then the bathroom was constructed and separated; the kitchen followed but was given no wall; neither had the house as such any surrounding walls.

Next he took, as the first toy person, the maid. Here, Zeeno was doubtful for a time—put the toy back and in a nervous manner touched the region of his penis. He looked around the room with a worried expression, then shifted to a street scene. First he placed the cars (the red racer and the green truck) and then outlined the street (just as in the house scene he had first placed the furniture and then built the walls of the rooms). Now he seemed able suddenly to continue more rapidly, obviously lost in that concentration characteristic of undisturbed play. He placed other cars in more rapid succession, then put people quickly and decisively at certain places, keeping males separate from females, and the daughter from the rest of the family.

2. *The Dramatic Scene.* When the observer entered the room, Zeeno exclaimed, "There is not enough space in this house," and added quickly and anxiously, as if he did not believe himself, "Shall I tell you why the son and the father sleep in one bed? Because the mother, of course, has to be near the kitchen, and the daughter sleeps in the dining room because the maid has to be near the kitchen, too. The green truck drives on the highway and the red racer has to stop suddenly. Here [pointing to the extreme left of the scene] is a fisherman. He is disturbed by a man with his four dogs who is looking for a lost lamb."

3. The manifest content of this use of the play material raises several analytic questions: Where is the dramatic scene which the subject was asked to construct? In the house everybody is asleep. Furthermore only those walls are built which separate people—not the outer walls which make a house and a home. The need to keep things separate is paramount: bed, wall, couch, wall; men, women, their positions only weakly rationalized. In the street a collision is prevented—a dubious dramatic element. Likewise the scene at the left at most only implies a drama, i.e., a lamb has been lost—an accident in the past, not a dramatic scene in the present. What is it that has to be separated and why? What does the subject's childhood memories suggest in regard to these ideas?

The biography calls our attention to the following event: "Zeeno used to sleep in the same room with a sister who died. . . . She died about three o'clock in the morning before the doctor arrived." He remembers "lying in bed not particularly concerned about this." Nevertheless the examiner to whom the subject tells this story reports that: "He has a little anxiety about this. He was silent for some time afterwards."

From dream interpretations we know that the dream often disguises the sleeper's deep inner participation in a scene by having him see himself as a "not particularly concerned" onlooker. The psychoanalyst of children can add to this well-confirmed interpretation the actual experience of having seen children accept a traumatic experience, especially the death of a relative, with complete calm, although every detail of a later neurosis may indicate the pathogenic importance of this same event. It is possible that a feeling of guilt may torment Zeeno in connection with this death, about which he denies any natural anxiety. Children who mourn in this "invisible" way are often deeply concerned with the idea that some aggressive or sexual act or wish of their own might have been the cause of the death of the ambivalently loved person.

Several times during the various interviews Zeeno voiced thoughts of death. When, in the conference, he was asked of what he was most afraid, Zeeno answered, "That I am not going to live terribly long." To one of the ink blots he said, "I immediately think of a skeleton and ribs, and on each side above I see two faces looking at each other, guarding these ribs with an austere expression, like twins"— a detail which may be significiant in considering the role which certain twins played in his life as can be read in his biography. He had shared the bedroom with his second sister after the first had died. At the very time of his sister's illness Zeeno remembers having had "mimic intercourse" with an older girl several times, either one of his sisters, or more probably one of their friends. Experiences with girls, however, and punishments connected with them seem to have come into associative connection with his sister's death. It may have been some such anxiety which he was trying to overcome by the repeated self-assurance: "I know a lot of people older than myself who have actually asked me to advise them on certain [sexual] subjects. This always made me think that my advice was pretty good."

When he talked about his actual sexual experiences, Zeeno's language became especially queer and detached: "I never mingle in intimate relations." . . . "I have never desired to indulge with a virgin." . . . "I decided I might indulge in sexual congress." . . . "Having found a suitable person, I took part in coitus on various occasions." In such carefully chosen expressions we see an effort to separate the experience from its affect, a tendency which is obvious both in Zeeno's thinking and living and in the formal elements of his play construction.

As for the search for the lost lamb, the part of the scene, which in spite of its inconspicuous position at the edge of the table, approached a dramatic content more nearly than any other part: I assume that it represented the unanswered question in the subject's mind, as to "what happened to the lamb," the little sister. Other details of this scene which could confirm our interpretation reveal more about the actual family constellation of the subject's childhood than is permissible to quote.

4. *General remarks.* In selecting and comparing certain elements of the subject's memories and of his play, we point to the *probable* importance of a certain event in his life. As a psychic reality, we assume, the theme of that traumatic event still imposes both its content, and certain structural elements as well, on the subject's autoplastic and alloplastic behavior, i.e., it imposes certain configurations upon an arrangement of toys on a table.[17] In Zeeno's case we suggest the interpretation that in his life as well as in his play construction he has to separate certain elements because their connection arouses anxiety in him, and that these elements correspond to the details of his experiences with his sister. In this short account we are forced to neglect the fact that in the formulation of every psychic theme it is possible to interchange active and passive, subject and object, without having the theme lose either its importance or its inner truth; that is to say, we may assume that Zeeno is afraid to die young (like his sister) according to the primitive notion of "an eye for an eye," or that he, the younger, felt himself to have been seduced by his sister, or shared some kind of guilt with her and was afraid of having to die as she did.

Other interpretations may suggest themselves to the careful reader of the subject's biography. Our conclusion is that he was unable to construct a dramatic situation but revealed only at the very edge the traumatic situation in his memory which struggled for expression when, at our authoritative suggestion "to play," a safety valve was opened and quickly closed again.

N: Berry

1. *Preparatory Period.* Without any hesitation Berry builds the form shown in Figure 11a. Then he changes the form and constructs a scene (playing with, contemplating, and at first rejecting the maid as did more than half of the group): The father and mother discover the son with the maid in the kitchen (Figure 11b). But he does not like this scene. He builds another house, without doors, in which the kitchen is separated from the living room and the son and maid from the parents, who, in addition, are completely shut in by a ceiling—the only one to be found in these constructions.

2. *The Dramatic Scene.* (Figure 11c) He explains the scene more impersonally than the other subjects do. "The owner of the house and his wife, a visitor in the kitchen." Behind the house in the garden sits "a member of the family," and on the street the policeman stops traffic in order to let the little girl pass safely.

3. *Comments.* Again where we vainly awaited a dramatic situa-

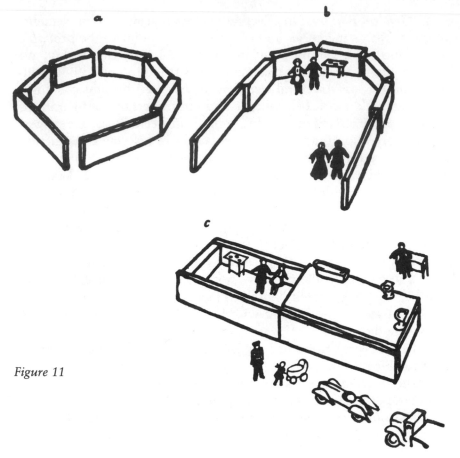

Figure 11

tion, we find only the indirect suggestion of drama which is implicit in the effort to avoid discovery and accident.

Among the subject's memories occurs the following scene: At the age of six—a garden behind the house, a little girl with whom he eats onions. He kisses the girl. One day the girl doesn't come back. She is not allowed to come any more. "Is this because of me?" he asks his mother. "I doubt it," is the answer. In this moment he says he learned what it meant to doubt—a statement which justifies our taking this scene seriously. An event recurring in his later childhood awoke in him this bitter feeling of doubt again and again, doubt of the justice of his parents. If he had a quarrel with his sister, the parents usually intervened in her favor.

Discovery, intervention, punishment appear in a rather decisive way in the material of the Clinic: For example, the subject relates that Hawthorne's vicar wears the black veil because he has discovered his brother with a woman. The vicar thus in wearing the veil punishes

himself for what he has seen. In the autobiography we find the statement "I had an exceptionally curious mind regarding sex matters
and read a great variety of medical books from the age of ten to
fifteen." This may throw light on a neurotic difficulty in reading.
This inhibition however had a prior history, Berry having developed
first an inhibition against play with girls or touching them at all,
especially his sister. Later this inhibiton extended to reading, in which
his curiosity obviously had found refuge. Visions of the past, so he
says, came between him and the reading matter; and it tormented
him that there should be so little personal feeling in these visions—
a subjective account of that separation of experience and affect which
we found in Zeeno.

His first house-form (Figure 11a) suggests a diagrammatic cross-
section of a female pelvis. Here he himself has formed that which he
perceives in the ink blot test: "Cross-section through a female body,
as one sees it in medical books." Other blots remind him of embryos
or portions of a miscarriage; others of ulcers and decomposed animals. Thus the house seems first to represent the (female) body, which
contains what he wants to know. It then takes the form of a real
house which contains the body which one wants to know about:
hence, man, maid, and intervention. But Berry remembers that if one
tries to enter and discover the secret, one is discovered oneself and
separated from the object of one's curiosity. Therefore, it seems better
to avoid discovery by separating all dangerous elements right at the
beginning. Thus, in his play construction, parents are enclosed so
that they are unable to discover the son (nor can he, we may add,
see what they are doing). This avoidance again (as in Zeeno's case)
has its parallel in a precaution on the street: the traffic is stopped in
order to let the little girl pass safely. In this way a traumatic outcome
is avoided, but at the same time a dramatic situation has become
impossible.

Separated and alone, "a member of the family" sits behind the
house in the special arrangement similar to Zeeno's "sister." She may
well be the girl in the garden behind the house of his childhood, the
girl whose disappearance caused or was caused by guilt. Certainly it
must be significant that through all of these constructions wherever
we are able to sense the persistence of concern for a person who
disappeared during childhood, this person is represented by a toy
which is placed outside of a closed house or room and always to the
right of the subject. In one case, the "best boy" of the group, a dead
rival-cousin, was even placed on another table where he "walked in
safety." One cannot help comparing this with the custom of some

primitive peoples who make a hole in their houses through which they push the corpses of their dead, only to close it again so that the dead cannot come back into the house. Neither Zeeno's nor Berry's house had doors and we find a house without doors in the constructions of the subjects in whose mind the idea of death and sex are closely linked: the dark room whence we come (the womb, the inside of the female body) and the one where we go (the tomb, the beyond). Symbolically these are one idea in primitive thought and may become permanently associated by a traumatic experience occurring at that age and stage of childhood for which this association, in an abortive form, is typical (the phallic-sadistic stage of libido-organization).

Here we might make another suggestion. So far as the first house-form represented a cross-section through a female body it contained a secret with which Berry was much concerned, as is suggested by his history as well as his ink blot fantasies of embryos and miscarriages. In his childhood he had heard that before he was born his mother had given birth to a girl who died—a fact which had strengthened his sexual and medical curiosity and influenced his mental development.

O: Asper

Because of its extreme emphasis on separation a construction which showed the most psychotic elements is of special clinical interest.

1 and 2. *Preparatory Period and Dramatic Scene*. (Figure 12) Asper places six peasants near one another like soldiers. Then he stares at them for several minutes, looking very unhappy, almost as if paralyzed. Thereupon he arranges some cars: In the green truck he puts a policeman; smaller cars and a man are approaching with a dog. Again follows a long, paralyzed hesitation, as if a single movement would bring about a catastrophe. Suddenly he crashes the red racer into a block so that it overturns. Immediately after this the subject seems freer, as if a magic word had been spoken, and completes the scene quickly. He puts the little girl into a corner and surrounds her by animals. He surrounds the policeman's car with peasants and turns the peasant with the dog so that he "leaves the field" (as Kurt Lewin would put it).

3. *Comments*. When the observer enters the room the subject says, "The imagination does not have enough to work on. Everything here is symbolical." About the little girl he adds: "She does not understand what it is all about. The animals are her pets." About the green truck: "An army truck. These men could easily be taken into the truck." (He puts them in.) . . . About the peasant: "He is immune to all of

Figure 12

us, he lives in the woods, he is outside, he can't be touched."

The subject in his nearness to mental disintegration (elsewhere he says that even the word " 'incongruous' becomes meaningless after a while") was the only subject who felt that his play construction was symbolic; while at the same time, paradoxically but significantly enough, he was the one who of the whole group felt most keenly that the dangers of playing were real. Nearer to "catastrophe" than any of the other subjects, he scarcely dared to move. He maintained a careful organization of cars and soldiers, gradually placed the soldiers closer and closer to the policeman, and felt easier only after he had rendered the red racer innocuous. The peasant with his dog goes silently away: "He is outside, he can't be touched."

Much could be said about the psychotic characteristics of this play construction:[18] how the danger of symbolic expression in infantile material is feared as if it were a real danger, how the plot shrinks to a mere spatial arrangement whose function it is to make everything, "right in time, right in space, not too late, not too soon, just right," as one of the inmates of the Worcester State Hospital remarked when he showed me his construction.

It is because of this need to maintain psychic barriers to protect themselves from infantile chaos that out of 40 normal, neurotic and psychotic adults and children the only person to protest against the test as "childish" was an inmate of the Worcester State Hospital. He had said that he could build an accident, but refrained from it. Instead, he merely placed the furniture, people, cars and animals in curved rows. At one point he started to put the little girl into a bed, but smiled thoughtfully and gave it up to arrange another long row of toys. Reminded by the observer that he wanted to build an accident, he said: "Well, well, well, a child might do that, if it cared to." Then for a moment he threw the cars around furiously, as if illustrating what a child would do. Thereupon he began setting the blocks two and two together, and said, "Some people forget their childhood, others go back to it." Then, as he built a solid square of block he said, "This could be the foundation for a house—or wharf. And this"—putting two blocks together—"is a breakwater. It is supposed to turn waves backwards." After a thoughtful moment he began to whirl the breakwater around as if it were helpless against the waves, and said slowly, "Do you think—a wave—can flow—backwards?"

II

"Let nothing happen to the girls and let nothing happen anyway" seemed to be the slogan of the small group of cautious subjects represented by Zeeno and Berry, who by the separation of dangerous play elements demonstrated to us the compulsive character's technique of prevention. "Let something happen but let it happen to the girl" is the slogan of the majority, whose spokesman we shall describe next.

P: Oriol

1. *Preparatory Period.* After receiving his instructions the subject jokes. He takes the toy toilet between his fingers and smiles broadly at the observer. Left to himself he grows serious: Let's see. Little girl? No. Maid? No. Baby carriage? No. (Highly dissatisfied.) Suddenly, with sweeping movements, he makes three piles—people, cars, blocks. He then finds excited satisfaction in taking single objects out of the piles and constructing his scene.

In the center of his construction he first puts a policeman standing on a block with four cars pointing straight at him from four directions. If real, this scene could represent only a suicidal demonstration against the authority of the state. And, although in the final scene he had turned the cars so that they were not pointing at the policeman,

Figure 13

his first remark when the observer entered the room continued the theme of revolt.

2. *The Dramatic Scene.* (Figure 13) "This is like the Place de la Concorde, where the riots were." Of the policeman, "He stands in his box higher than the other people" (suggesting probably something like the Napoleon column in the Place Vendôme). The little girl is run over—thus suffering the fate for which at first the policeman was destined—"because the maid chats with an old friend of her mother and does not watch the girl." The parents, by coincidence, arrive at this moment and are witnesses to their daughter's death.

On leaving, the subject again takes the toilet, laughs and says, "I suppose some people use this to express their ideas. I haven't come to that stage."

3. *Comments:* Though the subject jokes twice about the toy toilet, he assures us, without being asked, that he does not use this medium through which he supposes "some people" express their ideas. This and his strange pleasure in piling the toys and in taking single pieces out of the piles, arouses a suspicion as to the psychic reality of a painful element in the subject's memories. At the age of eight (an unusually advanced age for the breaking through of aggression in this direction) Oriol was found *smearing feces*. This story is often repeated at home to family intimates, much to his discomfort, and is advanced by his family as a reason for wondering how he ever got into college.

In addition to the riot topic and the hints regarding the *anal riot* of his childhood, there are in his construction spatial arrangements which indicate what may be the main psychic and physiological quandary of his life, i.e., to retain or release. First he builds one street, then a square with four entrances, and finally points out explicitly that the square has many exits. We may add that no one who had heard the subject talk would fail to remark his speech, which often approaches an *oral riot*—a flow of intellectually defiant words which he releases continuously. He is said to have learned to talk very late.

Oriol likes to play with the idea of running away from home; but he has decided to run away only intellectually. He keeps silent when with his father, but remains intellectually his own boss, and says so to whoever wants or does not want to listen. While his memories are full of humiliating experiences, his confessions express the wish to overcome humiliation through greatness, and to overcome unclean tendencies by producing beauty. "If I could remodel the world I would like to be the greatest writer." But, "I am afraid of life and afraid of death." Sure to be humiliated whenever he expresses his immature and unconsolidated impulses, he must choose masochistic wish fulfillments in order to gain satisfaction. He wants to be a poet—but he wants to be a martyr poet. "I want to expose myself and suffer." Here, even were it not suggested by other constructions as well, one would suspect that the girl in the accident represents the subject himself whose parents thus witness his suffering.

Of his construction, Oriol is right in saying, "I haven't come to the stage where I would use the toilet to express my ideas," for he obviously prefers a suicidal accident to a riot, after the fecal riot of his past (playing with feces) is suggested to him by the stimulus situation of being asked to play. But in spite of his objection, he must repeat the event he wants to avoid in the formal elements of his construction (piling: playing).

4. *Second Construction.* A year later Oriol was asked to construct another dramatic scene. In evaluating such a repetition we must remember that the earlier construction had taken 20 minutes, had not been understood by the subject as "meaning" anything, and had not been mentioned to him by anybody afterwards. Again Oriol piles the blocks before he starts. This time his square is first round with one exit leading to the water. A truck coming from the direction of the water is headed straight for the policeman. There is a dog in front of the truck. "It will not be run over," the rebellious subject says, a fact which we shall recall later when, in reviewing the construction of the well-educated and pious Mauve, a dog is run over. In changing the square, all form is abandoned, the blocks and furniture appear in piles. Again the memorial for a revolutionist takes the center and

this time it is a communist worker. Quite independent of this scene, another part of the table is supposed to be the inside of a house. Here a little girl stands in front of a mirror "admiring herself and stubborn." "She is defiant. She does not like people. Later, she will go to the maid, who cannot tell her to 'shut up!' " This parallel to the communistic orator on the memorial characterizes well the state of continuous, narcissistic, and oral revolt in which our subject lives.

When the observer reenters the room, Oriol has the red racer in his hand. After having given his other explanations, he adds it to the scene, remarking as if excusing himself, "This one does not mean anything." Then, in going out, he says: "I left the bathroom empty. I would be embarrassed—" Thus he seems to follow the pattern of his first construction which he had left with the words, "I suppose some people use this [the toilet] to express their ideas. I haven't come to that stage." We have seen how far this last negation really was a double affirmation; we may assume the same about the protested unimportance of the red racer.

5. *Remarks.* Oriol's construction shows the confusion which can extend to the adolescent mind from childhood experiences in an almost tragi-comic way. Only with weak negations does he separate himself from the most embarrassing childhood situations. A need to expose himself must have been decisive in this construction.

Oriol did not talk when he was expected to; he still soiled when he was no longer expected to do so—and this "stubbornness" (which might well be based on a constitutional or early traumatic factor) still pervades everything he says and does with typical pregenital ambivalence. Not independent enough to do without love and protection, he still is not able to return love because this would have meant in childhood the unconditional surrender of the jurisdiction over parts of his body and now would mean the final socialization of modes of behavior which are derived from those organic functions. Oriol does not soil, because he is neither child nor psychotic; nevertheless, elimination and retention in their characterological and mental aspects are his problem. What is presented here by Oriol, in his chaotic way in regard to anal-sadistic characteristics, differs only quantitatively, not qualitatively, from the general problems facing our whole group of late adolescents. Did their genitality make itself independent of regressive association with the psychobiologically significant drives of childhood? We know that the absence of genital consolidation necessitates a continuous state of defense against the guerila warfare of infantile impulses which still resist "don'ts" which have long since become senseless, infantile impulses, which promise nonexistent paradises, and which urge the individual to subdue love objects or to surrender to them—in an oscillation between love and hate.

Since we may be criticized for the clinical predilections in our observation of a group of individuals who did not come as patients, it might be of special interest to compare with the illustration of Oriol's fixation on oral and anal-sadistic autoerotism the construction of Mauve, who was perhaps the best organized personality in the group. His construction shows a typical attempt to overcome the pregenital ambivalence menacing the best organized young men in their relationships with the other sex. Between Oriol and Mauve lies the problem of the whole group: how, in a society, which with moral and economic means discourages unbroken psychosexual progress, can one adapt without sacrificing one's genital masculinity; how develop without rebellion; how wait without regression; how love without suspicion, fear and hate; in a word, how overcome ambivalence, the counterpart of obedience? This is the moral problem of adolescence which various cultures deal with in various ways.

Q: Mauve

1. *Preparatory Period.* Mauve took off his coat and, obviously pleased with himself and ready to serve scientific purposes, began his construction like a good organizer, quickly and without interruption. A growing excitement was evident—he got caught by his ideas.

2. *The Dramatic Scene.* (Figure 14) Mauve explains: "The green truck is running over a dog—it is the little girl's dog." A car coming after it bumps into the truck, a second one is just turning over, a third one tries to avoid the crash. In the kitchen "the maid is fainting; she has a little dog herself and this is the reason why she feels like that." In the living room we see "a young lady on the couch in the first stage of pneumonia. Something very emotional in this scene. Her fiancé and her doctor are looking down on her. The mother does not feel well and has gone to bed."

3. *Comments:* This is the only time a dog is run over instead of a woman; we are therefore interested to hear Mauve in another interview say: "Women are faithful, they are dogs. They have been dogs for so many centuries." In his outlook on life, as well as in his conception of himself, we see him separate himself from the "animal in us." "My standards are high and I intend to keep them." Woman and drives belong to another, an animalistic world which is separated from the young man's world of clear standards.

Figure 14

On the other hand, standards are derived from his education by his mother and other women. Many years younger than the father, the mother is deeply attached to the son and he accounts for their emotional relationship in the most explicit œdipus fantasy offered by any of the group.[19] Over-obedient to her wishes, he says, he "almost dedicated his life to the avoidance of drinking, smoking and swearing." And yet certain circumstances in his relationship to his mother seem to draw him deeply into ambivalence towards the weaker sex.

His mother is "handicapped by a disease which periodically disables her completely" and she always tried to keep the healthy, active boy close to home, of which he complains, though taking care of his mother in a most touching manner. If, in the "dog running on the street," we want to see a symbolic rebellion of the son against all the careful obedience which a physically weakened authority is imposing on him, we may understand that it is his drive, the "animal in us," which is punished by being run over. On the other hand— the dog represents the group of human beings to whom something happens: i.e., women.

If we confront this subject's outbreak with his remarks about women on the one side and his educational indebtedness to his mother and other women on the other, a conscious or unconscious duality of attitude towards women, quite common in our civilization, is represented: men easily identify women with the wishes which they stimulate. If they learn to have contempt for "lower" drives (and their pregenital components) they may also have contempt for women so far as they are the objects of their wishes. As beings, however, held in high esteem ("mother, aunt, teacher") women are also identified with the strictest and most idealistic concepts of conscience. "Angels" or "dogs"—women awaken uncomfortable ambivalent feelings, feelings which spoil the perspective of sex life. A not unusual type of rather well adapted young men (whom Mauve seems to represent) learns to live and to care for a world of achievements which have "nothing to do with women"; it is characteristic of this type that in order to satisfy his conscious and potent genital wishes he goes "to Paris"—as Mauve says he plans to do. There, then, women are neither angels nor dogs; they are French. The girl who does not belong to one's own culture or class (in other constructions often the girl who does not belong to the family, namely, the maid) is the object of more conscious fantasies.

4. *General remarks.* We may ask, however, what the little girl, to whom the subjects pay so much damaging attention, might represent. It is hard to give the reader an impression of the uncanny regularity with which these young men whether normal, neurotic or psychotic examined the little girl and, as if they were following a ritualistic duty, seriously put her under the green or red car, or placed a policeman in the center of the scene to protect her. The majority of the subjects who failed to have this theme in their final scene at least considered it and rehearsed it during the preparatory period. A great number of problems must be evoked by this little girl and the crux of the problem must be symbolized by the accidents which happen to her.

Some of the possible explanations, all suggested by material which cannot be quoted here in full are:

a.) The little girl may represent a little girl of importance (i.e., a sister) in the subject's childhood. The uniform and typical handling of this toy suggests, however, that she represents rather a symbol than an historical individual.

b.) The little girl, as the youngest among the toys, might appear to be the representative of "the child," the most endangered and therefore the most protected human being in traffic. Can we assume that in spite of the abundance of dramatic moments in life and literature, movies and newspapers, accidents resulting in the deaths of children are emotionally important enough to be the dramatic scene par excellence for the majority of twenty Harvard students? In that case, our psychoanalytic explanations are less valuable, though not entirely worthless since they show the unconscious meaning of this accident in its relationship to other unconscious concepts of "what happens to children."

c.) The emphasis may lie on *girl*. Since, according to common infantile theories, girls are made into girls, not born as such, some violence is assumed to exist in sexual matters. The accident, then, which belongs to the "complex" of related symbols dominating our construction, may represent the act of violence of which girls are the victims.

d.) Since, beside the little girl, the victims in these accidents are always and only female toys, the little girl may represent a *pars pro toto*, namely, the female world, in which case it might have been selected because it provokes the least conscious aggressive fantasies and allows the subject to feel himself consciously free of any participation in the committed violence. We shall presently come back to this point.

e.) The little girl may represent a *totum pro parte*. Freud, in the *Interpretation of Dreams* (p. 338), remarks that in dreams "children often signify the genitals since men and women are in the habit of referring to their *genital organs* as 'little man,' 'little woman,' 'little thing.' To play with or to beat a little child is often the dream's representation of *masturbation*." It is a big step from our first tentative explanation to this interpretation; but the reader will have to decide to make this step with us tentatively—or to leave the question open. Psychoanalytic method, waiting for the most part for associative material in order to interpret any product of the mind, uses only a few "established" symbols, uniform "translation" of which has proved to be necessary and suitable in long and exhaustive studies.

Two of these symbols with which we are concerned here are put together by Freud in a title to the interpretation of a woman's dream which states bluntly: "The 'little one' as the genital organ. Being run over as a symbol of sexual intercourse." (*Op. cit.*, p. 342.) Dream interpretation thus suggests that what the subjects do with the little girl corresponds in their unconscious with ideas of autoerotic and alloerotic sexual acts, in which something happens to the partner's or the subject's own sexual organs. There is nothing in their strange behavior which a priori could devaluate such a strange notion.

f.) We cannot avoid pointing to a sociological factor, namely, the sexual life typical for such a group of biologically mature individuals as our subjects. Their sexual activities are autoerotic, or else consist of a kind of mutual (heterosexual) autoerotism, more or less sanctioned by society. The danger of this form of gratification is the conditioning of masculine impulses by the repetition of a situation with infantile characteristics. Whenever the mature drive is aroused, *the impulse of masculine intrusion* and certain related sadistic tendencies are mobilized with all the other impulses which participate in the pattern of complete sexual satisfaction. In mere sex play they fail to be satisfied and—as it were—to be disarmed. It is, I think, this frustrated intrusive component of masculinity, which, though continuously stimulated in our subjects, has not yet found its wholesome amalgamation with the other factors of heterosexual partnership, and which therefore in their secret fantasies appears in a certain *homicidal and suicidal* rudeness—which, we may add here, has an important sociological counterpart in certain adolescent and cruel forms of public sensationalism not dissimilar in content to our constructions.

g.) Female subjects who constructed scenes with the same toys showed as a common factor the criminal man (father). The five college girls among them (the same age as our subjects) constructed the following scenes:

R: A father, who was a deserter in war and lives in shameful exile, picks up on the street a little girl who has been run over by a truck. She is his daughter.

S: A selfish father, who has neglected his wife and children for years, comes home and finds everything destroyed and everybody killed by a flood.

T: A father, supposedly away in an insane asylum, comes home to murder his family.

U: A landowner strangles his wife. His servant's daughter, to whom he has made advances, testifies against him at the trial.

V: Robbers steal a table out of a house in the middle of the night.

It would be interesting if further studies would substantiate that to the main theme of our male subjects ("Something happens or is prevented from happening to a girl"), there corresponds a female one: "A man is (or is prevented from being) criminally aggressive." The fact that—with a few exceptions—both sexes place a member of the opposite sex in the center of the construction, points clearly to a sexual component in scenes which on the conscious level refer to danger and death.

W: Krumb

1. *Preparatory Period and Dramatic Scene.* Krumb considers for a while the problem of whether to use one or two tables. He decides

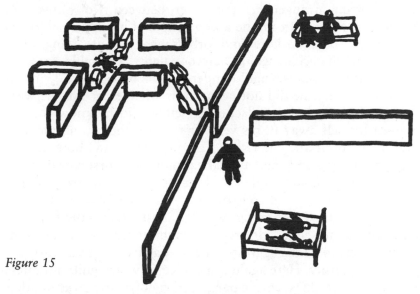

Figure 15

on one. With two blocks he builds a wall, puts the red racer at an angle of 45° toward it and then makes a small opening in it. Then he puts the father into the house so that the red racer, if driven, would run through the hole in the house and hit the father in the back. (Figure 15.) After this his doubts disappear. He obviously gets a funny idea and, laughing, puts the son and the maid together into a bed. The scene is completed quickly as seen in Figure 15. The father finds the son in bed with the maid and forbids intercourse. "Nothing homosexual is going on in the other room," adds the subject. The little girl is caught between two cars and the red racer speeding dangerously around the corner means one more danger for her. He seems not quite sure about which is the front and which the back of the racer, so that in reality it would, if "speeding dangerously," hit door and father.

2. *Comments:* This subject, the only one to put a boy and girl in a bed together, is a manifest homosexual—a fact which without any help from the rich but disorganized and complicated material of his life history, makes it possible for us to understand the meaning of the almost topological description of his inner conflicts in his scene; the living between two alternatives, both dangerous.

"Last year I had affairs with about three women and some fifteen men. Now it is only with men that I can find happiness. Being homosexual makes it possible for me to repress sexual impulses (?). I wish I could repress my feelings of guilt also."

It seems that Krumb tries to appease his growing feeling of guilt by the following arrangement: the father, between two rooms with a couple of the same sex in one and a couple of heterosexual lovers in the other, turns to the latter and forbids what they are doing. Thus the father himself decides against heterosexuality. The subject assures us that "nothing homosexual" happens in the other room, without our asking. In fact, he did not even know whether or not we were informed of his sexual predilections. Neither did he know that he had given himself away in his very first move: the arrangement of the racer, the door and the father. [Because we know] how often a house symbolizes a body and a car the genitals, this first construction represents the form and mode of a homosexual act: intercourse per anum. (See Oriol's second construction.) His indecision, then, as to which direction the car is going (whether crashing into the father or into the already mutilated girl) represents the alternative to the homosexual choice: to be the aggressive or the passive, the sadistic or the masochistic, partner. Here again is a choice, in which guilt doubtless drives him into the masochistic part, as many of his remarks in other interviews indicate, i.e., "The moving picture *Death Takes a Holiday* made me in love with death."

We have to leave it to the reports on their biographies to emphasize the complicated psychological aspects of the struggle of conscience in the individual subjects. If we could report more examples it would be worthwhile to define and to compare the different ways in which a conflict of conscience appears in the preparatory period, with the outcome as represented in the final scene. In the succession of toys which the subjects take and refuse at the beginning, one notices a peculiar alternation of symbols of repressed (maid, etc.) and repressing forces (policeman, etc.). The streeet seems always to offer a welcome opportunity for shifting the problem to the impersonal. The subjects show all varieties of guilt-feelings from the anxiety of losing love and protection (i.e., in building harmonious scenes with the mother at the table and the maid at the stove—entirely forgetful of the instructions) to the fear of catastrophe (policeman regulating traffic and preventing accidents as the only "dramatic" element) to various forms of self-punishment. It is as if these subjects, in the slow tortuous process of civilized maturation, had to find a painfully individual substitute for that sacrifice of a tooth or other symbol which "cruel" primitives in their puberty rites inflict uniformly and once and for all on the boys of their community.

Second Construction. One year after this construction (it might be well to state here again that not one word of interpretation was given to the subjects) Krumb was again asked to construct a scene.

He immediately asked: "May *two* things happen?," thus taking up again the dualism of the first construction. He builds first two houses, then one house with two parts, two rooms in each part. Again males and females are separated. The father, he says, has a homosexual crush on a severely wounded soldier and is in the bathroom—while in the street the red racer is wrecked by the green truck. "I have a feeling," the subject remarks, "that I have repeated my last construction. I struggled for three minutes to overcome the feeling that I did the same thing. Then I did—and found that I had expressed homosexuality this time, which it seems I could avoid last time." Finally, Krumb gives a confirmation of our first assumption, which no doubt to many readers seemed hazardous, namely, that the small hole in the house of the first construction symbolized the homosexually attacked rectum; the house of the second construction, again, and at the same place, has a small hole. Krumb remarks about it: "The house is badly built, *bad odors* come out of here."

III. X: Vulner

This is the construction of the only subject to whom the suggestion "dramatic scene" implied a scene on a stage.

During the *Preparatory Period* Vulner is very hesitant. He takes the son first, then the father, but puts them back and seems to think seriously. He accidentally drops the son, plays with the policeman, in serious thought, head dropped forward. Should he take the cow? No. Then he takes the son again and acts quickly.

The *Dramatic Scene* represents the corner of a room. The mother is sitting in a chair, the father stands in front of her. In a doorway stand son and daughter.

"The head minister is handing in his resignation. The day before he had talked with the queen about the question of the crown prince's marriage to a commoner. He had decided against it. In the meantime he has learned that it is his daughter whom the prince wishes to marry." Asked what the outcome will be, the subject replies, as if he were finishing a fairy tale told to a child, "He will probably marry her."

Analytic Remark: The most interesting aspect of this "really dramatic" construction is that there is very little to say about it. The scene possibly contains some hints in regard to the subject's family situation; he has one sister, no brother. But essentially the scene is a dramatic cliché and does not suggest any detail of the subject's biography, except that his mother is a writer and that as a boy he had often participated in dramatic plays.

IV.   (Final Remarks)

Having asked out subjects for a dramatic scene, we find a product of traumatic tension; instead of tragedy we find accident.

Dramatic and traumatic moments have one psychological element in common. Both are events which transgress the boundaries of the human ego, the first in widening it beyond individuation, the second in nearly extinguishing it. In other words, in a truly dramatic moment the individual is confronted with a choice which may make him the heroic or tragic master of human fate in its eternal aspects; he is allowed one chance to overcome the bondage of gravity and repetition. The traumatic moment destroys individuation, chance and choice, and makes the individual the helpless victim of repetition compulsion.

To be sure, in offering the little toys for a dramatic task we probably asked our subjects to take a too difficult step from the ridiculous to the sublime. In offering play material we ourselves have provoked the spirit of infantile conflict, since play "presupposes a psychic substance which is not quite structuralized yet."[20] The specific conflicts appearing in the constructions indicate that the subjects when confronted with toys, continued where they had left off in their childhood play with the attempt to overcome traumatic experience by active repetition in play.

In describing these results we naturally do not characterize individuals in their conscious and rational individuation. The psychoanalytic microscope first focuses on neurotic material in its specific psychosexual characteristics. It shows us the inner frontier where the rational human mind—whether in the state of infancy, savagery or civilization—is constantly faced by the wilderness of the irrational.

The set-up of this particular study is not of any general value and is not recommended as a psychological experiment. But the results of this accidental undertaking may be of some interest in regard to the psychology and the psychopathology of play (important for the treatment of patients who cannot or do not want to speak): we can observe directly the structuralization of a given space in accordance with the qualities of a traumatic configuration, which imposes on the subjects' autoplastic and alloplastic behavior spatial elements of a past event or of the way in which the subject has armed himself against the (irrational) danger of its recurrence.

Further deciphering of play hieroglyphs—especially in the legitimate sphere of childhood—may offer valuable keys for the understanding of the prelinguistic and alinguistic strata of the human mind.

Notes

[1] Anna Freud. *Introduction to the Technic of Child Analysis.* Nervous and Mental Disease Monograph Series 40, (1928), 43.

[2] Robert Wälder, "The Psychoanalytic Theory of Play." *Psychoanalytic Quarterly*, 2 (1933), 208–24.

According to the current theories of play, either the past, "a pressure exerted by unfinished processes," leads the playing child's mind to the *mastery through repetition* of traumatic experiences: "adding an *active counterpart to the passive experience*" (Freud); or the present is in the lead insisting on the *discharge of surplus energy*, on the fulfillment of wishes here and now, or on *functional pleasure* (Buehler, in Wälder's formulation: "pleasure experienced in pure performance without regard to the success of activity"); finally, it may be the future and its tasks for which the child may be training himself in the trials, errors and victories of his play experimentation (Groos).

[3] Sigmund Freud, *Introductory Lectures on Psychoanalysis* (London, Allen & Unwin, 1922), 128.

[4] George Santayana, *The Last Puritan* (New York: Charles Scribner's Sons, 1936), 98–99.

[5] As to the development relationship of biting and focusing, see Chapter III, B, page 105.

[6] *Zeitschrift für psychoanalytische Pädagogik*, IX (1935).

[7] See part 3 of this note page 102.

[8] In concluding a letter to his mother, J wrote instead of "Love, J," "Left, J."

[9] See, however, case P (Oriol) in Chapter IV, page 124.

[10] See case E, page 85.

[11] When the author first used the scheme to be presented on the following pages in order to explain certain play phenomena in a seminar in Boston, in 1934, he did not know of F. Alexander's "vector analysis." (See the publications of the Chicago Psychoanalytic Institute.) For the limited purpose of these notes, it seems better not to discuss Alexander's conclusions.

[12] A sixth mode, ◉   digestive-assimilative "building-up" is vaguely put "inside the body." It will have to be replaced by whatever may in the future best represent the knowledge of the complicated relationships and connections (4, 5, 6) of the inner organs to the social organs, which will prove to be of some importance in regard to connection of body-ego and play structuralization.

[13] A later, mature level of this correlation, characterologically and pathologically not independent from this first pregenital level, may be seen in the circle of conception (more or less active incorporation) pregnancy and parturition (more or less retentive or eliminative) and lactation (in which the woman accomplishes more or less the long desired equivalent of intrusive generosity). Men find a fulfillment of this correlation in the sublimation of creative work.

[14] Margaret Mead, *Sex and Temperament* (New York: William Morrow & Co., 1935), 27.

[15] The experimental or interview procedures of the Harvard Psychological Clinic mentioned in this report are:

1. *Conference.* (Dr. Henry A. Murray) The first session for the subject was the Conference. The subject sat down at a table with the 5 members of the Diagnostic Council. He was asked questions and given certain tests to perform in their presence.

2. *Autobiography.* (Dr. Henry A. Murray) The subject was asked to write for 2 hours about his early life and development. He was presented with an outline to guide him.

3. *Childhood Memories.* (H. Scudder Mekeel) The subject was given a questionnaire pertaining to family relations, and he was interviewed twice (each session one hour) and asked to give as many memories as possible of his childhood and adolescence.

4. *Sexual Development.* (Dr. William G. Barrett) The subject was asked to lie on a couch and say what came to his mind. Later, he was asked various questions about his sexual development.

5. *Hypnotic Test.* (Robert W. White) In two sessions, an attempt was made to hypnotize the subjects and a numerical score assigned representing his susceptibility to hypnosis. On a

later day, a different interviewer encouraged him to discuss the test at length.

6. *Thematic Apperception Test.* (Christiana D. Morgan) The subject was shown a series of dramatic pictures. He was asked to make up a story for which each picture might be used as an illustration.

7. *Imaginal Productivity Test.* (David R. Wheeler) (a) Beta Ink Blot test. The subject was asked to tell what forms he could make out in the ink blots. (b) Similes test. The subject was asked to make up similes for certain words (presented to him in succession by the E). (c) Minister's Black Veil test. The subject was asked to spend an hour writing a story using as a theme the appearance of a minister in the pulpit with a black veil over his eyes. (Hawthorne).

[16] Unfortunately such a partial report as this one cannot convincingly demonstrate this specificity. The skeptical reader is referred to the Clinic's forthcoming publication which, in addition to further reports of procedures with the same subjects, contains detailed biographical studies. (The names used in this report are those used in the Clinic's material.)

[17] In Kurt Lewin's terms: A "structuralization of the life-space" represented in play, a material which is less "refractory" than actual life.

[18] See also Saul Rosenzweig and David Shakow, "Play Technique in Schizophrenia and Other Psychoses, II. An Experimental Study of Schizophrenic Constructions with Play Materials." *American Journal of Orthopsychiatry*, VII (1937), 36.

[19] See the Clinic's publication [page 749, item 6].

[20] Wälder, *op. cit.*

Studies in the Interpretation of Play: Clinical Observation of Play Disruption in Young Children (1940)

I. Orientation

The purpose of this monograph is a modest and elementary one. Specimens of a psychotherapist's experience, namely, the observation of the first play enacted by young patients in his office, are reviewed, as it were, in slow motion. Two aspects are isolated as far as clinical material permits: What, to this psychotherapist, are the outstanding attributes of a play observation? What conscious considerations lead him to the "meaning" on which he bases his first diagnostic decisions?

This primitive inquiry marked the initial phase of a study of neurotic episodes and incipient neuroses in the pre-school child.[1] Unfortunately, however, simple purpose does not necessarily make for simple reading; and the concentration on small specimens in a field with such vast connotations and (recently) such general appeal necessitates a rather general introduction.

The problem of play lies at the intersection of a variety of educational and clinical interests. In reaction to an era which hoped to develop

First published in *Genetic Psychology Monographs*, 22 (1940): 557–671.
References are cited by bracketed numbers in the text. For full citations see listing of references at the conclusion of this paper.

virtues in children by clipping the wings of their spontaneity, modern education wishes to develop and to preserve, modern psychotherapy to utilize the benevolent powers which are said to emanate from the child's "creative" activities.

The contribution of psychoanalysis to this development is a singular one. It not only assumes, with others, a vague—self-teaching, self-healing—function in play but also detects a detailed correspondence between central personality problems and both the content and the form of individual play creations.

The clinical psychoanalysis of play, however, has shared the methodological limits of other psychoanalytic media with which Freud did not concern himself in detail (as he did with dreams, slips, witticisms, etc.). Their discernible phantasy content is welcome as something vaguely similar to and therefore useful substitutions for memories, dreams, and other media which are not plentiful in contacts with a small child; their *specific variables*, however (such as, in play, the variables of extension in actual space), have not been considered worth any special methodological consideration. Responsibility for this neglect seems to lie in the same general attitude among psychoanalysts which induced Freud to complain in regard to the interpretation of dreams, the oldest *via regia* to the human mind: *"Die Analytiker benehmen sich als wäre die Traumlehre abgeschlossen."* (7)

Tenaciously as the clinical worker may cling to standardized habits of interpretations and may try to see by means of a new medium only that which he had learned to see through older ones, his experience is never the same; new variables of changed experience constantly force him to imply new concepts or a different use of old ones. The clinical observer not only shares a particularly elusive *personal* equation with all those who observe with the naked eye and ear. His work also underlies the *practical* equation derived from the necessity to influence sooner or later the very material under observation. Finally, something like a *cultural* equation expresses the influence on his work and thought of his constantly changing function in science and society. Whatever scientific ore, therefore, may be present in the clinical experience (made elusive by technical, personal, practical, and cultural changes) comes to light mainly through the therapist's constant *efforts at making explicit some of the implicit (preconscious) steps of selecting, associating, and reasoning* which constitute his clinical "intuition" at a given time and in a given technique.

This being our object, we shall be forced to risk tiring the reader with details, details which will seem superfluous to the play technician whose optimism is satisfied with shortcuts, and senseless to the psychoanalyst who has learned to view pessimistically any attempts at demonstrating psychoanalytic experience to the "outer world."

In adult life (10) *"talking it out"* is the simplest autotherapeutic measure employed during tense periods by individuals who are not too asocial. Religious and psychiatric sects ritualize it in varying degrees by providing at regular intervals an authoritatively sanctioned listener who gives undivided attention and, sworn to neither censure nor betray, bestows absolution by explaining the individual's problem as belonging in a greater religious, ethical, sociological, medical context. The method finds its limitations where the clinical situation loses the detachment in which life can mirror itself and becomes the center of a passionate conflict as expressed in a too dependent (if not sexual) or too hostile attitude toward the therapist. In psychoanalytic terms: the limitation is set by the tendency (especially strong in neurotics) to superimpose one's basic conflicts on every new situation, even the therapeutic one. This leads to a *transference* which temporarily makes the therapeutic situation a disturbing factor in the patient's life. The patient is in resistance; in a war to end all wars, he becomes more deeply embroiled than ever. At this point non-psychoanalytic efforts are given up; the patient, it is said, does not want to get well or is too inferior to comprehend his obligations in treatment. Therapeutic psychoanalysis at this point systematically begins to make use of the knowledge that no neurotic is undivided in his wish to get well and by necessity transfers his dependencies and hostilities to the treatment and the person of the therapist; in revealing these "resistances" he points the way to *his* treatment.

"To play it out" is the most natural autotherapeutic measure childhood affords. Whatever other role play may have in the child's development (and I do not think that these roles are adequately known), the child also uses it to make up for defeats, sufferings, and frustrations, especially those resulting from a technically and culturally limited use of language. This, the "cathartic" theory of play, is one of the many play theories, all of which agree only in assuming an untimely tension. If not a *catharsis* for excessive (traumatic) stimulation in the past, play is considered the expression of a *surplus energy* for which there is no more "practical" use at the moment; with untimeliness projected into phylogenetic dimensions, play becomes a *recapitulation* of (now useless) phylogenetic leftovers or the *preparatory* expression of what in the future will be useful activity.

In Spencer's classic words, wherever circumstances allow or suggest play, those tendencies are *"simulated"* which are *"unusually ready to act, unusually ready to have their correlative feelings aroused"* (14) (but at the same time are *not any more* or *not as yet practicable* in connection with their real goal).

Of all organisms the human child is probably the one who has to learn to postpone temporarily and permanently the most formidable array of tendencies which because of his slow maturation and his higher aspirations are precocious or definitely out of place. Some of them (as Freud has recognized in neurotics) remain "unusually ready to have their correlative feelings aroused" throughout life. Our new knowledge of such unconscious and subverbal "readinesses" gives the previous theories of play a new and specifically human meaning. In all its slow maturation and long defenselessness, the human child, so we learn, lives through periods of diffuse, culturally and biologically impracticable impulses of a sensual and aggressive nature, which he cannot help attaching to the narrow circle of his very originators, protectors, and educators—his family. The task of maturation, then, is to outgrow in the most constructive manner these premature emotional and instinctual attachments while outgrowing the need for protection. But this is a slow and partly indefinite process; and the human animal not only plays most and longest but also remains ready to become deadly serious in the most irrational contexts.

Modern play therapy is based on the observation that a child made ambivalent and insecure by a secret hate against or fear of the natural protectors of his play (family, neighborhood) seems able to use the protective sanction of an understanding adult, in professional elaboration the play therapist, to regain some play peace. The most obvious reason is that the child has the toys and the adult for himself, sibling rivalry, parental nagging, and routine interruptions do not disturb the unfolding of his play intentions, whatever they may be.

The observing adult's "understanding" of such play, then, is a beneficial factor even where it finds only an intangible minimum of expression in the child's presence, while its value for an indirect use in advice and guidance can hardly be over-estimated. The peace provided by solitary play or by play in the presence of a sympathetic adult often radiates for some time, often long and intensively enough to meet the radiation of recognition and love from some source in the environment, a necessary factor in all psychological cures. The chances therefore seem better where the mother too has an opportunity to relieve in conversations her ambivalence toward the child and is prepared to respond to his improvement.

As we shall demonstrate, however, the phenomenon of *transference* in the work with the playing child, as well as with the verbalizing adult, marks the point where simple measures fail, namely, when an emotion of such intensity as to defeat playfulness forces an immediate and only thinly-veiled discharge into the play and into the relationship to the play observer. The failure is characterized by what is to be described in this monograph as *play disruption*, i.e., the sudden and complete or diffused and slowly spreading inability to play.

Recent work in this country has emphasized the alternatives of "passivity" or "activity" on the part of the play observer, the extreme passive attitude representing a certain seductive lifelessness, a kind of play hostess attitude, the extreme active one an animated encouragement of the child to "release aggression" against toys named after members of the child's family. Where a child can follow this latter suggestion without immediate or delayed play disruption we have no reason to be worried about the child, although the "release" theory implied in such procedures seems tenable only in clearly "traumatic" cases and there only theoretically, as the thorough analysis of such cases shows. The clinical problem seems to be solved only be the establishment of permanent and sufficient everyday release channels and not by a momentary release under special conditions. Much of this "release" ideology as well as certain forms of purely symbolic and purely sexual interpretation seems to be a revival of the most primitive techniques of the early psychoanalysis of adults—now transferred to the new field of play therapy.

Those children who transfer not the solution but the insolvability of their problems into the play situation and onto the person of the observer need to be induced by *systematic interpretation* to reconsider, on a more verbal level, the constellations which have overwhelmed them in the past and are apt to overwhelm them when reoccurring. Where *this* goal is given, child psychoanalysis begins.

Child analysis proper, in the cases which are its domain, seeks to provide the child with opportunity for catharsis only in the frame of an intimate therapeutic contact in which *repeated interpretation* furthers the *verbal communication* of inner dangers and the establishment of a *supremacy of conscious judgment* over unmanageable or incompletely repressed tendencies. To interpret means to reveal to the patient, at a *dynamically specific moment*, meanings which he can fully admit to himself only under the guidance of the therapist. Such interpretation is impossible without a technique which systematically and consistently reveals the *dynamics of the developing therapeutic situation*, especially the forces of transference and resistance.

Its application is useless or dangerous where there is not time enough to follow the patient and to give new interpretations until a lasting ability is secured to express in a more conscious and social, more humorous and more useful manner that which he first could only admit to verbalization under the guidance of a therapist. Interpretation waits for a specific moment; it needs preparation and after-treatment; it does not claim success until a general and lasting increase of constructive vitality seems secured.

As the treatment proceeds and as the child's verbal powers increase, play observation loses much if not most of its exclusive importance. For the age group reported, however, the investigation of the child's play is a natural first step which coincides with the first step of a variety of treatments; while it can be abandoned or deferred without damage, it can also be pursued and developed without break.

As stated above, this monograph demonstrates the analytic method merely in so far as it permits one to locate through play observation the approximate "seat" and extent of an emotional disturbance before definite clinical procedure is decided upon. This procedure may or may not be child psychoanalysis. Only in the last case to be reported will an effort be made to demonstrate the function of therapeutic interpretations. I should like, however, at least in the introduction, to transgress the scope of this monograph and to indicate briefly some views in regard to the wider problem of psychoanalysis.

Psychoanalysis, besides being a psychotherapeutic method, is a method of research, a system of psychological and "metapsychological" concepts and a social phenomenon. It rests on observation, on speculation, and on professional organization.

Freud's unconventional eye gave *clinical observation* a new focus and a new scope. The new focus was neurotic man at the intersection of nature and culture, the scope so vast that the neurologist Freud, in conceptualizing the peculiar logic of a neurosis, found himself referring to such seemingly and academically remote phenomena as the primitive's superstition, the child's wishes, the artist's imagination. However, in doing so Freud painstakingly emphasized the fact that the everyday basis of his expanding system was and remained the observation of the forces most clearly operating in the clinical situation; namely, tranference, resistance, repression, regression, etc. The clinical observer of a verbalizing adult sees his personality outlined in the way in which his feelings, memories, hopes, etc., do or do not cross the threshold of verbalization, once this threshold is emphasized by the suggestion to associate freely. He has to evaluate a *dynamic scale* of representations, on which a single idea or complex of ideas alternately appears remembered, re-enacted, dreamt, avoided, projected on others, repudiated, joked about, etc., each time with specific *disguises* and *omissions* and accompanied by a *specific quantity and quality of awareness.*

Psychoanalysis emphasizes the fact that the non-clinical fields such as psychology, anthropology, child development, etc., overlap one another precisely in as far as they are psychological. This could be demonstrated either by a changing of focus of their own methods, which would make it possible to find in their material the facts which Freud found in his neurotics, or by an adaptation of the psychoanalytic method to their material, i.e., through methods which use in these non-clinical situations whatever forces in them correspond to the clinical forces of resistance, regression, and transference.[2]

Thus one will see how individuals and groups defend themselves against ideas and needs which are considered dangerous to the commanding ideas and needs of their reality, and how the *suppressed, the expressed, and the aspired to are interwoven.*

In the application of psychoanalysis to the study of children, the variations in the individual's quantity and quality of verbalized awareness obviously cannot provide the proper dynamic scale because children, on the whole, cannot obey the rule of free association. Of the scales to be applied instead, two will be elaborated in this monograph, namely, the correlation of the individual's *verbal* behavior with his *spatial* expression and his recognizable changes of *affect.*[3]

There are a number of facts which, for better or worse, are constantly re-established by daily psychoanalytic experience; the discrepancy between the representation in verbalized consciousness and the motivating power of certain ideas (repression); the priority among these ideas of those concerning the child's first bodily (sexual) orientation in the world of physical and social facts; their disguised expression in various metaphoric ways; the sexual deficiencies and the defensive personality changes resulting from them, etc. All these facts are taken for granted here although they are, of course, considered subject to further scientific observation. The observation of these facts, however, and the theory of transference, resistance, and repression imply and have led to many concepts of what Freud calls "metapsychological" nature.

Freud and the first psychoanalysts were faced with the task of conceptualizing a field which had almost no tradition. They were erudite men who had at their disposal modes of thought from a variety of the scientific and extrascientific fields which in the past had monopolized man's conduct, such as theology, philosophy, and art. In the psychoanalytic system not only the superficial evidence of an occasional term such as *Oedipus Complex* points into the past, but, more important, such sweeping conceptual configurations as the free floating in the body of a *libido* with its *cathexis* and *catharsis*; in the mind, the struggle of an ego between an *id* and a *superego*; and in the world at large, a gigantic melting of life and death instincts.

The libido concept, for example, might be suspected of having fallen heir to the Greek interpretation of hysteria; there the *uterus* wandered about in the body, selecting its organ for interference. In Freud's system it is not the uterus but the *libidinal cathexis of the psychic representation of the genitals* which is displaced to the representation of other parts of the body which then show conversion symptoms. The same libido, if cathexing the therapist's representation in the patient's mind (and reinforced by the transference of the cathexis of the father image to that of the therapist's), creates the favorable condition for the influence of the therapist on the patient as the *animal spirits* of the last century did while still actually crossing the space between patient and therapist.

In spite of his antiphilosophic sentiments, Freud on occasion referred, not without sovereign pleasure, to such similarities between his concepts and those of prepsychological thinkers, the last example being the identity of the *life and death instincts* with Empedocles' *philia* and *veikos*. (7) His "*id*" he early recognized as a kin of Schopenhauer's *will*. Both *id* and *will*, several steps further back in the history of conceptual configurations, take on personal shape, appear as the *devil*.

Freud has traced these and many other ancient images from their projection onto the periphery of man's world back to where they originated, in *man's mind*, where observed with dynamic tools they become a subject of psychology. He draws these images closer to the scientific thinking of his day (and nearer to observation and, ultimately, experiment) by making them *quantitative* and *genetic*. Thus, the libido theory on the one hand becomes something like a theory of *preservation of psychic energy*; on the other hand, the theory of the fate of the libido directly contacts the *theory of evolution*.

Freud's historical habit of weighting a particular observation with whatever standard of conceptualization seemed adequate to further its clarification has led to the use in psychoanalytic literature of a disturbing variety of, as it were, terminological currencies which alternately represent human data in terms of the mythology of millennia, the philosophy of centuries, and the scientific methods of decades. Freud implies that in time all these currencies will be exchanged, at their face value, into one based on the clinical and experimental standard of the day.

The real danger, however, of the pre-scientific ancestry of revolutionary thought in psychology has proved to be and will, at least for a while, be a group-psychological one. A certain idea, by fitting into an ancient, possibly long-suppressed mode of thought, to some appears immediately convincing and pertaining to the nature of the experience: "this I have always known." The same mode of thought being alien (perhaps repressed) to others may deter them from consideration of the same idea even if it is already well on its way to substantiation: "this I have always avoided." In such development observation is often little consulted; group identification replaces scientific method; and a regression takes place to conflicts in ancestral thinking and to spiritual and philosophic leftovers and leftouts.

This third influence in the formation of a system, namely, the group psychological meaning derived from the organization of its adherents, has been especially powerful in the history of psychoanalysis for another reason intrinsic in its nature.

When Freud, in the good faith of scientific ethos, first revealed the hitherto undescribed manifestation on which he focused his attention, and the unheard of selections and associations of his mind which made him focus on them, he was met with an overwhelmingly ugly response from the scientists of his day. Partially understandable as a Victorian reaction against a bold mind and his sovereign habits of deduction, this response nevertheless had certain qualities in common with the behavior and the argumentation of a cornered patient: it forced Freud to realize that his era was going to resist as one patient the Freudian kind of enlightenment. He proceeded, however, to recognize and to conceptualize this *"resistance" as an attribute of living psychological matter*. Freud's observations had struck at the specific illusion which had reached its climax in his era, namely, that there was no psychological limit to the subordination of sex and aggression to will, belief, and reason. Resistance, in the larger sense, is human inability to accept any theory which makes the current conception of "free will" relative.

The ever-renewed detection and therapeutic utilization of the selective, repressive, projective mechanisms in the human mind are the tools which Freud gave to psychotherapy and psychology; they point beyond systems and schools, for they insist on pursuing resistance wherever it chooses to hide in the evolution of human consciousness, and no school can avoid for long becoming a hiding place for collective regressions—not even the psychoanalytic one from which groups of adherents necessarily aim to derive a secondary gain by ascribing to themselves more than a relative freedom from resistance and privileges such as methodological isolation.

But there is no reason to doubt that all these phenomena will gradually and permanently become subject to the developing psychoanalytic method itself. Always proceeding along the line of most resistance, it will stimulate clinical observation and its application, and will make it possible to understand conceptual and group psychological process such as marked the beginning of its own history.

Freud has not analyzed children himself. He based the reconstruction of psychosexual development in childhood on the systematic analysis of the verbalizations of adult neurotics and on a wealth of corroboratory, although unsystematic, observations of childhood. When it became apparent that clinical contact with small children was possible, Freud left this field to others (and expressly to his women pupils). The few references to direct child observation to be found in his work (8) make apparent the loss which this Victorian fact implies for child psychology.

Anna Freud's cautious and clear *Introduction to the Technique of Child Analysis* (5) still seems to be the only safe technical statement in regard to the application of psychoanalysis to clinical work with children. However, detailed discussions of her Vienna seminar, which represented the most significant expansion of her basic technical ideas, have not been published. The field has thus been left to clinical abstracts and to one most ambitious systematic attempt, namely, Melanie Klein's *The Psychoanalysis of Children* (11).

Mrs. Klein has enriched our thinking by concentrating on some neglected features of infantile, and especially female, phantasy life, such as the preoccupation with the body interior. Her book, however, abounds in methodologically irresponsible statements referring to what its author is supposed to have "shown" in regard to the psychology of normal childhood. From these "demonstrations" she and her followers derive the license not only to reconstruct earliest psychic development where it is least approachable, but also to convey such reconstructions to child patients. Their interpretations, fairy tales stripped of all artistry, seem to fascinate children and are said to cure them. The author of this paper cannot, at the present time, overcome a suspicion as to the final adpatation of the child cured by this method to any environment, except that which cultivates a special type of psychoanalytic outlook.[4]

In some of the contributions to the child analysis number of the *Psychoanalytic Quarterly* (1), a new living relationship between disturbed child and understanding adult (a kind of doctor-aunt who helps the child to find words for unspeakable experiences) is lucidly described.[5] As far as smaller children are concerned, such descriptions seem most convincing where the historical tool of psychoanalysis, namely, "making conscious," is not assumed a priori to have been applied. While the concepts of resistance and transference when applied to smaller children lose little of their value as tools of investigation, repression, because of the lack of dependable verbal contact between therapist and child, becomes a somewhat meaningless concept; by inferring it, one often misses the opportunity to observe stages in which what is later to be called repression is just about to happen, and by treatment seems prevented rather than made retroactive. It is exactly this prevention of a disastrous gap between verbal and subverbal experiences in childhood which promises to become the most useful contribution of psychoanalysis to a future era (and promises to have been the most poignant criticism of the passing one).

However, we have not always been conscious enough of the fact that in the humanities premature reconstruction has to resort to medieval images. In some of our writings Freud's tentative abstractions of a topology, a genetics, and a mechanics of psychic life are inadvertently colored by visions and clothed in moods. What the child's ego is said to experience and to do often goes even beyond the concept of a persona in a person; it implies an organism with a sensory and motor system of its own within the organism—indeed, a human-like being between a devil- and a god-like one. Like *diaboli* of old, these parts of the psyche reflect and act, avoid effort and gain satisfaction with sly and dialectic skill. Similarly, in the conceptualization of inaccessible parts of childhood there occur *homunculi* of synthetic babies who are complete miniature editions of adult cannibals or psychotics; or reconstructed newborns laden with *primordial images* of sin and guilt. Thus residues of the intellectual past and by-products of extra-scientific ideologies of today are used to draw prematurely into a developmental synthesis of "the child," striking observations as well as moods, beliefs, and divinations from many planes.

Any description of a prolonged period of child psychoanalytic treatment seems to find a powerful obstacle in the fact that the child, relatively more than the adult, is constantly changing under the influence of extratherapeutic factors. Therapeutic influences act at best as accelerators and inhibitors on a continuum of maturational processes which, *in their normal or, let us say, extra-clinical manifestations, for the most part have never been properly studied and described*. The intimate changes observed during a child's treatment therefore are too easily explained as a function of the treatment; while the danger implied in attempts to influence by means derived from clinical work the as yet unknown factors in the maturation of the child must be obvious. Thus the early possibility of basing a reconstruction of the child's normal inner development on present clinical data and applying such premature syntheses to the philosophy and practice of education seems doubtful. But it will be as rewarding as it is time-consuming to apply child-psychopathological knowledge to research in "normal" childhood, i.e., the development and inner life of children whom neurosis has not isolated from the supporting field of group values.

II. The Initial Situation and Its Alternatives

Every psychotherapist has certain vague expectations in regard to what a disturbed child entering his room for the first time may be expecting of him and may do. Against this generalized picture the behavior of a single child stands out in its dramatic individuality.

Our young patient usually arrives hand in hand with his mother. He can be expected to have made a mental note of the fact that our office is in a "hospital-like" institution. On entering the waiting room he finds a friendly secretary and is then invited into an inner room about half of which (signified by "adult furniture") is set aside for the therapist's plainly non-medical business, the other half (signified by floor space and an array of ordinary toys) for a child's play. He is told sooner or later that he is expected to let his mother withdraw to the waiting room and to allow the connecting door to be closed; the therapist and the toys are then to be at his disposal.

This situation confronts the young patient with a maze of conflicting possibilities. We would like to describe it as consisting of several overlapping fields of ambiguity which are created by the child's relation to mother, therapist, toys, and inner conflict.

There is first of all his *mother*. He may hold on to her hand or body, insist on staying with her in the waiting room, demand that the door remain open, or stubbornly remain near the door which has closed between her and him. If he does this, the situation is for him still related mainly to one goal, his mother, and through her the way home from a vague danger. This idea, however, is rarely unequivocally pleasant. Our small patient usually has reached a deadlock with his mother, who cannot understand why he does not "simply drop" his problem; while the home atmosphere, in which he, in most cases, has been subjected to varying educational methods, has become charged with unsolved conflicts. Thus, frightened as he may be, he feels attracted by the *doctor possibilities*, the second field, and one which offers possible escape from the unbearable pressure of the domestic situation. Something which the mother or somebody else has said usually has created a slight hope in the child that the therapist may be a person who understands the conditions and the tempo in which a symptom of fear can be gradually abandoned without giving place to chaos within or more trouble without. Many a child has learned also to expect that he will be able to play for time by repeating to this new therapist what has satisfied the old ones. On the other hand the therapist has been called a "doctor" and the medical implications of the surroundings add to the mere strangeness of the situation and create the expectation in the child that some kind of surprise attack is to be made on his physical or moral inviolacy. The mother, with the best intentions, often transfers the negative aspects of the "mother field" into the field of doctor possibilities; she insists, for example, on reporting in the child's presence latest developments, on admonishing, or even threatening him, or on trying to secure the therapist's promise of diagnosis and advice. Literally and psychologically, therefore, the mother has to be referred to the waiting room; the child must feel that time has another quality in the doctor sphere, in which paradoxically, there is no hurry about getting well.

In the meantime, a third ambiguous field[6] has competed with mother and therapist in dominating the child's expectancies, namely the *toys*.[7] For the child they open another haven, in which space too has another quality, and the therapist usually is quite glad to resign for a while in favor of this quasi-free sphere. Indeed, "what would we do without toys," has become a common exclamation now that we have relaxed our efforts to ignore this most natural tool. The toys evoke in the child that remainder of playful explorativeness which his neurosis and the present doctor situation [have] not been able to submerge; and once he has started to select and manipulate, we can be sure that the temptation to play and to be the unquestioned and inviolable master in a microcosmic sphere will be great. However, we again see the child manifest hesitation. He has experienced too often the fact that the imagined omnipotence in the toy world only makes him feel his impotence the more keenly when he is suddenly interrupted. Playfulness does not rule until (and then only as long as) pressing purposes and fears have lost their compelling power. Thus the child often begins to play with hesitation, with selection, with one eye on the therapist or the door—but he begins to play.

Peace seems to reign. The mother is comfortably seated in the waiting room and has promised "not to go away"; the doctor has been diagnosed as a person who will not make surprise attacks on one's bodily or moral reserve; the toys, sure not to question or to admonish, promise a time of "unpurposeful" play.

However, it is at this point that the most dangerous field of ambiguity—namely, the child's reluctance to confess and his need to communicate his *conflict*—takes possession of the peaceful situation. Whatever it is that drives the child—an urge to get rid of some past or to prepare himself for some future, or both—the ever-present gestalt of the life task which has proved too much for him appears in the metaphoric representation of the microsphere. It is here that our "sign-reading" sets in, and that the tools which Freud gave us become indispensable; for they make us realize that in the playful arrangement which the child is driven to superimpose on the inventory of toys we offer him, he offers us an outline of the "inner maze" in which he is caught. Our small patients either show an anxious care in excluding this or that toy from their play or they work themselves toward a borderline where they themselves suddenly find their own doings unsafe, not permissible, unworkable, or unsatisfactory to the point of extreme discomfort. They cannot go on playing in peace—a phenomenon which we shall call play disruption.

I shall give a brief example of the place of such a play disruption in the four fields of ambiguity, governed as they are by the changing valences of the parent who is present, the therapist, the toys, and the shadow of inner conflict.

A girl of four still withstands toilet training. When put on the toilet, she seems unable to "let go"; later she soils her bed. Recently she was knocked down by an automobile; this has increased her inaccessiblity and her pale stubbornness. (As is obvious from her utterances at home, a small neighborhood dog is, at the moment, important in her phantasy life. It is female like herself, and not housebroken, and recently was knocked down by an automobile too; but unlike herself, it is frequently beaten for soiling, was badly hurt in the accident [it lost a leg]. This little dog apparently represents to her all that "is coming to her.")

Very pale, the little girl has finally left her mother in the waiting room. She stands near the door of my room, sucking her finger, neither willing to play nor wanting to go back to her mother. I try to help her by outlining with some blocks a few rooms on the floor (an approach I use only on rare occasions). A little girl lies in a bed and a woman stands in the middle of the bedroom from which a door leads into a bathroom. There is a garage with a car and a man. After a while the little girl suddenly warms up, approaches with flushed cheeks and kicks the woman doll so that it falls over, closes the bathroom door and goes to the toy shelf to get three shiny red cars for the man in the garage. May we say she expresses a dislike for what must mean to her a mother in front of the little girl's bed and for the demand of the open bathroom door; and that she shows a readiness to give whatever the cars mean to the man (father). At this point, however, she bursts into tears and anxiously asks, "Where is my mummy?" In panicky haste she takes three red pencils from my desk and runs out of the room to present them to her mother. Then she sits down beside her, pale and rigid, determined not to return to me. (The mother wants to give back the pencils, but she is told that the child is free to return them another time.)

The patient has scarcely reached home when she seems to feel guilty about having taken my pencils and shows signs of despair at not being able to bring them back until the next day. However, when the time for her next hour has arrived, she sits in the waiting room clutching the pencils in one hand, some unknown object in the other. She refuses to come with me. After a while it becomes noticeable that she has soiled herelf. When she is picked up to be led to the bathroom, the pencils fall to the floor and with them a little toy dog, one of whose legs has been broken off.

If we undertake to interpret this example properly, we would be led to consider in detail the patterns of guilt-feeling in this child: Having manifested aggression toward the woman in the play setup, she experienced the fear of the possible loss of her mother's love; in hurrying to bring her an equivalent of what she had given to the man in the play, she happened to snatch objects which belonged to me, thus provoking a situation which would again ask for acts of rectification and which would imply an element of desire for punishment. (As if under compulsion to do or to allude to that which brings punishments, she held on to my property, brought the toy dog with a damage identical with her dog friend's injury, and soiled in my room—transferring a "symptom" for which she had never been punished in a way either quantitatively or qualitatively equal to the hostility it expressed, as subsequently became apparent.)

What interests us here first of all is the traffic between the fields outlined above and the play disruption's place in them. The little girl, moderately sure that her mother would not leave and somewhat loosened by the playful way in which the therapist approached her problem, got as far as to say in the language of play signs that she did not like the idea of the lady standing there near the open bathroom door but was willing to give the reddest cars to the man, when she must have experienced what Adam did when he heard God's voice: "Adam, where art thou?" Her play suddenly seemed all-visible in the mother-field and she went to atone for her deed not, however, without stealing my pencils and thus innocently establishing a new goal in the doctor sphere. The trip home again increased the stubbornness against mother and bathroom demands and, consequently, the importance of the goal she had established in my sphere. The next day, back in my office and faced with the necessity and possibility of making everything come out even, she is caught by emotional paralysis, and her symptom expresses for her what she did not dare to express in her play; namely, the inability "to give" to an ambivalently loved person.

It is this very inability which in this case called for analysis and re-education. However, we shall have to resist the temptation to describe the little girl's treatment at this point. Instead we concentrate on some further aspects of the described play situation.

We may call the toy scene on the floor *microcosmic*, i.e., *an arrangement of small objects in such a way that their configuration signifies a configuration of conflicting forces in the child's life*, in this case the child's retentive attitude toward her mother and her generous attitude toward the father. That the woman in the play really signified her mother (and that the man, perhaps, already indicated a father transference on the therapist) became plain when the microcosmic play was disrupted and she tried to rearrange another sphere in such a way that it represented a reversal of the "guilty" microcosmic configuration: she gave to her mother—and robbed me. Such *rearrangements of the child's relationship to the real persons or the life-sized objects present in the therapeutic situation* we shall designate as *macrocosmic*. In this case the traffic from what we shall call, for short, the *microsphere* to the *macrosphere* implied a play disruption which, of course, is not always necessarily the case. Such a shift can take place as a playful expansion, perhaps with a transition from solitary play to a game, especially if another person is induced to play a role in the desired macrocosmic arrangement. (Using, for example, with an omnipotent gesture, a chair for a horse to ride on and to order about would be the macrocosmic play equivalent to the microcosmic form of making a toy rider hop along the floor.)

Beside the microcosmic and macrocosmic "spheres" of representation we can discern an autocosmic one: *the sphere of dramatization by means of an interplay of body parts and organ systems*. The little girl's soiling belongs here: it was a *symptom in the autosphere*. There is also *autocosmic play*, i.e., the original play in the growing world of the child's expanding body consciousness and the mutual enchantment of its parts.

The antithesis of play disruption is a phenomenon which we shall call "play situation." If play "succeeds," i.e., if it is not disrupted from within or interrupted from without, it has an effect on the child comparable to a few hours of good, long-needed sleep—everything "looks different." I do not doubt that it is this autotherapeutic function of play which we are restoring in many cases by creating for a child regular and undisturbed periods of play, no matter how we rationalize what is happening during such a "cure." In contrast to the little girl's macrocosmic outbreak after the microcosmic disruption we sometimes see microcosmic play satiation lead directly into a macrocosmic play or game in which the rearrangement achieved in small dimensions is tried out (and this often too courageously for the child's own anxiety) on big objects and people. I shall give here a non-psychiatric example of this normal phenomenon.

I once visited a boy of four a few hours after he had undergone an ear operation. He was, of course, most uncomfortable, insisted that many parts of his body hurt and that he wanted to urinate and defecate but was unable to do so. Three questions were most apparent in his complaints: first, whether or not the doctors were going to stick more instruments into him; second, why it was that only the doctor could remove the bandage around his head; third, whether his ear was still under the bandage.[8]

An understanding doctor had given him a roll of adhesive tape shortly before and he had held it, clutched in his hand, ever since. The tape was wound on a tin spool which fitted into a tin cylinder. Only one end of the spool could be inserted into the cylinder because the rim on the other end extended beyond the cylinder and served to fasten the two pieces together. The boy removed the spool from

Figure 1   **A**   **B**

its container and suggested the following play: "You try to put this (A) into that (B)" (Figure 1). Accidentally I tried it the wrong way,[9] whereupon he said with startlingly emphasis, "It's much too big!" Since he kept repeating these words with a vague expression of pleasure, I cooperated by not accomplishing the deed, and by repeating my mistake over and over again, giving him the repeated opportunity to pronounce the magic phrase, "It's much too big." Each time I had failed to fit the spool and cylinder into one another, he took the two objects and, fitting them correctly, said with much emphasis, "Now it's closed." The repetition of this ritual of pretending that *only he could stick A into B* already seemed to influence his general condition considerably.

Suddenly he said, "Let's pretend this is a leg and it's sore." He attempted to unwind the roll of adhesive tape, but found he could not separate the layers. Disappointed, he asked me to unwind it. I played that it was very difficult to unwind, whereupon he said with glee, "We need a giant for that." I pretended to phone the nurse to send up a giant, then left the room and reappeared as the giant. However, I had a white coat on which made the play situation resemble too much the actuality (he was a patient expecting a doctor). He asked anxiously why the giant had an apron on. He quickly recovered, however, and, after the giant's initial help, began to remove the tape from the spool (to which task, as had now been proved, only a giant's strength was equal). Pieces of it were placed around the cylinder, which was now serving as the "leg."

There was much joyful concentration on the completion of the "bandage." But a few tiny spots of red inscription were not covered by the tape and he now concentrated on them. "Look! There's a toe sticking out. And here is another toe, and another toe." I asked, "Shall we put the bandages around the toes, too?" He replied enthusiastically, "Yes," and put the tiny bandages over the toes. While doing so he began to sing and already felt quite cool. It was evident that he felt no pain.

When the entire surface of the cylinder was fully bandaged, the patient inserted the spool into it and taped over the whole configuration. "Nobody can take this off." He asked his mother and me to remove the bandage, but, of course, "we couldn't." Whereupon he proudly repeated that, first, *nobody but he could remove the bandage or the spool;* that, second, *he was not going to do it.* Our "requests" were of no avail.

It will already have become evident to the reader that the patient arranged the play objects in such a way that they expressed in sign magic his active mastery over the situation victimizing him at the time. That only he could stick Object *A* into Object *B*, a pleasure provided by the nature of the toy (which, as we shall see, was subsequently bandaged), may have had a quite general meaning of mastery, although it may have already implied the more specifically satisfying idea that nobody (i.e., the physicians) could stick more objects into his head. The fact that he was obliged to wait until the physician was willing to remove his bandage was reversed by the game wherein only a giant could remove the adhesive tape from the spool and only the child remove the bandage from the cylinder (but would not do it). Finally, since he himself had covered the "toes" so carefully, he knew that these "extremities" were there and that he himself had covered them—an arrangement which might have been reversing the actual situation wherein the physician had covered his ears and would not allow him to see whether or not they were still there.

After approximately half an hour of such play the patient was smiling and singing. He fell asleep after I left. When he woke up again, he smiled mischievously and said to his mother, who was sitting beside his bed, "Let's put some bandage over the doctor's eyes when he comes in; let's put it all over him. The big bad wolf—only then we wouldn't have enough bandage left if Charlie[10] hurts his leg."

Leaving aside the last "altruistic" remark in which the patient already visualized a time when he might be providing bandages for his brother (who had by then become the medical victim), we see in the remark about the doctor being covered all over by the bandage a *typical omnipotent rearrangement in phantasy of the macrosphere in accordance with a previous microcosmic rearrangement.* First, only the patient could make and remove bandages, and now the doctor himself becomes the victim of bandaging to a degree ("all over him") surpassing the discomfort he had created for the child.

This wishful and wileful restructuralization in play of the child's most immediate sphere of discomfort uses, of course, all the mechanisms which Freud showed were governing factors in play, in his classical example of a boy who had to adapt to his mother's absence:[11] the working over of an experience in which one had been a *passive* victim by its representation in such a way that one becomes the active aggressor against a toy or a partner. As for microcosmic play, the traumatic experience is caught in a *small* and *simple* configurational frame (an accessible *Beutefeld*), and is to be reprojected in its all-too-simple formulation into the bigger world, which consequently becomes a macrocosmic play-and-error field for microcosmic theories.

In the little girl's case the microsphere represented "a family"; in the case of the hospital patient, endangered parts of the body, ear, head, etc. Thus a variety of segments of the pressingly immediate life situation may be projected into this least refractory of all spheres of representation. A child concerned about "the body as a whole" or even about "life as a whole" may build corresponding configurations both as wishful arrangements and as traumatic repetitions. Illustrations of this will follow.

Of special interest is one of the intermediate steps between the spheres of representation, namely, behavior with *extensions of the autosphere*. Play belongs in this category wherever it is clear that an isolated object is used as a means to extend or intensify the mode of expression of an organ or an organ-system and does not become a part of an extrabodily microcosmic arrangement. Let us say a block, if replacing the finger as an object of licking, is a part of an autocosmic extension; it would still be one if rhythmically banged against another block, while it would become a part of a microcosmic arrangement when, with consideration for its physical laws and its usual connotation, it is placed on another block so that together they may form a building.[12]

These spheres of representation and dramatization can help us where it is advisable to neglect social connotations, such as what is considered to be a play act, a serious deed, a habit, a symptom, etc., and to find instead in corresponding configurational properties the common denominator for the various parts within the complicated unit of a clinical contact. Our girl patient, for example, manifested the quandary of cooperative retention and elimination on the one side and hateful retention and ejection on the other (plus their relationship to mother and father) in all the three spheres mentioned.

As for the traffic between these spheres of representation we observe that just as an organ, the whole body, a family constellation, or a conception of life as a whole can be represented by a microcosm, so sucking, banging, defecating, etc., when they are prolonged habits, can often be understood as dramatizing social situations and attitudes.

We will readily see that especially for the disturbed child from three to six years old (the age range in our study) autocosmic manifestation leads back easily into the sphere of regressive habits, while macrocosmic expansions make the child try out the environment in a manner both surprising and displeasing to attending adults. There remains then, by force of age preference and expediency, the microsphere as a haven for overhauling the boats before taking further trips into the unknown. Our disturbed children approach this sphere, break down or hesitate before they reach it, experience a disruption in it, or suffer a belated disruption after having over-estimated the omnipotence provided by it. The "sign-magic" used during such behavior seems to us to outline where in the child's life the sphere of relative tolerance borders on the danger sphere of unbearable pressures.

Among such manifestations, that of extrabodily representation of organ-modes, which is the subject of early and special environmental interference, is of outstanding importance for the understanding of preschool play and also for that of all emotionally disturbed older children.

As diagrammatically developed in a previous article (2), the orificial organ-modes incorporation, elimination, retention, and intrusion and the body apertures which are their "models" par excellence—namely, mouth, sphincters, and genitals—are combined to normal mutual emphasis in successive stages, namely, the stages described by Freud as pre-genital. In each of these stages there is an interrelation between the sensitization and training of a *vital orifice* and the growing *periphery of mastery* (a) oral-(respiratory)-sensory-tactual, (b) anal-(urethral)-muscular, (c) genital-(urethral)-motor. This interrelation can express itself in mode-behavior both *centrifugally as generalization* of the mode, i.e., the mode of the dominant zone becomes the dominant mode of behavior in general, or *centripetally* as a *specialization* of the zone (i.e., a general tendency can express itself in the habits of one zone). For example, the retentive mode may first find emphasis in sphincter-habits and then appear as a general retentive tendency in many aspects of behavior; or it may become noticeable in other habits (such as keeping food in the mouth and neither swallowing nor returning it) and then find its most intensive expression in sphincter-habits. We thus can speak of *mode-fixations* and of *zone-fixations,* the first being a carrying over of one mode from its model-zone to other zones where it is as it were a gesture without functional logic or in the use of one zone for several untimely and displaced modes. Some of these generalizations and specializations are only observable in a limited number of temporarily or permanently fixated children.

"Surveying the field of zone experience and mode manifestation, one finds that what Freud had described as pre-genitality is the development through a succession of narcissistic organ cathexes of impulses and modes of behavior the final integration of which implies all the possible relationships of a body and an object and thus the basic spatial modalities of experience. Led (or confused) by zone experience as well as growing capacity children experiment more or less playfully in space with all the possible relationships of one object to another one and of the body as a whole to space." To modes which in their bodily, spatial, or social expression are curtailed by inhibiting experiences "the organism offers a limited range of safe displacements in habits and minor symptoms. Reality allows for certain systems of subjectified perception; society permits a number of odd social habits and, more or less queer traits. To the child especially the world of play affords opportunity to experiment with organ-modes in extrabodily arrangements which are physiologically safe, socially permissable, physically workable and psychologically satisfying."

Between displacements within the body (habits, symptoms) and the free external displacement in play, we find various arresting combinations. The following example, a previously published (2) non-psychiatric observation, illustrates the way in which the dominance of simple organ-modes during training may for a while govern a child's spheres of behavior. A little boy, *H,* two and one-half years of age, who struggled rather belatedly against enuresis, began to take to bed with him little boxes, which he held closed with both hands. When a box opened during the night, sometimes apparently with his unconscious help, he would cry out in his sleep or awaken and call for someone to help him close it. He would then sleep peacefully, even though not necessarily dry. But he continued to experiment.

During the day he looked around for suitable boxes—obviously driven by an urge to materialize an image of "closedness." Finally he found what seemed to fit the image, a cardboard cylinder which had been the center of a roll of toilet paper. He put two cardboard caps from milk bottles over the openings of the roll. All through the night he would try to hold this arrangement firmly together with both hands—as an animistic guardian of the retentive mode. But no sooner had his training achieved a relative success in closing his body during sleep than he began, *before* going to sleep, to throw all available objects out of the window. When this was made impossible, he stole into other rooms and spilled the contents of boxes and bottles on the floor.

Clearly, the first act, namely holding a closed box as a necessary condition for sleep, resembles a compulsive act originating in the child's fear of failing to retain because of his weakness or because of his wish to expel. Emptying objects, on the other hand, or throwing them out of the window is "delinquent" and the result of the fear of being overpowered by the claims of *society to which he surrenders the zone but not the impulse.* The impulse appears on other levels of representation, where it betrays itself through configurations representing the retentive and eliminative modes.

To prevent the little boy from throwing things out of the window, it was opened from the top. Thereupon he was found riding on it, leaning out into the night. I do not think he would have fallen out; he probably wanted only to show himself "master of openings," as compensation for the surrender of the free use of his excretory openings to society. When, in consequence, his mother kept his window closed until he was asleep, he insisted that the door be left ajar.

Thus not only sections of one's body and toys, but also the body as a whole in its spatial relationship to the whole room or to the whole house, may serve the displaced expression of the impulse in various degrees of compulsive, naughty, or playful acts.

The animal psychologist, having seen rats (whom he had made hungry) learn to run mazes (which he had built) toward food (which he had put there) comes to the conclusion that "the environment takes on for the physiologically aroused organism, by dint of his innate endowment and past experiences, the character of a hierarchy of to-be-sought and to-be-avoided superordinate and subordinate objects" (15).

Essentially, our diagnostic confidence is based on the same expectation, which, however, is derived from the repeated clinical experience that the hierarchy of actually sought-after and avoided toys (offered as stimuli and supports) allow us to draw conclusions in regard to what *has aroused or is arousing the playing organism physiologically and what has happened to it environmentally.* That we cannot consider play an intermission or a vacation from urgent life but rather a continuation of it on a sign level is only our serious adaptation to the serious way in which (given our therapeutic setup) the child behaves with strict selectivity, creates meaningful sign coherence, and by his emotions betrays a "purpose" where "play" has been suggested.

In describing to the reader, by way of introduction, some of the significant alternatives with which the child is faced on entering the therapeutic situation, and some of the therapist's useful expectancies, we by no means hope to induce him to share what may seem a radical determination. Illustrations can only convince him who already believes that those selected are representative. Therefore I can close this introduction only with the rather inhuman suggestion that a publication like the present one should be read at least twice. Only after the comparison of several cases has made the reader more familiar with the nature of the inventory of possible kinds of behavior from which the individual child makes his choices will he begin to believe that even if presented with different supporting objects the individual child patient could not have produced configurations essentially dissimilar to those which are described in the following pages.

III. Studies in Play Interpretation

A. METHOD OF REPRESENTATION

Our material is divided into *contacts* (visits), which in turn consist of *behavior items*. These items are described and discussed in five categories, *A, B, C, D, E,* which indicate the shifting foci of the analytic attention; their peripheries overlap.

A gives a common-sense description of what happens before the observer's eyes; *B* and *C* demonstrate (in slow motion, as it were) two concurrent tendencies in the observer's mental activity: *B* is directed toward a future exact description in areas which can also be explored and measured under other than psychiatric conditions; *C* toward the clinician's age-old right and duty to allow himself to be led by subjective factors. The reader should visualize the relationship of *B* and *C* and their intervention between *A* and *D* in the following manner (Figure 2).

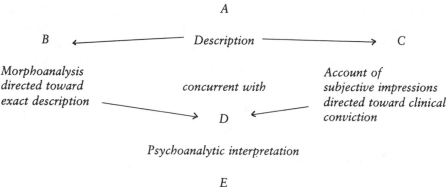

Figure 2

"A"

The "behavior item to be analyzed" represents as nearly as possible the span between the moment when we observe that the child has turned his attention to a toy, a person, or a conversational manner and the moment when we notice that he turns to the next one. This is, of course, a crude concept of an "observational unit"; however, it is the one naturally used in a therapeutic situation in which the task is to infer from the *selective attractions and aversions created by a standard environment* what the patient's relationship may be to certain classes of ideas and thus to discover the pathogenic associations of his mind—which he may keep hidden, which may be unconscious to him, or whose reference and importance may not be understood by him.

"B"

Morphoanalytic description emphasizing the configurations manifested in four areas of behavior:

1. *Affective:* The patient's manifested emotional *interest in and withdrawal from* the object of the behavior item.

2. *Ideational:* Verbalized content, acted out *themes*, etc.

3. *Spatial: Configurations* and *modes* in the three spheres of representation.

4. *Verbal:* Mode of *expression*; speech, voice.

"C"

Observer's Impressions, Associations, and Reflections. While in B the therapist attempts an approximation of objective configurational analysis of what he sees and hears in the currently manifest, in C he *gives impressions* ("it was as if . . .") and *associates past impressions*— previous observation on the child in question or on other children, data communicated to him by the parents, etc.—and he *reflects on latent possibilities,* i.e., the possibility that his associations may correspond to a genetic or associative connection in the child's mind between what he is doing under the observer's eyes and what he is said to have done in other situations.

"D"
Psychoanalytic Interpretation.

1. His observational and reflective reactions lead the observer to various *interpretational hints.* A *symbolic equation* or metaphor may make it possible to recognize a play act as alluding to and *standing for an otherwise manifestly avoided* item (person, object, or idea); or a *play arrangement* may prove to represent a specific effort on the part of the child to rearrange "in effigy" his psychological position in an experienced or expected danger situation. Such an arrangement usually corresponds to the child's defense mechanisms (6).

2. If these first hints survive the sifting processes of further observation and investigation, they will sooner or later grow together and create a conviction and an image in the observer's mind in the form of the *reconstruction of a genetic sequence* or of a *dynamic configuration* pertaining to the patient's inner or outer history.

3. The observer may proceed to convey parts of these reconstructions to the child whenever he feels the time has come to do so. This, then, is the *therapeutic interpretation.*

"E"
Confirmation of interpretation gained after the contact, and further speculation reaching out beyond the evidence offered by the behavior item.

B. A SIX-YEAR-OLD BOY'S SECRET: JOHN
The observation of the first of our "specimens" led to the discovery of a later verifiable fact, namely, a conscious *secret* kept hidden from the therapist (and his predecessors) by both the child patient and his mother.

John is six years old and a sailor's child. Years of psychiatric investigation have failed to throw light on his impulse to soil himself when overcome by a strange state of rage and sexual excitement. This infantile habit in its importance for the environment has remained the center of a general emotional arrest and of a system of petty delinquency. The mental test shows traces of disintegration and extreme fatigue rather than retardation in his only slightly subnormal intelligence. When he is brought to my attention John is at a hospital where he has undergone (with negative results) an examination of his eliminative organs and an encephalogram; he has also been circumcised. Thus unlike all the other patients to be presented here, John is not brought by his mother. On the contrary (and this is a variation of our model "field situation"), the way back to his mother leads through a successful relationship with me, knowing, as he does, that I will have a word in the final decisions as to his placement, further treatment, etc.

The day before the first regular contact, John had been casually introduced to *Ps*.[13] He had a toy gun in his hand and a dagger at his side and had exclaimed, "I am a cop." When asked, "Who are you going to shoot?" he had replied, "The bad guy." "Who is the bad guy?" "Me."

Today *Ps* brings him some Plasticine because he was told that John had been sad about the fact that none of the hospital toys were "his own." *Ps* therefore expected John to spend valuable time on the question of which of *Ps*'s toys he would be allowed to take to his room, a common technical problem which can be solved only from case to case and often is of diagnostic value in itself. However, *Ps* did not want to lose any time in this instance and assumed that once the ownership of the play medium was settled *Pt* would concentrate more quickly on whatever he needed to express. *Ps* also considered Plasticine to be a fitting "support" for the phantasies of a child who soiled and played with feces.

1. First Contact

John appears, armed again and looking pale, forlorn, and somewhat scared; he accepts the Plasticine with surprised eagerness but without thanks, and immediately concentrates on making an "aeroplane," which, as he says with a shy smile, "brings people from across the ocean." This smile quickly gives way to serious concentration, during which he ignores *Ps* for a while.

"A"
BEHAVIOR ITEM TO BE ANALYZED
Plasticine: Balls
John makes small *balls of Plasticine.*
With three blocks he builds *a grocery store.*

"You are the grocery man; I am a truck driver." John fills the truck with the balls and then, elaborately and with a "motor noise" approaches the store, finally dumping the truck's contents into a corner. When asked, "How much does the grocery man owe you?" John refuses payment (as if the delivery represented a present to the grocery man). This is repeated.

Suddenly he calls one Plasticine ball *mother nut*. Then he takes a smaller ball of the same color and calls it *baby nut*. He then makes of another color Plasticine a long row of balls equal in size to the first one and calls them *brother nuts*. "Whose brothers are they? "My mother's brothers." "You mean uncles?" John becomes very pale, sways as if he were going to faint, and leaves the room hurriedly.

After a while he comes back, obviously from the toilet for he refers to his general state with the words "This is the way I feel when I soil." *Ps* asks once more, "Now tell me, who are your mother's brothers?" John, with a desperate look, "Me."

"B"

MORPHOANALYSIS OF MANIFESTED CONFIGURATIONS

1. *Affect as manifested in interest and withdrawal:* The interest in the Plasticine is first one of hungry *taking* into *possession*. Then follows a short period of quiet *play concentration* out of which suddenly emerges the idea for a *game*. The expression increasingly becomes one of eagerness to play in *cooperation with Ps* and to play *at giving him something*. At the height of this contact-seeking the phantasy of the nut family appears. Some implication of this phantasy then brings about a sudden and vehement play disruption; an anxiety attack and the symptom of sudden defecation make an end to play and game. (What is the dangerous implication of the nut family phantasy?)

2. *Ideational content:* (a) Balls are being made; (b) groceries are delivered without pay; (c) a nut family is represented which consists of a mother, a baby, and many "brothers." (What relation is there between balls, delivery, and the members of a family?)

3. *Spatial expression:* After having put aside his weapons and prepared the balls, *Pt* seeks intimate *spatial contact with Ps*, trying to win him for a game in which they concentrate together on the microcosmic elaboration of *Pt*'s phantasies. This game is dominated by the configuration of *delivering and dumping*. After the disruption the autocosmic sphere takes the lead and the patient defecates.

It will be seen that the microcosmic play and the autocosmic symptom have in common the *eliminative mode*, the difference being that the balls are dumped as presents in the context of a general contact seeking, the feces eliminated in anxiety, followed by a general closing up. (What is to be delivered in friendliness, what retained in anxiety?)

4. *Verbal expression:* (a) There is probably more than one meaning in the "nuts" which he delivers, the most obvious being that the family

he has in mind is "nuts"; (*b*) the "me" the day before manifestly expressed the "turning against himself" of the weapons originally intended for "bad guys." Today it turns my questions in regard to the uncles back to him. (Bad uncles in a crazy family? Who are they?)

"C"

IMPRESSIONS, ASSOCIATIONS, REFLECTIONS

John, apparently too starved for gifts to smile or express thanks, accepts the Plasticine the way a hungry man reaches for food. (This "aeroplane bringing people from across the ocean" could be equally well associated with either John's absent sailor father or *Ps*, whose accent indicated he had come from far away. Is this the beginning of a transference, i.e., does this express the need for a father?)

John had been described to *Ps* as a very friendly, accessible, and even voluble boy who craved for a good contact, especially with men. However, at a certain point he would always close up without any real understanding having been reached. When would he close up in the game with the balls which seemed to mean more and more to him as he proceeded?

He made balls, then seemed very eager to play in cooperation with *Ps* and to deliver something to him, a mode underscored by the refusal of payment which would naturally belong to the commercial play content. This "delinquent" boy who steals and hides what belongs to others and does not even give his feces at the requested time wants to deliver something to *Ps* (a father substitute?).

The nuts turn into a family, a mother, and a baby. Is he homesick? One automatically expects next a father and a brother (to complete approximately the actual family constellation), but John lets about fifteen "brothers" follow who are different in color. The number makes *Ps* suspicious and asks who they are. The answer, "mother's brothers," could still mean, for example, the many brothers which he expects his mother to produce now that she has started on that line. To make sure which kind of brothers he means, *Ps* gives him the term for a mother's real brothers.

The word "uncle" seems to hit him like a blow, causes panic with organic symptoms, including the urge to defecate, and ends the game. "Uncles," of course, is not always a correctly used term, and the "different color" suggests that these uncles may not be real relatives, may be outsiders, strangers—John's father is a sailor and the mother has many nights without a husband.

After the disruption and John's return from the toilet, he had answered *Ps*'s last question with "me"—just as he had done that day before when asked, "Who are you going to shoot?" In other words, when asked about the subject of admitted aggressive tendencies, *Pt* had evaded the issue by putting himself jokingly into the role of the "guy" whom he wanted to harm. Today, in a much more serious way, he acts as a victim (internalizes somatically) when asked for the identity of somebody who is characterized as "mother's *many* brothers" who in the play family appear in the *father's place* and cause panic when called *"uncles."* If our reflections point in the right direction, John has been made the victim (and has gone on making himself a victim) of an unbearable secret which he does not dare convey, namely, his mother's infidelity or maybe prostitution.

As to our expectation that in John's handling of the clay we would find expressed something of the retentive-eliminative problem which builds the basis of his main symptom, namely his untimely elimination of feces: We see him all-giving where he plays in delivering the clay balls, apparently unconsciously "giving away" more than he wanted to. Then he tried to close up—and defecates (just as the little girl above had done when deciding to hold on to the pencils). As for the fact that the patient's eliminative system has become the means of expressing ambivalence, constitutional and historical factors will have to be considered. From the anamnesis one fact suggests itself: John was hard to train and his mother beat him often. When, as we assume, he was a witness to his mother's infidelity, i.e., saw her do "dirty" secret and sexual things herself, it is conceivable that he was overcome by hate against the deceitful M out of love for whom he had fought himself in an effort to become clean, asexual, and truthful. However, more important at this moment than any reconstruction is the recognition of the conscious factors which block the access to the *Pt*'s confidence.

"D"
PSYCHOANALYTIC INTERPRETATION

1. *Symbols.* (*a*) The *balls* (dumped in playful cooperation) correspond in *consistency* and mode of use to feces (which he ejects in anxiety and anger). (*b*) The *balls* ("mother nut," "baby nut" on the one side, many "brother nuts" on the other) correspond in their most obvious differentiations—namely *color* and *number*—to a traumatic family constellation (mother and baby on the one side, many strangers on the other).

2. *Defensive arrangements:* The two sets of symbols correspond to the two main problems (both eliminative-retentive) of the therapeutic situation: (*a*) to the symptom which is to be removed; namely, the untimely elimination of feces; (*b*) to the first requirement for its removal, namely, the giving away of the mother's secret, which John has succeeded in keeping isolated from all therapeutic confessions made during previous treatment. That *Ps*, instead of asking embarrassing questions, has brought John a present and plays with him probably increases the (conscious) feeling in John that to be fair with *Ps* he should verbally deliver the secret and thus make the first step toward a new life in which he would learn to retain his feces. For various reasons, some of which will be made apparent only by further analysis, the patient first resists the overwhelm-

ing need to deliver his secret. His defenses are: (*a*) to use the play support offered by *Ps* for the substitution of the delivery of the secret with a delivery in a game. This defense fails when the patient's conversation unconsciously gives away a hint by delivering the strange nut family. (*b*) Noticing this, he uses his second and usual defense; he closes up, as far as the secret behind the hint is concerned, while the eliminative urge expresses itself at its original zone, the eliminative organs. As this happens the conflict between the eliminative and retentive modes and his masochistic tendency to express aroused emotions in a regressive, autocosmic, and punishment-provoking way get the better of him.

3. At the end of this first contact, *Ps* makes only an intentionally vague statement to *Pt*, for which the latter thanks him with a smile. More cannot be done, since it remains necessary to disclose what may be proven to be fact in these "communications," in this case a too delicate investigation with which to burden a child. If the information proves correct, the mother has to be urged to give John permission to talk about *all* his experiences, including those involving her. Only then can we decide how "deep" we have to go to locate the possible damage to John's inner defenses.

"E"
CONFIRMATION AND FURTHER SPECULATION

During *Ps*'s next conversation with the patient's mother, she confessed that there were certain episodes she had urged John not to tell the doctors about, and had added, "Daddy surely would kill me if he heard about it." She asked for psychological help for herself and released John from the promise of secrecy which had blocked previous therapeutic efforts.

The following rudely clinical excerpts from a previous publication (2) may serve to characterize John's further treatment.

The first barrier which psychoanalysis was forced to attack was the castration fear, which, after the *circumcision, had suppressed his soiling without sublimating the impulse.* Expecting new physical deprivations, the boy would continue to appear equipped with two pairs of eyeglasses on his nose, three knives on a chain hanging out of his trousers and a half dozen pencils sticking out of his vest pocket. Alternately he was a "bad guy" or a cross policeman. He would settle down to quiet play only for a few moments, during which he would choose *little objects* (houses, trees and people) no larger than two or three inches high, and make *covers* for them out of *red Plasticine.* But again and again he would become very pale and ask for permission to go to the bathroom.

In describing an automobile accident he had witnessed, in which the chief damage was a *flat tire*, John almost fainted. He felt equally sick when I asked him about certain sleeping arrangements. It appeared that he had seen (in crowded quarters) a man perform intercourse with a woman who sat on him, and he had observed that the man's *penis looked shorter* afterwards. His interpretation of this had been entirely *anal*. Maybe the woman, whose face seemed flushed, had defecated into the man's umbilicus and had done some harm to his genitals. Or the man had, as it were, eliminated a part of his penis into the woman's rectum out of which she later would deliver, i.e., again eliminate, the baby. In addition to the *enlightenment* given that semen and not a part of the penis remained in the woman, the circumcision was talked over and reassurances given for the more important remainder of his genitals.

His first concentrated skillful and sustained play was the following: A caterpillar tractor slowly approached the rear end of a truck, the door of which had been opened. A dog had been placed on the tractor's chain wheels in such a way that he was hurled into the truck at the moment the tractor bumped into it. Obviously he wanted to make sure by *experimenting* with his toys that the pleasant idea of something being thrown into another body without hurting either the giver or the receiver was sensible and workable, although his unresolved anal fixation (no doubt in cooperation with certain common "animalistic" tendencies and observations) did not allow him to conceive of intrusion in any other way than from behind. But it was not as before brown stuff or mud which was thrown, it was *something living* (semen).

Outside the play hours, the eliminative impulse made its reappearance in John's life in macrocosmic fashion. The whole house, the whole body, the whole world was used for the representation of an impulse which did not yet dare to return to its zone of origin. In his sleep, he would start to throw the belongings of other people, and only theirs, out of the window. Then, in the daytime, he threw stones into neighbors' houses and mud against passing cars. Soon he deposited feces, well wrapped, on the porch of a hated woman neighbor. When these acts were punished, he turned violently against himself. For days he would run away, coming back covered with dirt, oblivious of time and space. He still did not soil, but desperation and the need for elimination became so all powerful that he seemed to *eliminate himself* by wild walks without any goal, coming back so covered with mud that it was clear he must have undressed and rolled in it. Another time he rolled in poison ivy and became covered with the rash.

When he noticed that, by a slowly narrowing network of interpretations, I wanted to put into words those of his impulses which he feared most—namely, elimination and intrusion in their relationship to his mother—he grew pale and resistive. He began a four-day period of fecal *retention*, stopped talking and playing, and stole excessively, hiding the objects. As all patients do, he felt rightly that verbalization means detachment and resignation: He did not dare to do the manifest, but he did not want to give up the latent.

He did not live at home at this time. After many weeks, he received the first letter from his mother. Retiring to his room, he shrank, as it were, physically and mentally, and soiled himself. For a while he did this regularly whenever his mother communicated with him. It was then possible to interpret to him his ambivalent love for his mother, the problems of his bowel training, and his theories concerning his parents' bodies. It was here also that his first free *flow of memories* and associations appeared, allowing us to verbalize much that had been dangerous only because it had been amorphous.

One day he suddenly expressed the wish to make a poem. If there ever was a child who, in his make-up and behavior, did not lead one to expect an aesthetic impulse, it was John. Nevertheless, in a *flood of words*, he now began to dictate song after song about beautiful things. Then he proposed the idea, which he almost shrieked, of sending these poems to his mother. The act of producing and writing these poems, of putting them into envelopes and into the mailbox, fascinated him for weeks. He *gave something to his mother* and it was *beautiful*! The intense emotional interest in this new medium of expression and the general change in habits accompanying it, indicate that by means of this act of sending something beautiful to his mother the eliminative impulse had found a higher level of expression: the zone submitted to training.

C. A NEUROTIC EPISODE IN A GIRL OF THREE

The second case should bridge to some extent the short and all too "obvious" first and the longer and very complex third examples. Among the writer's Boston notes, he finds the following encounter with a charming but badly scared little girl who was friendly enough to provide a basis for diagnosis in *two contacts*. We shall call her Mary.

The complaint was that shortly before her third birthday Mary had developed nightmares during which she struck about wildly; at about the same time, after a dozen visits to a play group organized by a group of mothers in a suburb, she had been overcome by violent anxiety attacks with uncontrollable crying. An attempt had been made to let Mary's mother stay in or near the nursery, but this arrangement had helped only temporarily. The routine situations of afternoon rest and going to the toilet seemed provocative factors in the outbreaks of anxiety.

It must be noted however, that Mary had no attacks during her first visits to the play group, although she showed some tenseness and some rigidity of posture and behavior. When the attacks began, the play group leader as well as the mother felt that something in the nursery must have frightened her. We shall concentrate on the way this complicated something was revealed during the first two contacts with me.

1. First Contact

Mary, dark-haired, attractive, is slight but well built. Her walk is somewhat stiff and her handshake rigid, but she seems well coordinated.

"A"

MOTHER

Holds mother's hand as she enters office. When she shakes hands with Ps, she gives him a brief smile, then immediately turns her head away and from then on tries not to look at him. She turns to her mother, puts arms around her, and keeps her near the open door. While M tries to encourage her to look at the toys, she closes her eyes tightly, hides her face in M's skirt, repeats in a babyish voice, "Mommy, mommy, mommy."

"B"

I

1. After a short glance into the room and a very short and slightly coquettish contacting of Ps in whom M tries to interest her, Mary withdraws to her mother.

2. Spatially keeping near the open door, she clings babyishly to M's body (adherence) as if she wanted to hide in it, and excludes Ps to the extent of closing her eyes very tightly so as not to see him (encasement). No selectiveness in regard to the toys is evident.

"C"

I

She first looks at me as if she wanted to see whether or not the new adult is going to understand fun. However, this feeler is quickly withdrawn; her flight to her mother seems somewhat dramatic. I am not sure that she is not hiding a smile. It seems that she did not show any similar reaction either to the secretary or to a lady who spoke to her in the waiting room; the first impression is that she is conscious of my being a man (doctor) and that there is a coquettish element in her behavior.

"A"

II

MOTHER AND DOLL

Pointing to a (girl) doll, Mary asks M several times, "What that, what that?" After M has explained that it is a dolly, Mary repeats in a babyish way, "Dolly, dolly, dolly," and suggests in words not understandable to

Ps that *M* take off the dolly's shoes. *M* tries to induce her to perform this act herself, but Mary simply repeats her demands again and again without listening to *M*.

"B"
II

1. Her interest in the doll is not able to overcome her reluctance to play; *she makes her mother play.*
2. The content: Mother dresses, undresses a *girl* doll's *feet.*
3. Thus Mary draws the doll into the mother adherence.
4. Her speech remains babyish, repetitious.

"A"
III

INTERRUPTION

M begins to feel embarrassed since the hour is assuming the character of an observation of her in her play with Mary. She asks, therefore, if it is not time for her to leave the room and to wait outside. *Ps* approves of her decision. Mary does not show any signs of fear when, the adherence to *M* being thus broken up, she suddenly finds herself without anybody to lean on.

"C"
III

Mary showed the same initial lack of anxiety when left by *M* in the nursery school. It seems either that something specific must happen to provoke manifest anxiety or that her anxiety typically remains latent for a while.

"A"
IV

DOLL

M has left the doll in Mary's hand. Mary grasps it firmly around its legs. Suddenly she smiles mischievously, her face flushes, and she begins to touch various things in the room with the doll's head. When a toy falls from the shelf, she laughs and begins to push smaller toys, always with the doll's head, in such a way that they fall too. Her excitement increases, manifested by chuckling and laughter. With special glee she pushes (with the doll's head) a toy train which is on the floor in the middle of the room. As one car overturns, she overturns them all. But then she suddenly stops and becomes very pale.

She leans with her back against the sofa, holds the doll over her genital region and drops it on the floor. She picks it up again, holds it over the same region, and drops it again. While repeating this from ten to fifteen times, she begins first to whine, then to cry, finally to yell, "Mommy, mommy, mommy."

(*M*, sure that the game is up, enters room to take Mary home.)

"B"
IV

1. The sudden hilarity and blushing aggressiveness immediately enter into a dramatic curve of quickly increasing excitement. This likewise suddenly reverts to pale inhibition and overt anxiety. Her blind screaming contacts her mother and restores the mother adherence.

2. The discernible content has been: *Pushing and throwing down* of things, not with her hand but with an extension of her hand; the *dropping* from the genital region of a doll (which before, as an extension of the hand, had been, as it were, a pushing tool).

3. Spatially, after the physical adherence to *M* is made impossible, the child turns in a diffused way to the room at large and to the small toys in it. Her play is of the *autocosmic extension* type with the doll used as an extension of the pushing hand. Only in pushing the train does she approach a possible *microcosmic theme* (train accident); whereupon she withdraws to the periphery of the room where she dramatizes the loss from the genital region of the doll which had been an extension of the aggressive hand. Paralysed by anxiety, she then contacts her mother, who leads her out of the conflict situation.

4. Corresponding to this aggressive and regressive behavior, her loud communication changes from coquettish chuckling to excited laughter, to pale silence, to anxious whining, to desperate screaming, "Mommy, mommy, mommy."

"C"
IV

The doll in Mary's hand is used in such a way as to appear that she does not dare touch or push the objects with her bare hand. One is reminded that in the play group her strange way of touching and lifting things ("never with the whole hand") was observed. This and a certain rigidity in the extremities suggest that Mary is (constitutionally or traumatically) disturbed in the manipulative and locomotor sphere.

The way in which she then seems unable to stop her own dramatization of something dropping from the genital region reminds one of the interpretation given to certain hysterical (grand mal) attacks in which the patient is supposed to represent both partners in an imagined scene, namely, the victim and the aggressor in a sexual act. Here it would be the robbed and the robber. Literally, the dropping of a doll from between the legs suggests "birth." The half-sitting position she assumes when dropping the doll suggests a "toilet situation." Birth and toilet situation have in common the "dropping" of (valuable) bodily content. While we know nothing about the events of Mary's toilet training period, it seems that in the nursery the toilet situations were factors in the outbreak of her anxiety. Finally the association with "extension" (and pushing?) suggests that she may be dramatizing the fact that she has no penis. It is most probable that on entering the nursery school Mary was given her first opportunity to go to the toilet in the presence of boys and to see boys' genitals. Is this the "loss" which she indicates?

"D"
IV

1. Symbols: The doll, first a baby (with shoes), is then used as (*a*) a hand extension (finger?); (*b*) a gential extension (penis or bodily content?).

Of defensive arrangements the following were recognizable: at the beginning and at the end of the hour self-protection by means of regressive M-adherence and denial of interest in toys and *Ps*; during the pushing episode, protection of extremity by the use of an (overcompensatory?) extension. The defense arrangement breaks down as Mary is overcome by the impulse to push and by some phantasy of the loss of the extension. We may therefore say:

2. Mary seems to be full of mischief (so far expressed as aggressive pushing), but is afraid of her impulses because she may damage her hand or lose something in the genital region if she does not restrict her sphere of expression and keep close to her mother.

3. The contact offered neither the opportunity not the appropriate moment for the administration of a therapeutic interpretation. If the mother had not interrupted (a behavior which throws some light on her part in the child's anxiety situations) *Ps* would have tried to get in some kind or verbal contact with the child.

2. Interview with Mother

In a conversation with M the child's total situation at the time of her visits to the nursery is discussed. M relates a fact which she had forgotten to tell me before: Mary had been *born with a sixth finger* which had been removed when she was approximately half a year old. Just prior to the outbreak in the play group Mary had frequently asked about the *scar* on her hand and had received the answer that it was "just a mosquito bite." The mother admits, however, that the child in somewhat younger years could easily have been present when her operation was discussed. Around the time of her anxiety Mary had been equally insistent in her *sexual curiosity*, a fact which speaks for the possible importance at that time of a "scar" association between the actually lost finger and the mythical lost penis.

Her curiosity had received a severe blow when, shortly before the outbreak of anxiety, her father, irritable because of an impending legislative decision, had *shown impatience with her during her usual morning visit* to him in the bathroom and had shoved her out of the room. She had liked to watch the shaving process and had also frequently on recent occasions (to his annoyance) asked about his genitals. It must be taken into account here that a strict adherence to a certain routine situation in which she could do, say, and ask the same thing over and over again always had been a necessary condition for Mary's inner security.

As to the child's physical condition at these particular times, it appears that bad dreams with violent kicking in sleep (which M tries to check by holding her tight and awakening her) and foul breath on awakening had been attributed by one physician to a *bad condition of the tonsils*. Another physician, however, had denied this. The mother and the first physician had engaged in a heated discussion (before Mary) as to whether she needed an immediate *operation*. Before we evaluate all these factors (which add the association "operation" to that of "scar" and explain both an increase adherence to M during F's irritable absent-mindedness and an increased fear of doctor-possibilities), we shall report Mary's second contact in order to see which of all these factors her further play will single out as subjectively relevant.

"A"
I
MOTHER

Mary again smiles bashfully at me, again turns her head away, holding on to M's hand and insisting that M come with her into the room. Once in the room, however, she lets her mother's hand go and as M and Ps sit down she begins to play peacefully and with concentration.

"A"
II
BUILDING A HOUSE WITH BLOCKS

Mary goes to the corner where the blocks are on the floor. She selects two blocks and arranges them in such a way that she can stand on them each time she comes to the corner to pick up other blocks. She carries the blocks to the middle of the room, where she has put a toy cow, and builds a very small house. For about 15 minutes she is completely absorbed in the task of arranging the house so that it is strictly rectangular and at the same time fits tightly about the cow. She then adds several blocks to the long side of the house in the following way (Figure 3).

At the point marked X she adds a sixth extension, shifting it several times to other places, but finally returning it definitely to X.

Figure 3

"B"
II

1. Today Mary peacefully concentrates on microcosmic play with a certain maternal quality of care and order. There is no climax of excitement, and the play ends on a note of satiation.

2. Her play has as subject (*a*) the building of a close-fitting stable for a toy cow; (*b*) adorning the stable building with six wings (five plus one).

3. Though *M* is present, Mary does not seem moved by impulses of adherence. She builds freely in the middle of the room, moving to the corner and back without hesitation.

Play again begins with an autocosmic extension—namely creating a base for the feet—and then is microcosmic throughout. The block configuration suggests, first, the female protective mode; second, a hand with a sixth finger or a foot with a sixth toe.

"C"
II

The mother has remained in the room, not "good technique," but before this can be changed, Mary has concentrated so deeply on her play that it seems better to let her finish it.

Mary, with all her rigidity, balances well standing on the two blocks and bending down. The fact that she has to create a foot extension (protection? overcompensation?) for herself before picking up blocks reminds us of the fact that during the previous contact she had to add an extension (the doll) to her hand before she pushed the objects in the room. Both these acts suggest, of course, the association: scar, operation.

The house is built with a special expression of maternal "care." The five wings, to which (after some doubt as to where to put it) a sixth is added, again remind one of the amputation of her sixth finger.

But this time, although again beginning with the representation of the extension of an extremity, Mary's play does not lead into an aggressive outbreak (and the subsequent representation of a catastrophe). It finds satiation in the building of a female protective configuration. There is a pervading femininity about today's behavior which serves to underscore in retrospect and by contrast the danger dramatized during the first contact, namely, the loss from the genital region of an object used for agressive pushing. The interesting combination of a handlike configuration with one which we are used to interpret as symbolizing the female organs of proceation furthermore suggests that a masturbation threat (harm to hand or genital if in contact) may be one of the specific experiences to which the little girl is reacting with anxiety.

"D"
II

1. *Symbols.* (*a*) blocks—protection—extension of feet—; (*b*) blocks—building—female protective configuration around animal—safe body content; (*c*) blocks—extensions of building—six fingers to a hand.

2. *Defensive arrangement.* Maternal herself and master of the microsphere, Mary restores her body's inviolability by representing as restituted the loss alluded to during the first contact: her feet are extended (protected?); the content of her female body (baby) is well protected; the sixth finger is returned to the hand. The play ends on a note of satiety.

"A"
III
GAME WITH Ps

Suddenly Mary looks teasingly at Ps, laughs, takes M's hand and pulls her out of the room, saying, "Mommy, come out."

Ps waits for a while then looks out into the waiting room. He is greeted with a loud and triumphant "Thtay in there!" Ps withdraws, whereupon Mary closes the door with a bang. Two further attempts on the part of Ps to leave his room are greeted in the same way.

(After a while, Ps opens the door slightly, quickly pushes the toy cow into the other room, makes it squeak and withdraws it again. Mary is beside herself with pleasure and insists that the game be repeated again and again until, finally, it is time for her to go home.

When she leaves she looks at Ps directly, shakes hands in a natural way, and promises to "come back").

"B"
III

1. After being satiated with peaceful building, Mary suddenly and teasingly turns to me to intiate a game. During the game it is noticeable that, in spite of her aggressive hilarity, she does not tend (as she did during the first contact) toward overdoing aggressiveness and then with-

drawing from it; Mary is in the real spirit of the game up to the time she has to leave.

2. The game has a content: A man (*Ps*) is teasingly locked into his room alone.

3. This game is macrocosmic indeed. Mary is the master, not only of both the waiting room and my office (and the connecting door), but also of her mother and especially of me. She takes *M* out of my space and locks me into it.

4. "Thtay in there" are the *first words* she has ever addressed to me. They are said clearly and in a loud voice.

"*C*"

III

Mary's provocative behavior came very suddenly and with determination, as if something in her had waited for the moment when she would be free enough to initiate this game. What does it mean? The day before I had asked the mother to leave the room in the middle of the hour. Has Mary anticipated the repetition of this, and has she arranged her triumphant going out of the room with *M* in place of my sending *M* out without Mary? The situation does not seem covered by this possible interpretation.

The words which Mary uses when initiating the game somehow resemble the words which the mother told me the father had used when locking the child out of the bathroom during his days of irritation. "Stay out of here," had been the father's angry words. "Thtay in there" is probably linked with it, although in addition to the transference to me a double reversal had taken place: from the passive to active (it it she who gives orders), and in regard to the vector (she "encloses" instead of being excluded). One remembers now that from the moment Mary came into my room at the beginning of the first contact she showed a somewhat coquettish and bashful interest in me. Since it can be expected that she would transfer to me (the man with the toys) a conflict which disturbed her usually playful relationship to her father, it seems possible that in this game she is repeating with active mastery ("You thtay in there") the situation of exclusion of which she has been a passive victim at home ("Stay out of here"). (This possibility came to me only after I had reacted to her play provocation, which, of course, I was prepared to do as soon as she would have chosen the moment and the theme. By my play acts I unconsciously took the role of the "good father" in a specific, symbolic way.)

"*D*"

III

1. *Arrangement*. After having assumed the good mother role (mother identification) and having protected and restored her body (restitution),

Mary is transferring to me the role of the bad father (father transference) in a rearrangement of the situation which created the conflict between them (reversal of active into passive).

2. We do not know why the second contact was peaceful. It oftens happens that once excessively fearful doctor-expectations are disproved (they are, of course, more easily disproved in less neurotic children), the problems which had been previously presented in all their horrors appear in the form of restitutions: peaceful and playful identification with her mother, protection and restitution of her body in play, and the teasingly revengeful restitution of the play relationship to her father in transference. The child, as it stands at the end of the second contact, has indicated that she wants to be sure of her mother as a haven of protection, of her father as an interesting masculine playmate, and of her body as an inviolable whole in spite of the (at the time intrusive) impulses it expresses and the bodily dangers (operation) experienced and anticipated.

"E"
III

After a play contact which gave the therapist some first insight and the patient some long needed partial play satisfaction, there remain the following therapeutic questions: how normal for her age are the child patient's problems, how much essential stability and adaptability has she betrayed, and how much support can she expect from her environment?

4. Etiological Speculations

We may now inquire into the factors in Mary's life to which our attention has been drawn by her play. Now, as at any deeper point of clinical investigation, we seek to gain insight into changes in the following three segments of the patient's life and into their particular functional relation; namely, into the *coincidence in time* and the *mutual aggravation* of (a) changes in the *physiological sphere* as they are brought about by decisive epigenetic steps in *growth and maturation*, or by some special disbalancing factor such as *sickness or accident*; (b) changes in the constellation or the enotional temperature in the *environment*; (c) changes in the person's *conception of his status* in the world, i.e., a subjectivation of causal judgment in terms of guilt, inferiority, projected intentions, etc.

We find in a disturbed adult's life history that a set of conscious and unconscious ideas (a "complex") is subjectifying his experiences, making all changes mutually aggravating, bringing about continuous libidinal disequilibrium and making the individual the easy "traumatic" victim of specific types of occurrences. Usually the "complex" dates far back—and, indeed, we can observe in still undisturbed children that it is one or the other normal maturational crisis, with its complex of wishful and fearful expectations, during which (given a certain lack of psychosomatic or social support) experiences of a specific type or combination become traumatic: perception is subjectified, anxiety increases, defensiveness stiffens.

Once the mechanisms of psychological homeostasis have been upset for a long time and the individual finally is forced to seek help from a representative of a healing method, content and morphology of his sickness show such a multiple relation to an endless number of factors seemingly making one another pathogenic that unlimited material is provided for the discussion of whether the condition has a physiological or psychological basis. Usually, reality forces a simple solution: whatever method by right or might can claim the patient, is able to secure a selection of data and, by interjecting its curative agent, is successful in breaking the vicious circle of pathogenic factors will also determine the only "evidence" of the circle's "beginning" which anybody will ever have.

We hope to approach such problems from a new angle through the study in normal or only temporarily disturbed children of those periods of lowered physiological resistance, those types of lowered environmental support, and those mechanisms of attempts at adjustment which, if occurring together, represent a combination producing traumatic strain.

Mary's disclosure of her personality in her present stage of maturation and state of anxiety shows her generally somewhat *timid*: in all her aggressiveness she likes to have the retreat to her mother well covered. She is *rigid* in the sense that changes of routine are in themselves upsetting. On the other hand, she is playfully *mischievous* and psychosexually *girlish*. There is no doubt that Mary is *dramatic* (an interesting hysterical contrast to some of her compulsive traits), lovable, playful, outgoing, coquettish if master of the situation; stubborn, babyish, and shut-in when disturbed.

Physiological changes: maturational. Mary's age and play suggest that she may be considered to be in the stage of childhood characterized (in both sexes) by a rapidly increasing power of *locomobility*, expanding *curiosity*, and *genital sensuality*, which in psychoanalytic literature is called the phallic stage and for which the author, in order to take into account certain developmental facts, has used the terms "locomotor-phallic" or "intrusive stage" (3).

The intrusive stage, in analogy to other stages, emphasizes sometimes silently, sometimes more noisily the following developmental potentialities:

1. The *impulse* of intrusion (epigenetically emerging with added vigor from the inventory of given impulses), the urge to force one's way into the object of interest and passion.

2. The *sensual (libidinal) experiences* of increased locomotor pleasure and (often masturbatory) indulgence in phantasies of instrusive conquest.

3. A channel for the *release* (catharsis) of *surplus tension* from various sources in relatively excessive activity, of an aggressive, curious, and masturbatory character.

4. Specific trial and error *experiments* in regard to how far one can go in physically and socially forcing one's way into the sphere of others.

5. A complex of *omnipotence and impotence phantasies* depicting the child either in the unlimited execution of the intrusive mode, and the unlimited mastery over its phantasy object (omniscient master of the universe, conquering the mysterious, taking revenge on giant enemies, etc.), or as the victim of other masters.

6. A new focus for the expectation of danger (*developmental fear*), i.e., an intolerance toward all interferences which may bring frustration to 1, 2, and 3, and danger to the organs involved. If increased by constitutional or environmental factors this intolerance may lead to an abnormal intensity or prolongation of 3 (i.e., excessive aggressiveness or masturbation) and severe anxiety and rage in the face of attempts to break it.

7. *Reaction* formations, i.e., changes in the personality which can be understood as permanent defensive reactions of the ego against those aspects of 1–5 which can be neither quite outgrown nor successfully used in socially approved action patterns.

To the future of the personality this stage (like all the others) provides a source of experiential wealth and power as well as of danger.

8. The personality is strengthened and enriched by (*a*) the successfully socialized use (sublimation) of the new impulse for such growing abilities and aspirations as are in accord with ego and environment: outgoingness and energy, courage in the face of the unknown, etc.; (*b*) by reliable *reactive* virtues binding some of the excessive energy and the unsuitable modes of the stage, such as self-restraint, protective attitudes, etc.

9. The danger consists in the potential *developmental fixation* which may build the basis for a future (periodic or permanent) *developmental regression*, such as the sadomasochistic dealing with partners in love or work. Reaction formations while creating virtues

under certain conditions may imply excessive and permanent inhibition of intrusive types of action, repression of corresponding thoughts and past experiences or more radical measures such as the "turning against oneself" of intrusive acts and thoughts, i.e., masochistic fantasies, often with organic concomitants, or with the provocation of bad treatment by others.

In every developmental stage there is a period when a momentary fixation threatens to become incompatible with progression—the most common kernel of neurotic episodes in childhood. Such neurotic episodes are, of course, similar in content and form to the manifestations of chronic neurotics.

The study of neuroses has shown us that special educational interferences with the general mode of the intrusive stage (such as Victorian tendencies to place special limitations on many forms of locomotor and curious expansiveness, and to react with disciplinary selectivity to sexual curiosity) result in a fixation on the idea of genital intrusion, making the genitals the subject of excessive cathartic acts or that of excessive curiosity and often the consequently excessive repression of both. Such fixation brings with it a prolonged emphasis on the idea and the fear of intruding and on the idea and fear of being intruded upon and, consequently, fears for the inside of the body (as a goal of intrusion) and for extremities and penis as the organs of intrusive aggressiveness. Such a body of fearful expectations becomes, then, a ready factor in the traumatic nature of corresponding experiences.

It must be obvious that this stage offers special problems to the girl. Led by the intersexual experiences of younger organisms, she too has reached a period of stronger intrusive tendencies, often observed as tomboyishness. During this period clitoral masturbation and phantasies of having or achieving a penis (with all the locomotor and mental prerogatives ascribed to it) are not infrequently admitted. We know that in certain types and under certain cultural conditions this wish remains dangerously determining for life, while often, in a way much less well known, the locomotor-phallic complex seems easily and, so to speak, noiselessly subordinated to the wish for a baby and all the prerogatives connected with *this* possibility. But the physiological and psychological conditions which the girl must accept while imagining for the first time becoming the object of intrusive impulses and developing and libidinizing the (not necessarily unaggressive or passive) impulses of inception make the problem of female masochism a cardinal one—for personality as well as for culture. Of the mature man and the mature woman we expect that both the sadistic and the masochistic aspects of sexual intrusion have been subordinated to a satisfactory mutuality. This ideal of sexual maturity presupposes the successful liquidation of the phantasies and fears of the intrusive stage, during which to the bewildered child "cruel" and "sexual" often seem synonyms (3).

Mary, as little as she told us so far, has revealed something of the conflict of the girl who does not know whether she wants to be a boy or a boy's girl—although she has done so with more grace and humor than we could expect from the chronic victims of this conflict.

We also understand that during her first contact Mary indicated to us that she had associated the intrusive impulses of the stage just outlined with the idea of *"danger to the extremities"*—an association probably preconsciously emphasized by the allusions to her *lost finger* and the imminent danger of an *operation*. However, during her second contact she dramatizes the development of a female identification and mastery of the fears of the intrusive stage.

In regard to the necessary attachment to one or both of her parents of these impulses and fears ("Oedipus Complex") we can only say that the therapist in this case naturally attracted the father-transference; there seems to be little doubt as to the importance at this time of the child's father as a partner in teasing games and as an object of sexual curiosity. The child's flight to her mother is by no means free of ambivalence, as further observation would quickly reveal.

Physiological changes: special physiological condition. Mary has not been sleeping well of late. She has severe panics (or tantrums) in her sleep, during which she yells, "No, no, no!" Whatever it may be that she is dreaming about, she awakens with a foul breath and there is a suspicion that the state of her *throat* causes irritation and contraction even if there is no indication for a tonsillectomy. She has heard of the possibility of an operation, which she seems to have associated with the loss of her finger.

Environmental changes. The sudden addition to her sphere of experience of the *play group* puts Mary for the first time in her life in the hands of an adult other than a near relative and into a play situation with boys (at home there is only an older sister). Both her *maturational* state and the *idea of an operation* as associated with the loss of the finger must give the observation of sexual differences (in children) at this moment, even if it has been observed before, a sudden specific pathogenic importance.

At *home* it seems to be the *father's irritability* which the child, not knowing the cause, must have misunderstood and connected with the place where it was first experienced (or because of obvious associations most intensely experienced); namely, the *bathroom*. Thus this experience, too, has been incorporated into the field of *mutually specific factors*.

We shall now offer a tentative diagrammatical summary, (*a*) comprising the interrelation of the historical, maturational, special physiological, and environmental changes with the impulses, ideas, and fears which we suspect of forming parts of the anxiety content; and (*b*) leading us back to the behavior items which "told us" of these impulses, ideas, and fears (Table 1).

What I have said about Mary represents the "mental note" which the psychoanalyst would make tentatively at the end of the two contacts. Some parts of the note would stand out in more clarity than others; however, we would expect him to have the courage to modify even his "clear impressions" if further observations demanded it.

As for Mary, the contacts were interrupted by a vacation period, after which the observer left Boston. Therefore Mary's situation was carefully discussed with her understanding parents, who accepted (and partly themselves suggested) the following recommendations. Mary's curiosity in regard to both her scar and her genitals required a truthful attitude. She needed to have other children and especially boys visit her for play at her home. The matter of the tonsils called for the decision of a specialist, which could then be candidly communicated to the chid. It did not seem wise to awaken and hold her during her nightmares; perhaps she needed to fight her dreams out, and there would be opportunity to comfort her when she awoke spontaneously. The child needed much locomotor activity; playful instruction in rhythmic movements might help her to overcome some rigidity with her extremities which, whatever the cause, presumably has been increased since she heard for the first time about the amputation of her finger.

A conversation with the parents a half year after the contacts described in this report did not seem to indicate the immediate necessity for further psychoanalytic observation. A tonsillectomy had proved unnecessary; the nightmares had ceased; Mary was making free and extensive use of the new play companions provided in and near her home. For various circumstantial reasons, she had, however, not visited the original play group again. She had asked for *Ps* often, wanting to know the color of the train he had taken when leaving town.

When Mary, a while later, paid *Ps* a short visit, she was entirely at home and asked *Ps* in a clear, loud voice about the color of his

TABLE 1 DIAGRAMMATIC SUMMARY

The diagonal (A–G) shows the historical, maturational, and environmental changes which seem to be of acute importance in the patient's present life situation.

Downward and to the left of the diagonal (AB–FG) the possibly and probably resulting emotional emphases are shown. Emphasis AB is the result of the mutual aggravation of change A and B; AC that of A and C; etc.

Upward and to the right of the diagonal (ab–fg) the play acts are shown which made us aware of the actuality and motivating power of the ideas and emotions shown in AB–FG: ab points to AB, ac to AC, etc. However, play acts are "overdetermined", i.e., correspond to several ideas and emotions.

A HISTORICAL: amputated finger	**ab** autosphere microsphere	**ac** hysterical dramatization: loss from genital region protective overcompensation: extensions of hand and foot restoration: female protective configuration and six-finger configuration	**ad**
AB 1. fear for (aggressive) extremities. 2. masochistic fantasies?	**B** MATURATIONAL I intrusive (phallic) vs. female protective impulses	**bc** defense bashfulness before play expression: exhibitionistic elements in hysterical dramatization transference: provocative mischievousness in play with Ps	**bd**
AC association scar-vagina	**BC** sexual curiosity and feeling of shame	**C** MATURATIONAL II curiosity vs. bashfulness	**cd** transference and sublimation: curiosity in regard to Ps train
AD theory that mother evades the scar-vagina issue because she caused these losses?	**BD** provocative mischievousness in play with father	**CD** curiosity in regard to father's body	**D** MATURATIONAL III need for (and fear of) father; need for (and jealousy of) mother "ambivalences")
AE association: amputation of finger—loss of penis—operation on tonsils	**BE** general fear of being intruded upon	**CE** fear of physical examinations	**DE** fear dreams ("no, no, no!")
AF theory of chirurgical punishment	**BF** guilt feelings for mischievousness	**CF** guilt feelings for curiosity	**DF** feeling of being rejected by father
AG feeling of having been robbed of important organs	**BG** mischievous intentions and anticipating fears in contacts with boys?	**CG** curiosity in regard to children's genitals	**DG** need for mother

ae	af	ag
be, ce, de mixture of coquetry (man) and fear (doctor)	bf, cf *defense:* mother adherence and shying away from toys	bg, cg
	symptom play disruption with new mother adherence	*symptom:* anxiety attacks in nursery
	df, ef *transference in macrocosmic play:* transformation of "doctor" situation into "playing with man" situation and "rejection" of *Ps* *(reversal)*	*dg, eg* *regression:* babyish mother adherence
E PHYSIOLOGICAL throat condition (threatened operation)		
EF feeling of impending danger	F ENVIRONMENTAL I father's temporary irritability	fg see dg
EG feeling of danger	FG devaluation of "big girl" hood; need for mother	'G ENVIRONMENTAL III new play group (with boys)

train. She addressed *M* and *Ps* alternately and entered *Ps*'s room without anxiety. Her play immediately centered on the cow again, which, with loving words, was given a tight-fitting stable.

D. ORALITY IN A BOY OF FOUR

Dick was brought to our attention by a physician from a nearby town who occasionally attended the meetings of our Yale study group. His mother, the physician's patient, had complained for the last year or so of a "queer trait" in her little boy; encouraged by our work, the physician, an extraordinarily good observer, familiar with the principles of psychoanalysis, decided to try her eye on the child's play. She invited the little boy, who had never seen her, to come to her office to play and reported to us the five contacts, the first three of which will be given here.

Dick on his fourth birthday was a physically healthy, attractive, and intelligent child who had a good appetite and slept well. However, he was often dreamy and withdrawn and, with strange indifference, would express rather queer fears and concepts. His parents, warned by outsiders, began to fear that "some day he might withdraw completely and not come out of it." They had had this in mind for some time when suddenly, at four years and two months of age, he calmly refused to speak for 24 hours and for some days after would only whisper. Such "spells" recurred.

It had started during a big family dinner. An uncle's completely bald head fascinated Dick. Innocently, he remarked, "You haven't any hair on your head." The adults smiled in embarrassment and hoped he would think of something else, but a few moments later he addressed the bald-headed man again. "Have you no comb at your house?" After more such remarks Dick's grandmother took him aside and told him that he was "not to talk about this any more." The child, without any display of emotion, became silent and remained silent for 24 hours, except for some whispered remarks in school the next morning.

Naturally, the parents were worried about such a radical reaction to an everyday occurrence such as the prohibition against talking about a seemingly unimportant matter. On the other hand, it was hard to judge the "seriousness" of Dick's reaction, for he seemed neither stubborn, nor worried, nor angry; he simply was far away, apparently uninterested in a means of communication which had proved so troublesome.

One remembered then that on several occasions Dick had been a radical representative of the biblical saying "If thine eye offend thee, pluck it out"—or rather its infantile form, "If thine eye offend thy parents, pluck it out." There had been, for example, a time (it was during one of his mother's pregnancies) when he was very proud of and liked to display and brag about his "nice fat tummy." Its unproductivity devaluated the possession of this part of his body, whereupon he remarked that he was going to throw it out of the window and was found pressing it against a hot radiator "to burn it off." Similarly, after one of his little sisters had been born and had taken supremacy in the family's attention, he seemed ready to cast away all the prerogatives of his age and sex. He began to creep, to use baby talk, and even to want his clothes and his belongings to be called "little." Again, he not only tried to deny a devaluated possession, this time his genitals, but was found attempting "to pull them off," and finally asked his distraught parents to do him this service.

It would be hard to say exactly whether and where all this transgresses the range of variations and episodic peculiarities of normal child behavior. To his intimate observers, Dick seemed to *experiment with reality* in a somewhat less playful and more deeply preoccupied way than most children do. He was interested in parts of the body (the "tummy" of a pregnant woman, the penis) which are of outstanding importance in some cases, but are missing in others without apparent disadvantage for either well-being or prestige. This preoccupation with missing things could take possession of him to such a degree that the majority of his remarks and questions during a given period would indicate a concept of the world in which *missing things* were not the exception but the rule and the dominant aspects. After he had been frightened by the sight of eyeglasses, he asked everyone, including perfect strangers, whether their eyes came out. After he had discovered that a certain old man had false teeth, he asked the same question about everybody's teeth. When he saw a sculptured bust, he remarked that it had "no feet"; on entering a room, he pointed to what looked to him like holes in the ceiling before he noticed anything else. To him, a person did not "have" a tummy or an arm, but "wore" them; an expression which clearly implied the suspicion that these parts could be taken off like clothes.

Thus, at times, his body image seemed to lack a certain integrity. But while his calmness suggested that this lack was simply the remnant of an earlier age—i.e., represented a maturational deficiency— his usual display of intelligence contradicted this interpretation. Consequently, it was necessary to assume that the boy experienced (or pretended to experience) rather something of a disintegration of his body image.

An attempt to test Dick's intelligence had the following result:

> In many instances the child appeared to be concentrating on the task at hand. At other times he seemed almost like a sleepwalker. The very much longer time required for the third trial of the Sequin form board may be attributed to the fact that two or three times he simply became fixated on a block and was unable to continue the activity. When a key was held out to him and he was asked to name it, he seemed to look right through it; several minutes later it was presented to him again and he quickly and easily gave the name. His successful responses (at the age of 44 months) were, for the most part, at the three-and-one-half and the four-year levels. One certainly has the impression that this is a potentially able child. [When brought in during one of his phases of not speaking,] he was very aloof and did not speak a word. He was fascinated by the bridge of blocks built for his own little car and smiled willingly, but would not try one himself; he sat down once or twice; but each time became uneasy and immediately pushed the chair away from him. He looked out of the window a good deal and remained in a teasing mood so that no satisfactory developmental picture could be obtained. He resented all efforts to help him and pushed the examiner's hand away. In general, he looked at everything with a curious combination of attention, and dreaminess. He was not eager to leave, but went passively when told to go.

That Dick really had a most emotional interest in the integrity of the objects to whose defects he referred casually became obvious when, during his spells of silence or whispering, he could be observed creating a private world in which he could inquire about missing things and be sure to get a comforting answer. Thus he could be overheard asking himself, "Has that car got a spare tire?" and answering himself, "Yes, it has, Dick." This (normal if transient) method of dealing with observable fact he used also in matters of conscience. "Dick, you must not do that.—But I want to do it.—It is better not to do it.—But I am going to do it." Whereupon the "adult" voice seemed to be giving in.

Dick seemed genuinely afraid that certain radiators were going to bite him, and it will be one of the tasks of our play analysis to find out why certain radiators seem to him to be animal-like, others not. This manifest fear that something inanimate might have a hidden mouth to bite him corresponded to the only recurrent dream he liked to report, namely of a certain being to whom he gave a strange name and of which he could only say that it had "no mouth." Incidentally, he spoke about dreams as if they were real. Visiting a friend, he would say, "I was here last night and played with you." We know that many children indicate that at least in answer to certain suggestive questions they are unable to differentiate verbally between dream and reality. What interests us about this child is that he preferred to talk about such borderline experiences, often to the exclusion of all other topics. Cars often seemed to be animate beings for him. "It is too bad that motorcars have to sleep out in the street." For some time he has been differentiating also between men-cars and lady-cars, basing the distinction partly on types of cars which were driven by men or women of his acquaintance. This differentiation, however, overlapped with the one applied to all objects and based on their "yes" or "no" aspects, namely, whether they have a hole (a sink for him is a "no thing") or outstanding parts (a comb is a manifold "yes thing").

All-or-nothing people, who seem ready literally to pluck out the eye which offends them, are hard to deal with. When asked to *keep* it they may insist with equal radicalness on using it. Thus when Dick's parents noticed that to the detriment of his development he had decided to become in all physical and mental respects the likeness of his sister, they initiated a campaign for masculinity, insisting that to have a penis was practical and desirable and nothing to be ashamed of. He took them at their word. He exhibited his penis and, this prohibited, began to shout around his word for penis in a voice the masculinity of which left nothing to be desired; he began to lift the skirts of little girls and finally annoyed adult women visitors by looking at them from the frog's eye-view. The fact that the shouting of the word for penis occurred and was prohibited shortly before he met and annoyed the man who had no hair explains some of the intensity of his reaction to the grandmother's prohibition. For him, *to have a thing, to show it, and to use the word for it* meant three inseparable aspects of its possession. It was obviously intolerable to him that after he had tried in vain to be everything people seemed to like better than a little boy (namely, a pregnant mother, a little girl, etc.) he should meet even more powerful interferences when acting on the suggestion that he become a boy. Not only did he, as we have heard, begin to whisper, but he also wrapped his head in a sheet at night, tried to force his head into a toilet, etc. Biting became the dominant idea in his play; he threatened to bite not only his sister, but also himself, and actually was observed biting a dog's tail.

From such scant material, which gives the mother's complaints (somewhat ordered by us according to areas of expression rather than chronologically), we derive the following preliminary outline of Dick's personality: He is overcome by his drives at one moment, by prohibiting forces at the next; each time, however, an all-or-none attitude takes possession of him; similarly he changes his roles of identification easily, although each time radically and completely. Thus in his subjective as well as his objective world he keeps roles changeable, and parts detachable, introjects easily and projects easily. What danger he may be trying to ward off (if what we describe are defensive mechanisms, and not merely regression and disintegration) is only hinted at in the content of his phobia: *He is threatened by a being with a mouth, which in his dreams* (according to the undistorted wish-fulfilling character of children's dreams) *appears without a mouth.* Mouth and throat become the "zonal" emphasis in a world of dangerous have-nots (have holes) and detachable parts: he has spoken of biting ever since his last experiment in masculinity—at the height of the phallic phase—failed.

We cannot publish a detailed chronological life history of this child. Whatever historical data come to our mind as we observe the child's play will be reported in that context. We must concentrate on tracing the outline in playful and fearful acts of a doubting and often despairing infantile mind which has been unable so far to settle down to a clear differentiation of certain borderlines of individual and social existence. We shall see him concerned with *the differentiation between male and female, between ego and object, between animate and inanimate, between bodily coherence and fluctuating environment,* etc. As psychoanalytic experience and theory would lead us to expect such basic uncertainty will prove to be linked with an *oral complex*, i.e., the fixation on an easy regression to the wishes and fears of one of the incorporative stages. Beyond showing how this reveals itself in the child's play, we will avoid drawing diagnostic or prognostic conclusions from childhood material we are just learning to approach.

Whether the fault lies with the circumstances under which this material was won, or its inner affinity to the early stages of personality development, it is hard to present and doubtless even more difficult to read. The patient reader, it is hoped, will reach some point which can serve him as a bridge from his adult thinking to that of a disturbed infantile mind—and to that of stubborn observers who cannot bring themselves to dismiss "queer" material as meaningless.

The circumstances of observation and the nature of the material make the following methodological changes necessary:

1. An account of the sequence of the child's acts will not be attempted. Instead, an inventory of behavior items (according to the classifications: toys, "life-sized" objects, people) will be given for each contact. Only occasionally will a reference be made which places an act nearer to the beginning or the end of a contact.

2. Except where a coherent plot becomes discernible there will be no attempt to account regularly for the ideational content in the patient's fleeting play.

3. In order to familiarize the reader with the character of this patient's play the inventory of the first three hours is given in toto before the single items are taken up for analysis.

1. Inventory of First Three Contacts

a. First contact. Dick, who has never seen the physician before, seems from the very start to accept her in a matter-of-fact way. Pressing into her room, he only asks in a casual way, "Are your eyes all right?" and then eagerly, "Where are the toys?"—He immediately piles all the toys (except for a large truck with doors) into one box and carries them to the couch.—His mother, who comes after him to ask if it will be all right for her to go away, has to repeat her question before he gives a casual, rather impatient "Yes." She says goodbye, but he pays no further attention to her.

(1). *Toys.* Dick takes or points to a number of toys, and with one exception merely makes remarks about them instead of playing with them. He looks from all possible angles at the toy cars, his head close to them, and repeatedly makes the following remarks. "They have no spare tires." "Are they broken off?" "Did they ever have them?" "They are not meant to have spare tires, are they?" "It's all right, they don't need them." "Don't you touch them." "I don't like those cars." "I don't want to play with them."

He treats the red wrecker with a satisfied smile. "This car has two spare tires." "I like this one." He associates to it: "Mother's car has a spare tire."

"There is no water in the toilet." "We will leave the cover up." "We had batter put it down again." "I don't have to go to the toilet." "Don't put any water in it."

Dick has left only one toy in the toy closet, a big red truck with doors. Near the end of the hour he says, "I can't have it, can I?" The physician says he can play with any of the toys. "No," he says, and closes the closet door. Later he takes the truck out, opens its back doors, shuts them, and puts the truck back, saying, "You mustn't touch it."

He builds a garage for two cars; puts doors on it and two roofs; is pleased with it. After a little, he opens the doors with the intention of putting in two cars, then knocks the whole structure down, saying, "I don't need it."

(2). *Big objects.* Dick says, "Does the chair come off?" The physician thinks he means the swivel top and replies, "No." Dick says, "Yes, it does," and demonstrates by lifting the chair. "The table comes off too. You were kidding me when you said it didn't, weren't you?" (He lifts the table.)

He looks at the radiator in an intently exploratory way, eyeing the two ends with some anxiety, and says, "There is no water coming out, is there? How does it work?" The physician offers to turn on the steam. He seems alarmed and cries, "Don't do it!" The physician says, "Tell me what you want to know about radiators." Dick presses against the physician's knees and says in a confidential manner, "I want to know about yellow radiators."

Near the end of the hour Dick says to the physician, "You mustn't take your dress off. I will spank you if you do."

b. Second (short) contact. Dick again presses eagerly into the room the minute the door is opened and goes instantly to the toys. His acts and words are almost identical with those of the first contact with the difference that he handles the cars with more freedom and only once or twice comments on the lack of spare tires.

About the girl doll he says: "She has no pants on. She has to go to the toilet. You make her sit on the toilet. She is all through." He puts her in front of the basin to wash her hands, then puts her in the bath tub. (Her dress is sewed on.) "She is a naughty girl to be in the tub in her dress. She mustn't take her dress off."

c. Third contact.

(1). *Toys.* About the cars Dick says over and over: "Do they have spare tires? Are they broken off?" He points to little knobs and calls them spare tires.—He says, "Have all wreckers two spare tires? I want to break them off."

He sets the bathroom set up several times, each time hesitating to play with it. His eyes wander to the dolls, but he turns away again. Finally, near the end of the hour, he announces: "The little girl needs a bath; she is sick." He asks the physician to let the water run into the tub; he seems pleased and excited.

He opens the truck doors and says, "I'd better shut them." He opens them again and puts half a dozen toys in. He removes them again.

Dick again builds a garage with closed doors and runs a small car against the door as if it wanted to enter. The physician remarks, "The car can't go through the closed door, can it?" Dick opens the door, runs a car in and out and in again, leaves it for a while, then takes it out again and abandons the garage with the doors open.

(2). *Big objects.* About the carvings on the arms of the chair Dick says: "They aren't feet, are they? They won't come off, will they?—they look like your hands."

"I am afraid it will bite me." The physician asks, "Who?" Dick replies, with glee, "The radiator downstairs."

(3). *Physician.* Pressing against the physician's knees, he points to big gold buttons (resembling large raspberries) on her dress and says several times: "I want to bite them." The physician asks, "Do you like to bite things?" He replies, "Yes, I like to bite sister. I am going to bite sister when I go home today."—Shortly afterward he says, "I want to eat my dinner. Have you any crackers?" Then he asks: "People can't go down people's lanes, can they?" The physician says, "You mean the red lane?" He replies, "The yellow lane. Sister calls it a red lane. I call it a yellow lane.—Yellow is my favorite color."

2. First Contact: Analysis

"A"

I

PHYSICIAN

Dick, who has never seen the physician before, seems from the very start to accept her in a matter-of-fact way. Pressing into her room, he only asks in a casual way, "Are your eyes all right?" and then eagerly, "Where are the toys?"

II

TOYS

He immediately piles all the toys (except for a large truck with doors) into one box and carries them to the couch.

III

MOTHER

His mother, who comes after him to ask if it will be all right for her to go away, has to repeat her question before he gives a casual, rather impatient "Yes." She says goodbye, but he pays no further attention to her.

"B"
I, II, III

No hesitance on seeing a stranger (doctor) is manifested. His mother's departure is even urged with slight impatience. His interest in the physician is fleeting and temporary. All his eagerness is directed toward *having all the toys at once.*

In the macrosphere we thus see an exclusion of the mother, a passing by the doctor, an eager intrusion into the strange room; in the microsphere, and eager collection of all the toys (with the exclusion of one large truck) in one place.

The sentence, "Are your eyes all right?" is *D*'s individual way of saying, "How do you do."

"C"
I, II, III

The impatience with which Dick leaves his *M* behind is in striking contrast to the usual mother adherence displayed by children brought for observation. One is immediately reminded of his reported tendency to deny pronouncedly his interest in persons, objects, or parts of himself to which he had clung the moment before.

His first likewise pronouncedly "casual" interest in *Ps*, then, concerns a part of her body which to his mind (how seriously we don't know) could "come off." This remark recalls an episode: A barber not long ago happened to inflict a slight cut on Dick's ear, whereupon the boy would go to barbers only on the condition that they *did not wear eyeglasses,* as if to imply that persons who have detachable parts are more apt to mutilate others. It may be in keeping with such an idea that he feels safer with a doctor if her eyes are "all right." However, all this seems, for the moment, overshadowed by his eagerness to see the toys.

"A"
IV–VIII
TOYS

Dick takes or points to a number of toys, and with one exception merely makes remarks about them instead of playing with them.

He looks from all possible angles at the toy CARS, his head close to them, and repeatedly makes the following remarks: "They have no spare tires." "Are they broken off?" "Did they ever have them?" "They are not meant to have spare tires, are they?" "It's all right, they don't need them." "Don't you touch them."

"I don't like those cars." "I don't want to play with them."

He treats the red WRECKER with a satisfied smile. "This car has two spare tires." "I like this one."

He associates to it: "Mother's car has a spare tire."

"There is no water in the toilet." "We will leave the cover up." "We had better put it down again." "I don't have to go to the toilet."

"Don't put any water in it."

(Dick has left only one toy in the toy closet, a big red TRUCK with doors.) Near the end of the hour: "I can't have it, can I?" (The physician says he may play with any of the toys.) "No." Closes the closet door.

Later he takes the truck out, opens its back doors, shuts them, and puts the truck back. "You mustn't touch it."

He BUILDS A GARAGE for two cars; puts doors on it and two roofs; is pleased with it. After a little, he opens the doors with the intention of putting in two cars, then knocks the whole structure down, saying, "I don't need it."

"B"
IV–VIII

Dick reveals his interest and withdrawal in the following scale of approaches and avoidances.

Having *piled up* all the toys most eagerly, he does not play with them. He shifts his interest from one to the other, only to *discard* most toys with one or more remarks of a negative character.

He is positive about ("*likes*") only the red wrecker (which has two spare tires where other cars have none) and *associates* to it his mother's car (the only reference to an object outside of the playroom).

He *manipulates* but does not play with the truck with two doors (which had been the only toy left behind in the closet).

He really *plays* only for a moment at building a two-door garage which, however, he *destroys* immediately.

At the same time he establishes a verbal adherence to the physician. In addition to referring to missing parts, he protests his disinclination to play with the toys and insists that such play is prohibited, either assumedly by the physician or expressly by himself.

"C"
IV–VIII

Dick's curve of interest and withdrawal recalls the strength of his initial attachment (eager incorporation) to persons and objects, and his seemingly unemotional dismissal and easy change of them.

As he wants to have all the toys but does not take the time to play with them, he insists on continuously talking with the physician without listening to her answers. His one-sided pursuit of a problem becomes most obvious where he dismisses as irrelevant permissions given by *Ps* and goes on establishing prohibitions. Thus, in spite of his confidential adherence and urgent inquisitiveness, Dick seems to be quite out of touch with the physician, while for the latter, it is hard to know not only what he means but also how seriously he is interested in what he means. Referring at random to the objects at hand, he is obviously speaking of some situation other than the one he presently shares with the physician.

A first hint as to what he may refer to is given in his questions in regard to parts coming off objects and to prohibited acts. These two classes of ideas in almost identical formulations are represented in the questions he asked his mother in rapid succession when she tried to assure him that his penis once and for all belonged to him: "Does sister have a penis?" "Did she lose it?" "Will she have one later?" "Did she do anything naughty to it?"

His assurances that the cars "aren't meant to have spare tires," that "they are all right," and "don't need them," correspond, then, to the answers the mother reports having given the boy: "Girls are meant to be the way they are," etc.

His whole attitude makes it probable that whatever he wants to discuss here is related to a conversation he had with an adult. That "the cars are all right" as well as the prohibitions "not to touch them" is brought forward in the way of a now reassuring, now admonishing adult. As we saw, he not only discards Ps's permission to play with (her) truck, but at the same time treats her as if she were not of age.

Thus, first eagerly interested in the toys, he gradually and individually denies his interest in any of them (except the wrecker with the double spare tires) and instead assumes the role of the adult who knows well that the play is forbidden, while the physician becomes a naughty girl with bad intentions. Are these intentions projected, i.e., do they represent his original play intensions? In any event, in creating this arrangement with an adult Dick goes one step further than he did in the monologues (overheard by M) and which he was two people all in one, the prohibiting adult and the stubborn child. He now assigns the infantile role totally to the physician while he becomes the prohibiting adult.

"D"
IV–VIII

The tentative nature of the first references to symbolic equations has been emphasized above. We are therefore stating them boldly here, going out from what seems to us the key to the patient's system of symbols.

Symbols. If small cars without spare tires are associated with *small human bodies with missing parts* (girls, sisters), a truck and a garage are larger bodies and potential *receptacles for smaller bodies* (women, mothers).

Arrangement. Dick, afraid to play because of the meaning the toys have for him, denies his interest in them; he takes unto himself the attitude of the selecting, prohibiting, and reassuring adult and assumes (projects?) naughty intentions in the physician.

"A"

IX, X, XI

Life-sized objects: Chair, Table, Radiator. "Does it *come off?* (CHAIR) (Physician thinks he means the swivel top and says "No.") "Yes, it does." He demonstrates by lifting the chair.

"The table comes off too. You were *kidding* me when you said it didn't, weren't you?" (He lifts the table.)

Looks at RADIATOR in an intently exploratory way, eyeing the two ends with some anxiety: "There is no *water coming out,* is there? How does it work?"(Physician offers to turn on the steam.) He seems alarmed, "Don't do it!"

(Physician: "Tell me what you want to know about radiators.") Dick presses against the physician's knees and says in a confidential manner, "I want to know about *yellow radiators.*"

"B"

IX, X, XI

On the whole, as we saw, avoiding microcosmic play, Dick gives a more courageous interest to some life-sized objects. He does not discard them as he did the smaller objects, but elatedly proves by lifting them that two of these objects (chair, table) "come off." However, when shifting his interest to the radiator, he withdraws: "Don't do it."

Thus in his general attempt at showing himself the courageous master of the macrosphere (i.e., of life-sized objects and of the physician) he fails when confronted with the radiator, *which has apertures and a watery, noisy inside.* When speaking of this, Dick develops a more intimate bodily adherence to the physician than he does during the rest of the contact.

Verbally, he *"kids"* her in the macrosphere as in the microsphere he has disciplined and reassured her.

"C"

IX, X, XI

In IV–VIII we understood Dick's first reference to the small toys to mean that parts are missing, have "come off." He now demonstrates to the physician that life-sized objects "come off" in toto. These objects have *four legs,* one similarity with animals. The radiator's similarity with animals rests on the fact that he has a *(warm, noisy, water-filled) inside and apertures for intake and release.* Dick dares to touch chair and table, but not the radiator.

This brings to mind the explanation Dick's mother had for his radiator phobia. It appeared, she reported, after a *nurse had kidded* Dick to the effect that *a certain radiator* (it was yellow and had four legs) would jump at him and *bite him.* Probably she used this as a threat in connection with some misdemeanor on his part.

It seems possible, therefore, that Dick in his first contact is introducing us to two aspects of one and the same problem, (*a*) can small objects (children) lose parts "which they need," (*b*) have big objects (animals? adults?) the intention of suddenly jumping at you (and biting)? These questions appear in a conversational context which betrays deep mistrust in and the anxious wish to experiment with adults' prohibitions, assurances, and jokes: His dealing with small objects seemed to lead back to a *reassuring conversation with his mother*, his dealing with big objects to refer to the *nurse's threat*.

"D"
IX, X, XI

1. *Symbols*. Chair, table, radiator; four-leggedness, occasional four-leggedness, apertures, warm touch, inner noise: Bodies which move and bite.

2. Years ago a nurse had said a radiator would bite him. *"She is only kidding,"* his mother had reassured him. This episode is represented with *displacement* (chair, table, which *do* come off, instead of radiator), reversal from passive into active (the physician is kidded and is shown that certain objects *do* come off), and *denial* (of his fear). The arrangement fails in the case of a radiator, the original object of his phobia. We see: Dick *believed in the nurse's threat more than in his mother's reassurances*.

"A"
XII

PHYSICIAN

Near the end of the hour, to physician: "You mustn't take your dress off. I will spank you if you do."

"B"
XII

After the short bodily adherence, Dick's interest in physician again appears fleeting, surprising, teasing. She is small and inclined to uncover herself; he is big, and assumes the punishing tone of an adult.

"C"
XII

During the first contact Dick's verbalized interest in the physician's body has proceeded from an organ extension (eyeglasses), which we assume to stand for the part they cover (eyes), to the clothes, which may be taken off, revealing the *whole body*. This reflects two of the three foci of interest in inanimate objects, namely, the *partial* focus, "coming-off" parts of small objects; and the *total* one: the "coming off" of big objects.

A third focus—namely, the "insides" of larger objects which could enclose the smaller ones—has not appeared in relation to the physician's body. But we have noticed that all the extreme moments of the contact referred to receptacles. It was the big truck that was *completely ignored* at the beginning of the contact when Dick was so eager to get all the toys (—and to ignore mother and physician). His *only play* concerned the two-door garage which he destroyed, and *open anxiety* was obvious only when the working inside of the radiator was referred to.—(Has his fear of certain radiators originally been the fear of woman's bodies? If yes, why?)

"D"
XII

Symbols. As there is a symbolic equation between toy cars and children, there is one between life-sized objects with four legs and animals or adults. The danger threatening the small beings is that something may "come off" them; the danger going out from big beings is that they may move and (at least so says his radiator phobia) bite.

Arrangement. The warning given the innocent physician not to take her dress off, again uses the projective-introjective arrangement which typified the whole hour. *He speaks as if she were intending to do the "naughty" thing he has in mind.* This is as far as the transference has developed during the first contact.

"E"
XII

If we review Dick's behavior with objects so far, we find three themes represented: (1) it is not permissible to touch small cars (children) with missing parts (genitals); (2) it is not permissible to touch big cars and other receptacles (women) which can harbor small cars (children); (3) it is dangerous to touch large inanimate objects (animals, women?) that have apertures and an inside. In order to see the dangerous ideas behind the avoided objects and acts we may connect tentatively: 1 and 2: a girl is being born from within a mother; 1 and 3: missing parts on small bodies have been bitten off by a dangerous big object; 2 and 3: inanimate and animate receptacles are female; both have insides and dangerous apertures.

3. Second (Very Short) Contact: Analysis
"A"
I

REPETITIONS

Dick again presses eagerly into the room the minute the door is opened and goes instantly to the toys. His acts and words are almost identical with those of the first contact with the difference that he handles the cars with more freedom and only once or twice comments on the lack of spare tires.

II

GIRL DOLL AND BATHROOM

"She has no pants on. She has to go to the toilet. You make her sit on the toilet. She is all through."

Puts her in front of the basin to wash her hands; then puts her in the bath tub. (Her dress is sewed on.) "She is a naughty girl to be in the tub in her dress. She mustn't take her dress off."

"B"

This is the longest interest Dick attached to any one toy so far. Ideational content: Dirty, *naughty*, exhibitionistic girl is taken care of and reproved. Microcosmically the girl is *put into a receptacle* (an act symbolically avoided the day before). This is done in cooperation with the physician.

"C"

Like Mary in her second hour, Dick is somewhat changed. The physician's impression is that he seems to accept in their existing form the cars without spare tires, an impression that goes well with his maternal play with the girl doll. He is motherly today, perhaps an identification with the physician who the day before disproved his fearful expectations and proved not to be a doctor but a maternal friend.

On the one hand, the girl dolly seems to be pretty naughty—whether she does or does not take off her dress. She has inherited the naughtiness which during the first contact appeared partly in denials and was partly projected on the physician.

"D"

Arrangement. Dick and physician are united in the maternal care for a naughty child. According to our expectations (which Mary did not disappoint) this more concentrated microcosmic interlude should free some expansive energy for a clearer macrocosmic representation of Dick's wishes.

4. Third Contact: Analysis

"A"

I

TOYS

Over and over: "Do they (CARS) have spare tires? Are they broken off?" Points to *little knobs* and *calls them spare tires.*

"Have all WRECKERS two spare tires? I want to break them off."

Sets BATHROOM SET up several times, each time hesitating to play with it. His eyes wander to the dolls, but he turns away again. Finally, near the end of the hour, he announces: "The little girl needs a bath, she is sick." Asks Ps to *let water run into the tub*, seems pleased and excited.

Opens TRUCK doors. "I'd better shut them." Opens them again and *puts* half a dozen *toys in.* Removes them again.

Dick again builds a GARAGE with closed doors and runs a small car against the door as if it wanted to enter. (Physician remarks, "The car can't go through the closed door, can it?") Dick opens the door, runs a *car in and out and in again,* leaves it for a while, then takes it out again and abandons the garage with doors open.

"B"
I

Dick's interest, though still fleeting and finally always discarded, remains with each item for one *positive* or *aggressive* statement or move *beyond the first contact's* self-imposed limits. The little have-not cars still have knobs that suggest the possibility there may have been or there some day may be more; while the proud wrecker tempts him to break off his double parts.—Toys are put into the truck, cars without spare tires into a garage, and a (sick) girl into the bath tub. Verbally there is an increase in positive statement.

"C"
I

Before he again disposes of the toys in his usual fleeting, listless way, Dick adds something positive or aggressive to his repetitions, as the following comparison shows:

FIRST CONTACT	THIRD CONTACT
Cars "They have no spare tires."	"Little knobs are spare tires."
Wrecker "He has two spare tires."	"I want go break them off."
Truck "I must shut it."	Puts toys in.
Bathroom "Don't put any water in it."	"Let water run into the tub."
Garage Destroys structure before putting cars in.	Runs a car in. (Does not destroy the garage.)

The evaluation of the car knobs, in the generally more hopeful atmosphere of this hour and if viewed in the context of the other symbolical treatment of toy cars, corresponds to a typical self-comforting infantile reaction to the observation of sexual differences: Little boys and girls often expect a penis to be growing inside the girl (the clitoris providing the girl with a tangible hope) while little boys expect all nipples to become breasts. Both vain hopes contain, as is so often the case, some biological truth. The hopeful reference to these knobs is, then, a belated symbolical expression of that one idea in the conversation with his mother which had not been taken care of in the first contact, namely, the question "Will she [sister] have a penis later?"

It is interesting that this item, in the context of a general slight expansion of *Spielraum** in this hour occurs in connection with a temptation to devaluate the overcompensatory red car by making him lose what was his distinction. Dick's inclination to sacrifice his proudest possessions (tummy, penis) in order to avoid friction and to atone for his aggressiveness against his sister must come to mind. (We remember he had tried to pull off his penis at the end of a supermasculine period when he had been told he was "hurting the girls' feelings.") This suggests a defense mechanism of equalization.

"A"
II
CHAIR, RADIATOR

About carvings on CHAIR'S arms: "They aren't feet, are they? They won't come off, will they?—They *look like your hands.*"

I am *afraid it will bite me.*" ("Who?") With glee: "The RADIATOR downstairs."

"B"
II

In the macrosphere (as in the microsphere) Dick's increasingly gleeful interest remains long enough with the subject to reveal further dangerous associations. (*a*) The association between a potentially detachable part of one of the life-sized objects (the chair's "hands") and a part of the physician's body is frankly pointed out; (*b*) the expectation of being bitten by a radiator is mentioned for the first time "with glee."

"C"
II

During the first hour it was already obvious that there was a correspondence between the spontaneous remarks made about the life-sized objects and those addressed to the physician, the idea of the big organism with dangerous intentions being the connecting association. It is in keeping with the aggressive expansion in the microsphere that in the macrosphere a connection is created between an inanimate, life-sized object and the physician's body. The first contact gave reason to suspect that the transference was developing along this line. (Remember Dick's first question: were the physician's eyes all right—which meant—or did they come off?)

The exalted feeling of "living dangerously" which accompanies today's adventurous expansion (in the microsphere it was represented by the idea of his wrecking the red wrecker) is climaxed in the queer pleasurable anticipation of the very event which is the center of his phobia, namely, to be bitten by the radiator. It is this glee in Dick which was always one

---

* Literally "play space" but meaning a sphere of active leeway for interaction.

of the most difficult traits to understand. There is little obvious "mas-ochism" in it; rather a playful question in view of the dangers of bi-sexuality: how would it be if the sexes could be interchanged—what would one lose, what win?

"A"
III
PHYSICIAN

Pressing against the physician's knees, he points to big, *gold buttons* (resembling large raspberries) on her dress and says several times: "I want to bite them." ("Do you like to bite things?") "Yes, I like to bite sister. I am going to bite sister when I go home today."

Shortly afterwards: "I want to eat my dinner. Have you any crackers?"

Shortly afterwards: "People can't go down people's lanes, can they?" ("You mean the red lane?") "The yellow lane. Sister calls it a red lane. I call it a yellow lane.—Yellow is my favorite color."

"B"
III

This is the longest and most serious concentration on the physician's person reported so far. With verbal frankness two themes are clearly revealed: a biting wish toward her "buttons" and a consideration of the question of whether one person can be swallowed by another. Spatially, then, both the themes which were first dramatized with inanimate objects have found their way to the human organism: parts of a whole being bitten by a whole; a whole being swallowed by a whole. Verbally the statements are clear and frank; he gives a direct answer to question, while he associates one of the home problems, his playful wish to bite his sister.

"C"
III

The expansion in positive statements makes him reveal a wish toward the physician's dress: to bite her buttons. If we confront this statement (as we did the preceding ones) with the corresponding remark during the first hour, we find opposed: First hour "Don't take your dress off"— This hour: "I want to bite the buttons." The impression is that this expresses an oral interest in the physician's breast (see *E*) although the surprising clearness of the statement can be expected either to hide an as yet undiscernible factor or to lead to bad consequences, such as a belated disruption.

At home Dick has voiced for weeks a wish to "bite his sister's tummy." If we remember that he talked first of his "nice fat tummy" when his mother was pregnant (and that his tummy became devaluated after an unproductive hospitalization for a tonsillectomy) we realize that tummy once meant the bulging aspects of femininity and probably included the breasts as the outside of that big inside out of which the babies come, the very idea which we felt he symbolically approached and avoided from the start.

"D"
III

1. *Symbols*: Little knobs on cars—potential (detachable) organs (penis, nipples) on girl's body.

Buttons on physician's dress—nipples on woman's body (which one wishes to bite).

Yellow lane in yellow radiators	=	red lane in bodies	=	nutritional canal

Life-sized, four-legged objects—female organisms (by whom one expects to be bitten or swallowed).

Arrangement: After having microcosmically arranged during the second contact for the little girl to be the naughty child and for the physician and himself to be identified in standards and function in regard to such children, Dick dares to rearrange the whole inventory outlined during the first contact. (*a*) He establishes equality of equipment among the sexes: the knobs of the have-nots will become sizable parts, the spare tires of the have-too-muches can be broken off. (*b*) The cars are put into the truck, the sick girl into the bath; of this the system of symbolic equation used so far admits only one interpretation: the small sister is put back into the mother. (*c*) People cannot be swallowed by others; he is not afraid of the radiator (the nurse was only fooling).

(Are these conditions under which he can express [in transference] his biting impulses toward his mother's body?)

"E"
III

1. On the afternoon of the day of this contact, Dick's nursery school teacher makes an observation which indicates that the interest in the female breast actually is uppermost in the patient's mind on this day and is on the surface of his consciousness, although already subject to the defense mechanism (introjection of prohibition) which we saw especially active during the first contact: Dick asked the teacher whether the buttons on her dress could be unbuttoned. Then he pulled her dress apart without unbuttoning it; he "seemed eager and tense." When the dress opened a little, he suddenly withdrew and said, "No, I can't look in."

2. The dominating conception in all this play seems to be: there are haves and have-nots in the biological world (yes-things and no-things) and these two groups, in various forms of intercourse, make use of their various extensions and inlets. This mutual use seems to imply a danger to the inviolability of the body as a whole: The mouth can suck and bite

the breast, the penis force itself into the body, the baby swell the "tummy" and force its way out of it. These possibilities appear doubly dangerous if one is ignorant or incredulous of the inner or outer laws which are said to inhibit adult bodies from destroying one another and, on the other hand, possessed by impulses—in this case an overwhelming compulsion to think and talk of biting and an equally overwhelming fear of being bitten and robbed.

3. One could have made an interpretational statement to the child at this point, indicating that behind his kidding terrifying ideas were hidden; that these secret ideas had given a traumatic reality to the nurse's "kidding"; that it would be worthwhile talking over what he meant by biting and what the nurse had meant, etc.

5. Fourth and Fifth Contact

After the third contact, in which he had just revealed to the physician certain wishes and fears concerning the *biting* and *swallowing* of one human being by another, Dick contracted *croup*. If not genetically meaningful, this event must have secondarily assumed an unfortunate meaning, namely *oral* (throat) *punishment* for him. When, ten days later, he arrived for his fourth contact, we find him *whispering*, shrinking from self-expression, and armed against temptations as well as punishment. It takes only one more contact, however, to bring him back on the road toward further oral revelations. In order to let his extreme form of shrinking, self-limitation, and encasement stand out against another unfolding of his biting fantasies (which are now familiar to us) we shall briefly contrast, without detailed analysis, the most interesting corresponding items of the two contacts.

6. Fourth Contact: Analysis

"A"

Dick is not as eager as usual to enter the room. He has not taken his heavy snow suit off, seems extremely pale and apathetic and *speaks only in whispers*.

The physician suggests that he take off his snow suit and offers her help. He refuses, whispering, "I will keep them on anyhow. I can sit out here until I take them off." From time to time he smiles at the physician, but stops as soon as she smiles back.

After a while he enters the room with all his clothes on. When asked whether he is hot, he whispers, "I don't want to take them off; just my sweater." Takes cap off so that sweater can be taken off; *puts cap on again* and keeps it on; he is plainly hot and uncomfortable for the duration of the contact. For the most part he wanders around, or moves back and forth on knees.

At one point he suddenly becomes more active; puts all square BLOCKS

IN A ROW, end to end, and producing aphonic noises shoves the line of blocks along the floor by pushing the rear blocks.

Then he builds a GARAGE, runs the little red wrecker into it, and shoves the line of blocks so that they *block the garage* and, lying on his stomach and whispering, gazes into it.

Looks under GIRL DOLL'S skirts and examines her sleeves. Puts her in the bath tub, then on the floor. Puts BOY DOLL beside her. Puts *boy in tub*. Puts a *block in front of the tub*.

Lying on back, examines TRUCK intently. Suddenly in a *loud, clear voice*: "That isn't a truck!" He points to a little wheel that hangs down from the underside of the truck. (Physician asks, "What is it then?") *Whispering* again: "It isn't anything."

"B"

His interest is first concentrated on *himself* and on keeping himself enveloped in clothes and excluded from the physician's room. Then in sudden moves, while still keeping himself in a fortress of clothes, he is playing for moments with more concentration and more independence than ever before. He does not destroy or discard, but (whispering) watches his play arrangements. Autocosmically enveloped and without voice, he puts the *wrecker* in the garage and the *boy* into the tub and *blocks* both with blocks.

Verbal. Whispering and aphonic noises. The statement, "I can sit out here until I take them off" contains a *self verdict* in complete identification with an illusory adult judge. The only loud statement contains a *complete negation*: A truck with a spare wheel isn't a truck—it isn't anything.

"C"

The interrogation and bodily adherence to the physician are broken in this hour. Withdrawn into himself and enveloped in his clothes, he is able to concentrate on longer independent microcosmic play than before. The play is, in a certain sense, *narcissistic* in that he represents in the microsphere what happens in the autosphere: the objects of interest (himself, wrecker, boy-doll) are encased.

(Is he afraid the physician will examine his throat? The past has not given him any reason to expect this, nor has he himself ever treated the observer as a "doctor.")

"D"

AUTOSPHERE	MACROSPHERE	MICROSPHERE
1. Head covered with cap. Body enveloped in clothes. Voice covered by whispering.	Detained in waiting room.	Beloved red wrecker and boy doll in receptacles with exit blocked.

The boy is unborn (not the girl).

2. *Arrangement.* Dick today is completely identified with the voice of conscience. In the first hour he had projected all guilt content onto *Ps*, in the second hour onto the girl doll. In the third hour he had admitted aggressive wishes while already offering atonement. He now arrives at a deadlock of complete self-restriction and revengeful stubbornness: If I am not going to take my clothes off, I cannot enter the room and play. Therefore, I am not going to take them off. Dick's mother reports that she had blamed his carelessness in running around with too few clothes for his croup. The self-encasement of this contact, therefore, seems over-determined, a queer mixture of self-annihilation (punishment for last hour's references to the physician's body and implicitly his mother's body), security in self-restriction (he cannot do any harm) and stubborn, vengeful overobedience (I am not supposed to have few clothes on.—I shall have too many on). That the overdetermination is necessary to produce the performance is obvious from the fact that this extreme be-havior does not occur at home (where his sickness spoke for him) but at the physician's office. It allows us to see some of the components of those "whispering" episodes because of which Dick was brought for treatment: the pious overdoing of a prohibition both as a defense against temptation and a veiled vengeful satisfaction. The whole mischievous energy pent up in such dramatized self-restriction becomes obvious in the following "criminal" features of the fifth contract.

7. Fifth Contact

"*A*"

Enters room, *lively, talkative*, with hand (through clothes) on genital. "The floor doesn't come off, does it?"

"You [PHYSICIAN] haven't any penis." ("That's right.") "Ladies haven't." "Sister hasn't any penis."

"I'll show you mine." *Exhibits himself.*

"You undress the GIRL [DOLL]. You bite her tummy, her hand, her arm, her head, her feet, her behind."

(Pointing to FATHER DOLL): "I am going to take his hat off!"

"*B*"

The relationship between the microcosmic behavior of the day before and this contact's macrocosmic behavior is clearly one of complete re-versal. Whether or not his self-encasement was a relieving atonement for the weakness of the flesh or—as an infantile Nirvana—a triumph of that weakness, today he manically challenges the dangers which he fears most deeply. His questioning and teasing in regard to things which "come off" or part of which "come off" assume a truly macrocosmic form: at least the floor on which we stand won't come off! Consequently the auto-cosmic fears only symbolically expressed in the previous contacts are now clearly referred to and disproved: I can touch and show my penis! Such safety assured, he not only does not shy away from the idea that girls have been robbed and are bitten by women but enjoys the idea.

It is interesting that it is in the context of such a disproval of autocosmic dangers that he pays attention, for the first time, to the father doll: he threatens to take off his hat (in dreams, according to Freud, a penis-symbol). Of further interest are the contemporaneousness of self-encasement and voicelessness in the fourth contact, and that of emancipation of voice and exhibitionism in the fifth. We remember that his first whispering spells occurred on the occasion of his being forbidden to talk about a man's hairlessness; this happened shortly after he had been denied the right at the height of his phallic period to show his penis, to shout his word for penis, and to look underneath the girls' skirts because "it hurt the girls' feelings." The voice which exhibited, as it were, the penis in word-magic and hurt the feelings of female beings had a phallic connotation in more than one sense: The shouting, it seems, had not only *exhibitionistically conveyed the content penis*, but also as a *functional expression dramatized the intrusive mode* (*intensity* of voice and probably *phonetics* of penis-synonym) with the sadistic connotation of hurting girls.

About the time of these contacts the writer met Dick under the following conditions. He went to Dick's town in order to observe him in his play group. While searching for the teacher he suddenly heard strange shouts and terrified yells. Looking into a nearby room, which proved to be the toilet, he saw the boy (Dick) *exhibiting his penis and at the same time shouting* into the ear of a girl of approximately his age. The girl was in a panic, he in a strange state of compulsive acting without much affective participation. (Being visual rather than auditory, the observer remembers Dick's facial expression but not the sounds of what he shouted.)

"D"

1. *Symbols*. Formerly symbolic ideas referring to the female lack of a penis and his own phallic pride appear undisguised. The modal synonymity between *shouting* and *exhibiting* and between *missing part and bitten off part* is expressed clearly.

2. *Arrangement*. Manic challenge, suppression of voice of conscience, denial of fears.

"E"

If the observation had been continued at this point, the challenging of the father figure would probably have proved to be the beginning of the revelation of a complex of ideas connecting his father with the radiator phobia. Other items which lead beyond the intended comparison between the fourth and the fifth contact have been omitted here.

Because in most case abstracts the reader is aware of the lack of detailed accounts transmitting the "feel" of the observational situation, we are concentrating here on a few detailed accounts at our disposal. The reader will now doubtless feel that his hard-won familiarity with Dick's mind should be rewarded with an abstract of his further treatment and development. This cannot be given here. Dick was recommended for thorough child-analytic treatment, for which it was necessary to wait until his family's impending move to a larger city. As this is being written the treatment is in process.

A second unsatisfactory aspect of a detailed clinical account would not have been improved by a continuation of our report. On closer observation clinical material becomes more elusive. Every moment of attention, every step in the analytic direction is apt to bring to light a new element which proves to have been all-pervasive from the beginning. Descriptive and analytic restatements are necessary; reconstructions and interpretations, as they gain in volume, change in structure.

What is it then that we have set out to show: the emergence of an all-pervasive and only intra-individually logical (i.e., psychological) complex of ideas which alone gives the single reported behavior items symbolic or metaphoric meaning. Play acts of the kind Dick produced before our eyes are, of course, continually produced by other children in other situations, where they may mean something else or nothing beyond their face meaning. Small cars can "mean" small cars—within less fixed and less rigid configurations asserting themselves over shorter periods and through fewer areas of expression: The *prolonged and expanded sacrifice of the "real meaning"* of surrounding objects for the sake of their metaphoric meaning within a vicious circle of magic ideas is the mark of an emotional arrest.

Dick's dominating ideas express an *"oral complex."* He not only often speaks of biting; but betrays, in addition to the world of physical facts as he knows them to be, an image of a world in which the biting wish is universal, its magic consequences unavoidable. When he is in panic, it is because of a radiator that will bite; when he dreams, it is of a being without a mouth. When proud, he shouts; when depressed or oppressed, he whispers. In demonstrating the emergence of this complex in play contacts, we hope to have demonstrated how, with little interference from the side of the physician, the dynamic interplay of two pairs of psychological powerfields forces the complex to the surface, namely, the interplay of *resistance and transference,* and that of the *level of fixation and the level of arrest.*

To begin with the latter pair: The level of fixation is that system

of ideas, wishes, fears, defense mechanisms, ways of thinking, differentiating, experiencing which belong to a certain earlier period of
childhood and the magnetic power of which is apt to exert again its
way of organizing experience and action whenever a consolidation
on a higher level of experience and action seems blocked. In Dick's
case the fixation level is the second oral (biting) period. His level of
arrest, on the other hand, is the intrusive stage, the developmental
stage which proves unsurmountable to him. Dick is so hard to understand not only because his level of fixation is genetically an early,
structurally a primitive one; the greatest difficulty arises from the
fact that his inner world combines and synthesizes contents and principles of organization derived from both the level of fixation and the
level of arrest. Thus we find phallic trends expressed in terms of the
oral level (of fixation): i.e., his phallic-locomotor aggressiveness and
the problems of sexual differentiation are represented as temptations
to bite female persons and the fear of being bitten in turn. It is the
intrusive mode which characterizes for him the functions of both the
fixation zone (biting mouth, hurting voice) and the zone of arrest
(the dangerous and endangered phallus). It could be argued that such
irradiation of the intrusive problem had its center in the phallic stage
and only regressively mobilized oral associations. Certain data which
cannot be produced here suggest that intrusion was a problem from
the start. However, as we would expect, the conflict of intrusion
found its climax and caused a general arrest and disintegration at
the intrusive stage.

Caught between the phallic and the oral complexes as though
between Scylla and Charybdis, Dick is unable to see how he can
avoid the point where these two complexes touch; namely in the idea
of hurting a woman, thus both losing protection and provoking punishment. The concept of the world which he reveals and which is not
understandable with ordinary adult logic is an attempt to *synthesize
the level of fixation and the level of arrest in order to derive a design
for self-preservation.*

In the contacts with the physician, then, this "private world" of
the child only slowly asserted itself against a *resistance* which tried
to isolate it by avoidances and to keep it in a symbolic and metaphoric
disguise; only gradually was it represented in connection with the
physician's person. We have seen that the various aspects of this
connection were *transferred,* in a certain disguise and with wishful
changes, from former experiences with relations to other women
(mother, nurse) and did not originate in the therapeutic situation,
except in so far as woman doctor—nurse—and mother—situations

have common attributes: they all favor associations such as: child's unsatisfied interest in woman's body, child's secret wishes in regard to woman's body, woman's investigation of child's body, threat to child's body, etc.[14]

The inventory of symbols revealed in Dick's developing play-manifestations rather clearly indicates the boy's concern with situations in which biological haves are threatened by the oral eagerness of the have-nots. Beyond this, only further analysis would reveal the syntax which in the patient's mind gives this inventory some kind of logical order. The reconstruction of what in the patient's mind is the cause of, the condition for, the temporal successor or predecessor of other factors, and how such psycho-logic compares with the historical sequence of events is a task accomplished only with painful slowness. Up to now we know approximately what the patient is talking about; but we do not know what he is saying, i.e., whether he is reporting the past or imagining the future, and whether he is representing what he is doing in such a picture or what is being done to him.

One example of a possible historical reconstruction would be this: The boy saw his sister nursed. He felt strange urges and aggressive impulses, only parts of which probably stood out consciously, as wish for the mother's breast, anger at the sister's favored position, aggression against his mother, etc. Factors of his stage of development (intrusive, locomotor, phallic), of his constitution (oral? schizoid?) and of his personality development (projective and introjective mechanisms) gave this wish dangerous connotations. For example, unlike his sister, he had teeth, a fact which may have been actually pointed out to him. This would be a danger threatening his mother.[15] However, his thoughts seemed also dangerous to his sister as it meant to take her nourishment away, an idea which fused with the other wish, namely, to send her back into the mother's body. His projective, introjective ways of experiencing, then, intensified by the oral problem he was faced with, not only caused him to experience what mother and sister would feel if victimized by him, but also made him expect that they wanted to do to him what he wished to do to them.

It may have been during attempts to experiment with and to synthesize in play, theories, phantasies, and strange habits, such ideas of attacks and counter-attacks (in which he alternately identified himself with a dangerous mother and a small, toothless, penisless baby) that the nurse helped by her threat to create a focus for all his anxieties in a radiator phobia. The idea that the radiator could jump and bite appealed to an always easily mobilized primitive level of the boy's mental life on which everything with noisy insides, a warm touch, pipe systems with water, etc., whether inanimate or animate, was somehow identical; while, like all objects of phobias, it also made more tangible, more impersonal, and more discussable, those vague and secret fears which could not be discussed with the protecting adults because they concerned just these adults: the radiator stands for what the child could expect the adult (mother) to do to him if she knew what he secretly wanted to do to her. On the other hand, while an unseen source of danger, this hypnotically attractive phobic object by no means created comfort, and the efforts at eradicating and denying the whole conflict could not relax. Dick dreams of a being which has no mouth at all and we recognized some of his phantasies as picturing a world in which there are no differences between the sexes and between big and little: everybody has and is everything and there need be no envy, no threat. Thus, beside a fear world in which vague dangers are pinned down to tangible objects and into a context with some kind of logical structure, we also see traces of a wish world, another synthetic product of the child's despairing ego.

Other observers and the reader may have arrived at other possibilities of reconstruction. But if we ask at this point who is right, there is only one answer: the patient. Only continued work with him could narrow down possibilities to probabilities and bring about that psychological insight, the formulation of which creates the feeling of high probability in the experienced reader, and if transmitted to the patient, clears his vision into the past and vitalizes his expectation of the future.

E. DESTRUCTION AND RESTITUTION IN AN "EPILEPTIC" BOY OF FOUR

With the following description we merely introduce the second phase of treatment, namely, the period following the decision to proceed with the psychoanalytic procedure proper, and the time of first interpretations. With the focus shifted, we shall abandon the detailed representation used so far.

Fred was entering the disquieting period of locomotor and sexual development usually associated with the age of four somewhat prematurely before his third birthday; we have tried to characterize this period briefly above. Mentally, his development ratio was 125; he was especially advanced in his verbal expression. Physically excellently developed and well nourished, he was easy to handle—especially if, as was often the case, he was given his own way. Certain sadistic characteristics mainly expressed in teasing and occasional tempers had been outspoken for years; but nothing would have induced either his parents or his pediatrician to suspect the clinical syndrome which now suddenly emerged, namely, "epilepsy."

For some time Fred had seemed to try in provocative games and social experiments to see how far he could go in playfully hurting others and in suffering their reactions. Although he enjoyed exploring by play and error the outer limits for the manifestation of an obviously pressing aggressiveness, he had a low tolerance for situations in which he actually hurt somebody or was actually hurt by somebody. As his silent paleness seemed to indicate, such events forced him to suppress in too short a time and to turn against himself the overwhelming aggression for which he was trying to find a social form.

The tension created by these manifestations, which were neither in quantity nor in quality really abnormal, was heightened when one day his grandmother arrived in town for a long visit. She was even more anxious than his mother lest he hurt himself or get hurt; and special restraint was put on Fred's activity because she was afflicted with a heart disease. Fred tried his best, but soon increasing complaints from the neighborhood indicated that he had found a new field of activity. When he hit a boy with a shovel, he was ostracized in the neighborhood. It was shortly after this social trauma that he again went too far in his teasing attacks on his mothers and, finally, on his grandmother.

One morning, in the presence only of the grandmother, he climbed on a windowsill and threatened to jump out of the window. Startled, the grandmother tried to reach him but fell on the floor, for the first time in his presence suffering one of her frequent heart attacks; she spent several months in bed, seemed to recover, but suddenly died. "When I saw him standing there, something hurt in here," she had kept repeating over and over.

A few days after the old lady's death, Fred's mother saw him pile up his pillows before going to sleep, in a way in which his grandmother had done in order to feel more comfortable. In the morning, at the exact hour he had been awakened five days before by his mother's crying over the grandmother's death, he was heard making strange noises and found in a terrifying attack. His face was white, his eyes glassy; he frothed at the mouth and gagged. Finally, he shook all over and lost consciousness. To his mother he looked like her dying mother, but the hurriedly called physician diagnosed his symptoms as convulsions, ascribed them tentatively to bad tonsils, and administered an injection.

Soon two further attacks (usually beginning with the twitching of the face and subsequent clonic convulsions on the right side) followed at intervals of four weeks and six weeks respectively. The first attack lasted 20 minutes, the second 45. Immediately after the third, which lasted more than two hours, Fred was admitted to the hospital where he was diagnosed as an "idiopathic epileptic." However, neurological examinations were entirely negative except immediately after the attack. Fred, they emphasized, was an excellently-developed and well-nourished boy of above average intelligence and remarkable sociability. Dismissed after a few days of rest and observation, Fred was free of attacks for several months until, after two relatively less violent seizures, he again had to be hospitalized because of an attack at the time of the anniversary of the grandmother's death. The diagnosis appeared gradually modified as *"Idiopathic epilepsy with psychic stimulus as precipitatng factor"* and the patient was recommended to the Department of Psychiatry and Mental Hygiene where he received treatment first from Dr. Felice Emery and then from this writer. During these treatments there were many minor (mostly staring) spells; major attacks occurred only five days after his psychiatrist "had gone on a long trip," i.e., had moved to another town, and again, a year later, five days after the present writer had "gone to the Indians," i.e., on a field trip.

I shall first report on the psychological development of the case and then quote a neurologist's interpretation of the medical data in the light of our study.

Fred's parents had tried to explain the grandmother's disappearance by saying she had gone on a long trip. The boy, in spite of having seen the coffin and having witnessed the family's mourning, accepted and clung to the version that the grandmother had not died at all. But children betray their knowledge of such over-eagerly accepted adult lies with an uncanny sense of humor. Thus, one day when his mother asked him for an object which he had mislaid he said, "I guess it has gone on a long trip." During the same period in his nursery school he was noticed building coffin-shaped houses whose openings he would barricade in a way corresponding to a death configuration, generally observable in play and in rituals of primitive people. It seemed clear that the boy "knew" and that his knowledge (or what he tried to do to it) was the "psychic stimulus" the physicians were looking for.

Before every major or minor attack, Fred's aggressiveness would increase. An object would fly out of his hands, sometimes creditably "without his being aware of it," and strike somebody's head. The usually affectionate and reverent boy at such times would indulge in violent attacks against parents and against God. "Did grandmother have a good heart when she was a child?" "The whole world is full of skunks." "I don't like you, mother." "I hate God." "I want to beat God." "I want to beat heaven." After the attack the boy would indicate that he had experienced his unconsciousness as death. He behaved as if he had been reborn, smiling, loving, obedient and reverent—an angelic child.

I shall first present excerpts from Dr. Felice Emery's notes in order to contrast the transferences which the boy established to this woman psychiatrist and then to me. The following development in play of two dominant ideas [namely, "burning and attacking psychiatrist" and "building a castle"] reflects, it seems, the *destructive-restitutive* conflict in the boy's mind.

1. Excerpts from the Patient's First Ten Contacts with Woman Psychiatrist

I

Fred, asking psychiatrist to smoke a cigarette, becomes extremely interested in the way it *slowly burns down*. He asks *Ps* to smoke two more cigarettes and watches intently. "Why don't *you smoke the burning end?*" he finally asks.

While watching *Ps*, he touches the telephone and she is forced to give him the instruction that the telephone is not an object at his disposal. Shortly afterward he suddenly reaches for the telephone and seeing that *Ps* is *startled*, he says teasingly, "I wasn't going to touch it; *I fooled you!*"

II

"I'm going to *make you smoke* every time I come." When *Ps* picks up a toy on the floor, he moves a screen so that it falls over her. In great excitement he crawls under the screen (which he calls a *blanket*), yelling, "I'm climbing up on top of you." Then he tries to stand on the screen but breaks through, dropping one and a half feet. He *crawls in and out* through the hole and calls it a window.

In the afternoon, at home, wandering around in a daze "as if hypnotized," he asks his mother what the difference between people and animals is and seems especially interested in *animals which jump at others*, such as tigers and dogs.

(He is coercive, aggressive, intrusive in thoughts and acts which imply: making *Ps* smoke the burning end of a cigarette, startling teasing, fooling her and climbing on top of her. A sexual meaning is discernible—underneath the screen he tries to climb "on top" of the psychiatrist calling the screen a "blanket." Is he afraid of the animal, the tiger, in *himself*?)

III

"When I put the *screen* over you, were you all *burning up*?" "Was your house ever burnt up?" "My house was never burnt up." "I want to go to the toilet."

(Note the associations—sexual act: burning; burning body; burning house; also the urinary urge at this moment.)

At home, just before falling asleep, he again refers to an animal aggression. "Cats are made the same as dogs and dogs are made the same as cats." "Can dogs climb trees?" "Why do they like to *chase cats*?"

IV

"I would like to set the whole *building on fire*." "I'm going to set fire to your skirt."

"Let's *build* a castle."

(Note the association—setting fire to building: setting fire to psychiatrist's skirt. In view of this repeated analogy, we may expect an analogy of—building a castle: building a body.)

In the evening, asking again where there are tigers, he says to his mother, "The night is attached to the day. The day is attached to the night. The sun is attached to the sky."

(The constructive idea of building a castle has a counterpart in that of a coherent universe.)

V

"Could you smoke the cigarette from the wrong (*burning*) *end*?"
"I'm going to *undress you*. I'm going to *burn you*."
"Let's build a castle."

VI

"I want to smoke" (takes one puff anxiously). "That's enough.—Do *firemen* ever get *on fire*?"

Hits a cigarette with a bar. "Is it *dead* now?" (burning: dying) "What part of a cigarette burns?—What parts of a house burn?" (burning cigarette = dying cigarette; burned house = dying house?; burned body = dying body?)

Stamps his feet and yells, "I am not going to leave till you build a castle."

VII

"You smoke a cigarette while you build a castle." (The destructive and the constructive ideas merge; see VIII and IX.)

"Would you turn into ashes if you would burn?"

He throws a ball of Plasticine at *Ps*, yelling "I will *hurt you* and you will hurt me." After she has "hurt" him, he puts the chair in front of her, "You are *in jail*."

"Please walk with a creepy walk."

"There was a lady *who fell out of the* hotel *window* and she broke her hands, her legs, her body, her head. Wasn't that terrible?"

"We don't need a castle today."

(He wants *Ps* to walk in a creepy walk, which means to be an old woman, and he makes her hurt him and be put in prison. Is this the inversion in play of the fear which governs him, namely, that he will be put in jail [coffin, dark place, tomb] for having killed his grandmother by playfully threatening to jump out of the window?)

VIII

He hits the castle, with the words, "Does that hurt?" (Confirms the association—house: body.)

IX

"You smoke four cigarettes at once and build a castle that is round and has a door at each end."

He tries to light a match by stroking *Ps* cheek and by placing a match in her nostril. "Let's have a big flame."

Three times *Ps* builds a castle and three times he steps on a table and jumps on the blocks. From there he tries to jump on *Ps*.

(Repetitions with "orgiastic" dimensions: four cigarettes burn; three castles are destroyed; he tries to jump on *Ps* and actually to set fire to her.)

On Day III, the first association of burning and coitus had been followed by the wish to go to the toilet. Ever since, the psychiatrist had noticed a certain genital excitability in the boy as manifested in his repeated sudden urge to urinate, and in his clutching his penis. She now gives him a first interpretation by way of asking him whether to burn something, to destroy something, and to scare or jump on a woman gives him sensations in his penis. She thus approaches what must be most unconscious and least communicable to him and, furthermore, can be assumed to be one of the outstanding etiological factors in his sickness, namely, the strong phallic-locomotor emphasis at the time of the grandmother's death (and ever since).

To this question, Fred, surprised, reacts much like Dick. "I wish I were a little girl," he says. Then, transferring this idea of partial self-destruction and self-victimization to the house, the representative in play of a restituted body, he points to one of the longer blocks on the castle and asks, "Why is this sticking out?" He pushes it back. "Will that hurt the castle?" "Have you got a saw? I want to saw this off." He pushes a long block against it. "Does that hurt the castle?"

(He thus seems to experiment with the two aspects of the possession of a penis: who is hurt more, the male who loses it, or the female against whom it is used?)

Ps does not give him this explanation but merely remarks, "A castle made out of blocks falls apart rather easily. It is different from a person's body which cannot fall apart in the same way." "Why doesn't it fall apart?" he asks. "Because the body has grown that way itself; every part is needed." He doubts, not without reason: "You need your eyes. Will your eye drop out?" "No—your eye won't drop out." "When it gets black and blue—what happens then?" "If your eye gets black and blue it heals."

In leaving *Ps* on this day, Fred says to his mother in an enthusiastic tone, "It's the biggest castle we have ever built."

(The castle was not bigger, but the interpretation had made the restitution more convincing.)

X

With this reassuring contact the themes of burning and building lose their central position in Fred's play with the therapist. Another content, more clearly betraying the fear of the dead grandmother, takes their place.

(We consider the fact that the content changes and approaches pathogenic material more courageously a sign that the right interpretation took place at the right time.)

Fred now plays that an imaginary *lady* who is far away tries to call up 15 times a day. He wants *Ps* to go over to the house of that lady and break her telephone because the lady tries to call and to tell him that she is going to come and set him on fire or that she is going to send a policeman to arrest him. (We remember he had tried to set the psychiatrist on fire and in Hour VII had jailed her, asking her to "walk with a creepy walk.") "We had better go off *on a long journey* so that when she comes *she won't find us here*. We had better take twelve gallons of gas."

While the imaginary overland connection to the lady takes the center of his play with the psychiatrist, at home his interest shifts to communication with *heaven*. "How does God tell you to be good? Heaven is higher than the clouds." As if incidentally, he also for the first time begins to ask about his *grandmother*, what she would look like now, would she look old, etc.

Soon *Ps* thinks the time has come to talk about the grandmother. Using his suggestion to write his name on a blackboard, she asks for his father's name, his mother's name, his grandmother's name, and when he pronounces the latter with special tenderness, she adds quietly, "Your *grandmother died*, didn't she?" Fred explodes, "No, she didn't die—she went away—*didn't she go away? Why did she die?* She was sick in my house. Did she die in my house? Is she in my house now? Well, where is she? Do you mean that I will never see her again? Let me see her."

Ps explains to him the impossibility of his wish and, in spite of his seeming to lose interest abruptly, insists on telling him that he must be thinking that he had done some harm to his grandmother. He answers decisively, "No—I didn't do anything to her," but then acts out his confession, as most children and some adults do: He climbs on the table (a conference table), stamps up and down the full length of it, and yells, "Who is making that noise? Can they hear it outside? What will they do if it disturbs them? If they did come in, I wouldn't be quiet." Then menacingly coming up to the end of the table where *Ps* is sitting, he suddenly crouches down, climbs into her lap, and says quietly and anxiously, "Why did I stop here?" *Ps* repeats her explanation.

In the evening of this day at home, the boy begins to mourn as if he had never heard before that his grandmother was dead. He cried incessantly, asked why the grandmother had died, and why they hadn't taken her to the hospital to save her. "I would like to open grandmother's grave and see what she looks like. I will bring all of the doctors in the world here to make her heart go again." And then, with a scientific sublimation of the destructive impulse, he explained: "I would like to cut her body to pieces and see what it looks like inside."

In the night he *soiled himself*. The next morning he didn't remember what day it was or what time of the day, and after having vomited, he slept far into the day. To his mother he said, "Supposing you would break your neck, you know what I would do? I would put it together again."

2.

Fred's treatment was not completed when his first psychoanalyst left the city. She had been able to bring back to his memory the details of his grandmother's death and to discuss with him the phallis-locomotor tension of his maturational stage, which had made him associate aggressive and phallic intentions as characterizing a bad boy. However, it was obvious that other sources of tension of the period in question had not been verbalized. Also, as the psychiatrist suggests, it may be that the playful aggression allowed to this child in analysis made the transference too realistic and permitted the accumulation in Fred of guilt feelings concerning the psychiatrist similar to those concerning the grandmother. In any event, after the psychiatrist had left town, Fred began to speak of her with the same words which he had always used to characterize his relationship to his grandmother ("Why has 'my friend' gone away?"), and had a severe *epileptic attack* (the first one since the beginning of the treatment) *five days* after the departure, thus repeating the pattern "dying five days after a beloved person whom one had attacked goes on a long journey."

After this attack, I took Fred over for treatment. The difference in the transference became obvious soon. Fred had a period of what one might call an infantile homosexual panic. After the first hour with me, he insisted in retrospect that at the time of his latest hospitalization *men nurses* had *taken his temperature* all night and didn't let him sleep. This of course did not correspond to the facts since he had been taken care of entirely by female nurses who had taken his temperature only once during the night. But to this phantasy there corresponded the first game he played with me during my first contact with him. Out of Plasticine he formed "snakes" or "worms" and tried to get behind me so that they could bite my buttocks. (Remember how, in his play with the woman psychiatrist in a similar twofold representation he had jailed the old lady, then phantasized that an old lady was going to jail him). Correspondingly, at home, his relationship to his father changed. He would without provocation repeat, "Don't touch me, Daddy," and especially when awakening from his nap he would experience and express moments of depersonalization—"I don't want you to come near me, Daddy. Where am I? Where is our home? I don't see well. Is everything all right? Everything looks bigger. Something is hanging from the walls awfully big and crooked." He also began to look intently at his father, remarking, "Grandmother looked just like Daddy." (We see that the man therapist not only attracted another [homosexual] transference but by his very existence brought about the manifestation of the corresponding [previously latent] conflicts at home).

In the meantime I questioned the mother again about the weeks preceding the first attack because it seemed that Fred's guilt feeling was not entirely covered by the explanation of the crime which he felt he had committed against the grandmother. Only against severe emotional resistance did the mother reveal an incident which had occurred about one week before the grandmother's dramatic heart attack. A toy had "inadvertently" flown from Fred's hand, hit his mother in the face and loosened one of her front teeth. Irritable as she may have been because of the special pressure which the grandmother's visit exerted on the home, and also worried for the precious front tooth, the mother had punished Fred corporally for the first time in his life. As she described this, Fred's transference to both the woman psychiatrist and to me appeared in a new light—the crime complex established in connection with the grandmother's death obviously had irradiated, in retrospect and prospect, to include guilt feelings toward both father and mother and expectations of danger for and from the side of both. (It will be remembered that against his father he never had dared to express aggression as he had so liberally done with women.)

I shall report here the way in which the transference of one of these irradiations manifested itself in his first epileptic (minor) spell in our offices.

During the first weeks of his treatment with me, we had in accordance with his wish played dominoes. The possession of the double black, so he had decided, determined who had the first move. If he were not in possession of it and whenever he lost a game, he became angry and pale. I tried (as far as he, a good player, let me) to increase the number of his defeats gradually, in the hope of being able to observe the coming and going of an attack under emotional conditions approximately known to me. One day the threshold seemed reached. Fred had lost again and at a time during the hour when he could not hope to make up for it. Suddenly he got up, took a rubber Popeye doll and *hit me* in the face with it; then he stiffened, got pale, his eyes stared for a fraction of a second, and he vomited. He had hardly recovered when he said in a most pathetically urgent tone of voice, "Let's go on playing." He hurriedly built up his domino figures in front of him in a rectangle and in such a way that the signs pointed inward; he, their possessor, would have to lie inside of his configuration (like a *dead person* in a coffin) in order to read them. Fully conscious, he now recognized the queer configuration and gave me the look of a cornered animal. I pointed out to him that every time he hit somebody he felt that he must die. He confirmed this by asking breathlessly, "Must I?" I explained to him the historical connection between these feelings and the death of his grandmother, whose coffin he had seen. "Yes," he said, a little embarrassed because up to now in spite of the mourning episode he had insisted that the grandmother had gone on a trip. I furthermore pointed to the similarity between his attack on my face during a game and the attack on his mother's face a week before the grandmother's fatal attack. It appeared that he could not remember the attack on his mother while he seemed never to have forgotten the episodes relating to his grandmother. That *the mother, too, might die* as a consequence of the (earlier) aggressive acts and phantasies was obviously the deepest danger threatening him. This, too, was pointed out.

Beginning with this episode a series of interpretations used *specific moments* to bring *his fear of death into relation with his strong impulses and his low anxiety threshold.*

The effect of such interpretational steps can best be illustrated by an episode which occurred a few days after the interpretation reported above. In the afternoon Fred's mother, fatigued, was lying on a couch. Fred stood in the doorway and looked at her. Suddenly he said slowly, "Only a very bad boy would like now to jump on you and step on you, only a very bad boy would want that, isn't that so, mummy?" The mother, to whom I had explained some of the boy's problems, laughed and replied, "Oh no, quite a good boy might *think* that, but, of course, he would know that he did not really want to do it." This conversation established a relationship between mother and son which made it increasingly possible for him to tell her, especially when he felt as if an attack were approaching, of his aggressions, anxieties, and religious scruples, all of which she learned to handle as well as her own attitude toward death permitted. At the same time she could apply in such instances certain preventive measures recommended by pediatricians.

We see what the interpretation had done. It had used the highly *affective moment (namely the repetition in transference of a scene which the memory resisted)* to verbalize for him his impulses against the protecting mother—impulses derived from the same source as those which had "killed" the grandmother and thus might bring about the mother's death. These impulses could now be admitted to consciousness, faced with the superior intelligence of his increased age, understood as more magic than real and even admitted to the mother, who, far from either wildly punishing or lightly approving, understood and offered help. Such experiences are an inducement to further transferences, confessions, and conversations, which of course included Fred's aggressions against his father which consequently were mostly consistently transferred to the therapist not without leading to a major attack five days after this therapist, too, had gone on a trip (from which he returned, however). Thus, while *historical reality* had emphasized the grandmother's death as the trigger stimulus mobilizing Fred's epileptic reaction, *analysis* proved Fred's sadistic wishes against his mother and death wishes against his father to be the *psychological reality* of his maturational stage which had made him susceptible for the traumatic event of the grandmother's death. The misunderstanding of the causal connection of what had happened to the grandmother and what he had done to her was transferred and interpreted first; what he was afraid might happen

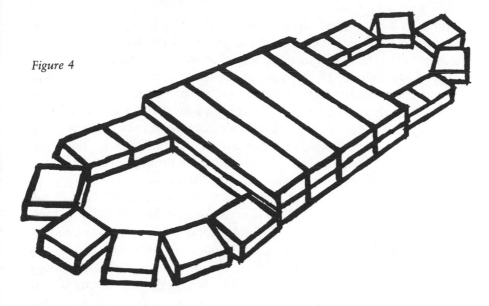

Figure 4

to the mother because of his deeds and wishes, next; while the most-dreaded and most deeply repressed aggression against the providers, father and God (the latter now united in heaven with the revengeful grandmother), could be approached only later. During this latter stage, his persistent attempts at building configurations of a safer body and a safer world led to the construction (Figure 4). At the same time he day-dreamed of a compromise with God: "Why not eliminate death and birth?" he asked him. "Let children grow up and down, up and down, indefinitely." The block construction says the same in spatial projection: from a firm fundament roads lead away in two directions, but both come back and close the circle of safety—an earthly infinity.

In the course of these events Fred's attacks became fewer and better predictable, drug applications could be reduced to a minimum and to well-circumscribed critical moments, and Fred recovered from minor spells more quickly and with less after-effect. We shall not predict that he will not have a minor attack now and again; but he may be spared major ones especially if the medical suspicion of a progressive lesion of the central nervous system proves unfounded. In any event, we have reason to consider it probable that psycho-somatic vigilance can help such a patient to lead a normal life in which possible rare attacks are well isolated and for the most part predictable events.

Fred's case was chosen as our last example because it combined dramatic brevity with all the ordinary attributes of a situation in which an interpretation is warranted: The play has failed; the child is about to be overwhelmed by the guilt and the danger of the situation which he wants most to forget or to avoid. All defenses have proved inadequate, all attempts at restitution and atonement futile. The therapeutic situation has become the pathogenic situation, the therapist only one more evil. What seems needed is more cruel self-suppression, deeper regression, more radical repression. At this point the patient suddenly finds his experience put into words. The most human way (which always had seemed most completely impossible), namely, communication, now proves to be open.

However, once the first interpretation is given and its startling effects lived through, the child is conscious of the fact that the therapist understands or wants to understand more than he has been told, and the patient is expected to cooperate in the verbalization of his suffering and what lies behind it. This brings with it complications and new resistances the description of which do not belong in this monograph.

3. Medical Note

During a short period of common affiliation with the institutions named below, I had the opportunity to discuss several case histories of epileptics with Dr. Frank Fremont-Smith, then Assistant Professor of Neuropathology in the Harvard Medical School and Associate Psychiatrist in the Massachusetts General Hospital. I have asked him to study my notes on "Fred" and to interpret the medical history in the light of the psychological study. I am indebted to him for the following abstract and statement:

1. The patient on first admission to the hospital was three years, one and one-half months of age. His family history showed nothing of significance to the present illness. Birth was full term, normal spontaneous delivery. The boy weighed 7.5 pounds, breathed and cried spontaneously. There was no cyanosis and no convulsions. The neonatal period was normal. No breast feeding. The developmental history too seems normal, with several attacks of sore throat and fever, once followed by a mild otitis media. At one and a half years of age and at two years of age the boy fell down a flight of stairs.

The first convulsion (five a.m.), two and half months before admission, lasted 20 minutes; the second convulsion one month later, 45 minutes. The third convulsion (at eighty-thirty p.m.) was described as follows: The patient cried out and vomited—twitching of eyes and mouth on right—then clonic convulsions of right arm and both legs—frothing at mouth—eyes turned to right—urinated—convulsion continued with vi-

olent twitching entire right side intermittently until morphine and sco-
polamine were given at eleven p.m. Twitching continued until admission
at one a.m.

On admission and on subsequent days, physical examination was
entirely negative with the exception that on admission, while in coma,
deep reflexes and cremasteric reflexes were temporarily absent and there
was a temporary *positive* Babinski reflex on the right. Laboratory studies,
too, including lumbar puncture and fasting blood sugar, were negative
with the exception of a moderate secondary anemia.

In the two and a half years following the first admission he had two
convulsions, the first after finding the body of a dead mole, and the
second immediately after inadvertently killing a butterfly. His sixth convulsion took place about a year later. He has continued to have "staring"
spells and also occasional periods when he seems frightened and dis-
orientated, usually preceded by vomiting. When he is entirely well he
gets excellent grades at school and appears to make a good social adjustment outside the home.

The diagnosis from the medical record is idiopathic epilepsy with
psychic stimulus as the precipitating factor and organic background not
unlikely.

On several occasions the convulsions were observed to begin in the
right hand, in twitching about the mouth, and once in the right eyelid.
Some of the attacks have involved the right side much more than the
left, especially the right arm, and the eyes have been observed deviated
to the right. During one attack the right pupil was greater than the left,
and after two attacks there was transient positive Babinski reaction, once
on the right and once bilateral.

2. The term "idiopathic epilepsy" is used to describe a syndrome,
fairly clearly defined clinically but, as the term "idiopathic" indicates,
etiologically obscure. Examination of the brain at autopsy in such cases,
may reveal congenital abnormality, the scar of birth injury or of postnatal injury or infection, or occasionally an unsuspected tumor, while
not infrequently careful study fails to demonstrate any abnormality which
could be considered as an etiological factor. The capacity to react with
a convulsive seizure is normal for man and for mammals in general, as
well as for many of the lower vertebrates, under appropriate stimulus
such as electrical or pharmacological stimulation. The threshold for the
convulsive response may be lowered by various irreversible structural
lesions (scars, brain tumors, etc.) or by reversible chemical alterations
(hypoglycemia, anoxemia, etc.).

An "epileptic" may be described as an individual whose threshold is
permanently or temporarily lowered so that stimuli which in the average
individual would not result in an attack (either grand mal or petit mal)
frequently precipitate a seizure. The onset of an acute infection and the
accentuation of an emotional conflict are common precipitating factors,

which may become effective in cases with gross pathology of the brain, such as scar or tumor, as well as in the cases in which the predisposing factors are much more obscure.

In the case of the four year old child here described no final decision can yet be reached regarding etiology. The convulsions are typical grand mal seizures and the minor attacks consistent with petit mal and psychomotor seizures. The tendency for the attacks to start on the right side and to be most prominent on the right, together with the right Babinski reflex observed once, immediately after an attack, and the inequality of the pupils observed in another attack suggest the possibility of cerebral pathology (congenital abnormality, old scar or slowly growing tumor) in the left hemisphere as a predisposing factor, while the clinical history and the special psychological studies make it clear that emotional conflict is frequently the precipitating factor.

Whether such conflict as this boy exhibited could precipitate a convulsion in a child without disturbance of the central nervous system other than that accompanying the emotional conflict itself must remain an open question. It should be pointed out, however, that whether the conflict results in convulsion or other bodily manifestations, insight into the psychodynamics of the conflict is essential to the understanding and treatment of the emotional immaturity and social maladjustment which are on the basis of the conflict itself. The seizures from this point of view, when induced by emotional stress, may be looked upon as psychosomatic crises which in other individuals, differently constituted, might become manifest through other organ systems, cardiovascular, gastrointestinal, etc., including the psychic sphere, as in "psychomotor attacks" and "epileptic fugues."

IV. Conclusion

The psychoanalytic attributes of our material are on the whole the mechanisms first described by Freud as resistance, transference, and regression. They appear in the interplay of social, verbal, spatial, and bodily forms of expression.

To begin with the verbal, the very first words spoken by our patients on meeting us, betrayed their dominant system of defense:

John, we remember, appeared armed to the teeth. Asked whom he was going to kill, he answered, *"me"*—with one monosyllable betraying the *"turning against himself"* of all the hate which his secret and other, less conscious reasons prevented him from expressing directly. *Mary*, however, did not say anything to the therapist until she had regained all her stubborn superiority. She only talked to her mother, in *lisping, whining* baby talk. We would not be surprised to find her use deliberate *regression* paired with stubbornness as a defense even in riper years. *Dick's* greeting "are your eyes all right?" makes the therapist the patient and the patient the therapist. It represents what Anna Freud calls "the identification with the (here potential) aggressor" and contains the *projective-introjective* mechanisms which prove so strong during later observations.—(*Fred's* first words are not recorded.)

Robbed or about to be robbed of the protective aura of maternal presence, how do our patients *act in space?*

John's mother is nowhere near. While his eyes are evasive, his skin pale, he moves with unafraid strides. But he has surrounded himself with a *layer of weapons.* (He is the delinquent, afraid of further castration. His recent circumcision had been explained to him as a consequence of the fact that he had "played with himself," a fact which will have to be analyzed immediately after the resistance nearest to consciousness—namely, the secret—is worked through.) *Mary,* on entering with her mother, throws one mischievous glance across the room toward the therapist, then closes eyes and ears and almost *disappears* in the maternal skirt, holding the mother near the door. (She acts with hysterical dramatization and phobic avoidance. Ambivalent flight to her mother after a play disturbance with the father and with boys in a play group will prove to be her problem.) *Dick,* however, with hurried determination leaves his mother and *passes by* the therapist as if not interested in her. (Interest in the female body will immediately begin to dominate his play.) *Fred,* finally after some diffused handling of the toys, goes *right for* the psychiatrist's body. (Playful attack, in his case, will prove to be the defense against his fear of being attacked and of suffering an "internalized" [epileptic] attack).

It is in the metaphoric and symbolical use of toys that all these defenses are first caught off guard; in the *microsphere* the child does what he does not dare to do in reality:

John, in the macrosphere *armed against* doctors and police, in playing *"delivers"* his secret, although only in *metaphoric* allusion. *Mary,* the *bashful* one, has a moment of *mischievous hilarity* in pushing the toys and finally the toy train, although using a *protective extension* in doing so. *Dick,* so *indifferent* toward mother and psychiatrist, has many *urgent questions* about the toy cars, in which he plainly *alludes* to the female body. *Fred,* the *killer,* passionately wants to build a house—to *restore a body,* as we were able to translate the *symbolism* of his play.

Each one of these *indirect admissions* in the microsphere is an element in a personal transference:

> *John*, in delivering his secret metaphorically, gives the therapist what in reality is the *father's*. *Mary* betrays her playful interest in her *father* and in boys and (during the second contact) takes revenge on the therapist for a scene in which her father had reacted with irritability to her interest in him. *Dick* takes a little longer to express the more regressive wish to bite the *mother's* body, in the words, "I want to bite your buttons." Fred, after having "hurt" the therapist, wants her to "walk with a creepy walk" like the *grandmother*.

It is a question, partly only of words, which of the tricks of play language we are to call symbolic or metaphoric, which to consider analogies or allusions. A symbol, it seems, should be definitely of a higher order, very condensed and abstracted in its form, superindividual in its meaning and treated with a high degree of affectual inhibition and sublimation.

> *Mary*, who suffered a play disruption when overturning the *toy train*, develops a raptured admiration for shining locomotives. Her first question on seeing me weeks later concerns the locomotive of the train which took me south. Her *F* in the meantime had regained her friendship by joint visits to trainyards. "Shining locomotive" has become a symbol of admired paternal power.

It will take some careful study to denote how early true symbols appear in play and what their fore-runners are. "Metaphoric" is an appealing parallel to "transference" (metapherein—to transfer); "allusion" has "play" in it (alludere—to play with). At the moment I would say that the play acts reported are analogies to conflict situations. The children unconsciously allude to them by transferring their ambivalence toward their parents onto the therapist and by representing other aspects of the conflict metaphorically in play.

But a child seems to be able to solve a problem in play or other activities only inasfar as the traumatic event alluded to mainly consisted of an *enforced passivity*, a violation by a superior force.

> *Mary*, whose indignation with her irritable father and fear of operation are greater than her guilt, can "solve" her problem on the second day, at least enough to meet constructively an improved home situation.

Inasfar as the trauma involves "blood guilt," the primitive feeling of having magically violated an ambivalently loved person, only a conscious, verbally communicated "yes, yes—no, no" can bring relief. This need, becoming urgent with the successful although first unconscious allusion to the conflict, drives some patients from the treacherous play back into symptom and regression. At this point we offer *interpretation* as a help toward communication.

John, asked to name the uncles, answers with his symptom (defecation) and reasserts his defense—"me." *Mary* becomes stiff, blind, and dumb with anxiety when the toy train overturns. *Dick*, after having confessed that he wanted to bite the therapist's buttons, appears wrapped in clothes, in silence and in apathy. *Fred* gives me the first opportunity to observe one of his minor epileptic spells after having hit me in the face as he had done to his mother.

The play, we see, indicates the need which is both intensified ("ready to have its correlative feelings aroused") and in a state of suppression; the *form of the disruption* alludes to the danger which would follow the fulfillment of the need.

John's "me" indicates, that once his secret was revealed, something terrible would happen and that he preferred to be the victim. *Mary* dramatizes that, if she is too much of a tomboy and dares to envy the male his anatomical share, something similar to what already has happened to foot and genitals will, on the occasion of the threatened operation, happen to other parts of her body. *Dick* indicates that according to "an eye for an eye" he wil be what his oral jealousy makes him wish his sister to be, namely, an unborn nothing. *Fred*, in his arrangement of dominoes, confesses his expectation of death as a punishment or atonement for aggression.

All of this, of course, gives us only a first impression and allows only for tentative conclusions in regard to the *degree of emotional arrest*, the *depth of regression*, the *weakness of the defenses*, the *rigidity of conscience*, etc. On the one hand we weigh these impressions against the obstacles and weaknesses in the environment as transmitted by the parents; on the other hand, we have to reconstruct the degree of development attained when the arrest and the regression occurred, and weight this positive aspect against the chances for our getting the environment ready to help the child beyond arrest and fixation when we succeed in making him set his face again toward the future.

That goal of this description was a presentation of empirical data which (*a*) would allow the therapist and his study group to account for some of their diagnostic habits, and (*b*) could be of didactic-comparative use for non-therapeutic psychologists. However, clinical description, even where more skillfully handled, can only approximate such goals; and once such approximation is attempted, the focus shifts from the larger theoretical implications to the details of observation on which first conceptual steps can be based.

It seems advisable in conclusion to point to some of the practical and therapeutic aspects of our material.

Our "short stories" may have given the reader the impression that the psychoanalysis of a child is characterized throughout by high tension and by a rapid succession of dramatic insights. This is not the case. After our interpretations have led to relieving communication and to promising improvement, long periods follow which are quiet, peaceful, even dull. The child plays, builds, paints, writes, and discusses whatever he pleases as long as his guilt and anxiety allow him to do so. Such periods mean recovery for the child, more intimate and slowly growing insight to the therapist. But the therapist by no means accompanies the child's acts with running interpretative commentary. Interpretations to children are rare and on the whole underlie the following guiding principles. They point out symptoms of disruption throughout the patient's life and sum up the problem behind them as it has been reconstructed on the basis of recent observation. However, they do not translate to the child the meaning of any playfully or skillfully accomplished act. Verbal self-consciousness in conditioning connection with playful activities is not desired; for these very activities must help the child later to contact the fields of cultural value, in which alone he can really find a recovery without self-consciousness. There are also no attempts at arguing for an interpretation by transmitting to the child the details of its derivation. The interpretation will be accepted by the child if both the child and the therapist are intellectually and emotionally ready for it; which means for the therapist if he is in the right mood and frame of mind to put his insight into coherent, constructive, and understandable words.

This point deserves emphasis in conclusion. Throughout a tedious piece of writing I have paid compulsive attention to details of clinical reasoning. An analytical instrument was to be demonstrated. But to learn to know the properties and the range of an instrument is one thing—to learn to use it unself-consciously and firmly, another. It is good to be explicit for the sake of training; for the sake of therapy, it is necessary to act with intuitive regard for implied probabilities and possbilities. The scientific world wants to know *why* we are so sure to be on the right track; the patients only *that* we are sure. Few patients (and they are apt to argue and doubt) want to know whether or not our interpretations are scientifically true; most patients are satisified that they feel true and that they *give meaning to suffering*. Except where the parent already has learned to expect this meaning from elaborate analysis and synthesis, increased scientific conscientiousness on the part of the therapist by no means necessarily conveys a feeling of security to him. Some groups of parents and adult patients, it is true, share the specialist's delight in new terminological, experimental, statistical rituals. The majority are bewildered by them. The conceptual frames of therapeutic habits, it must often seem to them, are like the microsphere in play, into which we project complex reality in order to have our wishes for omnipotence come true according to the less refractory microcosmic law and language. By reprojecting our interpretation into the macrosphere of social reality, we are able to observe whether or not it provided constructive meaning within the patient's culture. By correlating it with those of other conceptual microspheres which have been longer and more consistently corrected by systematic experimental reprojection into physical reality we may see how scientific we are. But only if and where science will prove dominant over other sources of psychological strength will the scientific attitude in therapy also necessarily be the efficient one.

It is an intriguing idea that even where nobody sees it or does anything about it children proceed to express their vital problems in the metaphoric language of play—more consistently and less self-consciously than they are able or willing to in words.

To be observed when playing is natural for children; it does not have to wait for the family's clinical surrender. If we can establish the language of play with its various cultural and age dialects[16] we may be able to approach the problem why it is that certain children live undamaged through what seem to be neurotic episodes and how early neurotic children may indicate that they have reached a deadlock.

This objective becomes important at a time when there is increasing awareness of both the extent of mental suffering and the impracticability and social deficiency of the alleviating techniques. Their results point to childhood as the possibly more economic time of correction.

The neurotic adult has usually made his choice of vocation and marriage companion on the basis of his neurosis. Both are endangered when that basis is reconsidered. The child's choices (except for that of his parents) are still preliminary; the changes we effect only replace changes which would occur with less planning. Furthermore, the adult patient usually develops a therapeutic dependency on his therapist, a dependency which every observing person will agree, often persists in the cured, and especially the much more frequent half-cured neurotic, in a form which differs from a neurosis only in the degree of terminological rationalization. One reason for this embarrassing fact undoubtedly is the impossibility, after one's analysis, of settling one's grievances with the childhood parents and of beginning life again, where the old road to isolation branched off. One has only one childhood. That which was merely repressed from consciousness, after having been reasonably developed and experienced, one may hope to liberate through analysis; but emotional impoverishment in childhood is incurable in later life, and to face the fact that one is crippled to the extent of having had the wrong childhood and to gain spiritually and intellectually from this fact is, after all, open to few.

The child's dependence, however, is his natural state. Transference in childhood has a different connotation; it is of shorter duration and less consistent, and what is transferred can usually be retransferred to the parents. The parents, in turn, are more accessible to correction and advice as long as they and the child are young, and small changes in the parents are often gratefuly responded to by the child with obvious and far-reaching improvements. Thus, what is delegated to the therapist can be returned to the home before the child's personality development is completed and before all chances have been exhausted of identifying thoroughly with parents who are enlightened and live up to their capacity to love.

References

1. *Psychoanalytic Quarterly*, 4, 1 (1935). Child analysis number.
2. E. Homburger Erikson, "Configurations in Play: Clinical Notes." *Psychoanalytic Quarterly*, 6 (1937), 138–214.
3. ———, "Problems of Infancy and Early Childhood." In *Cyclopedia of Medicine, Surgery, and Specialties* (Philadelphia: Davis, 1940).
4. L. K. Frank, "Projective Methods for the Study of Personality." *Journal of Psychology*, 8 (1939), 389–413.
5. Anna Freud, *Introduction to the Technique of Child Analysis*, auth. trans. by L. Pierce Clark. Nervous and Mental Disease Monograph Series No. 48 (New York: 1928), 59.

6. ——, *The Ego and the Mechanisms of Defense* (London, Hogarth, 1937), 196.
7. S. Freud, "Analysis, Terminable and Interminable." *International Journal of Psychoanalysis*, 18 (1937), 373–405.
8. ——, *Beyond the Pleasure Principle*, auth. trans. from 2d German ed. by C. J. M. Hubback (New York: Ballou, 1924), 90.
9. ——, "Neue Folge der Vorlesungen zur Einführung in die Psychoanalyse." In *Gesammelte Schriften*, vol. 12 (1934), 151–345.
10. M. Gitelson et al., "Clinical Experience with Play Therapy." *American Journal of Orthopsychiatry*, 8 (1938), 466–78.
11. Melanie Klein, *The Psychoanalysis of Children* (New York: W. W. Norton, 1932), 393.
12. J. W. Macfarlane, "Studies in Child Guidance." Society for Research in Child Development Monographs, 3, 6 (1938).
13. H. A. Murray et al., *Explorations in Personality* (New York: Oxford University Press, 1938), 775.
14. H. Spencer, *Principles of Psychology*, 3d ed. (New York: Appleton-Century, 1892). 2 vols.
15. E. C. Tolman, *Purposive Behavior in Animals and Men* (New York: Appleton-Century, 1932), 463.
16. R. Wälder, "The Problem of the Genesis of Psychical Conflict in Earliest Infancy: Remarks on a Paper by Joan Riviere." *International Journal of Psychoanalysis*, 18 (1937), 406–73.

Notes

[1] The members of the Study Group were Felice Begg-Emery, M.D.; E. H. Erikson; Edith B. Jackson, M.D.; Marion C. Putnam, M.D., in the Department of Psychiatry and Mental Hygiene: and Ruth W. Washburn, Ph.D., in the Department of Child Development, Institute of Human Relations and School of Medicine, Yale University.

These studies and their publication were aided by a grant to the Institute of Human Relations, Yale University, from the Josiah Macy, Jr. Foundation.

[2] For example, the anthropological observer with psychoanalytic training learns to understand, one is tempted to say, the culturality of a cultural entity from the way a given complex of ideas is repreented on the dynamic scale of a culture's collective consciousness: in one variation as historical memory and in another as mythological history; in one disguise re-enacted in heavy rituals, in another in light games; in a third entirely represented by avoidance. The complex may be recognizable in culture pattern dreams or in individual dreams; in humorous or in hateful projections on the neighbor, on the prehuman race, or on the animal world; it may be represented in deviating behavior designating either the select or the damned or both.

[3] A future psychoanalysis of play will be based on material allowing the weighing of an individual's play against that of his age and culture group.

[4] For the most comprehensive criticism of the "English School of Child Analysis" see Robert Wälder (16).

[5] The author wishes to recommend especially the papers by Bertha Bornstein and Steff Bornstein (1).

[6] I must acknowledge here the influence of Kurt Lewin's terminology, although my grasp of it does not seem to go beyond the recognition of a most valuable reformulation which gives certain modern modes of thinking terminological recognition.

[7] In regard to the influence of the presence of these toys on the total situation, an animal psychologist's remark comes to my mind: "Whenever a rat is placed within sight or smell of food, it appears quite obvious and therefore it tends to remain unremarked that his selectiveness as to the surrounding means-objects are thereby affected." (10)

[8] Worries of this type are, of course, common among hospitalized children. The increased

specialization which makes it necessary that before and after an operation the child is contacted by a great number of experts, each of whom has his own little method of "talking the child's language,' brings with it a disturbing variety of assurances, reassurances, promises, back-slaps, playful threats, etc., which may often make the psychological safety a reverse function of the physiological one said to be achieved by the specialistic perfection. As our patient was being prepared for his operation one attending individual had referred to his "beautiful eyelashes" and jokingly threatened that upon waking up he would find them removed from his eyes and attached to hers.

9 That he had the spool and that I made a mistake have to be considered as (regularly present) *supporting factors* in the particular development of what, in view of its coherent manifestation must be considered the "contemplated" play configuration.

10 The patient's brother.

11 The reader is urged to read this description and its discussion (8).

Freud, *Beyond the Pleasure Principle, loc.* cit.

12 A schizophrenic patient at the Worcester State Hospital was asked to build a house. He looked into space, grasped one block firmly and "tasted it" with his fingers; then he took a block in the other hand and did the same thing. With an expression of recognition, he bent his head forward, then brought first one then the other block to his mouth, snapping at them, making sounds of "tasting" and exclaiming "Good!," "Good!" He did not touch them with his lips; nor was he able to put more blocks on top of one another than the two which he could hold in his two hands. Similarly, when given toy cars, he could (with much delight) push them so that they flew over the edge of the table, but he could or would not "direct" them in any way. He manifested a stage of play organization between the autocosmic extension use of toys and their use in the microsphere.

13 Ps = psychoanalyst or psychiatrist, Pt = patient.

14 In Mary's case we saw how the image "man who plays with me" overcame the doctor association and favored the transfer of her conflict with the temporarily less playful father; while John, armed against all doctors, could not help delivering the secret to me which belonged to his father. But the material, especially in regard to the confession compulsion expressed in "A," *is* influenced by the intitial "doctor"-expectations of the child. In the psychoanalysis of adults, too, there is a situational connection between the patient's very first associations and memories with the enforced infantile position into which he is asked to revert: the position of lying down, the sacrifice of upright and aggressive motility, the suggestion to lay himself open psychologically before a person who in his turn guards his integrity, the suggested lowering of the critical threshold and of cultural standards in expressing uncritically the flow of asso-ciation. If not a verbal suggestion, all this certainly represents a situational emphasis which should be kept in mind when evaluating the first selection of childhood material emanating from the patient's associations and resistances.

15 The first 20 hours of Dick's psychoanalytic treatment were signified by the fact that he had every toy bite every other toy, with two exceptions: *a baby doll and a toy cow never bit one another.*

16 In connection with Jean Walker MacFarlane's guidance study (12) I am having the oppor-tunity to collect in regular intervals microcosmic constructions of two hundred unselected children of the pre-adolescent age and to enter into a developmental and statistical appraisal of some of the play metaphors first encountered in clinical work. What sort of test can be based on such material is still a debatable question. At any rate my contribution to H. A. Murray's *Explorations in Personality* (13) is not as it has been titled a "Dramatic Production *Test*" but a clinical exploration.

The Dream Specimen
of Psychoanalysis (1954)

I. Orientation

Before we embark on advanced exercises in the clinical use of dream interpretation, it seems an attractive task to return, once more, to the "first dream ever subjected to an exhaustive interpretation." This, of course, is Freud's dream of his patient Irma (6). While Freud has by no means published a full account of his exhaustive analysis, he, nevertheless, has offered this dream to his students as the original dream "specimen." For this reason (and for others, only dimly felt up to the time when Freud's letters to Fliess [9] were published) the "Irma Dream" had imprinted itself on the minds of many as a truly historical document; and it seems instructive to discuss this dream once more with the specific purpose of enlarging upon some aspects

First presented in 1949, in the form of two lectures, in the Seminar on Dream Interpretation of the San Francisco Psychoanalytic Institute. Somewhat enlarged after the publication of Freud's letters to Fliess.
First published in the *Journal of the American Psychoanalytic Association*, 2 (1954), 5–56. Reprinted in *Psychoanalytic Psychiatry and Psychology. Clinical and Theoretical Papers: The Austen Riggs Center*, I, eds. Robert P. Knight and Cyrus R. Friedman (New York: International Universities Press, 1954), 131–70.
   References are cited by bracketed numbers in the text. For full citations see listing of references at the conclusion of this paper.

of dream interpretation which we today, half a century later, would consider essential to an exhaustive analysis.

As we review in our minds the incidents of dream analysis in our daily practice and in our seminars and courses, it must be strikingly clear that the art and ritual of "exhaustive" dream analysis have all but vanished. Our advanced technique of psychoanalysis, with its therapeutic zeal and goal-directed awareness of ever-changing transference and resistances, rarely, maybe too rarely, permits that intellectual partnership, that common curiosity between analyst and patient which would take a good-sized dream seriously enough to make it the object of a few hours' concerted analysis. We know too well that patients learn to exploit our interest in dreams by telling us in profuse nocturnal productions what they should struggle and learn to tell us in straight words. And we have learned (or so we think) to find in other sources what in Freud's early days could be garnered only from dreams. Therefore, we feel that even a periodic emphasis on dreams today is wasteful and may even be deleterious to therapy. But let us admit that such restraint, more often than not, is a policy of scarcity rather than abundance; and that the daily choice of dream data, made necessary by such restraint, is more arbitrary and often whimsical than systematic. The truth is that the privilege of using choice and restraint in the interpretation of dreams must be earned; only sufficient regard, at least during the years of training, for the art of total dream analysis, brought up to date at each stage of the development of psychoanalysis, can help a candidate in psychoanalytic training to graduate to that much more advanced practice (now freely granted to beginners) of picking from a patient's daily dream productions whatever dream fragments, symbols, manifest images, and latent dream thoughts support the prevalent trend of interpretations. It stands to reason that a psychoanalyst can know which dream details he may single out for the purposes of the day only if, at least preconsciously, he has somehow grasped the meaning of the whole dream in relation to the course of the analysis and in relation to the course of the patient's life.

Such grasp can become a firm possession of the analyst's preconscious mental activity only if he has acquired by repeated exercise the potential mastery of the whole inventory of manifest leads, associational trends, and relevant life data which make up a whole dream. If he can learn this in his own analysis, so much the better. Some must learn it later, when dream analysis becomes the main vehicle of self-analysis. In the course of formal training, however, "exhaustive" dream analysis can best be studied in connection with those seminars, usually called "continuous," in which the study of the history of a whole treatment permits a thorough assessment of the inventory of forces, trends, and images in a patient's life—including his dream life. I propose that we prepare ourselves for the task of this total analysis by taking up once more Freud's dream of his patient Irma.

To reinterpret a dream means to reinterpret the dreamer. Let me, therefore, discuss first the spirit in which we undertake such a reinterpretation.

No man has ever consciously and knowingly revealed more of himself, for the sake of human advance, than did Freud. At the same time, he drew firm lines where he felt that self-revelation should come to an end, because the possible scientific gain was not in proportion to the pain of self-exhibition and to the inconvenience of calumny. If we, in passing, must spell out more fully than Freud did certain latent dream thoughts suggested by him, we are guided by the consideration that the most legitimate didactic use of the personal data of Freud's life concerns a circumscribed area of investigation, namely, the dynamics of creative thought in general and, specifically, in psychoanalytic work. It seems to us that the publication of Freud's letters to Fliess points in this direction (2).

In reviewing the dream of Irma, we shall focus our attention, beyond the fragmentary indices of familiar infantile and neurotic conflicts, primarily on the relation of this very dream to the moment in Freud's life when it was dreamed—to the moment when creative thought gave birth to the interpretation of dreams. For the dream of Irma owes its significance not only to the fact that it was the first dream reported in *The Interpretation of Dreams*. In a letter sent to his friend Fliess, Freud indulges in a fancy of a possible tablet which (he wonders) may sometimes adorn his summer home. Its inscription would tell the world that "In this house, on July 24, 1895, the Mystery of the Dream unveiled [enthüllte] itself to Dr. Sigm. Freud" (9). The date is that of the Irma Dream. Such autobiographic emphasis, then, supports our contention that this dream may reveal more than the basic fact of a disguised wish fulfillment derived from infantile sources; that this dream may, in fact, carry the historical burden of being dreamed in order to be analyzed, and analyzed in order to fulfill a very special fate.

This, then, is our specific curiosity regarding the dream of Irma. We can advance this approach only in the general course of demonstrating the dimensions of our kind of "exhaustiveness" in the interpretation of dreams.

But first, the background of the dream, the dream itself, and Freud's intepretation.

II. The Irma Dream, Manifest and Latent

The dreamer of the Irma Dream was a thirty-nine-year-old doctor, a specialist in neurology in the city of Vienna. He was a Jewish citizen of a Catholic monarchy, once the Holy Roman Empire of German Nationality, and now swayed both by liberalism and increasing anti-Semitism. His family had grown rapidly; in fact, his wife at the time was again pregnant. The dreamer just then wished to fortify his position and, in fact, his income by gaining academic status. This wish had become problematic, not only because he was a Jew but also because in a recent joint publication with an older colleague, Dr. Breuer, he had committed himself to theories so unpopular and, in fact, so universally disturbing that the senior co-author himself had disengaged himself from the junior one. The book in question (*Studies in Hysteria*) had emphasized the role of sexuality in the etiology of the "defense neuropsychoses," i.e., nervous disorders caused by the necessity of defending consciousness against repugnant and repressed ideas, primarily of a sexual nature. The junior worker felt increasingly committed to these ideas; he had begun to feel, with a pride often overshadowed by despair, that he was destined to make a revolutionary discovery by (I shall let this stand) undreamed-of means.

It had occurred to Freud by then that the dream was, in fact, a normal equivalent of a hysterical attack, "a little defense neuropsychosis." In the history of psychiatry, the comparison of normal phenomena with abnormal ones was not new: the Greeks had called orgasm "a little epilepsy." But if hysterical symptoms, if even dreams, were based on inner conflict, on an involuntary defense against unconscious thoughts, what justification was there for blaming patients for the fact that they could not easily accept, nor long remember, and not consistently utilize the interpretations which the psychiatrist offered them? What use was there in scolding the patient, as Bernheim had done: "vous vous contre-suggestionez, madame?" "Defense," "transference," and "resistance" were the mechanisms, the concepts, and the tools to be elucidated in the years to come. It was soon to dawn on Freud that in order to give shape to these tools, a basic shift from physiologic concepts (to which he was as yet committed) to purely psychological ones, and from exact and sober medical and psychotherapeutic techniques to intuitive observation, even to self-observation, was necessary.

This, then, is the situation: within an academic milieu which seemed to restrict his opportunities because he was a Jew; at an age when he seemed to notice with alarm the first signs of aging, and, in fact, of disease; burdened with the responsibility for a fast-growing family—a medical scientist is faced with the decision of whether to employ his brilliance, as he had shown he could, in the service of conventional practice and research, or to accept the task of substantiating in himself and of communicating to the world a new insight, namely, that man is unconscious of the best and of the worst in himself. Soon after the Irma Dream, Freud was to write to his friend Fliess with undisguised horror that in trying to explain defense he had found himself explaining something "out of the core of nature." At the time of this dream, then, he knew that he would have to bear a great discovery.

The evening before the dream was dreamed, Freud had an experience which had painfully spotlighted his predicament. He had met a colleague, "Otto," who had just returned from a summer resort. There he has seen a mutual friend, a young woman, who was Freud's patient: "Irma." This patient, by Freud's effort, had been cured of hysterical anxiety, but not of certain somatic symptoms, such as intense retching. Before going on vacation, Freud had offered her an interpretation as the solution of her problems; but she had been unable to accept it. Freud had shown impatience. Patient and doctor had thus found themselves in a deadlock which made a righteous disciplinarian out of the doctor and a stubborn child out of the patient: not a healthy condition for the communication of insight. It was, of course, this very kind of deadlock which Freud learned later on to formulate and utilize for a working through of resistance. At the time, Freud apparently had heard some reproach in Otto's voice regarding the condition of the patient who appeared "better, but not well"; and behind the reproach he thought to detect the stern authority of "Dr. M.," a man who was "the leading personality in our circle." On his return home, and under the impression of the encounter, Freud had written a lengthy case report for "Dr. M.," explaining his views on Irma's illness.

He had apparently gone to bed with a feeling that this report would settle matters so far as his own peace of mind was concerned. Yet that very night the personages concerned in this incident, namely, Irma, Dr. M., Dr. Otto, and another doctor, Dr. Leopold, constituted themselves the population of the following dream (6, pp. 196–197).

A great hall—a number of guests, whom we are receiving—among them Irma, whom I immediately take aside, as though to answer her letter, and to reproach her for not yet accepting the "solution." I say to her: "If you [*du*]¹ still have pains, it is really only your own fault."—She answers: "If you [du] only knew what pains I have now in the throat, stomach, and abdomen—I am choked by them." I am startled, and look at her. She looks pale and puffy. I think that after all I must be overlooking some organic affection. I take her to the window and look into her throat. She offers some resistance to this, like a woman who has a set of false teeth. I think, surely she doesn't need them [*sie hat es doch nicht nötig*].— The mouth then opens wide, and I find a large white spot on the right, and elsewhere I see extensive grayish-white scabs adhering to curiously curled formations which are evidently shaped like the turbinal bones of the nose.—I quickly call Dr. M., who repeats the examination and confirms it. Dr. M. looks quite unlike his usual self; he is very pale, he limps, and his chin is clean-shaven [*bartlos*]. . . . Now my friend, Otto, too, is standing beside her, and my friend Leopold percusses her covered chest and says: "She has a dullness below, on the left," and also calls attention to an infiltrated portion of skin on the left shoulder (which I can feel in spite of the dress). M. says, "There's no doubt that it's an infection, but it doesn't matter; dysentery will follow and the poison will be eliminated." . . . We know, too, precisely [*unmittelbar*] how the infection originated. My friend, Otto, not long ago, gave her, when she was feeling unwell, an injection of a preparation of propyl . . . propyls . . . propionic acid . . . trimethylamin (the formula of which I see before me, printed in heavy type). . . . One doesn't give such injections so rashly. . . . Probably, too, the syringe [*Spritze*] was not clean.

I must assume here that Freud's associations to this dream are known to all readers, in all the literary freshness which they have in *The Interpretation of Dreams,* and in all the convincing planlessness of true associations, which, unforeseen and often unwelcome, make their determined entrance like a host of unsorted strangers, until they gradually become a chorus echoing a few central themes. Here I must select and classify.

Irma proves, first of all, to be the representative of a series of *women patients.* Freud remembers a number of *young women* in connection with the question whether or not they were willing to accept their therapist's "solution." Besides Irma, who we now hear is a rosy young *widow,* a *governess* comes to memory, also of youthful beauty, who had resisted an examination because she wanted to hide her false teeth. The dreamer remembers that it had been this governess about whom he had had the angry thought (which in the dream he expresses in regard to Irma), namely,*"Sie hat es doch nicht nötig"* (incorrectly translated as, "She does not need them"). This trend of association establishes an analogy between women patients who will not accept solutions, who will not yield to examination, and who will not submit to advances, although their status promises an easy yielding: young widows, young governesses. Fifty years ago as well as today, suspicions concerning young women patients and especially "merry widows" found their way into medical wit, humor, and scandal. They were accentuated at the time by the common but not officially admitted knowledge that the large contingent of hysterical women was starved for sexual adventure. On the sly it was suggested that the doctor might as well remove their inhibitions by deeds as well as words. It was Freud who established the fact that the hysterical patient transfers to the doctor by no means a simply sexual wish, but rather an unconscious conflict between an infantile wish and an infantile inhibition. Medical ethics aside, neither satisfaction nor cure could ensue from a sexual consummation of the transference.

But then other kinds of patients—men, women, and children—impose themselves on the dreamer's memory: "*good ones*" who fared *badly*, and "*bad ones*" who, maybe, were *better off*. Two hysterical ladies had accepted his "solutions" and had become worse; one had died. As to *obstreperous* patients, the dreamer must admit that he thinks of a very occasional patient, his own wife, and he must confess that even she is not at ease with him as the ideal patient would be. But are there any easy, any ideal patients? Yes, *children*. They do not "put on airs." In those Victorian days, little girls were the only female patients who undressed for examination matter-of-factly. And, we may add, children oblige the dream interpreter by dreaming simple wish fulfillments where adults build up such complicated defenses against their own wishes—and against the interpretation of dreams.

In speaking of his *men patients,* the dreamer is ruthless with himself and his memories. Years ago he had played a leading role in research which demonstrated the usefulness of cocaine for local anesthesia, especially in the eye. But it took some time to learn the proper dosage and the probable dangers: a dear friend died of misuse of cocaine. Other men patients come to mind, also *badly off*. And then there are memories concerning the *dreamer himself* in his double role as patient and as doctor. He had given himself injections for swelling in the nose. Had he *harmed himself*?

Finally the dreamer, apparently looking for a friend in his dilemma, thinks of his oldest and staunchest admirer, a doctor in another city, who knows all his "*germinating ideas,*" and who has fascinating ideas regarding the relationship of *nose* and *sexuality* and regarding the phasic aspect of conception; but, alas, he too has a *nasal affliction*. This far-away doctor is no other than Dr. Fliess, whom Freud at the time was consulting, confiding his emotions and his ideas, and in whom he was soon to confide his very self-analysis.

To state the case which Freud at the time wished to make we shall quote from his lengthy summary (6, pp. 204–207).

The dream fulfills several wishes which were awakened within me by the events of the previous evening (Otto's news, and the writing of the clinical history). For the result of the dream is that it is not I who am to blame for the pain which Irma is still suffering, but that Otto is to blame for it. Now Otto has annoyed me by his remark about Irma's imperfect cure; the dream avenges me upon him, in that it turns the reproach upon himself. The dream acquits me of responsibility for Irma's condition, as it refers this condition to other causes (which do, indeed, furnish quite a number of explanations). The dream represents a certain state of affairs, such as I might wish to exist; *the content of the dream is thus the fulfillment of a wish; its motive is a wish.*

This much is apparent at first sight. But many other details of the dream become intelligible when regarded from the standpoint of wish fulfillment. I take my revenge on Otto. . . . Nor do I pass over Dr. M.'s contradiction; for I express in an obvious allusion my opinion of him: namely, that his attitude in this case is that of an ignoramus ("Dysentery will develop, etc."). Indeed, it seems as though I were appealing from him to someone better informed (my friend, who told me about trimethylamin), just as I have turned from Irma to her friend, and from Otto to Leopold. It is as though I were to say: Rid me of these three persons, replace them by three others of my own choice, and I shall be rid of the reproaches which I am not willing to admit that I deserve! In my dream the unreasonableness of these reproaches is demonstrated for me in the most elaborate manner. Irma's pains are not attributable to me, since she herself is to blame for them in that she refuses to accept my solution. They do not concern me, for being as they are of an organic nature, they cannot possibly be cured by psychic treatment. —Irma's sufferings are satisfactorily explained by her widowhood (trimethylamin!); a state which I cannot alter. —Irma's illness has been caused by an incautious injection administered by Otto, an injection of an unsuitable drug, such as I should never have administered. —Irma's complaint is the result of an injection made with an unclean syringe, like the phlebitis of my old lady patient, whereas my injections have never caused any ill effects. I am aware that these explanations of Irma's illness, which unite in acquitting me, do not agree with one another; that they even exclude one another. The whole plea—for this dream is nothing else—recalls vividly the defense offered by a man who was accused by his neighbor of having returned a kettle in a damaged condition. In the first place, he said, he had returned the kettle undamaged; in the second place, it already had holes in it when he borrowed it; and in the third place, he had never borrowed it at all. A complicated defense, but so much the better; if only one of these three lines of defense is recognized as valid, the man must be acquitted.

Still other themes play a part in the dream, and their relation to my non-responsibility for Irma's illness is not so apparent. . . . But if I keep all these things in view they combine into a single train of thought which might be labeled: concern for the health of myself and others; professional conscientiousness. I recall a vaguely disagreeable feeling when Otto gave me the news of Irma's condition. Lastly, I am inclined, after the event, to find an expression of this fleeting sensation in the train of thoughts which forms part of the dream. It is as though Otto had said to me: "You do not take your medical duties seriously enough; you are not conscientious; you do not perform what you promise." Thereupon this train of thought placed itself at my service, in order that I might give proof of my extreme conscientiousness, of my intimate concern about the health of my relatives, friends and patients. Curiously enough, there are also some painful memories in this material, which confirm the blame attached to Otto rather than my own exculpation. The material is apparently impartial, but the connection between this broader material, on which the dream is based, and the more limited theme from which emerges the wish to be innocent of Irma's illness, is, nevertheless, unmistakable. I do not wish to assert that I have entirely revealed the meaning of the dream, or that my interpretation is flawless. . . .

For the present I am content with the one fresh discovery which has just been made: If the method of dream-interpretation here indicated is followed, it will be found that dreams do really possess a meaning, and are by no means the expression of a disintegrated cerebral activity, as the writers on the subject would have us believe. *When the work of interpretation has been completed the dream can be recognized as a wish-fulfillment.*

We note that the wish demonstrated here is not more than pre-conscious. Furthermore, this demonstration is not carried through as yet to the infantile sources postulated later in *The Interpretation of Dreams*. Nor is the theme of sexuality carried through beyond a point which is clearly intended to be understood by the trained reader and to remain vague to the untrained one. The Irma Dream, then, serves Freud as a very first step toward the tasks of the interpretation of dreams, namely, the establishment of the fact that dreams have their own "rationale," which can be detected by the study of the "work" which dreams accomplish, in transforming the latent dream thoughts into manifest dream images. Dream work uses certain methods (condensation, displacement, symbolization) in order to derive a set of manifest dream images which, on analysis, prove to be significantly connected with a practically limitless number of latent thoughts and memories, reaching from the trigger event of the preceding day, through a chain of relevant memories, back into the remotest past and down into the reservoir of unconscious, forgotten, or unclearly evaluated, but lastingly significant, impressions.

Our further efforts, then, must go in two directions. First, we must spell out, for the Irma Dream, certain latent connections, which in *The Interpretation of Dreams*, for didactic reasons, are dealt with only in later chapters: here we think primarily of the dream's sexual themata, and their apparent relation to certain childhood memories, which in Freud's book follow the Irma Dream by only a number of pages. And we must focus on areas of significance which are only implicit in *The Interpretation of Dreams* but have become more explicit in our lifetime. Here I have in mind, first of all, the relationship of the latent dream thought to the dream's manifest surface as it may appear to us today after extensive studies of other forms of imaginative representation, such as children's play; and then, the relationship of the dream's "inner population" to the dreamer's social and cultural surroundings.

I propose to approach this multidimensional task, not by an immediate attempt at "going deeper" than Freud did, but, on the contrary, by taking a fresh look at the whole of the manifest dream. This approach, however, will necessitate a brief discussion of a general nature.

III. Dimensions of the Manifest Dream

The psychoanalyst, in looking at the surface of a mental phenomenon, often has to overcome a certain shyness. So many in his field mistake attention to surface for superficiality, and a concern with form for lack of depth. But the fact that we have followed Freud into depths which our eyes had to become accustomed to does not permit us, today, to blink when we look at things in broad daylight. Like good surveyors, we must be at home on the geological surface as well as in the descending shafts. In recent years, so-called projective techniques, such as the Rorschach Test, the Thematic Apperception Test, and the observation of children's play, have clearly shown that any segment of overt behavior reflects, as it were, the whole store: one might say that psychoanalysis has given new depth to the surface, thus building the basis for a more inclusive general psychology of man. It takes the clinical psychoanalytic method proper to determine which items of a man's total behavior and experience are amenable to consciousness, are preconscious, or unconscious, and why and how they became and remained unconscious; and it takes this method to establish a scale of pathogenic significance in his conscious and unconscious motivations. But in our daily work, in our clinical discussions and nonclinical applications, and even in our handling of dreams, it has become a matter of course that any item of human behavior shows a continuum of dynamic meaning, reaching from the surface through many layers of crust to the "core." Unofficially, we often interpret dreams entirely or in parts on the basis of their manifest appearance. Officially, we hurry at every confrontation with a dream to crack its manifest appearance at if it were a useless shell and to hasten to discard this shell in favor of what seems to be the more worthwhile core. When such a method corresponded to a new orientation, it was essential for research as well as for therapy; but as a compulsive habituation, it has since hindered a full meeting of ego psychology and the problems of dream life.[2]

Let us, then, systematically begin with the most "superficial": our first impression of the manifest dream. After years of practice one seems to remember, to compare, and to discuss the dreams of others (and even the reports given to us of dreams reported to others) in such a matter-of-fact manner that one reminds himself only with some effort of the fact that one has never seen anybody else's dream nor has the slightest proof that it ever "happened" the way one visualizes it. A dream is a verbal report of a series of remembered images, mostly visual, which are usually endowed with affect. The dreamer may be limited or especially gifted, inhibited or overeager in the range of his vocabulary and in its availability for dream reports; in his ability to revisualize and in his motivation to verbalize all the shades of what is visualized; in his ability to report stray fragments or in the compulsion to spin a meaningful yarn; or in his capacity or willingness to describe the range of his affects. The report of a dream, in turn, arouses in each listener and interpreter a different set of images, which are as incommunicable as is the dream itself. Every dream seminar gives proof that different people are struck by different variables of the manifest dream (or, as I would like to call them, by dream configurations) in different ways, and this by no means only because of a different theoretical approach, as is often hastily concluded, but because of variations in sensory and emotional responsiveness. Here early overtraining can do much harm, in that, for example, the immediate recognition of standardized symbols, or the immediate recognition of verbal double meanings may induce the analyst to reach a premature closure in his conviction of having listened to and "understood" a dream and of understanding dreams in general. It takes practice to realize that the manifest dream contains a wealth of indicators not restricted to what the listener happens to be receptive for. The most important of these indicators are, it is true, verbal ones; but the mere experiment of having a patient retell toward the end of an analytic hour a dream reported at the beginning will make it quite clear to what extent a verbal report is, after all, a process of trying to communicate something which is never completely and successfully rendered in any one verbal formulation. Each completed formulation is, of course, a complete item for analysis; and one it is told, the memory of the first verbal rendering of a dream more or less replaces the visual memory of it, just as a childhood experience often retold by oneself or described by others becomes inextricably interwoven with the memory itself.

I pause here for an illustration, the shortest illustration, from my practice. A young woman patient of German descent once reported a dream which consisted of nothing but the image of the word S[E]INE (with the "E" in brackets), seen light against a dark background. The patient was well-traveled and educated and it therefore seemed plausible to follow the first impression, namely, that this image of a word contained, in fact, a play of words in a variety of languages. The whole word is the French river SEINE, and indeed it was in Paris (France) that the patient had been overcome with agoraphobia. The same French word, if heard and spelled as a German word, is SEHN, i.e., "to see," and indeed it was after a visit to the Louvre that the patient had been immobilized: there now existed a complete amnesia for what she had seen there. The whole word, again, can also be perceived as the German word SEINE, meaning "his." The letter "E" is the first letter of my name and probably served as an anchorage for the transference in the dream. If the letter "E" is put aside, the word becomes the Latin SINE, which means "without." All of this combined makes for the riddle "To see (E) without his . . . in Paris." This riddle was solved through a series of free associations which, by way of appropriate childhood memories of a voyeuristic character and through the analysis of a first transference formation, led to the visual recovery of one of the forgotten pictures: It was a "Circumcision of Christ." There she had seen the boy Savior without that mysterious loincloth which adorns Christ on the Crucifix—the loincloth which her sacrilegious eyes had often tucked at during prayers. (The dream word SEINE also contains the word SIN.) This sacrilegious and aggressive curiosity had been shocked into sudden prominence by the picture in the Louvre, only to be abruptly repressed again because of the special inner conditions brought about by the state of adolescence and by the visit to the capital of sensuality. It had now been transferred to the analyst, by way of the hysterical overevaluation of his person as a therapeutic savior.

The presence of meaningful verbal configurations in this dream is very clear. Less clear is the fact that the very absence of other configurations is equally meaningful. That something was only *seen*, and in fact focused upon with the exclusion of all other sensory experiences (such as spatial extension, motion, shading, color, sound, and, last but not least, the awareness of a dream population), is, of course, related to the various aspects of the visual trauma: to the symptom of visual amnesia, to an attempt to restore the repressed image in order to gain cure by mastery, and to a transference of the original voyeuristic drive onto the person of the analyst. We take it for granted that the wish to revive and to relive the repressed impulse immediately "muscles" its way into the wish to be cured. That the dream space was dark and completely motionless around a clear image was an inverted representation of the patient's memory of the trauma: an area with a dark spot in the center (the repressed picture) and surrounded by lively and colorful halls, milling crowds, and noisy and dangerous traffic, in bright sunlight. The lack of motion in the dream corresponds to the patient's symptoms: agoraphobia and immobilization (based on early determined defense mechanisms) were to end the turmoil of those adolescent days and bring to a standstill the struggle between sexual curiosity and a sense of sin. There was no time dimension in the dream, and there was none in the patient's by now morbid psychic life. As is often the case with hysterics, a relative inability to perceive the passage of time had joined the symptom of spatial avoidance, just as blind anxiety had absorbed all conflicting affects. Thus, all the omitted dimensions of the manifest dream, with the help of associations, could be made to converge on the same issues on which the one overclear dimension (the visual one) was focused. But the choice of the manifest dream representation, i.e., the intelligent use of multilingual word play in a visual riddle, itself proved highly overdetermined and related to the patient's gifts and opportunities: for it was in superior esthetic aspirations that the patient had found a possible sphere of conflict-free activity and companionship. In the cultivation of her sensitive senses, she could see and hear sensually, without being consciously engaged in sexual fantasies; and in being clever and witty she had, on occasion, come closest to replacing a son to her father. This whole area of functioning, then, had remained more or less free of conflict, until, at the time of accelerated sexual maturation and under the special conditions of a trip, sacrilegious thoughts in connection with an esthetic-intellectual endeavor had brought about a short-circuit in her whole system of defenses and reasonably conflict-free intellectual functions: the wish to see and feel esthetically, again, converged on sexual and sinful objects. While it is obvious, then, that the desublimated drive fragment of sacrilegious voyeurism is the force behind this dream (and, in this kind of case, necessarily became the focus of therapeutic interpretation) the total dream, in all of its variables, has much more to say about the relationship of this drive fragment to the patient's ego development.

I have temporarily abandoned the Irma Dream for the briefest dream of my clinical experience in order to emphasize the fact that a dream has certain formal aspects which combine to an inventory of configurations, even though some of these configurations may shine only by their absence. In addition to a dream's striving for *representability*, then, we would postulate a *style of representation* which is by no means a mere shell to the kernel, the latent dream; in fact, it is a reflection of the individual ego's peculiar time-space (2), the frame of reference for all its defenses, compromises, and achievements (3). Our "Outline of Dream Analysis" (Chart I), consequently, begins with an inventory of Manifest Configurations, which is meant to help us, in any given dream or series of dreams, to recognize the interplay of commissions and omissions, of overemphases and underemphases. As mentioned before, such an inventory, once having been thoroughly practiced, must again become a preconscious set of general expectations, against which the individual style of each dream stands out in sharp contour. It will then become clear that the dream life of some (always, or during certain periods, or in individual dream events) is characterized by a greater clarity of the experience of *spatial* extension and of motion (or the arrest of motion) in space; that of others by the flow or the stoppage of *time*; other dreams are dominated by clear *somatic* sensations or their marked absence; by a rich *interpersonal* dream life with an (often stereotyped) dream population or by a pronounced aloneness; by an overpowering experience of marked *affects* or their relative absence or lack of specificity. Only an equal attention to all of these variables and their configurations can help the analyst to train himself for an awareness of the varieties of manifest dream life, which in turn permits the exact characterization of a given patient's manifest dream life at different times of his treatment.

CHART I: OUTLINE OF DREAM ANALYSIS

I. Manifest Configurations

VERBAL
general linguistic quality
spoken words and word play
SENSORY
general sensory quality, range and intensity
specific sensory focus
SPATIAL
general quality of extension
dominant vectors
TEMPORAL
general quality of succession
time-perspective
SOMATIC
general quality of body feeling
body zones
organ modes
INTERPERSONAL
general social grouping
changing social vectors
"object relations"
points of identification
AFFECTIVE
quality of affective atmosphere
inventory and range of affects
points of change of affect
SUMMARY
correlation of configurational trends

II. Links between Manifest and Latent Dream Material

ASSOCIATIONS
SYMBOLS

III. Analysis of Latent Dream Material

ACUTE SLEEP-DISTURBING STIMULUS
DELAYED STIMULUS (DAY RESIDUE)

ACUTE LIFE CONFLICTS
DOMINANT TRANSFERENCE CONFLICT
REPETITIVE CONFLICTS
ASSOCIATED BASIC CHILDHOOD CONFLICTS
COMMON DENOMINATORS
   "wishes," drives, needs
   methods of defense, denial, and distortion

IV. Reconstruction

LIFE CYCLE
present phase
corresponding infantile phase
defect, accident, or affliction
psychosexual fixation
psychosexual arrest
SOCIAL PROCESS: COLLECTIVE IDENTITY
ideal prototypes
evil prototypes
opportunities and barriers
EGO IDENTITY AND LIFEPLAN
mechanisms of defense
mechanisms of integration

As for Part II of our "Outline" (Links between Manifest and Latent Material), the peculiar task of this paper has brought it about that the dreamer's associations have already been discussed, while some of the principal symbols still await recognition and employment.

IV. Verbal Configurations

In the attempt now to demonstrate in what way a systematic use of the configurational analysis of the manifest dream (in constant interplay with the analysis of the latent content) may serve to enrich our understanding of the dream work, I find myself immediately limited by the fact that the very first item on our list, namely, "verbal configurations," cannot be profitably pursued here, because the Irma Dream was dreamed and reported in a German of both intellectual and colloquial sophistication which, I am afraid, transcends the German of the reader's high school and college days. But it so happens that the English translation of the Irma Dream which lies before us (6) contains a number of conspicuous simplifications in translation, or, rather, translations so literal that an important double meaning gets lost. This, in a mental product to be analyzed, can be seriously misleading, while it is questionable that any translation could avoid such mistakes; in the meantime we may profit from insight into the importance of colloquial and linguistic configurations. Actually, what is happening in this translation from one language into another offers analogies with "translations" from any dreamer's childhood idiom to that of his adult years, or from the idiom of the dreamer's milieu to that of the analyst's. It seems especially significant that any such transfer to another verbal system of representation is not only accidentally to mistranslate single items, but to become the vehicle for a systematic misrepresentation of the whole mental product.

There is, to begin with, the little word *du*, with which the dreamer and Irma address one another and which is lost in the English "you." It seems innocent enough on the surface, yet may contain quite a therapeutic burden, a burden of countertransference in reality and of special meaning in the dream. For with *du* one addressed, in those days and in those circles, only near relatives or very intimate friends. Did Freud in real life address the patient in this way—and (a much more weighty question) did she address the Herr Professor with this intimate little word? Or does the dreamer use this way of addressing the patient only in the dream? In either case, this little word carries the burden of the dreamer's sense of personal and social obligation to the patient, and thus of a new significance in his guilt over some negligence and in his wish that she should get well—an urgency of a kind which (as Freud has taught us since then) is disadvantageous to the therapeutic relation.

To enumerate other verbal ambiguities: there is a very arresting mistranslation in the phrase "I think, surely she doesn't need *them*" which makes it appear that the dreamer questions the necessity for Irma's false teeth. The German original, *"sie hat es doch nicht nötig,"* means literally, "she does not need *it*," meaning her resistive behavior. In the colloquial Viennese of those days a richer version of the same phrase was *"das hat sie doch gar nicht nötig, sich so zu zieren,"* the closest English counterpart to which would be: "Who is she to put on such airs?" This expression includes a value judgment to the effect that a certain lady pretends that she is of a higher social, esthetic, or moral status than she really is. A related expression would be the protestation brought forth by a lady on the defense: *"Ich hab das doch gar nicht nötig, mir das gefallen zu lassen";* in English, "I don't need to take this from you," again referring to a misjudgment, this time on the part of a forward gentleman, as to what expectations he may cultivate in regard to a lady's willingness to accept propo-

sitions. These phrases, then, are a link between the associations concerning patients who resist "solutions" and women (patients or not)
who resist sexual advances.

Further mistranslations continue this trend. For example, the fact
the Dr. M.'s chin, in the dream, is *bartlos*, is translated with "clean-
shaven." Now a clean-shaven appearance, in the America of today,
would be a "must" for a professional man. It is, therefore, well to
remember that the German word in the dream means "beardless."
But this indicates that Dr. M. is minus something which in the Europe
of those days was one of the very insignia of an important man, to
wit, a distinctive beard or mustache. This one little word then denudes
the leading critic's face, where the English translation would give it
the luster of professional propriety; it is obvious that the original has
closer relations to a vengeful castrative impulse on the part of the
dreamer than the translation conveys.

Then, there is that little word "precisely" which will become rather
relevant later in another context. In German one would expect the
word *genau*, while one finds the nearly untranslatable *unmittelbar*
("with a sense of immediacy"). In relation to something that is suddenly felt to be known (like the cause of Irma's trouble in the dream)
this word refers rather to the degree of immediate and absolute conviction than to the precise quality of the knowledge; in fact, as Freud
points out in his associations, the immediacy of this conviction really
stood in remarkable contrast to the nonsensical quality of the diagnosis and the prognosis so proudly announced by Dr. M.

There remains the brief discussion of a play of words and of a
most relevant simplification. It will have occurred to you that all the
mistranslations mentioned so far (except "precisely") allude to sexual
meanings, as if the Irma Dream permitted a complete sexual interpretation alongside the professional one—an inescapable expectation
in any case.

The word play "propyl . . . propyls . . . propionic acid," which
leads to the formula of trimethylamin, is so suggestive that I shall
permit myself to go beyond the data at our disposal in order to
provide our discussion of word play in dreams and in wit with an
enlightening example. Freud associated "propyl" to the Greek word
propylon (in Latin *vestibulum*, in German *Vorhof*), a term architec-
tonic as well as anatomic, and symbolic of the entrance to the vagina;
while "propionic" suggests *priapic*—phallic. This word play, then,
would bring male and female symbols into linguistic vicinity to allude
to a genital theme. The dream here seems to indulge in a mechanism
common in punning. A witty word play has it, for example, that a

mistress is "something between a mister and a mattress"—thus using a linguistic analogy to the principal spatial arrangement to which a mistress owes her status.

Finally, a word on the instrument which dispenses the "solution." The translation equips Dr. Otto with a "syringe" which gives the dream more professional dignity than the German original aspires to. The German word is *Spritze*, which is, indeed, used for syringes, but has also the colloquial meaning of "squirter." It will be immediately obvious that a squirter is an instrument of many connotations; of these, the phallic-urinary one is most relevant, for the use of a dirty syringe makes Otto a "dirty squirter," or "a little squirt," not just a careless physician. As we shall see later, the recognition of this double meaning is absolutely necessary for a pursuit of the infantile meaning of the Irma Dream.

The only verbal trend, then, which can be accounted for in this English discussion of a dream reported and dreamed in German induces us to put beside the interpretation of the Irma Dream as a defense against the accusation of medical carelessness (the dispensation of a "solution") and of a possible intellectual error (the solution offered to Irma) the suggestion of a related sexual theme, namely, a protest against the implication of some kind of sexual (self-) reproach.

In due time, we shall find the roots for this sexual theme in the dream's allusion to a childhood problem and then return to the dreamer's professional predicament.

We will then appreciate another double meaning in the dream, which seems to speak for the assumption that one link between the medical, the intellectual, and the sexual themes of the dream is that of "conception." The dream, so we hear, pictures a *birthday reception* in a great hall. "We receive" stands for the German *empfangen*, a word which can refer to conception (*Empfängnis*) as well to reception (*Empfang*). The dreamer's worries concerning the growth of his family at this critical time of his professional life are clearly expressed in the letters to Fliess. At the same time, the typical association between biological *conception* and intellectual *concept formation* can be seen in the repeated reference to "germinating ideas."

V. Interpersonal Configurations in the Dream Population

For a variety of reasons, it will be impossible to offer in this paper a separate discussion of each of the configurational variables listed

SELECTED MANIFEST CONFIGURATIONS

| | I
Interpersonal | | II |
THE DREAMER	THE POPULATION		AFFECTIVE
1. WE are receiving	WIFE receives with him		Festive mood?
2. I take Irma aside I reproach her	IRMA has not accepted the solution		Sense of urgency Sense of reproach
3. I look at her	Complains, feels choked		Startle
4.	Looks pale and puffy		
5. I think			Worry
6. I take her to window I look I think	Offers resistance		Impatience
7.	THE MOUTH opens		
8. I find, I see organic symptoms			Horror
9. I quickly call Dr. M.	Dr. M. confirms symptoms		Dependence on authority
10.	Looks pale, limps, is beardless		
11.	OTTO, LEOPOLD, join examination		
12.	LEOPOLD points to infiltration		
13. I "feel" infiltration			Fusion with patient. Pain?
14.	Dr. M. gives nonsensical reassurance		Sense of reassurance
15. WE know cause of infection			Conviction, faith
16.	OTTO gave IRMA injection		
17.			
18. I see formula			
19. (judges)			Sense of righteousness
20.	THE SYRINGE was not clean		

in our "Outline." The medical implications of the sequence of *somatic* configurations must be ignored altogether, for I am not sufficiently familiar with the history of medicine to comprehend the anatomical, chemical, and procedural connotations which the body parts and the disease entities mentioned in the dream had in Freud's early days. The *sensory* configurations happen in this dream to fuse completely with the dreamer's *interpersonal* activities. Only once—at a decisive point in the middle of the dream—there occurs a kinesthetic sensation. Otherwise, at the beginning as well as at the end of his dream the dreamer is "all eyes."

Most outstanding in his visual field, so it seems, is, at one time,

III	IV
SPATIAL	TEMPORAL
Spacious hall	Present
Constricted to a "space for two"	Present
	Past reaches into
	Present, painful
Close to window	" "
	" "
	" "
Constricted to parts of persons	
	Present co-operative effort
	Present co-operative effort
	Present co-operative effort
	Present co-operative effort
	Future brighter
	" "
	Past guilt displaced
	Present, satisfactory
	Past, guilt localized

Irma's oral cavity, and, at another, the formula trimethylamin, printed in heavy type. The infinite connotations of these two items of fascination become clearer as we see them in a variety of dimensions.

The Irma Dream, to me, suggests concentration on the dreamer's interaction with the people who populate his dream, and relate this interaction to changes in his mood and to changes in his experience of space and time. The chart above lists contemporaneous changes in the dream's *interpersonal, affective, spatial,* and *temporal* configurations.

Given a diagrammatic outline, we have the choice between a horizontal and a vertical analysis. If we try the vertical approach to the first column, we find the dreamer, immediately after having abandoned the receiving line, preoccupied with an intrusive and coercive kind of examination and investigation. He *takes* the patient aside, reproaches her, and then *looks* and *thinks*; finally he finds what he is looking for. Then his activities of examining fuse with those of the other doctors, until at the end he again *sees*, and this time in heavy type, a formula. It is obvious, then, that investigation, in isolation or co-operation, is the main theme of his manifest activities. The particular mode of his approach impresses one as being *intrusive*, and thus somehow related to phallic.[3] If I call it a singularly male approach, I must refer to research in another field and to unfinished research in the field of dreams. Observations on sex differences in the play construction of adolescents (4) indicate that male and female play scenes are most significantly different in the treatment of the space provided, i.e., in the structuring of the play space by means of building blocks and in the spatial vectors of the play activities. I shall not review the criteria here, because without detailed discussion a comparison between the task, suggested by an experimenter, of constructing a scene with a selection of building material and toys, is too different from the inner task, commanded by one's wish to sleep, to represent a set of images on the dream screen. Nevertheless, it may be mentioned that Dr. Kenneth Colby, in following up the possibility of preparing an analogous kind of psychosexual index for the formal characteristics of dreams, has found temporal suddenness, spatial entering, the sensory activity of looking, concern with authority, and a sense of ineffectuality, to be among the numerous items which are significantly more frequent in male dreams.[4] Dr. Colby has been able to isolate some such regularities in spite of the fact that the dream literature at the moment indulges in every possible license in the selection, description, and connotation of dream items. It seems to me that such studies might prove fruitful for research and technique, especially if undertaken in the frame of a standardized inquiry into the variables of dream experience, as suggested in our inventory of configurations. It is possible that the dream has hardly begun to yield its potentialities for research in personality diagnosis.

But now back to the "interpersonal" configurations, from which we have isolated, so far, only the dreamer's activities. If we now turn to the behavior of the dream population, it is, of course, a strangely intrapersonal social life which we are referring to: one never knows whether to view the cast of puppets on the dreamer's stage as a microcosmic reflection of his present or past social reality or as a "projection" of different identity fragments of the dreamer himself, of different roles played by him at different times or in different situations. The dreamer, in experimenting with traumatic reality, takes the outer world into the inner one, as the child takes it into his toy world. More deeply regressed and, of course, immobilized, the dreamer makes an autoplastic experiment of an alloplastic problem: his inner world and all the past contained in it becomes a laboratory for "wishful" rearrangements. Freud has shown us how the Irma Dream repeats a failure and turns to an illusory solution: the dreamer takes childish revenge on Otto ("*he* did it") and on Dr. M. ("he is a castrate and a fool"), thus appeases his anxiety, and goes on sleeping for a better day. However, I would suggest that we take another look at the matter, this time using the horizontal approach to the diagrammatic outline, and correlating the dream's changing interpersonal patterns with the dreamer's changing mood and perspective.

The dreamer, at first is a *part of a twosome*, his wife and himself, or maybe a family group, vis-à-vis a number of guests. "We receive," under festive circumstances in an opulent spatial setting. Immediately upon Irma's appearance, however, this twosomeness, this acting in concert, abruptly vanishes. The wife, or the family, is not mentioned again. The dreamer is suddenly *alone* with his worries, vis-à-vis a complaining patient. The visual field shrinks rapidly from the large hall to the vicinity of a window and finally to Irma's oral aperture; the festive present is replaced by a concern over past mistakes. The dreamer becomes active in a breathless way: he looks at the patient and thinks, he looks into her throat and thinks, and he finds what he sees ominous. He is startled, worried, and impatient, but behaves in a punitive fashion. *Irma*, in all this, remains a complaining and resistive vis-à-vis, and finally seems to become a mere part of herself: "*the mouth* opens." From then on, even when discussed and percussed, she does neither act nor speak—a good patient (for, unlike the proverbial Indian, a good patient is a half-dead patient, just alive enough to make his organs and complexes accessible to isolation and probing inspection). Seeing that something *is* wrong, the dreamer calls *Dr. M.* urgently. He thus establishes a *new twosome*: he and the "authority" who graciously (if foolishly) confirms him. This twosome is immediately expanded to include a professional group of younger colleagues, Dr. Otto and Dr. Leopold. Altogether they now form a small community: "*We know. . . .*"

At this point something happens which is lost in the double meaning of the manifest words, in the German original as well as in translation. When the dreamer says that he can "*feel*" the infiltrated portion of skin on the (patient's) left shoulder, he means to convey (as Freud states in his associations) that he can *feel this on his own body*: one of those fusions of a dreamer with a member of his dream population which is always of central importance, if not the very center and nodal point of a dream. The dreamer, while becoming again a doctor in the consenting community of doctors, thus at the same time turns into his and their *patient*. Dr. M. then says some foolish, nonsensical phrases, in the course of which it becomes clear that it had not been the dreamer who had harmed Irma, not at all. It is clear with the immediacy of a conviction that it was Dr. Otto who had infiltrated her. The dream ends, then, with Otto's professional and moral isolation. The dreamer (first a lonely investigator, then a patient, now a *joiner*) seems quite righteous in his indignation. The syringe was not clean: who would do such a thing? "Immediate" conviction, in harmony with authority, has clarified the past and unburdened the present.

The study of dreams and of culture patterns and ritualizations reveals parallels between interpersonal dream configurations and religious rites of conversion or confirmation. Let me repeat and underscore the points which suggest such an analogy. As the isolated and "guilty" dreamer quickly calls Dr. M., he obviously *appeals for help from higher authority*. This call for help is answered not only by Dr. M., but also by Dr. Leopold and Dr. Otto, who now, together with the dreamer, form a group with a *common conviction* ("we know"). As this happens, and the examination proceeds, the dreamer suddenly feels as if he were the sufferer and the examined, i.e., he, the doctor and man, fuses with the image of the *patient* and *woman*. This, of course, amounts to a surrender analogous to a spiritual conversion and a concomitant sacrifice of the male role. By implication, it is now *his* mouth that is open for inspection (passivity, inspiration, communion). But there is a *reward* for this. Dr. M. (symbolically castrated like a priest) recites with great assurance something that makes *no logical sense* (Latin, Hebrew?) but seems to be *magically effective* in that it awakes in the dreamer the *immediate conviction* (faith) that the causality in the case is now understood (magic, divine will). This common conviction restores in the dream a "We-ness" (congregation) which had been lost (in its worldly, heterosexual form) at the very beginning when the dreamer's wife and the festive guests had disappeared. At the same time it restores to the dreamer a *belongingness* (brotherhood) to a hierarchic group *dominated by an authority* in whom *he believes implicitly*. He immediately benefits from his newly won *state of grace*: he now has sanction for *driving the devil* into Dr. O. With the *righteous indignation* which is the believer's reward and weapon, he can now make *"an unclean one"* (a disbeliever) out of his erstwhile accuser.

Does this interpretation of the Irma Dream as a dream of conversion or confirmation contradict that given by Freud, who believed he had revenged himself on the professional world which did not trust him? Freud, we remember, felt that the dream disparaged Dr. M., robbing him of authority, vigor, and wholeness, by making him say silly things, look pale, limp, and be beardless. All of this, then, would belie as utterly hypocritical the dreamer's urgent call for help, his worry over the older man's health,[5] and his "immediate" knowledge in concert with his colleagues. This wish (to take revenge on his accusers and to vindicate his own strivings) stands, of course, as the dream's stimulus. Without such an id wish and all of its infantile energy, a dream would not exist; without a corresponding appeasement of the superego, it would have no form; but, we must add, without appropriate ego measures, the dream would not work. On closer inspection, then, the radical differentiation between a manifest and a latent dream, while necessary as a means of localizing what is "most latent," diffuses in a complicated continuum of more manifest and more latent items which are sometimes to be found by a radical disposal of the manifest configuration, sometimes by a careful scrutiny of it.

Such double approach seems to make it appear that the ego's over-all attitude in dream life is that of a withdrawal of its outposts in physical and social reality. The sleeping ego not only sacrifices sense perception and motility, i.e., its reactivity to physical reality but also renounces those claims on individuation, independent action, and responsibility which may keep the tired sleeper senselessly awake. The healthy ego, in dreams, quietly retraces its steps; it does not really sacrifice its assets, it merely pretends that, for the moment, they are not needed.[6]

I shall attempt to indicate this systematic retracing of ego steps in a dream by pointing to the *psychosocial criteria* which I have postulated elsewhere (2) (3) for the ego's successive graduations from the main crises of the human life cycle. To proceed, I must list these criteria without being able to enlarge upon them here. I may remind the reader, however, that psychoanalytic theory is heavily weighted in favor of insights which make dysfunction plausible and explain why human beings, at certain critical stages, should fail, and fail in specific ways. It is expected that this theory will eventually make adequate or superior human functioning dynamically plausible as well (12,13). In the meantime, I have found it necessary to postulate tentative criteria for the ego's relative success in synthesizing, at critical stages, the timetable of the organism, and the representative demands and opportunities which societies universally, if in different ways, provide for these stages. At the completion of infancy, then, the criterium for the budding ego's initial and fundamental success can be said to be a Sense of *Basic Trust* which, from then on, promises to outbalance the lastingly latent Sense of *Basic Mistrust*. Such trust permits, during early childhood, the critical development of a Sense of *Autonomy* which henceforth must hold its own against the Senses of *Shame* and *Doubt*, while at the end of the oedipal phase, an unbroken Sense of *Initiative* (invigorated by play) must begin to outdo a more specific Sense of *Guilt*. During the "school age," a rudimentary Sense of *Workmanship* and Work-and-Play companionship develops which, from then on, must help to outbalance the Sense of *Inferiority*. Puberty and Adolescence help the young person sooner or later to consummate the selective gains of childhood in an accruing sense of *Ego Identity* which prevents the lasting dominance of a then threatening Sense of *Role Diffusion*. Young adulthood is specific for a structuring of the Sense of *Intimacy* or else expose the individual to a dominant Sense of *Isolation*. Real intimacy, in turn, leads to wishes and concerns to be taken care of by an adult Sense of *Generativity* (genes, generate, generation) without which there remains the threat of a lasting Sense of *Stagnation*. Finally, a Sense of *Integrity* gathers and defends whatever gains, accomplishments, and vistas were accessible in the individual's life time; it alone resists the alternate outcome of a Sense of vague but over-all *Disgust*.

This, of course, is a mere list of terms which point to an area still in want of theoretical formulation. This area encompasses the kind and sequence of certain universal psychosocial crises which are defined, on the one hand, by the potentialities and limitations of developmental stages (physical, psychosexual, ego) and, on the other, by the universal punctuation of human life by successive and systematic "life tasks" within social and cultural institutions.

The Irma Dream places its dreamer squarely into the crisis of middle age. It deals most of all with matters of *Generativity*, although it extends into the neighboring problems of Intimacy and of Integrity. To the adult implications of this crisis we shall return later. Here we are concerned with the dream's peculiar "regression." The doctor's growing sense of harboring a discovery apt to *generate new thought* (at a time when his wife harbored an addition to the *younger generation*) had been challenged the night before by the impact of a doubting word on his tired mind: a doubting word which was immediately echoed by self-doubts and self-reproaches from many close and distant corners of his life. At a *birthday* party, then, the dreamer suddenly finds himself *isolated*. At first, he vigorously and angrily asserts his most experienced use of one of the ego's functions: he examines, localizes, diagnoses. Such *investigation in isolation* is, as we shall see later on, one of the cornerstones of this dreamer's sense of *Inner Identity*. What he succeeds in focusing on, however, is a terrifying discovery which stares at him like the head of the Medusa. At this point, one feels, a dreamer with less flexible defenses might have awakened in terror over what he saw in the gaping cavity. Our dreamer's ego, however, makes the compromise of abandoning its positions and yet maintaining them. Abandoning independent observation the dreamer gives in to a *diffusion of roles*: Is he doctor or patient, leader or follower, benefactor or culprit, seer or fumbler? He admits to the possibility of his *inferiority in workmanship* and urgently appeals to "teacher" and to "teacher's pets." He thus forfeits his right to vigorous *male initiative* and guiltily surrenders to the inverted solution of the oedipal conflict, for a fleeting moment even becoming the feminine object for the superior males' inspection and percussion; and he denies his sense of stubborn *autonomy*, letting *doubt* lead him back to the earliest infantile security: childlike *trust*.

In his interpretation of the Irma Dream, Freud found this trust most suspect. He reveals it as a hypocritical attempt to hide the dream's true meaning, namely, revenge on those who doubted the dreamer as a worker. Our review suggests that this trust may be overdetermined. The ego, by letting itself return to sources of security once available to the dreamer as a child, may help him to dream well and to sustain sleep, while promising revengeful comeback in a new day, when "divine mistrust" will lead to further discoveries.

VI. Acute, Repetitive, and Infantile Conflicts

I have now used the bulk of this paper for the demonstration of a few items of analysis which usually do not get a fair share in our routine interpretations: the systematic configurational analysis of the manifest dream and the manifest social patterns of the dream population. The designation of other, more familiar, matters will occupy less space.

Our "Outline of Dream Analysis" suggests next a survey of the various segments of the life cycle which appear in the dream material

in latent form, either as acutely relevant or as reactivated by associative stimulation. This survey leads us, then, back along the path
of time.

OUTLINE OF DREAM ANALYSIS

III. Analysis of Latent Dream Material
Acute sleep-disturbing stimulus
Delayed stimulus (day residue)
Acute life conflicts
Dominant transference conflict
Repetitive conflicts
Associated basic childhood conflicts
Common denominators
  "wishes," drives, needs
  methods of defense, denial, and distortion

The most immediately present, the *acute dream stimulus* of the
Irma Dream may well have been triggered by discomfort caused by
swellings in nose and throat which, at the time, seem to have bothered
the usually sound sleeper; the prominence in the dream of Irma's
oral cavity could be conceived as being codetermined by such a stimulus, which may also have provided one of the determinants for the
latent but all-pervading presence in the dream of Dr. Fliess, the oto-
laryngologist. Acute stimulus and *day residue* (obviously the meeting
with Dr. Otto) are associated in the idea as to whether the dreamer's
dispensation of solutions may have harmed him or others. The *acute
life conflicts* of a professional and personal nature have been indicated
in some measure; as we have seen, they meet with the acute stimulus
and the day residue in the further idea that the dreamer may be
reproachable as a sexual being as well.

Let us now turn to matters of childhood. Before quoting from
The Interpretation of Dreams, a few childhood memories, the relevance of which for the Irma Dream are beyond reasonable doubt, I
should like to establish a more speculative link between the dream's
interpersonal pattern and a particular aspect of Freud's childhood,
which has been revealed only recently.

I must admit that on first acquaintance with regressive "joining"
in the Irma Dream, the suggestion of a religious interpretation persisted. Freud, of course, had grown up as a member of a Jewish
community in a predominantly Catholic culture; could the over-all
milieu of the Catholic environment have impressed itself on this child

of a minority? Or was the described configuration representative of a basic human proclivity which had found collective expression in religious rituals, Jewish, Catholic, or otherwise?

It may be well to point out here that the therapeutic interpretation of such patterns is, incidentally, as violently resisted as is any id content (5). Unless we are deliberate and conscious believers in a dogma or declared adherents to other collective patterns, we dislike being shown to be at the mercy of unconscious religious, political, ethnic patterns as much as we abhor sudden insight into our dependence on unconscious impulses. One might even say that today when, thanks to Freud, the origins in instinctual life of our impulses have been documented and classified so much more inescapably and coherently than impulses rooted in group allegiances, a certain clannish and individualist pride has attached itself to the free admission of instinctual patterns, while the simple fact of the dependence on social structures of our physical and emotional existence and well-being seems to be experienced as a reflection on some kind of intellectual autonomy. Toward the end of the analysis of a young professional man who stood before an important change in status, a kind of graduation, a dream occurred in which he experienced himself lying on the analytic couch, while I was sawing a round hole in the top of his head. The patient, at first, was willing to accept almost any other interpretation, such as castration, homosexual attack (from behind), continued analysis (opening a skull flap), and insanity (lobotomy), all of which were indeed relevant, rather than to recognize this dream as an over-all graduation dream with a reference to the tonsure administered by bishops to young Catholic priests at the time of their admission to clerical standing. A probable contact with Catholicism in impressionable childhood was typically denied with a vehemence which is matched only by the bitter determination with which patients sometimes disclaim that they, say, could possibly have observed the anatomic difference between the sexes at any time in their childhood, or could possibly have been told even by a single person on a single occasion that castration would be the result of masturbation. Thus, infantile wishes to belong to and to believe in organizations providing for collective reassurance against individual anxiety, in our intellectuals, easily join other repressed childhood temptations—and force their way into dreams. But, of course, we must be prepared to look for them in order to see them; in which case the analysis of defenses gains a new dimension, and the study of social institutions a new approach.

The publication of Freud's letters to Fliess makes it unnecessary to doubt any further the possible origin of such a religious pattern in Freud's early life. Freud (9) informs Fliess that during a most critical period in his childhood, namely, when he, the "first-born son of a young mother," had to accept the arrival of a little brother who died in infancy and then the advent of a sister, an old and superstitiously religious Czech woman used to take him around to various churches in his home town. He obviously was so impressed with such events that when he came home, he (in the words of his mother) preached to his family and showed them how God carries on (*"wie Gott macht"*): this apparently referred to the priest, whom he took to be God. That his mother, after the death of the little brother, gave birth to six girls in succession, and that the Irma Dream was dreamed during his wife's sixth pregnancy, may well be a significant analogy. At any rate, what the old woman and her churches meant to him is clearly revealed in his letters to Fliess, to whom he confessed that, if he could only find a solution of his "hysteria," he would be eternally grateful to the memory of the old woman who early in his life "gave me the means to live and to go on living." This old woman, then, restored to the little Freud, in a difficult period, a measure of a sense of trust, a fact which makes it reasonably probable that some of the impressive rituals which she took him to see, and that some of their implications as explained by her, appear in the Irma Dream, at a time when his wife was again expecting and when he himself stood before a major emancipation as well as the "germination" of a major idea. If this is so, then we may conclude that rituals impress children in intangible ways and must be sought among the covert childhood material, along with the data which have become more familiar to us because we have learned to look for them.

For a basic childhood conflict more certainly reflected in the Irma Dream, we turn to one of the first childhood memories reported by Freud in *The Interpretation of Dreams* (6, p. 274):

> Then, when I was seven or eight years of age another domestic incident occurred which I remember very well. One evening before going to bed I had disregarded the dictates of discretion, and had satisfied my needs in my parents' bedroom, and in their presence. Reprimanding me for this delinquency, my father remarked: "That boy will never amount to anything." This must have been a terrible affront to my ambition, but allusions to this scene recur again and again in my dreams, and are constantly coupled with enumerations of my accomplishments and successes, as though I wanted to say: "You see, I have amounted to something after all."

This memory calls first of all for an ethnographic clarification, which I hope will not make me appear to be an excessive culturalist. That a seven-year-old by "satisfies his needs in his parents' bedroom" has sinister implications, unless one hastens to remember the technological item of the chamber pot. The boy's delinquence, then, probably consisted of the use of one of his parents' chamber pots instead of his own. Maybe he wanted to show that he was a "big squirt," and instead was called a small one. This crime, as well as the punishment by derisive shaming, and, most of all, the imperishable memory of the event, all point to a milieu in which such character weakness as the act of untimely and immodest urination becomes most forcefully associated with the question of the boy's chances not only of ever becoming a man, but also of amounting to something, of becoming a "somebody," of *keeping what he promises*. In thus hitting the little exhibitionist in his weakest spot, the father not only followed the dictates of a certain culture area which tended to make youngsters defiantly ambitious by challenging them at significant times with the statement that they do not amount to much and with the prediction that they never will. We know the importance of urinary experience for the development of rivalry and ambition, and therefore recognize the memory as doubly significant. It thus becomes clearer than ever why Dr. Otto had to take over the severe designation of a dirty little squirt. After all, he was the one who had implied that Freud had promised too much when he said he would cure Irma and unveil the riddle of hysteria. A youngster who shows that he will amount to something is "promising"; the Germans say he is *vielversprechend*, i.e., he promises much. If his father told little Freud, under the embarrassing circumstance of the mother's presence in the parental bedroom, that he would never amount to anything—i.e., that the intelligent boy did not hold what he promised—is it not suggestive to assume that the tired doctor of the night before the dream had gone to bed with a bitter joke in his preconscious mind: yes, maybe I did promise too much when I said I could cure hysteria; maybe my father was right after all, I do not hold what I promised; look at all the other situations when I put dangerous or dirty "solutions" in the wrong places. The infantile material thus adds to the inventory of the doctor's and the man's carelessness in the use of "solutions" its infantile model, namely, exhibitionistic urination in the parents' bedroom: an incestuous model of all these associated dispensations of fluid.

But it seems to me that this memory could be the starting point for another consideration. It suggests not only an individual trauma, but also a pattern of child training according to which fathers, at significant moments, play on the sexual inferiority feelings and the smoldering oedipal hate of their little boys by challenging them in a severe if not viciously earnest manner, humiliating them before others, and especially before the mother. It would, of course, be difficult to ascertain that such an event is of a typical character in a given area or typical for a given father; but I do believe that such a "method" of arousing and testing a son's ambition (in some cases regularly, in some on special occasions) was well developed in the German cultural orbit which included German Austria and its German-speaking Jews. This matter, however, could be properly accounted for only in a context in which the relation of such child-training patterns could be demonstrated in their relation to the whole conscious and unconscious system of child training and in their full reciprocity with historical and economic forces. And, incidentally, only in such a context and in connection with a discussion of Freud's place in the evolution of civilized conscience could Freud's inclination to discard teachers as well as students (as he discards Dr. O. in his dream after having felt discarded himself) be evaluated. Here we are primarily concerned with certain consequences which such a cultural milieu may have had for the sons' basic attitudes: the inner humiliation, forever associated with the internalized father image, offered a choice between complete submission, a readiness to do one's duty unquestioningly in the face of changing leaders and principles (without ever overcoming a deep self-contempt and a lasting doubt in the leader); and, on the other hand, sustained rebellion and an attempt to replace the personal father with an ideological principle, a cause, or, as Freud puts it, an "inner tyrant."[7]

Another childhood memory, however, may illuminate the personal side of this problem which we know already from Freud's interpretation of the Irma Dream as one of a vengeful comeback.

I have already said that my warm friendships as well as my enmities with persons of my own age go back to my childish relations to my nephew, who was a year older than I. In these he had the upper hand, and I early learned how to defend myself; we lived together, were inseparable, and loved one another, but at times, as the statements of older persons testify, we used to squabble and accuse one another. In a certain sense, all my friends are incarnations of this first figure; they are *revenants*. My nephew himself returned when a young man, and then we were like Caesar and Brutus. An intimate friend and a hated enemy have always been indispensable to my emotional life; I have always been able to create them anew, and not infrequently my childish idea has been so closely approached that friend and enemy have coincided in the same person; but not simultaneously, of course, nor in constant alternation, as was the case in my early childhood [6, p. 451].

This memory serves especially well as an illustration of what, in our "Outline," we call *repetitive conflicts*, i.e., typical conflicts which punctuate the dreamer's life all the way from the infantile to the acute and to the outstanding transference conflicts. The fact that we were once small we never overcome. In going to sleep we learn deliberately to return to the most trustful beginning, not without being startled, on the way, by those memories which seem to substantiate most tellingly whatever negative basic attitude (a sense of mistrust, shame, doubt, guilt, etc.) was aroused by the tiring and discouraging events of the previous day. Yet this does not prevent some, in the restored day, from pursuing, on the basis of their very infantile challenges, their own unique kind of accomplishment.

VII. Transference in the Irma Dream

Among the life situations in our inventory, there remains one which, at first, would seem singularly irrelevant for the Irma Dream: I refer to the "current transference conflict." If anything, this dream, dreamed by a doctor about a patient, would promise to contain references to countertransference, i.e., the therapist's unconscious difficulties arising out of the fact that the patient may occupy a strategic position on the chessboard of his fate. Freud tells us something of how Irma came to usurp such a role, and the intimate *du* in the dream betrays the fact that the patient was close to (or associated with somebody close to) the doctor's family either by blood relationship or intimate friendship. Whatever her personal identity, Irma obviously had become some kind of key figure in the dreamer's professional life. The doctor was in the process of learning the fact that this made her, by definition, a poor therapeutic risk for him.

But one may well think of another kind of "countertransference" in the Irma Dream. The dreamer's activities (and those of his colleagues) are all professional and directed toward a woman. But they are a researcher's approaches: the dreamer takes aside, throws light on the matter, looks, localizes, thinks, finds. May it not be that it was the Mystery of the Dream which itself was the anxious prize of his persistence?

Freud reports later on in *The Interpretation of Dreams* (6) that one night, having exhausted himself in the effort of finding an explanation for dreams of "nakedness" and of "being glued to the spot," he dreamed that he was jumping light-footedly up a stairway in a disarray of clothes. No doubt, then, Freud's dreams during those years of intensive dream study carry the special weight of having to reveal something while being dreamed. That this involvement does not necessarily interfere with the genuineness of his dreams can be seen from the very fact, demonstrated here, that Freud's dreams and associations (even if fragmentary and, at times, altered) do not cease to be fresh and almost infinitely enlightening in regard to points which he, at the time, did not deliberately focus upon.

In our unconscious and mythological imagery, tasks and ideals are women, often big and forbidding ones, to judge by the statues we erect for Wisdom, Industry, Truth, Justice, and other great ladies. A hint that the Dream as a mystery had become to our dreamer one of those forbidding maternal figures which smile only on the most favored among young heroes (and yield, of course, only to sublimated, to "clean" approach) can, maybe, be spotted in a footnote where Freud writes, "If I were to continue the comparison of the three women I should go far afield. Every dream has at least one point at which it is unfathomable; a *central point*, as it were, connecting it with the unknown." The English translation's "central point," however, is in the original German text a *Nabel*—"a navel." This statement, in such intimate proximity to allusions concerning the resistance of Victorian ladies (including the dreamer's wife, now pregnant) to being undressed and examined, suggests an element of transference to the Dream Problem as such: the Dream, then, is just another haughty woman, wrapped in too many mystifying covers and "putting on airs" like a Victorian lady. Freud's letter to Fliess spoke of an "unveiling" of the mystery of the dream, which was accomplished when he subjected the Irma Dream to an "exhaustive analysis." In the last analysis, then, the dream itself may be a mother image; she is the one, as the Bible would say, to be "known."

Special transferences to one's dream life are, incidentally, not exclusively reserved for the author of *The Interpretation of Dreams*. In this context I can give only a few hints on this subject. Once a dreamer knows that dreams "mean" something (and that, incidentally, they mean a lot to his analyst), an ulterior *wish* to *dream* forces its way into the *wish to sleep by way of dreaming*. That this is a strong motivation in dream life can be seen from the fact that different schools of dynamic psychology and, in fact, different analysts manage to provoke systematically different manifest dreams, obviously dreamed to please and to impress the respective analysts: and that members of primitive societies apparently manage to produce "culture pattern dreams," which genuinely impress the dreamer and convince the official dream interpreters. Our discussion of the style of the Irma Dream has, I think, indicated how we would deal with this phenomenon of a variety of dream styles: we would relate them to the respective cultural, interpersonal, and personality patterns, and correlate all of these with the latent dream. But as to the dreamer's transference to his dream life, one may go further: in spurts of especially generous dream production, a patient often appeals to an inner transference figure, a permissive and generous mother, who understands the patient better than the analyst does and fulfills wishes instead of interpreting them. Dreams, then, can become a patient's secret love life and may elude the grasp of the analyst by becoming too rich, too deep, too unfathomable. Where this is not understood, the analyst is left with the choice of ignoring his rival, the patient's dream life, or of endorsing its wish fulfillment by giving exclusive attention to it, or of trying to overtake it with clever interpretations. The technical discussion of this dilemma we must postpone. In the meantime, it is clear that the first dream analyst stands in a unique relationship to the Dream as a "Promised Land."

This, however, is not the end of the transference possibilities in the Irma Dream. In the letters to Fliess, the impression is amply substantiated that Freud, pregnant with inner experiences which would soon force upon him the unspeakable isolation of the first self-analysis in history—and this at a time when his father's death seemed not far off—had undertaken to find in Fliess, at all cost, a superior friend, an object for idealization, and later an (if ever so unaware and reluctant) sounding board for his self-analysis. What this deliberate "transference" consisted of will undoubtedly, in due time, be fully recorded and analyzed. Because of the interrelation of creative and neurotic patterns and of personal and historical trends in this relationship, it can be said that few jobs in the history of human thought call for more information, competence, and wisdom. But it furthers an understanding of the Irma Dream to note that only once in all the published correspondence does Freud address Fliess with the lone word *Liebster* ("Dearest"): in the first letter following the Irma Dream (August 8, 1895). This singular appeal to an intellectual friend (and a German one at that) correlates well with the prominence which the formula for trimethylamin (a formula related to Fliess' researches in bisexuality) has in the dream, both by dint of its heavy type and by its prominent place in the play of configurations, for it signifies the dreamer's return to the act of independent observation— "I see" again.

The Irma Dream, then, in addition to being a dream of a medical examination and treatment and of a sexual investigation, anticipates Freud's self-inspection and with it inspection by a vastly aggrandized Fliess. We must try to visualize the historical fact that here a man divines an entirely new instrument with unknown qualities for an entirely new focus of investigation, a focus of which only one thing was clear: all men before him, great and small, had tried with every means of cunning and cruelty to avoid it. To overcome mankind's resistance, the dreamer had to learn to become his own patient and subject of investigation; to deliver free associations to himself; to unveil horrible insights to himself; to identify himself with himself in the double roles of observer and observed. That this, in view of the strong maleness of scientific approach cultivated by the bearded savants of his day and age (and represented in the dreamer's vigorous attempts at isolating and localizing Irma's embarrassing affliction), constituted an unfathomable division within the observer's self, a division of vague "feminine yielding" and persistent masculine precision: this, I feel, is one of the central meanings of the Irma Dream. Nietzsche's statement that a friend is a lifesaver who keeps us afloat when the struggling parts of our divided self threaten to pull one another to the bottom was never more applicable; and where, in such a situation, no friend of sufficient superiority is available, he must be invented. Fliess, to a degree, was such an invention. He was the recipient of a creative as well as a therapeutic transference.

The "mouth which opens wide," then, is but the oral cavity of a patient and not only a symbol of a woman's procreative inside, which arouses horror and envy because it can produce new "formations" but also the investigator's oral cavity, opened to medical inspection; and it may well represent, at the same time, the dreamer's unconscious, soon to offer insights never faced before to an idealized friend with the hope that (here we must read the whole dream backwards) *wir empfangen*: we receive, we conceive, we celebrate a birthday. That a man may incorporate another man's spirit, that a man may conceive from another man, and that a man may be reborn from another, these ideas are the content of many fantasies and rituals which mark significant moments of male initiation, conversion, and inspiration (11); and every act of creation, at one stage, implies the unconscious fantasy of inspiration by a fertilizing agent of a more or less deified, more or less personified mind or spirit. This "feminine" aspect of creation causes tumultuous confusion not only because of man's intrinsic abhorrence of femininity but also because of the conflict (in really gifted individuals) of this feminine fantasy with an equally strong "masculine" endowment which is to give a new and original form to that which has been conceived and carried to fruition. All in all, the creative individual's typical cycle of moods and attitudes which overlaps with neurotic mood swings (without ever coinciding with them completely) probably permits him, at the height of consummation, to identify with father, mother, and new-born child all in one; to represent, in equal measure, his father's potency, his mother's fertility, and his own reborn ideal identity. It is obvious, then, why mankind participates, with pity and terror, with ambivalent admiration and ill-concealed abhorrence, in the hybris of creative men, and why such hybris, in these men themselves, can call forth all the sinister forces of infantile conflict.

VIII. Conclusion

If the dreamer of the Irma Dream were the patient of a continuous seminar, several evenings of research work would now be cut out for us. We would analyze the continuation of the patient's dream life to see how his inventory of dream variations and how his developing transference would gradually permit a dynamic reconstruction of the kind which, in its most ambitious version, forms point VI of our "Outline":

IV. Reconstruction
LIFE CYCLE
   present phase
   corresponding infantile phase
   defect, accident, or affliction
   psychosexual fixation
   psychosexual arrest
SOCIAL PROCESS: COLLECTIVE IDENTITY
   ideal prototypes
   evil prototypes
   opportunities and barriers
EGO IDENTITY AND LIFEPLAN
   mechanisms of defense
   mechanisms of integration

In the case of the Irma Dream, both the material and the motivation which would permit us to aspire to relative completeness of analysis are missing. I shall, therefore, in conclusion, select a few items which will at least indicate our intentions of viewing a dream as an event reflecting a critical stage of the dreamer's life cycle.

As pointed out, the Irma Dream and its associations clearly reflect a crisis in the life of a creative man of middle age. As the psychosocial criterion of a successful ego synthesis at that age I have named a Sense of Generativity. This unpretty term, incidentally, is intended to convey a more basic and more biological meaning than such terms as creativity and productivity do. For the inventory of significant object relations must, at this stage, give account of the presence or absence of a drive to create and secure personal children—a matter much too frequently considered merely an extension, if not an impediment, of genitality. Yet any term as specific as "parental sense" would not sufficiently indicate the plasticity of this drive, which may genuinely include works, plans, and ideas generated either in direct connection with the tasks of securing the life of the next generation or in wider anticipation of generations to come. The Irma Dream, then, reflects the intrinsic conflict between the partners and objects of the dreamer's intimate and generative drives, namely, wife, children, friends, patients, ideas; they all vie for the maturing man's energy and commitment, and yet none of them could be spared without some sense of stagnation. It may be significant that Freud's correspondence with Fliess, which initiates an *intellectual intimacy* of surprising passion, had begun a few months after Freud's marriage: there are rich references to the advent and the development of the younger generation in both families, and, with it, much complaint over the conflicting demands of family, work, and friendship. Finally, there is, in the material of the Irma Dream, an indication of the problem which follows that of the generative conflict, namely, that of a gradually forming *Sense of Integrity* which represents man's obligation to the most mature meaning available to him, even if this should presage discomfort to himself, deprivation to his mate and offspring, and the loss of friends, all of which must be envisaged and endured in order not to be exposed to a final Sense of Disgust and of Despair. The fact that we are dealing here with a man of genius during the loneliest crisis of his work productivity should not blind us to the fact that analogous crises face all men, if only in their attachments and allegiances to trends and ideas represented to them by strong leaders and by coercive institutions. Yet again, such a crisis is raised to special significance in the lives of those who are especially well endowed or especially favored with opportunities, for the "most mature meaning available to them" allows for deeper conflict, greater accomplishment, and more desperate failure.

A discernible relationship between the dreamer's acute life problem and the problems left over from corresponding infantile phases has been indicated in Section VI. Here I shall select two further items as topics for a final brief discussion: psychosexual fixation and arrest; collective identity and ego identity.

In our general clinical usage we employ the term fixation alternately for that infantile stage in which an individual received the relatively greatest amount of gratification and to which, therefore, his secret wishes persistently return and for that infantile stage of development beyond which he is unable to proceed because it marked an end or determined slow-up of his psychosexual maturation. I would prefer to call the latter the point of *arrest*, for it seems to me that an individual's psychosexual character and proneness for disturbances depends not so much on the point of fixation as on the *range* between the point of fixation and the point of arrest, and on the *quality* of their interplay. It stands to reason that a fixation on the oral stage, for example, endangers an individual most if he is also arrested close to this stage, while a relative oral fixation can become an asset if the individual advances a considerable length along the path of psychosexual maturation, making the most of each step and cultivating (on the very basis of a favorable balance of basic trust over basic mistrust as derived from an intensive oral stage) a certain capacity to experience and to exploit subsequent crises to the full. Another individual with a similar range but a different quality of progression may, for the longest time, show no specific fixation on orality; he may indicate a reasonable balance of a moderate amount of all the varieties of psychosexual energy—and yet, the quality of the whole ensemble may be so brittle that a major shock can make it tumble to the ground whereupon an "oral" fixation may be blamed for it. Thus, one could review our nosology from the point of view of the particular field circumscribed by the points of fixation and arrest and of the properties of that field. At any rate, in a dream, and especially in a series of dreams, the patient's "going back and forth" between the two points can be determined rather clearly. Our outline, therefore, differentiates between a point of psychosexual fixation and one of psychosexual arrest.

The Irma Dream demonstrates a great range and power of pregenital themes. From an initial position of phallic-urethral and voyeuristic hybris, the dreamer regresses to an oral-tactual position (Irma's exposed mouth and the kinesthetic sensation of suffering through her) and to an anal-sadistic one (the elimination of the poison from the body, the repudiation of Dr. Otto). As for the dreamer of the Irma Dream (or any individual not clearly circumscribed by neurotic stereotypy), we should probably postpone any over-all classification until we have thought through the suggestions contained in Freud's first formulation of "libidinal types." In postulating that the ideal type of man is, each in fair measure, narcissistic *and* compulsive *and* erotic, he opened the way to a new consideration of normality, and thus of abnormality. His formulation does not (as some of our day do) focus on single fixations which may upset a unilinear psychosexual progression of a low over-all tonus, but allows for strong conflicts on each level, solved by the maturing ego adequate to each stage, and finally integrated in a vigorous kind of equilibrium.

I shall conclude with the discussion of ego identity (2,3,5). This discussion must, again, be restricted to the Irma Dream and to the typical problems which it may illustrate. The concept of identity refers to an over-all attitude (a *Grundhaltung*) which the young person at the end of adolescence must derive from his ego's successful synthesis of postadolescent drive organization and social realities. A sense of identity implies that one experiences an over-all sameness and continuity extending from the personal past (now internalized in introjects and identifications) into a tangible future; and from the community's past (now existing in traditions and institutions sustaining a communal sense of identity) into foreseeably or imaginable realities of work accomplishment and role satisfaction. I had started to use the terms ego identity and group identity for this vital aspect of personality development before I (as far as I know) became aware of Freud's having used the term *innere Identität* in a peripheral pronouncement and yet in regard to a central matter in his life.

In 1926, Freud sent to the members of a Jewish lodge a speech (8) in which he discussed his relationship to Jewry and discarded religious faith and national pride as "the prime bonds." He then pointed, in poetic rather than scientific terms, to an unconscious as well as a conscious attraction in Jewry: powerful, unverbalized emotions (*viele dunkle Gefühlsmächte*), and the clear consciousness of an inner identity (*die klare Bewusstheit der inneren Identität*). Finally, he mentioned two traits which he felt he owed his Jewish ancestry: freedom from prejudices which narrow the use of the intellect, and the readiness to live in opposition. This formulation sheds an interesting light on the fact that in the Irma Dream the dreamer can be shown both to belittle and yet also temporarily to adopt membership in the "compact" majority of his dream population. Freud's remarks also give added background to what we recognized as the dreamer's vigorous and anxious preoccupation, namely, the use of *incisive intelligence* in *courageous isolation*, the strong urge to investigate, to unveil, and to recognize: the Irma Dream strongly represents this ego-syntonic part of what I would consider a cornerstone of the dreamer's identity, even as it defends the dreamer against the infantile guilt associated with such ambition.

The dream and its associations also point to at least one "evil prototype"—the prototype of all that which must be excluded from one's identity: here it is, in the words of its American counterpart, the "dirty little squirt," or, more severely, the "unclean one" who has forfeited his claim to "promising" intelligence.

Much has been said about Freud's ambitiousness; friends have been astonished and adversaries amused to find that he disavowed it. To be the primus, the best student of his class through his school years, seemed as natural to him ("the first-born son of a young mother") as to write the *Gesammelten Schriften*. The explanation is, of course, that he was not "ambitious" in the sense of *ehr-geizig*: he did not hunger for medals and titles for their own sakes. The ambition of uniqueness in intellectual accomplishment, on the other hand, was not only ego-syntonic but was ethno-syntonic, almost an obligation to his people. The tradition of his people, then, and a firm inner identity provided the continuity which helped Freud to overcome the neurotic dangers to his accomplishment which are suggested in the Irma Dream, namely, the guilt over the wish to be the one-and-only who would overcome the derisive fathers and unveil the mystery. It helped him in the necessity to abandon well-established methods of sober investigation (invented to find out a few things exactly and safely to overlook the rest) for a method of self-revelation apt to open the floodgates of the unconscious. If we seem to recognize in this dream something of a puberty rite, we probably touch on a matter mentioned more than once in Freud's letters, namely, the "repeated adolescence" of creative minds, which he ascribed to himself as well as to Fliess.

In our terms, the creative mind seems to face repeatedly what most men, once and for all, settle in late adolescence. The "normal" individual combines the various prohibitions and challenges of the ego ideal in a sober, modest, and workable unit, well anchored in a set of techniques and in the roles which go with them. The restless individual must, for better or for worse, alleviate a persistently revived infantile superego pressure by the reassertion of his ego identity. At the time of the Irma Dream, Freud was acutely aware that his restless search and his superior equipment were to expose him to the hybris which few men must face, namely, the entry into the unknown where it meant the liberation of revolutionary forces and the necessity of new laws of conduct. Like Moses, Freud despaired of the task, and by sending some of the first discoveries of his inner search to Fliess with a request to destroy them (to "eliminate the poison"), he came close to smashing his tablets. The letters reflect his ambivalent dismay. In the Irma Dream, we see him struggle between a surrender to the traditional authority of Dr. M. (superego), a projection of his own self-esteem on his imaginative and far-away friend, Fliess (ego ideal), and the recognition that he himself must be the lone (self-) investigator (ego identity). In life he was about to commit himself to his "inner tyrant," psychology, and with it, to a new principle of human integrity.

The Irma Dream documents a crisis, during which a medical investigator's identity loses and regains its "conflict-free status" (10, 13). It illustrates how the latent infantile wish that provides the energy for the renewed conflict, and thus for the dream, is imbedded in a manifest dream structure which on every level reflects significant trends of the dreamer's total situation. Dreams, then, not only fulfill naked wishes of sexual license, of unlimited dominance and of unrestricted destructiveness; where they work, they also lift the dreamer's isolation, appease his conscience, and preserve his identity, each in specific and instructive ways.

Bibliography

1. E. H. Erikson, "Studies in the Interpretation of Play," *Genetic Psychology Monograph*, 22 (1940), 557–671.
2. ———, *Childhood and Society* (New York: W. W. Norton & Co., 1950).
3. ———, "Growth and Crises of the 'Healthy Personality.' " For Fact-Finding Committee, Midcentury White House Conference (New York: Josiah Macy Jr. Foundation, 1950). Somewhat revised in *Personality in Nature, Culture and Society*, eds. C. Kluckhohn and H. R. Murray (New York: Knopf, 1953).
4. ———, "Sex Differences in the Play Constructions of Pre-Adolescents." *American Journal of Orthopsychiatry*, 21 (1951), 667–92.
5. ———, "Identity and Young Adulthood." Presented at the Thirty-fifth Anniversary of the Institute of the Judge Baker Guidance Center in Boston, May 1953 (to be published).
6. S. Freud, "The Interpretation of Dreams," In *The Basic Writings of Sigmund Freud* (New York: Modern Library, 1938).
7. ———, "The History of the Psychoanalytic Movement." In *The Basic Writings of Sigmund Freud* (New York: Modern Library, 1938).

8. ———, "Ansprache an die Mitglieder des Vereins B'Nai B'rith" (1926). In *Gesammelte Werke*, vol. 16 (London, Imago Publishing Co., 1941).
9. ———, *Aus den Anfängen der Psychoanalyse* (London: Imago Publishing Co., 1950).
10. H. Hartmann, "Ichpsychologie und Anpassungsproblem." *Internationale Zeitschrift für. Psychoanalyse und Imago*, 24 (1939), 62–135. Translated in part in Rapaport (13).
11. E. Kris, "On Preconscious Mental Processes." *Psychoanalytic Quarterly*, 19 (1950), 540–60. Also in *Psychoanalytic Explorations in Art* (New York: International Universities Press, 1951).
12. ———, "On Inspiration." *International Journal of Psychoanalysis*, 20 (1939), 377–89. Also in *Psychoanalytic Explorations in Art* (New York: International Universities Press, 1952).
13. D. Rapaport, *Organization and Pathology of Thought* (New York: Columbia University Press, 1951).

Notes

[1] German words in brackets indicate that the writer will question and discuss A. A. Brill's translation of these words.

[2] "Formerly I found it extraordinarily difficult to accustom my readers to the distinction between the manifest dream-content and the latent dream-thoughts. Over and over again arguments and objections were adduced from the uninterpreted dream as it was retained in the memory, and the necessity of interpreting the dream was ignored. But now, when the analysts have at least become reconciled to substituting for the manifest dream its meaning as found by interpretation, many of them are guilty of another mistake, to which they adhere just as stubbornly. They look for the essence of the dream in this latent content, and thereby overlook the distinction between latent dream-thoughts and the dream-work. The dream is fundamentally nothing more that a special *form* of our thinking, which is made possible by the conditions of the sleeping state. It is the dream-work which produces this form, and it alone is the essence of dreaming—the only explanation of its singularity" (6, pp. 466–467).

[3] See the chapter "Zones, Modes, and Modalities" in (2).

[4] According to a report presented to the Seminar on Dream Interpretation in the San Francisco Psychoanalytic Institute.

[5] In another dream mentioned in *The Interpretation of Dreams* (6), Freud accuses himself of such hypocrisy, when in a dream he treats with great affection another doctor whose face ("beardless" in actuality) he also alters, this time by making it seem elongated and by adding a yellow beard. Freud thinks that he is really trying to make the doctor out to be a seducer of women patients and a "simpleton." The German *Schwachkopf*, and *Schlemihl*, must be considered the evil prototype which serves as a counterpart to the ideal prototype, to be further elucidated here, the smart young Jew who "promises much," as a professional man.

[6] See Ernst Kris' concept of a "regression in the service of the ego" (11).

[7] As pointed out elsewhere (2), Hitler, also the son of an old father and a young mother, in a corresponding marginal area, shrewdly exploited such infantile humiliation: he pointed the way to the defiant destruction of all paternal images. Freud, the Jew, chose the way of scholarly persistence until the very relationship to the father (the oedipus complex) itself became a matter of universal enlightenment.

Sex Differences in the Play Configurations of American Preadolescents (1955)

In previous publications,[1] the writer has illustrated the clinical impression that a playing child's behavior in space (i.e., his movements in a given playroom, his handling of toys, or his arrangement of play objects on floor or table) adds a significant dimension to the observation of play. And, indeed, three-dimensional arrangement in actual space is the variable distinguishing a play phenomenon from other "projective" media, which utilize space either in two-dimensional projection or through the purely verbal communication of spatial images. In an exploratory way it was also suggested that such clinical hints could be applied to the observation of older children and even of adults; play constructions of college students of both sexes[2] and of mental patients were described and first impressions formulated.[3] In all this work a suggestive difference was observed in the way in which the two sexes utilized a given play space to dramatize rather divergent themes; thus male college students occupied themselves to a significant degree with the representation (or avoidance) of an imagined danger to females emanating from careless drivers in street traffic, while female college students seemed preoc-

First published in the *American Journal of Orthopsychiatry*, 21, (1951), 667–92. Reprinted in a shorter version in *Childhood and Contemporary Cultures*, eds. Margaret Mead and Martha Wolfenstein, (Chicago: University of Chicago Press, 1955), 324–41.

cupied with dangers, threatening things and people in the interior of houses, and thus from intrusive males. The question arose whether or not such sex differences could be formulated so as to be useful to observers in a nonclinical situation and on a more significant scale; and whether these differences would then appear to be determined by biological facts, such as difference in sex or maturational stage, or by differences in cultural conditioning. In 1940 the opportunity offered itself to secure play constructions from about 150 California children (about 75 boys and 75 girls), all of the same ages.[4] The procedure to be described here is an exploratory extension of "clinical" observation to a "normal" sample.[5] The number of children examined were, at age eleven, 79 boys and 78 girls, at age twelve, 80 boys and 81 girls, at age thirteen, 77 boys and 73 girls. Thus the majority of children contributed three constructions to the total number of 468 (236 play constructions of boys and 232 constructions of girls), which will be examined here.

On each occasion the child was individually called into a room where he found a selection of toys such as was then available in department stores (122 blocks, 38 pieces of toy furniture, 14 small dolls, 9 toy cars, 11 toy animals) laid out on two shelves. There was no attempt to make a careful selection of toys on the basis of size, color, material, etc. A study aspiring to such standards naturally would have to use dolls all made of the same materials and each accompanied by the same number of objects fitting in function and size, and themselves identical in material, color, weight, and so on. While it was not our intention to be methodologically consistent in this respect, the degree of inconsistency in the materials used may at least be indicated. Our family dolls were of rubber, which permitted their being bent into almost any shape; they were neatly dressed with all the loving care which German craftsmen lavish on playthings. A policeman and an aviator, however, were of unbending metal and were somewhat smaller than the doll family. There were toy cars, some of them smaller than the policeman, some bigger; but there were no airplanes to go with the aviator.

The toys were laid out in an ordered series of open cardboard boxes, each containing a class of toys, such as people, animals, and cars. These boxes were presented on a shelf. The blocks were on a second shelf in two piles, one containing a set of large blocks, one a set of small ones. Next to the shelves the stage for the actual construction was set: a square table with a square background of the same size.

The following instructions were given:

I am interested in moving pictures. I would like to know what kind of moving pictures children would make if they had a chance to make pictures. Of course, I could not provide you with a real studio and real actors and actresses; you will have to use these toys instead. Choose any of the things you see here and construct on this table an *exciting* scene out of an *imaginary* moving picture. Take as much time as you want, and tell me afterward what the scene is about.

While the child worked on his scene, the observer sat at his desk, presumably busy with some writing. From there he observed the child's attack on the problem and sketched transitory stages of his play construction. When the subject indicated that the scene was completed, the observer said, "Tell me what it is all about," and took dictation on what the child said. If no exciting content was immediately apparent, the observer further asked, "What is the most exciting thing about this scene?" He then mildly complimented the child on his construction.[6]

The reference to moving pictures was intended to reconcile these preadolescents to the suggested use of toys, which seemed appropriate only for a much younger age. And, indeed, only two children refused the task, and only one of these complained afterward about the "childishness" of the procedure: she was the smallest of all the children examined. The majority constructed scenes willingly, although their enthusiasm for the task and their ability to concentrate on it, their skill in handling the toys, and their originality in arranging them varied widely. Yet the children of this study produced scenes with a striking lack of similarity to movie clichés. In nearly five hundred constructions, not more than three were compared with actual moving pictures. In no case was a particular doll referred to as representing a particular actor or actress. Lack of movie experience can hardly be blamed for this; the majority of these children attended movies regularly and had their favorite actors and types of pictures. Neither was the influence of any of the radio programs or comic pictures noticeable except in so far as they themselves elaborated upon clichés of western lore; there were no specific references to "Superman" and only a few to "Red Ryder." Similarly, contemporary events of local or world significance scarcely appeared. The play procedure was first employed shortly before the San Francisco World's Fair opened its gates—an event which dominated the Far West and especially the San Francisco Bay region for months. This sparkling fair, located in the middle of the bay and offering an untold variety of spectacles, was mentioned in not more than five cases. Again, the approach and outbreak of the war did not increase the occurrence of the aviator in the play scenes, in spite of the acute rise in general estimation of military aviation, especially in the aspirations of our boys and their older brothers. The aviator rated next to the monk in the frequency of casting.

It has been surmised that in both groups the toys suggested infantile play so strongly that other pretensions became impossible. Yet only one girl undressed a doll, as a younger girl would; she had recently been involved in a neighborhood sex-education crisis. And while little boys like to dramatize automobile accidents with the proper bumps and noises, in our constructions automobile accidents, as well as earthquakes and bombings, were not made to happen; rather, their final outcome was quietly arranged. At first glance, therefore, the play constructions cannot be considered to be motivated by a regression to infantile play in its overt manifestations.

In general, none of the simpler explanations of the motivations responsible for the play constructions presented could do away with the impression that a play act—like a dream—is a complicated dynamic product of "manifest" and "latent" themes, of past experience and present task, of the need to express something and the need to suppress something, of clear representation, symbolic indirection, and radical disguise.

It will be seen that girls, on the whole, tend to build quiet scenes of everyday life, preferably within a home or in school. The most frequent "exciting scene" built by girls is a quiet family constellation, in a house without walls, with the older girl playing the piano. Disturbances in the girls' scenes are primarily caused by animals, usually cute puppies, or by mischievous children—always boys. More serious accidents occur too, but there are no murders, and there is little gun play. The boys produce more buildings and outdoor scenes, and especially scenes with wild animals, Indians, or automobile accidents; they prefer toys which move or represent motion. Peaceful scenes are predominantly traffic scenes under the guiding supervision of the policeman. In fact, the policeman is the "person" most often used by the boys, while the older girl is the one preferred by girls.[7] Otherwise, it will be seen that the "family dolls" are used more by girls, as follows functionally from the fact that they produce more indoor scenes, while the policeman can apply his restraining influence to cars in traffic as well as to wild beasts and Indians.*

---

* Editor's Note: At the conclusion of this paper, there appear a series of case illustrations excerpted from another article by Erikson (1958, p. 299.) These illustrations provide vivid examples of the emergence of sex differences through spatial relationships.

The general method of the study was clinical as well as statistical; i.e., each play construction was correlated with the constructions of all the children as well as with the other performances of the same child. Thus *unique elements* in the play construction were found to be related to unique elements in the life-history of the individual, while a number of *common elements* were correlated statistically to biographic elements shared by all the children.

In the following three examples, the interplay of manifest theme and play configuration and their relation to significant life-data will be illustrated.

Deborah,[8] a well-mannered, intelligent, and healthy girl of eleven, calmly selects (by transferring them from shelves to table) all the furniture, the whole family, and the two little dogs, but leaves blocks, cars, uniformed dolls, and the other animals untouched. Her scene represents the interior of a house. Since she uses no blocks, there are no outer walls around the house or partitions within it. The house furniture is distributed over the whole width of the table but not without well-defined groups and configurations: there is a circular arrangement of living-room furniture in the right foreground, a bath-room arrangement along the back wall, and an angular bedroom arrangement in the left background. Thus the various parts of the house are divided in a reasonably functional way. In contrast, a piano in the left foreground and a table next to it (incidentally, the only red pieces of furniture used) do not seem to belong to any configuration. Taken together, they do not constitute a conventional room, although they do seem to belong together.

Turning to the cast, we note, within the circle of the living-room, a group consisting of a woman, a boy, a baby, and the two puppies. The woman has the baby in her arms; the boy plays with the two puppies. While this sociable group is as if held together by the circle, all the other people are occupied with themselves: clockwise, in the left foreground, the man at the piano, the girl at the desk, the other boy in the bed in the left background, and the second woman in the kitchen along the back wall.

Having arranged all this slowly and calmly, Deborah indicates with a smile that she is ready to tell her story, which is short enough: "This boy [in the background] is bad, and his mother sent him to bed." She does not seem inclined to say anything about the others. The experimenter (who must now confess that, at the end of this scene, he permitted himself the clinical luxury of one nonstandardized question) asks, "Which one of these people would you like to be?" "The boy with the puppies," she replies.

While her *spontaneous story* singled out the lonely boy in the farthest background, an *elicited afterthought* focuses, instead, on the second boy, who is part of the lively family circle in the foreground. In all their brevity, these two references point to a few interpersonal themes: punishments, closeness to the mother and separation from her, loneliness and playfulness, and an admitted preference for being a boy. Equally significant, of course, are the themes which are suggested but not verbalized.

The selective references to the boy in disgrace and to the happier boy in the foreground immediately point to the fact that in actual life Deborah has an older brother. (She has a baby brother, too, whose counterpart we may see in the baby in the arms of the mother.) We have ample reason to believe that she envies this boy because of his superior age, his sex, his sharp intellect, and his place close to the mother's heart. Envy invites two intentions: to eliminate the competitor and to replace, to become him. Deborah's play construction seems to accomplish this double purpose by splitting the brother in two: the competitor is banished to the lonely background; the boy in the foreground is what she would like to be.

We must ask here: Does Deborah have an inkling of such a "latent" meaning? We have no way of finding out. In this investigation, which is part of a long-range study, there is no place for embarrassing questions and interpretations. Therefore, if in this connection we speak of "latent" themes, "latent" cannot and does not mean "unconscious." It merely means "not brought out in the child's verbalization." On the other hand, our interpretation is, as indicated, based on life-data and test material secured over more than a decade.

But where is Deborah? The little girl at the desk is the only girl in the scene and, incidentally, close to Deborah's age. She was not mentioned in the story. She is, as pointed out, part of a configuration which does not fit as easily and functionally into a conventional house interior as do the other parts. The man at the piano, closest to the girl at the desk, has in common with her only that they share the two red pieces of furniture. Otherwise, they both face away from the family without facing toward each other; they are parallel to each other, with the girl a little behind the father.

In life, Deborah and her father are close to each other temperamentally. Marked introverts, they are both apt to shy away in a somewhat pained manner from the more vivacious members of the family, especially from the mother. Thus they have an important but negative trend in common. Just because of their more introvert natures, they are unable to express what unites them in any other way than by staying close to each other without saying much. This, we think, is represented spatially by a *twosome in parallel isolation.*

In adding this theme to the two verbalized themes (the *isolated bad boy* and the identification with the *good boy in the playful circle*), we surmise that the total scene well circumscribes the child's main life-problem, namely, her isolated position between the parents, between the siblings, and (as yet) between the sexes. In a similar but never once identical manner, our clinical interpretation arrives at a theme representative of that life-task which (present or past) puts the greatest strain on the present psychological equilibrium. In this way, the play construction often is a significant help in the analysis of the life-history because it singles out one or a number of life-data as the *subjectively most relevant* ones and adds a significant key to the dynamic interpretation of the child's personality development.

We may ask one further question: Is there any indication in the play constructions as to how deeply Deborah is disturbed or apt to become disturbed by the particular strain which she reveals? Here a clinical impression must suffice. Deborah uses the whole width of the table. She does not crowd her scene against the background or into one corner, as according to our observations, children with marked feelings of insecurity are apt to do; neither does she spread the furniture all over the table in an amorphous way, as we would expect a less mature child to do. Her groupings are meaningfully and pleasingly placed; so is her distribution of people. The one manifest incongruity in her groupings (father and daughter) proves to be latently significant; only here her scene suffers, as it were, a symptomatic lapse. Otherwise, while there is a simple honesty in her scene, there certainly is no great originality and no special sparkle in it. But here it is necessary to remember the surprising dearth of imagination in most constructions and the possibility that only specially inclined children may take to this medium with real verve.

In one configurational respect Deborah's scene has much in common with those produced by most of the other girls. She places no walls around her house and no partitions inside. In anticipation of the statistical evaluation of this configurational item, we may state here an impression of essential femininity, which, together with the indications of relative inner balance, forms a welcome forecast of a personality potentially adequate to meet the stresses outlined.

In addition to the arrangement on the table and its relation to the verbalization, clinical criteria may be derived from the observation of a child's general approach to the play situation. Deborah's approach was calm, immediate, and consistent; her selection of toys was careful and apt. Other typical approaches are characterized by prolonged silence and sudden, determined action; by an enthusiasm which quickly runs its course; or by some immediate thoughtless remark such as, "I don't know what to do." The final stage of construction, in turn, can be characterized by frequent new beginnings; by a tendency to let things fall or drop; by evasional conversation; by the need to find room for all toys or to exclude certain types of them; by a perfectionist effort at being meticulous in detail; by an inability to wind up the task; by a sudden and unexplained loss of interest and ambition, etc. Such time curves must be integrated with the spatial analysis into a space-time continuum which reflects certain basic attributes of the subject's way of organizing experience—in other words, the ways of his ego.

In the spatial analysis proper, we consider factors such as the following:

1. The subject's approach, first, to the shelves and then to the table, and his way of connecting these two determinants of the play area.

2. The relationship of the play construction to the table surface, i.e., the area covered, and the location, distribution, and alignment of the main configurations with the table square.

3. The relationship of the whole of the construction to its parts and of the parts to one another.

Let us now compare the construction of calm and friendly Deborah with that of the girl most manifestly disturbed during the play procedure. This girl, whom we shall call Victoria, is also eleven years old; her intelligence is slightly lower than Deborah's. She appears flushed and angry upon entering the room with her mother. A devout Catholic, Victoria had overheard somebody in the hall address this writer as "Doctor." She had become acutely afraid that a man had replaced the Study's woman doctor at this critical time of a girl's development. This she had told her mother. The mother then questioned the writer; he reassured both ladies, whereupon Victoria, still with tears in her eyes but otherwise friendly, consented to construct a scene in her mother's protective presence.

Victoria's house form (she called it "a castle") differs from Deborah's construction in all respects. The floor plan of the building is constricted to a small area. There are high, thick walls and a blocked doorway; and there is neither furniture nor people. However, there seems to be an imaginary population of two: "The king," says Victoria, letting her index finger slide along the edge of the foreground, "walks up and down in front of the castle. He waits for the queen, who is changing her dress in there" (pointing into the walled-off corner of the castle).

In this case the "traumatic" factor seems to lie, at least superficially, in the immediate past; for the thematic similarity between the child's acute discomfort in the anticipation of having to undress before a man doctor and, in the play, the exclusion of His Majesty from Her Majesty's boudoir seems immediately clear. High walls and closed gates, as well as the absence of people, all are rare among undisturbed girls; if present, they reflect either a general disturbance or temporary defensiveness.

One small configurational detail in this scene contradicts the general (thematic and configurational) emphasis on the protection of an undressed female from the view even of her husband. In spite of the fact that quite a number of square blocks were still available for a high and solid gate, Victoria selected the only rounded block for the front door. This arrangement, obviously, would permit the king to peek with ease if he were so inclined, and thus provides, for this construction, the usual (but always highly unique) discrepant detail which reveals *the dynamic counterpart to the main manifest theme* in the construction. Here the discrepant detail probably points to an underlying exhibitionism, which, in this preadolescent girl, may indeed have been the motivation for her somewhat hysterical defensiveness; for her years of experience with the Study had not given her any reason to expect embarrassing exposition or willful violation of her Catholic code. We note, however, that Victoria's construction, overdefensive as it is in its constricted and high-walled configuration and theme, is placed in the center of the play table and does not, as we have learned to expect in the case of chronic anxiety, "cling" to the background; her upset, we conclude, may be acute and temporary.

Lisa, a third girl, has to deal with a lifelong and constant problem of anxiety: she was born with a congenital heart condition. This, however, had never been mentioned in her interviews with the workers of the Guidance Study. Her parents and her pediatrician, although in a constant state of preparedness for the possibility of a severe attack, did not wish the matter to be discussed with her and assumed that they had thus succeeded in keeping the child from feeling "different" from other children.

Lisa's scene consists of a longish arrangement, quite uneven in height, of a number of blocks close to the back wall. On the highest block (according to the criteria to be presented later, a "tower") stands the aviator, while below two women and two children are crowded into the small compartment of a front yard, apparently watching a procession of cars and animals. Lisa's story follows. We see in it a metaphoric representation of a moment of heart weakness—an experience which she had never mentioned "in that many words." The analogy between the play scene and its suggested meaning will be indicated by noting elements of a moment of heart failure in brackets following the corresponding play items.

"There is a quarrel between the mother and the nurse over money [anger]. This aviator stands high up on a tower [feeling of dangerous height]. He really is not an aviator, but he thinks he is [feeling of unreality]. First he feels as if his head was rotating, then that his whole body turns around and around [dizziness]. He sees these animals walking by which are not really there [seeing things move about in front of eyes]. Then this girl notices the dangerous situation of the aviator and calls an ambulance [awareness of attack and urge to call for help]. Just as the ambulance comes around a corner, the aviator falls down from the tower [feeling of sinking and falling]. The ambulance crew quickly unfolds a net; the aviator falls into it, but is bounced back up to the top of the tower [recovery]. He holds on to the edge of the tower and lies down [exhaustion]."

Having constructed this scene, the child smilingly left for her routine medical examination, where, for the first time, she mentioned to the Institute physician her frequent attacks of dizziness and indicated that at the time she was trying to overcome them by walking on irregular fences and precipitous places in order to get used to the dizziness. Her quite unique arrangement of blocks, then, seems to signify an uneven fencelike arrangement, at the highest point of which the moment of sinking weakness occurs. That the metaphoric expression of intimate experiences in free play "loosens" the communicability of these same experiences is, of course, the main rationale of play therapy.

These short summaries will illustrate the way in which configurations and themes may prove to be related to whatever item of the life-history, remote or recent, is at the moment most pressing in the child's life. A major classification of areas of disturbance represented in our constructions suggests as relevant areas: (1) family constellations; (2) infantile traumata (for example, a twelve-year-old boy, who had lost his mother at five but had seemed quite oblivious to the event, in his construction revealed that he had been aware of a significant detail surrounding her death; this detail, in fact, had induced him secretly to blame his father for the loss); (3) physical affliction or hypochrondriac concern; (4) acute anxiety connected with the experiment; (5) psychosexual conflict. Naturally these themes interpenetrate.

We shall now turn to a strain which is by necessity shared by all preadolescents, namely, sexual maturation—a "natural" strain which, at the same time, has a most specific relation to the clearest differentiation in any mixed group, namely, difference in sex.

Building blocks provide a play medium most easily counted, measured, and characterized in regard to spatial arrangement. At the same time, they seem most impersonal and least compromised by cultural connotations and individual meanings. A block is almost nothing but a block. It seemed striking, then (unless one considered it a mere function of the difference in themes), that boys and girls differed in the *number* of blocks used as well as in the *configurations* constructed.

Boys use many more blocks, and use them in more varied ways, then girls do. The difference increases in the use of ornamental items, such as cylinders, triangles, cones, and knobs. More than three-quarters of the constructions in which knobs or cones occur are built by boys. This ratio increases with the simplest ornamental composition, namely, a cone on a cylinder; 86 per cent of the scenes in which this configuration occurs were built by boys. With a very few exceptions, only boys built constructions consisting *only* of blocks, while only girls, with no exception, arranged scenes consisting of furniture exclusively. In between these extremes the following classifications suggested themselves: towers and buildings, traffic lanes and intersections, simple inclosures, interiors without walls, outdoor scenes without use of blocks.*[9]

CONFIGURATIONAL ANALYSIS SCALE

I. Block configurations.

A. *Sidewalk.* One or more blocks lying flat, the length being at least one unit length long. (One unit length and one unit width are measured with the lengths and the widths of the large standard blocks.)

B. *Freestanding wall.* One or more blocks forming a wall. This wall is not a part of any configuration described in categories C to L, but is freestanding and at least one unit long. It may be straight or form an angle.

C. *A lane.* This configuration consists of two parallel A's or B's. The

---

* Editor's Note: A Configurational Analysis Scale and associated block configuration drawings have been added to help illustrate these classifications (Erikson, 1951, see References, p. 310).

distance between the parallels should be smaller than their length.

D. *A tunnel.* A lane with a roof.

E. *A crossing.* Consists of lanes which cross one another.

F. *Miscellaneous partitions.* Walls dividing a given space without forming configurations *A* to *E*.

G. *Inclosures.* In general, while configurations *A* to *F* have more the character of dividing a space in such a way that objects are kept apart or channelized, the emphasis in *G* (and partially also in *H* and *J*) is on the enclosing of a given space on four sides. The background may form one of these sides.

H. *Building.* A house representation in which an interior is not only enclosed on four sides, but also covered with a roof which furthermore bears ornaments such as smokestacks or towerlike additions. In this category another basic general configurational trend is added to the previously mentioned tendencies toward *dividing, channelizing,* and *enclosing,* namely, the tendency toward *elevating* and *elaborating,* which in an increasing measure dominates categories *H, J,* and *K.*

J. *Tower.* At least twice as high as it is wide. At least half of its height transcends the rest of the construction.

K. *Miscellaneous structures* not included under *A* and *J,* such as façades, boats, trains, bridges, and so on.

L. *Ruin.* A pile of blocks arranged to indicate that it represents a destroyed structure.

II. Configurations of furniture without any use of blocks.

A. One room.

B. More than one room.

III. Configurations of animals without any use of blocks.

IV. Configurations of cars without any use of blocks.

The most significant sex differences concern the tendency among the boys to erect structures, buildings and towers, or to build streets; among the girls, to take the play table to be the interior of a house, with simple, little, or no use of blocks.

The configurational approach to the matter can be made more specific by showing the spatial function emphasized in the various ways of using (or not using) blocks. This method would combine all the constructions which share the function of *channelizing* traffic (such as lanes, tunnels, or crossings); all elaborate buildings and special structures (such as bridges, boats, etc.) which owe their character to the tendency of *erecting* and *constructing*; all simple walls,

Block Configurations

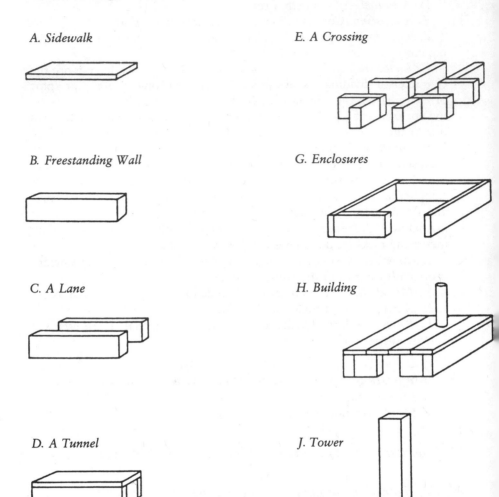

A. Sidewalk

B. Freestanding Wall

C. A Lane

D. A Tunnel

E. A Crossing

G. Enclosures

H. Building

J. Tower

which merely *inclose* interiors; and all house interiors, which are without benefit of inclosing walls and are thus simply *open interiors*.

In the case of *inclosures*, it was necessary to add other differentiations. To build a rectangular arrangement of simple walls is about the most common way of delineating any limited area and, therefore, is not likely to express any particular sex differences. But it was found that, in the case of many boys, simple inclosures in the form of front yards and back yards were only added to more elaborate buildings or that simple corrals or barnyards would appear in connection with outdoor scenes. In this category, therefore, only more detailed work showed that (1) significantly more boys than girls build inclosures only in conjunction with elaborate structures or traffic lanes; (2) significantly more girls than boys will be satisfied with the exclusive representation of a simple inclosure; (3) girls *include* a significantly greater number of (static) objects and people within their inclosures; (4) boys *surround* their inclosures with a significantly greater number of (moving) objects.

Height of structure, then, is prevalent in the configurations of the boys. The observation of the unique details which accompany constructions of extreme height suggests that the variable representing the opposite of elevation, i.e., *downfall*, is equally typical for boys. Fallen-down structures, namely, "ruins," are exclusively found among boys,[10] a fact which did not change in the days of the war when girls as well as boys must have been shocked by pictorial reports of destroyed homes. In connection with the very highest towers, something in the nature of a downward trend appears regularly, but in such a diverse form that only individual examples can illustrate what is meant: one boy, after much indecision, took his extraordinarily high tower down in order to build a final configuration of a simple and low character; another balanced his tower very precariously and pointed out that the immediate danger of collapse was in itself the exciting factor in his story, in fact, *was* his story. In two cases extremely high and well-built façades with towers were incongruously combined with low irregular inclosures. One boy who built an especially high tower put a prone boy doll at the foot of it and explained that this boy had fallen down from its height; another boy left the boy doll sitting high on one of several elaborate towers but said that the boy had had a mental breakdown and that the tower was an insane asylum. The very highest tower was built by the very smallest boy; and, to climax lowness, a colored boy built his structure *under* the table. In these and similar ways, variations of a theme make it apparent that *the variable high-low* is a *masculine variable*. To this generality, we would add the clinical judgment that, in preadolescent boys, extreme height (in its regular combination with an element of breakdown or fall) reflects a trend toward the emotional overcompensation of a doubt in, or a fear for, one's masculinity, while varieties of "lowness" express passivity and depression.

Girls rarely build towers. When they do, they seem unable to make them stand freely in space. Their towers lean against, or stay close to the background. The highest tower built by any girl was not on the table at all but on a shelf in a niche in the wall beside and behind the table. The clinical impression is that, in girls of this age, the presence of a tower connotes the masculine overcompensation of an ambivalent dependency on the mother, which is indicated in the closeness of the structure to the background. There are strong clinical indications that a scene's "clinging" to the background connotes "mother fixation," while the extreme foreground serves to express counterphobic overcompensation.

In addition to the dimensions "high" and "low" and "forward" and "backward," "open" and "closed" suggest themselves as significant. Open interiors of houses are built by a majority of girls. In many cases this interior is expressly peaceful. Where it is a home rather than a school, somebody, usually a little girl, plays the piano: a remarkably tame "exciting movie scene" for representative pre-adolescent girls. In a number of cases, however, a disturbance occurs. An intruding pig throws the family in an uproar and forces the girl to hide behind the piano; the father may, to the family's astonishment, be coming home riding on a lion; a teacher has jumped on a desk because a tiger has entered the room. This intruding element is always a man, a boy, or an animal. If it is a dog, it is always expressly a boy's dog. A family consisting exclusively of women and girls or with a majority of women and girls is disturbed and endangered. Strangely enough, however, this idea of an intruding creature does not lead to the defensive erection of walls or to the closing of doors. Rather, the majority of these intrusions have an element of humor and of pleasurable excitement and occur in connection with open interiors consisting of circular arrangements of furniture.

To indicate the way in which such regularities became apparent through exceptions to the rule, we wish to report briefly how three of these "intrusive" configurations came to be built by boys. Two were built by the same boy in two successive years. Each time a single male figure, surrounded by a circle of furniture, was intruded upon by wild animals. This boy at the time was obese, of markedly feminine build, and, in fact, under thyroid treatment. Shortly after this treatment had taken effect, the boy became markedly masculine. In his third construction he built one of the highest and slenderest of all towers. Otherwise, there was only one other boy who, in a preliminary construction, had a number of animals intrude into an "open interior" which contained a whole family. When already at the door, he suddenly turned back, exclaimed that "something was wrong," and with an expression of satisfaction, rearranged the animals along a tangent which led them close by but away from the family circle.

Inclosures are the largest item among the configurations built by girls, if, as pointed out, we consider primarily those inclosures which

include a house interior. These inclosures often have a richly ornamented gate (the only configuration which girls care to elaborate in
detail); in others, openness is counteracted by a blocking of the entrance or a thickening of the walls. The general clinical impression
here is that high and thick walls (such as those in Victoria's construction) reflect either acute anxiety over the feminine role or, in
conjunction with other configurations, acute oversensitiveness and
self-centeredness. The significantly larger number of open interiors
and simple inclosures, combined with an emphasis, in unique details,
on intrusion into the interiors, on an exclusive elaboration of doorways, and on the blocking-off of such doorways seems to mark *open
and closed* as a feminine variable.

Interpretation of Results

The most significant sex differences in the use of the play space, then,
add up to the following picture: in the boys, the outstanding variables
are height and downfall and motion and its channelization or arrest
(policeman); in girls, static interiors, which are open, simply inclosed,
or blocked and intruded upon.

In the case of boys, these configurational tendencies are connected
with a generally greater emphasis on the outdoors and the outside,
and in girls with an emphasis on house interiors.

The selection of the subjects assures the fact that the boys and
girls who built these constructions are as masculine and feminine as
they come in a representative group in our community. We may,
therefore, assume that these sex differences are a representative
expression of masculinity and of femininity for this particular age
group.

Our group of children, developmentally speaking, stand at the
beginning of sexual maturation. It is clear that the spatial tendencies
governing these constructions closely parallel the morphology of the
sex organs: in the male, *external* organs, *erectible* and *intrusive* in
character, serving highly *mobile* sperm cells; *internal* organs in the
female, with vestibular *access*, leading to *statically expectant* ova.
Yet only comparative material, derived from older and younger subjects living through other developmental periods, can answer the
question whether our data reflect an acute and temporary emphasis
on the modalities of the sexual organs owing to the experience of
oncoming sexual maturation, or whether our data suggest that the
two sexes may live, as it were, in time-spaces of a different quality,

in basically different fields of "means-end-readiness."[11]

In this connection it is of interest that the dominant trends outlined here seem to parallel the dominant trends in the play constructions of the college students in the exploratory study previously referred to. There the tendency was, among men, to emphasize (by dramatization or avoidance) potential disaster to women. Most commonly, a little girl was run over by a truck. But while this item occurred in practically all cases in the preliminary and abortive constructions, it remained a central theme in fewer of the final constructions. In the women's constructions, the theme of an insane or criminal man was universal: he broke into the house at night or, at any rate, was where he should not be. At the time we had no alternative but to conclude tentatively that what these otherwise highly individual play scenes had in common was an expression of the sexual frustration adherent to the age and the mores of these college students. These young men and women, so close to complete intimacy with the other sex and shying away only from its last technical consummation, were dramatizing in their constructions (among other latent themes) fantasies of sexual violence which would override prohibition and inhibition.

In the interpretation of these data, questions arise which are based on an assumed dichotomy between biological motivation and cultural motivation and on that between conscious and unconscious sexual attitudes.

The exclusively cultural interpretation would grow out of the assumption that these children emphasize in their constructions the sex roles defined for them by their particular cultural setting. In this case the particular use of blocks would be a logical function of the manifest content of the themes presented. Thus, if boys concentrate on the exterior of buildings, on bridges and traffic lanes, the conclusion would be that this is a result of their actual or anticipated experience, which takes place outdoors more than does that of girls, and that they anticipate construction work and travel while the girls themselves know that their place is supposed to be in the home. A boy's tendency to picture outward and upward movement may, then, be only another expression of a general sense of obligation to prove himself strong and aggressive, mobile and independent in the world, and to achieve "high standing." As for the girls, their representation of house interiors (which has such a clear antecedent in their infantile play with toys) would then mean that they are concentrating on the anticipated task of taking care of a home and of rearing children, either because their upbringing has made them want to do this or because they think they are supposed to indicate that they want to do this.

A glance at the selection of elements and themes in their relation to conscious sex roles demonstrates how many questions remain unanswered if a one-sided cultural explanation is accepted as the sole basis for the sex differences expressed in these configurations.

If the boys, in building these scenes, think primarily of their present or anticipated roles, why are not boy dolls the figures most frequently used by them? The policeman is their favorite; yet it is safe to say that few anticipate being policemen or believe that they should. Why do the boys not arrange any sport fields in their play constructions? With the inventiveness born of strong motivation, this could have been accomplished, as could be seen in the construction of one football field, with grandstand and all. But this was arranged by a girl who at the time was obese and tomboyish and wore "affectedly short-trimmed hair"—all of which suggests a unique determination in her case.

As mentioned before, during the early stages of the study, World War II approached and broke out; to be an aviator became one of the most intense hopes of many boys. Yet the pilot shows preferred treatment in both boys and girls only over the monk, and—over the baby; while the policeman occurs in their constructions twice as often as the cowboy, who certainly is the more immediate role-ideal of these western boys and most in keeping with the clothes they wear and the attitudes they affect.

If the girls' prime motivation is the love of their present homes and the anticipation of their future ones to the exclusion of all aspirations which they might be sharing with boys, it still would not immediately explain why the girls build fewer and lower walls around their houses. Love for home life might conceivably result in an increase in high walls and closed doors as guarantors of intimacy and security. The majority of the girl dolls in these peaceful family scenes are playing the piano or peacefully sitting with their families in the living-room; could this be really considered representative of what they want to do or think they should pretend they want to do when asked to build an exciting movie scene?

A piano-playing little girl, then, seems as specific for the representation of a peaceful interior in the girls' constructions as traffic arrested by the policeman is for the boys' street scenes. The first can be understood to express *goodness indoors*; the second, a guarantor of safety and *caution outdoors*. Such emphasis on goodness and safety, in response to the explicit instruction to construct an "exciting movie scene," suggests that in these preadolescent scenes more dynamic dimensions and more acute conflicts are involved than a theory of mere compliance with cultural and conscious ideals would have it. Since other projective methods used in the study do not seem to call forth such a desire to depict virtue, the question arises whether or not the very suggestion to play and to think of something exciting aroused in our children sexual ideas and defenses against them.

All the questions mentioned point to the caution necessary in settling on any one dichotomized view concerning the motivations leading to the sex differences in these constructions.

The configurational approach, then, provides an anchor for interpretation in the ground plan of the human body; here, sex difference obviously provides the most significant over-all differentiation. In the interplay of thematic content and spatial configuration, then, we come to recognize an expression of that interpenetration of the biological, cultural, and psychological, which, in psychoanalysis, we have learned to summarize as the *psychosexual*.

In conclusion, a word on the house as a symbol and as a subject of metaphors. While the spatial tendencies related here extend to three-dimensionality as such, the construction of a house by the use of simple, standardized blocks obviously serves to make the matter more concrete and more measurable. Not only in regard to the representation of sex differences but also in connection with the hypochrondriac preoccupation with other growing or afflicted body parts, we have learned to assume an unconscious tendency to represent body and its parts in terms of a building and its parts. And, indeed, Freud said fifty years ago when introducing the interpretation of dreams: "The only typical, that is to say, regularly occurring representation of the human form as a whole is that of a house."[12]

We use this metaphor consciously, too. We speak of our body's "build" and of the "body" of vessels, carriages, and churches. In spiritual and poetic analogies, the body carries the connotation of an abode, prison, refuge, or temple inhabited by, well, ourselves: "This mortal house," as Shakespeare put it. Such metaphors, with varying abstractness and condensation, express groups of ideas which are sometimes too high, sometimes too low, for words. In slang, too, every outstanding part of the body, beginning with the "underpinnings," appears translated into metaphors of house parts. Thus, the face is a "façade," the eyes "front windows with shutters," the mouth a "barn door" with a "picket fence," the throat a "drain pipe," the chest a "bone house" (which is also a term used for the whole body), the male genital is referred to as a "water pipe," and the rectum as the "sewer." Whatever this proves, it does show that it takes neither erudition nor a special flair for symbolism to understand these metaphors. Yet, for some of us, it is easier to take such symbolism for granted on the stage of drama and burlesque than in dreams or in children's play; in other words, it is easier to accept such representation when it is lifted to sublime or lowered to laughable levels.

The configurational data presented here points primarily to an unconscious reflection of biological sex differences in the projective utilization of the *play space*; cultural and age differences have been held constant in the selection of subjects. As for *play themes*, our brief discussion of possible conscious and historical determinants did not yield any conclusive trend; yet it is apparent that the material culture represented in these constructions (skyscrapers, policemen, automobiles, pianos) provides an anchor point for a reinterpretation of the whole material on the basis of comparisons with other cultures. In such comparisons *houses again mean houses*; it will then appear that the basic biological dimensions elaborated here are utilized at the same time to express different technological space-time experiences. Thus it is Margaret Mead's observation that in their play Manus boys who have grown up in huts by the water do not emphasize height, but outward movement (canoes, planes), while the girls, again, concentrate on static houses. It is thus hoped that the clear emphasis in this paper on the biological will facilitate comparative studies, for cultures, after all, elaborate upon the biologically given and strive for a division of labor between the sexes and for a mutuality of function in general which is, simultaneously, workable within the body's scheme and life-cycle, meaningful to the particular society, and manageable for the individual ego.

Case Illustrations*

Now as I show you some pictures, I wish you would pay attention to whether there are blocks at all, or whether there aren't; if there are blocks, whether they make for high buildings or low buildings, whether the buildings are open or closed, whether the whole construction is in the foreground or in the background; and whether the

* Excerpted from "Sex Differences in Play Construction of Twelve-year-old Children." In *Discussions on Child Development*. General Proceedings of the Third Meeting of the World Health Organization Study Group, 3, eds. J. M. Tanner and B. Inhelder (New York: International Universities Press, 1958)

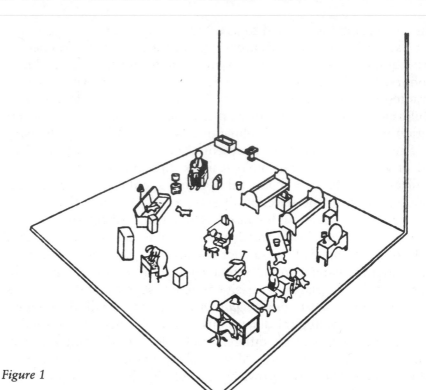

Figure 1

94

buildings contain people and animals or are surrounded by people and animals. The sex differences lie in these simplest spatial relationships.

Fig. 1, I would classify as an open interior. There are no walls around the house, nor walls separating the different rooms of the house. This is a kind of construction which occurs significantly more often in girls' scenes.

Fig. 2 is what I would call a "low inclosure." A low inclosure is one that is only one block high, has no ornaments, no roof, no tower, but on occasion an "elaborate front door." This again is on the whole a feminine construction. Boys build such inclosures primarily in connection with more complicated structures. In this case, the low inclosure is attached to the background, in fact, it opens up toward the wall.

Fig. 3 is a very feminine configuration. There are not only no walls, but a round arrangement of furniture, with either an animal or a male breaking into the circle. Sometimes both appear—such as father coming home on a lion and right behind him, upholding a semblance

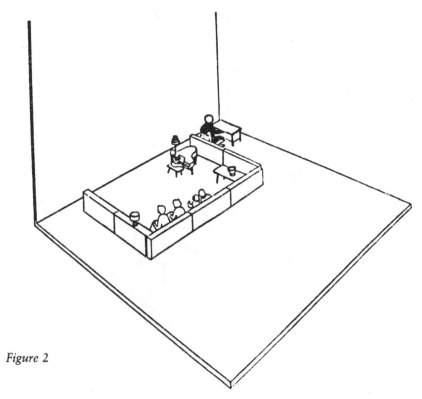

Figure 2

of law and order, a policeman. The Fig. 3 configuration was done by an Italian-American girl. You see how visibly excited that family is. The child spent quite some time turning their arms up in the air. The exciting thing is that a little pig has run into the family house, and in this case it is not the policeman but the dogs who are trying to protect the house.

Fig. 4 is a boy's construction: a locomotive constructed out of blocks. I would definitely call this an "elaborate building," and as a building it is very masculine construction. Yet, when I asked the boy, "What is so exciting about it?" he said that is a very, very narrow bridge which that train has to squeeze through. This boy had an acute and painful phimosis. Thus what dominates at the moment as a discomfort or a conflict enters by way of a unique detail in what otherwise is a normal and in fact outstanding performance.

Fig. 5 is a typical boy's construction. There is an Indian who wants to attack a fort, which, as you see, has many guns. Boys, more often than girls, erect buildings, cover them with roofs, provide them with ornaments and other items which stick out: towers, guns, etc.

I do not need to point out that *Fig. 6* is a boy's construction. It is

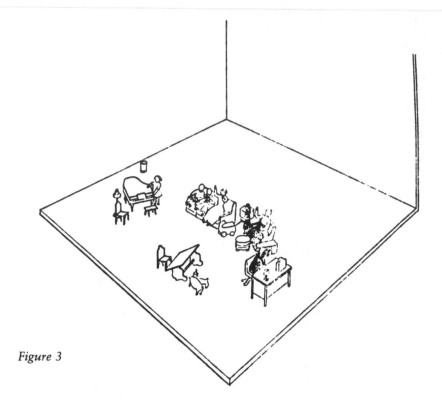

Figure 3

almost too masculine. It isn't just height that is masculine. In connection with the highest towers and buildings there is in the exciting
or unique element a downward trend, as if such height went too far.
He "stuck his neck out." In this case, the exciting element is that the
proud boy sitting on top of the world is really insane, and in fact,
on top of a sanatorium.

Fig. 7 is by a boy who at the time was highly dependent on his
mother, and with a certain "façade" of aloofness. This is expressed
by a high façade, leaning against the background. But not only that.
When I asked him, "What is the exciting element?" he said that this
man (the "father") has placed some bombs underneath that façade.
You can see the cylinders. So here again, his high façade, if you
pushed slightly, would collapse. But now let's see how such a theme
may develop as time passes.

Fig. 8 shows his later construction, again a façade, this time well
founded, but still against the background. The boy standing there,
high and mighty. The same cylinders which before had represented
bombs are now out here, each one kept by a peg from rolling towards

Figure 6

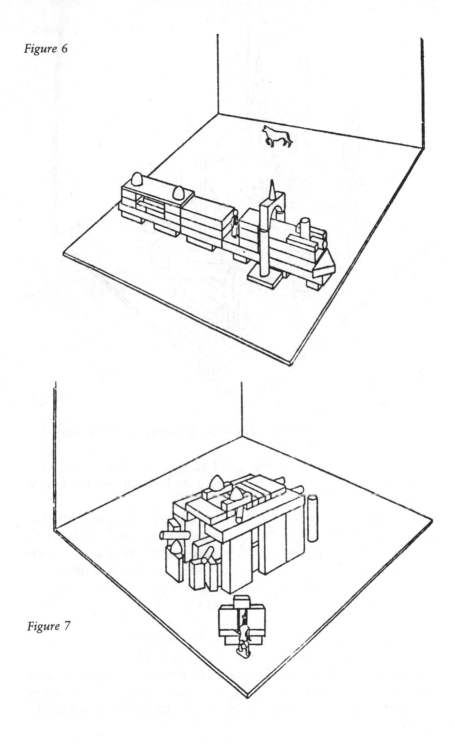

Figure 7

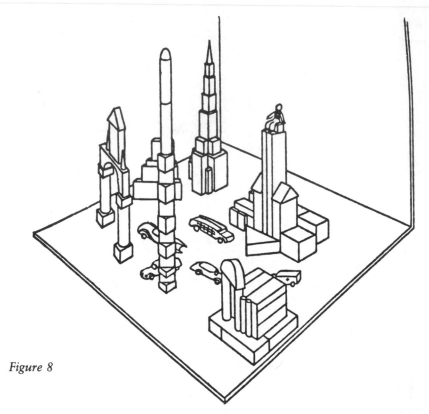

Figure 8

the building. So he has regained safety. I cannot go now into that
critical year in the family history.

Fig. 9 you may also find too good to be true. Here is the only
child whose mother came in with her. I had to ask the mother to
wait outside.

This child builds a boardwalk against the back wall, and another
one coming out into space. Not a diagonal then, but two separate
tendencies, to hang on to the background and to come out. Let me
show how the repetition of a theme underlines this configuration.
Here is a cowboy guarding a bull. Here is a policeman guarding a
bear, a tiger and a lion. Here is an Indian guarding the baby. So that
you see that in content and form the emphasis is on the "Mother
watches over me, I hang on to her." In this particular case, attempt
at a symbiosis with the mother was clinically evident.

Incidentally, only two children ignored the table altogether. One
was this girl, the other a very meek little black boy. He built under
the table. He nearly made me cry. He didn't dare to build where the
others did.

Fig. 10 is the construction made by the same girl half a year later. The conflict over emancipation from the mother is now more clearly counterpointed. There is a "tower," hugging the background, and there is a boardwalk reaching out, and the children sit and watch the world go by. Such changes in configuration often correspond to clear-cut changes in the interview material secured by other workers. Incidentally, the only high towers built by girls are in the back third of the table, and the highest tower built by any girl was built on the shelf back behind the table.

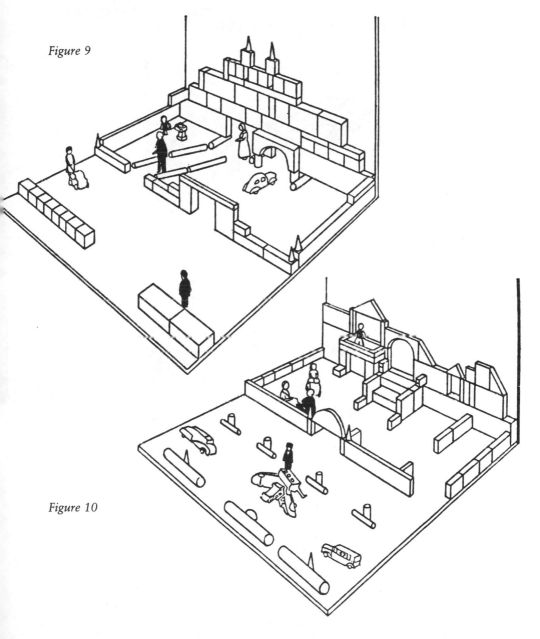

Figure 9

Figure 10

Fig. 11 is an example of the development of one theme during one session. This boy was an enuretic. He started with this phallic tower out in the foreground. Then he took the tower down. His configuration then went downward and backward to *Fig. 12.* He moved it into the background, and made it a low inclosure such as is typical for girls. At the same time, his final story "regressed," as it were, for it concerned a sleeping baby.

Yes. In later constructions he overcame these trends. Here in *Fig. 13* is his brother, at the time more "outgoing" and more masculine. The similarity of initial configuration is uncanny. I do not believe that he could have possibly known what his brother had built. He

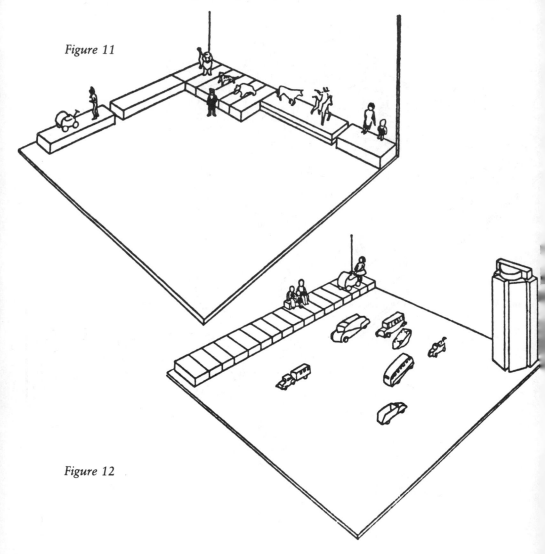

Figure 11

Figure 12

starts with a phallic tower of more moderate height. But then *(Fig. 14)* he builds outward, retaining the tower, and adds what I call a "barrier"—an exclusively male configuration. By the same token his story is concrete and up-to-date; this represents the entrance to the San Francisco World's Fair.

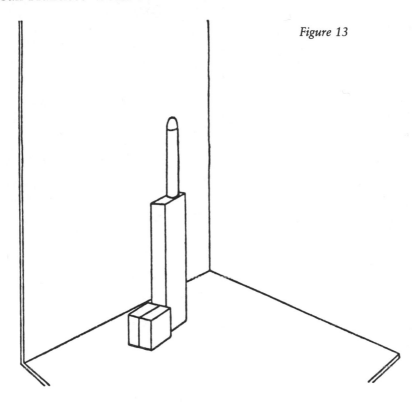

Figure 13

Figure 14

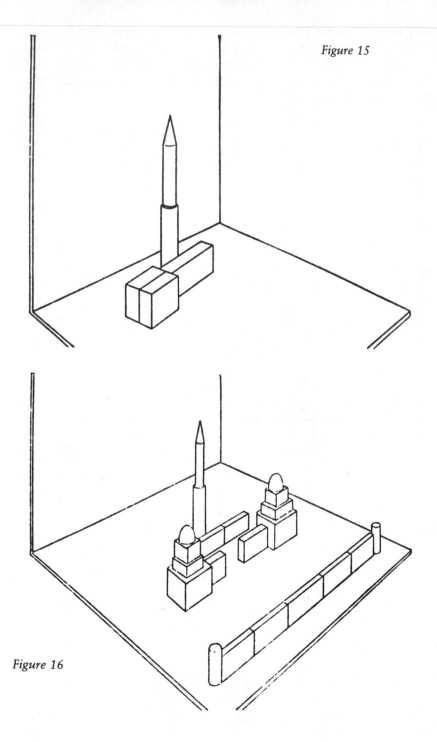

Figure 15

Figure 16

Notes*

[1] Erikson, 1937, 1938, 1940.

[2] Erikson, 1938.

[3] Erikson, 1937; see also Rosenzweig and Shakow, 1937.

[4] The author is indebted for this opportunity to Dr. Jean W. Macfarlane, director of the Guidance Study, Institute of Child Welfare, University of California, Berkeley. The Guidance Study, in the words of its director, is "a 20-year cumulative study dedicated to the investigation of physical, mental, and personality development" (Macfarlane, 1938). Its subjects were "more than 200 children arbitrarily selected upon the basis of every third birth during a given period in Berkeley, California." The children were matched at birth on certain socioeconomic factors and divided into a guidance group and a control group. The study thus provided for "cumulative observation of contemporaneous adjustments and maladjustments in a normal sample."

[5] At the time of this investigation, the author was not familiar with the much more comprehensive "world-play" method of Margaret Lowenfeld in England (Lowenfeld, 1939).

[6] The emphasis on the element of "excitement" warrants an explanation. In the exploratory study mentioned above (Erikson, 1938), Harvard and Radcliffe students had been asked to build *"a dramatic scene."* All English majors educated in the imagery of the finest in English drama, they were observed to build scenes of remarkably *little dramatic flavor.* Instead, they seemed to be overcome by a kind of infantile excitement, which—on the basis of an extensive data collection—could be related to *childhood traumata.* Conversely, a group of psychology students in another university, who decided to employ a short cut by asking their subjects to build *"the most traumatic scene* of their childhood," apparently aroused resistance and produced scenes characterized by a remarkable lack of overt excitement of any kind, by a dearth in formal originality, and by the absence of relevant biographic analogies. These experiences suggested, then, that we should ask our preadolescents for *an exciting scene* in order to establish a standard against which the degree and kind of dramatic elaboration could be judged, while this suggestion as well as the resistance provoked by it could be expected to elicit lingering infantile ideas.

[7] Honzik, 1951.

[8] All names are, of course, fictitious, and facts which might prove identifying have been altered.

[9] An analysis of the sex differences in the occurrence of blocks and toys in the play constructions of these preadolescents has been published by Dr. Marjorie Honzik. For a systematic configurational analysis and for a statistical evaluation see the original article (Honzik, 1951). The writer is indebted to Dr. Honzik and also Drs. Frances Orr and Alex Sherriffs for independent "blind" ratings of the photographs of the play constructions.

[10] One single girl built a ruin. This girl, who suffered from a fatal blood disease, at the time was supposed to be unaware of the fact that only a new medical procedure, then in its experimental stages, was keeping her alive. Her story presented the mythological theme of a "girl who miraculously returned to life after having been sacrificed to the gods." She has since died.

[11] For an application of the configurational trends indicated here in a masculinity-femininity test cf. Franck, 1946. See also Tolman, 1932.

[12] Freud, 1922.

* For full citations, see List of References that follows.

List of References

ERIKSON, ERIK HOMBURGER. 1937. "Configurations in Play," *Psychoanalytic Quarterly*, VI, 2, 139–214.

———. 1938. "Dramatic Productions Test." In *Explorations in Personality*, ed. H. A. MURRAY. New York: Oxford University Press.

———. 1940. "Studies in the Interpretation of Play. I. Clinical Observation of Play Disruption in Young Children." *Genetic Psychology Monographs*, XXII, 557–671.

———. 1951. "Sex Differences in the Play Configurations of Preadolescents," *American Journal of Orthopsychiatry*, XXI, 4, 667–92.

FRANCK, K. 1946. "Preference for Sex Symbols and Their Personality Correlation," *Genetic Psychology Monographs*, XXXIII, 2, 73–123.

FREUD, S. 1922. *Introductory Lectures on Psychoanalysis*. London: Allen & Unwin.

HONZIK, M. P. 1951. "Sex Differences in the Occurrence of Materials in the Play Constructions of Preadolescents," *Child Development*, XXII, 15–35.

LOWENFELD, M. 1939. "The World Pictures of Children: A Method of Recording and Studying Them," *British Journal of Medical Psychology*, XVIII, Part I, 65–101.

MACFARLANE, J. W. 1938. *Studies in Child Guidance*. I. *Methodology of Data Collection and Organization*. ("Society for Research in Child Development Monographs," III, 6.)

ROSENZWEIG, S., and SHAKOW, D. 1937. "Play Technique in Schizophrenia and Other Psychoses," *American Journal of Orthopsychiatry*, VII, 12, 32–47.

TOLMAN, E. C. 1932. *Purposive Behavior in Animals and Men*. New York: Century Co.

Play and Actuality (1972)

Maria Piers's benevolent planning has made me the last speaker in this series of symposia and permits me to do two things—one hardly dreamt of, the other habitual throughout my professional life. I never dreamt of having the last word after Konrad Lorenz, Jean Piaget, and René Spitz. And I welcome the opportunity after numerous digressions to turn once more to the play of children—an infinite resource of what is potential in man. I will begin, then, with the observation of one child's play and then turn to related phenomena throughout the course of life, reflecting throughout on what has been said in these symposia.

In the last few years Peggy Penn, Joan Erikson, and I have begun to collect play constructions of four- and five-year-old children of different backgrounds and in different settings, in a metropolitan school and in rural districts, in this country and abroad. Peggy Penn acts as the play hostess, inviting the children, one at a time, to leave their play group and to come to a room where a low table and a set of blocks and toys await them. Sitting on the floor with them, she

Presented at a symposium sponsored by Loyola University of Chicago and the Erikson Institute for Early Education. Other conference participants were Jean Piaget, Peter H. Wolff, René A. Spitz, Konrad Lorenz, and Lois Barclay Murphy. First published in *Play and Development* ed. Maria W. Piers, (New York: W. W. Norton, 1972), 127–67.

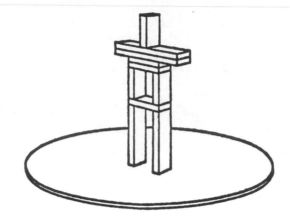

Figure 1

asks each child to "build something" and to "tell a story" about it. Joan Erikson occupies a corner and records what is going on, while I, on occasion, replace her or (where the available space permits) sit in the background watching.

It is a common experience, and yet always astounding, that all but the most inhibited children go at such a task with a peculiar eagerness. After a brief period of orientation when the child may draw the observer into conversation, handle some toys exploratively, or scan the possibilities of the set of toys provided, there follows an absorption in the selection of toys, in the placement of blocks, and in the grouping of dolls, which soon seems to follow some imperative theme and some firm sense of style until the construction is suddenly declared finished. At that moment, there is often an expression on the child's face which seems to say that *this is it*—and it is good.

Let me present one such construction as my "text." I will give you all the details so that you may consider what to you appears to be the "key" to the whole performance. A black boy, five years of age, is a vigorous boy, probably the most athletically gifted child in his class, and apt to enter any room with the question "Where is the action?" He not only comes eagerly, but also builds immediately and decisively a high, symmetrical, and well-balanced *structure*. (See Fig. 1). then does he scan the other toys and, with quick, categorical moves, first places all the *toy vehicles* under and on the building. Then he groups all the *animals* together in a scene beside the building, with the snake in the center. After a pause, he chooses as his first *human doll* the black boy, whom he lays on the very top of the building. He then arranges a group of adults and children with outstretched arms (as if they reacted excitedly) next to the animal scene.

Finally he puts the babies into some of the vehicles and places three men (the policeman, the doctor, and the old man) on top of them. That is it.

The boy's "story" follows the sequence of placements: "Cars come to the house. The lion bites the snake, who wiggles his tail. The monkey and the kitten try to kill the snake. People came to watch. Little one (black boy) on roof is where smoke comes out."

The recorded sequence, the final scene as photographed, and the story noted down all lend themselves to a number of research interests. A reviewer interested in sex differences may note the way in which, say, vehicles and animals are used first, as is more common for boys; or he may recognize in the building of a high and façade-like structure something more common for urban boys. Another reviewer may point to the formal characteristics of the construction—which are, indeed, superior. The psychoanalyst will note aggressive and sexual themes not atypical for this age, such as those connected here with the suggestive snake. The clinician might wonder about the more bizarre element, added almost as a daring afterthought, that of men of authority (doctor, policeman, old man) being placed on top of the babies. Such unique terms, however, escape our comprehension in this kind of investigation, and this usually for lack of intimate life data.

In looking for a theme unique for this boy and unitary in its dominance, I would first focus on the block construction itself, "topped" as it is by a black boy. The meaning of this configuration emerged as we listened to Robert's teachers. One said, "Physically, this boy can compete with boys much older than he. But when he is unhappy, he becomes quite detached and dances a two-step around the classroom with his arms stretched out sideways." As the teacher mimicked his posture, the boy's structure revealed itself as a body image: legs, torso, outstretched arms, and head. Another teacher gave a second clue: she had once congratulated the boy on his athletic ability, but he had responded with a despairing gesture, saying, "Yes, but my brain is no good." She had assured him that body and brain can learn to help each other. This must have impressed him as a formula for the solution of whatever some inner conflict had come to mean to him, or his blackness, or his age, or all three. At any rate, the theme of a dancing body with a black boy as head literally stands out by priority, prominence, and centrality.

It would take a comparison of a wide variety of such constructions to make the probable meaning of this one construction convincing. Today we must accept this one performance as an example of a five-year-old's capacity to project a relevant personal theme on the *microcosm* of a play table.[1]

Our model situation, then, owes its relevance to the observation that one child after another will use a few toys and ten to twenty minutes' time to let some disturbing fact of his life, or some life task, become the basis for a performance characterized by a unique style of representation. Let me try to give some added dignity to the matter by merely mentioning that other play constructions done by the same child over a period of time show an impressive variation as well as a continuity of themes. And if I ever doubted that such continuity is a witness of unifying trends close to the core of a person's development, I learned better when quite recently I had an opportunity to compare the play constructions done in the manner just described thirty years ago by children in their early teens with the dominant themes in their subsequent lives.* History, of course, assigned unexpected roles to many of these persons who are now in their early forties; and yet many of these constructions decades later can be clearly seen as a condensed statement of a theme dominant in a person's destiny.

In studying such specimen, such condensed bits of life, the observer is loath to fit them into the theories to which he and others at different times and under other conditions have subordinated related phenomena. True, the themes presented betray some repetitiveness such as we recognize as the "working through" of a *traumatic* experience, but they also express a playful *renewal*. If they seem to be governed by some need to *communicate*, or even to *confess*, they certainly also seem to serve the joy of *self-expression*. If they seem dedicated to the *exercise* of growing faculties, they also seem to serve the *mastery* of a complex life situation. As I would not settle for any one of these explanations alone, I would not wish to do without any one of them.

Rather, I would not quote one of my predecessors in this symposium in order to underline one of the basic principles bequeathed by him to the Erikson Institute.† Declaring that he is an "interactionist," Piaget said: "What interests me is the creation of new things that are not preformed, nor predetermined by nervous system maturation alone, and not predetermined by the nature of the encounters with the environment, but are constructed within the individual him-

---

* As recorded in the Institute of Human Development of the University of California.
† Quotations from preceding symposia are taken from the original transcripts.

self." Piaget concluded by suggesting a liberating methodology in all teaching. "Children," he said, "should be able to do their own experimenting and their own research." Such experimenting, however (as I felt strongly when watching Baerbel Inhelder in Geneva induce children to be experimental), relies on some playfulness and, in fact, on an interplay of the child's inner resouces with the nature of the task and the suggestiveness of interviewers who are "game." "In order for a child to understand something," Piaget concluded, "he must *construct it himself*, he must *re-invent* it."

Piaget, of course, spoke of cognitive gains. But let me suggest in passing that such play procedures as the one described may well facilitate in a child an impulse to recapitulate and, as it were, to reinvent his own experience in order to learn where it might lead. If there is something to this, then we may entertain the dim hope that some such play procedure may become an adjunct to early education rather than remain a method in the service of the clinic or of research only.

But what seems to be the *function of playfulness* in the children's responses both to Piaget's cognitive challenge and to our expressive one? The most general answer necessarily points to a quality of all things alive, namely the restoration and creation of a *leeway of mastery* in a set of developments or circumstances. The German language has a word for it: *Spielraum*, which is not conveyed in a literal translation such as "playroom." The word connotes something common also for the "play" of mechanical things, namely *free movement* within *prescribed limits*. This at least establishes the boundaries of the phenomenon: where the freedom is gone, *or* the limits, play ends. Such a polarity also seems to adhere to the linguistsic origins of the word *play*, which connotes both carefree oscillation and a quality of being engaged, committed. Language, furthermore, conveys any number of destructive and self-destructive nuances such as playing *at* something or *with* somebody, or playing oneself *out*; all these and other kinds of play connote the limits which end all play.

But if I should now make the first of a number of comparative leaps and ask where I would look for the closest analogy to our play constructions in adult life, I would point to the dramatist's job. If, in this small boy's life, the classroom and the home setting are an early equivalent of the sphere of adult actuality with its interplay of persons and institutions, then his solitary construction is the infantile model of the playwright's work; he, too, condenses into scenes of unitary place and time, marked by a "set" and populated by a cast, the tragic (and comic) dilemma of representative individuals caught in the role conflicts of their time.

Before turning to the sphere of human playfulness in later life, let me touch on some of its fundamentals in man's ontogenetic beginnings. Here I can point to René Spitz's discussion of "basic education." He, who has given us classical studies of the tragic consequences of a restriction of sensory *Spielraum* in early childhood, now has returned to specify what that deprivation consists of. He tells us that it is the gift of *vision* which first serves to integrate the "unconnected discreet stimulations" of taste, audition, smell, and touch. To him, the maternal person, visually comprehended, is both the earliest environment and the earliest educator, who "enables the child—all other things being equal—to achieve the capacity to learn." She seems to do so by truly letting her face shine upon the newborn's searching eyes, and by letting herself be thus verified as one "totality." I would prefer to speak of wholeness rather than of totality, in order to indicate the very special Gestalt quality of that visual integration which permits the infant to extend what I have called his *auto-sphere*, and to include the inclined human face and the maternal presence in it. As Joan Erikson puts it in her essay "Eye to Eye": "We began life with this relatedness to eyes. . . . It is with the eyes that [maternal] concern and love are communicated, and distance and anger as well. Growing maturity does not alter this eye-centeredness, for all through life our visual intercourse with others is eye-focused: the eye that blesses and curses."[2]

Spitz now ascribes to organized vision the role of a first ego nucleus, anchored "in a special sector of man's central nervous system, which permits a first integration of experience." It will be obvious that a certain playfulness must endow visual scanning and rescanning, which leds to significant interplay as it is responded to by the mother with playful encouragement. This, in turn, confirms a sense of mutuality in both partners. It is such *interplay*, I would believe, which is the prime facilitator of that "ego nucleus."

If these matters are reminiscent of religious images such as the inclined face of the Madonna and the aura of her oneness with the Christ child, I also believe that the phenomena which René Spitz (and Joan Erikson) refer to *are* the ontogenetic basis of faith, a fact which remains both elemental and fateful in man's whole development. Let me illustrate this theme with an example from art history.

In our seminar on Life History and History at Harvard, Professor Helmut Wohl enlarged on some autobiographic notes left by Michelangelo. The great sculptor right after birth had been given a wet nurse because his mother was too sick to take care of him. To farm an infant out to wet nurses was, it seems, not atypical in the lives of men and women of that time; in fact, the patron of our meeting, St. Loyola, was brought up by a blacksmith's wife. The "other woman" in Michelangelo's case was the daughter and wife of stonemasons; and his first environment, being adjacent to a stone quarry in Settignano, must have had an inescapable auditory quality. At any rate, Michelangelo acknowledged that while his mother had given him life itself, the wet nurse ("perhaps joking or perhaps in earnest") gave him "delight in the chisel, for it is well known that the nurse's milk has such power in us . . . by changing the temperature of the body."[3] That chisel eventually (and under the protectorate of a fatherly patron, Lorenzo de' Medici) became for him the executive tool of his very identity. When he created young David, Michelangelo equated "David with the sling" and "I with the chisel."[4]

But if Michelangelo had two mothers, he, alas, lost both early. He was separated from the wet nurse when he returned to his mother and then his mother died when he was six years old. Wohl presented to us the sequence of Madonna images that Michelangelo sketched, painted, or sculptured, the first in his late teens and the last in his late eighties. His Madonnas always show a marked distance between mother and child, beyond the Renaissance theme of the willful boy Jesus straining away from his mother's arms; here the Madonna herself is looking away from her child, her eyes remaining inward, distant and almost sightless. Only the very last of Michelangelo's preserved sketches of the Madonna portrays, in Wohl's word, a nearly "conflictless" image of mother and child. The Madonna holds the child close to her face and he turns to her fully, attempting to embrace her with his small arms. So it took the closeness of death for Michelangelo to recover what he had lost early in life, and one cannot help connecting this, the old man's refound hope, with St. Paul's saying, "For now we see through a glass darkly: but then face to face: now I know in part; but then shall I know even as also I am known."[5]

This, of course, would seem to be only a subsidiary theme in Michelangelo's gigantic confrontations. He not only hammered away at his strangely tortured sculptures, sovereignly transcended by irate Moses but also painted his own vision of Adam and the Creator and of Christ at the Last Judgment in the Sistine Chapel. In a sonnet, he describes how, at the crippling expense of his whole physique, he gazed up at the ceiling, lifting arm and brush: "my beard toward

Heaven, I feel the back of my brain upon my neck."⁶ But whether or not a mighty compensatory force intensified Michelangelo's creative furor, we may well pause to wonder at the very fact of the singular fascination which these artistically created visual worlds painted on hallowed halls hold for us. Could all this be ontologically related to the singular importance of that playfully structured visual field in the beginnings of childhood?

As we proceed, I will refer to other visualized spheres endowed with a special aura. I already have mentioned the theater. The dictionary says that the root of the word is *thea*—a sight, which, in turn, is related to *thauma*—that which compels the gaze. Maybe, the "legitimate" theater is only a special case, a condensed version of all the imagined, depicted, and theorized spheres (yes, there is *thea* in *theory*, too) by which we attempt to create coherencies and continuities in the complexity and affectivity of existence.* And we will not forget that the late Bertram Lewin spoke of a "dream screen" on which we experience our nightly visions.

But I must now ask a theoretical and terminological question. If, as we are apt to say, the maternal caretaker is the first "object" playfully engaged by the scanning eyes, who are the "objects" in later stages, up to St. Paul's finite recognition? Are they, as some of us would be all too ready to say, "mother substitutes"?

First a word about the term *object*. Within a theory of cognition it makes sense to speak of object constancy as the goal of the newborn child's gradual comprehension of the coherence and the continuity of what he perceives. It makes sense within a theory of sexual energy called libido to speak of a growing capacity to "cathex" the image of a comprehensively perceived person and thus to become able to love. And it makes sense to describe with clinical shorthand as "object loss" the various deficiencies or regressions which make it impossible

---

* I owe to Gerald Holton a number of suggestive references to Einstein's meditations on the nature of his mathematical inspiration. It is said that Einstein was not yet able to speak when he was three years old. He preferred communing with building blocks and jigsaw pieces. Later (in 1945) he wrote to Jacques Hadamard: "Taken from a psychological viewpoint, this combinatory play seems to be the essential feature in productive thought—before there is any connection with logical construction in words or other kinds of signs which can be communicated to others."⁷ And, again: "Man seeks to form for himself, in whatever manner is suitable for him, a simplified and lucid image of the world (*Bild der Welt*), and so to overcome the world of experience by striving to replace it to some extent by this image. That is what the painter does, and the poet, the speculative philosopher, the natural scientist, each in his own way. Into this image and its formation he places the center of gravity of his emotional life, in order to attain the peace and serenity that he cannot find within the narrow confines of swirling personal experience."⁸

for a person to maintain either a cognitive sense of another person's wholeness or the capacity to wholly love and accept the love of other persons. All this describes the conditions for, but it neither explains nor guarantees that interplay by which the growing person and those attending him are capable of maintaining and expanding the mutuality of "basic education."*

Today, I think we would agree on three points. Cognitively seen the first *object wholeness* experienced by the infant must somehow coincide with the first *subject wholeness*. This means that the coherence and the continuity of the object world are a condition for the coherence and continuity of the "I" as observer. This joint sense of being both subject and object becomes the root of a sense of identity.

Secondly, if for its very "'basic education" the child depended on a mothering supported by a family and a community, so will it, all through life, depend on *equivalents* (and not on *substitutes*) of the constituents of the early mutuality. I would emphatically agree with Peter Wolff that on each stage of development a child is "identified by the totality of operations he is capable of"; and I would conclude that the early mother's equivalent in each later stage must always be the sum of all the persons and institutions which are significant for his wholeness in an expanding arena of interplay. As the radius of physical reach and of cognitive comprehension, of libidinal attachment and of responsible action—as all these expand, there will, of course, always be persons who are substitutes for the orginal mother. But that, as we know, can be a hindrance as well as a help, unless they themselves become part of that wider sphere of interaction which is essential for the increasing scope of what once was basic education. In our five-year-old's play construction we saw reflected, in addition to impulses, fantasies and familial themes, the teacher and the school environment in the widest sense of an encounter with what can be learned. But so will, in adolescence, the peer generation and the

* The questioning of terms easily becomes part of wider concern about conceptual habituation. What we have now heard of the importance of vision must make us wonder to what extent the "classical" psychoanalytic technique itself may have helped shape some of our concepts. For if vision is, indeed, the basic organizer of the sensory universe and if the beholding of one person's face by another is the first basis of a sense of mutuality, then the classical psychoanalytic treatment situation is an exquisite deprivation experiment. It may be the genius of this clinical invention that it systematically provokes the patient's "free" verbal associations at the expense of a visual word, which, in turn, invites the rushing in of old images seeking a healing mutuality with the therapist. But sooner or later every field must become aware of the extent to which its principal procedure codetermines the assumed nature of the observed and the terms decreed most appropriate to conceptualize that nature.

ideological universe become part of the arena which is the equivalent of the early mother. In adulthood the work world and all the institutions which comprise the procreative and productive actuality are part of the arena within which a person must have scope and leeway or suffer severely in his ego-functioning. Thus on each step what had been "in part" will now be recognized and interacted with in its wholeness, even as the person comes to feel recognized as an actor with a circumscribed identity within a life plan. In fact, unless his gifts and his society have on each step provided the adult with a semblance of an arena of free interplay, no man can hope to reach the potential maturity of (presenile) old age when, indeed, only the wholeness of existence bounded by death can, on occasion, dimly recall to him the quality of that earliest sensory matrix.

What we so far have vaguely called interplay can be made more specific by linking it with the problem of ritualization which was discussed on the last occasion when Konrad Lorenz and I served together on a symposium.[9] His subject then was the ontogeny of ritualization in animals, and mine, that in man. Julian Huxley, the chairman of that symposium, had years ago described as ritualization in animals such instinctive performances as the exuberant greeting ceremonials of bird couples, who, after a lengthy separation, must reassure each other that they not only belong to the same species but also to the same nest. This is a "bonding" procedure which, Huxley suggested, functions so as to *exclude ambiguity* and to facilitate unimpaired *instinctive* interplay. Lorenz, in turn, concentrated on the ritualizations by which some animals of the same species given to fighting matches make peace before they seriously harm each other. It was my task to point to the ontogeny of analogous phenomena in man. But with us, so I suggested, ritualization also has the burden of *overcoming ambivalence* in situations which have strong *instinctual* components (that is, drives not limited to "natural" survival), as is true for all important encounters in man's life. Thus the ontologically earliest ritualization in man, the greeting of mother and baby, adds to the minimum facial stimulation required to attract a baby's fascination (and eventually his smile) such motions, sounds, words, and smells as are characteristic of the culture, the class, and the family, as well as of the mothering person.

Konrad Lorenz, the foster mother of the goose child, Martina, has rightly gained fame for his ability to greet animals as well as humans in a bonding manner. In the present symposium you had the opportunity of seeing and hearing him demonstrate the lost-and-found game, which in German is called guck-guck da-da and in English, peek-a-boo. Let me call all these and similar phenomena in man *ritualized interplay*. This extends from the simplest habitual interaction to elaborate games, and, finally, to ornate rituals.* Today when so many ritualizations so rapidly lose their convincing power, it is especially important to remember that in this whole area of ritualized interplay the most horrible dread can live right next to the most reassuring playfulness. Little Martina was running and falling all over herself for dear survival when she pursued Konrad Lorenz, and any accidental interruption of the ritualized behavior by which animals do away with ambiguity can lead to murder. As to man, we only need to visualize again small children who cannot smile, or old persons who have lost faith, to comprehend both the singular power and the vulnerability of ritualized reassurance in the human situation.

Yet, what constitutes or what limits playful ritualization in man is as hard to define as play itself; maybe such phenomena as playfulness or youthfulness or aliveness are defined by the very fact that they cannot be wholly defined. There is a reconciliation of the irreconcilable in all ritualizations, from the meeting of lovers to all manner of get-togethers, in which there is a sense of choice and ease and yet also one of driving necessity: of a highly personalized and yet also a traditional pattern; of improvisation in all formalization; of surpise in the very reassurance of familiarity; and of some leeway for innovation in what must be repeated over and over again. Only these and other polarities assure that *mutual fusion* of the participants and yet also a simultaneous *gain in distinctiveness* for each.

Before moving on to adolescence, let me stop, in passing, to recount an experience which illustrates the relevance of all this for the school age. We recently visited a Headstart School in Mississippi, in an area where sniping nightriders and arson were then still expectable occurences whenever Blacks consolidated a new kind of community life with outside help. As visitors, we were called up to concentrate on how and by whom the children were taught and what they were learning. But we were equally struck by how these people had ritualized both "school" and "learning." With our academic eyes it was, in fact, not quite easy to know to what extent they were playing at being a school or actually were one. Obviously the arrangements for learning and singing together, but also those for eating and conversing constituted new roles under new conditions: to grow into the

---

* It specifically excludes, of course, the symptomatic "rituals" of isolated neurotics, as well as all derisive uses of the word *ritualization* as synonymous with repetitiveness and rigidification. All these, in fact, connote symptoms of deritualizations in our sense.

spirit of these roles seemed to be the heart of the matter. This, then, was ritualized interplay in the making; and only the whole milieu, the whole combination of building and equipment and of teaching mothers and of motherly teachers, of learning children and of helpful fathers and neighbors were a collective guarantee of the survival of what was being learned—whether, at this beginning, it was much or little. We could not help thinking of other schools, more easily certified on the basis of grim accomplishment where much is learned by inexorable method but often with little spirit. And yet, the final assimilation of what has been learned would always seem to depend on any "school's" cultural coherence with a growing environment.

The life of all schooling depends on all this; but so does the fate of the children who soon will enter the stage of adolescence—the stage when the young themselves must begin to offer each other traditional ritualizations in the form of spontaneous improvisations and of games—and this often on the borderline of what adults would consider the license of youth: will they then have learned to be playful and to anticipate some leeway of personal and social development?

Children cannot be said or judged to be "acting" in a systematic and irreversible way, even though they may, on occasion, display a sense of responsibility and a comprehension of adult responsibility which astonish us. Young people, on the other hand (as we realize in our time more than ever before), are apt to continue to play and to play-act in ways which may suddenly prove to have been irreversible action—even action of a kind which endangers safety, violates legality, and, all too often, forfeits the actor's future. And, in recent years, youth closer to adulthood has begun on a large scale to usurp responsibility and even revolutionary status in the arena of public action. This had resulted in lasting consequences even where the action itself may not have been much more than a dare or a prank on a stage of imagined power. Never before, then, has it been more important to understand what is happening in that wide area where juvenile play-acting and historical action meet.

The return in adolescence of childlike and childish behavior in the midst of an increasing anticipation of and participation in adulthood has been treated in unnumerable textbooks. They point to the impulsivity of sexual maturation and of the power of the aggressive equipment and yet also to the vastly expanded cognitive horizon. There is the intensity of peer-group involvement at all costs, a search for inspiration (now often forfeited to drugs), and yet also the desperate need (yes, an ego need) for an ideologically unified universe sanctioned by leaders who would make both freedom and discipline meaningful. To all this, I have added the discussion of identity—and of fidelity. In my book such postadolescent "virtue" is meant to represent a minimum evolutionary requirement rather than a maximized ideal.* Actually the formulation of such successive virtues was intended to follow the clinical formula (quoted in Konrad Lorenz's paper) of our lamented friend Donald Hargreaves: "What is the normal survival function of the process here disturbed?" In other words, I have emphasized fidelity because I think I have observed the fateful deficit in ego-strength resulting from the absence of such commitments as would permit youth to anchor its readiness for loyalty in social reality; and the equally fateful deficit in meaningful social interplay resulting from a state of society in which old fidelities are being eroded. I would, therefore, follow Konrad Lorenz in asserting that all through man's socio-genetic development, rites and rituals have attempted to attract and to invest that fidelity. Where and when both generations can participate in them with affective and cognitive commitment, these rites, indeed, are performing "functions analogous to those which the mechanisms of inheritance perform in the preservation of the species." Today, as we all agree, a deep and worldwide disturbance exists in this central area of ritualized interplay between the generations.

But let me again take recourse in an observation which every reader can match with variations from his own experience. A few years ago I was invited to attend a confrontation between the trustees and the students of a great university which, months before, had been one of the first to undergo what for a while became obligatory crises on a number of campuses: occupation of the administration's citadel and "liberation" of captive documents; brutally effective police intervention followed by a rapidly spreading student strike; a confused arousal of the faculty; and finally a widespread bewilderment and depression on the part of almost all concerned, including the most learned and the most politically adept minds.

At this meeting there were old and wealthy men, the trustees; there were learned men and guests like me; there were some students (however selected); and there were specialists in group meetings who lent a certain technical expertise to what could have been a natural mixture of reticence and spontaneous confrontation. After a few days of

---

* I must repeat this in view of such well-meant pictorial presentations of my stages of life as that of the Sunday *Times* of New York, where the successive virtues were posed by models who, indeed, look "virtuous" in a class-determined and even racist way: blond and blue-eyed, healthy and well kempt, and obviously brought up on a mental health food.

plenary speeches and more or less strained small group discussions, the students decided to present their case in their own way and to confront the trustees with an improvisation. The setting was a kind of amphitheater. One young man with long blond hair played a leading part; he had the words *Jesus Saves* printed in strong colors on his sweat shirt. He exhorted the elders to "give in gracefully" to certain nonnegotiable demands. Another young man, having embraced the first in brotherliness, took him by the arm and led him before some of the men of the Establishment, one by one. Pointing to the flaming motto on his friend's sweat shirt, he asked these men whether the inscription meant anything to them—and what had they done recently for their neighbors? Now, there are probably few groups of men who (in the light of their community's standards of charity) have done more for their "neighbors," both openly or privately, than have some trustees of our colleges. But, of course, the students had intended to confront them with their sins against the university's actual neighbors in the poor housing areas surrounding the campus and owned by the university. And they made it clear that they did not expect answers other than confessions of guilt. The old men, in turn, tried desperately to understand, because that was what they had come for. The situation became extremely tense, some students themselves (as they said later) beginning to feel like "freaks." Some faculty and some visitors began to show bitter annoyance.

A scene such as this leaves the viewer in doubt as to whether he is witnessing a theatrical improvisation, a mocking demonstration, or, indeed, an act of religious ritualization. To me, it was all of this and I said so: there were ceremonial fragments assembled in a manner half-mocking and half-deadly serious, flaunting as well as protesting such themes as brotherly love, charity, and sacrifice. But what had kept the performance from coming off was a failure of ethical nerve; the students had, with total righteousness, demanded that everyone should admit his sins except themselves, thus using Jesus to mock the elders; a mere turnabout of punitiveness, however, could never lead to a meaningful covenant.

I saw in this act (even/and) just where it failed, a combination of themes for which our time must find new forms, whether or not the leaders and organizers of such events consciously intend such renewal. The students, in fact, had succeeded (at the price of taking chances with their own credibility) to elucidate an overweening problem; they had played with a ritual fire which youth alone cannot possibly contain in a new universal form, and which in changing times can emerge only from a joint adulthood willing to take chances with new roles and that means: to play where it counts.

Let me now turn to a historical example. One of the most noteworthy revolutionary ritualizations of recent times has been the founding of the Black Panther Party—noteworthy in our context as an illustration of youthful political imagination on the very border of disaster. Such ritualization can go to the core of history, whether it "succeeds" or not; it is successful if it makes an unforgettable point and if it has the flexibility to go on from there.

Much of the Panthers' history has happened in the dark of the ghetto as well as in that legal twilight which confuses and scares the "law-abiding." Yet, there is no denial of a certain genius in the translation of values which Huey P. Newton (he was twenty-two years old at the time) and Bobby Seale displayed when they cast themselves and other young blacks in totally new roles, and this at a time when black youth in this country needed new images of dignity and of heroism. The fact that this new image included gun-carrying in public seemed revolting to many, while it is, in fact, a traditional historical stance in formerly exploited and belittled minorities: the autonomous man with his own gun, a man ready to use it both as a symbol and as a weapon for the defense of his and his people's dignity—this stance has been true of the first American revolutionaries as well as in the radically different contexts of the modern Jews and the Diaspora,* and the erstwhile British Indians, all youths whom successful revolutions are apt to forget. Sometimes, there is a book involved as well as a gun: a book which testifies both to tradition and to the power of literacy. In Newton's case, it was a law book such as that found on the street on the night in Oakland when a policeman (himself only twenty-three years old) lost his life in a scuffle never clearly reconstructed. Newton survived and prevailed through years of solitary confinement with a healthy body and with undaunted stature. The image he created was based on the usurpation of the black American of the oldest right of all (other) Americans (a right engraved on the imaginations of our young and the young abroad by way of Western movies), namely to bear arms in the creation of a semblance of legality in an area not yet defined in its traditionalities.

* Eldridge Cleaver at one time acknowledged this parallel by saying that "psychologically" black people in America had "precisely the same outlook" as Eastern European Jews had under Theodor Herzl (*New Outlook*, December 1970).

Originally young Newton not only insisted on the traditional legality of the arming of citizens, but also attempted to sanction it with a new uniform and a discipline which, I think, even Gandhi might have acknowledged (if with some sadness) as a necessary step toward a nonviolent approach—necessary for the simple reason that he who would not know how to use a gun both well and with restaint would not know how and when not to use it. But Newton, in addition to protesting dramatically the negative identity of his own people as the meek and helpless victims of the lynch law and its daily ramifications, established as the enemy of his people the very uniformed men who had become to them representatives of a lawless law employed to protect usurped privilege rather than legality and to punish powerlessness as much as illegality. Thus he attempted to turn the very image of the protectors of such law into a negative identity, namely, that of victimizers of the poor. The Black Panthers, then, are of interest precisely because, according to Newton's intent, this original "violence" was to be contained in a new code of discipline.

Revolutionary activity, however, is always beset with the dilemma of defining who and what is the law, and what disruptive act, when, and where, is political rather than criminal. There may be also the proud and mocking creation of a new "species," as attested to by the very party name, which, in the case of the Panthers, is that of an animal said to be ferocious primarily in defense, and the relentless and publicist verbal weapon of calling men of the "legitimate" police force "pigs." Such debasement of the opponent is a moral violence which not only can arouse murderous hate in the defamed, it can also become a retrogressive stance in the defamer. In the American Black, of course, such defamation is grounded more than in any other social group, both in a common history of daily and total defenselessness (or what Newton refers to as the "truly oppressed") and in an explosive folk language long the only outlet for in-turned aggression—and in fact used with mocking as well as murderous abandon against other Blacks. The original imagery of the young leaders of the Black Panther movement (and I am talking about these origins of the movement and not about the tedious stance of its propagandistic habituation) surely contained, therefore, the possibility of creating a new set of roles, which often may have appeared to be all too grandiosely staged, but which did link past and future by recapitulating historical images in a radically new setting. True, certain titles of command seemed rather florid in the absence of an assured body of followers; but it must be remembered that revolutionary language—at total risk to itself—always challenges history to confirm what has already been claimed as certain. This is, of course, compounded where the revolutionaries are young, for youth and revolution both play with that theater of action where personal conversion and radical rejuvenation confirm each other, to the point that history's agreement is taken for granted. And sometimes, history assents. Our black revolutionaries differ from others in that they are not rebelling against a father generation. Their symbol of the Establishment is "the man"; yet, both examples given remind us to look for the adult counterplayers in attempted ritualizations demanding new kinds of generational transfer. And there we often find glaring vacancies in the cast required for the fulfillment of the script—vacancies impossible to fill by excitable police or by uncomfortable judges.

This is the "gap," then; Konrad Lorenz would convince us that it exists not only because of a combination of historical and technological changes, but because of a misdevelopment of evolutionary proportions. He reminds us of the pseudotribal character of much of the present-day rebellion; and to him the widespread and truly "bizarre distortions of cultural behavior" represent a new "infantilism" and a regression to a primitivity which he considers analogous to a "disturbance of the genetic blueprint." Looking at revolutionary youth from the point of view of an evolutionary ethologist, apparently he feels that humanity has reached a critical point when the changes in social norms necessary within the period between generations have begun to "exceed the capacity of the pubertal adapting mechanisms."

Lorenz introduces into the discussion a term which I used at the London symposium where I drew attention to the phenomenon of cultural psuedospeciation—meaning the tendency of human groups to behave as if they were *the* chosen species. Lorenz discusses the matter vividly:

In itself, it is a perfectly normal process and even a desirable one. . . . There is, however, a very serious negative side to it: pseudo-speciation is the cause of war. . . . If the divergence of cultural development has gone far enough, it inevitably leads to the horrible consequence that one group does not regard the other as quite human. In many primitive languages, the name of the tribe is synonymous with that of man—and from this point of view it is not really cannibalism if you eat the fallen warriors of the hostile tribe! Pseudo-speciation suppresses the instinctive mechanisms normally preventing the killing of fellow members of the species while, diabolically, it does not inhibit intra-specific aggression in the least.

Before coming to the implications of pseudospeciation for youth and adulthood, however, let me ask what importance it may have for the problem of play. In the animal world, obviously the play of the young is linked with the adaptation of the species to a section of the natural environment. The play of the human child, however, must orient him within the possibilities and the boundaries first of what is imaginable and possible, and then to what is most effective and most permissible in a cultural setting. One of the playing child's tasks, then, is to try out some role pretensions within what he gradually learns is his society's version of reality and to become himself within the roles and techniques at his disposal. No wonder, then, that man's play takes place on the border of dangerous alternatives and is always beset both with burdening conflicts and with liberating choices.

At the same time, however, human play as well as adult ritualizations and rituals seem to serve the function of adaptation to the "pseudo" aspects of human "reality," for, as I will point out in some detail later, man, in addition to making gigantic strides in learning to know nature and the uses it can be put to, has . . . striven to maintain prejudged assumptions concerning the ordained excellence of particular versions of man. Thus, his playful imagination not only does serve all that is and could be but also is forced to endow that which, so he is clearly taught, must be if he is to be judged sane and worthy. Youthful rebellion always attempts to create new leeway for new and potential roles in such assumed realities; but the very condition of pseudospeciation has made man's playfulness a matter both of freedom and of bondage, both of enhanced life and of multiplied death.

I have attempted to illustrate the way in which youthful play-acting and the assumption or usurpation of historical roles can border on each other. But we must now account for the fact that new ritualizations are, indeed, apt to miscarry because of the "horrible fact that the hate which the young bear us is tribal hate." And, indeed, it seems that the shift in the overall ecological and technological conditions of mankind has led, at least within the orbit of the American industrial world culture (which includes the World War II enemies of the United States), to a new grouping of pseudospecies: on one side all the young people across the borders of former empires and on the other the whole "old" generation.

It is obvious enough that the young reject, above all, the insignia and the attitudes which have marked their victimization and heroification as soldiers serving one of the pseudospecies extant now. Because they carry this protest literally on the sleeve, we can now add to the subjects to be reviewed the ritual importance of human *display*, for we are reminded of the prominence, in all of classical warfare, of the resplendent uniforms, topped by animal plumage, which was intended to unite and divide the young men of the world into warriors serving either the right and godly or the wrong and evil species: that the display of physical insignia signifying human pseudospeciation imitate those of animal speciation is only too obvious. And it begins to make sense that the rebellious youth of today is displaying, instead, an impressive array of self-contradicting insignia, often mocking all uniformity by mixing fragments of military uniforms (and even of flags) with the ornaments of relaxed brotherhood. For youth attempts to create not only new arenas for involvements and commitments, but also such new types of heroes as are essential to the emergence of a whole "human being" representative of mankind itself—if and when the old have abrogated their pseudospecies, or have been destroyed. In the meantime, youth often seems to feel that it can enforce basic changes only by mockingly insistsing on a moratorium without end and an unlimited arena of its own, and it is often only with drugs that they can aver the remaining boundaries and simulate a free territory within. This is a state of affairs open to all kinds of group retrogressions as well as personal regressions.* But, then, adolescent regressions always have been, to some extent, semideliberate recapitulations of childhood fantasy serving the adaptive purpose of reviving what infantile playfulness was sacrificed to the established order for use on new ideological frontiers. Similarly, large-scale historical retrogressions often seem to be semideliberate attempts to invoke the revolutions of the past in the name of a future revolution as yet neither defined nor localized nor fixed in time. But the extremes noted here may be necessary aspects of shift, the outcome of which can only be appraised when it will be clear where such playful trends combine with the discipline and the competence necessary for sustained change.

If one accepts the theory of a shift from the pseudospecies mentality to an all-human one (and this is the hopeful aspect on which Konrad Lorenz and I would agree), one may well see in the radical display

---

* In a paper on dissent, I have offered a topology of such semideliberate retrogression, relating them to the stages of life and thus indicating both their potentially prophetic and their potentially dangerous significance for the individuals involved.[10]

of youth an upheaval necessary for an elemental regrouping which transvaluates past ideals of excellence and heroism in the service of a more universal speciation. To be sure, much horrible hate and much resultant paralysis is thus transferred to the intergenerational struggle where it appears to be hopelessly raw and untrained in comparison to the age-old stance and stamina of uniformed and disciplined military behavior. This probably is the cause of occasional enactments of totally "senseless" cruelty and of dramatic murder for the sake of a vindictive illusion of extinguishing the established.

But we may well remind ourselves of two momentous developments characteristic of the other, the adult side of playing history. The first is the fact that adult man, with the help of the most creative expansion of scientific and organizational leeway (remember Einstein's playfulness), has created a world technically ready to eliminate mankind in one instant for the sake of one nation or another that cannot stop playing empire. Is it any wonder that some of the most romantic and the most destructive behavior in modern youth seems to mock us by anticipating the day when the nuclear holocaust *has* occurred?

The second fact is the disintegration of paternalistic dominance, both in familiar relations and in the "minds of man." For this again we blame primarily the antipaternal attitude of the young. Following Freud we have obediently persisted in referring to the origins of the rebellious complex in childhood as the Oedipus Complex. But (as Dr. Piers has also pointed out in these symposia) we have thus immortalized as inescapable only the behavior of the son Oedipus, who unknowingly slew his father as the Oracle had predicted, while we have paid little attention to the fact that this father had such faith in the Oracle's opaque announcement and in his own interpretation of it, that he was willing to dispose of his son. But maybe Laius did only more openly and more dramatically what may be implicit in circumcisions, puberty rites, and "confirmations" of many kinds. As a prize for certified adulthood, the fathers all limit and forestall some frightening potentialities of development dangerous to "the system." And they all strive to appropriate the new individual for the pseudospecies, marking and branding him as potentially dangerous, initiating him into the prescribed limits of activities, inducting him into a preferred service, and preparing him for being sacrificed in holy wars. Maybe they only underscore ritually what human development and the structure of human society accomplish anyway. For after having played at a variety of choices, most adults submit to so-called reality, that is, a consolidation fo established fact, of acquired methods, of defined roles, and of overweening values. Such consolidation is deemed necessary not only for a style of acting and interacting, but, above all, for the bringing up of the next generation of children. They, it is hoped, will, from their childhood play and their juvenile role experimentation, move right into the dominant means of production and will invest their playfulness and their search for identity in the daily necessity to work for the higher glory of the pseudo-species.

Today, Laius and Oedipus face one another in a different confrontation. For even as the youth of divergent countries begin to look, talk, and feel alike—and this whether they are rebelling against industrial civilization or are, in fact, rapidly learning the prerequisite skills—so does the older generation appear to become more and more alike and stereotyped. For they impersonate a new and universal type, the efficient member of an organized occupation or a profession, playing free and equal while being at the mercy of mass-produced roles, of standardized consumership, and of rampant bureaucratization. But all these are developments which, in fact, take the play out of work—and this not (or not only) because of a Calvinistic choice to separate the two for the sake of righteousness, but because it can't be helped. And this seems to be the message of much of the mockery of the young, that if there must be defined roles, it may be better to go on playing at choosing them than to become their ready puppets.

A concluding section on play in adulthood can only be an opening section for another, a future essay. For here we enter both the twilight of what is called "reality" and the ambiguities of the word *play*—and these two assuredly are related to each other. Even as man protests the pure truth just because he is the animal who can lie—and pretend to be natural—so he strives to be in tune with hard reality just because he so easily falls for illusions and abstractions. And both truth and reality are at issue when man must define what he means when he says he is playing—or not playing.

The poet has it that man is never more human than when he plays. But what must he do and be, and in what context, to be both adult and playful; must he do something in which he feels again as if he were a playing child, or a youth in a game? Must he step outside of his most serious and most fateful concerns? Or must he transcend his everyday condition and be "beside himself" in fantasy, ecstasy, or "togetherness"?

Maybe an epigenetic view makes it unnecessary to categorize so sharply. The adult once was child and a youth. He will never be either again; but neither will he ever be without the heritage of those former states. In fact, I would postulate that, in order to be truly adult, he must on each level renew some of the playfulness of childhood and some of the sportiveness of the young. As we have seen, the child in his play and games as well as the young person in his pranks and sports and forays into politics, protected as they both are, up to a point, from having their play-acting "count" as irreversible action, nevertheless are dealing with central concerns both of settling the past and of anticipating the future. So must the adult, beyond playful and sportive activities specified as such, remain playful in the center of his concerns and concerned with opportunities to renew and increase the leeway and scope of his and his fellow man's activities. Whatever the precursors of a specifically adult playfulness, it must grow with and through the adult stages even as these stages can come about only by such renewal. But here we are faced with a threefold dilemma: the adult's marked inner separation (repression and all) from much of his childhood; the limitations of adolescent identity development in terms of available roles; and a certain intrinsic intolerance in adult institutions to the renewal of the identity crisis. Adult institutions want to ban the turmoil of youth even as they want to banish the thought of decline and death. This leaves adulthood in a position of double defensiveness and with a need to bolster the boundaries of what to a given generation of adults seems "real."

"Creative" people know this, and the poet Frost said it. In an encounter with two tramps who see him chopping away at some wood and remind him of the fateful division of work and play, he intones:

> But yield who will to their separation
> My object in living is to unite
> My avocation and my vocation
> As my two eyes make one in sight.
> Only where love and need are one,
> And the play is work for mortal stakes,
> Is the deed ever really done
> For heaven and the future's sakes.[11]

We may for the moment ignore the fact that the men thus addressed were looking for work; we know that one man's play and work may be another's unemployment. But taking Frost's creativity as a measure, we may add to his formulation the postulate that the adult, in combining vocation and avocation, creates leeway for himself while creating leeway for those within his scope of mutuality.

At the beginning of this essay, I compared a child's solitary play construction with the function of a dramatic performance in adulthood: in both, a theme and a conflict, dominant in the "big" world, are meaningfully condensed into a microsphere and into a spectacle and a speculum, a mirror of inner and outer conditions. (The stage play is a tragedy, where a representative person is shown as one who can envisage greater freedom for his time and age but finds that he has forfeited it for lack of inner and outer *Spielraum*.) The dimly lit theater thus deals with the reflection and individual fate of all those areas of public action which occur in "all the world," in the light of day. But if man, as pointed out, calls these spheres "theaters," "spectacles," and "scenarios" one wonders sometimes which is metaphorical for what. For man endows such spheres of highest reality, too, with a ceremonial and procedural aura which permits him to get engaged with a certain abandon, with intensified loyalty, and often with increased energy and efficiency, but also with a definite sacrifice of plain good judgment. Some of these special spheres are endowed with rituals in super-real halls, be they cathedrals, courts, or castles. But their hypnotic power as a visionary sphere transcends all locality and institutionalization; we may think here of the monarchy or the presidency, of the law courts or the seats of government; all these, while denoting an obligation of superhuman excellence, are also apt to cover, with everybody's connivance, a multitude of contradictions and pretenses accepted as the "rules of the game." Any observing visitor to a legislative chamber or a chief executive's mansion will not escape an occasional eerie sense of unreality in such factories of decision which must determine irreversible shifts in what will seem compellingly real to so many, and in what to generations to come will seem worth living, dying, and killing for—remember the Iron Curtain! Most fateful for mankind as a species (we cannot say this too often) is the tendency to redivide the political scene in such a way that those "on the other side" suddenly appear to be changed in quality, reduced to statistical items and worthy only of "body counts." However, the aura of some (if not all) of these spheres is being diminished in our very time by the production through the media of new spheres of vision, with their strange interplay of service, truth, and business. Some such spheres, as the "national scene," or the "forum of public opinion," or the "arena of politics," are also being studied in their major dimensions by social science; but we know as yet little about their dynamic influences on personality, on identity, and, indeed, on sanity—either in individuals or in cliques, in organized groups or in the masses. The fact is that such phenomena, in turn, can only be studied by "fields" of approach and "schools" of thought and by theoretical systems which themselves fascinate by their ability to organize appearances and to make visible the factual truth. But science, at least, perseveres in an in-built critique of science itself as well as of the scientist; and this in terms increasingly accessible to all "species" of men. If factuality is the soul of all search for reality, then mankind is on the way to agreeing to a joint reality; and if truth can only emerge from an all-human actuality, all men may, someday soon, be "in touch" with each other.

I am suggesting for a future occasion, then, that we take a new good look not only at those occasions when adults claim that they are playing like children, or play-acting on the legitimate stage, but also at such other occasions when they insist with deadly righteousness that they are playing for "real" stakes and yet, sooner or later, appear to have been role-playing puppets in imaginary spheres of "necessity."

If at the beginning of this paper I made a "leap" from play construction to theater, let me now make one back from adult reality to infancy. Could it not be that all these spheres have a place in adult man's life equivalent to that visual sphere which in the very first year of life provides, all at once, an integrated sensory universe, a mutuality with a maternal person, and a beginning of inner order, and thus provides the basic leeway for growth, action, and interaction? I do not wish to overdo this; in adulthood such visualized spheres obviously overlap with concrete areas of established power and organized technique which have their own rationale of continuity and growth. Yet they all share in that quality of vision which not only renders experience vastly more comprehensible, but also provides man with collective and individual affirmations of an emotional kind. And, indeed, the vision is often attended to by some kind of goddess (made visible as Nike in graceful flight, or Freedom baring her breast to the storm of revolution, "blind" Justice, or somber and selfless Truth, not to speak of "smiling" Success) which, indeed, gives recognition in turn for having been recognized. These visions, it must be repeated, can bring out the best in man as they encourage, with a greater leeway, courage and solidarity, imagination and invention. The human tragedy has been and is that the highest of these goddesses are overshadowed by the demands of the pseudospecies, which eventually employs even the most heroic deeds and the most sincere gains in knowledge, for the exploitation and enslavement, the denigration and annihilation, or, at any rate, the checkmating of other "kinds" of men. As any visual order must always discriminate as well as abstract, it is hard for man not to make himself more real and his world more comprehensible without envisaging others as expendable or nonexistent—even eight hundred million Chinese behind a bamboo curtain.

And then, there are the great adults who are adult and are called great precisely because their sense of identity vastly surpasses the roles foisted upon them, their vision opens up new realities, and their gift of communication revitalizes actuality. In freeing themselves from rigidities and inhibitions they create new freedoms for some oppressed categories of men, find a new leeway for suppressed energies, and give new scope to followers, who, in turn, feel more adult for being sanctioned and encouraged. The great, we say, are "gifted" with genius; but, of course, they often must destroy, too, and will seem evil to those whom they endanger, or whom they exclude.

Freud, in freeing the neurotics of his repressed era from the onus of degeneracy, invented a method of playful communication called "free association" which has taught man (way beyond the clinical setting) to play back and forth between what is most conscious to him and what has remained unverbalized or become repressed. And he has taught man to give freer play to fantasies and impulses which, if not realized in sexual foreplay or "sublimated" in actuality, help only to narrow his *Spielraum* to the point of explosions in symptomatic actions.

But as Freud "took morality for granted," he also treated adulthood and reality as matters on which all enlightened men would agree. Yet, I think, he made the point that only when man has faced his neurotic isolation and stagnation is he free to let his imagination and his sense of truth come up against the existential dilemmas which transcend passing realities.

Marx, it is interesting to recall, spoke of a *coming* adulthood of the species. At the celebration of Marx's 150th birthday in Trier, Robert Tucker pointed out that "self-realization, or becoming fully human, was not for Marx a problem that an individual person could solve on his own. It could only be solved within the framework of the self-realization of the species at the end of history."[12] Marx referred to history both as an *Entfremdungsgeschichte* that made of man an alienated creature, and as a *growth process of the human race*, an *Entstehungsakt*; only a kind of rebirth could overcome the submersion of the aesthetic production "according to the laws of beauty" and the deadening of all playfulness by unfree labor. Tucker suggested that we may today well be in a final "maturation crisis." "If so," he added, "the most serious aspect of the crisis is the . . . tendency of most people and even the leaders of nations to assume that no great change is called for, that we immature humans are already grown up."

Now, a few years later, it is obvious that this awareness, while maybe not yet accessible to "most people" and their leaders, has spread at least to the point where the young people deny that the older ones have grown up. In fact, there is a pervasive suspicion of the whole idea of growing up; and there is also an increased awareness of history, which among other things teaches that the revolutionary leeway gained yesterday can become the obsession and the suppression of today, and this for reasons immanent in greatness itself as well as in adulthood itself. If great men inspire vast changes with a creative playfulness both driven and (necessarily) destructive, their followers must consolidate change, which means to take the risk out of it. Neither the task of a Marxian critique of unconscious "historical" motivation nor the Freudian one of an inner enslavement to the immaturity both of impulse and of conscience can be said to be accomplished in any foreseeable future.

But the method of yesterday can also become part of a wider consciousness today. Psychoanalysis can go about defining its own place in history and yet continue to observe its traditional subject matter, namely the symptoms of repressions and suppressions—including their denial. It can study successive re-repressions in relation to historical change; there can be little doubt but that our enlightened age has set out to prove Freud wrong by doing openly and with a vengeance what he said were secret desires, warded off by inhibitions. We can learn to find out how we have contributed to such developments by our exclusive reliance (also culturally and historically determined) on the "dominance of the intellect" which often made the acceptance of psychoanalytic theory and vocabulary the measure of a man's adaptation. We know now (and the study of play confirms us in this) that the comprehension of Freud's *Wirklichkeit* must go beyond one of its meanings, namely reality, and include that of actuality.[13] For if reality is the structure of facts consensually agreed upon in a given stage of knowledge, actuality is the leeway created by new forms of interplay. Without actuality, reality becomes a prison of stereotypy, while actuality always must retest reality to remain truly playful. To understand this fully we must study for each stage of life the interpenetration of the cognitive and the affective as well as the moral and the instinctual. We may then realize that in adulthood an individual gains leeway for himself, as he creates it for others: here is the soul of adult play.

In conclusion, we must take note of another "gap" in our civilization which only partly coincides with the generational one. It is that between a grim determination to play out established and divisive roles, functions, and competencies to their bitter ends; and, on the other hand, new kinds of group life characterized by a total playfulness, which simulates vast imagination (often drug-induced), sexual and sensual freedom, and a verbal openness often way beyond the integrative means of individuals, not to speak of technological and economic realities. In the first area, that of habituated pragmatism, leading individuals make a grim effort at pretending that they are in full command of the facts and by no means role-playing—a claim which in fact gives them a vanishing credibility. The playful crowd, on the other hand, often seems to play all too hard at playing and at pretending that they are already sharing a common humanity, by-passing those techincal and political developments which must provide the material basis for "one world." But man is a tricky animal; and adults playing all too hard at role-playing or at simulating naturalness, honesty, and intimacy may end up being everybody and yet nobody, in touch with all and yet not close to anybody.

Yet, there are also signs that man may indeed be getting ready to renounce his claims on the ancient prerogatives of special pseudo-species, such as the abuse of others and the waste of resources in the environment and in inner life. Psychoanalysis, at this juncture, must remain vigilant in regard to the anxieties and rages aroused where a wider identity will endanger existing styles of instinctuality and identity and traditional visions of morality and reality.

But we must always also be receptive to new forms of interplay; and we must always come back to the children and learn to recognize the signs of unknown resources which might yet flourish in the vision of one mankind on one earth and its outer reaches.

Notes

¹ Erik H. Erikson, *Childhood and Society*, 2nd ed. (New York: W. W. Norton, 1963).
² In *The Man-Made Object*, ed. Gyorgy Kepes (New York: Braziller, 1966).

[3] Ascanio Condivi, *Vita di Michelangiolo Buonarotti* (Rome, 1553). Here translated by Alice Wohl.

[4] Charles Seymour, *Michelangelo's David: A Search for Identity* (Pittsburgh: University of Pittsburgh, 1967), 7.

[5] I Corinthians 13:12.

[6] Creighton Gilbert, *Complete Poems and Selected Letters of Michelangelo* (New York: McGraw-Hill, 1965), 5.

[7] Jacques Hadamard, *The Psychology of Invention in the Mathematical Field* (Princeton: Princeton University, 1945), 142–43.

[8] Quoted in Holton, "On Trying to Understand Scientific Genius," *The American Scholar*, 41, 1 (Winter 1971/72).

[9] Erik H. Erikson, "A Discussion of Ritualisation of Behavior in Animals and Man," organized by Sir Julian Huxley, F.R.S., *Philosophical Transactions of the Royal Society of London*, Series B, 772, 251 (1966) 337–49.

[10] "Reflections on the Dissent of Contemporary Youth," *International Journal of Psychoanalysis* 51, 11 (1970).

[11] Robert Frost, "Two Tramps in Mud-Time."

[12] Robert Tucker, *The Marxian Revolutionary Idea* (New York: W. W. Norton, 1969), 215.

[13] Erik H. Erikson, *Insight and Responsibility* (New York: W. W. Norton, 1964), chap. 5.

III.
WAR
MEMORANDA

On Nazi Mentality (1940)

The so-called Canadian project for the study of German prisoners in Canada was initiated by the Committee for National Morale before the United States entered the war.

It will be remembered that the press early in this war reported on a new type of prisoner: an arrogant, unfeeling robot, who mechanically spouted Nazi ideology and on occasion rioted in obscene ways. The most recent of these news items concerned a former English brigadier general who had been court-martialed because, during the Battle of Flanders, he had struck two Nazi prisoners. "They spat on the floor, spat on my shoes, and then spat on me, and called me a bloody English swine."*

Naval intelligence data and personal communications from individual officers, while less sensational, nevertheless confirmed noteworthy attitudes on the part of German prisoners. A Canadian officer expressed it this way: "They all look alike; they all talk alike. It is impossible to know what they think. Today they swear that they are

Written for the Committee on National Morale (for the Coordinator of Information), 1940. Published here for the first time. Some of the other renowned participants on the Committee for National Morale were Gordon Allport, Gregory Bateson, Edwin Boring, Kurt Lewin, Margaret Mead, Gardner Murphy, and Henry A. Murray.
* New York Times, February 21, 1942.

Nazis; tomorrow that they are not. Both times they have the same bland facial expression."

Such attitudes were noted, derided, explained as a reflection of Nazi mentality but never studied and interpreted by students of personality.

The Committee for National Morale recognized that the study of available specimens of the future enemy's mentality was an essential preparation for total war—as essential as the study by military observers of mechanized warfare on the battlefronts. It, therefore, offered its services to the authorities concerned, both in the United States and in Canada. With their approval and active interest the necessary arrangements were made, and preparatory studies of documents undertaken.

The entry of the United States into the war has restricted the availability of Nazis for personal observation and has thus emphasized the soundness of the Canadian project itself. On the other hand, it may have altered the status of the original plan. This report puts our preparatory considerations at the disposal of whatever agency may not be entrusted with this work. Preparatory considerations, it will be realized, are a somewhat personal matter. They are determined by a worker's particular experiences and expectations. There will be no attempt to deny their tentative nature.

A Clinical Analogy

As the clinician looks back on Germany's defeat and its resurrection in Hitler's imagery, he is haunted by an analogy: It is as if the German nation as a whole could be likened to a not uncommon type of adolescent who turns delinquent. Gifted, ambitious, proud, he is at the same time possessed by wild drives, is immature in his social ideas, unsure of his ideals, and morbidly suggestible. During a period of rapid growth and strong aggressiveness he suffers a severe humiliation. He disavows his primitive tendencies and attempts to adjust abruptly to his neighbor's standards. This personality, however, is not ready to sustain the change; he "overadjusts." Nor is his "environment" decent or prudent enough to back him up. Adjustment becomes self-debasement. Anxiety within, disappointment without are the result. The adolescent finds that he has relinquished his old self without gaining a new one in his adjustment to the conflicting demands of his environment. As he begins to mistrust them, he mistrusts the values which he has just begun to share with them. At this point he meets a leader and a gang who proclaim that the adolescent is always right, that aggression is good, that conscience is an affliction, adjustment a crime. He throws off his conscience. He closes up against the people he has loved and the values he has recognized. There is only one goal: To be himself, even if there is little he can call self and even if this means social isolation and dependence on the gang and its leader. He is seduced into acts of defiance which he can justify before himself only by further acts of defiance. He must constantly act.

The analogy fades out when it comes to therapy. Germany's "environment," it is true enough, acted as do the relatives of a delinquent adolescent: They lost invaluable time in trying to decide whether to punish him or to love him more, to restrain him or give him rope, to ignore his "attention seeking" or to cater to it. But beyond this, Germany's direct neighbors could hardly be compared to an adult environment, unless one conceives of its diplomacy and strategy as overadult, senile.

The analogy, however, becomes almost reality if we apply it to the psychological mechanisms involved in the change of mind taking place in every German participant of the Nazi revolution. The adolescent defenses described have an affinity to the Führer's personality and to that of many of his sub-Führers. They explain some of the power of these people over German adolescents and over those numerous Germans who (as pointed out) never overcome a certain adolescent conflict.

We expect, then, to find among deeply indoctrinated Nazis: (1) adolescents; (2) men in whom a barely repressed adolescence was resurrected; (3) men who for economic or other reasons feel deeply enough for national socialism to sacrifice their potential individual maturity; (4) men who have become convinced that national socialism is successful, or at any rate not opposed by any potent enemy, and who on this basis try their best to live up to its adolescent imagery.

But to point to the elaboration in a cultural system of preadult potentialities does not mean to belittle it. Infantile and adolescent experiences are the psychological raw material which every human being brings to his culture. Every culture by child training and education makes a selection of infantile experiences and modes of acting and thinking; it favors some, suppresses others, and allows a third type to manifest itself only under special personal or social conditions. The adolescent potentiality is not less powerful than are other preadult potentialities. On the contrary, it is this very potentiality which ancient and modern adolescence rites have tried to suppress, to modify, or to sublimate. There are parallels so close between these rites and those of national socialism that in an anthropological interpretation Hitler can be said to lead the emancipation of the adolescent. So far in history the adolescent had to sacrifice solemnly some of his blood, some of his teeth, or a part of his genitals, or had to admit his sinfulness and bow his knee, in order to confirm his intention to become a man in his father's world. In Hitler's Germany he marches with his emancipated equals, led by a leader who never sacrificed his will to any father.

The acceptance of an adolescent imagery by a whole nation, however, does not mean that every single member of that nation can be suspected of having—as an individual—no more latent maturity, intelligence, and decency than does an adolescent. It means only that more mature traits are suspended or perverted beyond recognition in as far as the individual takes part in a powerful adolescent group response to common dangers, national or irrational.

Our first group alone–namely, the adolescent grown up under nazism—finds himself in complete inner harmony with the imagery of the Third Reich. He would rather die than relinquish this imagery. He probably will have to die.

The other groups, however, can be assumed to possess a tendency to identify with the values of the civilized world. Propaganda, police, prudence, and pride may keep this tendency in the unconscious and in hiding. But for some time, at least, it will remain a psychological reality. If one takes the viewpoint of evolution, one cannot see how it can ever disappear.

This latent reality, however, does not change the necessity to fight the Germans mercilessly until they are ready to envisage the advantages of Allied victory. In as far and as long as they fight with and for an adolescent imagery, they will expect and respect only powerful self-preservation on the part of their enemies; almost any words, at this time, would be understood as signs of weakness or as an attempt to repeat "Wilson's betrayal."

What will break down a delinquent adolescent within himself, and in a nation will bring about a break between "real" delinquent adolescents and potentially mature men, is the combination on the part of a superior power of proven outer strength and that inner strength called understanding.

As the clinician considers the possibility of our propagandists' getting in touch with these Germans, he can conclude with only the following—maybe quite impracticable—remarks. There is no use denying to Germans that the Third Reich is a magnificent realization of collective adolescent dreams for the sake of gang leaders. There is no use denying to ourselves that the common German man temporarily has identified himself with that cause and, at present, cannot visualize any other course. But as he is fought successfully, he should be told what the Allied world stands for.

For Wilsonian promises, however, of certain almost forgotten freedoms, the German common man at present has no stomach, no training, and no use. They lead him only to the conclusion that all governments produce empty lies, and therefore, he will do just as well to keep the homegrown variety.

It is the imagery of the family as the basis of cultural life which would be the greatest contrast with the Hitlerian imagery. Our propagandists should secure detailed data on episodes, processes, and statistics in Germany which endanger the family and subordinate old and young to the delinquent adolescent and his gang leader. They should present these arrogant and indifferent Germans with a cool picture of what German "world domination" would mean to the life of their children, based as it would be on eternal wars, i.e., on the eternal disruption of German family life. Biographic sketches of ordinary Germans as well as of German leaders, presented by way of radio and leaflet in serial form, would probably help formulate more clearly what German wit already attacks in isolated cases. Statistics could be presented to show the disintegration of the idea of the family in young people.

One should endeavor to dramatize the central role of the family in anything we have called culture on this earth so far. The point is to secure the facts and, without propagandistic pathos, to weave them into an impressive whole which will be before the eyes of some Germans at the moment when our world has proven itself strong enough to promise alternatives.

This propagandistic approach is suggested by our preliminary considerations. As we succeed in collecting firsthand data for the research project contemplated, we may be able to modify this approach and to suggest details with more assurance.

A Memorandum Concerning the Interrogation of German Prisoners of War (1943)

The Council on Intercultural Relations has asked me for a memorandum concerning the psychological study of German prisoners of war.

I am not acquainted with the organization and the methods of the United States Army and Navy Intelligence Services which deal with prisoners of war. I do not know, therefore, whether what I say agrees or conflicts with the present official policy.

Intelligence work in this field commonly has the purpose of eliciting from the prisoners:

1. *Military* facts
2. Data concerning the enemy's *morale*
3. Such knowledge of the prisoners as is necessary to maintain *discipline* among them

In addition, Nazi prisoners must be considered carriers of *indoctrination*; they are the only specimens available to American social and clinical scientists for the testing, by observation, of those innumerable theories of the *psychology of nazism* which have developed in this country and some of which will, for better or for worse, influence vital military and diplomatic decisions.

Written for the Committee on National Morale (for the Council on Intercultural Relations), 1943. Published here for the first time.

Nazi prisoners seem to be tough customers for both interrogators and internment administrators. I assume, however, that the extraordinary behavior of these prisoners has not changed this country's determination to abide by the rules of the Geneva Convention and to avoid methods which would give Germany cause to institute "equivalent" reprisals against American prisoners in German hands. Outlawed methods are, in the words of the Geneva Convention, "inhuman," "violent," and "insulting" ways of exerting pressure "to obtain information regarding the situation in their armed forces or in their country."

It is conceivable that for this very reason, intelligence agencies in this country would shy away from employing "psychiatric" or similar sinister-sounding approaches, which connote the use of hypnotic power or drugs. And yet clinical social psychology in this country has developed procedures which are far from being cruel, dangerous, or undignified and provide a technique which can be used in situations in which individuals and groups are not willing or are unable to reveal their thoughts and their knowledge in verbal communication.

In speaking of clinical social psychology, I have in mind the work of a group of American psychiatrists, psychologists, and sociologists who, during the last two decades, have applied the knowledge of psychiatry beyond its original field of individual pathological deviation to cultural and national differences and to the pathology of group life. In their original psychiatric observations, these observers have recognized that what the individual undergoing study answers in response to a specific question is only a fraction (and often the least revealing part) of what he gives away in his total bearing, in his facial expression, and in his gestures; in involuntary sounds, inflections, and grammatical deviations; in what he says about seemingly unrelated subjects; and in what he does or says after the questioning is over. In other words, they have learned to observe people under special conditions; to work with indirection where the direct approach is useless; and to employ patient observation where active-coercive methods are impractical.

It seems, therefore, that their experience should be valuable in a situation in which the subject of interrogation not only is unwilling to talk but is also protected by international law from being coerced to talk.

To analyze the situation, German prisoners of war are:
1. *Men*, of a certain *age*, condition of *health*, personality *type*, *family status*, *economic* and *educational* background, *religious* and *class* affiliation

2. *Reichs-Germans*, with a specific *regional* background
3. *Soldiers*, of a certain *rank*, in one *military category*
4. *National Socialists*, of varying *degrees of indoctrination*
5. In three standard situations:
   a. Recent capture
   b. Transportation
   c. Internment

Clinical social psychologists are obviously best equipped to evaluate the interaction of all these personal, national, and situational factors.

The situation of recent capture, for example, offers a specific dynamic situation which the clinical psychologist can define. It is a traumatic situation for the soldier—i.e., he suffers from mental shock. It is a conflict situation: His loyalty and his military oath are in opposition to his feeling of relaxation, of relief from danger, and of freedom from the accustomed supervision; hostility against and contempt of his captors are in opposition to his fear of and submissiveness to them; fear, suspicion, and caution in opposition to his wish to communicate, to speak his mind, to appease those who now have him in their power.

In the case of Germans, these universal conflicts are intensified by:
1. Their often fanatic, often studied contempt of their captors
2. Special training, which has prepared them for the more common methods of interrogation and warned them of the pitfalls of being interrogated
3. Their suspicion that Gestapo agents may be among them and even among their captors, ready to denounce them after the war if they do not show the contemptuous aloofness befitting Nazi soldiers.

It seems impossible that this intensified conflict, even if covered by extreme arrogance, should not lead, in every individual captive, to symptomatic behavior which would allow the clinical psychologist to separate "promising" from "useless" subjects and, at any rate, to make relevant observations concerning the Nazi mentality. In the state of humiliation, of fear, of the sudden lack of familiar supervision, what these prisoners do may, in some way, indicate the reactions to be anticipated when parts of Germany disintegrate. Then, one hears, there are those Germans, often of high rank, who throw off the whole burden of fear and fanaticism and open up (just as fanatically). Their personalities and their background should be studied clinically, for whatever motivated them to surrender psychologically may be latent in others who, if spotted, might easily be led to do the same.

Similarly, whole Nazi crews, teams, and units, when suddenly robbed of their group coherence, seem to reveal symptoms of pathological regression and of group disintegration. The rifts thus appearing, as well as the consequent spontaneous new clique formations, are apt to reveal some of the dynamic factors behind Nazi group psychology. Their analysis may suggest means to accelerate disintegration of Nazi morale.

Internment is an abnormal situation which causes its specific group phenomena and individual pathological reactions, summed up in the term *barbed wire disease*. One could argue that the just-captured or the long-confined Nazi is not a normal Nazi. All the more, however, can he be understood only by specialists such as clinical social psychologists, who have learned to take circumstantial distortions into account and to generalize from special cases. (The psychiatric patient, for example, is not a normal being, and still, since he has a special reason to be communicative, he will reveal psychological mechanisms which can then be detected, in less pathological forms, in less disturbed individuals. (The reservation Indian is not the "real" Indian, and still he serves, and must serve, for the study of Indian personality.) As a matter of fact, just because they are set aside from normal life, prison camps (those "cities of futility") are well-definable social situations, almost of experimental character. Nazis, then, will behave in this situation, both as prisoners and as Hitler-Germans: they will develop special forms of "barbed wire disease"—and special defenses against it. This should become obvious, not only in their relationship to their captors and guards but also in their attitudes toward one another and in their individual behavior. Suspicions and hostilities; cliques, friendships, and sexual attachments should be telling expressions of Nazi mentality.

As to the possible official status of clinical psychologists in interrogation and internment agencies, I do not know whether there is any objection to their being employed as administrators, interrogators, entertainers, instructors, guards, censors, etc. in such a way that their routine duties will permit them to make, to record, to discuss, and to abstract psychological observations. Be that as it may, I should like to point to one article in the Geneva Convention which could be interpreted as justifying the open presence of clinical psychologists as mental hygienists and psychiatric observers in clinical units on the front and in internment camps.

Article 4 of the convention says that "differences in treatment between prisoners are permissible . . . if such differences are based on . . . the physical or mental health . . . of those who benefit from them."

Since prisoners of war have a claim to the hygienic and therapeutic facilities offered by the interning country to its own soldiers, German prisoners should not be denied psychiatric attention in all those matters in which, according to this country's advanced methods, psychological factors play a role. From the list of those matters, not even persistent colds can be definitely excluded, much less sluggish digestions or run-down moods. If the clinical personnel chosen for this task partakes of the sociological orientation and the clinical methods of observation which characterize what I have defined as clinical social psychology, they will unavoidably make observations relevant both to the treatment of the prisoners and to the knowledge of Nazi psychology.

Their findings should, of course, be coordinated in field research stations, as well as in a central coordinating agency which will provide workers with further questions and suggestions and give results to the agencies entrusted with strategy and propaganda.

Finally, there is an angle to this matter which makes use of advanced clinical observation in internment camps an outright national necessity. Many American prisoners now in enemy hands will be in need of mental rehabilitation after their return. It is doubtful (as it was after the last war) whether the few medical men employed to take care of absolute necessities in our internment camps will have the time and the opportunity to study the various versions of this war's "barbed wire" symptoms with modern methods. It will be necessary to study what is available—i.e., the Nazi version (and the Japanese version) of these symptoms—in such a way that the generalizations derived have both specific value (for the understanding of Nazis) and general value (for the understanding of "barbed wire" symptoms in general). It must also be borne in mind that American soldiers returning from Nazi prison camps, in addition to being victims of internment proper, will have been the subjects of crude or subtle ideological propaganda. This will erect special problems of rehabilitation, calling for men trained in the psychiatric implications of indoctrination.

No better use can be made of our Nazi prisoners than to study them as extensively as practical, humane, and legal considerations will permit.

Comments on Hitler's Speech
of September 30, 1942
(1942)

To an observer who has always emphasized that Hitler's lack of taste, of logic, and of truth should not be used as arguments against the man as a propagandist; to one who has attempted to analyze the strong magic imagery hidden in Hitler's most illogical, obnoxious, and morbid statements, this Sportspalast speech contains welcome signs. The magic spell is being broken.

Hitler's performances are, of course, always a mixture of shrewd, planned, directed elements and of unplanned, impulsive, emotional ones. Goebbels lets him loose as a trainer does a tamed beast: with some instructions as to how to act, in accordance with the German propaganda strategy of the moment, but also with the knowledge that the beast can be relied upon to produce a certain (by now standardized) sequence of "wild" gestures which throw a singular magic spell over a German audience.

As pointed out in my paper,* this spell is based on a historically well-founded synthesis of the following beliefs and facts:

1. "Fate" has selected Hitler to be the first undefeated representative of the *German adolescent imagery*. He usurps the power of

Written for the Committee on National Morale (for the Council on Intercultural Relations), 1942. Published here for the first time.
* "Hitler's Imagery and German Youth." *Psychiatry*, (5 November 1942), 475–493.

the fathers but does not (as revolutionaries are apt to do), in the end, emulate their weaknesses.

2. In combining German romanticism with the least dreamy and most efficient German type—namely, the German soldier—he heals the split between the *spiritual* and the *militaristic* aspects of Germany's chauvinism.

3. This treatment is expressed, both spiritually and materially, in the blitzkrieg, which frees the Germans (a) from military-political encirclement and (b) from the old conflict between oversuggestibility to and stubborn defensiveness against the surrounding cultures.

The morale issue now is: If 1918 is not repeated, then it will cease to count. It will have been merely a trick of Fate, temporarily subservient to World Jewry. *A repetition of 1918*, however, *would make manifest Fate out of a lapse of history*. Hitler therefore has to convince himself, the German people, and Fate itself that there really are no parallels between 1917 and 1942. The mere thought of such a parallel would make it appear that all his tremendous successes served only to enlarge Germany's Middle European prison but have not broken it. Repetition would turn his victorious challenge into a final and definite proof of the (so hotly denied) war guilt and into an absolute confirmation of defeat. This, it seems to me, is the portent of his speech.

The background is the Sportspalast. Great popular successes were gained here, and here were made many boastful predictions which Fate chose to verify. Before Goebbels and Hitler enter the hall, Field Marshal *Rommel* takes a seat beside Field Marshal Keitel. He receives an ovation matched only by that later given to Hitler himself. It must be remembered that neither Keitel nor Rommel is an officer of the aristocratic caste. Furthermore, Rommel is probably the least compromised field marshal. Never having shared his African headquarters with the autodidact Hitler, and probably relatively independent in his decisions, he was the last German general to lead a campaign to the point where a final victorious thrust could be expected to hit the heart of the enemy's resistance. His fight "under Africa's sun" was a romantic symbol of the fact that German *encirclement* was broken and that the *lifeline* of the British Empire was in acute danger. And Rommel had been singled out by Churchill for a tribute in the House of Commons—a body of parliamentary critics to whose criticism Hitler is so amazingly sensitive. (Now that Rommel is defeated and the British lifeline, augmented by the United Nations lifeline, is reaching across the Atlantic and through the heart of Africa, have the shortwaves reminded the Germans of Rommel's appearance at the Sportspalast? German memory is short. The magic spell must be worn down by ceaseless reminders, finally causing an inescapable memory.)

Goebbels opens the meeting with a slip of the tongue. "In October and November 1942," he says (in September 1942), "the National Socialist movement entered the decisive phase of its struggle for power." He meant to say 1932, for in 1932 the National Socialist party, after having lost two million votes, regained its power, in spite of "ridiculous and spiteful rumors." This, Goebbels claims, is going to happen again in 1942. But his slip betrays the issue mentioned above—namely, that one defeat may be an accident, but that two defeats are Fate.

Goebbels then turns against the British claim that Germany is "triumphing itself to death." "Never in history has the *succession of victories led to final defeat*," shouts Goebbels, rather daringly denying the dangerous parallel which even a short memory could provide.

As if seeing a powerful enemy in British propaganda (to listen to which is, after all, supposed to be strictly "verboten"), Goebbels introduces Hitler's consequent counterpropaganda. The enemies' promises of *postwar reconstruction really* represent a *bad copy of the National Socialist program*, he says; that program which, after all, has not developed beyond a prelude solely because of the lack of living space and the war emergency.

Then Goebbels introduces the *Winterhilfswerk*, which he calls the *"principal account of the German socialism of action,"* although it is obviously nothing but a good old capitalistic collection of money, reinforced by the coercive methods of the party. Furthermore, in spite of the admission that not even "half of those Germans earning an income are members of the party," he says that two-thirds of the money collected is turned over to the National Socialist Volksbund.

Most of this money is given to the organization Mother and Child, one-third of it for *Heime*. (Did anybody ask the Germans next day what kind of *Heime* is meant: birth clinics for "state" children? By mentioning this part of the *Hilfswerk* first, Goebbels himself gives an opening for the propagandistic discussion of the family under national socialism.)

Then Hitler enters, greeted as "a great bridge between the warfront and the home front." He ceremoniously shakes hands with Field Marshal Rommel—and speaks.

Two-thirds of Hitler's speech is devoted to derisive and sneering remarks of the kind which he is said to deliver with skill. It soon becomes obvious that he has reserved *two different sets of sarcastic images* for the Anglo-Saxons and for the Russians respectively.

His images are essentially identical with those discussed in the chapters "Father," "Jew," "Soldier," of my previous analysis of Hitler's images.* The *Anglo-Saxon* elder statesmen are depicted as senile, feudal, paralytic drunkards, the younger ones as spoiled braggarts, and both types as being too snobbish to understand the modern world. The *Russians*, on the other hand, are denied recognition as human beings; their undeniable power is attributed to their being subhuman beasts, or Asiatics. As is his habit, against such a background Hitler sets the image of the *German soldier*.

The first Anglo-Saxons to be mentioned are Churchill and Roosevelt, as representatives of a decadent feudal system. Churchill's white silk shirt tuxedo (*kluft*, meaning "formal dress"), and sombrero are mentioned in connection with his extensive travels during recent months. Here Hitler uses a "sour grapes" technique concerning travels, which really are witness to the fact that Hitler's enemies can move freely in a large part of the world while he is still hammering at Germany's prison walls. Just as he does with Churchill's tuxedo, he deliberately overlooks the cultural connotation of the fireplace, sitting beside which Roosevelt speaks to Americans (or rather, spoke before Pearl Harbor). In referring to *Plaudereien am Kamin* (in itself a verbatim translation of "fireside chat," but also the title of a German book of the Victorian era), he replaces the American symbolism of the autonomous individual home with a strictly upper-bourgeoisie meaning, for only castles and mansions have *Kamine* in Germany. Next he introduces Mr. Duff Cooper and Mr. Eden. If one were to count how often Hitler mentions these gentlemen, one would think either that he considers them especially dangerous or that the Germans—even on penalty of death—have developed the habit of turning on the radio whenever Duff Cooper or Eden speaks to them. Actually, these men seem to be selected rather for the purpose of representing the "rich boys from next door," slick braggarts with a comlete lack of principles and personality; in other words, the kinds of *feudal sons* which one could expect fathers like Roosevelt and Churchill to produce. He calls them nobodies, blusterers, blockheads, and worthless fellows, in spite of which he seems to be much more concerned about *their opinion concerning the Russian campaign* than about Stalin's. Those who know Hitler have said that he really admires the British. Still, it is hard to believe that his technique is only personal

* See note page 351.

revelation; he tries to devaluate Western conscience and to counteract feelings of inferiority, not only in himself but also in every German. In elevating Duff Cooper and Eden to an allegedly exclusive representative position, he at the same time ignores the spiritual and political changes in the British people. As a matter of fact, by depicting the Anglo-Saxons as effeminate bourgeois, and the Russians as beasts born in the mud, Hitler tries to *isolate the two national components of the "little man"* who is standing up against him in all countries. Apparently afraid of the spiritual power expressed in British and Russian tenacity, and in American grimness, Hitler makes a wordplay out of the various meanings of the word *belief*. Men, he says, who "believed" that Dieppe was a success could not be expected to "believe" in the principles they profess, and he ends this play with the catchphrase "but *we* 'believe' that we have to beat the enemy."

In his further campaign for the recognition of the *somberly obvious*, he then continues Goebbels's reasoning: that nobody ever met defeat after a continuous succession of victories. He enumerates all his successes, adding derisively each time (more than a dozen times in all) that in British eyes, "all this means nothing at all." To this observer, the emotional and repetitive way in which Hitler repeats these fateful words, "*dann ist das öben nichts*," he betrays his and his countrymen's sneaking fear that Fate may actually have snared him.

He does not make any promises; victory is a rare word in this speech. Against senile, feudal Churchill he has nothing to hold out but the old role of the *defiant adolescent* depicted in the very first chapter of *Mein Kampf*. "Mr. Churchill, you have never been able to scare me." (It will be noted that, in a following speech, just having been informed of "Roosevelt's invasion" of Africa, he said: "From my boyhood, I have kept the bad habit of having the last word.") It is obvious that only an anachronistic magic spell (as partially analyzed in my above-mentioned paper can explain the reliance of a modern people on such immature personal statements.

While nervously answering imaginary critics in England, Hitler now and again drops a word indicating his line of *psychological defense against the Russians*. They seem to count not as men and critics but merely as a dangerous, dirty mass of bestiality, suddenly rising up from Dostoyevsky's depths and attacking the pure German knight, while the British gentlemen in tuxedos look on and snicker. When first mentioning Russia, Hitler crossly defines her as a country which "permits a decent, reasonable war only for a few months at a time." He repeats the old phrase of "General Winter," avoiding any reference to Russian leaders. When speaking of Stalingrad, he adds that the name does not matter. Finally, when forced to admit that the Russians seem to be doing quite well with their nonexisting net of streets and railroads, he explains that the Russian is something like a swampman, born in mud and thriving on it. It is obvious that he thus adds a Russian image to that of the Jew, who, so far, has had a monopoly of an entirely subhuman or, rather, metahuman, phenomenon—superordinate even to Fate.

Thus again Hitler employs adolescent thinking, according to which the young hero in the outer world fights a double danger, which is also within himself: the tyranny of the old men; from whom he derived his inhibited conscience; and the temptations of the lower strata of human life, which appeal to his own rebellious drives. This, as I pointed out in "Hitler's Imagery," are his old standbys.

What really bothers Hitler in the Russians, he betrays in a slip of the tongue: *"Es ist die Angst vor dem Regime, das Millionen Menschen"*—corrects himself—*oder die Millionen Menschen—noch immer erfüllt."* The equivalent in English would be as follows: "It is the fear of the *regime which* still holds and pervades—I mean, the *fear which* still holds and pervades millions of Russians." So it is the unbreakable *Russian spirit* which this man cannot take and which he "tears into the mud." What do the German officers and soldiers think about this lack of soldierly spirit as expressed in Hitler's tendency to deny a courageous enemy human recognition?

For there is another conscience to be considered, one which Hitler cannot afford to push aside with ridicule and defamation: the conscience of the German officer. The general staff must have fought a stubborn and courageous fight with this Austrian adventurer. For, in the midst of his adolescent harangue, a mature note appears: "It always was a *sober* scope of aims—*audacious where it had to be audacious*, prudent where it was possible to be prudent, circumspect when there was time, cautious where we believed that we had to be cautious under all circumstances—but "—he repeats this like an obedient pupil—" we also have been quite daring where only boldness would save us." This observer does not believe that Hitler wrote this paragraph, but that it represents the line to be pursued by the German general staff from now on. The line is prudent enough; however, it upsets the whole psycho-logic of Hitler's inventory of magic tricks; it confines, as it were, the delinquent adolescent to his room, asking him to think it over and to be sensible. How much Hitler suffered under the military education which he received last winter at such a tremendous price to the German people can be seen from the typically adolescent projection with which he sneers at the above-mentioned "rich boys" in England who, having "*no military schooling*," thought he had made a mistake in invading Russia. He, the former corporal, in Field Marshal Rommel's presence, even calls the British generals idiots—words which he is now forced to eat.

About the fateful winter of '41 and '42, he says: "Worse cannot and will not happen," which implies that it would if it could. Goebbels, too, has said that the worst was behind the German people. One wonders what is intended by such reassuring words, especially when they are immediately followed by sinister threats as to the terrible fate in store for the Germans should they ever lose their nerve and give in to panic. One has the feeling that the severity of the winter of '41 and '42 is almost played up against a complete playing down of such future threats as the bombing raids from England. American industrial mobilization, and Russian preparations for an offensive. "The Anglo-Saxon leaders promise only sweat, blood, and tears." The German leaders seem to believe that the Germans would not stand for more winters like that of '41 and '42, if they had to anticipate and to visualize their recurrence, while they will bear any hardship once it has become an irrevocable fact.

Where is the threat of *American industrial mobilization*? It also is played down and belittled, and this against the background of the German genius for organization, as manifested in the rebuilding of the Russian road and railway system. Immediately after having exhorted such feats, he calls enemy tanks, airplanes, and other weapons "rubbish," "shabby stuff" (*Gelump*), which he would not dare ask German soldiers to use. Here his language disintegrates completely, and he becomes thoroughly adolescent, especially when he claims that Americans think that every weapon which they produce is "*the* invention of the *world*," as if American industry were a child playing superman. This part of his speech ends with the following logic: Having denied that American airplanes and tanks are better than German ones, he adds "*but, at any rate,* ours are the greater heroes." Can this be understood as anything but an (unconsciously admitted) adolescent denial of the fear of American equipment at a time when the first Flying Fortresses are shooting down his newest fighter planes? Does he—or does he not—remember the surprise experienced during the First World War by the superbly prepared German soldiers when, after years of victory, they found themselves opposed by better armament and a higher spirit?

Hitler therefore answers America's industrial threat by counter-threatening that he will produce weapons superior every time to those of his enemies. He adds that "the insane man in the White House," by involving America in the war, has only brought anti-Semitism to America and that the American Jews will cease laughing, just as the German Jews have done. One wonders whether the spread of *anti-Semitism* is not the *secret weapon* primarily employed by Hitler's agents in this country at this time. The possibility has been considered that the saboteurs recently executed may conceivably have been planted by the Gestapo in order to deflect American attention from a much more thorough scheme of ideological sabotage.

As Hitler is apt to do with apparent personal satisfaction and with popular success, he turns from the image of the grinning Jew (who will not grin for long) to the image of the *German soldier*. As far as coherence, form level, and sincerity are concerned, this is the best part of Hitler's speech. He even becomes paternal and human when he speaks of the anxiety of the young recruit who enters battle for the first time. To Hitler, as for many Germans, his identification with the "lonely infantrist" who does not ask questions is as basic as the identification with the "little man" is for Henry A. Wallace or Wendell Willkie. One seriously doubts that Hitler sees any other meaning in the universe than the sufferings and triumphs of the German infantrist. He probably likes to live near the front, and he will stay there for longer and longer periods because the concern with everyday strategic problems probably appeases his conscience and his worries. His whole speech reflects a narrow attention to whatever is immediately ahead—now that the Jews and Roosevelt have created this situation. In asking the German people also to identify with the German soldiers, he implicitly and explicitly suggests that they forget about war guilt and war aims and try to make the best of the situation as it is. Then, however, he introduces a new trend. It will be remembered that both Goebbels and he earlier accused Germany's enemies of usurping some of the National Socialist doctrine and of trying to take the wind out of National Socialist sails. As could have been predicted, whenever Hitler plays the suspicious accuser, he is already preparing, on his part, to realize the intention of which he suspects his adversaries. He emphasizes the new *democracy* which will be born from the experience of the German soldier, whose deeds represent "a certificate of blood (*Bluturkunde*) which is going to replace the certificates of origin, of position, of possession, and of education (*unsere sogenannte Bildung*). He even promises that Germany is going to be the land of *unlimited opportunities* for the German, thus stealing America's chief appeal to the German masses, who refer to the United States as the land of *unbegrenste Möglichkeiten*.

There are other, minor indications that Hitler gives careful attention to the American way of thinking (or to what it seems to him or to Goebbels to be). Some of his warm, intimate references to German soldiers seem to be fashioned after a propaganda technique used by Roosevelt in several of his last speeches—namely, the bridging of the gap between home front and war front—by giving intimate descriptions of the difficulties surmounted by certain categories of the armed forces. In the other direction, he tells the army the story of "a bombed town in Friesland." Also, he tries to create a slogan by saying that every simple sentence (*Satz*) in the army's communiqués really means tremendous personal risks (*Einsatz*): *"Jeder Satz ein Einsatz."*

There is no denying that the German soldier combines the oldest tradition with the most streamlined modern techniques and even a new democratic spirit. Here Hitler is most sincere, and so are the Germans. Before long, however, Hitler probably will be promising some kind of democracy in a purified and dominant Germany. The Anglo-Saxon founders of democracy, he probably will say, also had a racial monopoly for democracy in mind; not democracy for Negroes, Jews, and British Indians. (From the counterpropagandistic point of view, an ominous parallel can be drawn between Hitler's and Goebbels's promises of bigger and better socialism and democracy after the war and the imperial and royal Prussian promises of reform toward the end of the last war. The failure of these promises partially prepared the way for Wilson's savior role.)

No speech of Hitler's would come up to Goebbels's expectations without some reference to rape. This theme undergoes many variations: Hitler's protective furor sometimes refers to Germany's being raped in Versailles or to the rape of the German minorities in the (now occupied) countries. It may well be significant that, in his last few speeches, the maltreated woman referred to is again the *German woman in persona within Germany*. Early this year, the "senile" German judiciary was blamed for not punishing sufficiently a man who maltreated a woman; now it is the good-for-nothing and criminal" who molest women going home from work at night. As always when speaking on this theme, Hitler becomes outraged to the point of universal destructiveness (the rape-and-castration themes being very dear to his heart, as pointed out by Ambassador Henderson as well as by psychoanalysts). Thus, unwittingly, he makes a strange statement: "We shall see to it that not only the decent man dies at the front [*dass nicht nur der Anständige an der Front stirbt, sondern*], but that the criminal and the indecent one at home under no circumstances survives this era." Such sentences cannot really be translated; so that the singular combination of *repetitious themes, sincere emotion, propagandistic shrewdness, bad grammar, and unconscious giveaway* characterizing Hitler's speeches is usually lost in the English translation.

However, this theme, too, has an important parallel in 1917 and '18. At that time rumors and reports of the German woman's infidelity at home swept the front and contributed to the breakdown of morale; it was an indication that women no longer believed in the cause for which they had sacrificed marital pleasures for years. Hitler, by denouncing promiscuity as rape and by promising the protection of the state, hopes to forestall the bad effects on morale of such rumors. Moreover, national socialism has done much to break down the family in Germany. All the more reason for counterpropaganda to refer unceasingly to the disintegration of German morals under nazism.

As has been amply pointed out in the press, the greatest change manifested in this speech concerns the repeated assurance that the *war will not be lost—* instead of the promise that it will be won. The sequence of Hitler's remarks, and the images used, confirm that Hitler means what he says. Thus, when declaring that the alternative to victorious endurance is extermination, he adds: "If a soldier did not know this, then you could not expect of him that he risk his life under such horrible circumstances." Does this thought alone keep the German soldier in the field?

This passage suggests that isolated Anglo-Saxon statements which suggest horror peace aims (such as the castration of all German males or the deportation of all German children for compulsory education) need to be refuted officially, explicitly, and repeatedly by Allied propaganda. It must be remembered that the Germans are guilty of aiding or tolerating comparable sweeping solutions of "population-and-indoctrination problems" and therefore can actually visualize alleged Allied plans which, to Americans, seem to be too ridiculous for refutation.

The most fundamental change in Hitler's imagery is the replacement of images of movement by those of *stationary endurance*. "We stand behind our soldiers, just as our soldiers stand in front of us. And together we stand in front of our people and in front of our

Reich and will not capitulize under any circumstances."

This imagery of standing guard is, of course, an old and universal one: *"Fest steht und treu die Wacht am Rhein."* It must be remembered, however, that the last war has compromised the guard on the Rhine, while this war's greatest German triumph was the defeat of the French stationary guard on the Rhine (the Maginot line) by the German blitz, which promised once and for all to forestall trench warfare and encirclement. As I (following many others) have pointed out in my paper on Hitler's imagery, the psychological structure of nazism stands and falls with the imagery of blitz warfare; furthermore, in this war Allied counteroffensive power ("artillery of the air," "Flying Fortresses") by far suprasses that of the last war. Stationary warfare is not even defensive warfare anymore. The grandiose United States policy of surrounding the Reich with an (at first seemingly unconnected) circle of springboards for an "all-around" air offensive therefore undoubtedly causes grave concern in Berlin.

This American plan, like the German blitz before it, is primarily based on military logic. However, it represents at the same time a sweeping synthesis of America's mechanical genius, industrial spirit, and traditional personality traits (as historically based on the hate of tyrants, the spirit of the advancing frontier, the impetus of the ranger, etc.)* Only such a synthesis will be tough enough to impress the Germans, for only a people that can synthesize, at a historical moment, acute necessity and traditional character structure has (as Hitler would put it) a claim on Fate.

---

* For present-day manifestation of the American personality structure, see: Margaret Mead, *And Keep Your Powder Dry.* (New York: William Morrow, 1942).

Comments on Anti-Nazi Propaganda (1945)

The clinical analysis of Hitler's imagery* is here concluded with a few remarks concerning the study and use of anti-Nazi imagery.

First: The suggested analogy between Nazi group phenomena and adolescent delinquency rests on the following psychological mechanism: If adolescent individuals or young nations find themselves unable to integrate their more civilized (or mature) values, they may, under certain conditions, repress these values and treat their existence in others with scorn and violence. This inner arrangement temporarily leads to feelings of safety, elation, and dominance, and permits the shrewd pursuit of antisocial goals.

In an individual case of this kind, the clinician must be able to demonstrate to the patient: (1) that he is invested with the power (or has influence over those invested with the power to put a stop to the delinquency and that he would not hesitate to use his influence or his power for the protection of the community; (2) that he understands delinquency as one potential outcome of universal human conflict and is willing to review with a brotherly and objective attitude

Written for the Committee on National Morale (for the Council on Intercultural Relations), 1945. Published here for the first time.
* See E. H. Erikson, "Hitler's Imagery and German Youth," *Psychiatry*, 5 (November 1942), 475–93.

the particular anxieties and aspirations which have induced the patient to turn against the values of his community; (3) that he has the power to protect the delinquent from irrational punishment, as well as from inner chaos, during a period of reconstruction following the demonstration by the delinquent of a sincere wish to give a new trial to the ways of his community. However, psychotherapy is applicable only in cases where the desirable values, although in a repressed state, do exist in the patient.

In the case of a whole gifted nation which has fallen prey to the delinquent-adolescent, the suggestions would be: (1) that those individuals who, because of their chronic adolescent personalities, or because of indoctrination during childhood or adolescence, are unable to visualize any other imagery be put out of action; and (2) that those individuals who have remained potentially sensitive to civilized values be given psychological support, so that they may gain the courage to reinstate these values and to reaffirm their educational and political responsibility.

Here, too, only demonstrated actual power, convincingly combined with the power of understanding and self-discipline, can become a decisive psychological influence.

So much for the analogy.

Second: The Germans expect and respect only signs of powerful self-preservation on the part of their enemies. They interpret any attempt to talk, *rather* than to act, as a sign of weakness or as an attempt to betray them again. For Wilsonian promises, the German common man, at present, has no stomach, no training, and no use. They lead him only to the conclusion that all governments produce empty lies and that, therefore, he may just as well keep his home-grown variety and defend his soil and his kin to the last.

Third: There is no use denying to Germans that the Third Reich, in many respects, is a magnificent realization of certain collective adolescent fantasies. As such, it has provided the German nation with the first modern synthesis of its national personality traits—a synthesis which replaced the general discontent in being German and which, so far, is not matched by any convincing vision of a synthesis of German anxieties and aspirations with those of the democracies. In fact, every alternative to nazism, at the moment, implies not only the threat of slaughter and of anarchy to the German but also that of individual psychological chaos. Therefore, there is no use denying to ourselves that the common German man temporarily has good reason to identify himself with the Nazi cause, either because he is obsessed or paralyzed or merely because he cannot visualize any other cause. But in preparation for the breakdown of this identification, the German must be told what the Allied world stands for. He must be told convincingly, because otherwise there is no saying where his inner chaos will lead.

Fourth: No matter what idea one wishes to get across to the Germans, it should be clothed in an imagery which, to them, sounds as familiar as—or, preferably, more familiar than—Hitler's imagery (the "familiarity" of which is pointed out in my paper). The very antithesis of Hitler's imagery is that of the *family*, the *township*, and the *region* as the basis of universal cultural life. This is the imagery on which all genuine cultural achievements in Germany were based; it is, at the same time, the only imagery with which true democratic experiences are associated (the integration of democratic ideas on a national scale having failed). This imagery undoubtedly exists in most Germans in a latent, bewildered, repressed form. Within Germany, however, it has no mouthpiece and no leader. It is being shouted down by the loud, boisterous, Reich-German voice in power. Therefore, cultural propaganda promises to be most successful where its verbal inventory is based on regional imagery. For example, the relationship to family, class, nation, or mankind differs in various regions (Prussian, Bavarian, Austrian, etc.) in the emotional emphasis on, let us say, categorical duty, mechanical efficiency, childlike sentiment, religious universality, affiliative sociability, righteous indignation, forgiving humor, moral and physical cruelty against the self and against others. Thus, while the most promising content of propaganda consists of truths (both in the sense of facts and in that of simple verities understood by the common man everywhere), these truths become most "evident" if selected and phrased according to the emotional requirements of regions and classes.

Fifth: Propaganda agencies probably have at their disposal detailed and accurate data on episodes and developments which show how, in Nazi Germany, the imagery of the family and the region is subordinated to or betrayed by the delinquent imagery of a gang leader. Such material could provide the Germans with a cool picture of what German world domination, even if possible, would mean to the moral future of their own children. Biographic sketches of ordinary Germans, as well as of German leaders, help to substantiate suspicions which, in the meantime, have already been spread by German rumor and folk wit.

Sixth: While the imagery of propaganda demands a knowledge of regions and classes which can be established only with the help of American natives of Germany, *it is imperative that the propaganda be American in character.* Not "This is one particular segment of Free Germany speaking to you from Washington, D.C., in the hope of regaining lost political power with the help of American battalions, *but* "This is the powerful American people speaking to the German people, with an understanding based on the fact that the American nation, while Anglo-Saxon in its guiding principles, is comprised of people from all the nations of Europe and therefore embodies now principles of national integration in the evolving industrial world."

Seventh: Essential goals are:

a. That only images be used which exist in strong, latent form in every German, but are neglected, suppressed, or cynically misused by Hitlerism

b. That only data be used which can be observed or substantiated by every German or which, at any rate, will surely not be found to be inaccurate

c. That these images and facts be woven into a simple, realistic, and artistic design

d. That this design receive its inner strength from the acts, intentions, and latent aspirations of the Allied nations, and especially of the United States

e. That alternatives to nazism be presented as integrated part solutions for universal evolutionary striving, rather than something which allegedy exists in its complete form in the allied world of today

A Memorandum
to the Joint Committee
on Post War Planning
(1945)

The questions of the Panel on Education arrived here about three weeks ago. Not having been in Germany proper since 1929, and having been unable to come to New York and to hear your experts on Nazi educational institutions in Nazi Germany, I had not much to say until a week ago when the psychiatric and anthropological memoranda arrived. I assume you are interested in individual reactions to your formulations, and I am sending you a spontaneous statement.

My paper "Hitler's Imagery and German Youth"* largely agrees with the more extensive formulations of such historically minded analysts and sociologists as Alexander and Parsons and, as your anthropologists indicated, with much of their cultural findings. However, my paper also proposes to take into account the deep changes which the Nazi revolution may have brought about in German thinking. (See page 480.)

Psychiatric-historical formulations need to be tested in close and systematic observation of available sections of contemporary history (analogous to what we are doing in the psychoanalysis of individuals).

Written for the Committee on National Morale (for the Conference on Germany After the War), 1945. Published here for the first time.
* "Hitler's Imagery and German Youth." *Psychiatry*, 5, (November 1942), 475–93.

In your statements there is no reference to source material concerning the various phases of German history under the Nazis. Such data are indispensable (1) as a test of the psychiatric-historical theories; (2) as a basis of efficient planning.

More than two years ago some of us made suggestions concerning the way in which the behavior of German prisoners of war might be studied immediately after capture and later, without violation of either word or spirit of the Geneva Convention. I do not know whether this opportunity to observe successive samples of Nazi mentality under defined and controlled conditions has been utilized. There are other sources, such as the study of changes in propaganda. My first question, therefore, would be: Is the committee in touch with agencies that are now in possession of relevent firsthand data concerning the behavior of Nazis during the various phases of this war?

Without such data I see a new Tower of Babel arising, not one with a disturbing number of languages but rather one with a small vocabulary (ego, libido, character structure, reeducation, neuropsychiatric, etc.) which, however, has a disturbing number of meanings and countless practical implications.

It is obvious that only history can change peoples. The question is not what discipline alone or what disciplines combined could solve this historical dilemma but rather: What combination of disciplines is *now well enough integrated* to present the Germans with a total situation which must convince them that their history, as they see and saw it, is over? Only an unequivocal change in its total historical situation will convince a people that its common panics and its traditional enthusiasms are outlived and that its habitual forms of self-assertion do not pay any longer. Only after such conviction has had time to sink in can changes in those family patterns and attitudes of child training be expected, which, according to everything we now know, is the model and basis for later education. In this sense, too, I am unable to answer the questions of the educational panel as to how home, school, college, etc. could each by itself be changed so as to produce "similar" results.

A few years ago, when H. S. Mekeel and I studied difficulties in the education of Sioux Indian children, we came to the conclusion that governmental education failed where economic changes had not been consolidated and child training had not changed in its basic attitudes. I cannot refrain from quoting myself: "The young American democracy lost its first battle with the Indians when it could not decide whether it was conquering, colonizing, converting, or liberating them, and when consequently it sent to the Indians a succession of representatives who had one or another of these objectives in mind. The Indians considered such historic doubt uncivilized and highly suspicious."

Let us assume for a moment that Germany's reeducation is an *American* problem: He who wants to reeducate another nation or "change" another nation's "basic character structure" has to be a part of an unequivocal historical force. This committee, a professional group within one nation, endeavors not only to play a useful part delegated to it by the usual executives of national history but also expressly wishes to suggest or to determine a scientifically planned history, based on a psychiatric master plan. My second question, therefore, would be: Is this committee informed about the nature of the concerted pressure that will be brought to bear on the German people, first by the three main occupying nations, secondly, by the various functionaries within each occupying nation? One may assume that Russian influence on the areas it occupies will perforce be uniform. In the case of the United States, are there any expectation and promise that there will be thorough agreement as to basic administrative and propaganda procedures within the military, diplomatic, political and commercial categories, on the one hand, and, on the other, the reeducational forces?

The general orientation of this committee is that of mental hygiene. Is mental hygiene an unequivocal historical force in the United States? Has it established a machinery of mutual collaboration with those who do the "dirty work" of history? If such machinery is not now established in this country, would it be sage to use defeated Germany as an experimental ground for psychiatric theories which may constitute a descriptively and theoretically promising beginning of a new discipline but which so far have no practional tradition?

It will not be enough during the coming days of German reconstruction for one American group, let us say the reeducational one, to claim that according to the American system at home it has no power over another group—let us say the potential carpetbaggers of the coming reconstruction era or the royalist diplomats. The Germans, trained to think totalitarian, and suggestible to paranoid historical concepts, will consider ideological disunity among the educational, the political, the military, the diplomatic, and the commercial forces of this country either another sign of democratic corruption or a gigantic pretense comparable to the Wilsonian principles, behind which they expect a new sinister scheme of cultural emasculation or economic exploitation, or both.

My third question: In the absence of a detailed machinery for the governmental execution of a psychiatric master plan, in the absence of research concerning the prospective acceptibility of such a plan to the American people, what useful subordinate role could mental hygiene play in specific, specialized tasks within the framework of the United Nations' policy? This, of course, may have been discussed. Yet the material sent to me so far and the questions which I have been asked to answer do not indicate either the information or the ready tools on which such far-reaching planning must be based. What impresses me in some formulations is their daydreamish totalitarian character. On occasion, I discern wolf Goebbels himself in psychiatric clothing.

Germany is a nation, not a tribe. If I were asked (in spite of the pitfalls inherent in such formulations) to state in the shortest possible fashion what difference between a tribe and a nation seems most relevant in this connection, I would say that primitive tribes attempt to arrive at a synthesis of economic and emotional safety on the most centripetal, exclusive basis: The tribe constitutes what is relevant of mankind. Modern nations are the outcome of a tendency to base such a synthesis on the inclusion by expansion or identification of ever-larger portions of mankind: regions, nations, classes, continents. This inclusion varies in focus, scope, tempo, and intensity: accordingly it burdens individuals and groups with varying specific problems of identification. The fact that wars are becoming ever more intensive and extensive probably is not so much the result of an insurmountable devilishness of human nature as rather of the fact that now and from now on, larger entities than ever before experience both the triumph of identification with one another and the fear of loss of identity. There are periods of consolidation of that which has been included but wherever the more inclusive tendencies periodically prove insufficient to allay (1) panic (fear of loss of collective safety and identity); (2) ego anxieties (fear of loss of libido and ego satisfactions within the cultural sanctions of one's childhood ideals) temporary regressions to quasi-primitive ideologies occur, all isolationist in character and accompanied by open sadistic horrors.

It will not do to call one nation psychiatric names. Every nation has particular regressive syndromes to which it is apt to revert when safety and identity are threatened. The Germans overdo this greatly, too, yet a neuropsychiatric theory of historical events should be universally applicable.

The idea of reeducating the Germans seems to be expressed alternately by the concepts of a basic character structure which has to be changed or a kind of collective affliction the existence of which could even be diagnosed in individuals. The concept of a basic character structure, by its use of the words *basic* and *structure*, seems to imply something very static, which fits tribes better than nations. Dynamically seen, much of what is described as character is often rather what in individuals we would call reaction formation, maintained with the more monomanic effort and the more panicky intensity, the more a collective loss of identity is threatened. In the so-called German character structure repressed guilt feeling toward mankind is discernible behind arrogance; all too clear insight behind defiance; and a great love for the non-German world behind paranoia and projection and hate. All this belongs to the basic character structure, too; in *every* German there is guilt feeling, insight, and love of progress, together with arrogance, defiance, and paranoid hate.

I venture to say that even in Germany a European spirit must be in the making. In most discussions on the subject of "reeducation," there is a strange assumption that those Germans who now make an impression of dependability on Anglo-Saxons are also the Germans who have the proper images, the insight born of bitter experience, and, most of all, the necessary training to build a progressive Germany. The condemnation of Nazi horrors should not keep observers from considering the possible evolutionary merits which may even be inherent in the Nazi movement in the sense that more than any other revolution, it has already begun to destroy the parental images which in the reports of this committee are ascribed to the German character structure. The Nazi movement, with its desperate totalitarian attempt to test the age-old German idea of German superiority against the whole world, may have prepared the unequivocal historical answer which the Germans have never been faced with before, largely because of the neglect of other nations that forgot that historical existence is and remains a constant test; there is no such thing as a world safe for democracy.

If one wants to weed out those Germans who will be useful in a democratic Europe and those who could not be, the last thing I would consider of importance is party membership. It is possible that some young Nazis (of the type which the Russians seem to be utilizing now in their committee of German officers and soldiers in Moscow) will be realistic and cynical enough to know a historical decision when they see one; that they more than any other German group have undergone a decisive break with the feudal and narrowly nationalistic concepts of pre-Nazi Germany; that they more than any others have learned to think in terms of scientific planning on a European scale. One fact which deserves study is the replacement in Germany of some of the old hierarchic values by *Volksggenosseuschaft* and party membership; while we may not like the Nazi party, still we ought to study the revolutionary change in the forms of mutual identification which this has brought about. This, after all, is the historically relevant question in revolutions. Incidentally, our advocates of psychocultural approach may find that intelligent Nazis rather than educated socialists speak their language and, in fact, have read their very papers.

Such Nazis are guiltly, of course, of having acquiesced with and, even more, of having planned and executed the machinery which crushed and tortured millions. Undoubtedly, they could not have obeyed and they could not have done their work as superbly as they did without mobilizing in themselves the last ounce of that German spirit which is now described as paranoid. Undoubtedly they fell prey to suggestions and drugged themselves with autosuggestion. But whether you can call their "paranoia" "learned" or not, *it probably did not keep them from learning*. In order to meet the requirements of their tasks they had to study other countries. They probably know more about the world now than Germany ever knew before. That to the last they are trying to uphold the racial fiction will make the lesson only the more final when the fiction breaks down. I think one should be ready with all the integrated theories and techniques of observation to observe Germany's defeat, and then one should observe and test these theories and adapt them. On the other hand, one cannot warn too much against the lip service that will be offered to the Atlantic Charter by some Germans who, because they have been excluded for a decade from the history of their country, actually have forgotten nothing and have learned little. Once before, Germany was permitted to turn its unique need for supremacy into a supremacy of masochism, priding itself that it had been elected by Fate to suffer and humiliate itself. It will be no triumph to make Germans admit that they are guilty, for they will do it with a feeling of being superior, because they were able both to commit such crimes and to atone for them into the bargain. Both defiance and atonement need time to crystallize into patterns of European action.

I wonder whether it is promising to view the problem in terms of "Germany" or "the German." The problem of Germany's reeducation seems to me neither a *national* nor an *individual* one. Maybe it ought to be *understood* as a *European* problem, and it ought to be *attacked* as a *regional* one.

European: Europe is not the Europe we knew. The recent catastrophe undoubtedly has created the core of a European spirit which alone will reeducate Europe and Germany with it. I personally have no sympathy with the world outlook in which Americans plan to emasculate Germany just in order to permit the rest of Europe "peacefully" to pursue monarchic or postmonarchic small-nation politics backed up by their three powerful big brothers. Beware of another Congress of Vienna. As far as I can discern, the future lies in cultural autonomy for regions and the economic interdependence for the continent, with an adjustment of borders and politics to this aim.

National: It probably would be a mistake to face the whole German nation with conditions which it would have to accept as a whole or not accept at all. Such an attempt may lead to passive resistance on a large scale.

Individual: While the problem has psychiatric aspects, it does not, to my mind, admit of a psychiatric practical approach. To weed out on a large scale untrustworthy Germans from trustworthy ones seems to me impossible. The analogy with army psychiatry is dynamically incorrect. Army psychiatrists select a man on the basis of whether they think that he will stand up in a situation which the majority of his pals have to endure and in which they exert pressure on him to be as good as they are and not let them down. Whether or not he would get panicky if his whole regiment were gripped by panic cannot be predicted on a neuropsychiatric basis. No matter what an individual German seems to be thinking now or to have thought in the past, his behavior under changing group pressure is hard to predict.

Regional: I therefore hope that the problem will be attacked *region by region*, community by community, in a *group psychological* manner. Promises as to freedom of self-government, free trade, and freedom of education etc. should probably be varied according to the nature of the region. Certain regions would probably yield at an early date and by their example and their consequent experience bring the pressure of example and identification to bear on other German regions and communities. (Military safeguards are, of course, not considered here.) Such a plan also would take care of the completely unpredictable fate of the various German regions between now and the as yet quite mythical unconditional surrender of the whole nation.

In order to bring educational pressure to bear on anybody, you have to make him desire education through identification. If faced with an unequivocal historical decision, German schools will change, I think. I would leave it to them how and when this will be done, merely establishing military safeguards and minimum requirements for the self-government and resumption of national and international trade for each region. On the positive side a European Institute of

Education for peace could be established which would at first admit only a limited number of Germans and which would foster discussion and research free enough to assure its graduates high status in Germany as well as in the schools of other countries. But I do not think that the United States should sponsor such an institute.

If you want more panels, I would suggest a panel on the status of women in Europe. It is not quite comprehensible that there is not an organization of European women in exile who would get together with the best (not the loudest) of American and British womanhood in order to study the ways and means by which German woman can be approached by propaganda now, and in which the women of Europe might be trained to help prevent wars in the future. Who more than the women would have the right and the duty to form a permanent congress for the preservation of human resources? But this will take long training, which should begin now.

The matter of reeducation will logically begin with women and small children through health centers and baby clinics. Here again, however, it will be necessary to be well informed about the Nazi methods of child care. Where their methods are efficient, or, on a general scale, more efficient, it is merely a problem of permeating child care with a new spirit of interest in every human child as against the strictly German interest in pure racial offspring.

As for the propaganda material which the panel may want to prepare, it would be quite necessary to tone down the oversimplified descriptions and diagnosis of the German character structure.* These diagnoses, after all, correspond to our case reports in psychiatric meetings. The case looks that way certainly, but the person often does not. When American soldiers in Africa saw their first Nazi prisoners, they found them to be "guys like us." I have heard the same statement from a Jewish member of the military police who guarded Nazi prisoners on a transport. There are, of course, other statements of United Nations' guards standing completely dumbfounded before the blind arrogance of German prisoners—a contrast which only shows how easily groups can turn off and on "paranoid" attitudes. When American soldiers, after having killed, captured, or driven into hiding the worst Nazis, come to see their

---

* On page 5 of the anthropological report "FEAR OF LOSS OF STATUS" is put in capitals as *the* major negative sanction in German society. Is this not too generally true to characterize Germans? Fear of loss of *domineering status* would seem more accurate, since status can give many prerogatives such as earthly possessions, a place in heaven, equality, the right to isolate oneself, the right to serve, the right to advance, etc. The German idea of status is that of the bicyclist: He bends down deeper in order to tread down harder.

first German villages, their first German mothers, and especially their first German girls, nostalgic feelings will join their surprise as to how human these Germans are after all. Add to this the by now proverbial American sentimentality toward the defeated, especially at a time when America will still be untouched by war while German homes will have been destroyed by American bombs and shells: The danger will be great that American occupational forces will consider everything that has been said in too vivid and too strong colors as propaganda (which it is). Then they will want to go home and forget the whole thing.

This leads to a last suggestion: Has this committee considered the "reeducation" which American soldiers may be going to receive when they occupy Europe, and especially Germany? The American soldier above all should be able to recognize in the United Nations' actions toward Germany a solidly unified policy. Otherwise, the breach now developloing between the Americans who fight actual Nazis and those who are planning at home will only widen.

IV.
CROSS-CULTURAL
OBSERVATIONS:
THE COMMUNAL
ENVIRONMENT

A Yurok Fisherman

Observations on the Yurok: Childhood and World Image (1943)

Explanatory note

When told of my wish to review some of his data on the Yurok [8]*
from the standpoint of psychoanalytic child psychology, A. L. Kroeber
advised caution and suggested action. "You say you want to interpret," he remarked. "You mean, of course, you have questions to
ask, further inquiries to make." With this he put his finger on the
weak spot in all attempts to interpret observations in which one has
had no part. But he did more. He accompanied me to the Klamath,
made me acquainted with the (not extensive) Yurok territory, and
introduced me to some of his old informants.

As I had observed during a similar short stay, with H. S. Mekeel,
among the Sioux [3], native informants, as if having missed such
questions, eagerly give information on the training of children in
their culture—a field until recently neglected and now hotly debated
in both psychology and anthropology. With some data on Yurok
childhood as it once was, I could return both to Kroeber's Handbook

First published by the University of California Publications in American Archaeology and
Ethnology, 35, 10 (1943), iii + 257–302, Berkeley: University of California Press.
* References are cited by bracketed numbers in the text. They may be found at the end of this
article.

and to my own sketchy material on Sioux childhood. Since Sioux education emphasizes the necessity of the dispersing of property whereas the Yurok make a point of amassing it, it seemed of interest to see in what respect Sioux and Yurok methods of early child training differ.

An anthropological publication usually aspires to documenting established fact with theoretical finality. Instead this paper presents one clinical worker's impressions and speculations. His criteria for publication (the same as for his paper on the Sioux [3]) were the following:

1. The available anthropological data on the tribe studied suggested a number of interpretations analogous to some that had previously been found meaningful in the clinical psychoanalytic study of human motivation.

2. The writer's brief experimental collecting of data on the tribe's child training seemed to confirm these interpretations.

3. The interpretations and the additional data obtained seemed plausible and suggestive to the anthropologist most familiar with the intricate folkways of the tribe.

These admittedly subjective criteria may be expected to seem valid only to anthropologists and clinical workers who share the following interests and assumptions. Therapeutic work with adult and young neurotics in our culture has made it necessary for the clinical worker to pay attention to the study of social phenomena and to make suggestive contributions to it, for the analysis of neuroses not only reveals the intricate ways of neurotic substitute adaptations but also points to the pathology of folkways which cease to give meaning and consistency to social strivings.

Child training is the basic regulator of social strivings. The infant's body is the first training ground. Long before the child has been provided with his culture's vocabulary, which stamps a selected number and kind of his experiences as official, he has begun to express himself through the medium of his expanding and maturing organ systems. His sensory, tactual, muscular, and motoric contacts with his environment, the urges of his vital and sensual body apertures and their particular organ modes (incorporation, retention, elimination, intrusion, inclusion) are unfailingly associated with responses from the selected individuals and small social units entrusted with his care [4]. These responses encourage, provoke, regulate, modify, and suppress; they make social events out of bodily sensations. They condition in the growing body a model configuration of the physical, emotional, and intellectual attitudes desired by the group. The infant's body thus is not only his first means of expression, his first experiment in physical existence but also the culture's first means of communicating with him. Since the maturing organism's needs remain essentially the same, our conscious and unconscious mental life remains filled with urges and aversions, with images and analogies which are the residues of the body's earliest experiences; this becomes abundantly clear in clinical work. It is the basis for the many references in this paper to bodily analogies in Yurok thinking. In fact, Yurok concepts seem more than usually determined by such analogies.

There was a time when even the trained observer could not detect any system of child training in the primitive tribes he visited. Rather, he observed a lack of restriction, especially in those respects in which he himself had been trained most rigorously; his response was either that of righteous horror or of romantic elation. Both attitudes made him imperceptive to the systematic methods and aims of primitive child training.

Our (maybe only slightly less romantic) assumption is that primitive systems of child training, far from being arbitrarily lenient or cruel, have a logic of their own. They reveal mechanisms of an automatic mutual regulation of child training, tribal preservation, and individual mental health. They represent unconscious attempts at creating out of human raw material that configuration of attitudes which is (or once was) the optimum under the tribe's particular natural conditions and economic-historic necessities [4].

Of particular interest to the clinician is the fact that in all their weirdness, which has such detailed similarities to the imagery of our neurotics, some of these systems seem able to avoid the early deep estrangement between body and self and between self and parents which characterizes much of the white man's most civilized and most neurotic accomplishments.

The conclusive study of these phenomena and their application to child training in our civilization demand thorough training in anthropology and sociology as well as intimate clinical knowledge. Since investigators with such well-rounded training do not yet exist in abundance, I shall not further apologize for this overstepping of professional lines. Instead, I shall try to make the best of the habits of clinical description. In the following, each section concentrates on strong personal impressions and pursues them conceptually as far as they will lead.

The methodology of anthropological and psychoanalytic interviewing overlaps at least in the sense that some experience in one should shorten the discrimination period and sharpen one's perception in the other. With further conceptual clarification of the questions that are practicable and meaningful in work with human beings, some of the more obvious sources of methodological error will be eliminated.

The tolerance shown by A. L. Kroeber and the Department of Anthropology at Berkeley was positive and liberal, and I wish to express my sincere gratitude to them. Also, I am grateful to Jean Walker Macfarlane, who arranged my work in the Guidance Study of the Institute of Child Welfare in such a way as to permit my making this investigation.

Institute of Child Welfare,
University of California
Berkeley, California

Introduction

Some two hundred miles north of San Francisco the Redwood Highway (U.S. Highway 101) enters the area from which its name is derived. Here the Pacific's humidity—creeping inland as fog, or beating coast and mountains with rains—permits evergreen forests at sea level. Before reaching the Oregon border, the highway crosses the elaborate estuary of the Klamath River and enters the town of Klamath. Here is the center of the ancient Yurok territory. The Yurok lived, and still live, on lagoons and at the mouths of small streams down the coast to Trinidad Bay and up the coast to Wilson Creek (about forty-two miles in all), and on ancient river terraces for about thirty-six miles upstream along the ever-narrowing, densely forested valley of the Klamath just beyond its confluence with the Trinity River. "Their principal highway was the river" [12], which made them somewhat acquainted with and allowed a certain amount of intermarriage with the Karok living on the upper Klamath and the Hupa living on the Trinity, neighbors sharing the essentials of Yurok culture although speaking different languages and having a different ethnic background. Otherwise the Yurok were not intimate with tribes that could not be reached by boat. Probably never more than a few thousand people, they lived a centripetal and exclusive life, refusing the status of a world to anything beyond that disk of territory of about a hundred and fifty miles diameter which is recognized in the Yurok inventory of names. They ventured neither into the interior of the country nor on the ocean (except for occasional daring trips to Redding Rock, five miles offshore). They concentrated much of their technical and spiritual faculties on the annual salmon run (the periodical gift of food sent to them from a mysterious source "across the ocean"), which to them meant not only sportive massacre but also supply for winter storage, fraternization of the tribe as a nation, and spiritual rebirth.

The ethos and peculiar logic of their life are still reverently and stubbornly conscious to a small number of older Indians. At first it seems as strange to our perception and sensation as is the tom-tom in the prairie or the remoteness of Acoma; but on further study the strangeness diminishes.

The history of these Indians' clash with white civilization is unique. Their modern frame houses are near the visible and still name-bearing house pits which once formed the subterranean part of what in its superterranean structure always had been a wooden frame house. It is true that the salmon today does not stand in the center of either their society or their economy; like other United States citizens the Yurok are obliged to accept certain seasonal restrictions and trade limitations. But unlike the buffalo hunter, who with the extinction of the game and the denudation of the prairie saw eradicated all the old modes and values of life, the Yurok still sees, catches, eats, and talks salmon. The modern Yurok, steering a raft of logs down the river or doing timberwork for the big companies, is a picture of relative historical and economic health; for his technology had been in large part that of a timberman: he had exported dugouts and prepared lumber for his own houses as well as for those of his neighbors outside the Redwood belt. Yurok women had spent most of their days in the gathering of acorns, wild bulbs, and grass seeds; they were even planting tobacco before the white man came; and so to cultivate vegetables and walnut and apple trees is not too far a step from old custom. Thus, one has the impression that at least in some essentials the Yurok does not have to relearn the ABC of his ancient economic mind and whatever of the past is still a part of his child training. Above all, these people had their own kind of money when the white man came. "The Yurok concerns his life above all else with property. When he has leisure, he thinks of money; if in need, he calls upon it. He schemes constantly for opportunity to lodge a claim or to evade an obligation. No resource is too mean or devious to essay in this pursuit" [8]. This "primitive" tendency the Yurok need not forget in the white world, and therefore their grievances with the government (for example, with the Howard-Wheeler

Act forbidding Indians to sell reservation land except to one another)
find other than the inarticulate, smouldering expression of the prairie
man's passive resistance. Where it flares up, it is the voluble hatred
of one group of citizens of the United States against, as they consider
them to be, another greedy group of citizens. As I was to learn, it is
expressed openly. The observing white man, however, who is at first
repulsed by the Yurok's money-mindedness and suspicious compulsiveness, cannot escape the final insight that his relations with the
Yurok lack alleviating romanticism because Yurok and white man
each understands too well what the other wants, namely, possessions.

I shall first report on my contact with a selected group of Indians
who had a high standing among Indians as well as whites. They were
living on idyllic spots above the very mouth of the river, in the town
of Requa, once the most populated of the Yurok towns.

According to habit, we shall proceed on clinical lines. Having read
Kroeber's "case history," and having been led by it to a certain
diagnostic impression, we approach the individuals we interview with
the expectation that they will demonstrate in changes of affect, in
gestures, in the selection of words and subjects how much of the
diagnostic preconception deserves to be formulated.

Our preconception is this: Yurok thinking, so far as it is magic,
tends to assimilate concepts derived from (1) observations of the
geographic and biological environment, that is, (a) the lower part of
a river valley with a mysterious periodical supply of fish, (b) a prey
(salmon) with a particularly dramatic biology; and (2) experiences
of the human body as a slowly maturing organism with periodical
needs. In the nonmagical sphere, of course, the Yurok reaches a
certain degree of logic and technique, as do all human beings; but
wherever magic behavior seems indicated—that is, wherever mysterious food sources beyond the Yurok's territory, technology, and
causal comprehension need to be influenced, or whenever vague human impulses and fears need to be alleviated—the Yurok tries to
understand nature around and within him by blending bodily and
geographic configurations, both of which become parts of one geographic-anatomical environment. In this environment the periodical
affluence of the waterway has a functional interrelation with the
periodicity of vital juices in the body's nutritional, circulatory, and
procreative systems. Therefore, the Yurok's main magic concern is
that vital channels be kept open and that antagonistic fluids be kept
apart from one another.

Into this unified environment, in turn, the Yurok's ethical orientation is blended. As we shall see, the groundwork for it is laid by the (unconscious) conditioning in early childhood training as well as in the formulated values of verbal education. (Probably a similar assimilation takes place in the Yurok's orientation in time: by a projection of typical childhood experiences into "prehistory" a unified time environment is created which again allows for oriented behavior.)

In demonstrating some configurations of Yurok culture which seem to express this mutual assimilation of geographic, anatomical, and ethical concepts, we do not propose to generalize that all people living along rivers with salmon runs do as the Yurok do, although some might in some particulars. Neither do we overlook the fact that almost every item of Yurok ethnology on which our demonstration can be based is shared by the Yurok's ethnic neighbors where it may have the same, a similar, a transformed, or a different meaning. Here, too, our attitude is clinical: we would expect an individual ego to synthesize individually experiences typical for many; similarly, we assume that a group ego (or whatever we choose to name the organized and organizing core of a culture situated as it is in its constituent individual egos) tends to take stock of and to synthesize what has been selected, accepted, and preserved. It is this *synthetic tendency* which in the following pages is to be demonstrated *within one culture*; we believe it to be an essential attribute, although not the explanation, of culture as such.

Generalizations, if they were our goal, would lead us to the psychology of the ego [5], and its synthetic functions [6], in the sense that a tendency toward a conceptual synthesis of the inner and the outer environment is a potentiality of the human mind—a potentiality which is developed as one of the infantile ego's methods of orientation in the world, and which in adult life either manifests itself in institutionalized human pursuits of magic, intuitive, and artistic character or makes itself psychotically independent of cultural and physical reality.[1] As a group-psychological phenomenon, however, we consider it to be an argument neither for the equation of phylogeny and ontogeny nor for that of "primitive," infantile, and psychotic thinking; we merely regard it as the (here well-integrated) use and organization of a mental potentiality for the sake of orientation, survival, mental economy, and self-expression.

I. The Mutual Assimilation of Anatomical and Geographical Concepts in the World Image of the Yurok

THE DOUBLE VECTOR

One of the first Indians to whom the writer was introduced was in a certain sense a colleague of his. F called herself, and was called by others, a "doctor." So far as she treated somatic disorders or used (the Yurok brand of) physiological treatment, the writer could not claim to be her professional equal. However, she also did psychotherapy with children, and in this field it was possible to "exchange notes." She laughed heartily about psychoanalysis, the main therapeutic principles of which, as will be shown presently, can be easily expressed in her terms. There is a radiant friendliness and warmth in this very old woman; if melancholy makes her glance and her smile withdraw behind the stone-carved pattern of her wrinkles, it is a dramatic melancholy, a positive withdrawal, not the immovable sadness seen in some faces of other Indian tribes.

As a matter of fact, F was in an acute state of gloom when we arrived. Some days before, on stepping out into her vegetable garden and glancing over the scene, a hundred feet below, where the Klamath enters the Pacific, she had seen a small whale enter the river, play about a little, and disappear again. This shocked her deeply. Had not Wohpekumeu[2] decreed that only salmon, sturgeon, and similar fish should cross the fresh-water barrier set by the creator? This breakdown of a barrier, this disturbance of a vector, could only mean that the world disk was slowly losing its horizontal position, that salt water was entering the river, and that a flood was approaching comparable to the one which once before had destroyed mankind. However, she told only a few intimates about it, indicating that perhaps the event could still become untrue if not talked about too much.

Except for facts bordering on taboo subjects, it was easy to converse with this old Indian woman because usually she was merry and quite direct. (During our first interviews Kroeber had sat behind us, listening and now and again interrupting. On the second day, I noticed that he was absent from the room for some time, and I asked where he had gone. The old woman laughed merrily, and said, "He give you chance to ask alone. You big man now.")

What are the causes of child neuroses (bad temper, lack of appetite, nightmares, delinquency, etc.) in Yurok culture? Yurok children are supposed to be able, after dark, to see the "wise people," a race of small beings which preceded the human race. If a child sees a member of this race, he develops a neurosis, and if he is not cured he eventually dies.

The "wise people" are described as not taller than a small child. They are always "in spirit," because they do not know sexual inter-course. They are adult at six months of age, and they are immortal. They procreate orally, the female eating the man's lice. The orifice of birth is unclear; however, it is certain that the "wise" female has not a "woman's inside," that is, vagina and uterus, with the existence of which, as well be shown later, sin and social disorder entered the world.

We observe that the "wise people" are akin to infants: they are small, oral, and magic, and they do not know genitality, guilt, and death; they are visible and dangerous only for children because children are still fixated on earlier stages and may regress when the stimulation of the daylight is waning—then becoming dreamy, they may be attracted by the "wise people's" childishness and by the narcissism with which they thought they could be wise and be magic without social organization. For the "wise people," as we shall see, were creative; but they knew not genitality and, consequently, what it meant to be "clean." (In this case a phylogenetic fantasy seems to *symbolize* ontogeny: the "wise" men, I think, are the projection of the [pregenital] state of childhood into prehistory.)

If a child shows disturbances indicating that he may have seen "wise people," his grandmother goes out in the garden or to the creek (wherever she has been informed that the child has played after dark), cries aloud, and speaks to the spirits: "This is our child; do not harm it." If this is of no avail, the grandmother next door is asked to "sing her song" to the child; every grandmother has her own song. (American Indians in general seem to have a fine understanding of ambivalence, which dictates that in certain crises near-relatives are of no educational or therapeutic use.) If the neighbor grandmother does not avail, F is finally appealed to and a price is set for the cure.

F says she often feels that a patient is coming:

Sometimes I can't sleep; somebody is after me to go and doctor. I not drink water, and sure somebody come. "F, I come after you, I never sleep last night, I come after you, I give you ten dollars." I say, "I go for fifteen dollars." "All right."

The child is brought by his whole family and put on the floor of F's living room. She smokes her pipe to "get into her power." Then, if necessary, the child is held down by mother and father while F sucks the first "pain" from above the child's navel. These "pains," the somatic "causes" of illness (although they, in turn, can be caused by bad wishes), are visualized as a kind of slimy, bloody materialization. To prepare herself for this task F must abstain from water for a given period. "As she sucks, it is as if her chin were going through to your spine, but it doesn't hurt," one informant reports. However, every "pain" has a "mate"; a thread of slime leads F to the place of the "mate," which is sucked out also.

We see that to the Yurok disease is bisexual. One sex is represented near the center of the body, which is most susceptible to sorcery, while the other has wandered to the afflicted part, like the uterus in the Greek theory of hysteria or the displaced organ cathexis in the psychoanalytic system.

Having swallowed two or three "pains," F goes to a corner and sits down with her face to the wall. She puts four fingers (omitting the thumb) into her throat and vomits slime into a basket. Then, when she feels that the "pains" she has swallowed are coming up, she holds her hands in front of her mouth, "like two shells," and with spitting noises, which I cannot characterize phonetically, spits the child's "pain" into her hands. Then, as she dances, she makes the "pains" disappear. This she repeats until she feels that all the "pains" have been taken out of the child.

Then comes the "interpretation." She smokes again, dances again, and goes into a trance. She sees a fire, a cloud, a mist, then sits down, fills her pipe anew, takes a big mouthful; and then has a more substantial vision which makes her say to the assembled family something like this: "I see an old woman sitting in the Bald Hills and wishing something bad to another woman. That is why this child is sick." She has hardly spoken when the grandmother of the child rises and confesses that it was she who on a certain day sat in the Bald Hills and tried to practice sorcery upon another woman. Or F says, "I see a man and a woman doing business [having intercourse] although the man has prayed for good luck and should not touch a woman." At this, the father or the uncle gets up and confesses to his guilt. Sometimes F has to accuse a dead person of sorcery or perversion, in which event the son or the daughter of the deceased tearfully confesses to his misdeeds.

It seems that F has a certain inventory of sins which, like many a psychopathological system of interpretations, simply attaches, under ritualistic circumstances, one of a given number of explanations to a certain disturbance and makes people confess tendencies which, in view of the structure of the culture, can be predicted, and which to confess is profitable for anybody's inner peace. Having an exalted position in a primitive community, F is, of course, in possession of enough gossip to know her patients' weaknesses even before she sees them and is experienced enough to read her patients' faces while she goes about her magic business. If she, then, connects a feeling of guilt derived from secret aggression or perversion with the child's symptoms, she is on good psychopathological grounds, and we are not surprised to hear that neurotic symptoms usually disappear after F has put her finger on the main source of ambivalence in the family and has provoked a confession in public.

When I asked F to tell me how she happened to become a shaman, she quickly and seriously said, "This cost twice a dollar." Anyone not prepared for the Yurok mentality could easily mistake this request for what it would mean among other Indian tribes, namely, an attempt to capitalize on what seems most interesting to the white man. Here, however, one receives the impression of a superindividual eagerness, a wish not for money but for the establishment of a certain ritual atmosphere. Like all activities of a higher importance, doctoring is highly paid among the Yurok: in American money, F receives as much as a psychiatrist (but has to return the fee when she is unsuccessful). Once the sanctity of the situation was established, a more intense level of Yurok experience opened up: F's seeming interest in money abruptly and surprisingly changed into "pity and terror." Soon she shed tears in recording how she was forced to become a doctor. However, we do well to restrain our sympathy until we understand more of the magic function of tears in Yurok culture.

> My mother says, "You be doctor." I say, "No." She say, "You much money, beautiful clothes; if not doctor, will have nothing." I again say, "No." She scold, she scold too rough; I go away from home, stay out at night, sleep with Nancy over in other village.

F's rejection, of course, concerns the more material aspect of Yurok doctoring, namely, the sucking from sick persons' bodies of "pains," which are described as being slimy and bloody and looking like a polliwog.

> There I dreamt a woman is coming, her hair is long, she has grass skirt and small basket. She say to me, "Come with me in there." I say, "All right," and she holds a basket. She say, "You look in there." I look, mist

closes sky, water dropping out of sky, white yellow black bloody nasty. [I later verified this as meaning: Through the mist I saw the sky come together. Out of the cleft I saw water dropping, white, yellow, and black. It looked bloody and nasty.]

She hold little basket out so water dropped in it; she turn around, I see stuff in basket, I kind of afraid, I turn around. She say, "You stay there." I go, I look back; she throw basket on me, it hit me on mouth; I swallow stuff, I no sense any more; I wake up with noise, Nancy wake me up. "You crazy," she says. I never tell I dreaming that night; not sleep again.

F knew why she did not tell Nancy about the dream, for in the dream she had swallowed the stuff of which pains are made. We see here one of those interesting mechanisms which are active in the institutionalization of what seem hysterical or psychotic phenomena. People, so I heard later, had predicted for years that F would be a shaman "because she slept so much," that is, had contact with prehistory, night, and death. In her dream F already submits to the social pressure which says that a woman of her personality make-up, being the daughter and granddaughter of doctors, should also become a doctor. By her terrified awakening she probably had already communicated her conflict to Nancy; but a dream is still a *private* symptom which one is able to keep to oneself. She does not dare go to sleep again, afraid as she is of the inner voice which, in the morning, forces her to speak a clearer language, namely, that of an *organ* symptom which cannot be hidden.

In the morning when eating breakfast I feel sick. I want to go outside, found huckleberry [a berry red, soft, and sweet, and of the size of a nipple]. Ate little bit, feel sick, worse; three o'clock fellow bring crabs, I cook and I eat, I vomit. Other women say, "Maybe you dreaming bad." "Why, I did." "Well, then you not drink water or else you never get well."

Water—so we can paraphrase—water, one of the most common Yurok taboos, should not touch the inside of the body, if anything goes on or is going to go on which implies a transmutation in the service of biological or spiritual change.

"Maybe you get [to be] doctor if [you] go to sweat house." "No." Ate crabs, all come out again, can't eat nothing; men-folk in sweat house make big fire; evening, women cook acorn.

The community has accepted the verdict of her symptoms and she in turn accepts their verdict as expressed in the preparations for her novitiate. Here F is at the crossroads of psychopathology and privileged social career.

The life history of another Yurok woman, now deceased, of which I was able to secure only fragments, indicates that flight at this moment may mean (or already signifies) lifelong neurotic suffering. The story paralleled F's up to the point reached in our account. Here, however, the woman objected and ran away. She became a very neurotic woman, with chronic indigestion. She vomited whenever she saw traditional Indian food such as acorn soup or salmon. One of her daughters acquired the mother's symptoms as a child, constantly needing laxatives, being finicky about food, and beginning to vomit at adolescence. Many factors may enter here; however, the old woman is said to have spoken incessantly of her interrupted novitiate; she had, psychologically, never developed beyond the point where it broke up.

If F took the alternative road to a social position of prestige and wealth, it has to be kept in mind that manifestly she did so with trembling and that even today, when she is by far the richest, best-dressed, and most esteemed Indian woman in her community, she has to call on her reservoir of pity and terror when relating the story.

Note the interplay of inception and ejection in this story. The mother had suggested curing, which means sucking and becoming rich. The daughter is overcome by loathing and runs away. In her dream she is forced by an old woman to swallow down into her stomach what she repudiated when awake. Awake again, she vomits involuntarily. Now, as we shall see, under a trance induced by the excitement of the community this involuntary vomiting of stomach content is transformed into an ability voluntarily to vomit the first "pain," then to swallow it again (but this time only deep enough to imbed it in slime), and to produce it again without throwing up food with it—a mastery over the oral-nutritional canal which will give her the power to cure people. This is common enough throughout primitive medicine. In Yurok culture, however, it seemed to be specifically related to other "double-vector" situations, that is, configurations in which an object entering a canal turns around and leaves it and by doing so creates a magic event of either beneficial or dangerous character. In geographic dimensions we saw such a double-vector arrangement in the behavior of the little whale who entered and left the mouth of the Klamath.

Three women and I; women make four acorn soups; I say put away; old men go to sweat house, pretty near dark. I get sick again, commence throw up, tell women I going outside. She says, "Put your head in there and maybe [it will] all come out [of you]." I say no; she says again; she give me her cap. I put my head in: oh, sick, sick; after while lots of stuff come out, spit, that's all. [She means she already vomits slime, not food.] Men in sweat house yet; when I get through [vomiting] I tell women, "I feel good now, maybe it come out"; put it on fire [light up the fire to see]; was dark; put it on fire and she holler, she says, "aw-w-w-w, you look, it is like worm, black." [F demonstrates that the worm, meaning the "pain," was as big as half her index finger.] Slimy, she gets neighbor woman doctor too; doctor she says; old man says, "Sweat house is too hot yet, dance in house, take it on hand" [he means the "pain"]; other woman put pain on his hand. Henry was boy, he see me that time.

This witness could not be reached; however, as mentioned before, another informant reported Henry as testifying that the "pain" looked like a clot of black blood and had the form of a polliwog.

Had to learn make noise. [F far back in her throat made a noise the repeated production of which ought to be sufficient to produce some blood.] Henry say, "I dance with you." Other women put it [the "pain"] back in my mouth; throw it in like that; it inside again; I fight, fight, mess up fire, spill acorn, no sense, just like no sense at all; after while I stop. Old man, mother's first cousin, take me to sweat-house dance; too dark in sweat house, everybody come in singing; I guess eleven o'clock [at night] I stop, time I feel tired; rest go back into house; I sleep in sweat house tired; one o'clock at night he says, "I going to wake up wife"; all women come back again singing again, oh I feel sick again, dance and dance, oh just daylight quit, I cover up face with hands like in house. [Here big tears roll down her cheeks, and her face expresses a reliving of what must have been the hardest days of her life.] Never drink no water. [Here she coughs.] Eat nothing. [Here her voice indicates a climax of her self-pity.] Noon go back to sweat house; well, I dance again, nothing come; I dance, tired in evening, I quit, go into house again. Old man my uncle says, "One o'clock you start again." Oh everybody so glad to sing. [Here, when she reports how her uncle tells her of the community's aproval and joy, her face begins to light up and she looks like a little child who smiles abruptly with tears in her eyes.] One o'clock, woman she wake me: "Come on." I dance again. [F's expression again becomes tired and resigned, but it changes abruptly.] But two o'clock I feel different, shaking inside, I like to dance; have basket, put hand in mouth again. [She demonstrates that she put the three middle fingers of her right hand into her mouth.] I throw up. I told, "Light, candle." I put in hand, two pains, slimy, black. [With joy in her voice:] Well, you know

Indians; when see it, cry; singing again, I stand up, I hold it again. [She demonstrates that she holds the two "pains" in her clasped hands.] Again I crazy; boy jump on me, hold arms around my body, makes me dance. Henry's mother pat my chest, pat my shoulder, make sound with pipe, pain come out [of me] again. If it come out four time, all right. Well, one fellow go after my mother. Mother says, "Won't come. She not be doctor, she not ask for money, she send patients away." [The mother indicates her doubt, probably ritually required, that the daughter will ever develop the self-confidence necessary to ask for a high fee.] He says, "You don't know what you say, you doctor yourself." Well, mother coming, father coming, and I see every time; I start again one o'clock at night, kick dance, I spit again, and oh my mother and father were crying so hard and my sister coming and her husband and old Spott, sweat house just full, all singing, and I never feel tired when all the fellows singing; looks [as if] I never get tired; eat acorns, never drink no water; used to be that way, everybody liked to singing, so from Johnson's up-river they coming, lots of work to feed them. I dance, dance, dance, sweat and hot, I again sick, I do it again that way. [She means she vomits.] After a while it comes out again. [This is the third "pain," and she now speaks with deep satisfaction.] Old Spott worse, cried; eight days blood he coming, all bloody over here into basket; next morning, four o'clock, pain is again and blood with it. [This is the fourth and final "pain."]

Six months never drink water; sleep in sweat house, not when blood comes out. [She means except when she menstruates.] Sometimes in sweat house I feel somebody no clean, he get out. [She means she feels that a man had intercourse with his wife at a time when she menstruated and therefore should not be near her. This taboo we shall explain later.] All winter I dance, go up to woods, clap hands [and say], "I will get lot money for doctoring" [that is, she prays in the Yurok way, stating, with or without tears, as a fact that which she wants to become true]. He say, "Now you doctor this rock. Just play this rock is sick, just as if doctor pretends." All way back past sweat house everybody sing, I dance; that's the time I drink water again.

As if asking for a fellow therapist's sympathy, F concludes:

Two years I doctor I get nothing. One time Johnson fellow says, "I give you three dollars." [Laughs merrily.] Three dollars! oh, I so proud.

One element, and a decisive one, is missing in F's story. Other Yurok say that her trouble began with her grandmother's taking a "pain" out of her mouth (the grandmother's) and making F swallow it. Why did F not mention this?

Several explanations are possible: either the grandmother story is something which the community only infers from the dream, according to which an old woman makes F drink blood or dirty stuff out of a basket or there is an amnesia for the orginal trauma, and this either in the primary sense, that F has actually repressed the occurrence represented in her dream, or in the secondary one, that the occurrence (although she did not choose to remember or at least to verbalize it at the moment when she started her story) is in F's preconscious mind and could be ascertained. Finally, the "amnesia" may be only an official one; that is, this most real and quite conscious aspect of her story is suppressed by a taboo.

Interestingly enough, however, this important omission has a certain configurational similarity with the very first issue which, as we observed, affected F's emotions deeply—the whale's entering of the river mouth. In both occurrences the wrong object took possession of the vector of permissible objects: the whale came in where only salmon (in Yurok: "that which is eaten") is permitted; the "pain" (a slimy substance looking like a polliwog) came in where only food should come in. Are we confronted here with an individual's complex? As we shall see, strong recurrent taboos among the Yurok concern the "contamination" (either by an inversion of vectors or by the meeting of antagonistic objects in the same aperture) of what floats in the water, what passes the nutritional system, and what flows in the body's veins. The "pain" swallowed by F forbids her to drink water. Venison, too, being "bloody," is antagonistic to water; after having eaten deermeat one ought not even to wash one's hands, but merely to wipe them. Salmon, water-born, would avoid a house which contained a menstruating woman. Money, the product of another "stream," is the successful antagonist of sexual intercourse: husband and wife meet outside the house to avoid its criticism. A man's oral contact with a woman's vagina (her "inside") will keep the flow of salmon and of money from the river, and will make all the Yurok weak: it is this perversion, small children are taught, that makes the mud hens so weak that they cannot fly. We see, therefore, that what the grandmother tries to make the girl do on the manifest (historical) as well as on the latent (dream) level somehow goes against the whole Yurok training of the mutual exclusion of what floats in the channels of geography and anatomy. If not easily refused and well repressed, this seduction therefore can only lead either to psychopathology (incomplete repression) or to sublimation in connection with a high social goal. The dream's disguise shows the force of repression. Not the grandmother, but a most impersonal "old woman," is offering the blood, which does not come out of her mouth but out of a gigantic cleft in heaven. Above all, F does not accept it, but is forced to swallow it.

A cleft dripping with an ugly and bloody substance does not, as could be suspected, represent a part of the sucking situation, since in reality (in Yurok reality) no slit or wound indicates the place on the body out of which a "pain" has been sucked. At worst, this place may show slight tooth marks. This dream element, therefore, must represent loathing of an opening other than the mere zone of "pain"-sucking. If it is the grandmother's mouth, then its "gigantic" ugliness still calls for explanation.

Under questioning, F stated that she was just about to menstruate at the time of her novitiate; and indeed the psychotherapist of our culture is accustomed to meet her symptoms in preadolescents. Certain hysterical girls are apt to express loathing of certain foods, of certain aspects of the maternal or paternal bodies, or of the bulging aspects of adolescent growth itself. However, the object of loathing maintains a strange attraction; it is sought with eyes and imagination until its perceived image causes vomiting. Such symptoms point to an (ontogenetically) primitive level of bodily experience in which the female genitals, as a newly developing organ system of inception, are unconsciously associated with the infantile model of inception, namely, the oral-nutritional system. Thus both the first embarrassing rush of inceptive eagerness and the repudiation of the idea of inception are experienced and dramatized in oral addictions and aversions. In the dripping cleft, therefore, we see a condensation of a kind common in dreams of the menstruating girl's "inside which drips blood," the grandmother's mouth which sucks bloody "pains," and the prospective patients' insides in which "pains" wait to be sucked out.

Let us see what modes of behavior the Yurok culture would have forced on F had she matured like any other girl. When menstruating the first time, she would have had to sit silent in a corner of the home for ten days, with her back turned to the fire pit. She would have been under an obligation to move as little as possible. On one daily trip to bring in firewood, she would have been obliged to look neither to left nor [to] right. She would be forbidden to eat at least the first four days, and longer if possible. If then overcome by hunger, she would have to take her food to a spot where any sound of man and animal, and even the song of birds, would be confounded by the noise of the river. In other words, when showing the signs of female maturation, that is, the readiness to conceive, the adolescent girl is forced to dramatize a general closing up to any substance (be it even a sound of nature) which may reach her from the outer world. At the end of this period her mother shows her what her inceptive organization is meant for: putting twice ten sticks in front of her, she calls half of them sons, the other half, daughters [8].

So far, we come to the conclusion that in F it is (1) the premenstrual stage and (2) a hysterical anticipation of shamanism (increased by an ambivalent attitude, probably of an oral character, to grandmother and mother) which make her react with loathing and with flight to the grandmother's suggestion of capitalizing on the magic potentialities of her oral system. But she receives help from the community which lifts her oral desires and aversions to a plane of magic usefulness.

As Kroeber points out, even such typical stories as that of F's novitiate are individually owned; the individual only does his duty if he puts his personal stamp on a story which he has inherited as a culture pattern. The comparison of such stories, then, shows especially clearly what elements remain consistent for the culture or the individuals concerned. In the following short comparison of F's story with the account of another novitiate, given in Kroeber's report [8], I shall underline consistent elements.

Kroeber's shaman is married when the novitiate is "imposed" on her. However, this does not seem typical; she must have provoked this imposition by some kind of devious behavior (comparable to F's inclination to sleep a great deal) in adolescence or childhood. In accordance with the dreamer's status and age, the dream content also differs: the *tempter* appears to this married woman in the image of an *unknown*, short-nosed man, who *forces her to eat* deermeat which is *black with blood* and at a later stage of the dream appears to have been *salmon*. Salmon dripping with the blood of venison: again a *reversal of a basic Yurok avoidance*. The morning after this dream, this woman too *is ill, cannot eat*, and dances in the sweat house until she is unconscious. The fact that she does not try to flee before she dances in the sweat house may be related to the fact that, more mature, in the Yurok sense, than the adolescent F, she more consciously wanted to become a shaman because she desired the doctor fees. But she, too, in a sudden craze *flees* through the smoke hole, runs to another sweat house, and goes on dancing. On the tenth day she so far gains control over her "pain" that she can swallow it even if it is put in a basket on the other side of the room. Then for her, too, there came a *period of daily walks* to gather sweat-house wood, while all through the winter she *sleeps in the sweat house*. She, too, *"thought of money"*; facing the door of the sweat house, she would say, "A long dentalium is looking at me" (dentalium shells are the ancient Yuork money, graded according to size); or, walking by the river, she would take pebbles in her mouth, spit them out, and say, "Pains will come into my mouth as cool as these stones; I shall be paid for that." She, too, refers to *menstruation*, although only indirectly: during her ten-day periods of sweating and refraining from water she would gash herself—an activity which to my knowledge is required only of men contaminated by intercourse with a menstruating woman. But then, as has not been emphasized yet, sleeping in a sweat house and praying for money are strictly male activities; similarly the sign and privilege of a shaman, namely, her pipe, is otherwise only used by men; so that, all in all, we may suspect that it is not only conflict over the inceptive role, but also a strong ambition to share male prerogatives, which makes a woman behave in such a way that the community will force her to become a shaman.

This conflict by no means seems permanently solved when the novitiate is completed. Both women report anxiety dreams. Kroeber's shaman says that she dreams in a sweat house of an uma'a (a mysterious thing with which one destroys others by sending it to them, sometimes by shooting it on the end of a miniature arrow). The uma'a had one leg straight, the other one bent at the knee. He walked on the knee as if it were a foot, and he had only one eye. (Remember that her male guardian spirit was "short-nosed.") The shaman shouted, fled, and was finally brought back unconscious.

F reports that sometimes she is disturbed by "nasty" dreams, dreams of snakes, which make her feel sick all over again.

> I dream I live here. Why! there is house, *all doors that way*. I think I will go around look in, see Indian house, *all doors that way, to river*. I run around. Oh! *snake* all over; I hit them all; over my arm, I bite them; I like crazy; I go to sweat house, I dance, everybody sing.

Thus she sometimes has to repeat her novitiate.

Let us see what the house doors in the dream may signify.

TWO HOUSES, THREE DOORS

There are two distinct Yurok house forms: the big or living house, where women and children sleep and are joined by the men only when oral or genital needs compel them, and a somewhat smaller sweat house, where men and boys above a certain age spend the time "meditating," purifying themselves, and trying to raise their spirits above the attractions of the female sex. Of these two house forms, the living house can have its only door on either side, as the house names "Doorway Up-river," "Doorway Down-river," "Doorway toward the Ocean" indicate. The entrance to the sweat house, however, always faces a creek or the river or the ocean. If F dreams with so much emotion of a house which had its doorway toward the river, it probably was a sweat house, that is, forbidden to women and harboring male secrets (snakes). This meaning becomes clearer if we concentrate for a moment on the structure of the two types of Yurok houses.

From outside, both houses present the view of a gabled roof of weathered redwood planks almost at the ground level since the real room is subterranean. One enters by creeping through a rounded hole about 2 feet in diameter cut through a strong end plank which alone bears ornamentation (wood carving). In creeping through this hole, one holds on (if a stranger, advisedly so) to a pair of stones placed inside the door, where a slippery, notched ladder leads down into the dugout, a dark, disorderly, and populated octagon. In the center of the floor of this octagon, which may be from 2 to 5 feet below the ground outside, there is a fireplace. The only ray of light comes from the "chimney," an opening in the roof (effected by the mere putting aside of one plank) above the fireplace. Underneath the roof is a huge crisscross of poles on which salmon is hanging in all possible states of age and eatenness, while a shelf bench between the dugout and the side walls is loaded with enormous baskets full of acorns and utensils in various states of use. The total impression is that of darkness, crowdedness, and endless accumulation. This is where women and children live; the man who comes to visit his home is careful not to sit on the floor, but on a block or stool of the form of a cylinder or mushroom. Otherwise, his place is in the sweat house, where he takes the older boys; there is one sweat house to six or seven living houses.

While similar in structure and in its exterior, if possible even more ragged than the living house, the sweat house is somewhat smaller and has no provision for storage. It is lighter because its entrance hole is horizontal. Its floor is all paved with carefully selected slabs of stone and is kept scrupulously clean. There is a sacred post near the center of the house, and a central fireplace. The only furniture consists of a few block pillows of redwood. In contrast to the one-doored living house, however, the sweat house has an additional exit at one of its small ends: an oval opening of not more than from 10 to 14 inches in diameter, at some 4 feet below the ground. This leads into a kind of well set with cobbles, from which one emerges—if indeed one can get through the hole. This little oval is the spiritual test of the Yurok world: only a nude man, moderate in his eating habits and supple with the perspiration caused by the sacred fire, can slip through this hole and, as is required, jump into the creek, river, or ocean in order to perfect the purification necessary for a successful fisherman or hunter. A woman, a fat man, or a bad sweater would not be able to get through the hole. A man who wishes to be successful and to add to the success of the tribe will pass this test every morning; if contaminated by contact with a corpse or by intercourse with a woman, he will do so on two or more consecutive mornings, being careful not to mingle with the purified workers in the meantime.

As we shall see, these two house forms not only serve woman and man, respectively, but also symbolize what the man's and the woman's insides mean in Yurok culture: the family house, dark, unclean, full of food and utensils, and crowded with babies, the place from which a man emerges contaminated; the sweat house, lighter, cleaner, more orderly, with selectivity over who and what may enter, a place from which one emerges purified. If it is true that the male sex envies the female her birth-giving function as she envies him his life-spending one, the Yurok succeeds in symbolically reproducing himself from a male womb every morning. This womb, however, as a configuration, is a tube with an entrance and an exit, not a sacklike form like the living house and like the woman's inside with its periodical blood flow, which to the Yurok is the dark side of anatomy as death is of life, night of day.

What do the Yurok women think about this dichotomy? They do not seem to question it or to be dejected about it. Rather, they do what women do everywhere: they manage in daily reality to exert a power which is officially denied them in special places and at special times. On the other hand, there are Yurok fables which find it necessary to impress on the little Yurok girls the ugliness of "masculine protest" in woman.

The quarrelsome blue jay who scoldingly jumps from branch to branch is a jealous woman; she got so angry with her husband she pulled her clitoris out and put it on her head (see?).

The crow was the eagle's wife. She did not take care of his child. She demanded the right to dance in the sweat house. But the old man does not even look at her; he just calmly, proudly flies his circles (see?).

Such narrative education may have sufficed for the "normal" girl. F, as we have seen, shares the male's horror of the female and wishes to share his prerogatives. In establishing power over the body's apertures, she becomes a sexless companion of men; equals the best of them in wealth, and surpasses them in magic power. In the context of Yurok configurations we first notice that procreation and cure are the only nonpathological arrangements in which a double vector occurs, that is, where substances go into and come out of one and the same aperture (F's vomiting is a pathological version which she learns to "control"). The woman is the source of procreation, of evil, and of cure. We shall see later that at the beginning of time the Klamath itself flowed up on one side, down on the other. Then the creator made the river flow down only, the salmon climb up only—and we remember F's horror of the whale that entered, turned around, and left the estuary of the Klamath: salmon, as salmon, only goes one way.

The general Yurok attitude toward the human body and nakedness reflects the one toward the woman's inside. Only the menstruating woman and the young girl between her first menstruation and her first child keep their bodies out of the sight of bathers; otherwise, everyone swims where and how he pleases. Men emerging from the sweat house to jump into the river may hold their hands over their genitals or they may not; this does not depend on who is crossing their way.[3] The surface of the body is pure and purifiable; but its deep inside is likely to be incurably contaminated and contaminating.

CENTRIFUGAL CREATION AND CENTRIPETAL LAW

1

R is a one-man historical society of his tribe. His ability to convey the quality of his culture in English words is outstanding; it would be interesting to explore his life history for the sources of such a gift. However, I know little about him. The gestures of his hands were strikingly different from anything I have seen among whites or Indians. As he sat before his little frame hut with the river mouth and the vast ocean before him, he seemed to conduct an orchestra of directions which slowly crossed and circumscribed the disk which is the Yurok world. To whatever periphery these directions set out, there to dissipate, they were gathered back to the course of the river and down the valley to its estuary. His head and his eyes in calm concentration kept turning toward the Pacific Ocean, but his hands (with no movement of the fingers) would make alive the particular system of Yurok directions in which there is no west nor east, north nor south, but only an "upstream," "downstream," "toward the river," "away from the river," "around behind," "behind in rear"— the last two connoting a movement up the river, away from the river, and an elliptic return to it. One was reminded of the way the Yurok say the sky was made:

> Wesonamegetol . . . took a rope and laid it down in an enormous circle, leaving one end loose at a certain place among the hills. Traveling off . . . and coming around from the south to the same spot again, he joined the two ends of the rope together. Then for days he journeyed back and forth over the hills, filling in and knotting the strands across each other. When the sky net was complete the hero took hold of it in two places and "threw it up"[12].

Kroeber summarizes the Yurok geographic concepts as follows:

> The Yurok, and with them their neighbors, know no cardinal directions, but think in terms of the flow of water. Thus pul is the radical meaning downstream; pets, upstream; hiko, across the stream; won, up hill, that is, away from the stream on one's own side; wohpe, across the ocean, and so on. Such terms are also combined with one another. If a Yurok says "east" he regards this as an English word for upstream, or whatever may be the run of the water where he is. The name Yurok itself—which in its origin is anything but an ethnic designation—means "downstream" in the adjacent Karok language. The degree to which native speech is affected by this manner of thought is remarkable. A house has its door not at its "western" but is "downstream" corner. A man is told to pick up a thing that lies "upstream" from him, not on his "left." The basis of this reckoning is so intensely local, like everything Yurok, that it may become ambiguous or contradictory in the usage of our broader outlook. A Yurok coming from O'men to Rekwoi has two "upstreams" before him: south along the coast, and south-southeast, though with many turns, along the Klamath. When he arrives at Weitspus, the Trinity stretches ahead in the same direction in the same system of valley and ridges; but being a tributary, its direction is "up a side stream," and the direction "upstream" along the Klamath suddenly turns north, or a little east of north, for many miles. Beyond their Karok neighbors the Yurok seem to have a sense that the stream comes from the east. At least they point in that direction when they refer to the end of the world at the head of the Klamath [8].

I asked R to tell me how the world was made. The Yurok are great storytellers and a peculiar historical sense is strongly developed among them. "Every story should have a foundation," R says, meaning a foundaiton in historical fact; "explain where something began and came from and if you do not know the foundation, do not try to teach." Every magic formula of theirs is an account of the historical event occurring when the formula was first used, and even today the Yurok indicate that, to them, to tell history means to do something real to the present. When I asked a Yurok who loved to tell obscene stories about Irishmen to tell me a few genuine obscene Yurok jokes, he became abruptly serious and said almost anxiously that nobody would dare to "make up" stories about sex among the Yurok; he would only tell the old stories giving the historical foundation of how sex came to be. For the make-believe story might be understood as concerning a living Yurok, which either would make it a lie or might mean "to swear" at the particular Yurok—"to swear" connoting a verbal offense against another person. This, incidentally, is taught early: children are forbidden to talk about sex as long as their parents are alive because to do this means to "swear" at the parents. Another time, when collecting the moral fables that represent a large part of Yurok education (see Part II), I noticed that there were stories concerning the panther, the eagle, the buzzard, the rabbit, the eel, etc., but none about salmon. I asked for a fable about this animal and immediately was given the same kind of negative answer: about salmon, "the food itself," no stories can be "made up"; only the old stories can be repeated which give the historical foundation of its origin, and by their mere repetition they represent a kind of prayer, an assurance that values are durable and immovable.

R became very serious when he began to relate the story of the creation of the world (recorded in the following section); it was almost as if he were reciting a ritual formula. However, while the Yurok have to present stories and formulas concerning vital issues with a *historical attitude*, they are by no means obliged even to pretend to *historical truth* throughout; in some respects every narrator has an exclusive right and even the duty to give his story a personal flavor. R's story of the creation follows.

2

Wohpekumeu was in search of another land. In the old one across the ocean his wife was dead. He walked on water right in here where now the river is [demonstration of tapping steps]. Everything was dark. He walked up to the place Kenek. He stood there. He cried and sang: "I want a land here. I want a land here."

In the Yurok beginning there was not "the word," but tears and a nostalgic song.

> Land appeared on both sides of where he stood. In the middle the river went up on one side, down the other.

We note that the original vector system in the river represented the double vector. The later concepts of the river correspond to the facts only in regard to its one-way flow out of the mouth, but keep its origin upriver unexplained; lakes, or another part of the ocean, are vaguely assumed to provide the water. Similarly the "later" concepts of the body take into account the anatomical fact of genital conception, while the earlier "wise women" conceived through the mouth and had no vagina; but "the facts" arouse irrational horror of their intrabodily location, with the creation of which, as we shall see presently, sin came into the world just as it did with the eating of the fruit of the tree knowledge in Paradise.

> He cried again. "I'm terribly lonely. I must have somebody to talk to. I want somebody to talk to." He wiped his tears like this.

Here, R wiped his eyes in a slow, ritualistic way, indicating that his method of wiping off tears was as important as the fact of crying.

> When he looked again, there was a waterspout coming up from the solid ground, slowly coming up to the height of his breast. He cried again. When he looked again the water was up to his brow. It was developed slowly into a woman. Head, breasts, arms, navel. The rest was water.

It is the shedding of the creator's tears which causes a waterspout to grow; in the beginning, there were the fluids. When the spout has reached human height, the solidification of the woman takes place in the opposite direction. However, in both directions there is a point of hesitation; the creator has to cry twice to make the water "grow" above a certain imaginary barrier on the level of his chest. Correspondingly, the solidification of the woman hesitates after she is formed down to the navel; above which, vaguely, is the area of sorcery, that is, the lethal pinching of the nutritional canal.

> The creator cried again: "I want a whole woman, I want a whole woman." The girl became solid, hips and vagina and all.

Then the widower cried for his son. He came and the widower gave son and woman into marriage.

Here the grave question arises, why the nostalgic widower abruptly becomes altruistic once a whole woman stands before him, for whom he has cried so untiringly.

Then he created grass, flowers. The son said, "We need food, too." So the creator made elks, rabbits, deer, grouse. Son wanted fish too. Father cries, goes down to the ocean and steps out to the mouth where salt and fresh water meet. He takes a fish out and puts it into the fresh water. That is where salmon, eels, sturgeon, steelhead, sea lion, etc., came from.

He omitted the whale; this is the reason for F's worries over the young whale's playing about in the river mouth.

As is the custom of creators, Wohpekumeu said to his son: "If I give you fish, you must work." Then the creator went upstream again, found his son fishing. Then he planted people and other rivers.

But then he became girl-crazy. He had only to look at a woman and she was in a family way. The girls were hiding from him.

What had become the matter with the creator? First, he could not enjoy the woman he had created; now, could he not stop creating, or was this sudden craze a displacement of his love for the daughter whom he had renounced so easily?

He tried tricks: made an elk come out of the woods and jump into the river, so the girls might get curious.

But people got wise. They kept houses closed, girls inside. So he planned a war dance. Pulled out some pubic hair, put it on his hand, and blew it into the air. The hair became boys. He took them up to the timberland and made them dance. While he watched them, a girl came out of a house, saw the old man, and ran back before he could look at her. He never tried to go into houses.

We notice that he is inhibited in regard to "intrusion," as he was when the woman he had created stood in front of him.

He then asked all the boys to come into his arms and made birds out of them. They are now "the pubic-hair birds."

When he came back to Kenek, he wanted his son's wife. He told his son the grandson needed a pet, and made him go up a tree for a chicken hawk. As the son was climbing, Wohpekumeu made a wind blow off all the branches and left him in the treetop. The son descended by making a rope out of Indian chewing gum, made from the inside of certain herbs.

Beginning with the creator's "tricks," we see that the story reveals elements of excess and warns of the dangers of periphery. The "creator" wants to lure the girls *out of the house and up to the timberland*. In order to impress them he makes *fast-flying birds* out of the boys. He sends his son *up a tree*. It is after such centrifugal acts that he seduces his daughter-in-law.

When the son came back, he met his son blind, shooting birds. The birds would fall right into his hands so that he would not have to search; dentalium, too, was flying into his hands. The boy had surprised the grandfather as he was approaching his mother. Already sexually excited, the old man had blinded the boy with semen.

Here is the first suggestion of the gifts which, later on, when *centripetal* laws are established, will flow from the peripheries of the world right into the crying Yurok's outstretched hands.

The son held his cane in all directions; *from every direction it bent back* except when he held it straight up. In that direction he threw his son, to the land of children and deer.

It is as if this bending back of the cane were making retroactive the tendency of centrifugality manifested by the old man's seductive antics. It showed the "natural" centripetal forces in the Yurok world.

The old man, repenting, swore never to have a woman again and to go home across the ocean. On his way down the coast he met many women, beautiful, naked, lying with legs apart. "No more," he would say. But finally he found one at Little River, shining like the sun; she had a good form. He lies down between her legs, starts to copulate. She closes her thighs tight and says: "Close your eyes and don't open them till I tell you. You will feel warm and very cold; you will feel a very hot wind and a very cold wind blowing, but don't open your eyes." She brought him back to his old country. She was the Skate woman. A skatefish looks like woman's inside.

When he was gone, the "wise people" tried to make the world better by law but could not help being like the old man.

They had a big flood. Now they live in the mountains [along the dangerous peripheries].

Finally, the son said to the people: "The wise people's and my father's laws spoiled it all. Now it's up to you: *Keep clean.*"

In Yurok mythology the creator is contrasted to another, a cleaner, "god," who only smoked but never ate, who spent all his time with men and never desired a woman, and who finally did the great historical deed of banning women from the sweat house.

This puritanical, compulsive image emphasizes by contrast the strange contradictions in the creator himself, who represents what we would call a hysterical character: he is nostalgic but sly; powerful but partly inhibited; godlike but unreliable. Egotistical where women are concerned, he is surprisingly unselfish and generous in regard to food: for although tricked away from the world by the Skate woman, he is said to have "liberated the salmon for the world," thus causing the annual gift from across the ocean of the salmon supply.

3

The story of the creator's expulsion suggests two trends of thought: (1) its meaning in the totality of Yurok culture, and (2) its relation to similar "creator" stories elsewhere. To the Yurok the creator image suggests dangers; centrifugal drivenness, homelessness, lack of restraining values, promiscuity, excess of individual power, etc. We may assume that these dangers had a part in the establishment of the "centripetal" rules of "clean" Yurok behavior, rules which under the deadly influence of time have developed into an intricate phobic system described in detail in Kroeber's chapter "The Yurok." We can only touch here on some major particulars in which mankind is "cleaner" than were those who created and preceded it.

1) A general *restriction of geographic radius* makes the peripheries of the world vague and inaccessible by deliberate self-inhibition: The well-bred Yurok does not "stray" in the directions from which the son's stick turned away, that is, the country upriver, or behind the river, or beyond the ocean. Wherever such tendency is noticed, bad breeding is assumed (in Yurok terms: one of the grandmothers of such an individual probably was not paid for in full). The horror of unrestricted radius is still expressed today, for example, in the Yurok's contempt for "gypises"; they anxiously call children into the houses, lock the doors, and hide property when gypsies appear, much as if the gypsies were "wise people"; at least to the children it must seem so.

2) An extreme *localization* of spatial and historical meaning is

another manifestation of the centripetal tendency of Yurok ethos. It is one of the strangest experiences when walking or driving along with an old Yurok suddenly to see him point to an old house pit barely visible and full of debris, and hear him say with the deepest pride, "This is where I come from," like a European nobleman pointing to the castle of his ancestors; or, better, like a son introducing his aged mother. The Yurok goes very far in denying any prominence to a place which has not become a named "locus" by being given a historical foundation. The gigantic redwoods all around him seem not mentioned in his myths; a height of several thousand feet does not assure a mountain a name. It is mainly along the creeks or the trails that rocks, pits, groups of trees, holes in the ground, etc., are named and give meaning to their neighborhood. The majority of house names denote the position of the house in the village or in relation to the river. What the old Yurok meant in saying he belonged to the pit was that, being born there, he participated in the name which the pit would keep as long as it was visible, and often much longer. Such place names are considered almost timeless, and in describing the history of the place the Yurok will calmly enter the realm of mythology without changing what he considers his "historical attitude."

3) The *substantiation* and *monetarization* of *values* are, in turn, akin to the trend of extreme localization; for money is value which can be grasped and handled. We remember F's request to increase the pay for information when a more sacred level of Yurok existence entered her report. "Every profession and privilege and every injury and offense can be exactly valued in terms of property. . . . There is no distinction between material and non-material ownership, right, or damage, nor between property rights in persons and in things" [8]. One has to see Kroeber's work for such outstanding examples as: the exactly fixed prices to be paid for a woman (and to be paid back, should she choose to leave her husband, according as she had borne him one child or two or three); or the much discussed compensation for the utterance of the name of a deceased person; or of an injury suffered on another man's property; or the price to be paid by a village to the "mourners of the year" before any major dance could be held.

4) Virtues of *acquisition* and *retention* of *possessions* are necessary for such a system. On the one hand, the Yurok thought of, talked about, and prayed for money constantly; on the other, "life was evidently so regulated that there was little opportunity for anyone

to improve his wealth and station in society materially"[1]. The highest communal occasions, such as the dances, were characterized by a display of wealth.

5) The *avoidance* of *political power* is an anarchy obviously based on the idea that where every value is substantiated and where everybody is out to maintain his possessions, motives and rights cannot be miscontrued and no interference of a "state" is necessary. "Such familiar terms as tribe, village, community, chief, government, clan can be used with reference to the Yurok only after extreme care in previous definition—in their current senses they are wholly inapplicable. The Yurok procedure is simplicity itself. Each side to an issue presses and resists vigorously, exacts all it can, yields when it has to, continues the controversy when continuance promises to be profitable or settlement is clearly suicidal, and usually ends in compromising more or less. . . . Justice is not always done; but what people can say otherwise of its practices?"[1].

It is hard for a white man to comprehend that Yurok lack of organization is not an organizational deficiency or lack of societal development, but organized phobic avoidance based on a certain mistrust of "free-floating" human motives. We expect such centripetal laws of behavior, localized and substantiated in all details, to create a kind of individual who may easily look unheroic, jealous of place, possessions, and prestige, bickering about values, stingy in his contributions to the community, anarchistic in his political leanings, mistrustful of his neighbor and phobic-compulsive in his avoidances. To these traists we shall return when we come to the description of Yurok childhood and of the way Yurok training strove to create the right cultural character for the life they tried to live. However, one has to see the Yurok among themselves—adults dancing through a night after the mourners have been paid off and the old treasures have been produced for exhibition by the dancers; or Yurok children at play—in order to visualize the pervading harmony and decency that can ensue from the cultural elaboration of mechanisms which we, as members of a different culture or of a psychiatric subculture, are used to meet only in pathological isolation in "queer" or "malicious" individuals.

4

The avoided peripheries of the Yurok world are at the same time the main concern of magic; their common denominator is "biological multiplication." The Yurok have no history of where they came from as a people; they have only a vague conception of a lake from which the waters of the Klamath flow; of a place "across the ocean" where salmon originates; of another one where the money's "home" is, as the sky is the home of deer. These peripheral wombs are joined by the human womb, which (with partial displacement to the house of origin) is treated with ambivalence and surrounded with avoidances and purifications. "Clean living" is orderly living on and with a system of mutually exclusive unobstructed and uncontaminated channels in which life flows; even that which is accumulated, namely, dentalium shells, is lined on strings and carried in oblong purses with a slit along their length. Similarly, the sweat house, as pointed out, is "morphologically" a tube, not a sack or a womb. But all these tubes are guarded by taboos and rituals which prevent possible cross-contamination: at certain places, signified by rocks, along the river, women have to leave a boat and can reenter it only after having walked around the rock; neither ocean nor river like[s] it if one eats on a boat; money does not tolerate sexual intercourse in one and the same house; deer will stay away from where its blood may be subjected to the contact with water; salmon will avoid the man who either is full of food or has been in contact with the woman's inside, etc. While, then, the whole world is a closed space, its inner freedom depends on its fluid ways. Geographically, the greatest danger to the Yurok world would be a blocking of the river in such a way that salmon could not ascend, fry not descend.

5

By now, it has probably occurred to the informed reader that by using Yurok cosmogony a case could be made for Freud's historical reconstruction of the murder of the primal father who claimed all the women in the horde, of the erection by his sons of laws which would prevent any of them from repeating the primal role, and of the feelings of guilt left in man's unconscious as a residue of that historical event which expresses itself alternately in irrational rebellion and in irrational expiation [7].

Many variations of this lost theme point to its existence somewhere in space and time. Its radical historical localization by Freud is thoroughly convincing only to a few; others cannot be convinced by a mere demonstration of more variations. Here again one might profitably emphasize a level of analysis which lies between description and interpretation, namely, the level of configurational analysis, which would allow the establishment, of *differences* between the divers variations of the primal-father theme, and, maybe, their specific dynamic place within their cultures of origin.

About the affectual tone of the story, as expressed in the creator's nostalgia and his use of tears, I shall speak later. Its ethical relation to the characteristics of basic Yurok laws has just been briefly discussed. In regard to the spatial characteristics of the story I can, I am afraid, only offer another "just-so" story; but, maybe, several such stories will blend into a real one.

Let us assume that the Yurok came from somewhere else; with no chance or wish to turn back, they found their way blocked by the Pacific. They settled along the river, and, noticing the periodical salmon run, became fishermen—in technique and in magic.

The human mind is likely to feel guilty and, if necessary, to construct a guilt when it finds itself faced with sudden environmental limitation; adapting, it learns to see a virtue in the necessity imposed by the limitation; but it continues to look into the future for potential recurrences or intensifications of the trauma of limitation, anticipating punishment for not being virtuous enough. In this sense, to the restricted Yurok, centrifugality may have become a vice in the past, centripetality a virtue; and the ocean's disfavor, anticipated punishment for centrifugal "mental sins" which Yurok ethics tries to avoid.

In the psychoanalysis of individuals we meet these mechanisms in examples like the following: a patient who had one arm paralyzed by poliomyelitis in early childhood began in adolescence to thank God that He had saved him from the potential badness of at least one arm. However, he developed a severe agoraphobia; he feared for the unimpaired arm, while the space around him normally reached and defended by the stricken arm "felt like danger." Only after the patient had remembered the bad things which the arm had been doing or wanted to do when the paralysis struck did his phobic symptoms improve. The arm, of course, was paralyzed; but the patient's constriction of space feeling, and thus an important cause of his agoraphobia, were relieved when in consequence of the removal of his psychological paralysis the stricken arm plus the space surrounding it again felt like "belonging" to the body. The point is that mishap increases guilt feeling (except in "moral masochists" so satiated with vague guilt that actual mishap its a relief).

In analogy, I think it possible that the Yurok's history which placed him where he is and made centrifugality impossible is one source of his centripetal conscience. In the story of the creator, then, if history at all, I would be inclined to see a blend of two or more historical traumata, or rather the fear of their recurrence (fears—as conditioning factors in collective ideas—being more easily passed on from generation to generation than are memories). These fears concern the danger of the return of centrifugal impulses both in the tribe as whole and in every individual trained to be centripetal: the widower, free and creative, becomes the primary antagonist of the society of centripetal sons; but his banishment implies the constant danger that the river will refuse food to a population blocked by non-Yurok and by the ocean.

The personification of all this danger in the creator must be a synthetic product of the culture; for if we do not want to assume that it represents an actual historical memory of one powerful man, then it can only be either a condensation of many primal fathers characteristic for one stage of prehistory or a projection, renewed by each generation and individual, of a father-son relation always again experienced as identical in its essentials. I shall have more to say about this image when we come to discuss Yurok childhood, although, in this paper, I shall not be able to state a clear decision concerning the father-, mother-, and child-images of which the personality of the creator is a queer composite: he feeds like a loving mother, is an irresponsible father, and cries like a child.

We have stated our belief that the ego, under certain circumstances, tries to understand and master geographic space by projecting the nearest environment, namely body feelings, onto it. Similarly, we may add now, it may be trying to structuralize history by projecting onto it typical experiences of childhood; and as the synthesis of the inner and the outer spatial environment results in one world system of magic causation, so the integration of history and childhood leads to one functionally interrelated time environment: with powerful and overbearing creators in the background; with thoughts and acts in the present which rebel against the creators but at the same time atone for rebellion and implore protection and provision; and with an outlook toward the future which wants to maintain this balance and prevent a recurrence of the past and its ontogentic and phylogenetic dangers. The keynote of this synthesis, is, of course, human helplessness.

Let us now consider the possibility that the biology of the salmon as a gift and a message from the creator had its say also in this unification.

The Salmon Run and the Fish Dam
The annual erection in early autumn of a weir, called a "fish dam," across the Klamath at Kepel was not only "one of the greater rituals of native northwest California, perhaps the greatest," but was also

"the largest mechanical enterprise undertaken by the Yurok or, for that matter, by any northwest California Indians, and the most communal attempt" [11].

The approximate schedule of this yearly affair was as follows. The "dam chief," or "doctor of the world," after some initial ceremonies at the mouth of the river, travels upstream to Sa'a. Under elaborate ceremonials he calls a "medicine" (a song supposed to cure the world) down-river while all human beings hide in their houses. The coming event being announced, preparations proceed all over the Yurok territory. About the twenty-third day, the dam building begins, and it is completed in ten days. The dam consists of a "wide fence of poles and stakes driven into the bed of the stream, strengthened and shored up with structural devices against the force of the current, and so carefully fabricated that salmon could not get through. At regular intervals along the course of this weir, openings were left leading into small enclosures which the Indians speak of as traps, corrals, or pens. . . . In their effort to get upstream, the salmon filled the Indian pens as fast as the fishermen could empty them. The fish were split and dried, and very large quantities were in this way preserved" [3]. For ten days salmon is taken. Then elaborate dances follow. The dam's destruction is left to the rain floods of early winter.

Waterman and Kroeber, in explaining the choice of the place for the fish dam, quote the Yurok as saying that they had to find the "right" spot by trial and error. In the accounts of two erstwhile assistants of the dam chief, this trial and error again appears as a kind of geographic-anatomical parallelism: they both describe how their ancestors at one and the same time found the right place for the dam in the valley and the right condition in the body for its erection, namely, no food in the stomach. "So they brought it up and made it here, and it was right. Now when they work on the dam, they know when to eat: they do without breakfast" [11]. My informant M, who claims to have been the last real dam chief in 1906, states that they found the right place for the dam by establishing how far the ocean could be heard inland on the stormiest day: where one did not hear any more the most powerful surf, there was the place for the fish dam. The anthropologists add the practical interpretation that "the river here is or was rather broad and shallow, with a gravel bottom which permitted the easy driving of stakes. . . . Upstream from Kepel the river is, generally speaking, narrow and deep, even close along the shore. There are numerous pools and eddies . . . where the salmon congregate and are readily taken with a dip net. . . . Such places are much more numerous upstream than down. . . . The dam was built in a locality where fishing places were few and not much good" [11].

The description of the river conditions at Kepel coincides with that given by biologists for places where the salmon likes to spawn [2]. It prefers, so they say, large, clean gravel beds (which hold and protect the eggs) and swift current (which provides a free flow of well-aerated water); so it may be that the salmon, "tasting" this place as a possible spawning place, behaves conspicuously around the gravel beds at Kepel, actually the last ideal spawning places in Yurok territory. Higher up, the river as far as it still flows in Yurok territory is much narrower and more rapid; many boulders form "pockets" which allow for the spawning of only smaller groups of salmon. Maybe it should be taken into account that the salmon's natural history clearly determines an optimum time and an optimum place for an attempt to catch a winter supply of the greatest possible nutritional value. The "normal" salmon (which has not participated in the earliest migration coming up the river, has little nutritional value, and is taboo to the Yurok) stores up a large supply of fat and protein before migrating into the river and before beginning the migrational fast which at one and the same time marks the beginning of the salmon's sexual development and the beginning of the end of its life. For the first ten days of its migration the salmon still draws on this capital, and during the second week it reaches the pink of condition, its flesh being dark red, its body consisting of a maximum of solids and fats and a minimum of cartilage and water. Later the fish has to draw on this capital both for its vigorous activity of swimming and jumping upstream and for its sexual development. Consequently, its optimum nutritional condition quickly decreases both in the individual salmon as it advances up the river and in the entire migrating population as the season progresses. The salmon stretches and shrivels and develops new cartilage to sustain an increasingly grotesque form. The optimum place and time for a mass catch of winter supply would therefore be the point where the greatest number of relatively early migrants reach a maximum of solids content.

It is often doubted whether "mere Indians" would be able to observe facts like these. Our contention is that they know it even when they cannot formulate cause and effect. They know it for all practical purposes even when they express this knowledge in magic terms which interpret what is observed outside as if it had originated in themselves—interpretations that may not preclude observations which to a less intuitive era have to be demonstrated by research. Provided, then, that they did observe: what did it mean to the Yurok that the salmon they knew, namely, the powerful salmon working its way up the river, had little or no food in its stomach and never was observed eating; that, furthermore, its vigor and its solids content decreased with its sexual development, and finally, that the male salmon, becoming adolescent and senescent at the same time, develops a grotesquely elongated snout? Since the salmon was sent from across the ocean (after having been liberated by the "widower across the ocean"), was the message it carried a code message saying: strong salmon—no food—little sex; weak salmon—hungry (prolonged snout)—strong sex? It seems at least that this observation may have participated in the Yurok's decision that in order to be as strong as his prey he had better abstain from sex and have no breakfast before he should begin to build on the dam, or, for that matter, begin any ordinary day's fishing.[4] (See Part II for an account of the Yurok's way of interpreting nature to children.)

Waterman also asks why the Yurok leave the dam to its fate after working on it for ten days and then using it for ten days. "The number ten," so he partly answers himself, is one of "the usual ritualistic numbers of the Yurok." A further and, it seems, extremely important answer must be that the Yurok as the inhabitants of the lower Klamath are, as it were, the wardens of their section of nature. It seems affirmed by experiment that the migrating salmon "strays" only little except where several small rivers combine to form a bay; the salmon's "homing instinct"[5] drives it to its birthplace which it had left, almost two years earlier, not one-twentieth of its adult size. The human beings living along the mouth and the lower part of the river, therefore, are the economic and—to their magic minds—spiritual guardians of a definite, self-propagating segment of nature, a closed shop which to an appreciable degree can only be impaired by them (namely, if they cut the salmon off from its spawning places upriver) but cannot be augmented by anything but magic behavior. The dam, therefore, while serving immediate practical purposes, also dramatizes and plays with the very idea of blocking the salmon, which means at one and the same time impaired supply during years to come, famine, and spiritual separation from the "creator"—if not, indeed, war; for the tribes upstream could not tolerate such an undertaking.

Waterman apparently believes that the dam, at least periodically, really closed up the river. However, not even for ten days could this have been done without having an unmanageable number of salmon pile up against the dam, especially at night when the fishing ceased. Actually, there were three gates under the surface of the water which were opened at night. (To meet every emergency, these gates were expressly forbidden to women.)

The following is the account of M, who claims to have been the last dam chief (in 1906). Whether he could have been dam chief at a time when the ecclesiastic hierarchy of the Yurok was in full force, it is hard to say, but there seems little doubt that he did supervise something like the erection of a dam and that informant A, in Waterman's and Kroeber's report, was my informant's assistant in 1906. However, M's report can in no way compete with the report of his former assistant; it is a conversational report which it seemed better not to interrupt. It is recorded here because "no ceremony could be learned completely from *one* Yurok; their narrations are too unsystematic"[11]. Also, it may be interesting to observe what time does to such a story (Kroeber recorded his account during the summer in which the present writer was born).

> We cannot do it any more. You need sixty young men, stout men, good fellows. Nowadays nobody can work any more.
> Everybody pays chief, throws in two bits, maybe $20 in all. X [a storekeeper] promised $15 extra, he still has it.

This is said with deep satisfaction as if no story of the good old days would be either good or old enough without the mention of a debt feud.

> From my home [near the mouth of the river] went to Sa'a. The sweat house was ready, on a river bar my helper had the blanket ready. A little fire on the river bar between Murek and Kepel, in the middle of the river. When the fire out we take the coals to Sa'a. Go into hole [old sweat-house pit] and blacken my face [with naïve enjoyment of his importance]. People don't supposed to see me; no matter how many people, all go into houses [everybody has to hide in order not to see the chief]. On top of sweat house holler five times upriver, five times down-river. Put rock on house. That rock goes clear up to heaven, down to dead people, out through ocean to tell all beings. Even the dead people come. Therefore no live people on south side, dead people watch there.
> Anybody [nobody is supposed to] watch me when I go. One boy watch me. Next year boy was dead. One man watch me. Next year man was blind. Mother was my cook [I think he meant his wife].
> Tomorrow we are going to finish fish dam! Every time they roll one down [people rolled pickets and bundles down from the heights of the

steep hills opposite Sa'a], they dance. Everything down, everybody ready, we finish the dam tomorrow. Now people come down from every place, they work, but not I, just sat down on one place, can't walk. Everybody give me pickets, that's my pickets, that high [shoulder]. I got to have two men and a boat to get my pickets from farther upriver. I see boat coming from across the river, it lands where I sit. I jump into boat, they go just as fast as they can go. Paddle just as fast as they can go. I got little basket in my hand, catch little water in middle of river, then we land where my roll [picket bundle] is. I jump out, I run around the roll, I have basket in my hand. I sprinkle that water on that roll, I pray before I start across. I turn around, grasp the roll with one hand, not two. I drag it to the boat with one hand; helpers, it takes four to put it into the boat, me, I do it with one hand. Take roll on my side. That's the time they bring all the rest of the rolls, takes big boat to carry one roll. We start in to work. My roll first and from there they all the time tie it, roll it, tie it, roll it; sometimes water helps them. Now [excited] you hear the water making noise going through the pickets. Now they put redwood brush clear along the bottom, they all dive.

Long ago they said, "We don't want no rattlesnakes on this side of Kepel." So they hunted all the rattlesnakes and put them on other side of river, but one broke loose and is there yet today.

Thousands of people are waiting for them fellows [divers] to come up. They take me back across again, waiting for that girl. About afternoon like this I hear the girl coming. Not married. Put blankets over her, she come around and go up again. Leaving a basket there with acorns in it, [she] turns back. I singing that song. Now everybody got a pole ready, everybody come (Jim Marks did it). Girl runs down clear to the end of bar and jumps into river. They are all up at Kepel flat now. I am the last one to come and four girls stand there before we come, shell dress on, I come, them people come from fish dam. I go into center of them, and I throw that basket up to tell them to go. Everybody throwing poles over me and three girls and everybody running away. When that finished they had a deerskin dance that night.

What these girls eat, bones, etc., kept and put away, nobody touch it. Next day them girls throw it into river, and them fishbones become alive, jump like trout. Next day dance all day deerskin dance, etc. And then we start in catching fish.

For one or two months not to go far away from dam till river has washed it away. Not go near ocean.

That's my story, I have done it myself, I'm alive yet. Me have done it. Picture you took yesterday put it in newspaper, say he is the world's doctor, he is the man who done this.

Both the pride and the restrained cruelty expressed by this informant were extraordinary indeed. He would demonstrate how he burned a little angelica root every night, holding it in all directions and thus curing the world. Without his doing this, the world would not fare well; and he did not tire of referring to the fate of individuals who had not been obedient to the laws governing relationships to him and had wasted away and died, been bitten by rattlesnakes, or gone blind. One item among his boasts seemed most interesting: he was the only Yurok, he would repeat over and over, who never cried. Even should his wife die, he would simply leave the house, never look at her, and not shed one tear. A *widower without tears*—one conceives here the possibility that there is a relation between the dam chief and the widower across the ocean, the nostalgic Wohpekumeu with the fertile flow of tears.

One of the innumerable items in Waterman's and Kroeber's report neglected by my informant is the following ritual (abstracted):

> In the sweat house in Sa'a there is a small hole in the wall which is called a door and which is stopped with a plug. After all preparations are completed, the dam chief takes out the plug. Then the wind blows in at that door and says, "When I blow in there, I am calling you." Then the dam chief begins his medicine. At this time everybody has to hide. When everybody is safely inside, the shaman goes along all the trails "talking his medicine." I presume he imitates in this way the search of the original individual for the necessary secrets. After this point in the ceremonies lo keeps himself concealed from the sight of the people [11].

The present writer proposes the consideration that the original meaning of this ritual was a dramatized repetition of the widower's visit, his centrifugal search, and his banishment, which cures the world for one year.

Let us see what the medicine is which the widower possesses and which he "hollers on top of the sweat house and in Sa'a, five times upriver, five times down-river" while "people don't supposed to see him." It begins with the following words:

> That is how it will be. If they do not make the dam, there will be no more people. That is what I cry for. I think, "Alas! the people." For nearly ten days, he always tried to catch him [as he passed], always heard him downstream beginning to cry, again [perhaps?] he passed by, again he did not see him.
>
> After nearly ten days, now he thought: "What shall I do about him?" On the trail he stood, he heard him downstairs beginning to cry, still he stood there [with his arms spread], in the middle of the night he felt like wind coming to his heart, he felt him soon baby as big as, soon he was

larger, when it was nearly day he was larger, he began to twist [to escape], soon it was day, then he spoke.

He said: "Let me walk, let me go. I am the one who at night only travels." He said, the one who was holding him: "Why do you constantly cry?" He said: "I will tell you. I am so sorry for that, that there will be no people because they do not make the dam. I will leave you my song, I will tell it to you, then you must let me go"[11].

Who is it that "downstream begins to cry," who "at night only travels," who "feels like wind coming to his heart," and with whom the dam chief "wrestles till the break of day," until he receives the medicine? One suspects it is the crying "creator" who returns in the salmon.

The ceremonies at Kepel are also called a world-renewal festival. If our inference is correct, then the lonely "creator" in beginning to wander and to cry again brings all the old danger back in the world; while the dam chief who arrests him (as the dam arrests the salmon) is the "world doctor" who has cured the world of its eternal evil and has made himself the only person powerful enough to be able to dispense with crying.

Institutionalized crying, which can be provoked in Yurok individuals as well as in groups at any time by the mention of a beloved dead person, can only be explained in connection with Yurok child training, which will be discussed farther on. A deliberate activation of infantile crying, it is, like all regressions, full of ambivalence as if its message were: "See, I am only a child. If I had bad wishes against you, they do not count. Therefore, since you [the dead] may be living now near the mysterious source of earthly goods, please help me." The compensation of the mourners before a dance, which our Western spirit tempts us to interpret as a clever device of the mourners to capitalize on their sorrow, undoubtedly has a different meaning if understood as a community action which tells the dead: "See, we have not forgotten you. We do not want to dance without remembering you." That this remembrance is expressed in money given to a particular person seems simply an expression of the general Yurok trait of substantiating and monetarizing values.

The ambivalence hidden in this crying, however, comes to relief in the invention of a creator who comes back to this world like a guilty child, nostalgic, crying, and full of pity for mankind—attitudes which one certainly would not expect of a god who has been tricked away from the joys of this world. The people hide, as they once did, when the creator was loose; for, as in the olden days, the creator may pretend to be mourning his late wife but actually may bring promiscuity, incest, lawlessness. The dam chief stops him, whereupon he alone may express the punishing, pitiless, ungenerous attitudes which one would expect the god to display.

This world rejuvenation, this annual relief of the world from guilt and ambivalence, allows all the dam builders for at least a few days to "make all kinds of play" and to request everybody not to cry. "If someone cried, they would not be alive in a year." As Waterman and Kroeber further report, "the end of the dam building is a period of freedom. Jokes, ridicule, and abuse run riot; sentiment forbids offense; and, as night comes, lovers' passions are inflamed." Here, then, the crying widower is made the victim of a mockery which is reminiscent of the satires of ancient European spring ceremonials:

> The old men say, "Well, I think someone has died here; I hear crying." Then they send a man to where the crying is. He comes back and says, "The man lost his wife; he is a redwood, and he wants pay before we dance again." They agree and send him obsidians. The messenger comes back to say, "He wants one more obsidian and a woman." The old men are prepared with obsidians, knowing how many will be needed. They also pick up a fair-sized rock, which they call a woman. This is taken to the tree, which says, "Good, I'll take her." Then everything is settled; they have been paid twice just like head men owning the dam at Turep. Then they dance again on the flat on the hillside opposite Kepel.
>
> The tree that lost his wife cries and says, "My wife is dead." The old men have picked out several who stayed at the trees when the rest went uphill after sticks, and have told them how to cry. One cries for his wife, another acts as his brother, and others as his relatives. As they cry, they take the mucus from their noses and rub it on the head of the one who acts the widower until it is covered, so that it looks as if he were really in mourning [11].

The creator is said to have liberated the salmon; *is* he the salmon? If so, he lives unharmed through the magic battle of Kepel, for the salmon says, "I shall not be taken." I shall "travel as far as the river extends. I shall leave my scales on nets and they will turn into salmon, but *I myself shall go by and not be killed.*"

II. Yurok Childhood and Yurok Character

There are several all-Yurok villages along the lower Klamath, the largest representing a late integration, in the Gold Rush days, of a number of very old villages. Situated on a sunny clearing, it is accessible only by motorboat from the coast, or over foggy, hazardous roads. When I undertook to spend a few weeks there in order to collect more data and to check what I had concerning Yurok childhood as given by the Requa "intellectuals," I met with the resistive and suspicious temperament of the Yurok as a group. It appeared that, at the coast, I had visited and eaten meals with deadly enemies of an influential upriver family. (The feud dated back to the last century.) Furthermore, it seemed that this isolated community was unable to accept my declaration of scientific intention. Instead, they suspected me of being an agent come to investigate such matters as the property feuds brought about by the discussion of the Howard-Wheeler Act. According to ancient maps (existing only in people's minds), Yurok territory is a jigsaw puzzle of community land, land with common ownership, and individual family property. Opposition against the Howard-Wheeler Act, which forbids the Indians to sell their land except to one another, had taken the form of disputing what the single Yurok could claim and sell, if and when the act should be repealed, and one of my suspected secret missions apparently was that of trying under false pretenses to delineate property rights which the officials had been unable to establish. In addition, the impending death of a young Shaker and the visit of high Shaker clergy from the north had precipitated religious issues. Shakerism was opposed at the time not only by the Yurok "doctors" but also by a newly arrived missionary, the only other white man in the community. In view of this general tension, as well as of my inexperience, and of the short time at my disposal, I was not able to make relevant observations on Yurok childhood as it is today. However, after having discussed their suspicions with some Indians, I found informants who clarified the outlines of traditional Yurok childhood. On the Fourth of July, when permitted to do my share in paying off "the mourners of the year" and to attend a Brush dance, I had an opportunity to see many children assembled for a whole night.

The Tradition Concerning Yurok Childhood

Yurok informants, in their accounts of Yurok childhood as it once was, express themselves tenderly, with serious amusement, and with enjoyment of the important task of representing Yurok decency to children. It goes without saying that, like other Indians, they lack that defeatism which dominates scientific accounts of children as beasts to be tamed or machines to be measured and kept in order. To them, children's needs coincide with the culture's needs; only a child disturbed by spirits, white people, or non-Yurok Indians could be in danger or temptation of falling out of the safety and the comfort of cultural conformity. And, indeed, the little I saw of the Yurok children upriver brought me to recognize even in these times of undeniable cultural disintegration something of the picture the old Yurok have of children: even-tempered, physically vigorous and graceful, and without any noticeable nervous tension.[6]

Whatever physiognomic similarities we may see between the Yurok and phobics, their attitudes toward childhood and their children should teach us that a well-institutionalized phobic system may help a people to uphold a total picture of peace, decency, pride, and physical fitness. Probably there are healthy cultures and defective or senile ones; but the phobic potentiality as such, if part of a cultural personality, has at least a chance of integrating the unknown, of clarifying daily goals, of distributing attention and energy, and of preserving vitality; while an individual phobic neurosis always disintegrates and devitalizes and, when it dominates parental attitudes, estranges children from the intimacy of their immediate surroundings.

Indians know, of course, that even the educated white man has always overlooked their educational systems and has mistaken what he saw for a complete lack of educational initiative on the part of Indian parents. The statements volunteered by Indians, therefore, represent a selection, not always meaningful and coherent to us, which not only is intended to convey the tribe's venerated educational ethos and its traditional opinion of children, but which also reflects a defensive attitude directed against the white man's supposed opinion of Indians and their children.

Eager as the clinical inquirer may be to get at certain facts which would provide similarities, counterparts, or polarities to abstractions conceived elsewhere, he has also learned not to interrupt too often the sequence of the first material offered to him, for it represents the informant's attitude toward the facts, and in education, at least, it would be hard to know exactly where fact begins and attitude ends.

In keeping with the ritual importance of the number ten, the Yurok insist that it takes a firstborn child ten months to be ready for birth, subsequent children adhering to the biological norm. The main concern of the Yurok mother is to secure for the child an easy birth and a basic inclination to wake up and live. The mother eats little, carries much wood, and does other work which forces her to bend forward so that the fetus will not "rest against her spine"; then, during the latter part of her pregnancy, she rubs her abdomen in the afternoon to keep the fetus awake, a custom which we have already mentioned as the prenatal representative of the concern lasting to the end of the Yurok "preschool years" that sleep in the afternoon may bewitch the child and make it a prey of the attraction of death. (It will be remembered that F was expected to become a shaman because she slept so much.)

The main postbirth taboos for the Yurok parents are of an *oral* character. The father and the mother eat no deermeat or salmon, but content themselves with acorn soup, until the child's navel heals. The importance attached to this taboo is evidenced by the contention that convulsions in childhood are the result of the parents' disregard for an eating or drinking taboo. The more "phallic" Sioux Indians think that a child's convulsions are a result of the parents' intercourse during pregnancy; the Yurok do not discourage such intercourse.

During birth, the mother, who is lying on her back and bracing her feet against an assistant, must shut her mouth; this makes it easier for the child to pass the vagina: apparently another manifestation of the "tube" configuration.

The newborn baby is steamed in the steam of wild ginger, the navel is covered with a paste made of pounded land snail (shell and all), and the navel cord is put into a split made in a branch of a pine tree. After a warm bath, the baby is wrapped in a deer hide and then placed in a basket. While, already *in utero*, boys are supposed to move harder, girls to be more restrained, the cradle further emphasizes the sex difference: the baskets for boys are wider at the shoulders, those for girls, at the hips; near the baby girl's head a small shell dress is hung, a small bow and arrow near the boy's. To prevent the baby from being bothered by too much light while in this first cradle, two hazel branches are crossed over its head and covered with deer hide.

The first postnatal period is of ten days, during which time the baby is not breast-fed but is given a kind of nut soup from a tiny shell. As among other Indian tribes, the colostrum is considered disadvantageous to the baby; the Yurok's period of "ten days" is, of course, practically as vague as our term "a fortnight." To make this period bearable, the mother softens her breasts over the steam of herbs, and causes the milk to flow out. Once nursing begins, there seems to be no atmosphere of restraint or worry; as for cuddling and other cutaneous contacts, however, it must be remembered that the cradle basket, not the baby, was held in the arms.

The babyhood of the Yurok child seems characterized by a relative encouragement to leave the mother's support as soon as this is possible and emotionally bearable. The baby is nursed a maximum of one year, which is at the minimum side of the nursing periods among American Indians in general. Usually around the sixth or seventh month (that is, the period of teething as well as of near-creeping), attempts are made to make the baby "forget" the mother's milk: the first solid food, consisting of salmon or deermeat, is given a positive valence by being well salted with seaweed. This, incidentally, remains the confection of the Yurok and their neighbors inland, who pay a high price for it. But should a baby, on reaching his first birthday, not have "forgotten" the mother's milk, she will go away for a few days, or, in especially obstreperous cases, she will put wild onion on the nipples to give them a definitely negative valence. (The unweaned baby should never drink water, which is antagonistic to milk; if during his bath he tries to get a sip of water, he is smilingly said to steal.) Again, from three o'clock until sundown the baby is kept awake so that death cannot close his eyes.

After only twenty days the grandmother begins to massage the baby's leg muscles; the Yurok cradle basket leaves the feet free. Furthermore, there is an especial premium on the baby's early having strong legs and being eager to creep, for it is in the period between his birth and his first energetic creeping that the parents are forbidden sexual intercourse. To remind them, the baby has a buckskin bracelet around one ankle; this, it seems, symbolizes his "tie" to the mother. (This interpretation would give some meaning to the very strong taboo, to be mentioned later, that children should never tie each other together.) The Yurok child's first postnatal "crisis," then, consists of a relationship in time of weaning, teething, encouraged creeping, and the mother's returning to old sex ways and new childbirths.

Bowel training is introduced as soon as a child can walk. To "do business" (which expression, incidentally, at least in the Yurok pidgin English, is also used by the man for his part in sexual intercourse), the child is led out of the house, not by the parents but by the older children.

Because of the psychoanalytic habit (to be discussed later) of referring to the love of possessions as "anal," especially if avarice is associated with compulsiveness, obstinacy, and retentiveness, I carefully inquired into a possible emphasis on the time, place, or way of defecation or into possible difficulties encountered in this part of child training. However, I only met with a rather bland expression, or even slight astonishment that anybody should see in these matters a problem *per se*; that a disturbed child may also show disturbances in this sphere was not denied. The only fable which concerned itself with evacuation emphasizes in its moral the need for cautious intake rather than any concern over the bowels; and, incidentally, illustrates blatantly the "tube" configuration in Yurok imagination:

> The bear was always hungry. He was married to the blue jay. One day they made a fire and the bear sent the blue jay to get some food. She brought back only one acorn. "Is that all?" the bear said. The blue jay got angry and threw the acorn in the fire. It popped all over the place and there was acorn all over the ground. The bear swallowed it all down and got awfully sick. Some birds tried to sing for him but it did not help. Nothing helped. Finally the hummingbird said, "Lie down and open your mouth," and then the hummingbird zipped right through him. That's why the bear has such a big anus and can't hold his feces.

The Yurok make the distinction between a non-sense age and a sense age, which latter marks, in its meaning, if not in its timing, our "school age"—a differentiation, as psychoanalysis has shown, which rests not only on the child's language and locomotor development but also on the development of conscience and the readiness, with the beginning of the "latency," to utilize sublimations. Whether a Yurok child belongs in one or the other stage is ascertained by the question repeatedly put to him, "Can you tell me what I told you yesterday?" If the child can remember with some regularity what he has been told, he is said to have sense, which means that the child can now be held liable for his mistakes, at least in the sense that his father can be sued for the child's offenses against Yurok laws. Verbal education can begin.

The first group of prohibitions and laws of conduct transmitted to the child as soon as this stage is reached concern the intake of food. He is told: "Eat slowly; don't grab food; never take food without asking for it; don't eat between meals; never eat a meal twice," and so on.

During meals a strict order of placement is maintained. Between the parents a space is always left for a potential guest. The girls sit near the mother, the boys near the father. The father teaches the boys and the mother the girls how to eat. They are told to take a little food with their spoon, to put it into their mouth slowly, to put the spoon back into the eating basket, and to chew slowly and thoroughly, meanwhile thinking always of becoming rich. Then the food is to be swallowed and the child may again reach, without haste, for the spoon. Nobody is supposed to talk during the meal, so that everybody can concentrate on thoughts of wealth. While there is still food in one's basket or in one's mouth, one does not ask for more. If a child eats too fast, the father or the mother silently takes his basket away from him and the child is supposed to rise silently and leave the house. Otherwise, the child is not allowed to leave ahead of any guest. Girls especially have to be patient; they remain sitting until first the guest, then the boys, then the father have left the room, and until, subsequently, the mother has cleaned the men's baskets with mussel shells, rinsed them with cold water, and has swept (toward the fire) the floor over which the males had walked.

In this compulsive way an attitude toward wealth is conditioned (in connection with the oral zone but not at the oral stage) which later on allows the Yurok to think of wealth at any time in an almost hallucinatory way. When sitting or walking alone, he will always try to think of money or salmon, and he can make himself see money hanging from trees, even eating leaves or swimming in the river. In this way also an attitude is conditioned which encourages the Yurok to subordinate drive as such to the pursuit of wealth so that later on it will be not only his appetite for food which he learns to restrain for the sake of amassing wealth, but also his sexual desires. As a matter of fact, he may sit in the sweat house and at the same time attempt to see in the river a dentalium shell as large as a salmon and try *not* to think of women.

There seems to be no end to the emphasis given to restraint in eating. When the young Yurok visits friends and is offered food, he speaks much and acts as if he did not see the food until he has been urged so much that not to eat would be an affront. As an adult, he will begin his day's work without breakfast and have his first meal only after the major work is done.

To "teach" younger children, the Yurok do not tire of pointing out faces and figures in rocks and imagining them to be former human beings who have become stone at a dramatic and instructive moment. Thus, one of the commonest threats to the Yurok child concerns a rock near Kenek which is said once to have been a child. That child did not mind his parents; whereupon the owl took hold of it and carried it up to that rock, where it can be seen sitting and crying: "I wish the rock would lean over across the river" (like a bridge on which the child could cross the river and return home).

As we saw in one example (the form of bear feces), certain physiognomic characteristics of the animal environment are used in "teaching fables" to make the culture's values immediately convincing to the imaginative senses of the young child; the keynote of these fables is the ugliness of lack in restraint and conformity. They represent a major part of the Yurok's elementary education, which is immediately followed by an induction into the techniques of adult everyday tasks. The following are examples of such Yurok fables:

1. The buzzard at one time could not wait for his food. He tried to eat the soup before it was cool enough. One day he was so hungry he put his whole head into the soup and scalded the top part of his head. Now he does not touch warm food any more. He waits, high up there, until everything gets so old it stinks.

2. Once a party of animals was waiting for the day when all the beautiful furs and feathers were going to be distributed. The evening before, they all went to sleep. The coyote stuck sticks in his eyes to make sure he wouldn't sleep and thus would be the first one in the morning to select a beautiful tail. He made fun of the sleepy animals and especially pointed to an ugly tail, saying, "I pity the one who will get that tail." But towards morning he fell asleep anyway and when he awoke only that tail was left.

3. The eel and the sucker were great gamblers one time. They bet everything they had, including their houses and wives. Finally the eel offered all his bones and the sucker won them. That's why he has so many, the eel none.

4. Wild dove was a gambler, too. One day when he was gambling, sad news was brought to him: his grandmother had died. He was just about to "deal" [shuffle the sticks] when he received the news. He said, "I will deal once more." He said, "I will remember my grandmother when the sun gets hot in summer." To this day he still sits high up on a tree in summer, mourning for his grandmother.

5. Cottontail wanted to be an elk [to have horns as large as an elk's; and got them]. "All right," the animals said "start running and let's see how much noise you can make" [crashing through the brush]. He left. But nobody heard anything [he could not budge because his antlers had caught in the branches].

6. The crow wanted to be the prettiest bird in the world, pretty as a woodpecker. The animals said to him, "We are going to blindfold you and you fly away and when you come to a high tree wait there." The crow flew and flew and when he finally opened his eyes he was sitting on a smoke hole all black. Now he lives on excrement.

7. The panther, the wolf, and the eagle represent the male ego ideal; they are said "always to sleep in the sweat house," that is, to act like great hunters and ascetic heroes. The wolf's song is: "I will eat the bones, too. I will eat the bones, too, whenever I kill the deer." They eat every bit of a slain animal or tell others (first their mates or cubs) where the rest is. For while one should show restraint in eating, one should not waste any food; Yurok children have to finish what is in their eating baskets. Correponding to this male ideal the deer is the image of femi-

ninity, sacrifice, and quiet insistence—the very opposite to the obtrusive and ill-tempered blue jay and the ugly-sounding crow: the Yurok suffragettes.

8. The panther had two wives, the blue jay and the deer. He always slept in the sweat house and the deer sent her daughter to him to bring him acorn soup. It was very, very nice soup, but, every time, the blue jay took the soup away and ate it. One day the panther felt sorry for his daughter and took the soup himself. It was the best he had ever tasted and from that day on he always ate it himself. The blue jay got jealous, sneaked over to the deer, and tried to find out how she made that soup. She saw the deer take a rock, hit her front leg with it, and let some marrow bone run into the soup. The jealous blue jay thought she could do likewise, but when she hit her leg only slime came out. (You can still see the knot on the blue jay's leg.) When the panther ate the blue jay's soup it tasted so bad that he paid no more attention to the blue jay. The blue jay got terribly jealous and jumped around all the time. One day the panther said, "What is the matter with you?" The blue jay got terribly angry, pulled her clitoris out, and put it on her head. See?

9. At one time the crow was the eagle's wife. They had a baby, but the crow scalded it and killed it. When the eagle came home, he asked, "Where is the baby?" "At his grandmother's," the crow answered. So the eagle went there, but he could not find the baby. "Where did my young one go?" he asked, and they sent him to an uncle. Finally, he went home and found the dead young one in a basket. He almost killed the crow, but then he silently flew away and decided never to speak to her again. Now he circles high up while the crow sits and thinks to herself, "The old man is still the same. The old man is still the same." At one time she tried to get the eagle back by insisting that women should be allowed to dance too, and have the right to sing, but he just paid no attention to her.

10. [To a girl.] The mouse, Negenich, was once a very pretty girl, but boys never fell in love with her because she stole. She had a sister; her name was Frog. Nobody could make her steal. She married, raised a family, minded her own business. But Negenich did not want to mind, so she left the country, swam, traveled one day and one night to a beach. The Indians there spoke a different language. She told them about the Brush dance. They understood that language; she danced the Fire Brush dance. While dancing she took a mat, put it under her arm, and jumped under a rock. So the people said she had to go back. She lives as a mouse now here.

In this last story (10) we see the hunger for possessions, which leads to stealing, paired with the centrifugal wish to "leave the country," which is properly punished.

One wonders whether these ingenious and witty fables for children are of later or even foreign origin, or whether they are different from myths and formulae because they are intended for children. At any rate, they are told today with an entirely different affective tone from the myths; namely, with true pleasure in confabulation. As mentioned before, this tone changes only when one asks for stories about salmon. Then the magic-phobic attitude seems to interfere even today. It will be remembered that on the score of the main emphasis of these fables, the salmon could not be ridiculed, for in the river he abstains altogether from food. And the first concern of Yurok education is to limit the lawless, individualistic, and too direct expression of avaricious intake. The wish for food and for possessions is strictly destined to remain within the channels of Yurok law and to remain in Yurok conscience as an obedient expression of an ethos, not of individual avarice.

Second in emphasis is the prohibition of swearing, that is, the verbal offense consisting of the use of the words "dead people," or "dead man's son," or "dead man's child"; or even of the question put to a stranger where his father or his mother is, because they may be dead; or of a reference to somebody's mourning necklace. Swearing is multiplied by an accompanying gesture of turning the palms of the hands, held outspread thumb to thumb, toward another person (ten): this is the way the dead swear. For oral swearing, nettles are put on the child's lips; for the "dead man's" gesture, they are put on his hands. "Just a few nettles," the Yurok explain smilingly, "and he won't do it again." One can assume that the Yurok child early becomes aware of the fact that certain utterances result in a hushed silence or sharp rebuke.

   Sex talk, too, comes under the heading of swearing because it may imply an intention to joke about the parents' sex life (an interpretation with which Freud would agree). Again, the informants refer to sex talk when one asks about habits or practices: they do not believe, or pretend not to believe, that children go further; or, maybe, they pay as little attention to it as possible. At any rate, brothers and sisters are not separated or restricted by any taboos such as are customary on the Plains. As long as the boys are not busy helping in the sweat house, boys and girls play together; as already mentioned, they also swim together naked, as do adults. Any urge to cover a part of the body as shameful exclusively concerns the female genital, especially the virginal one after the menarchy.

Yurok children love to play wife purchase and to build miniature brush houses. Underneath the roof they hang sprouts of salmonberry representing drying salmon. The leaves of the firecracker flowers make good purses, their flowers, money. The girls make dolls out of blue mud and put them into little cradle baskets; but they must not put two dolls together in one cradle—a prohibition probably originating in the Yurok's dislike for twins, who they think may have committed incest *in utero*. (To warn them, children are told that once long ago some people put two dolls in a basket and the ocean flooded the world.) The girls play cooking and feeding the dolls, using wild celery as food.

While the boys may play with dolls once in a while, girls are definitely forbidden to play with boys' toys, namely, small dugouts made of the bark of bull pines, and bows and arrows. The boys were warned not to put toy canoes into the real creek or the river or even near the ocean. They have to build their own body of water somewhere inland, but must not spill or waste any good drinking water. To scare them away from the creek they are told that a large snake is lying at its bottom. One of their severest misdeeds is to urinate into the creek or river—a contamination which may make salmon angry, and the child sick.

To both sexes it is forbidden to tie their wrists together or to tie themselves to dogs. Again a story is told fixing the "cause" of this prohibition in history and geography.

> One day a bad boy went to a sweat house in the middle of the day. His two grandfathers slept there. He tied their hair together. Then he stepped back and woke them up by shouting. Soon afterward, many people died. This happened in Orek.

To teach older children, teachers are selected by acclamation. If enough people say about him, "He has good sense," a man with special skills in hunting, fishing, paddling through dangerous water, etc., is entrusted with the task of showing a group of from five to seven children "how to live right." In contrast to medicine men, shamans, midwives, etc., the teachers are not paid but are often invited for meals. When old, they are fed by their former pupils. The teacher does not receive any formula from his kin, but repeats stories and skills which are general property. It is interesting that again the parents are kept out of the educational process. The only "test" which the child has to undergo is a questioning by the grandfather in regard to the stories and skills which the child is supposed to be learning at the time.

One informant remembered a teacher who was a slave. He was

not an outcast like a thief, but "merely" had gambled away his freedom. When the men speared salmon, his position was behind the free men, but "he always knew when he saw a salmon come up to catch breath where it would come up the next time," and he speared it from his disadvantageous position; so he was made a teacher in salmon spearing.

If a child was not well-behaved "in school" (the informants say that three out of ten or possibly two out of six children would live through such a period of nonconformity), the explanation was simple. The child was neither inferior, nor sick, nor bad; but he had seen spirits of a special kind—bad ones, who had committed crimes in their time. Spirits of this type were especially small, had blue-black skin, a long white beard, very long fingernails, "Chinese" eyes, and would dance on their heads or on one leg. They would induce the child to make faces and to joke and laugh at the wrong moment. The treatment was equally simple. The teacher would say to the child, "Go to your folks and tell them I could not teach you." The child would be back soon and conform. If not, a doctor would be called: as we saw, a woman with control over double vector and ambivalence. She did what earlier F was described as doing: she relieved ambivalence and guilt in the child's environment while applying a suggestive treatment to his body.

There is little to say about adolescence beyond what has been said already about the ceremonies which seem to remind the girl to keep her senses closed to any temptations not likely to lead to the proud possession of ten boys and ten girls. Sexual irregularities in adolescence are neither denied nor condemned in a too personal way. The punishment rather concerns premarital pregnancy, which diminishes the girl's monetary value if paternity is not established; and if it is established, it is expensive for the boy. While adolescence is "marked" for the girl, there are no rituals or ceremonials for the boy: his gradual induction into the sweat house marks his fraternity with all men and institutionalizes his suspicion of female attraction as a potential stimulus to do something economically unwise. His adolescence rites, as it were, are lifelong: every morning he is purified from the contaminating contact with the sex which gave him birth.

If asked any specific questions about the symptoms which are the causes of many of our worries and our warfare with children in homes and nurseries, the Yurok smile and refuse to believe that any child for any length of time would be able to stand up against friendly cultural pressure and would insist on nonconformity where conformity is so pleasant and secures a full place in Yurok life, which, after all, is the best of all lives.

However, there is the individual with a female ancestor who was never paid for in full. One understands, now: the male ancestor was unable to subordinate a sentimental or sexual attachment to the economic ethos; he was weak. His children and children's children are apt to be weak, too; they, of course, behave "different," which is "too bad"—an attitude as pitilessly final if not so consciously cruel as our verdicts of "constitutional inferiority." Such environmental doubt naturally drives the individual in question deeper and deeper into mischief; he is avoided, and his line is apt to die out, which, in turn, "proves" that the general attitude toward bastards is justified.

But that a child as such could be inclined to be regressive or asocial is an idea which does not occur to a Yurok. Only children who have seen spirits may be temporarily disoriented.

TRADITIONAL CHILDHOOD AND CULTURAL CHARACTER

The majority of items volunteered by the Yurok informants, and at the same time those most vividly emphasized, concern the oral zone, namely, primarily the intake of food, both at the beginning of life and at the beginning of the "sense period"; and then the release of swear words. Should we suspect that the Yurok informants repress or suppress items concerning other zones of the body and other periods of development, or shall we take their selection at its face value?

In order to review our suspicions and, where necessary, revise our preconceptions, we shall take the data available (they are—to repeat this—data of verbal convention, not of actual observation), and shall state what configurational resemblance and what causal connection we see between the first experience of the small child and the cultural character of the adult Yurok. In doing so, we follow a theory based on Freud's work, introduced by Abraham for character pathology [1] and by Margaret Mead for comparative characterology [9]. According to this theory, individual as well as group differences in character not only resemble, but are the conditioned results of, specific differences characterizing the various types of the inescapable traumatization of the human baby.

I have stated in a previous paper [3] the opinion that a combination of three factors in training are genetically important for the Sioux child's final cultural personality. One is very late weaning, which is often postponed to the point where the child weans the mother or where the child after having been weaned returns to the mother's breast when she suckles a younger brother or sister. A second factor is the Sioux mother's strong physical reaction when the child, used to indulgence, tries to satisfy on the mother's nipples his biting wishes. This sudden and harsh deprivation within an experience otherwise characterized by extreme generosity seems to create the Sioux child's first temper tantrums, which are considered normal and "are looked at with the same pride with which many white parents listen to the voice of a yelling, red-faced baby and say, 'It will make him strong.' " We may assume that the violence and the lasting impression of these temper tantrums are increased by the third factor, namely, the Plains cradleboard, which does not allow the child to move his body. While the smaller child seems to find comfort and protection in so narrow an enclosure, the child with increasing muscle energy and with a need for a catharsis of anger may be assumed to feel rather frustrated. It seems to me that it is this unchannelized energy of frustrated impulses to bite and kick which is the contribution of the Sioux's child training to his cultural personality; it contributes to the urge for communal temper outbursts such as endless centrifugal "parties" setting out to hunt, kill, steal, and rape; to the Sioux Indians' proverbial cruelty both against enemies and against himself; and it finds its most exalted expression in the scene during the Sun dance when "little sticks driven through the breasts of the dancers and connected by strings to the Sun Pole, were pulled free so that the flesh was ripped open": a sacred turning against himself of the former Sioux child's biting wishes.

The importance of the biting impulses for Sioux personality is furthermore believed to be shown by the outstanding "bad habit" of the Sioux child, which involves the play of teeth and fingernails (or substitutes of similar texture) but, as far as I could observe, rarely the lips and the fingers. On the basis of such material, I suggested a systematic psychoanalysis of Sioux culture which should take into account both the Sioux's sadistic and self-punishing and his oral depressive traits, his generosity as well as his "biting" gossip, and finally his demanding dependence on the United States government.

Such observations are based on preconceptions which might be formulated as follows. We expect a human child to bring into life personality potentialities, that is, a variety of potential trait configurations based on the organism and the organization in time and space of its basic needs. These potentialities are limited by (1) the evolutionary state of the organism and any characteristics which the racial history may have been able to impress on it, and (2) the laws of psychological displacement which say that in a human being only a limited and delineated impulse modification is tolerable (libido-economy).

Child training, under the influence of an integrated and integrating cultural ego, systematically narrows the number of these potentialities by creating hypertrophies and atrophies the integration of which is the *cultural* trait configuration characterizing all members of the group. It does so by utilizing that basic polarity of human childhood which makes child care and child training necessary, namely, initial helplessness and prolonged dependence, on the one hand, and insatiable desire for independence, mastery, and investigation, on the other. Concentrating on a few areas of the child's infantile interests, child training develops and then channelizes or suppresses them, blocking regression and encouraging sublimation; thus it creates a specific ontogenetic trauma, a typical kind of expulsion from paradise in every new member's early childhood. The areas of special educational pressure (probably themselves the result of phylogenetic traumata) remain arsenals of strong and conflicting impulses and determine the cultural trait configuation as well as the nature of individual variations. (Of this total cultural trait configuration, anthropological investigation is apt to secure only one aspect, namely, a *traditional* trait configuration held together by the particular verbal logic of the tribe in question; while psychological observation tends to describe a *comparative* trait configuration based on the search for analogies to what we have come to formulate in regard to child training in our culture.) Strange as the methods of child training may seem, they are one expression of a tendency toward trait synthesis which assures cooperative efficiency and prevents irrational anxiety in most of the members of a homogeneous culture. What we finally may call *individual* trait configurations are, then, individual ways of succeeding or failing in synthesizing personal variations and limitations with the cultural trait configuration and with the culture's sanctioned opportunities for behavior variation; it is this, the ego *against* the culture, which primarily has been described in clinical literature, with a great emphasis on the little individual's painful adjustment to the big, bad "environment," and with little emphasis on the pleasures and opportunities which homogeneous environment gives to an organism eager for love and expression, not to speak of mere survival.

If it seems fruitful to apply the concepts derived from psychopathological observation to the phenomena of culture, it is because cultural synthesis as well as cultural rigidity and regression use, in every constituent member, potentialities the same as, or analogous to, those which are also elaborated in individual neurosis. However, as will be pointed out, once this similarity is recognized and has led to fruitful problems, the differences in the organization of these potentialities within such different settings as a culture or a neurosis need to be reemphasized.

This seems the more important as, in establishing analogies between culture and neurosis and causal links between child training and cultural character, psychiatric philosophy leads to the dangerous illusion that psychiatric-anthropological master minds could perhaps not only prevent neurosis, but, by decreeing ideal methods of child training, could help create assorted desirable cultures. As in homunculus fantasies of old, the mothers and the imponderables they stand for are overlooked. A successful preverbal child training reflects the homogeneity, not the verbosity, of a culture.

The Yurok baby is nused long and generously enough to acquire a basic feeling of being loved and provided for; the memory of a paradise is a prerequisite of cultural striving. Primary oral conditioning, then (a secondary one follows at the beginning of the "sense" stage), emphasizes the crossroads between the two oral modes, sucking and biting.

Yurok child training, in contrast to Sioux training, weans early, well before the child is one year old, and this at a time when his teeth develop and his encouragement to early locomotor activity bears fruit.

This tendency to wean early, as we saw, reaches into prenatal existence, where the fetus is discouraged from "resting against the maternal spine" and from sleeping when the evening shadows creep over the mountains. The centrifugal tendency of leaving maternal support is furthermore emphasized by the massaging of the leg muscles, which must accelerate the child's eagerness and ability to creep and to "stand on its own feet." The boy, especially, can join the men early; he has periods when he plays with other children, but he is early encouraged to carry wood for the sweat house. (If he is allowed to stay, he must only promise on his return home to let the father tell the stories told in the sweat house and not to interrupt or correct him.) According to our assumptions in regard to the vicissitudes of instincts, such "expulsion," even though it may be gradual and induced by the establishment of positive goals, should leave a residue of potential nostalgia in the child; and indeed, as we have seen, the Yurok can call on this nostalgic talent whenever he needs to influence the paternal powers behind the visible world. This is accompanied by other attributes of the first oral stage: the hunger cry, the complaint of helplessness, and the simple "hallucinatory wish fulfillment" implied in the habit of assuming that to say with tears, "I see salmon," is a way of getting it. It will be remembered that even the creator made the world out of nostalgia. "I am lonely," he said, and accelerated the high points of cosmogony by an ever-renewed flow of tears. Yurok songs, too, in their content as well as in their phonetics seem to be cries of desire and longing and in this are quite different from the martial cries of the Sioux.[7] The difference between Yurok and Sioux weaning would be that the Yurok at the time of his teething loses the nursing situation *in toto*, whereas the Sioux baby nurses throughout the biting period, thus being forced to suppress an ever-stimulated biting wish without being able to abreact his initial temper through violent movements of the limbs. The *energy* of the biting stage is, it seems, in Yurok training partly absorbed by the early-provoked muscular and locomotor interest in the environment. Its mode reappears in the economic mastery of this environment, that is, in the snaring of deer and the netting of fish, and in the most sublime technical and spiritual elaboration of the fish dam with its two closing "jaws." This interpretation, at least, gives additional meaning to the fact that it is necesary for the Yurok to imagine both salmon and deer as immortal: according to the Yurok brand of Platonism, the "ideas" of salmon and deer remain untouched while of their own volition they send their edible objectivation into the human traps. "I like this house," a deer will say, "I shall go into that man's snare." "I shall travel as far as the river extends," the salmon says, "I shall leave my scales on nets and they will turn into salmon but I myself shall go by and not be killed" [8].

The Yurok relation to the salmon and its metaphysical source, characterized as it is by tearful prayer before the capture of the prey, and, after its destruction and devouring, by the protestation that not the whole, not the life itself of the animal, has been destroyed, represents a parallel to the Yurok baby's oral experience which taught him: as long as you had no teeth, you only had to cry and the mother came; as soon as you began to use your teeth, the mother went away and you were taught "to forget the milk." Therefore, it seems better to pretend that you are a toothless baby, and if you did bite, to say that you bit only the edible representation of an immortal and invulnerable being which not only does not mind but expressly desires your bite.

This parallelism of what we assume to be the Yurok's relation, on the one hand, to the first ontogenetic source of food, namely, the mother, and, on the other, to the metaphysical source of "the world's" food supply is repeated in an anatomic-geographic parallelism. Like every one of the "helpless" individuals populating it along its central lane, the whole Yurok world has, as it were, its mouth open toward the yearly present of salmon, and it is ready to close the jaws of nets and dams as soon as the salmon is "in the bag"—whereupon the crying ceases, no offense is taken, and sexual restraint relaxes. It is as if the fish dam represented a play, with the greatest danger both in phylogenetic reality (the end of the salmon supply) and in onto-genetic fantasy (the loss of parental love because of one's oral sadism), and is therefore strictly ritualized at the beginning and enjoyed with manic lawlessness at the end.[8]

The secondary oral education at the "school"-age (a period fostering development of conscience, verbal intelligence, and sublimated curiosity) puts the finishing touches on this transformation of oral desire; it uses the situation of daily food intake to condition at one and the same time restraint in oral impulses and a disciplined desire for prey and wealth. Interestingly enough, the fables which are called on to reinforce the general attitude of considerate intake, and which are about the freest form of confabulation found in Yurok culture, use a mental potentiality which, according to another vague theory of psychoanalysis, represents the intellectual elaboration of the biting mode, namely, the appreceptive isoltion, the singling out of outstanding parts of the environment. With a sharp eye, they grasp one characteristic of each animal (the buzzard's bald head, the blue jay's crest, the bear's excrement) to substantiate their point, namely, the danger of avarice and inconsiderate intake. The general Yurok habit of isolating points and of localizing events probably uses the same mental potentiality, which may be called the "partialistic" mode of apprehending and organizing the environment.

The trianing of the oral-tactual-sensory organization thus contributes to the Yurok's cultural character two generalized modes, namely: (1) preambivalent nostalgia directed toward the personified food sources behind reality, this nostalgia being prevented from turning into a vague exploration of the geographic periphery by the "restriction of radius"; (2) sublimated, highly institutionalized "biting off" of circumscribed objects and events out of the mass of space and the stream of time.

The "object relation" to the mother or both parents, as built up during the oral stages, contributes the following relations of the Yurok to the beings surrounding him: (1) ambivalent avoidance of women and their houses, possibly with a projection of the "catching" mode into them, that is, a fear of being held and weakened; (2) a displacement of preambivalent trust into substitute parents behind the visible world from whence an eternal supply is flowing; (3) anarchic mistrust of earthly parent substitutes, such as political officials.

In his daily social contact with his fellow men the Yurok's receptivity becomes definitely more aggressive, challenging, claiming, and complaining:[9] comparing it with the attitude toward metaphysical beings, one is immediately reminded of the way in which a whining child, now so touchingly helpless in the presence of the mother, uses an instant of her absence to turn on his sibling and to protest that this or that object—anything will do—is his. Not that we would expect to find this behavior more extreme among Yurok children than among our own (short of murder, it hardly could be); we again have in mind a comparison between the typical Yurok child's typical expulsion from oral paradise and the typical Yurok's cultural character. A child, in a noncontraceptive culture, if weaned early will early be aware of a new tie between father and mother and will soon find a sibling baby in the place which was his. His protestation, even if suppressed, will easily combine the "biting" characteristics of the second-oral and the retentive ones of the anal stage; and indeed, to claim angrily the right to get what he has not got (often in connection with the sorrow over a loss or an alleged offense), and to hold to the last to what he has got, are the only techniques by which the Yurok can hope to gain a little more than he could by relying on his work technique or his ability to produce, raise, and sell worthy girls.

This channelization, this positive use of oral craving, has, as we saw, allies in negative institutions such as oral taboos and the prohibition of swearing. The earliest taboo is the prohibition given to the breast-feeding baby not to drink ("steal") water.

In our own culture swearing at a person has an admixture of displaced anality. We like to use "dirty" terms for a form of defamation which often seems like an elimination in the direction of the defamed or even identifies him with the eliminated. The meaning of Yurok swearing seems different. What he loosely translates as "swearing" is solely a verbal reference to a dead person. One wonders whether the temptation suppressed by this prohibition is that of calling the dead dead, powerless, gone, in other words, of eliminating them without remorse and anxiety.

The anthropologist who has lived long enough among a people can tell us whether or not what its informants care to enlarge upon, and what the culture cared to formulate, are representative for categories which can be observed as attracting most attention and arousing most emotion in daily and yearly life. But there is rarely available the material which would indicate whether or not traditional traits (such as nostalgia or avarice or retentiveness) are also dominant personal traits in typical individuals. Take the Yurok's ability to patnomime a crying helpless being or a deeply offended mourner. Does it mean that the Yurok anywhere within his technology is more helpless, more paralyzed by sadness, than are members of a tribe which does not develop these "traits"? Certainly not; his institutionalized helplessness *eo ipso* is neither a trait nor a neurotic symptom. It is an infantile attitude which the culture chose to preserve and to put at the disposal of the individual, to be used by him and his fellow men in a limited area of existence. Such an institutionalized attitude neither spreads beyond its defined area nor makes impossible the development to full potency of its opposite; it is probable that the really successful Yurok was the one who could cry most heartbreakingly or bicker most convincingly in some situations and be full of fortitude in others, that is, the Yurok whose ego was strong enough to *synthesize orality and "sense."* In comparison, the oral types whom we may be able to discern today in our culture and to whom (for purposes of simplicity in scientific and ethical orientation) we would be inclined to liken what we have said about the Yurok so far, are bewildered people who find themselves victims of an overgrown and insatiable potentiality without the corresponding homogenous cultural reality.

If we know the character potentialities required for the successful participation in the official part of a certain culture, we stand only at the beginning of a personological inquiry; for each system—let us say of generosity or avarice—admits in its own way certain additions to and deductions and exemptions from individual avarice or generosity. The Yurok of today is little help in this matter, which can only be studied in living primitive cultures; but our speculations insist that no consistent integrated cultural emphasis can develop without a specific conditioning—a specific variation of the universal expulsion from paradise—in early childhood; and that such a conditioning, in order to create people who can function as useful members of even the strangest culture, must aim for what we vaguely call a "strong ego," that is, a personality core both firm and flexible enough to maintain cultural and psychological *homeostasis*.

No student of psychoanalytic literature could avoid the impression that many of the Yurok "traits" correspond to the "anal character" as described by Freud and Abraham [1]. Compulsiveness, suspiciousness, miserliness, etc., are said to characterize "anal-neurotic" individuals, that is, individuals with an infantile history of preoccupation with excretion, with a narcissistic holding on to the "treasures" of the cloaca, and with a sadistic identification of other individuals with an expelled waste product:[10] a sad asocial picture.

In the psychoanalytic observation of adult patients, it has been emphasized [1] that it is hard to reconstruct orality because in retrospect one finds it buried under a layer of traits and fantasies developed during the anal period. The archaeological picture used here, as so often, is too static to fit the nature of developmental facts. If one begins with the beginning, it seems equally as difficult to discern with safety the onset of clear anal traits in a child; for, as we increasingly find in clinical work with small children, what has been called one of the main criteria of anality, namely, retentivity, may be already well developed in connection with orality; and it is my contention that the same is true for most if not all typical Yurok traits.

We may pause here to ask what our criteria are for calling an activity oral or anal. The only real criterion is, of course, the zone criterion, namely experiences at the zone in question or strong emotions immediately associated with zonal sensations and frustrations. All the other criteria seem secondary and have to be traced back to the first one in order to be considered valid. Such secondary criteria would be: first, the *mode* criterion, that is, the fact that the mode for which the zone in question is the modal zone (as the mouth is for receptivity, the anus for retentiveness and elimination) is either generalized (i.e., retentive personality) or displaced to another zone (i.e., genital retention)—and this in such a way that it can be traced back to the original zone. This mode criterion has a companion in the *countermode* criterion, that is, in the generalization or displacement of a mode counteracting another mode (i.e., retention as countermode of elimination). A further criterion would be the *affect* or *attitude* criterion, that is, the generalization of a typical behavior (experienced as affect and observable as an attitude) which has originated in the zonal experience in question (i.e., the affect and attitude of helplessness or nostalgic craving in connection with originally oral situations, or the affect and attitude of stubbornness originally in connection with the demand to regulate defecation).

So far as we know now, the Yurok does not seem to focus any interest, pleasurable or phobic, on feces; and such reaction formations as regularity or compulsive orderliness do not seem to transgress what could be expected of people with a craftsmanship of Yurok level. Anal character in our culture often appears to be a result of the impact on a retentive child of a certain type of maternal behavior in Western civilization, namely, a narcissistic and phobic overconcern with matters of elimination. This attitude helps to overdevelop retentive and eliminative potentialities and to fixate them in the anal zone; it creates the strongest social ambivalence in the child, and it remains an isolating factor in his social and sexual development. Forms of "individualism" in Western culture which represent a mere insistence on the privilege to sit in isolation on possessions can be suspected of representing just such an inroad of anality into cultural and political life. Otherwise it seems that cultural life and anality contradict one another.

What could be interpreted as counteranal traits among the Yurok rather concern all eliminations, be they oral (vomiting), anal, urethral (urination into the river, etc.), or genital (especially menstruation).

The affect and attitude criteria of what is called anal often seem to fit the official Yurok personality. His "pleasure of final evacuation and exhibition of stored-up material" is most conspicuous at dances, when, toward morning, the Yurok with a glowing face produces his fabulous treasures of headwear ornamented with woodpecker scalps or of obsidians. However, the institutionalized obstinacy which allowed him to accumulate these treasures seems counteracted by the highly social experience of seeing his treasures enhance the prestige of the whole tribe. At least ceremonially, they belong to everybody. Such ceremonial occasions put a great burden of free hospitality on the small villages where they take place. (F, even during one of her tearful descriptions of her novitiate, could not omit the statement that it cost a good deal to feed all the visitors; but this increased her importance at the time and thus her power now. As a hostess F is most gracious.)

These remarks are not to be understood as denying the possibility that in some cultures anality is quite developed according to all the criteria which we have enumerated, but we would expect its influence on cultural character to be different from that of anal fixation in our culture. Yurok retentiveness seems alimentary rather than anal; it is a tendency to accumulate creatively for the sake of making the most of the collected values, which belong to the whole social system where it gives communal pleasure, prestige, and permanence in turn.

The main body zone emphasized in Yurok child training is the oral-nutritional one; the modes stressed are reception and retention. Yurok child training and the Yurok's identification of world and body focus on the *alimentary* zone, in the sense of "the tubular food-carrying passage extending from the mouth to the anus," with a positive educational emphasis on the mouth. The rest of the body is subordinated to the concern with this zone; in particular, areas and modes of elimination are avoided.

The groundwork for the genital attitudes desired in Yurok culture is laid in the child's earlier conditioning which teaches him to subordinate drive to economic considerations; within the established limits of these considerations sex as such is viewed with leniency and some humor. Masturbation, for example, is admitted, but said to yield to a mild discouraging attitude. The Yurok do not expressly approve of, nor are they insensitive to, the habits of self-indulgence which have so prominent a place in the clinical complaints of parents in our culture; on the other hand, it seems that cultures which make for a gradual exchange of social for physical satisfaction render unnecessary—or can afford to ignore—a certain amount of autoerotic satisfaction. What seems to drive many of our children into self-indulgence is the accumulated frustration and repression throughout the various childhood stages; it is especially the feeling of having lost with the mother's availability, reliability, and firmness any possibility of deriving, through her, cultural compensations for sacrificed infantile satisfactions, which makes autoeroticisms in our culture indispensable addictions. Otherwise, every society which we know so far, demands a certain amount of subordination of gential drive to the particular libido organization favored and expressed by the culture.

In adolescence, when the relationship to the opposite sex becomes important, the young Yurok can look back on a childhood of free play with other children during which at least the body surface of the other sex had in no way remained a secret. By the time the girl has passed the menarchy and in some ways becomes more secretive (a mystification which must increase both her positive and negative fascination), the heterosexual relationship has already found a firm place within the established system of property values, based as it is on the modes of considered intake and clever retentiveness. A girl strives to be worth a husband who can pay well, and she knows that all her own and her children's and her children's children's happiness depends on the amount of wealth she will actually bring in; she must retain her good name and her value—if not her virginity—until this goal is reached. They boy, on the other hand, has to be able to wait until he has accumulated enough wealth to buy a worth-while wife; or at least has to be restrained enough never to be caught in heterosexual pursuits before this goal is reached. Again we see retention emphasized, both in the sense that the Yurok remains virtuous in order to retain value and possessions and in the sense that the Yurok man must project into the woman a tendency to "catch" him.[11]

Among neurotics this retentiveness is common enough: it interferes with psychosexual development and genital potency. But here again the comparison between the cultural and the neurotic character ends; for, on this level too, the strong Yurok is he who never risks, over sexual matters, his property or his luck in hunting or fishing, but who would still be man enough to use with unimpaired sexual potency opportunities without danger of commitment. The understanding between the sexes in these matters goes so far (or can go so far) that one informant defined a "nice girl" as one who always tells the boy beforehand when she is menstruating, thus saving him ritual trouble and subsequent loss of working time.

As for the woman's sexual potency as we have come to understand it, namely, the ability to reach a full orgasm during intercourse, nothing can be said. This writer did not stay long enough with the Yurok to talk with any woman about this matter; men, when asked about the woman's general sexual response, merely showed an astonished smile. "After all," they would say after a moment's silence, "our women were bought." Indian women, while modest and girlishly simple, certainly do not impress one as being sexually immature or inhibited, at least so far as basic genital satisfaction is indispensable to marital and paternal harmony; however, the female orgasm seems not to be represented among verbalized facts and certainly has not the connotation of a female achievement (of an almost masculine character) which it often assumes with modern white women.

In a primitive culture, the cycle of the year as well as that of every day, the smallest personal emotion as well as the great events of religious life, more consciously focus on the pursuit of food than we would permit our cultural life to do expressly—which speaks for a greater admitted importance in their culture of the laws and taboos of food intake than we would like to admit in our child training. If people like the Yurok seem to lose their concern for their children so much earlier than we do and, as a matter of fact, emphasize least the period which seems to be the one appearing as most critical in our clinical experience, namely, the "Oedipus" peirod, we have to remember that after a relatively longer period of closeness to their mother Indian children rapidly become members first of the cliquelike subcultures of other children and then of economy and culture itself: their reward for imitating the gestures of those around them is merely the feeling of a participation in group life, which we underdevelop in our children because in our increasingly specialized culture we create isolated places for childhood. Only he who has seen Indian children sitting through a night of dances can understand the possibility that rituals and myths by acknowleding unspeakable feelings in more than verbal representations take care of the impulses and fears of a period of childhood when our children still fight their lonely battles with the Oedipus provocations of an every-family-for-itself culture. We may suspect that sex and aggression in their widest sense, and within the basic laws of libido-economy, can be easily subordinated to cultural reality to the extent to which its economy and its child training, its mythological expression and its provisions for individual variations, are well synchronized. This seems to be true to a high degree in American Indian cultures.

On the whole, it is the woman's position in the culture which remains mysterious, and this on the basis of a strange paradox of which this last chapter should help to make us aware. Faced with the taboos and avoidances of a people like the Yurok, one cannot help wondering again and again what the woman thinks of the entirely negative role which she seems to play in the formalized part of her culture. Manifestly, she does not seem to take these laws either too literally or too seriously in a personal sense; she does not seem to question the fact that it is the man's job both to create and to uphold taboos and that it is hers to encourage her children to adhere to them; and she seems to derive a feeling of belongingness from them, as if she had long forgotten what they really mean—if, indeed, all the avoidance does not flatter her feeling of being dangerously attractive. Maybe she can act this way because in turn her powerful position in everyday life is not questioned by the men, and does not seem less convincing to them because so much of it evades verbalization and rationalization—the only criteria we (and this, unfortunately, includes an influential type of mother in our culture) seem to accept as denoting cultural importance. The homogeneity of a culture seems to depend to a large degree on mothers who peacefully, and firmly, and wordlessly mediate between themselves (as the child's original object of love and anxiety) and his later goals and gods—for many of which, after all, the mothers are the models. But the mothers cannot do their part without a homogeneous culture.[12]

In the Yurok world, homogeneity rests on an integration of ethical with economic, geographical, and physiological concepts, for all of which the ground work is laid in the training of the young organism.

The relationship of the whole body to the whole world is that of a vigorous strong-limbed physique assigned to strictly localized tasks within a circumscribed world with forbidding horizons: centripetality as against centrifugality.

Of the zones of the body, the alimentary canal is outstanding in ethical importance; of organ modes, incorporation is emphasized.

The mouth, beyond the everday tasks of verbal communication, utters cries and songs of helplessness and of grief, convincingly states wishes and claims, and keeps from releasing swear- (death-) words; as for its function as an organ of food intake, it is trained to choose food carefully, to avoid contamination, to chew slowly, and to subordinate oral craving to the craving for wealth. Vomiting, if uncontrolled, evokes horror; although, if controlled for the purpose of materializing "pains," it is considered magically beneficial.

The nutritional canal is in danger of being pinched together by sorcery which suffocates the individual. With respect both to vomiting and to sorcery, it is the one-way flow through the nutritional tube which is obstructed or averted.

The anus seems to be considered merely as the other end of the tube, with the function of releasing what was not needed and should remain eliminated.

The vagina, however, representing a saclike organ with a double vector and an inescapable contamination of fluids (blood, urine, and semen), has to be avoided or counteracted by purification. In contrast, the penis, also being the end of a tube, is considered without horror, except in its contact, or directly after its contact, with the enclosing vagina.

The configurational emphases of bodily existence thus are: the receptive opening has to be kept uncontaminated; the tube has to be kept unconstricted; the sac has to be avoided.

The geographic world consists primarily of a central lane dividing into two equal parts a disk of territory which is surrounded by ocean. In front of the river mouth, ocean and river fishes are divided; the main river fish, namely salmon, during one period of the year can be observed making a trip upriver from which it does not return. The middle part of the river, near the navel of the world, is obstructed by the yearly erection of a fish dam which is accompanied by sacred ceremonies and represents the most communal enterprise and the most advanced technical accomplishment of California Indian cultures. After its confluence with the Trinity River, the Klamath enters that territory at the periphery of the world disk which is avoided by every Yurok of good breeding: where the river comes from, where the money comes from, how the salmon procreates are problems which the Yurok considers not belonging in his world; he assigns them to imaginary wombs beyond the ocean.

The fate of the salmon as understood by the Yurok fits into his world outlook, for this strong animal never eats and has no food in its nutritional system. Its sexual development leads to loss of strength and to death. Its procreation and its source "beyond the ocean" are mysterious. Whether the old Yurok knew that the fry which descends the river is the product of the salmon which ascended it, we do not know; at any rate, this double vector aspect of the salmon's life is ignored, the territory where it takes place avoided.

Yurok architecture allows a dramatization of daily life, which represents both a magic adaptation to and a magic mastery of world and salmon as he sees them. The living house, the saclike place of storage and of gestation, and the place of double vectors and inescapable contaminations, forces purification on the man. In order to achieve this, he enters the sweat house, which is morphologically a tube, and leaves it through a narrow exit. This exit is the "obstruction" test of the Yurok world, in that it may represent a pinching of the tube if it is too small (i.e., for fat men), while it represents unobstructedness if the man is slim and sweaty enough to get through, in which case he is not offensive to the river.

These configurations are a limited but, it is hoped, not unrepresentative selection of truly "primitive" Yurok concepts. They seem to express the general idea that by being a good warden of his nutritional system and a good warden of the river, and by guarding strength and wealth, the Yurok is clean enough to perform the miracle of his existence, namely, to eat his salmon and have it next year too.

References Cited

(By bracketed numbers in the text)

1. Karl Abraham, "Psycho-Analytical Studies on Character-Formation." In *Selected Papers* (London: Hogarth Press and Institute of Psycho-Analysis, 1927).
2. F. A Davidson and E. O. Shostrom, *Physical and Chemical Changes in the Pink Salmon During the Spawning Migration*. U.S. Bureau of Fisheries, Investigation Report No. 33 (1936).
3. E. Homburger Erikson, "Observations on Sioux Education," *Journal of Psychology*, 7 (1939).

4. ———, "Clinical Studies in Childhood Play." In *Child Behavior and Development: A Representative Course of Studies,* eds. Barker, Roger, and others (New York: McGraw-Hill, 1943).
5. Anna Freud, *The Ego and the Mechanisms of Defense.* (London: Hogarth Press and Institute of Psychoanalysis, 1937).
6. Sigmund Freud, "On Narcissism: An Introduction." In *Collected Papers,* vol. 4 (London: Hogarth Press and Institute of Psycho-Analysis, 1925).
7. ———, *Totem and Taboo* (Vienna: Internationaler Psychoanalytischer Verlag, 1920).
8. A. L. Kroeber, "The Yurok." In *Handbook of the Indians of California,* Bureau of American Ethnology, Bulletin 78 (1925).
9. Margaret Mead, "The Use of Primitive Material in the Study of Personality." In *Character and Personality,* 3 (1934).
10. E. B. Powers, "The Spawning Migration of the Salmon." *Science,* 92 (1940), 2390.
11. T. T. Waterman and A. L. Kroeber, "The Kepel Fish Dam." University of California Publications in American Archaeology and Ethnology, 35 (1938), 49–80.
12. T. T. Waterman, "Yurok Geography." University of California Publications in American Archaeology and Ethnology, 16 (1920), 177–314.

Notes

[1] See the case study "Orality in a Boy of Four" [4]. The plumbing system of a house, connected as it is with food intake and excrementa, in the mind of a child can become an annex of his own organism as well as an object for the projection of what the child thinks other organisms are and feel like.

[2] Anything preceding the human race and the world as it is now is alternately attributed to the doings of Wohpekumeu the "widower across the ocean," sometimes called "the creator"; and of the woge, a race of "first people" or "spirits" or "wise people." We shall come back to them.

[3] To the "phallic" Sioux this would be unthinkable. The only occasion on which he would exhibit his genitals even to a man would be to his enemy, just before battle, in order to infuriate him [3].

[4] The more one thinks about a possible identification of the Yurok with the salmon, the more do certain comparisons become suggestive, and one wonders how much the Yurok may have guessed of the salmon's natural history. He certainly shares its "high degree of homing" and its disinclination to "stray from the parent stream." Furthermore, the Yurok so far favored intercourse in summer (when the salmon spawns) that most of their babies were born in the spring (when the salmon eggs hatch). This Kroeber explains exclusively as a result of the fact that the money in the house does not like intercourse and that all but the warmest summer weather forbids it in the open. However, in the pursuit of intercourse one would expect a tribe if not influenced by magic considerations to find other technical solutions than mere omission. Another point of interest is the fact that between June and September the salmon migrates both ways, the old ones heading upstream, the fry migrating toward the ocean. Here the double vector, which we found twice in anatomy (in procreation and in cure), occurs in geography.

[5] E. B. Powers, of the University of Tennessee, offers [10] the following interesting explanation of what has been called the salmon's homing instinct. (1) Fish respond to a carbon dioxide tension gradient. (2) There is an increase in protein metabolism in the salmon when approaching sexual maturity. Increased protein metabolism tends toward acidosis, that is, lowering of the alkali level of the blood. This brings about a response to a lower carbon dioxide tension of the water. (3) There is a carbon dioxide tension gradient from the mouth of rivers outward to the extent of their diluting influence in the ocean. This area would in turn be bounded by water having carbon dioxide tensions higher than the carbon dioxide partial pressure of the atmosphere. (4) The salmon finds the spawning streams by following the carbon dioxide tension

gradient. The steeper the gradient, that is, the greater the volume flow of the stream, and the nearer the approach to sexual maturity, the more vigorous the response of the salmon. When the salmon reach the mouth of the river, they respond to the current and ascend the spawning streams.

One feels that this is a kind of explanation of a "parent-stream fixation"—which Freud visualized when he said: "All our provisional ideas in psychology will some day be based on an organic substructure. We take this probability into account when we substitute special forces in the mind for special chemical substances" [6].

6 Because of the summer season, I was unable to visit any schools, and I found only one white teacher who confirmed this view; however, she in turn seemed a white woman extraordinarily free from prejudice and inhibition and apparently accepted by the majority of the Indians. This teacher confirmed my impression that the Yurok child, under proper treatment, has a much shorter way to go in adaptation to white standards than does the child of other tribes.

7 Early one fifth of July, during the last stages of a Brush dance which had lasted all night, songs were improvised; I could obtain only two translations: a girl sang, "I think of the time when I thought of you, but now it seems I have thrown you away"; a boy, "I think of the time when, down in Requa, I had two bottles of whiskey."

8 In the last analysis, the configuration of the salmon entering the river to deposit food without being destroyed itself, corresponds to infantile images of both the mother's nipple and the father's penis, the two highly cathexed organs which enter a mouth in order to deposit life-giving fluids.

9 In characterizing the Yurok's institutionalized claiming of recompense, Kroeber, during a few minutes of one seminar evening, used the expressions "whining around," "fussing," "bickering," "crying out," "self-pity," "excuses a child might give," "claimants who make themselves nuisances," etc.

10 That the prohibition of swearing may (or may not) be an oral counteraction of the death wish, the wish "to eliminate" rivals, has been suggested.

11 This fantasy of the vagina as a snare is expressed in the fate of the creator who, we remember, when finally succumbing to the Skate woman, finds his penis inclosed and himself abducted.

12 The process of civilization (of which we, the observers of primitive and transitory cultures and of neurotics in our own, are a part) seems to aspire at a psychological homeostasis on the level of a more universal synthesis, oriented toward an image of a supertribal and supersexual man in a superregional world. Advocating progress and rationality rather than tradition and belief, all-embracing universality rather than rigid exclusion, civilization endangers the remnants of tribal synthesis for the sake of an unknown future standard for all. The revolutions of today seem to represent attempts at consolidating human gains somewhere midway, with race or class replacing tribe, and world domination or world revolution replacing universality. The fate of democratic and rational education will depend on the degree to which rationality will make for a new and more universal cultural homogeneity.

Childhood and Tradition in Two American Indian Tribes (1945)

Some years ago the writer, a psychoanalyst then studying infantile neuroses, had the double good fortune of accompanying the anthropologist H. Scudder Mekeel to a Sioux reservation on the Plains, and of visiting with A. L. Kroeber some Yurok Indians on the Pacific coast.

The original conditions and cultural systems of these two tribes differed strikingly. The Sioux were belligerent nomads, roaming the North Central plains in loosely organized groups, pursuing "dark masses of buffalo." Their economic life was dominated by the conviction that "you can't take it with you"—either here or there. Their possessions were few and changed hands readily. Generosity and fortitude were their cardinal virtues. The Yurok, on the other hand, lived in a narrow, densely wooded river valley which steeply descends into the Pacific. They were peaceful and sedentary, gathering acorns, fishing, and preparing themselves spiritually for the annual miracle of the salmon run, when an abundance of fish enters and ascends their river, coming like a gift from nowhere beyond the ocean. They owned real estate along the river, considered that to be virtuous which

First published in *The Psychoanalytic Study of the Child*, Vol. I (New York: International Universities Press, 1945), 319–50. Reprinted in *Personality in Nature, Society and Culture*, eds. Clyde Kluckholn and Henry A. Murray (New York: Alfred A. Knopf, 1948), 176–203.

led to the storage of wealth, and gave monetary value to every named item in their small world.

A. L. Kroeber has written of the anthropology of the Yurok, H. S. Mekeel and others that of the Sioux. It was the purpose of the writer's trips to collect additional data concerning the rapidly disintegrating systems of child training in both tribes; and this, in order to throw further light on present-day difficulties of reeducation among the Sioux, and for the Yurok, to interpret some of the compulsive weirdness of their ancient tradition. This he did in two impressionistic and speculative papers[1] a comparative abstract of which follows.

Today Indian tribes are American minorities. Remnants of their old concepts of childhood are compromised by attempts at acculturation, whether successful or not. But these remnants, whether still practiced or hardly remembered, are all that will ever be known. For in the past child-training was an anthropological no-man's land. Even discerning white observers preferred to assume—with contempt or with elation—that Indian children were untrained "little animals." The Indians in the meantime have silently clung to items of child training which, as questioning quickly discloses, are of great emotional importance to them. In discussing "mental hygiene" problems in Indian reeducation, white educators, too, reveal unofficial observations and private prejudices of great potency. In order to understand the cultural equation in his data the author found it necessary to review some of the successive images of themselves and of one another which the two groups had developed since they had first met.

The original image of the Sioux is that of the warrior and the hunter, endowed with manliness and mobility, cunning and cruelty. The very image of the Plains Indian with feather trophies in his bonnet now adorns the American "nickel" (as trophy or as ideal?). But since the olden days the Sioux has been beset by an apocalyptic sequence of catastrophes, as if nature and history had united to declare total war on their all-too-manly offspring. Only a few centuries before the whites settled among them, the Sioux had left their original home territory further East and had adjusted their lives to one creature: the buffalo.

It is said that when the buffalo died, the Sioux died, ethnically and spiritually. The buffalo's body had provided not only food and material for clothing, covering and shelter, but such utilities as bags and boats, strings for bows and for sewing, cups and spoons. Medicine and ornaments were made of buffalo parts; his droppings, sun-dried, served as fuel in winter. Societies and seasons, ceremonies and dances, mythology and children's play extolled his name and image. (S. p. 106.)

The whites, eager for trade routes and territory, upset the hunting grounds and slaughtered buffalo by the hundred thousands. Eager for gold, they stampeded into the Black Hills, the Sioux' holy mountains, game reservoir, and winter refuge. The Sioux tried to deal with the U.S. generals, warrior to warrior, but found that the frontier knew neither federal nor Indian law. Forced to become cowboys, the Sioux soon found their grasslands destroyed by erosion, their herds decimated by selling booms and depressions. Finally there was nothing left but abhorred homesteading within the confines of reservations—on some of the poorest land in all the states. No wonder, then, that some missionaries convinced the older Sioux that they were the lost tribe of Israel.

During this historical period the Sioux encountered successive waves of white men who typified the restless search for space, power and new ethnic identity. The roaming trappers and fur traders seemed acceptable enough to the nomadic Sioux; certain American generals were almost deified for the very reason that they had fought them well; the Negro cavalry, because of its impressive charges, was given the precious name "Black Buffaloes." The consecrated belief in man demonstrated by the Quakers and missionaries did not fail to impress the dignified and religious leaders of the Sioux. But as they looked for fitting images to connect the past with the future, the Sioux found least acceptable the class of white man who was destined to teach them the blessing of civilization, namely, the government employee.

> The young American democracy lost a battle with the Indian when it could not decide whether it was conquering, colonizing, converting, or liberating, and sent successive representatives who had one or another of these objectives in mind—a historical doubt which the Indians interpreted as insecurity, much as children do when faced with their parents' vacillations. The discrepancy between democratic ideology and practice, furthermore, is especially pronounced in the hierarchy of a centralized bureaucracy, for which fact the older Indian, who had been reared in the spirit of a hunter democracy leveling every potential dictator and every potential capitalist, had a good, if not malicious eye. (S. pp. 123–124.)

The destitute, malnourished, disease-ridden Indian of today has little similarity to his original image. Life on the reservation seems depressively arrested, like a slow-motion picture. While conversations with older individuals restore the impression of ancient decency and dignity, the tribe as a whole behaves in a fashion analogous to an oral-dependent compensation neurotic: the victim of a one-time catastrophe has adjusted to "government rations" and refuses to feed himself.

> It seems only yesterday, especially for the older Indians, that the three inseparable horsemen of their history's apocalypse appeared on their horizon; the migration of foreign people, the death of the buffalo, and soil erosion. Somehow they still seem to expect that tomorrow the bad dream will be over. . . . They have asked the United States Supreme Court to give back the Black Hills, the buffalos, the gold—or to pay for them. Some day, they expect, there will be a notice on the bulletin board at the agency announcing that the court has heard them and has made them rich. In the meantime, why learn to farm? (S. pp. 103–104.)

Thus the Indians' detailed problems of today are seen against a historical background:

> Time for the older Indian, one gathers in talking with him, is empty waiting except for those vivid bits of the present in which he can be his old self, exchanging memories, gossiping, joking, or dancing, and in which he again feels connected with the boundless past wherein there was no one but himself, the game, and the enemy (the not-himself who could be fought). The space where he can feel at home is still without borders, allows for voluntary gatherings, and at the same time for sudden expansion and dispersion. He was glad to accept centrifugal items of white culture such as the horse and the gun. . . . But so far he has shown little eagerness for the centers of centripetal existence and accumulation: the fireplace, the homestead, the bank account. For these the educator encourages him to strive; they represent what the educator wants most for himself in life—although preferably far away from Pine Ridge. (S. p. 104.)

As for the younger Sioux of today:

> In their *early childhood* they were educated by members of the two older groups for whom the future is empty except for dreams of *restoration*. In their *later childhood* they were set an example of *reform* by the white man's educational system which was increasing in vitality and in perfection of organization. But the promise of vocational perfection, since it had a place neither in the individual's early impressions and childhood play nor among the virtues extolled in tales, cannot easily become generally meaningful. (S. pp. 115–116.)

Therefore: Our curiosity in regard to the educational difficulties in the Indian Service was focused first on those psychological realities in both groups in the light of which they characterize persons of the same or the other groups as difficult, disturbed, or abnormal. (S. p. 116.)

The Sioux lack any sense of property, whites say, and indeed, to the original Sioux, a "hoarder" was the poorest kind of a man because, apparently, irrational anxiety caused him to mistrust the abundance of the game and the generosity of his fellow men. The remnants of the old virtues of generosity, however, obviously not only represent a hindrance to federal indoctrination but also most practically interfere with attempts to help the Indian by special rations and subsidies. Recipients of relief are often beset by neighbors and relatives who, good-naturedly and with the best of cultural conscience, demand that they provide for them as long as the supplies last. The Sioux are unclean, others complain; hygiene on the prairie was based on the principle that sand, wind and sun take care of the contaminating waste products of the body. Child-birth took place on a sand pile, excrements were deposited in the sunny outdoors, and corpses were left on scaffolds for the sun to dry. Mekeel knew of old Indians who when sick insisted on living in "draughty" tepees behind their new "hygienic" frame houses. The little Indian girl, however, who, on entering a white school, is made to feel that she is dirty, and who learned to start the day with a shower, on returning home during late adolescence, is found to be "dirty" by her elders because she has not learned to observe avoidances during menstruation. One of the outstanding complaints brought against Indian children is that they withdraw into themselves or become truant; in the nomadic days, not only families moved from place to place but children also moved from family to family, calling all their aunts "Mother" and all their uncles "Father," thus having at their disposal the welcome of a wide and generous family system. The tendency to pack up and leave when things get tense seems so "natural" to Indian parents that the truant officer finds them utterly indifferent to his complaints.

Every expressed white complaint has a silent counterpart in what the Indians consider the white man's immoral, lazy and dirty nature. The Indian feels that the white man is tense and thus a bad advertisement for his principles of conduct. Above all he beats his own children and is rude to them: an obvious sign of utter lack of "civilization." The Sioux used never to threaten their children with corporal punishment or abandonment. They told them that somebody was going to "come and get them," maybe the owl—and maybe "the white man." This judgment has its counterpart in the opinion of an experienced white educator who claimed that Indian parents "love their children less than animals do." He based his opinion on the fact that the notoriously shy and reticent Sioux parents, after not having seen their children for years, neither kiss them nor cry when they come to get them.

The more confidential a conversation with white or Indian, the more irrational became the accusations concerning the harm which each group assumed the other was deliberately planning to do to children on both sides. Representative is the Indian opinion that white people *teach* their newborn babies to cry, because they do not want them to enjoy life; and the opinion, voiced by several whites, that Indians *teach* their children to masturbate, because they do not want them to crave higher things.

Thus, in trying to understand the grievances of both races, the author encountered "resistances" which, he believes, are based not on malice or entirely on ignorance, but rather, on anachronistic *fears of extinction*, and *fear of loss of group identity*; for the Indian is unwilling to part with the past that provided him with the last cultural synthesis he was able to achieve.

> But necessities change more suddenly than true virtues; and it is one of the most paradoxical problems of human evolution that virtues which originally were designed to safeguard an individual's or a group's self-preservation become rigid under pressure of anachronistic fears of extinction and thus can render a people unable to adapt to changed necessities. (S. pp. 117–118.)

Most whites, on the other hand, find it difficult to face a minority problem that endangers what synthesis their hardly-won status seems to promise.

> Every group, of whatever nature, demands sacrifices of its members which they can bear only in the firm belief that they are based on unquestionable absolutes of conduct. Thus the training of an effective and dependable government employee naturally tends to exclude automatically the ability to tolerate certain classes of people, their standards and habits. (S. p. 119.)

Such resistances—as the Office of Indian Affairs well knows—cannot be overcome by administrative and moral coercion but only by gradual enlightenment and by planned historical change. Otherwise,

> Plains tribes (not privileged as are the Pueblos to seclude themselves on self-sustained islands of archaic culture) will probably at best join the racial minorities in the poorer American population. Unavoidably, the psychological effects of unemployment and neurosis will be added to tuberculosis, syphilis, and alcoholism which the Indians have acquired so readily. In the long run, therefore, only a design which humanizes modern existence in general can deal adequately with the problems of Indian education. (S. p. 152.)

As for the "mental hygiene" problems encountered, the author suggests

> . . . that it is necessary to confront a possible list of problems as the educator sees them with two other lists, namely those vices which can be traced to old virtues, and new virtues which, if adopted by Indian children, become behavior problems in the eyes of their elders. (S. p. 118.)
>
> This, it seems, is the most astonishing single fact to be investigated: Indian children can live for years, without open rebellion or any signs of inner conflict, between two standards which are incomparably further apart than are those of any two generations or two classes in our culture.
>
> We have been led to consider such discrepancies to be among the strongest factors in individual maladjustment. However, as far as the latent psychological prerequisites are concerned, it seems that at the moment there is more inclination towards delinquency, both in the narrower sense of actual juvenile delinquency and in the form of a general and intangible passive resistance against any further and more final impact of the white standards on the Indian conscience than toward neurotic tension, such as self-blame in the service of the white standards. In any event the Indian child of today does not seem to find himself confronted with a "bad conscience" when, in passive defiance of the white teacher, he retreats into himself; nor is he met by unsympathetic relatives when he chooses to run home. (S. p. 124.)

In introducing the data on Sioux childhood, the author points to the various resistances which stand in the way of conceptualizing a child as a gradually conditioned rather than a ready made member of his tribe, race, or nation. Pre-scientific narcissism caused man to project himself—in the form of Adam—into the beginning of the world; and made him assume the fetus in its beginning to be a tiny, but complete man; these images have given way to the insight into evolution, and into epigenetic development. We now want to learn how a child *develops* into a white or an Indian, a member of a clan or of a class.

In a recent article I found it helpful to base what we have learned from Freud about the critical periods in early childhood on an analogy between the effects of environmental interference with the first extrauterine impulse manifestations and those of experimental or accidental interference with fetal development. In both, modification or damage affected in the (epigenetically created) organization depends on the developmental time of interference. Any accidental or experimental interference in a given period of growth will change the rate of growth of the system "just budding up," and in doing so will rob this system of its potential supremacy over "its" period, thus endangering the whole hierarchy of developing systems. Furthermore, the whole organism as well as any of its systems is most deeply affected by interference so timed as to hit its first unfolding; at a later stage it might be restricted in its expression, but could not be destroyed as a potentiality (C. R. Stockard).

Educational environment, by choosing a focus for its interference with the unfolding set of given human elements, by timing this interference, and by regulating its intensity, accelerates and inhibits the child's impulse systems in such a way that the final outcome represents what is felt to be—and often is temporarily—the optimum configuration of given human impulses under certain natural and historic conditions. In thus creating "anthropological" variations of man, instinctive education apparently uses, systematically although unconsciously, the same possibilities for modification which become more spectacularly obvious in the abnormal deviations brought about by deficiency or accident. (S. pp. 132–133.)

In making this statement, however, the author, to say the least, falls prey to semantic inertia. For environment cannot be said to "interfere with unfolding human elements." There is no social vacuum in which human elements could for a little while develop all by themselves, in order then—as similar phrases go—to be molded or "channelized" by society.

The libido-theory delineates the quality, the range of potentialities and the limitations of the psychological energy available at a given state of development. To be transformed into expressive and adaptive behavior, however, this energy needs a cultural medium; to develop human elements, i.e. to survive, a baby needs the seductive qualities of human organization. The same acts which help the baby to survive help the culture to survive in him; and as he lives to grow, his first bodily sensations are also his first social experiences.

The initial "vocabulary" of social experience, in turn, is dictated by epigenetic facts: the successive erogeneity of orifices and peripheral systems, and the step for step expansion of mastery over space. The ready receptivity of mouth and senses (including the skin) establishes the organ-mode of incorporation. The muscle system (including the sphincters) expresses the discrimination between retention and elimination. The locomotor system and the genital organs serve the establishment of intrusion and (in girls) inception.[2]

Incorporation and assimilation, retention and elimination, intrusion and inception are some of the basic problems of organismic existence. Emotional and intellectual, as well as physical, self-preservation demand that one accept, keep, digest, and eliminate; give and receive; take and be taken in *fair ratio*. This ratio is the firm foundation for the later development of the infinite variability and specialization of human existence.

Before the Sioux child was born his mother's relatives and friends for many months gathered the best berries and herbs the prairie produced and prepared a juice in a buffalo bladder which served as the baby's first nursing bottle. A carefully selected woman stimulated his mouth with her finger and fed him the juice while two other selected women sucked the mother's breast till it was ready to give the real stuff of life in generous quantities. Thus the baby was saved the exertion of stimulating his mother's breasts and of digesting the colostrum which precedes the generous flow of milk. Once the baby had begun to enjoy the mother's breast, he was nursed whenever he whimpered and was permitted to play freely with the breast. The Sioux Indians did not believe that helpless crying would make a baby strong, although, as we shall see, they considered temper tantrums in the older child beneficial. Boys in particular, and especially the first boy, were breast-fed generously for a period of from three to five years, during which time the father was supposed not to interfere by making sexual advances to the mother; intercourse was said to spoil the milk. The author points out that if the "length" of the breast-feeding period is a questionable concept if applied to a people like the Sioux, where the advent of a new baby often only temporarily interfered with the first child's breast-feeding: Even where a child had already learned to depend upon other food, he still was permitted to draw an occasional sip from his mother's or (for that matter) any other woman's breasts.

However, this paradise of a long and generous feeding history contained a forbidden fruit. Sioux grandmothers recount what trouble they had with these indulged babies when they began to bite with habitual abandon; how they would "thump" the baby's head and how he, in turn, would fly into infantile rage. The mother's apparent amusement with these tantrums was justified by the explanation that rage makes a child strong. They apparently fostered it. The author makes two observations in this connection. He wonders how well the Sioux infant was able to abreact rage in muscular movement while still strapped in the traditional cradle board. While it is un-doubtedly true that this tight container permitted the newborn to find a comfortable approximation of the fetal state, the author con-siders the possibility that inhibited expressions of provoked rage established a lasting reservoir of biting and muscular aggression which may well have contributed to the much described "trait" of anger and cruelty in Sioux character. The frustration of the biting period was also reflected in the most common nervous habit, the existence of which was admitted by the older Indians and was still observable in the younger ones:

> At any time, anywhere, one sees children (and adults, usually women) playing with their teeth, clicking or hitting something against them, snap-ping chewing gum or indulging in some play which involves teeth and finger nails on one or both hands. This seems rarely combined with thumb-sucking; the lips, even if both hands are as far inside the mouth as is at all possible, do not participate in this Sioux habit par excellence. (S. p. 139.)

The author sees in the history of the Sioux child's pre-verbal con-ditioning an ingenious arrangement which would secure in the Sioux personality that combination of undiminished self-confidence, trust in the availability of food supply, and ready anger in the face of interference, the co-existence of which was necessary for the func-tioning of a hunter democracy. We shall come back to this point in connection with the conditioning of the Yurok child, the child of "capitalist" fishermen. As will be seen then, in both tribes, the first trauma in relationship to the mother is dramatized in the rituals considered to be of highest spiritual meaning.

> It seems to me that it is this unchannelized energy of frustrated impulses to bite and kick which is the contribution of the Sioux's child training to his cultural personality; it contributes to the urge for communal temper outbursts such as endless centrifugal "parties" setting out to hunt, kill, steal, and rape; to the Sioux Indian's proverbial cruelty both against enemies and against himself; and it finds its most exalted expression in

the scene during the Sun dance when "little sticks driven through the breasts of the dancers and connected by strings to the Sun Pole, were pulled free so that the flesh was ripped open": a sacred turning against himself of suppressed—and long forgotten—wishes. (Y. p. 291.)[3]

The generosity manifested in the mother's initial handling of the child was continued in the family's respect for his property and the renunciation of adult claims wherever a conflict arose.

While a Sioux could not refuse a request for a gift, he could refuse to give away his child's possessions; the emphasis, however, was on the honor that would come to the child when he, of his own accord, would relinquish his property. The child was not taught that property was "bad," but given an example of extreme generosity by the parents, who even today, to the traders' horror, are willing to let the child waste money that should buy needed supplies.

The first strict *taboos* expressed verbally and made inescapable by a tight net of ridiculing gossip did not concern the body and physical habits, but were of a social nature and first applied to the relationship of brother and sister: When a certain age after the sixth year was reached, brother and sister were not to speak with one another any more, and parents as well as the older siblings would urge the girl to confine herself to female play and to stay near the mother and tepee while the boy was encouraged to join the older boys in cowboy and hunter games. (S. p. 142.)

From then on, the daily patterns for boys and for girls differed radically. The boy was to become restless, brave and reckless; the girl, reticent, industrious and chaste. Boys used miniature bows and arrows and later ropes for an initial imitation and, as soon as possible, the real activation of a hunter's or cowboy's existence. Of interest are the "bone horses," small bones of phallic shape taken from killed animals and called "horses," "buffaloes," "cows," "bulls," etc. The author believes that the constant fingering of these dolls by small boys tended to connect the masturbatory tendencies of the phallic-locomotor stage with fantasies of becoming great hunters or cowboys. While thus sadistic, intrusive tendencies are cultivated in the boy, in the girl, corresponding inhibitions are used to teach her "an extreme state of passivity and fearfulness." Girls were taught to sit modestly, to walk in small, measured steps, later to sleep with their thighs tied together, and not to go beyond a certain radius around the tepee or the camp. It was understood by both sexes that any girls who habitually overstepped such restrictions could be raped by boys without their incurring punishment. The girl, however, who learned to conform could connect fantasies of the brother's greatness as a hunter with the skills she learned. She knew that the brother, as an adult, would be obliged to bring to her the best of what he could rob or hunt; she would butcher the buffalo and, on occasion, the enemy killed by him; her skill in embroidery would come to full display when she would be called upon to ornament the cradles and layettes of his wife's children. Moreover, at certain ceremonies, she would sing of his bravery, and in the Sun Dance she would assist him during his tortures. This is an example of the way in which homogeneous cultures pay in the currency of prestige for whatever restrictions they feel they have to impose. The girl was taught to serve hunters, to be on guard against them, but also to become a mother who would be willing and able to instill into her boys the fundamental traits of the plains hunter. The first basic avoidance between brother and sister thus used the energies of the phallic-locomotor stage and of potential incestuous tendencies to establish a model of mutual respect and generosity among all the "brothers and sisters" of the extended kinship.

The author notes that such relationships were established without that estrangement between body and self which is effected by the idea of sin, and without that estrangement between parents and children which is caused where parents are the sole arbiters of seemingly arbitrary rules. Instead, older children would, with ridiculing comment, enforce rules basic to the whole pattern of Sioux existence.

The psychopathologist will be especially interested in the way individuals were treated who for one reason or another were unable to conform to these clear-cut differentiations between masculinity or feminity. It seems that conformance, wherever humanly possible, was urged by ridicule. However, for the sincere nonconformer there was a ritual way out—right through the ridicule. The disturbed boy would seek a vision quest in lonesomeness and self-torture. The inventory of such visions were standardized and yet his vision had to be personally convincing to secure the deviant public recognition. One such role was the "Heyoka." A boy would dream that he had seen the Thunderbird, whereupon his father would tell him that he "must go through with it" or be struck by lightning. He was then obliged to behave as absurdly and clownishly as possible until his elders felt that he had cured himself of the curse. Descriptions of such activities make it plain that they are analogous to the involuntary self-debasing exhibitionism in neurotic men in our society. However, in further analogy to the more or less voluntary and conscious role played by great comedians in our culture, a Heyoka, in spite of the contempt freely bestowed upon him, could prove himself so victoriously funny that he would end up a leader among his people. Correspondingly a girl might dream that she must choose between certain objects that are typical for men's and women's activities. After that, it would be recognized that she must be "Witko," which means "crazy." She then would throw to the winds all feminine restraint and probably become a prostitute, sometimes a famous one. A boy may dream that the moon has two hands and tries to make him choose between certain objects, but that suddenly the hands cross and try to force the burden strap of a woman upon him (T. S. Lincoln). If the dreamer fails in his resistance, he is doomed to be like a woman. Such a man is called a "berdache"; he dresses like a woman and does woman's work. He is not necessarily a homosexual (although warriors before going on the war path are said to have visited such men in order to increase their own ferocity). Sometimes, because of his position between the sexes, a berdache could excel in the arts of companionship, cooking and embroidery.

Thus the dreamer's deepest urges present themselves to him as a prophecy and as a command from a spiritual source. The abnormal was not permitted to escape the elastic net of cultural meaning.

The author's first anthropological impressions thus seemed to confirm Geza Roheim's classical thesis that there is a "correlation between the habitual infancy situation" and "the dominant ideas of a group." However, he cannot conceive of the second as being "derived" from the first or of primitive societies as being solutions of specific infantile conflicts. Such quasi-causal formulations lead, it is true, to the hen-or-egg question—what came first, the culture or the individual, specific infancy situation or dominant ideas. History, however, has beginnings only in myths; in reality it fuses into prehistory. And whatever the pre-human may have looked like, human beings always have attempted to derive a condensed design of group living that guarded against the *combined* dangers of physical harm (hunger, pain), group disintegration (panic), and individual anxiety; and had as their further goal: survival, accomplishment, self-expression. The treatment of children and other manifestations of a primitive culture evolve from an increasing synthetic tendency in the group-ego, situated as it is in its constituent individual egos. This tendency can be demonstrated somewhat more clearly in primitive societies because they represent condensed and homogeneous ways of dealing directly with one segment of nature. As we shall see later, the synthetic cultural tendency becomes less transparent where (1) tradition, i.e. previous syntheses, become a complicated "environment" that resists resynthesis; (2) where the means of production as a whole lose their concreteness to the individual, and only segments of the economic system are immediate enough to permit practical and magic adaptation; (3) where consequently antagonistic social entities are created within the total group—with some entities in their particular segment bent on making other entities subservient to their syntheses.

For a member of such a complicated society it is, therefore, instructive to see how a homogeneous group like the American Indian tribes dealt with human existence. Let us compare the Sioux concepts of childhood with those among the Yurok. These two tribes stand in opposition in almost all the basic configurations of existence. The Sioux roamed the plains and cultivated spatial concepts of centrifugal mobility, the horizons of their existence coinciding with the limits of the buffalo's roaming and the beginnings of enemy hunting grounds. The Yurok not only lived largely in or at the mouth of a narrow, mountainous, densely-forested valley, but, in addition, limited themselves within arbitrary borders. They considered a disc of about 150 miles in diameter, cut in half by the course of the Klamath river, to include all there was to this world. They ignored the rest and ostracized as "of ignoble birth" anyone who showed a marked tendency to venture into territories beyond. Instead they cried and prayed to their horizons which they thought contained the supernatural "homes" from which generous spirits sent the stuff of life to them: above all, salmon. The limitation of this world was manifested in its cardinal directions: there was an "upstream" and a "downstream," a "towards the river," and an "away from the river," and then, at the end of the world, an elliptic "in back and around."

Within this restricted radius of existence, extreme localization took place. Old Yuroks proudly point to hardly noticeable pits in the ground as their ancestors' home. Such pits retain the family name. The whole environment exists only in as far as human history has named certain locations. Their myths do not mention the gigantic redwoods which impress white travelers so much; yet the Yurok will point to certain insignificant looking rocks and trees as being the "origin" of the most far-reaching events. This localization finds its economic counterpart in a monetarization of values. Every person, relationship or act can be exactly valued and becomes the object of pride or ceaseless bickering. The acquisition and retention of possessions is and was what the Yurok thinks about, talks about and prays for.

This little well-defined world had, in the author's words, its "mouth open" towards the ocean and lived both in its practical and its magical pursuits for the yearly, mysterious appearance of tremendous numbers of salmon which came out of the ocean, climbed up the river, and usually having left an abundance of food supply in the Yurok's nets, disappeared up the river. The author debates the question as to whether the Yurok knew the complicated life history of the salmon, which, on reaching the spawning territory up river, procreates and dies; while some months later its diminutive progeny descends the river, disappears out in the ocean and two years later, as mature salmon, driven by a "homing instinct," returns to its very birthplace to fulfill its life cycle. The salmon, before entering the river, stops eating and therefore when caught has an empty stomach. As he ascends the river, his sexual organs develop and his fat content diminishes; at the optimum of his physical prowess and nutritional value, then, the salmon has ceased eating and has not commenced procreating. When the Yurok goes to catch him, he purifies himself as we shall see, from contact with procreation and abstains from food.

It is the author's thesis that the Yurok show one extreme type of conceptual integration:

> Our preconception is this: Yurok thinking, so far as it is magic, tends to assimilate concepts derived from (1) observations of the geographic and biological environment, that is, (a) the lower part of a river valley with a mysterious periodical supply of fish, (b) a prey (salmon) with a particularly dramatic biology; and (2) experiences of the human body as a slowly maturing organism with periodical needs. In the non-magical sphere, of course, the Yurok reaches a certain degree of logic and technique, as do all human beings; but wherever magic behavior seems indicated—that is, wherever mysterious food sources beyond the Yurok's territory, technology, and causal comprehension need to be influenced, or whenever vague human impulses and fears need to be alleviated—the Yurok tries to understand nature around and within him by blending bodily and geographic configurations, both of which become parts of one geographic-anatomical environment. In this environment the periodical affluence of the waterway has a functional interrelation with the periodicity of vital juices in the body's nutritional, circulatory, and procreative systems. Therefore, the Yurok's main magic concern is that vital channels be kept open and that antagonistic fluids be kept apart from one another. (Y. p. 259.)

. . . Every item of Yurok ethnology on which our demonstration can be based is shared by the Yurok's ethnic neighbors where it may have the same, a similar, a transformed, or a different meaning. Here, too, our attitude is clinical: we would expect an individual ego to synthesize individually experience typical for many; similarly, we assume that a group ego (or whatever we choose to name the organized and organizing core of a culture situated as it is in its constituent individual egos) tends to take stock of and to synthesize what has been selected, accepted, and preserved. It is this *synthetic tendency* which in the following pages is to be demonstrated *within one culture.* (Y. p. 259.)

One example of such primitive synthesis is the pervading importance of the "tube" configuration in Yurok thinking. According to Yurok mythology, the Klamath in prehistoric times flowed up on one side and down on the other. Now, it flows only in the downward direction and salmon ascend upward. To be sure that the river is open on both sides and thus an inviting waterway for the energetic salmon, the Yurok, magically concerned, attempts to keep all tubelike things within and around him unobstructed and all fluid-ways uncontaminated. He abhors the double-vector, i.e. a sac-like configuration which is entered and left through the same opening. Points in question are Yurok architecture and the Yurok concept of the human body.

The Yurok have two kinds of houses, the living house and the sweat house. Both are subterranean with a roof a few feet above the ground. The "doors" consist of oval openings just above the ground which admit one creeping human being at a time. The living house, however, has only one such opening (sac) while the sweat house has two (tube). The living house is a very crowded affair:

Underneath the roof is a huge criss-cross of poles on which salmon is hanging in all possible states of age and eatenness, while a shelf bench between the dugout and the sidewalls is loaded with enormous baskets full of scorns and utensils in various states of use. The total impression is that of darkness, crowdedness, and endless accumulation. This is where women and children live; the man who comes to visit his home is careful not to sit on the floor, but on a block or stool of the form of a cylinder or mushroom. Otherwise, his place is in the sweat house, where he takes the older boys; there is one sweat house to six or seven living houses. . . .

These two house forms not only serve woman and man, respectively, but also symbolize what the man's and woman's insides mean in Yurok culture: the family house, dark, unclean, full of food and utensils, and crowded with babies, the place from which a man emerges contaminated; the sweat house, lighter, cleaner, more orderly, with selectivity over who and what may enter, a place from which one emerges purified. (Y. p. 268.)

Living house and female anatomy are associated. After contact with either, the man has to pass the "test" of the sweat house. This he enters through the normal-sized door. However, he can leave it only through a very small opening which will permit only a man moderate in his eating habits and supple with the perspiration caused by the sacred fire to slip through. He is required to conclude the purification by swimming in the river. The conscientious fisherman passes this test every morning thus denying his contact with women and, as it were, giving daily rebirth to himself through a tube-like womb.

What the Yurok calls "clean" living is an attempt to keep vectors clear, channels unobstructed, and to avoid the wombs of multiplication: woman; the lake upriver from which he thinks the waters of the Klamath flow; the place across the ocean where salmon originate; the origin of his shell money up the coast. The author describes an old Indian woman's melancholic apprehension when she saw a whale enter, play around in, and leave the mouth of the Klamath; the river should serve only one vector: that of ascending salmon. For that which flows in one channel of life is said to be most eager not to come in contaminating contact with the objects of other channels or with "sac-like" configurations. Salmon and the river dislike it if food is eaten on a boat. Deer will stay away from the snare if deer meat has been brought in contact with water—even posthumously by washing the eating bowls. Salmon demands that women on their trip up or down river, at specified places, leave the boat and walk around a rock. Salmon also dislikes the man who is full of food, or, as we saw, has been in contact with the "woman's inside," and money will leave the house if intercourse took place while it was there. (Shell money is strung on thongs and carried in oblong tube-like purses.)

Only once a year, after the salmon run, these avoidances are set aside. At that time, following complicated ceremonies, a strong dam is built which obstructs the ascent of the salmon and permits the Yurok to catch a rich winter supply. The dam building is "the largest mechanical enterprise undertaken by the Yurok or, for that matter, by any California Indians, and the most communal attempt." After ten days of collective fishing, orgies of ridicule and of sexual freedom take place alongside the river, reminiscent of the ancient Satires of European spring ceremonials.

The author finds indications that these ceremonials dramatize the return, the ridicule, and the re-banishment of a "primal father" figure. For the Yurok's centripetal world was created by a most centrifugal and irresponsible father: The old man Wohpekumeu (the "widower from across the ocean") stood in the middle of the river which went up on one side and down on the other, and cried and claimed that he was lonely. Land appeared on both sides of him. He cried more. A water spout was rising in front of him, slowly coming up to the height of his breast. He cried again. The water came up to his brow. Upon further crying, the spout slowly developed into a woman, first her upper half and then, upon his further tearful insistence ("I want a whole woman") the lower part as well. After having created the rest of the world, the widower gave this woman to his son together with plenty of food, under the condition (which seems habitual with creators) that he must work. Later, however, he seduced his daughter-in-law and became so girl-crazy that he had to be banished. His sons decided that they would also overcome all centrifugal tendencies among themselves, henceforth love clean in their restricted, compulsive and phobic world.

This hysterical God, nostalgic but sly, powerful but inhibited, God-like but unreliable, is the originator across the ocean of the yearly salmon supply. In contrast to him, there is a more compulsive character, a "clean" God, who smoked but never ate, who never desired a woman, and accomplished the great historical deed of banning women from the sweat house. He represents all that the Yurok call "clean." And yet they know that they need a continuous, cautious, well-ritualized contact with the widower who provides food. The author interprets the rejuvenation ceremonial connected with the annual fish dam as dramatizing an early return of the primal father, who, having brought all the salmon (on a deeper level he is the salmon) is ceremoniously defeated by the dam chief, and after much ridicule, banned again. Whereupon the world for a short while is free of phobic restriction, sexual and otherwise. But then the Yurok again begins the "clean" life which helps him to be a conscientious warden of his segment of nature.

This interesting version of the primal father myth suggests some speculation concerning historical elements in its variations.

Let us assume that the Yurok came from somewhere else; with no chance or wish to turn back, they found their way blocked by the Pacific. They settled along the river, and, noticing the periodical salmon run, became fishermen—in technique and in magic.

The human mind is likely to feel guilty and, if necessary, to construct a guilt when it finds itself faced with sudden environmental limitation; adapting, it learns to see a virtue in the necessity imposed by the limitation; but it continues to look into the future for potential recurrences or intensifications of the trauma of limitation, anticipating punishment for not being virtuous enough. In this sense to the restricted Yurok, centrifugality may have become a vice in the past, centripetality a virtue; and the ocean's disfavor, anticipated punishment for centrifugal "mental sins" which Yurok ethics tries to avoid. (Y. p. 276.)

Thus an ontogenetic trauma (the banishment from the mother's body and house) and a historical task would appear synthesized, analogous to the spatial synthesis of geography and anatomy.

In his attempts to gather information on the Yurok's ancient child training system, the author, in some areas, found himself among hostile, contemptuous and resistive people who apparently suspected him of trying to get information on their property rights. He thus not only met some of the old money-mindedness and suspicion but he also was quite aware that the inner distance between Yurok and whites is not so great as that between whites and Sioux. For there was much in the A. B. C. of Yurok life that did not have to be relearned when the whites came. The Yurok lived in frame houses and in fact now lives in super-terranean structures next to pits in the ground which once contained his ancestors' subterranean dwellings. Unlike the Sioux, who, in the buffalo, lost overnight the focus of his economic and spiritual life, the Yurok still sees, catches, talks and eats salmon. When the Yurok man today steers a raft of logs, or the Yurok woman grows vegetables, their occupations are not too far removed from the original manufacture of dugouts, the gathering of acorns and the planting of tobacco. Above all, the Yurok concerned his life with property. "He schemed constantly to lodge a claim or to evade an obligation." According to the author, the Yurok need not forget this "primitive" tendency in the white world, and therefore his grievances with the United States find other than the inarticulate, smoldering expression of the prairie man's passive resistance. In fact, upriver, only twenty miles from a major U.S. highway, the author found himself treated (and saw visiting white officials treated) as definitely unwelcome white minority.

From a few wise old informants, however, the author gathered this information: The birth of a baby is surrounded with oral prohibitions. Father and mother eat neither deer meat nor salmon until the child's navel heals. Disregard of this taboo causes convulsions in the child. (The more "genital" Sioux thinks that a child's convulsions are caused by the parents' intercourse during pregnancy.) During the birth, the mother must shut her mouth. The newborn is not breast-fed for ten days, but given a nut soup from a tiny shell. The breast-feeding begins with Indian generosity. However, there is a definite weaning time around the sixth month, that is, around the teething period. Yurok breast-feeding thus is maintained for a minimum period among American Indians. Weaning is called "forgetting the mother" and is enforced, if necessary, by the mother's going away for a few days. This relative acceleration of weaning seems to be part of a general tendency to encourage the baby to leave the mother and her support as soon as this is possible and bearable—and not to return. From his twentieth day on, the baby's legs, which are left uncovered in the Yurok version of the cradle board, are massaged by the grandmother. Early creeping is encouraged. The first postnatal crisis for the Yurok child, therefore, occurs much earlier than that of the Sioux, and consists of a relationship in time of enforced weaning, teething, and encouraged creeping. The shorter nursing period, of course, accelerates the advent of a second crisis, namely, the mother's next pregnancy.

We have referred to the contribution made by the Sioux baby's oral training to Sioux character structure. The Yurok child, as we saw, is weaned early and abruptly, before the full development of the biting stage, and after having been discouraged from feeling too comfortable with his mother. The author suggests that this expulsion—in its relation to other items—contributes to the Yurok character, a residue of potential nostalgia which consequently find its institutionalized form in the Yurok's ability to cry while he prays in order to gain influence over the food-sending powers behind the visible world. There is something of an early oral "hallucinatory wish fulfillment" implied in the adult Yurok's conviction that tearful words, such as "I see a salmon," will cause a salmon to come. It is as if he had to pretend that he had no teeth so that his food supply would not be cut off. In the meantime, however, he does not forget to build nets.

This concentration on the sources of food is not accomplished without a second oral training at the "sense" stage, i.e. when the child can repeat what he has been told. He is admonished to eat slowly, not to grab food, never to take it without asking for it, never to eat between meals and never to ask for a second helping—an oral puritanism hardly equaled among other primitives. During meals, a strict order of placement is maintained and the children are taught to eat in prescribed ways; for example, to put only a little food on the spoons, to take the spoons up to their mouths slowly, to put the spoon down while chewing the food—and above all, to think of becoming rich during the whole process. Nobody speaks during meals so that everybody can keep his own thoughts on money and salmon. Thus a maximum of preverbal avarice and need for intake, which may have been evoked by the combination of early weaning, not only from the breast but also from contact with the mother and from babyish ways in general, is "tamed" and used for the development of those attitudes, which to the Yurok mind, will in the end assure the salmon's favor. The Yurok makes himself see money hanging from trees and salmon swimming in the river during off season. He learns to subordinate genital drives to the pursuit of money. In the sweat house the boy will learn the strange feat of thinking of money and at the same time *not* thinking of women.

These fables told to children in an interesting way underline the ugliness of lack of restraint. They isolate one outstanding item in the physiognomy of animals and use it as an argument for "clean behavior." The buzzard's baldness is the result of his having put his whole head into a dish of hot soup. The eel gambled his bones away. The hood of the angry bluejay is her clitoris which she tore off in "masculine protest." One fable which concerns itself with feces also emphasizes the need for cautious intake and incidentally illustrates the tube concept.

The bear was always hungry. He was married to the blue jay. One day they made a fire and the bear sent the blue jay to get some food. She brought back only one acorn. "Is that all?" the bear said. The blue jay got angry and threw the acorn in the fire. It popped all over the place and there was acorn all over the ground. The bear swallowed it all down and got awfully sick. Some birds tried to sing for him but it did not help. Nothing helped. Finally the hummingbird said, "Lie down and open your mouth," and then the hummingbird zipped right through him. That's why the bear has such a big anus and can't hold his feces. (Y. p. 286.)

Second in emphasis to cautious intake is the prohibition of swearing, that is, verbal offense committed especially by reference to death and dead people; i.e. verbal elimination.

In accordance with the Yurok's tendency to rush their children along on the path of maturation, they have an interesting concept of regression. It is bad for the child, they say, to sleep in the afternoon, for there is an affinity between dusk and death. In its time the fetus. was kept awake in the afternoon by the mother's rubbing of her abdomen. At dusk, children are hurriedly called into the house, because then they may see some "wise" people, i.e. members of the race that inhabited the earth before the Yurok took possession of it. The description of these "wise" people seems to mark them as a materialization of pregenitality, their attraction as a regressive tendency. They are adult at six months of age. They procreate orally and have no genitals. They do not know what it means to be "clean" and they never die. The child who seems a member of this race develops symptoms such as lack of appetite, nightmares, disobedience. He may waste away if he is not given treatment.

There are various forms of treatment. The parents themselves should stay out of it; maybe the grandmother next door will sing the proper songs. In severe cases, however, a psychotherapist is consulted. The author was able to interview the last of these women shaman. Her techniques embrace the psychosomatic, the bisexual and the ambivalent nature of neurosis. The shaman sucks two "pains" out of the child's body—one residing always above the child's navel (where it obstructs the nutritional tube) and its "mate" from wherever the child feels pain. Then follows the interpretation and the group therapy. The child is laid on the floor and his parents and relatives gather around in a circle. After elaborate rituals, the shaman has a vision and describes it. She will see, for example, a man who had made a vow of abstinence nevertheless have intercourse with a woman. Or she will see an old woman sitting in the hills trying to "sorcerize" somebody. Whatever it is, one or the other of the child's relatives will get up and confess that he has committed that crime. The fact that this procedure is said to result in cures can be attributed to the shaman's intuitive skill in making the child's relatives confess to whatever secret guilt caused ambivalent tension in the home and anxiety in the child, both of which are thus ameliorated.

The very healing power of the shaman is derived from a potentially pathogenic set of events.

Long before F., the daughter and granddaughter of shamans, reached puberty, people had predicted that she probably would turn into a shaman too because "she slept so much," that is, had a neurotic inclination to regress. During her premenarche, her grandmother tested her by taking a "pain" out of her own mouth and trying to make F. swallow it. F. ran away from home. The following night, however, she had an anxiety dream in which an old woman threw a basket over her mouth in such a way that she swallowed its "yellow, black bloody, nasty" content. She woke up in extreme anxiety but kept this dream to herself because she realized that people would force her to become a shaman if they knew that her grandmother's suggestion had invaded her dream life. At breakfast, however, she gave herself away by vomiting, whereupon the community made her confess and in great excitement prepared her novitiate. She now had to learn to transform this involuntary vomiting of stomach content into the ability to swallow and to throw up "pains" without throwing up food with it—a mastery over the oral-nutritional tube which gives F. the power to cure people. Here the abhorred double-vector becomes beneficial.

Unlike F., the ordinary Yurok girl when menstruating the first time is forced to "close up" all around. Silently sitting in the corner of her home with her back turned to the fire, she moves as little as possible. On leaving the house once a day, she does not look about. For four days or longer, she abstains from food. Then she takes her food to a spot where she can not hear any sound except the noise of the river. To the girl who has thus learned to guard her receptivity, her mother demonstrates the purpose of her inceptive organization by putting in front of her twenty sticks, calling ten of them sons, and ten, daughters.

F., however, acquired all the prerogatives forbidden to other women. She could sleep in the sweat house, pray for money, and smoke a pipe. She became as rich as any man and stronger in magic power. From F.'s and other shaman's dreams, the author concludes that F. was destined to become her mother's successor because she, alone among her sisters, early showed hysterical traits of "masculine protest" which are promoted to a plane of magic usefulness by the community. The author secured fragments of the case history of another woman who had fled her home just as F. had, when the career of a shaman was suggested to her. However, no inner pressure made her produce ("against her will") either a dream or the symptom of vomiting, the two involuntary affirmations of shamanism that alone convince the people of a shaman's calling. This woman had lifelong chronic indigestion and compulsively spoke of her interrupted novitiate until her death.

The author discusses the relationship of such institutionalized infantile behavior as the Yurok's crying and bickering to the problem of tribal character and to neurosis. The Yurok is, of course, helpless only in his magic protestations, not in his activities. He builds snares and nets and accomplishes the technical feat of the fish dam. The author believes that the closing of the two gigantic jaws of the dam is analogous to the Sioux Sun Dance in two respects: it is the event of highest collective significance in the tribe's life; and it dramatizes the oral (biting) taboo. The Yurok finds it necessary afterwards to assure his trapped prey that no malice was intended. In fact he claims that he really cannot harm his prey. "I will," says the salmon— according to Yurok Platonism—"leave my scales on nets and they will turn into salmon, but I, myself, will go by and not be killed." It is as if this combination of crying, snaring and protesting innocence represented a collective play with the greatest dangers of both ontogeny and phylogeny: the loss of the mother at the biting stage; the mythical banishment of the creator from the women of this world; and historically: the loss of salmon supply during bad years. There are further indications that the salmon (the food which refuses to enter the month of the world if you desire it too voraciously) is associated with nipple and penis, the too highly cathexed life-giving organs.

Toward his fellow men, however, the Yurok's receptivity loses all its helplessness. He claims, demands, whines, fusses, bickers, and alibis—as the author puts it, "like a jealous child who, now so touchingly helpless in the presence of the mother, uses an instant of her absence to turn on his sibling and to protest that this or that object—anything will do—is his." As for the ontogenetic basis of this behavior, we mentioned that a child who is weaned early will find himself in the company of a younger rival.

It obviously would take detailed studies to establish the Yurok's collective character, including the way in which a Yurok manages to be an individual. For it is only within the official character of a given people that a personological inquiry can begin. Each system, whether it emphasizes generosity or avarice, admits of additions and exemptions of individual avarice and generosity. To know a people's character one has to know their laws of conduct and the way they circumvent them.

The author believes that neurosis and culture, although using the same inventory of human potentialities, are systematically different phenomena. Sioux "sadism" does, of course, not keep a Sioux man from being a devoted lover and husband. As for the Yurok's "helplessness":

Does it mean that the Yurok anywhere within his technology is more helpless, more paralyzed by sadness, than are members of a tribe which does not develop these "traits"? Certainly not; his institutionalized help-lessness *eo ipso* is neither a trait nor a neurotic symptom. It is an infantile attitude which the culture chose to preserve and to put at the disposal of the individual, to be used by him and his fellow men in a limited area of existence. Such an institutionalized attitude neither spreads beyond its defined area nor makes impossible the development to full potency of its opposite: it is probable that the really successful Yurok was the one who could cry most heart-breakingly or bicker most convincingly in some situations and be full of fortitude in others, that is, the Yurok whose ego was strong enough to *synthesize orality and "sense."* In comparison, the oral types whom we may be able to discern today in our culture and to whom we would be inclined to liken what we have said about the Yurok, are bewildered people who find themselves victims of an overgrown and insatiable potentiality without the corresponding homogeneous cultural reality. (Y. pp 295–296.)

In contrast, an oral neurosis is non-adjustive and tends to be all inclusive. Most important, it interferes with the development of genital primacy in the individual.

Among our neurotics this retentiveness is common enough: it interferes with psychosexual development and genital potency. But here again the comparison between the cultural and the neurotic character ends; for, on this level too, the strong Yurok is he who never risks, over sexual matters, his property or his luck in hunting or fishing, but who would still be man enough to use with unimpaired sexual potency opportunities without danger of commitment. The understanding between the sexes in these matters goes so far (or can go so far) that one informant defined a "nice girl" as one who always tells the boy beforehand when she is menstruating, thus saving him ritual trouble and subsequent loss of work-ing time. (Y. p. 298.)

Wherever the emphasis of the ontogenetic trauma lies, every cul-ture must insure that the majority of its members will reach a certain amount of genitality—enough to support a strong personal ego and to secure a group-ego; but not more than is compatible with group living.

This applies to other pregenital factors as well. The collective or official character structure of the Yurok shows all the traits which Freud and Abraham found to be of typical significance in patients with "anal fixations", namely compulsiveness, suspiciousness, reten-tiveness, etc. The author, however, was unable to find in Yurok childhood an emphasis on feces or on the anal zone that would fulfill the criteria of a collective "anal fixation." He feels that Yurok attitude toward property is alimentary in its incorporative aspects and, in its eliminative ones, rather concerns the total inside of the body with its mixture of excreta. This may be true for most primitives.

Anal character in our culture often appears to be a result of the impact on a retentive child of a certain type of maternal behavior in Western civilization, namely, a narcissistic and phobic overconcern with matters of elimination. This attitude helps to overdevelop retentive and eliminative potentialities and to fixate them in the anal zone; it creates the strongest social ambivalence in the child, and it remains an isolating factor in his social and sexual development. Forms of "individualism" in Western culture which represent a mere insistence on the privilege to sit in isolation on possessions can be suspected of representing just such an inroad of anality into cultural and political life. Otherwise it seems that homogeneous cultural life and anality contradict one another. (Y. p. 297.)

The ground work for the Yurok's genital attitudes is laid in the child's earlier conditioning which teaches him to subordinate drive to economic considerations. Within such basic limits sex is viewed with leniency and humor. The fact that sex contact necessitates purification seems to be considered a duty or a nuisance, but does not reflect on sex as such or on individual women. There is no shame concerning the surface of the human body; it is its "inside" which, by implication, is covered when the young girl between menarche and marriage avoids bathing with others. Otherwise, everybody is free to bathe in the nude. But the girl knows that virtue, or shall we say an unblemished name, will gain her a husband who can pay well and that her status and that of her children and her children's children will depend on the amount her husband will offer to her father when asking for her. The boy, on the other hand, wishes to accumulate enough wealth to buy a worthwhile wife. If he were to make an unworthy girl pregnant, he would have to marry her. Above all, habitual deviant behavior is usually explained as a result of the delinquent's mother or grandmother not having been "paid for in full." This, it seems, means that the man in question was so eager to marry that he borrowed his wife on a down payment without being able to pay the installments; he thus proved that his ego was too weak to integrate sexual needs and economic virtues.

Exactly how genital the average genitality of any group can be said to be is debatable. The Sioux has an elaborate courtship during which, by restraint and the use of the love flute, he demonstrates to his girl that he has more than rape in mind. She, to be sure, brings a small knife along. Beyond this, intercourse in both tribes is mentioned by the men (of today!) as a primitive act of copulation without any aspiration to artfulness or with any consciousness of a female orgasm. "After all," one Yurok said, "our women were bought." Since highly male societies restrict the verbal consciousness of women it probably would have been difficult under ancient circumstances to elicit data on female sex attitudes; at and during the time of the author's short trips, it was impossible.

As we saw, Sioux and Yurok children learned to associate both locomotor and genital modes with those of hunting and fishing. The Sioux, in his official sexuality, was more phallic-sadistic in that he pursued whatever roamed: game, enemy, woman. (Just as he could "count coup," i.e., gain prestige points by merely touching an enemy, a Sioux man could claim to have taken a girl's virtue by touching her vulva.) The Yurok was more phobic-compulsive in that, in his sexuality, he identified with his prey. He avoided being "snared" by the wrong woman or at the wrong time or place—*wrong* meaning any circumstances that would compromise his assets as an economic being. To this end he is said to have had intercourse in the open, outside the configuration of the living house, ostensibly in order to avoid offending the money in the house. The Yurok woman, in turn, took care not to be bought too cheaply. The snaring configuration occurs in one final item of the primal father story: having promised to be a good god, but venturing down the coast, he found the skate woman lying on the beach, invitingly spreading her legs.[4] ("The skatefish looks like a woman's inside.") He could not resist her. But as soon as he had inserted his penis, she held on to him with vagina and legs and abducted him. On the basis of an analogous equation (fish that looks like woman's inside = female genitals = woman) the author has tentatively assumed that the oblong salmon sent by the gods also represents the god's phallus and the god. In the fishdam ceremonials, then, all three are snared—without being harmed. Thus the symbolic meaning of catching the unwilling penis is added to that of holding on to the elusive nipple. This seems to enhance the enjoyment of the rejuvenation orgies for both sexes; for it gives reassurance that the incestuous and sadistic fantasies emphasized in the Yurok version of childhood dependence have not only not offended either the ontogenetic or the phylogenetic providers, but have been successfully applied to the common good for one more year. This permits the Yurok to accomplish a most precarious feat, namely, to eat their salmon and have it next year, too.

As these excerpts show, the author's data are largely data of verbal tradition, not of observation. They reflect what women remembered doing or saying to their children. There is no reason to doubt, however, that this selection, as far as it goes, is representative. To be sure, there is a great emphasis on feeding procedures; yet it may well be that in human groups that concentrate as homogeneous entities on a direct hand-to-mouth contact with one segment of nature, there is a communal and magic emphasis on first ontogenetic feeding problems.

In the primitive child's later childhood, as it fuses into community life, there probably is a diffusion of those pathogenic tensions that are typical for our each-family-for-itself training. It is in experiences connected with good that the primitve child is closest to his family, and especially to his mother, on whom falls the task on feeding him of laying the basis for his attitude toward the world as a whole. Some consciousness of this mission, which gives female functions and modes equality in cultural importance with those of men, may prevent the vast majority of primitive women from resenting their restricted participation in the more spectacular activities of men.

The instinctive mental hygiene measures of homogeneous cultures are impressive: parent-fixations are diffused in extended families; children are largely educated by other children, are kept in check by fear of ridicule rather than by the bite of guilt feelings, and are encouraged to be virtuous by the promise of tangible and universal prestige points. On the plains at least, no threat of violence or abandonment estranges parent and child, no talk of sinfulness, body and self. As we consider our means of child rearing in a planned democracy, it may pay to ponder over the polarity of child training:

> The Sioux baby is permitted to remain an individualist (for example, in the way he weans himself from his mother) while he builds an unequivocal trust in himself and in his surroundings. Then when strong in body and confident in himself, he is asked to bow to a tradition of unrelenting public opinion which focuses on his social behavior rather than on his bodily functions and their psychological concomitants. He is forced into a stern tradition which satisfies his social needs and conspires with him

in projecting any possible source of sin and guilt into the supernatural. As long as he is able to conform, he can feel free. (S. pp. 152–53).

In comparison,

the dominating classes in the Anglo-Saxon world tend more and more to regulate early functions and impulses in childhood. They implant the never silent metronome into the impressionable baby to regulate his first experiences with his body and with the immediate physical surroundings. After the establishment of these safety devices, he is encouraged to become an individualist. He pursues masculine strivings but often compulsively remains within standardized careers which tend to substitute themselves for communal conscience.

However, as just demonstrated, child training is not an isolated field governed or governable by attitudes of malice or love of children, insight or ignorance; it is a part of the totality of a culture's economic and ideational striving. The systematic difference between "primitive" and "civilized" cultures almost forbids comparison of details. What follows are reflections with some bearing on the study of childhood by clinical psychoanalytic means.

As we have seen, primitive cultures are exclusive. Their image of man coincides with their consciousness of being a strong or "clean" Yurok or Sioux. We do not know how and how long they would have succeeded in remaining homogeneous if left alone. In civilization the image of man is expanding and is ever more inclusive. New syntheses of economic and emotional safety are sought in inclusive formations of new entities and new identities: regions, nations, classes, races, ideologies. These new entities, however, overlap, and anachronistic fears of extinction cause some areas to seek archaic safety in spasms of reactionary exclusion. The viciousness of the battlefields is matched in that of the wars of standards (including those of child training) and in the conflicts which individuals wage with themselves.

Primitive tribes have a direct relation to the sources and means of production. Their techniques are extensions of the human body; their magic is a projection of body concepts. Children in these groups participate in technical and in magic pursuits; body and environment, childhood and culture may be full of dangers, but they are all one world. The expansiveness of civilization, its stratification and specialization make it impossible for children to include in their ego synthesis more than a section or sections of their society. Machines, far from remaining an extension of the body, destine whole classes to be extensions of machinery; magic becomes secondary, serving intermediate links only; and childhood, in some classes, becomes a separate segment of life with its own folklore. Neuroses, we find, are unconscious attempts to adjust to the heterogeneous present with the magic means of a homogeneous past. But individual neuroses are only parts of collective ones. It may well be, for example, that such mechanical child training as western civilization has developed during the last few decades harbors an unconscious magic attempt to master machines by becoming more like them, comparable to the Sioux' identification with the buffalo, the Yurok's with the river and the salmon.

According to the author, clinical descriptions, i.e. the description of one or several successive segments of a historical process, defines every item of human behavior according to at least three kinds of organization:

(1) The biological one, which reflects the nature of the human organism as a space-time organization of mammalian organ-systems (evolution, epigenesis, pregenitality)

(2) The social one, which reflects the fact that human organisms are organized into geographic-historical units

(3) The ego-principle, reflecting the synthesis of experience and the resulting defensive and creative mastery (ego development)

None of these principles can "cause" a human event; but no human event is explained except by an investigation that pursues the Gestalten evoked by each principle in constant relativity to the two others.

In the psychoanalysis of the individual Freud has introduced this threefold investigation in the dynamic concepts of an id, a superego, and an ego.

What psychoanalysis has contributed to the knowledge of childhood, step by step, depended on the shifting foci of its theoretical attention. The id and its few basic drives were studied first. The initial focus of a science, however, threatens to impose its form on all further findings. Thus the next focus of study, namely the superego, which represents the first conceptualization of the influence of society on the individual, was primarily conceived of as an anti-id; it was said to be observable only when the id forced it to act. At best it behaved like the Victorian mother (quoted by Anna Freud) who sits in the parlor and periodically sends the nurse upstairs to tell the children not to do whatever it is they are doing. This mother never goes upstairs herself to tell the children what they *may* do—or even to do it with them. But this is what cultures, parents, neighborhoods do—and at least some of the ego's guiding ideals result from it. The ego, in turn, was at first conceived of as an ego both against the id and against the culture "with much emphasis on the poor little fellow's painful adjustment to the big bad environment" and with little emphasis on the fact that only a supporting society and a loving mother can make a functioning ego.

In his last writings Freud formulated the id and the superego in historical terms:

> During the whole of a man's life . . . the superego . . . represents the influence of his childhood, of the care and education given to him by his parents, of his dependence on them—of the childhood which is so greatly prolonged in human beings by a common family life. And in all this what is operating is not only the personal qualities of these parents but also everything that produced a determining effect upon themselves, the tastes and standards of the social class in which they live and the characteristics and traditions of the race from which they spring. Those who have a liking for generalizations and sharp distinctions may say that the external world, in which the individual finds himself exposed after being detached from his parents, represents the power of the present; that his id, with its inherited trends, represents the organic past; and that the superego, which later joins them, represents more than anything the cultural past, of which the child has to pass through, as it were, an after-experience during the few years of his early childhood.*

We are now studying the relationship of the ego to the "power of the present," that is the experience of perpetual change from the immediate past to the anticipated future.

In her book *The Ego and the Mechanisms of Defense*, Anna Freud asks whether or not the ego invents its defenses all by itself. She comes to the conclusion that the form of defense depends on the id content to be warded off, but does not discuss the relationship of ego mechanisms to the historical present.[5]

Anna Freud reports a case of altruism by identification and projection. A patient seems to have renounced all earthly pleasure. But far from being a Puritan, she does not insist that everybody else renounce these pleasures too. On the contrary, wherever possible she helps other people, even rivals, to enjoy what she herself seems neither

---

* Sigmund Freud, "An Outline of Psycho-Analysis." *International Journal of Psycho-Analysis*, XXI (1940), 82.

to demand nor to need. This is called a defense mechanism, although at times it must have approached a symptom, and around it a personality must have been built. Beyond asking what infantile drives made such a mechanism necessary, and indeed pleasurable, we could inquire: Why, and at what stage of the patient's life, did this mechanism develop and who was its model? Was it the parent of the same or of the other sex? Was it an ancestor, a priest, a teacher, a neighbor? Within what kind of a communal environment was this mechanism developed and within what kind of culture change? In what sections of her environment and at what period of her life did this kind of altruism secure to the patient glory and a halo, or shame and defamation, or indifference?

The need for clinical reconstructions that include the correlation of critical psychosexual phases with contemporaneous social changes becomes especially apparent—but it is by no means restricted—to American patients of psychoanalysis. This, I assume, is one major reason for the fact that the discussion of "social factors" that were energetically sought by some European workers in the field has become more systematic and decisive in this country. This change of focus—like preceding ones—is accompanied by apologies and apostasies, and this for reasons intrinsic in the psychoanalytic movement, but not to be discussed here.

This dynamic country, by its very nature, subjects its inhabitants to more extreme contrasts and abrupt changes during a lifetime or a generation than are normally the case with other great nations. The national character is formed by what we hope will ultimately prove to be fruitful polarities: open roads of immigration and closed areas of settlement; free influences of immigration and jealous islands of tradition; outgoing internationalism and defiant isolationism; boisterous competition and self-effacing cooperation; and many others. Which of the resulting contradictory slogans has the greatest influence on the development of an individual ego probably depends on the relationship of critical growth periods to the rate of change in the family history.

It was customary in some psychiatric circles in Europe to discuss what appeared to be a relative "ego weakness" in American patients. There are indications that in the depths of their hearts American neurotics, beyond seeking relief for guilt and inferiority feelings, desire to be cured of a basic vagueness and confusion in their identifications. Often they turn to psychoanalysis as a savior from the discrepancies of American life; abroad, they were willing to dissimulate their American identity for the sake of what promised to be a more comfortable one, made in "the old country."

The less neurotic American,[6] however, as long as he does not feel endangered by some too unexpected turn of events, paradoxically enough receives his very ego strength from a kind of proud refusal to settle on any form of group-ego too early, and too definitely. To be sure, he acknowledges some fundamental decencies and some—incredibly fleeting—common experiences on crossroads. Otherwise premature harmony disconcerts him; he is rather prepared for and willing to tackle discontinuities. In the meantime he lives by slogans which are, as it were, experimental crystallizations—a mode of life that can, of course, turn into perverse shiftiness.[7]

Such slogans as "let's get the hell out of here," or "let's stay no matter what happens"—to mention only two of the most sweeping ones—are in the sphere of ethos what rationalizations are in that of the intellect. Often outmoded, and without any pretense of logic, they are convincing enough to those involved to justify action whether within or just outside of the law insofar as it happens to be enforced. Slogans contain time and space perspectives as definite as those elaborated in the Sioux or Yurok systems—a collective ego time-space to which individual ego defenses are coordinated. But they change.

A cartoon in the *New Yorker* not long ago pictured an old lady who sat in her little garden before a little colonial house, knitting furiously but otherwise ignoring enormous bulldozers excavating the ground a hundred feet deep around her small property, to make space for the foundations of skyscrapers. Many a patient from Eastern mansions finds himself regressing to such an *ego-space*, with all the defense mechanisms of exclusiveness, whenever he is frightened by competition outside, or by unbridled impulses from within.

Or take a patient whose grandparents came West "where never is heard a discouraging word." The grandfather, a powerful and powerfully driven man, seeks ever new and challenging engineering tasks in widely separated regions. When the initial challenge is met, he hands the task over to others, and moves on. His wife sees him only for an occasional impregnation. According to a typical family pattern, his sons cannot keep pace with him and are left as respectable settlers by the wayside; only his daughter is and looks like him. Her very masculine identification, however, does not permit her to take a husband equal to her strong father. She marries a weak man and settles down. She brings her boy up to be God-fearing and industrious. He becomes reckless and shifting at times, depressed at others: somewhat of a juvenile delinquent now, later, maybe, a more enjoyable Westerner, with alcoholic moods.

What his worried mother does not know is that she herself all through his childhood has belittled the sedentary father; has decried the lack of mobility, geographic and social, of her marital existence; has idealized the grandfather's exploits; but has also reacted with panicky punitiveness to any display of friskiness in the boy, which was apt to disturb the now well-defined neighborhood.

In the course of a psychoanalysis patients repeat in transferences and regressions not only infantile instinctual tensions and ego defenses, but also their abortive (and often unconscious) infantile ego-ideals. These are often based on conditions and slogans which prevailed at the period of the family's greatest ascendancy. Specific conflicts and resistances result: the patient, on the one hand, is afraid that the brittleness of his ideal identity will be uncovered; on the other, he wishes the psychoanalyst, no matter with what means or terminologies, to free him from the ambiguity of his background and to provide him with the deceptive continuity of a magic psychoanalytic world.

This, however, is not the social function of psychoanalysis.

The individual is not merely the sum-total of his childhood identifications. Children—perhaps more pronouncedly in a highly mobile society—are early aware of their parents' position in the community; of their reactions to friends, servants, superiors; of their behavior in pleasant, pious, angry or alcoholized company; of Saturday nights in town and of mild enthusiasms and panics pervading neighborhoods, not to speak of lynchings and wars. If not impoverished too early by indifferent communities and selfish mothers, children early develop a nucleus of separate identity. Anxiety may cause them to sacrifice this individual awareness to blind identifications with parental persons. In the psychoanalytic treatment of adults this nucleus shoudl be recovered. The patient, instead of blaming his parents (i.e. turning his positive over-identifications into negative ones), should learn to understand the social forces responsible for the deficiencies of his childhood.

In our clinical attempts to reconstruct the childhood of adult patients we have studied "id resistances" as derivatives of the infantile fear of being deprived of urgent satisfactions; we have studied "super-ego resistances" as representatives of the infantile fear of being overpowered by such needs. The change in ego-potential or both these fears during maturational and psychological crises is well known to us. We perceive of the ego as a central regulator which, closest to the history of the day, guards a measure of safety, satisfaction and identity. As we add to our knowledge and technique the understanding of resistances that originate in contemporary conflicts of ego-ideals, we cannot fail to make new and, in a sense, perpetual contributions to the study of childhood in a world characterized by expanding identifications and by great fears of losing hard-won identities.

Notes

[1] "E. H. Erikson, "Observations on Sioux Education," *Journal of Psychology* (1939) 101–56; and *Observations on the Yurok: Childhood and World Image* (Berkeley and Los Angeles: University of California Press, 1943).
In the following, S, after a quotation refers to the first paper, Y, to the second.
[2] For a diagrammatic representation of the interrelations of zones and modes see the author's contribution to Margaret Mead's chapter in the forthcoming edition of the *Handbook of Child Psychology*.
[3] The author also considers the possibility that the remnants of such conditioning and its reflection in historical traits may contibute to the oral-depressive way in which the Sioux accept their—admittedly almost hopeless—lot.
[4] This may indicate that the Yurok position in intercourse was the same as the most usual one among Indians and whites today.
[5] See, however, A. Freud and D. T. Burlingham, *Infants Without Families.* In *The Writings of Anna Freud*, (New York: International Universities Press, 1944), vol. III, 543–664.
[6] His elusive nature is only now being defined by anthropologists. See Margaret Mead, *And Keep Your Powder Dry* (New York: William Morrow, 1942), for an attempt at such definition and for a relevant bibliography.
[7] What is popularly called an "ego" in this country, seems to be the defiant expression of the owner's conviction that he is somebody without being identified with anybody in particular.

Psychoanalysis and Ongoing History: Problems of Identity, Hatred and Nonviolence (1965)

The advance summary which I was asked to submit earlier this year to the American Psychiatric Association explains that at that time I was in India. It will be understood, then, that in spite of the promising title, my remarks cannot cover recent events in this country. In trying to trace Gandhi's activities in the city of Ahmedabad in 1918, I missed ongoing—and, in fact, on-marching—history in Selma, U.S.A. But I hope that our heightened awareness of matters both of hatred and of nonviolence makes it permissible to submit here some work in progress and some reflections on the evolutionary and historical background of aggressive and pacific trends in man.

My study concerns an event in the year 1918, when Gandhi took over the leadership of a mill strike in the city of Ahmedabad, a textile center since ancient times and the city with the highest percentage of organized labor in India today. This was one of the very first applications of Gandhi's method in India proper, a method and a discipline best known in the West as "nonviolence" and earlier as "passive resistance," but conceived by him as *Satyagraha*, that is, "truth force."

Written while living in India. Read at a joint meeting of the Section on Psychoanalysis, APA, with the American Psychoanalytic Association, at the 121st annual meeting of the American Psychiatric Association, New York, May 3–7, 1965. First published in the *American Journal of Psychiatry*, 122 (1965), 241–50.

I emphasize "India proper," for he had returned only a few years before to his homeland from South Africa where he had spent 20 years. He was approaching 50; and those of you who happen to know of my work will rightly suspect that this study is an older counterpart to *Young Man Luther*(4)*; my students have already dubbed it "Middle-Aged Mahatma." And indeed, my interest does concern the way in which this 50-year-old man staked out his sphere of generativity and committed himself systematically not only to the trusteeship of his emerging nation, but also to that of a mankind which had begun to debase its civilized heritage with the mechanized and organized mass slaughter of world wars and totalitarian revolutions.

Some of you will remember the awe with which we, as young people in the 1920's, heard of this "half-naked Fakir" who took on the British Empire without weapons, and who in seeking to influence the great refused to desert the poor and the lowly in that most impoverished of all big countries. In South Africa he had, as some might say, found his much delayed identity.

The once shy, if secretly willful, Indian boy and the equally shy, and yet deeply determined, young barrister—"made-in-England"— had found a new function and a new courage (12). This courage was really a configuration of attitudes based on traditional Hindu and Christian values as well as on family trends and personal conflicts. But at the same time it made a strength and a discipline out of what had become his countrymen's weaknesses in the eyes of others: the capacity for suffering and for passive forms of resistance and aggression.

In 1915, then, he had returned to India, imposing on himself a delay of political action (his probation, as he called it) during which he studied the condition of the masses of India by traveling among them. Then he plunged in; in 1916 he made his famous speech to the students in the Hindu University at Benares (*his* Wittenberg church door). In 1917, he instituted his first nonviolent campaign among some peasants in the Himalayan foothills; and in 1918, (a year before he became a political leader on a large scale) he led the nonviolent strike which is the subject of my study.

It was no accident, of course, that in that revolutionary period the saintly politician staked his future first on a *peasants'* and then on a *workers'* struggle. Some of the men and women who worked with

---

* References are cited by bracketed numbers in the text. For full citations see listing of references that follow article.

and against him at that time are still alive, and the fact that I may claim their friendship or acquaintance induced me to try to elucidate the dynamics of that event in their lives as well as in Gandhi's and in the cultural and economic conditions of that day.

Gandhi, who had become convinced that the workers' demands for higher wages were just, was able to impose on a poor, plague-ridden, illiterate and as yet unorganized labor force principles of nonviolent conduct which bore full fruit, not only in the fulfillment of immediate demands, but also in a permanent change of the relationship of workers to owners in that city and in India. To keep the workers to their strike pledge, however, Gandhi undertook his first public fast, that much-abused method of coercion by suffering which he later perfected as a political tool for creating the conviction that about some most simple and concrete and yet highly symbolic issues, a truly religious man is in dead earnest.

How this "poor" leader within the year established himself as *the Mahatma* of the Indian masses as well as the undisputed leader of a political elite—that is the wider framework of my study. It encompasses issues universal to ideological leadership. In Gandhi's case, however, the specific question arises as to whether his consummate style of pacification and his conviction that there was a dormant "truth-force" ready for activation in all human beings can be said to find any verification in what psychology has learned about history and about evolution since Gandhi's death.

But first, a few theoretical considerations. Is it at all a psychoanalyst's business to reconstruct and reinterpret historical events? And even where a relative competence is conceded, is the psychoanalyst not apt to focus on the psychopathology apparent in historical crises— the morbid motivation in the lives of the daring innovator as well as his fanatic followers, not to speak of the anxiety and the perversity which fill the vacuum left by a weakening or dying leader? I believe that the psychoanalyst's competence can find a specific application in the study of history because he faces, on a different level, a phenomenon analogous to the "resistance" well studied in his daily clinical work, namely, the phenomenon of historical memory as a gigantic process of suppresing as well as of preserving data, of forgetting as well as remembering, of mystifying as well as clarifying, of rationalizing as well as recording "fact."

If Albert Einstein said of Gandhi that "generations to come may find it hard to believe that such a man as this ever in flesh and blood walked upon this earth," we can observe that our generation—and in India, too—already seems unable to preserve the spirit of the pacific genius whose corpse they carried to the funeral pyre on a gun carriage drawn by uniformed men. The mills of history grind fast and fine; and the mechanisms of historical repression and regression, rationalization and readaptation would seem to be a fit study for the psycho-historian trained in psychoanalysis. He may do so, I believe, not only by comparing the divergent memories of the individuals who together made up an event, but also by comparing styles of documentation.

It is fascinating to behold the emergence of Gandhi's charisma before 1920; and to contrast it with the totem meal now in general progress which disposes of this man's presence—complex and yet straightforward, sometimes tediously moralistic and yet often gay, ascetic and yet of animallike agility and energy—by dissolving it in a mush of adoration or masticating it into role-fragments: was he *really* saint *or* politician, Indian *or* Westerner, obvious masochist *or* hidden sadist?

Imbedded in this historical process the psychoanalyst may then find data close to his clinical experience. He has concepts with which to explain how great innovators, on the basis of their own unresolved childhood conflicts, overtax themselves as well as their elite of lieutenants and their masses of followers, imposing on them as moral demands what perhaps only the genius can manage and only in his unique way, in one lifetime.

It is well known that Gandhi, before instituting his truth-force in South Africa, had committed himself, his family and his small community of Paulinian followers to a life of *Brahmacharya*, of chastity and austerity, systematically developing in himself a style of universal *caritas* both feminine and masculine. The confused and confusing consequences which this had for him at the stage of senile despair and for his public image well beyond his death will not concern us today, although the possible connection between his sexual or rather antisexual preoccupations (far beyond traditional asceticism) and his leadership in a nonviolent view of life certainly is part of any psychoanalytic study. But this part has become almost too pat for us and this especially since men like Gandhi, men who use intimate confession as a political tool, play right into our clinical habituations.

Yet, even as we judge the extent and nature of a patient's pathology by mapping out what he might do with his capacities and opportunities at the stage of development and under the social conditions in which we encounter him, so we can only study a great man's role in the light of the activation of adaptive, creative and destructive forces in him and in his period of history (6). In Gandhi's work, we see the translation of ancient precepts of spiritual love into an entirely new discipline and a method of economic and of political action. This method, obviously, could and does move some tough mountains, while it did not and could not work under all conditions. It always depends on a very specific complex of motivations both in those who employ this pacific technique and in those against or toward whom it is being employed. In studying the details of Gandhi's daily behavior, however, I have come to believe what events in this country must have suggested to many of you, namely that his "truth in action" contains psychological and historical verities which we may attempt to express in dynamic terms (2) in order to bring our knowledge as well as our convictions and sympathies into joint play.

Original Biological Orientation

To seek contact first with the original biological orientation in psychoanalytic theory, let me quote from Freud's famous letter to Einstein: "Conflicts between man and man are resolved in principle by the recourse to violence. It is the same in the animal kingdom from which man cannot claim exclusion" (8). This, for much of popular and educated opinion, still settles the matter. Yet, recent research suggests that some animals may justifiably beg exclusion from the human kingdom.

The recent book by Konrad Lorenz, *Das Sogenannte Boese* (10), summarizes what is known of intraspecies aggression among some of the higher animals and corrects the easy conviction that our "animal nature" explains or justifies human forms of aggression. Lorenz describes, of course, both threatening and murderous behavior on the part of animals that are hungry and go hunting; that must settle competitive questions of territorial occupation or utilization; or that are cornered by a superior enemy. The question is, under what conditions hatred and murder make their appearance among animals, and whether violence of the total kind—that is, of the kind characterized by irrational rage, wild riot or systematic extermination—can be traced to our animal nature.

Within the social species closest to man (wolves, deer and primates), Lorenz describes ritualized threatening behavior which, in fact, prevents murder, for such mutual threats usually suffice to establish an equal distribution of territory governed, as it were, by instinctive convention. Out in the wild, so he claims, such threatening behavior only rarely escalates into injurious attack; and one may well say—as is, indeed, the case with some human primitives who share the institution of highly ritualized warfare—that some "aggressive behavior" prevents war.

Lorenz furthermore summarizes observations which must make us again question the omnibus concept of an aggressive instinct. A hungry lion when ready for the kill (and he kills only when hungry) shows no signs of anger or rage; he is doing his job. Mutual extermination is not in nature's book; wolves on the chase do not decimate healthy herds but pick out the stragglers that fall behind.

It is from among the habits of wolves, also, that one of the most dramatic observations of *pacific rituals* is taken. Wolves, Dante's *bestia senza pace*, are, in fact, capable of devoted friendship among themselves. When two wolves happen to get into a fight, there comes a moment when the one that is weakening first bares his unprotected side to his opponent, who, in turn, is instinctively inhibited from taking advantage of this now nonviolent situation.

The ritual elaboration of this instinctive behavior (Lorenz goes so far as to call it an autonomous instinct) is illustrated also by the antler tournament among the Damstags (*Dama dama*) during which the crowns are alternately waved back and forth and loudly thrust against each other. (These antlers, incidentally, have become otherwise obsolete armament in extraspecific defense.) The tournament is preceded by a parade *à deux*: the stags trot alongside one another, whipping their antlers up and down. Then, suddenly, they stop in their tracks as if following a command, swerve toward each other at a right angle, lower their heads until the antlers almost reach the ground and crack them against each other. If it should happen that one of the combatants enters this second phase earlier than the other, thus endangering the completely unprotected flank of his rival with the powerful swing of his sharp and heavy equipment, he immediately puts a brake on his turn, accelerates his trot and continues the parade. When both are ready, however, there ensues a powerful but harmless wrestling which is won by the party that can hold out the longest, and conceded by the other's retreat. Such concession normally stops the attack of the victor.

Lorenz suggests an untold number of analogous rituals of pacification among the higher animals. We should add, however, that deritualization at any point can lead to violence to the death.

These observations, I am sure, rank high among those post-Darwinian insights which we owe not only to new methods of extending our photographic vision into the animal's own territory, but also to a new willingness to let observation correct what Freud called our instinct mythology. In this sense, I fail to be properly grateful to Lorenz's belated acceptance of Freud's early conceptual model of an "aggressive instinct" and its inhibition, for in the description of concrete situations, he must continuously dissolve "instinct" into drives, impulses and needs.

What we admire in the genius of new observation is, in fact, the refined description of the kinds of behavior elicited (and then stopped, displaced or replaced) in given inner states and under given external conditions. For, as Lorenz says so characteristically, *"Jawohl, ein Trieb kann angetrieben werden"*; yes, indeed, a drive can be driven, an instinct, instigated—that is, by compelling circumstances; and a drive can also remain latent, and yet at a moment's provocation impel competent action.

The very use of the word "ritual"[1] to describe the behavior of the stag seems to characterize the described scene as something which does not fit the simple model of naked and then inhibited aggression. Obviously, the ritualization already demands a preselection of partners of nearly equal strength, endowed with the same readiness for the clocklike display of a whole set of scheduled and reciprocal reactions of which the final turning away is only the conclusion, and a capacity to assume either one of the terminal roles convincingly and effectively. Much of animal aggression is already thus ritualized. I have never been able to watch the interactions of the angry-sounding seagulls in ethologist N. Tinbergen's films, for example, without thinking that they would long have burned up from sheer emotion were not their behavior an instinctive "convention," invested with only small doses of the available drive and emotion.

Lorenz sees in such ritualization the instinctive antecedents of man's morality and *its* ritualization. But human aggression and human inhibition are of a different order. It is precisely our insight into the paradoxical and maladaptive results of human inhibition (in evolution, through the generations and in the individual) which makes us question the term "inhibition" when used to explain the pacific behavior of animals and, by retransfer, that of truly peaceful men. And, indeed, Lorenz's reapplication of instinct theories to humanity remains, as he would be the first to admit, incomplete.

Let me note, however, the importance which Lorenz most suggestively ascribes to the invention, in the course of human evolution, of tools and weapons. For all this we know has evolved together: inventiveness and psychological complexity, social evolution and hatred, morality and violence. But we should ponder the fact that from the arrow released by hand to the warhead sent by transcontinental missile, man, the attacker, has been transformed into a technician and man, the attacked, into a mere target, while both are thus removed from encounters such as the higher animals seem to have achieved, namely, opportunities to confront each other not only as dangerous but also as pacific opponents within one species. On the contrary, man, the mere target, becomes the ready focus for hateful projections arising from irrational sources.

Man has, of course, developed ritual forms of undoing harm by means of peace settlements (which also carefully prepare future wars) and of preventing threatening harm by means of negotiation; and we pray that our diplomatic, technical and military caretakers will continue to build preventive mechanisms into the very machinery of overkill. But we also realize that a deep and nightmarish gap has developed between man's technological and his humanist imagination—a gap (and this is my point) which in the long run cannot be bridged with avoidances (prevention, deterrence, containment) alone, even as our theories cannot fathom it with concepts restricted to a model of "natural" aggression counteracted only by defense and inhibition.

Instinctual Drive vs. Instinctive Pattern

Lorenz speaks of a *hypertrophy of human aggressivenss*, and here lies one prime dividing line between animal-in-nature and man-in-culture: the rift between the animal's adaptive competence and man's florid and paradoxical drive-equipment. In order to adhere in theory to a certain integration of ethological data with Freud's initial observations, I find it useful to ask whether the assumption of an instinct in any described item of behavior is meant to convey the existence of an *instinctive pattern of adaptive competence*, or a *quantity of instinctual drive* in search of satisfaction, whether adaptive or not. It becomes clear, then, that Freud, for the most part, meant an *instinctual craving* even if he is translated as saying: "The slaughter of a foe gratifies an instinctive craving in man" (8); for the instinctual drives described by him more often lead man away from, rather than closer to, manifestations of instinctive competence [see also (9)].

Man is natively endowed only with a patchwork of instinctual drives, which, to be sure, owe much of their form and their energy to inherited fragments of instinctive animality, but in the human are never and cannot ever be in themselves adaptive or consummative (or, in brief, "natural"), but are always governed by the complexities of individuation and of cultural form, even though in our time we have come to visualize rational and cultural modes of being more natural.

The evolutionary rationale for this basic *separation of instinctual drive from instinctive pattern* is not hard to find. We are, in Ernst Mayr's (11) terms, the *"generalist" animal*, set to settle in, to adapt to and to develop cultures in the most varied environments, from the Arctic to the steaming jungle and even to New York. To perform this feat we have a long childhood, characterized by a minimum of instinctive pattern and maximum of free instinctual energy available for investment in a growing variety of *basic psychosocial encounters* which will, if we are lucky, bind our energy in patterns of mutuality, reliability and competence (13). These processes alone make the human environment what Hartmann calls an "average expectable" one (9). But, alas (and with this Freud has contronted mankind), man's instinctual forces are never completely bound and contained in adaptive or reasonable patterns; they are repressed, displaced, perverted and often return from repression to arouse *human* anxiety and rage. We, thus, can never go "back to nature;" but neither can we hope for a utopian culture not somehow forfeited to its past as rooted in the childhood of all individuals and in the history of groups.

Most of all, and here I begin to come back to the subject of hatred and conciliation, *sociogenetic evolution has split mankind into pseudo-species*, into tribes, nations and religions, castes and classes which bind their members into a pattern of *individual and collective identity*, but alas, reinforce that pattern by a *mortal fear of and a murderous hatred for other pseudo-species*. Only thus does man become uniquely what even Freud ascribes to our animal ancestry when he invokes the old saying: *homo homini lupus*.

Many of the earliest tribal names mean *"the* people," the only mankind, implying that others are not only different but also unhuman and in league with the Id as well as the Devil. Here, then, we face the problem of the *negative identity* (5). Identity has become a term used so vaguely as to become almost useless, and this because of our habit of ignoring dynamics when we describe normality. Yet, in any "normal" identity development, too, there is always a negative identity, which is composed of the images of that personal and collective past which is to be lived down and of that potential future which is to be forestalled.

Identity formation thus involves a continuous conflict with powerful negative identity elements: what we know or fear or are told we are but try not to be or not to see; and what we consequently see in exaggeration in others. In times of aggravated crises all this can arouse in man a murderous hate of all kinds of "otherness," in strangers and in himself. The study of psychosocial identity thus calls also for an assessment of the hierarchy of positive and negative identity elements given in an individual's stage of life and in his historical era.

Racial Struggle in U.S.

We can observe the gigantic human contest between positive and negative identities in our own ongoing history, for the racial struggle only accentuates a universal problem. In our colored population we see often manifested man's tendency to accept as valid negative images cruelly imposed on him not only by moralizing parents but also by overweening neighbors and economic exploiters. Such acceptance (and we see it in all minorities which are discriminated against) causes that double estrangment, that impotent hate of the despised self which can lead to paralysis or indirect defiance, to destructive or, indeed, self-destructive rage. As history changes, all manner of values are revised. That treasure of melodious warmth and gentle tolerance so characteristic of colored people and so eagerly borrowed by whites starved for sensuality and rhythm becomes associated with submissive Uncle Tomism. Powerful aspirations of developing dormant intelligence often appear to be inhibited by the prohibition (impressed on generations of children) to identify with the aims of the master race—a traditional prohibition now fully anchored in a negative identity.

Fanatical segregationism, on the other hand, only gives loud expression to a silent process in many, for the Southern identity, cultivating its slower and gentler ways against the dominant image of breathless Northern superiority (or, at any rate, power), had to reinforce itself with a sense of distance from the "lazy colored folk," for whose tempo and intimacy (shared by many whites as children and in hidden ways) there remains an unconscious nostalgia. In guarding that delineation with murderous hatred, however, the extremist excludes himself and his community defiantly from the identity of a Christian in an advancing society. During the rapid changes of a long overdue emancipation all *such images change their values*; and only positive historical change can rebind them in a new and wider identity promising a sense of inner freedom.

Whatever we can discern here as personal conflict has, of course, a side accessible only to the sociologist, for all communities fortify [as Kai Erikson (7) has clarified] the boundaries of their communality by defining (and keeping out-of-bounds) certain types as deviants. But when history changes, so do the images of deviancy, and individual men, with their positive and negative self-images, are often hopelessly lost in the change.

In the event of such aggravated personal and historical crises, furthermore, an individual (or a group) may suddenly surrender to *total doctrines and dogmas*, in which a negative identity element becomes the dominant one, defying shared standards which must now be sneeringly derided, while new mystical identities are embraced. Some Negroes in this country, as well as some untouchables in India, turned to an alien Allah, while the most powerful historical example of a negative identity attempting to become positive is, of course, that of the highly educated German nation despised by the world and debased by the Treaty of Versailles turning to mystical Aryanism in order to bind its shattered identity fragments.

In such cultural regression, we always recognize a specific rage which is aroused wherever identity development loses the promise of a traditionally assured wholeness. This latent rage, in turn, is easily exploited by fanatic and psychopathic leaders; it feeds the explosive destructiveness of mobs; and it serves the moral blindness with which decent people can develop or condone organized machines of destruction and extermination.

History, however, does provide a way by which negative identities are contained or converted into positive ones. Nietzsche once said that a friend is the lifesaver which holds you above water when your divided selves threaten to drag you to the bottom. In human history, the friendly and forceful power which may combine negative and positive identities is that of the *more inclusive identity*. In the wake of the great men and great movements, the inclusion of new identity elements supersedes the struggle of the old—positive and negative—images and roles. Often, this coincides with territorial or technological, intellectual or spiritual, expansion which sets free untold latent energies.

In political history, what we may call the *territoriality of identity* supersedes, I think, that of geographic territories, as may be seen in the mutual identification of the diverse constituents of the Roman empire, the Roman church or the British empire: all "bodies" characterized by new images of man as well as by territorial boundaries. The traditional themes of the *Civitas Romanus* or the *Pax Romana* have been accepted all too easily as mere matters of conquest, pride or power, although all three of these help. But we can locate the nexus of psychological and historical development in those more inclusive identities which help an era to bind the fears, the anxieties and the dread of existence.

In all parts of the world, the struggle is now for the *anticipatory development of more inclusive identities* whether they comprise the communality of the peasant-and-worker, or of all nonwhites, the joint interests of common markets and of technological expansion, or the mutual trusteeship of nations. The goal of imaginative and psychologically intuitive leadership, in each case, is the setting free of untold new forces; the price for the default of such leadership, malaise, delinquency and riot. In this sense, some of our activist youth today attempt to confront us with more inclusive images, in which old hatreds must wither away; and we are stunned to see how much we have ignored and have left to them who seem to sense that the species is the only identity inclusive enough.

You have, on the other hand, heard of the riots of Indian students over the issue as to what language is to replace English as a *lingua franca* so that a national link between the different language regions may be established. Thus, India is still struggling for the fundamentals of an all-Indian identity. Nehru once said that what Gandhi had accomplished for his country was primarily "a psychological change, almost as if some expert in psychoanalytic method had probed deep into the patient's past, found out the origins of his complexes, exposed them to his view, and thus rid him of that burden." Whatever you think of Nehru as clinical theorist, you know what he means.

A student of Indian politics (and a former co-worker of mine), Susanne Rudolph, has reviewed diverse self-images of India under the British Raj, and has concluded that Gandhi:

> resurrected an old and familiar path to courage, one that had always been significant to the twice-born castes, but had fallen into disrepute. By giving it new toughness and discipline in action, by stressing the sacrifice and self-control which it required, by making it an effective device of mass action, by involving millions in it, he reasserted its worth with an effectiveness that convinced his countrymen. . . . In the process of mastering his own fear and weakness, he reassured several generations that they need not fear those who had conquered them. (12)

But now they must learn to "conquer" themselves.

Before coming back to the essence of Gandhi's approach, however, let me answer one question which puzzles many. In the terms employed here what (beyond the obvious difference between violence and nonviolence) would differenciate the effectiveness of a Gandhi from that of a Hitler? Did the latter not also do for the Germans what the first is said to have done for India? The difference, I think, lies exactly in the emphasis on the *more inclusive identity*. Gandhi opposed British colonialism but he did so often by taking recourse to British fairness, even as he remained staunchly Christian in a Paulinian and universal sense, while denouncing Christian missionaries. His goal was an All-India, as an independent part of the British empire. His *inclusion of his opponent in all his plans* went so far that Kenneth Boulding could say recently that Gandhi had done more good to the British than to the Indians.

I need not detail the opposite: Hitler's desperate creation of an ahistorical ideal was based largely on the exclusion and annihilation of a fictitious Jewish culture which had become synonymous with his own negative identity (as Loewenstein and others, using other terms, have shown). His, then, was a totalitarian attempt at creating an *identity based on totalistic exclusion*. This, too, can work for a while and can mobilize the energies of a desperate youth.

If, at last, I try to sketch a convergence between Gandhi's nonviolent technique and the pacific rituals of animals, it should be remembered that I have used the bulk of my presentation to *differentiate* phenomena of social evolution from those of evolution proper. I have discussed man's instinctuality, his positive and negative identity and the moralism which springs from his guilt—all providing dangerous motivations for a creature now equipped with armament refined by means of scientific knowledge and technological knowhow. But it seems that in his immense intuition in regard to historical actuality and in his capacity to assume leadership in what to him was "truth in action," Gandhi was able to recognize some of those motivations in man which, in their instinctual and technical excess, have come between him and his pacific propensities; and that Gandhi created a social invention (*Satyagraha*) which transcends those motivations under certain conditions.

In Ahmedabad (3), as on other occasions, Gandhi, far from waiting to be attacked so he could "resist passively" or prove his "nonviolent love," moved right in on the opponent, in this instance the mill owners, by announcing what the grievance was and what he intended to do; *engagement at close range* is of the essence in his approach. He also saw to it that the issue was joined as an inevitable decision *among equals*. He explained that the mill owners' money and equipment and the workers' capacity to work depended on each other, and, therefore, were *equivalent* in economic power and in the right to self-esteem. In other words, they shared an inclusive identity.

In this sense, he would not permit either side to undermine the other; as the mill owners became virulent and threatening, he forbade his workers to use counterthreats. Or rather, he exacted from these starving people a pledge that they would abstain from *any destruction*, even of the *opponent's good name*. He thus not only avoided physical harm to machines or men (and the police withdrew all firearms on the third day of the strike) but also refused to let moralistic condemnation aggravate guilt feelings, as if he knew (what we know as therapists) that it is never safe to ally yourself with your opponent's superego.

He refused, then, to permit that cumulative aggravation of *bad conscience, negative identity* and *hypocritical moralism* which characterizes the division of men into pseudo-species. In fact, he conceded to the mill owners that they were erring only because they misunderstood their and their workers' obligations and functions and he appealed to their "better selves." He invited his main opponent, the leading mill owner, to lunch with him daily in a tent on the ashram grounds in order to discuss their respective next moves. In thus demonstrating perfect trust in them, he was willing to proceed with daily improvisations leading to an interplay in which clues from the opponent determined the next step.

Thus, he gave his opponent the maximum opportunity for an informed choice, even as he had based his demands on a thorough investigation of what could be considered fair and right; he told the workers not to demand more than that, but also to be prepared *to die* rather than to demand less. To strengthen their resolve, he distributed leaflets describing the sacrifices of the first Indian *Satyagrahis* in South Africa and thus provided them with *a new tradition*. It was when they nevertheless began to feel that he demanded more suffering from them than he was apparently shouldering himself that he declared his first fast. The *acceptance of suffering* and, in fact, of death, which is so basic to his "truth force," constitutes an *active choice without submission* to anyone; whatever masochism we may find in it, it is the highest affirmation of individualism in the service of humanity. It is at once a declaration of nonintent to harm others, and (here the parallel to Konrad Lorenz's stags is most striking) an expression of a faith in the opponent's inability to persist in harming others beyond a certain point, provided, of course, that he is convinced that neither his identity not his rightful power is in real danger.

Such faith, if disappointed, could cause the loss of everything—

power, face, life—but the *Satyagrahi* would, indeed, have chosen death rather than a continuation of that chain of negotiated compromises which eventually turn out to be hotbeds of future strife and murder. Here the Gandhian approach parts ways with the military approach, although Gandhi insisted that for anyone who did not have the nonviolent kind of courage, it was better to have a soldier's courage then none at all. (I doubt, however, that he would have included in this the "courage" of overkill by pushbutton.)

This is a somewhat "technical" summary of what I would consider to be certain essentials of Gandhi's technique (1). I wish I had time to describe the mood of this event, which was pervaded by a spirit of *giving the opponent the courage to change* even as the challenger changes with the events. The "technique" described was totally inbedded in a style of presence and of attention; the whole event, as many others in Gandhi's life, is the stuff parables are made of. For at such periods of his life he was possessed of a Franciscan gaiety and of a capacity to reduce situations to their naked essentials, thus helping others to discard costly defenses and denials and to realize hidden potentials of good will and energetic deed. Gandhi thus emerges amidst the complexity of his personality and the confusion of his times as a man possessing that quality of *supreme presence* which can give to the finite moment a sense of infinite meaning, for it is tuned both to the "inner voice" and to historical actuality, that is, to the potentialities for a higher synthesis in other individuals or in the masses. This I do not reiterate as an appeal to "higher" emotions in order to hide the methodological incompleteness of our work; rather, I want to submit that we know as yet little of the ego strength in such presence and of the ego needs of those who partake of it as followers.

Gandhi, of course, often "failed," and often "compromised;" and since great victories also contain ultimate failures, he did not escape the final despair of one who "in all modesty" (a favorite expression of his) had experimented with India, the British empire and Existence. At the end he claimed only that he had made a unique and systematic attempt to translate age-old spiritual insights into political action. In this, I believe, his initiative will survive him and his time as well as some of the irrelevant and undisciplined uses of his technique in our time, both here and in India. It must and will find applications in accord with changing history and technology.

If it can be said by a political scientist (1) that Gandhi's technique is based on "a psychologically sound understanding" of human suffering and of "the capacity of man to change," we may well recognize the fact (which we cannot elaborate on here) that Gandhi's "truth force," in all its Eastern attributes, corresponds in many essentials to what we have learned in the West about human suffering and the human capacity to change—learned from the psychiatric encounter as initiated by Sigmund Freud.

References

1. J. V. Bondurant, *Conquest of Violence* (Princeton, N.J.: Princeton University Press, 1958).
2. ———, "Satyagraha Versus Duragraha: The Limits of Symbolic Violence." In *Gandhi: His Relevance for Our Times*, eds. G. Ramachandran and T. K. Mahadevan (Bombay: Bharatiya Vidya Bhavan, 1964).
3. M. H. Desai, *A Righteous Struggle* (Ahmendab; Navajivan Publishing House, 1951).
4. E. H. Erikson, *Young Man Luther* (New York: W. W. Norton, 1958; paperback, Norton Library, 1964).
5. ———, "Identity and the Life-cycle," Monograph 1, *Psychological Issues, 1 (1959)*, 1–171.
6. ———, *Insight and Responsibility* (New York: W. W. Norton, 1964).
7. K. Erikson, *Wayward Puritans* (New York: Wiley and Sons, in press).
8. S. Freud, "Why War?" In *Collected Papers*, vol. 5 (New York: Basic Books, 1959).
9. H. Hartmann, *Ego Psychology and Adaptation* (New York: International Universities Press, 1958).
10. K. Lorenz, *Das Sogenannte Boese* (Vienna: Dr. G. Borotha-Schoeler-Verlag, 1964).
11. E. Mayr, "The Determinants and Evolution of Life: The Evolution of Living Systems," *Proceedings of the National Academy of Science*, 51 (1964), 834–41.
12. S. Rudolph, "The New Courage," World Politics, 16 (1963), 98-217.
13. R. W. White "Ego and Reality in Psychoanalytic Theory," Monograph 11, Psychological Issues, 3 (1963), 1–210.

Note

[1] Ritualization in animals and men is the subject of a forthcoming issue of the *Proceedings of the Royal Society* to which, among others, Konrad Lorenz and the writer have contributed.

Remarks on the
"Wider Identity" (1966)

The following remarks represent an attempt to link the problem of our national identity with the need for a future all-human identity. They were made at two altogether different meetings in the late sixties. One was a dinner of senators at the Washington home of one of them; the other, a kind of convocation at the Catholic Worker to which I sent a written contribution because I could not attend myself. For both, it so happens, the suggested theme had been a "Wider Identity." I probably would not today say all that follows here in the way I said it then. But it is interesting to see how we were preparing then for the nuclear crisis.

I would like to make it plausible in a few words that it takes a great people to be called upon to face and to solve such a crisis as ours and that such a call is well in line with the fact that Lincoln, with his passionate restraint, called America the "almost chosen people." However, one professional worker can contribute only such insights as he can grasp with the concepts at his disposal. In my case, the concept of "identity crisis" is being used rather widely—so widely

This article, published here for the first time, represents two talks that have been combined for the purpose of this volume. First presented to the Catholic Worker in Tivoli, New York, and at a senatorial dinner in Washington, D.C., 1966.

that it is already being made fun of in an occasional cartoon—no small recognition for a clinical term, or at any rate for the readiness of wide circles to find it suggestive. I have had reason to point out, however, that I might not have thought of this term, or be listened to, if I had not come to this country.

A well-known priest of poetic temperament and radical persuasion wrote to me a few days ago wondering (as friends will) what I would do next, having completed a book on Gandhi. And, as others do, he proceeded to suggest that I do what obviously he himself would like to do. "Could you undertake," he wrote, "something infinitely more complex, because too near for comfort—the spasm of the American soul, as it both resists and works toward birth, even as a new man is at stake?"

Here is an exponent of a world religion and of a supernational orientation; why would he expect to find the locus of the rebirth of the new man in the American soil? And why would I, foreign-born and one author of a book on the great Asian peacemaker, agree with him?

Along the lines of your subject I will answer this in terms of identity, leaving aside the relation of soul and identity—except by suggesting that to attend to one's soul (the existential sense of I and We) means to come to grips somehow with one's earthly identity: the sense of self and others, in a given place in history and geography.

May I assume, then, that you want to discuss man's wider, more inclusive identity because, as Catholics, you are used to thinking in terms of man's widest identity? And that you agree that at this point in history, for better *and* for worse, America has become the perpetrator and the guardian of a new and wider identity with which we as well as all other peoples will have to come to grips? At this point in history, meaning mankind's first and possibly already last chance to become what it is: one species?

To suggest a fateful reason for the fact that man has not yet accepted his specieshood I must introduce another term which provides the evolutionary background for the whole identity problem. The term is *pseudo-species*. I have invented it not for the purpose of sounding erudite and Darwinian but because the two little words state a basic fact in man's nature. Instead of a consciousness of being the one species he is, man has, as far back as we know, imagined his tribe or his nation, his caste or his class, and, yes, even his religion to be a superior species, a claim which he has always reinforced with systematic distortions of history and reality—sometimes poetic and sometimes heroic and often just vain—for which I cannot find any more polite term than the word *pseudo*.

In order to justify its self-election, it is true, each pseudo-species has also made special moral and ritual demands on itself which indeed resulted in a degree of brotherly love among those included in the assumed superiority. Unfortunately, however, the ensuing righteousness has also served to sanction the exclusion of other "species," often to the extent of their annihilation and, at any rate, of their assumed perdition in eternity.

I have now introduced this matter of pseudo-species in order to indicate that identity is an issue reaching much deeper than the conscious choice of roles or the rhetorical demand for equality.

Our sense of identity coincides with our pseudo-specieshood to such a degree that a danger to one is a threat to the other. In fact, exactly when we are working toward a wider indentity, our narrower identities are in such mortal danger that a sense of threatening extinction can take hold of us. Furthermore, as you have seen in the history of your own church, even a venerable example of a wider identity which truly began as a family of new men aspiring for the then widest identity which was embodied in Christ also developed all the aspects of a new and vainglorious pseudo-species. What nevertheless seems (to me, as a psychologist) to have perpetuated the Catholic "soul" is the humility engendered by the individual awareness of sin, the ideal of charity, and the communal certainty of grace. You stand for that.

But now, how about the "soul" of America? Why must America at this point in history and for the sake of mankind learn to know itself and acknowledge the necessity of humility, charity, and grace—all terms almost diabolically antithetical to some of its dominant aspirations and roles?

First of all, America, by its very history and nature, is the first great attempt to build a self-made nation out of immigrants coming from all the extant pseudo-species of the world. This has been most popularly expressed as the "melting pot" idea—an idea that is not free of some sinister meanings. For what is melted together forms a conglomerate in which the constituent parts are lost in a nondescript new mass except, maybe, for some stubborn fragments which resist dissolution. Luckily, one can also say that, on the contrary, a new kind of national genius took over America—namely, that of the self-made man in a new tradition created by self-chosen immigrants on an empty continent ready for vast and joint improvisation.

The "dream" of a new pseudo-species, of course, left out the Indians, who had inhabited the emptiness, and the blacks, whose migration was anything but self-chosen. Such oversights, we recognize today, have been part and parcel of the American "way of life," which has glorified the type of man who forcefully grasps given opportunities in order to make something of himself. According to this way of life, such a man has a natural right to exploit those not so inclined by temperament or not so favored by opportunities until they, in turn, learn to raise a loud enough scandal so that the existing laws of equality will be enforced and the "checks and balances" reinstated.

When I first wrote of the American identity twenty years ago, I pointed out that America's problem is that of having to reconcile one *too wide* identity with many *too narrow* ones. As a friend put it in a definitive illustration of the too wide identity, "I love mankind, but I hate folks." Well, those Americans caught in the second kind, the narrower identities of ethnic origin or preferred neighborhood, of occupation or profession, of organization or association, have truly learned to get along with their own kind of folks, but they are apt to resist the demand that they should identify with mankind.

So far this is simply an immigrants' world and a frontier world shared by many for the sake of a common dream: that the colossal gamble which has included all those unbelievable hardships now almost forgotten by affluent America would provide unlimited opportunities for an unimaginable variety of human types from all those "old countries." And this, by God, it has done.

The complications which have gradually added a way of death to the original way of life are (I think) the result of America's also becoming an industrial empire. The self-made American also became the master of "know-how," and technological proficiency seemed to provide him with such impersonal equipment and such impartial procedures as (who could doubt it?) were a gift of fate. Expansion and exploitation with such technical means did not need to be guided by conscious hate or by a conscious disdain for those who were pushed aside or exploited.

Nor was it perceived as any kind of imperialism if, wherever American know-how spread, fragments of the American superidentity (of which the supermarket is a fitting symbol) came along in a package deal or if periodical wars would lead to the consolidation of world markets and the spread of the American ideals of production and consumption. In fact, we were so convinced of the goodness of mechanical efficiency and the objectivity and neutrality of him who wields it that today we are naïvely surprised to find that not only brutal Germans but also nice Americans can participate in mechanical defoliation and extermination. Yet we still have not fully awakened to the fact that we have contributed to the modern version of what Loren Eiseley calls the lethal element of the universe by having decided to use the atomic bomb first.

Maybe one could say that the American Way of Life, with its industriousness and teamwork, its precision and amiability, its brand of courage and its competitiveness and showmanship, reached its pinnacle in the televised visit on the *moon*—a pinnacle made vainglorious only by that voice which pronounced this to be "the greatest moment since creation." The American Way of Death, which means the passionless use of overkill against other "species," reahced its climax in *Hiroshima*. In these two events the American pseudo-species overreached its own comprehension of itself and thus denied all of us, and especially our youth, a chance for a plausible identity and to a commitment to a *daily* way of life which would have meaning in itself without finding itself, sooner or later, an aimless and voiceless detail in a design without boundaries. Change as such could as yet become part of a planned world fit for a wider identity and a new adulthood on earth, but not by way of the cosmic coercion of gadgetry and the mere pressure of masses.

But moralistic horror alone does not help. As you, as Catholics, know, America has simply stepped into the center of the existential dilemma which empires have successively faced throughout historical time, and the rest of the world, while sometimes attempting to vilify us, has eagerly accepted our technological and commercial ideals, even as their radical youth has joined ours in a rebellion that can be understood only as an attempt to create a new and all-human identity by first resembling and aspiring to everything the parents were not. Maybe the old countries will learn to recombine these ideals with their traditions; in the meantime, however, this country alone must face the responsibility that much of the industrial way of life *is* its tradition and that its history *has* been self-chosen and that it must help create, beyond a technological civilization, an all-human culture.

This is the challenge with which the youth of the world are confronting us. For the moment—and at times—they do so by establishing, in all manner of mocking and serious display, a new cross-national and seemingly ahistorical pseudo-species consisting of all those who happen to be young and declaring all others to be defunct. This at least refurrows the ground of future identities. And so I have found myself recently, like some latter-day Diogenes, going around with a conceptual searchlight, asking people of different ages, occupations, and preoccupations: "Do *you* know what an *adult* is?" And a new and universal image is only conceivable out of a new synthesis of youthful imagination and such competence and insight as we are able to hand on convincingly.

I see from your program that you intend to investigate the conflict of various identities which "belong" to different anatomical, economic, historical, and geographic settings. Therefore, in conclusion, let me restate the way in which I, as a developmental psychologist, have come to reformulate the golden rule: An adult should strive to do to another what will enhance the other's growth (at his age, in his condition, and under his circumstances) while at the same time enhancing his, the doer's, own growth (at his age, in his condition, and under his circumstances). For this, of course, we have to know a lot, but such knowledge today is within our grasp, and at any rate, such knowledge of each other today is a condition for a wider identity.

Now, I know as well as the next man that individual and collective ethics have different structures. Yet collective ethics can be visualized and verbalized only by recourse to what the individual stands for. And so I think that groups living in the same period of history at different stages of collective development may well learn to strive along analogous "golden" lines.

A truly wider identity, however, includes not only the capacity for empathic identification with other people—and especially with people at first perceived as incomprehensively "other"—but also the willingness to understand the otherness as well as the all-too-familiar in ourselves. For to ourselves we are always the example of humanity closest at hand.

Environment and Virtues
(1972)

Many an anthropologist, it seems, has a deeply personal and enduring relationship to the culture, or the territory, which he studied first. There his identity as a researcher became irreversibly attuned to the uniqueness of the environmental setting as well as to that of the value system of a tribe or a people. I have always considered it decisive for my comprehension of the human environment that I had the good fortune within the space of a few years to accompany two anthropologists to their "favorite" tribes: first H. Scudder Mekeel to a Sioux Indian reservation on the Great Plains, and then the venerable Alfred Kroeber to the Yurok Indians on the Pacific Coast of northern California.[1]

My own, mostly clinical, training had taught me to understand human malfunctioning—and functioning—in terms of the developmental "givens" least subject to cultural relativity. The immediate purpose of the first trip was, in fact, a clinical one; namely, to investigate the difficulties encountered in the education of Sioux children in the prairie schools maintained by the United States Indian Service. As for the Yurok, Alfred Kroeber had always been interested in understanding aspects of their behavior and of their mythological

First published in *Arts of the Environment*, ed. Gyorgy Kepes (New York: Braziller, 1972), 60–77.

imagination which, so it seemed, had a certain weird similarity to the magic and phobic preoccupations of compulsive and obsessive individuals studied in our culture. In both instances, however, my anthropologist friends and I soon found ourselves discussing the powerful influence of the human environment, and that means the natural setting as perceived and transformed by a culture, and the values and virtues which have proven "fitting." This, it appeared, was made more poignant by my lucky choice of friends, for the original conditions and cultural systems of their favorite tribes differed strikingly, and systematically.

The Sioux were belligerent nomads, roaming the North Central Plains in loosely organized groups, in pursuit of "dark masses of buffalo." Their economic concepts were dominated by the conviction that "you can't take it with you"—either in this world or the next. Their possessions were few and changed hands readily. Generosity— as expressed in ceremonial give-away fasts—and fortitude in hunt and battle were their cardinal virtues. The Yurok, on the other hand, lived in a narrow, densely wooded river valley which descends steeply into the Pacific. They were sedentary and peaceful to the point of ignoring warring neighbors. They gathered acorns, fished along the river, and prepared themselves spiritually for the annual miracle of the salmon run, when an abundance of fish enters the mouth of the Klamath and ascends the river, coming like a gift from powerful spirits beyond the ocean. They owned "real estate" along the river, cultivated virtues which led to the storage of wealth, and gave monetary value to every named item in their small world. To me, the sharp-eyed Plains Indian and his endless horizons had served to reinforce the original image of "the Indian" acquired in my childhood days. Now I had to adapt myself to Indians who would point solemnly to a hardly discernible pit in the ground and call it their ancestral home.

Already then, of course, both the Sioux and the Yurok had ceased to function as living cultures and had become American minorities of a special historical and sociological kind. Remnants of their old value systems and of their child-training methods had been compromised by attempts at acculturation and federal education. But these remnants, whether still practiced or hardly remembered, were all that would ever be known. For in the past child training had been an anthropologist's no-man's-land. Even discerning early observers preferred to assume—with contempt or with elation—that Indian children were "untrained animals"; and, indeed even otherwise well-informed white educators quickly revealed strong private prejudices of long standing. The Indians in the meantime had silently clung to fragments of traditional values which, as questioning disclosed, were of great emotional importance to them. In order to understand the remaining values of the ancient child-training systems, which we now reconstructed, and to compare them with the modern values unsuccessfully imposed by the government, we found it necessary to review some of the successive images of themselves and of one another which the two Indian groups and their white caretakers had developed since they had first met.

The original image of the Sioux—and indeed the very image of the Plains Indian which came to adorn the American "nickel"—is that of the warrior and hunter, endowed with manliness and nobility, cunning and cruelty. But for a long time the Sioux had been beset by an apocalyptic sequence of catastrophes, as if nature and history had united to declare total war on their all-too-manly offspring. Only a few centuries before the whites settled among them, the Sioux had left their original home territory further east and had adjusted their hunting methods and their daily lives to one creature: the buffalo. This animal's body had provided food as well as material for clothing, covering, shelter, and for all manner of utilities. Medicine and ornaments were made of buffalo parts; and buffalo droppings, sun-dried, served as fuel in winter. Societies and seasons, ceremonies and dances, mythology and children's play extolled the buffalo's name and image. But the whites, eager for trade routes and territory, upset the hunting grounds and slaughtered buffalo by the hundred thousand. In search of gold, they swarmed into the Black Hills, the Sioux's holy mountains and winter refuge. Eventually forced to become cowboys, the Sioux soon found their grasslands destroyed by erosion, and their markets menaced by selling booms and depressions. In the end, nothing was left but abhorred homesteading within the confines of reservations—on some of the poorest land in all the states. When the buffalo died, it was said the Sioux died.

During this period the Sioux encounterd successive waves of white men who typified the restless search for space, power, and new ethnic identity. The roaming trappers and fur traders seemed acceptable enough to the nomadic Sioux; certain American generals were almost deified for the very reason that they fought well; the Negro cavalry, because of its impressive charges, was given the precious name of "Black Buffaloes." The consecrated belief in man demonstrated by the Quakers and missionaries did not fail to impress the dignified and religious leaders of the Sioux. But as they looked for fitting images to connect the past with the future, the Sioux found least acceptable the class of white man who was destined to teach them the blessings of civilization, namely, the government employee. The young American democracy thus lost the chance for a true re-education of the Indian when it could not decide on its guiding values: in pressing westward and in improvising transient settlements on changing frontiers, was America conquering or colonizing, converting or liberating, establishing a new way of life for all, or only for some?

The Indians found themselves in a cultural vacuum. For the older ones it seemed only yesterday that the three inseparable horsemen of their history's apocalypse had appeared on their horizon: the migration of foreign people, the death of the buffalo, and soil erosion. Somehow they still seemed to expect that tomorrow the bad dream would be over. They asked the United States Supreme Court to give them back the Black Hills, the buffaloes, the gold—or to pay for them. Someday, they expected, there would be a notice on the bulletin board at the agency announcing that the Court had heard them and made them rich. In the meantime, why learn to farm? Time for them, one gathered, was empty waiting except for those vivid moments of the present in which the Indian could be his old self, exchanging memories, gossiping, joking, or dancing, and in which he again felt connected with the boundless past where there was no one but himself, the game and the enemy (the not-himself who could be fought). The space where he could feel at home was still without borders, allowed for voluntary gatherings from all "corners" of the prairie, and at the same time for sudden expansion and dispersion. He had been glad to accept centrifugal items of white culture such as the horse and the gun, but he had little comprehension for the centripetal world image of the kind of men who were sent from mysterious Washington to re-educate him.

And, indeed, the very world image implicit in the Sioux Indian's tradition, forced us, the visitors, to study the structure of the environment and the values of "our" administrators and teachers. They, of course, had not come as students; nor had most of them come to stay. On the contrary, their passing contact with the Indians had been dictated more in consideration of careers which would eventually lead them elsewhere, namely, back to a class-structured world and its status escalation, with the hope of settling down on the highest social level attainable, as far from any Indians as possible. All the more did they cling to the world image they had brought along. They preached with defensive righteousness a life plan with centripetal and localized goals: home, real estate, bank account—all of which, however, receive their meaning from a sense of time in which the past immigrant and migrant must be overcome and even the full measure of fulfillment in the present is sacrificed to an increasingly higher standard of living in the ever distant future. The road to this future is indefinite adjustability, perpetual inner reform, and economic "betterment." Thus we learned from the whites, too, that geographic-historic perspectives and economic goals and means contain all that a group has learned from its history, and therefore dominate concepts of reality and ideals of conduct which cannot be questioned or partially exchanged without a threat to identity itself.

The younger Sioux had been brought up in their *early childhood* by the first group, the members of the tribe for whom the future was empty except for dreams of *restoration*. In their *later childhood* they were set an example of *reform* by the white man's educational philosophy. But, since it had a place neither in the individual's early impressions and childhood play (and among the virtues extolled in tales) nor in tangible expectations of any access to the white career pattern, the promise of vocational perfection could not become generally meaningful.

In trying to understand the grievances of both races, then, we encountered resistances to each other which were based not on malice or entirely on ignorance, but rather on anachronistic *fears of extinction*, and on the *fear of loss of group identity*; for the Indian could not part with a past that provided him with the last cultural synthesis he was able to achieve, and he could not identify with a white system that offered no new synthesis. We were faced with world images, each of which demanded sacrifices of its members which they could bear only in the firm belief that they were based on unquestionable absolutes of conduct. Virtues, so we learned, which originally were designed to safeguard an individual's or a group's self-preservation become rigid under pressure of anachronistic fears of extinction and the anxiety aroused by threatened identity loss, and can render a people unable to adapt to changed necessities. Most whites thus found it difficult to face a minority problem that endangered what synthesis their dearly-won status in a federal bureaucracy seemed to promise. In fact, the very training of an effective and dependable government employee tended to exclude automatically the ability to tolerate certain classes of people, their standards and habits—unless, of course, special training or special insight helped him to identify with the environment and the values of his clients. Without such empathy, however, the passive fortitude of Indian children seemed as infuriating as it was incomprehensible. Their misconduct at first rarely erupted into open "juvenile delinquency" but more often smouldered in the form of a general and intangible passive resistance against any further and more final impact of white standards on the Indian conscience—such as self-blame in the service of betterment. The Indian child did not seem to find himself confronted with a "bad conscience" within himself when, in passive defiance of the white teacher, he retreated into himself; nor was he met by unsympathetic relatives when he chose to run home.

Let us now turn from the evidence of cultural pathology to the hidden indices of past cultural functioning; that is, the imbeddedness of the Sioux in their environment and the environment's "indwelling" in their value system. To connect these two, it is best to introduce *developmental time*; for all men, at any given moment, live through stages of life in which their changing needs and developing capacities must be reintegrated with their institutions. The "environment" of an individual at a given stage of life, therefore, includes all those individuals and institutions who have meaning for him on the basis of his growing needs and capacities *and* who, in turn, need him and are able to include him in communal tasks.

To fathom the genius of culture it is necessary to trace the implanting of the dominant value system into each newborn member of a primitive community; and sensitive, older Indians knew very well what we were looking for. As the erstwhile guardians of an old world image, they, too, were aware of the fact that through its agents, the parental persons, a culture establishes in the young and very young a basic social grammar which is rooted in early bodily experience. At the very beginning, the maternal persons follow a sequence and alternation of indulging and denying, of accelerating and inhibiting infantile wishes and aspirations. They underscore but never derange the unfolding set of impulses and capacities in such a way that the eventual outcome promises to be the optimum configuration of human potentials under given natural and historical conditions. At the very beginning—and I can only point here to the early phase of life—the ever-expanding readiness of mouth and eyes, of sensory equipment and of musculature come to interact with the administrations of those who attend, train, and judge; thus, basic cultural variations are established in the universal set of infantile experiences.

Indeed, the Sioux child's preverbal conditioning can be seen as an ingenious arrangement which would first secure in him a safe combination of undiminished self-confidence and of trust in the availability of food supply, and then an ever-ready anger in the face of interference, for both trust and aggression seem necessary for the functioning of a hunter democracy. The most basic of developmental facts, of course, is that the newborn must learn to know the world by receiving and accepting both food and warmth in closeness to the mother, and then must learn to let go of her: the ontogenetic loss of paradise. Even before the Sioux child was born his mother's relatives and friends gathered the prairie's best berries and herbs and prepared a juice in a buffalo bladder which would serve as the baby's first nursing bottle. An expert woman stimulated his mouth with her finger and fed him the juice while other women sucked the mother's breasts until they were ready to give the real stuff of life instead of the less digestible colostrum. Once the baby had begun to enjoy the mother's breast, he was nursed whenever he whimpered: the Sioux did not believe that crying would make a baby strong, although they considered temper tantrums in the older child desirable. Boys in particular, and especially the first boy, were breast-fed generously for a period of from three to five years, during which time the father was to refrain from making sexual advances to the mother; intercourse was said to spoil the milk. The eventual advent of a new baby, however, did not totally preclude access to the maternal breast; even where he had already learned to depend on other food, the Sioux child was permitted to draw an occasional sip from his mother or (for that matter) from any other available woman.

This paradise of a long and generous feeding history, however, contained a forbidden fruit. Older Sioux women recount what trouble they had with these indulged babies when they began to teethe and bite. The mother would then "thump" the infant's head and he would fly into a rage. The women's habitual amusement with these tantrums was justified with the assertion that rage makes a child strong. One might wonder how well the Sioux infant was able to "abreact" rage while still strapped in the traditional cradle board. While this tight container permitted the newborn to find a comfortable approximation of the fetal state, it may also have inhibited in the infant the muscular expression of provoked rage and thus helped to establish a lasting reservoir of aggression that contributed to the much described "trait" of anger and cruelty in the Sioux character.

But such matters are by no means to be understood as a oneway "conditioning" of the individual child; only pervasive cultural values can give meaning to such items in child training. Thus (to follow this one trend) the generosity manifested in the mother's initial treatment of the child was continued in the family's respect for the child's possessions. While an adult Sioux could not refuse another's request for a gift, he could refuse to give away his child's things, for much honor would come to the child when he, of his own accord, would later relinquish his property on ceremonial occasions. He who had been given so much now became the giver. And it should be noted in passing that the child was not taught primarily by being told that property was "bad," but by being given an example of extreme generosity by his elders. All of these are, of course, cultural prescriptions only approximated in actual behavior, while under disintegrating conditions, prescribed virtues can become economic vices. At the time of my observations, to the trader's horror, parents were willing to let a child buy sweets and toys with money that was desperately needed for basic supplies.

The first strict *taboos* expressed verbally and made inescapable by a tight net of shaming applied to the relationship of brother and sister. After the sixth year of life brother and sister were not to address each other directly anymore. The girl would be urged to confine herself to female play and to stay near the tepee while the boy was encouraged to join the older boys in hunting games. From then on, the daily patterns for boys and girls differed radically. The boy was to become restless, brave, and reckless; the girl, reticent, industrious, and chaste. Boys used miniature bows and arrows and later ropes for an initial imitation, and as soon as possible, the real activation of a hunter's or cowboy's existence. While intrusive and sadistic tendencies were cultivated as masculine, corresponding inhibitions were invoked in the girl, as is typical for cultures catering to an extreme masculine ideal. Girls were taught to sit modestly, to walk in small measured steps, later to sleep with their thighs tied together, and not to go beyond a certain radius around the tepee or the camp. It was understood by both sexes that older girls who habitually overstepped such restrictions might be raped by the boys with impunity. Functioning cultures, however, cannot afford to distort the self-image of women and to take chances with their capacity to integrate their social and personal lives—if for no other reason than they must continue to support fully and effectively the development of well-functioning boys and girls. We have seen how the mothers were made to feel that to them fell the task of laying the foundation for the Sioux's basic attitudes toward the world as a whole. Such consciousness of a mission may have given female functions and modes equality in cultural and economic importance with those of men, and may have prevented the vast majority of women from resenting their restricted participation in the more spectacular male activities. But, in addition, the girl who learned to conform to these restrictions knew that as an adult her brother would be obliged to bring to her the best of what he could hunt or catch. She would butcher the buffalo and, on occasion, mutilate an enemy he had killed. Her skill in embroidery would come to full display when she would be called upon to ornament the cradles and layettes of his children. At certain ceremonies she would sing of his bravery and in the sun dance she would assist him during his prescribed self-torture. This is an example of the way in which homogeneous cultures—here a culture with an extreme elaboration of male fortitude and of female solicitude—attempt to pay in the currency of prestige for whatever exploitation they have come to impose.

A modern viewer of such a culture would do well, of course, to restrain his enthusiasm for its inner logic: for roles are so rigidly defined, and deviations held in check by such ridicule, that any habitual dissenter would soon find himself in unbearable isolation, if not in danger of perishing. Nevertheless, one must acknowledge a certain genius in the cultural assimilation to each other of somatic, social, and personal patterns and in the creation of a communal identity which, in turn, is indispensable to any individual identity. Such integration can exploit somatic patterns (such as the differences of sex, age, and type) only within limits which assure health and vitality to most; it can make demands on personal adaptation only within the limits which guard a manageable and, in fact, energizing degree of anxiety and of conflict; and it can dictate social roles only up to the point where a sense of communality can make up for the sacrifices in individual autonomy.

Let us now compare the environment and the virtues of the Sioux with those of the Yurok. As described, the Sioux roamed the plains and cultivated spatial concepts of centrifugal mobility, the horizons of their existence coinciding with the buffalo's roaming and the hunting grounds of superior enemies. The Yurok lived largely in or at the mouth of a narrow, mountainous, densely forested valley, and, as if making a virtue of a geographic pattern, confined themselves within strict territorial borders. To them, "the world" was a disc of about 150 miles in diameter, cut in half by the Klamath River, and defined by cardinal directions: there was an "upstream" and a "downstream," a "towards the river" and an "away from the river," and then, at the end of the world, an elliptic "in back and around." The Yurok ignored the worlds beyond and ostracized as "of ignoble birth" anyone who showed a marked tendency to venture into alien territories. Instead, they "cried" and prayed to their horizons which they thought contained the supernatural regions from which generous spirits sent the stuff of life to them: above all, salmon.

Within this restricted radius of existence, extreme localization took place. I have referred to the ancestral pits in the ground which for generations retained a family's name. In fact, the whole environment was noteworthy only in so far as mythological events had given names to circumscribed locations. Yurok myths do not mention the gigantic redwoods which overshadow their towns and fishing places; but they do refer to certain undistinguished rocks and trees as being the "origin" of the most far-reaching events. This localization found its economic counterpart in a monetarization of values. Every person, relationship, or act could be exactly valued and became the object of pride and of ceaseless bickering. Thus, when I asked a venerable shaman woman to tell me how she happened to become a shaman, she quickly and seriously said, "This cost twice a dollar." Anyone not prepared for Yurok mentality could easily mistake this request for an attempt to capitalize on what the white man considers valuable. In this instance, it is (also) a ceremonial duty.

The acquisition and retention of possessions were, above all, what the Yurok thought about, talked about, and prayed for. In fact, *this* "primitive" tendency the Yurok did not need to forget in the white world, and therefore their grievances with the government found expression other than the inarticulate smouldering of the prairie man's passive resistance. Where it flared up, it was the voluble anger of one group of citizens of the United States against what they, in turn, considered another greedy group. The observing white man, however, who may at first be repulsed by the Yurok's money-mindedness and suspicious compulsiveness, cannot escape the final insight that relations with the Yurok lack alleviating romanticism just because Yurok and white man understand too well what the other wants, namely, possessions.

This well-defined Yurok world, seen as a whole, seems to have its "mouth open" toward the ocean and toward the yearly, mysterious appearance of salmon which enter and climb up the river, and, usually leaving an abundance of food supply in the Yurok's nets, disappear upriver—as science tells us, to spawn and to die. Some months later its diminutive progeny descends the river, and disappears in the ocean—to come back two years later as salmon and climb (as if driven by a "homing instinct") back to its very birthplace, in order to fulfill its life cycle. From direct observation, the Yurok could only know that before entering the river, the salmon stop eating and therefore when caught have an empty stomach. As they ascend the river, their sexual organs mature, while their fat content begins to diminish. At the pink of their condition and nutritional value, then, the salmon have ceased eating and have not commenced procreating. To gain sympathetic power over such prey the Yurok fishermen make a special point of purifying themselves from contact with women, and of abstaining from food.

The Yurok "environment" consequently is magically conceptualized on the basis of

1) observation of the geographic and biological environment, that is, the lower part of a river valley and a mysterious periodical supply of a prey with a particularly dramatic biology; and

2) experience of the human body as a slowly maturing organism with periodic needs. In the nonmagical sphere, of course, the Yurok reached a certain degree of logic and technique, as do all human beings. Magic thought and behavior, however, seemed indicated wherever mysterious food sources beyond the Yurok's power and comprehension needed to be influenced, or whenever vague human impulses and fears needed to be alleviated, in which cases the Yurok tried to understand nature around and within them by blending bodily and geographic configurations into one geographic-anatomical environment. Thus, the periodic affluence of the waterway has a functional interrelation with the periodicity of vital juices in the body's nutritional and procreative systems, and therefore, the Yurok's main magic concern is that vital channels in nature be kept open by the strict regulation of such bodily events as eating and defecation, menstruation, intercourse, and childbirth.

One example of such primitive synthesis is the pervading importance of the "tube" configuration in Yurok thinking. According to Yurok mythology, the Klamath in prehistoric times flowed up on one side of its bed and down on the other. Now, it flows only in the downward direction and salmon ascend upward. I will never forget the same old shaman woman's apocalyptic apprehension when, from her home high up on a dune, she saw a small whale enter, play around in and leave the mouth of the Klamath. The river could safely serve only one vector of animal motion, that of ascending salmon. For that which flows in one channel of life is said to be most eager to avoid contaminating contact with the objects of other channels with "saclike" configurations. Both salmon and river dislike food to be eaten on a boat. Deer will stay away from the snares if deer meat has been brought in contact with water. Salmon demand that women on a trip up or down river leave the boat at specified places and

walk around a sacred rock. Salmon also dislike the man who is full
of food; and money will leave the house if intercourse takes place in
its vicinity. What the Yurok calls "clean" living, then, is an attempt
to keep vectors clear and channels unobstructed, and that means, to
avoid the wombs of multiplication—including the lake upriver from
which the waters of the Klamath flow; the place across the ocean
where salmon originate; and the beaches up the coast, where shell
money is collected.

The Yurok have two kinds of houses, the living house and the
sweat house. Both are sunk into the ground, with their roofs a few
feet above it. The "doors" consist of oval openings which admit one
creeping human being at a time. The living house, however, has only
one such opening while the sweat house has two, a bigger and a
smaller one. The living house is dominated by the activities shared
by men and women; it is full of food and utensils, crowded with
babies, and is for sleeping—and sleeping together. Living house and
woman are thus associated: after contact with either, the man has
to pass the "test" of the sweat house. This he enters through the
normal-sized door; but he must leave it through the very small opening which will let only such men slip through as are moderate in
their eating habits and supple with the perspiration caused by the
sacred fire. The men must then conclude the purification by swimming in the river. The conscientious fisherman passes this test every
morning, giving daily rebirth to himself through a tube—like through
a man-made womb.

Only once a year the whole system of magic avoidances is set aside
and superior mechanical invention takes over. Following complicated
ceremonies, a strong dam is built which obstructs the ascent of the
salmon and permits the Yurok to catch a rich winter supply. The
dam building according to Alfred Kroeber is the largest mechanical
enterprise undertaken by the Yurok or, for that matter, by any California Indians, and the most communal event. After ten days of
collective fishing, orgies of ridicule and sexual freedom take place,
reminiscent of ancient European spring rites.

We have referred to the contribution made by the Sioux infant's early
training to the dominant virtues as well as the dominant images of
the Sioux world. What, in comparison, happens in Yurok infancy?

Breast feeding begins with typical Indian generosity, however, there
is a definite weaning time around the sixth month, the teething period.
This acceleration of weaning seems to be part of a general tendency
to encourage the baby to leave the mother and her support as soon

as this is possible and bearable—and not to return. Weaning, in fact, is called "forgetting the mother" and if necessary is enforced by the mother's going away for a few days. As for muscular development, the baby's legs (in the Yurok version of the cradle board) are left uncovered from his twentieth day on and are massaged by the grandmother; creeping is encouraged. Such early locomotor autonomy seems to result in a physique capable of vigorous perambulation—within territorial limits. However, there also remains a lifelong and later minutely ritualized preoccupation with food and a capacity for a nostalgia utilized in ritual "crying." At the "sense" stage (that is, when the child can repeat what he has been told) he is admonished to eat slowly, not to grab food, never to take it without asking for it, never to eat between meals and never to ask for a second helping—an oral puritanism hardly equalled among other Indians. During meals, a strict order of placement is maintained and the children are taught to eat in prescribed ways: to put only a little food on the spoon, to lift the spoon up slowly, to put it down again while chewing the food—and, above all, to think of becoming rich during the whole process. Nobody speaks during meals so that everybody can keep his own thoughts on money and salmon. In fact, the adult Yurok during meals was supposed to make himself see money hanging from trees and salmon swimming in the river during off season. Thus a maximum of avarice and nostalgia is first provoked by the combination of early weaning (not only from the breast but also from contact with the mother) and is then "tamed" and used for the development of such "ideal" attitudes as will, to the Yurok mind, in the end, assure fate's favor. Even the fables told to children use the characteristic appearance of some animals in the natural surroundings to underline the ugliness of lack of restraint. They isolate one outstanding item in the physiognomy of animals to underscore the necessity of "clean behavior": the buzzard's baldness is the result of his having voraciously put his whole head into a dish of hot soup; the eel lost all of his bones by gambling them away; and the bear has such a big anus (as testified by the form of its feces) because he habitually overeats.

The groundwork for the Yurok's sexual attitudes, too, is laid in the child's earlier conditioning which teaches him to subordinate drive to economic considerations. The Sioux man, in his pronounced masculinity, was more phallic-sadistic in that he pursued whatever roamed: game, enemy, woman. The Yurok was more phobic-compulsive in that he cultivated avoidances, such as not being "snared" by the wrong woman or at the wrong time or place—wrong meaning under any circumstances that would compromise his assets as an economic being, so he could buy a worthwhile wife. If he were to make an unworthy girl pregnant, he would have to marry her. In the sweat house, he had to learn the strange feat of thinking of money and of *not* thinking of women.

Within such basic limits, however, sexuality was viewed with leniency and humor. The fact that sexual contact necessitated purification seemed to be considered a duty or a nuisance, but did not reflect either on sexuality as such or on women in general. It was the body's inner system of fluid ways which, by implication, was avoided when the menstruating young girl was constrained to bathe alone; the surface of the human body aroused no shame, and everybody was free to bathe in the nude. But the girl knew that virtue, or shall we say an unblemished name, would gain her a husband who could pay well and that her status and that of her children and her children's children would depend on the amount her husband would offer to her father when asking for her. Weakness of character or habitual deviancy was usually explained as a result of the delinquent's mother or grandmother not having been "paid for in full." This, it seems, meant that a woman and a man became involved prematurely and had to marry on a down payment and then maybe were unable to pay the installments. Such people were not "clean."

A few glimpses into the dynamics of what could be reconstructed as a Sioux and a Yurok value system have now shown us two examples of how the "primitive" consciousness of being human coincides with an exclusive image of being a "strong" Sioux or a "clean" Yurok. Each tribe was dominated by the conviction that its virtues marked it as *the* people in *the* world. The two cultures thus are specimens of what I have called *pseudo-speciation*—a term I can introduce here only briefly.[2] It refers to the conceptualization of human groups' attempts to create a unique and exclusive way of life pleasing to "their" supernatural powers, superior to any other way of life, and at least matching the ethological adaptation of the animal world. By a magic unification, what is known (and not known) of the human body's workings is integrated with what is known (and not known) of the ecology of the environment. The human propensity to invent, to plan, and to "grow" appropriate virtues becomes part of a *cultural style* with pervades the whole ensemble of designs, from the weaving of a blanket to the telling of stories, and from mythologizing to ceremonial behavior. Thus truly one world is presented to the growing individual at every step.

———————————

Any attempt to apply such observations as I have described here to modern civilizations cannot escape being contrived. Each observer, therefore, would do well to concern himself with generalizations which have the most immediate meaning in his own field. Let me come back, then, to the question of why the logic of primitive ideation and behavior so often seems to resemble the hidden logic of neurotic behavior in our own culture. For example, a clinician could claim to recognize in the Yurok's ceremonial obsession to cleanse themselves from contact with "the woman's inside" a parallel to the phobic avoidance of dirt, the abhorrence of sexuality, and the "washing ceremonials" of neurotic individuals in modern society. Or he could suspect behind the boisterous exhibitionism of the Sioux brave a hidden fear for his masculinity comparable to the unconscious "castration fear" in some of our most outspoken masculinists. But it must be clear by now that it is not the "savage" in his unified and communal world who resembles our neurotics, but rather modern neurotics who, in their failure to master discrepancies in their environment and in their values, become lonely caricatures of our primitive ancestors. That is, neurotic symptoms are not only partial regressions to infantile stages, in ontogeny but also diffuse retrogressions to mental and emotional mechanisms belonging to mankind's more magic and more homogeneous past.

All of us are, of course, apt to consciously romanticize or abhor primitive ways. Men and women in those early cultures seem to have an innocent and direct bodily and physical relation to the sources of food. Their tools and weapons are extensions of the human body; their magic is a projection of the logic of the body. Children participate in technical and in magic pursuits; body and environment, childhood and culture may be full of dangers, but they are all one world. In contrast, the expansiveness of our civilization and its social stratification and technical specialization make it almost impossible to base any personal synthesis on more than a section or a few sections of society. Machines, far from remaining an extension of the body, destine whole classes to become extensions of machinery, and the ruthless arbitrariness of man-made systems (rather than the will of moody and yet comprehensible gods) determines man's "environment." No wonder that on a collective level, too, we unconsciously grasp for magic solutions. Such mechanical child training, for example, as for a while was one of the prevailing patterns in Western civilization may be seen as a magic attempt to master a mechanized world by becoming more like machines, in analogy to the Sioux's identification with the buffalo of his hunting grounds, and the Yurok's with the river and the salmon. Thus we all carry ancient forms of magic adaptation into our technological present.

Man today, of course, is becoming aware of his indivisible spe-cieshood and he has no choice but to design an all-human environ-ment on the basis of universal science and technology. Such common specieshood has been prepared throughout the history of civilization by the gradual or violent inclusion of smaller pseudo-species into bigger and wider identities: nations, creeds, empires, markets—all promising, at least for their territory, an irreversible humanist sense of world community. Man has come to master technologically forces that he once feared as magic or evil. He has learned to study in minute detail what he once could only contemplate in awe. He enjoys—up to a point—a cultural heterogeneity that he was once mortally afraid of. He includes in his sense of human dignity other "pseudo-species" which he once considered contemptible if not ex-pendable. And, finally, he gains insight into what, in all his evolution, he had kept repressed in himself. There are dangerous limits, how-ever, to the integration of all these avenues of progress; and the very fear of identity extinction which we found in the whites and the Indians facing one another on the prairie leads in ever bigger theaters of encounter to more anachronistic fears of extinction. Paired with diabolically perfected means of annihilation, such fears can drive men to violent attempts at seeking archaic safety in *reactionary pseudo-species* formation, by which one nation, one creed, one type of man— and yes, one sex—defend the illusion of having been chosen to dom-inate. The calculated murder of the battlefields is matched by the viciousness of contending standards and by the paralyzing value con-flicts which individuals wage within themselves. No wonder that our time is preoccupied with the question of ultimate remedies and cures: the war to end all wars, the revolution that will end all class struggle, the political reforms and the therapeutic insights that will end both social and inner conflicts. We must suspect much magic thinking in all these utopias as well.

As we saw, the "primitive" modes of adaptation, which are the deepest layers of our socio-evolution, in "their time" helped to unify two essential aspects of cultural cohesion: an imbeddedness in the mastered environment and the ability to integrate the growth of the young with the values that served that mastery. In contrast, civilized controversies over the preferable training of children—whether pu-nitive, mechanical, or permissive—are all characterized by a defensive denial of the fact that the modern world has not as yet been able to integrate its man-made environment with the creative resources newly born with each generation of children.

At this moment in socio-genetic evolution, however (or maybe at the moment when socio-genetic evolution as we know it threatens to ensure its own demise), a remarkable development is "happening." A new kind of people has begun, often mockingly, to play pseudo-species not on a regional and traditional, but on a worldwide and futuristic basis: youth, now a self-appointed interracial, supra-national "people," questioning the "species" parent.

The enlightened youth of the industrialized and prosperous countries of today look at and into themselves and find themselves unprepared for true cultural integration; and they look at the disorganized and unplanned environment and find it unintegratable. Some, in many nations, aspire again to a tribal communality, sometimes wearing the very insignia of headbands and beads, and they give hope to visionary adults who would lead them in a regreening of the world. But, alas, theirs is all too often not only a counterculture, but an anticulture beclouding itself with utopias (reinforced by drugs) which, in turn, facilitate both individual regression and group retrogression. They leave it to some miracle of leadership—and to the working masses—to preserve or to restore the unity of production and consumption in this irreversibly technological world.

It is between this new utopian revolution of youth and the threat of an all too familiar reaction that a new conception of the human environment must come to unify the technological demands of modern living. And, indeed, since my anthropologist friends introduced me to the Indian worlds, we clinicians have had to expand our clinical awareness to include the necessity for a new unity of the outer (and now to be radically planned) environment and the identity needs of man. Some prophets, among the technological architects, expect such new identity to come from a newly conceived total design for man's surroundings, and would make the leap to a determination "to reform the environment instead of trying to reform man."[3] But one can also appreciate Constantines Doxiadis' warning that the task of the future requires us to be "very revolutionary when dealing with new systems and networks," but "very conservative when dealing with man."[4] I take "conservative" here to be an apolitical term applicable to my field which deals with man's unconscious, and thus with that aspect of our evolutionary heritage which (next to our biological make-up probably can change only at the slowest rate and is always beset with the danger of regressions. The question, then, is not only in how many ways man can, indeed, stretch and alter himself when his environment is redesigned for him, but also what he will be able to integrate in depth, with some vitality and creativity to spare. The fact is that man's fantastic capacity to learn and to invent is not equaled by his insight into those mental and emotional miscalculations which have made him what Loren Eiseley calls "the lethal element in the universe."

What (if I am not mistaken) the youth revolution is really after is a new and all-human kind of adult; and I think that they are learning that man can never reverse his inventions, his knowledge, and his insight. Knowledge and technique, of course, are self-perpetuating and self-accelerating. For that very reason they are apt to leave behind what it is always easiest for man to go back on: his insights into himself. For in all his cultural syntheses so far, the very fact that his most "mature," most "adult," most "successful" self-images were based on some pseudo-species also enforced massive denials and self-delusions, such as his superiority over all animal species (Darwin), his class superiority (Marx), and his mastery over his own instinctuality (Freud). And only today when the human species is ready for technological suicide, are we about to recognize man's greatest illusion, namely his denial of mortality by the ever-renewed insistence on belonging to some "chosen" species which guaranteed immortality to its heroes and gave their followers the license to exploit, demean, and annihilate other kinds of men.

We can only conclude (with an obligatory brevity which belies the complexity of the task) that the designers of an all-human environment would do well to pay equal attention to the way nature grows and spoils, the way technique synthesizes and destroys, and the way man develops and retrogresses. Men and women, as well as adults, youths, and children living in different social coordinates, experience space and time differently—a fact which designers must consider if they wish to minimize inner resistances to new forms and maximize a sense of active participation in a new communal environment. Above all, every growing young person lives, at every stage of his development, in a developmental space-time which denotes the limitations and fears of his age, and yet also the optimum of active experience possible in that period of growth. It would seem, then, that future man can grow into a planned world only if the designs literally *make space* for specific periods of human growth—and this in a way which combines ancient intuition for form, modern knowledge of details, and a commitment to equal rights for all growing beings.

Notes

[1] The data excerpted here were first reported (with references to H. Scudder Mekeel's and Alfred Kroeber's work) in my papers:
"Observations on Sioux Education," *Journal of Psychology*, 7 (1930), 101–56, and *Observations on the Yurok: Childhood and World Image* (Monograph). University of California, Publication of American Archaeology and Ethnology, 35 (1943), 257–301.
[2] "The Ontogeny of Ritualization in Man," *Philosophical Transactions of the Royal Society of London*, Series B., 772, 251 (1966), 147–526.
[3] "R. Buckminster Fuller," in *Who's Who in America*, (1968–1969), 13–14.
[4] Constantinos Doxiadis, "The Coming Era of Ecumenopolis," *Saturday Review* (March 18, 1967).

Thoughts on the City
for Human Development
(1973)

The life-cycle is a dominant theme in Doxiadis' work that has not been taken up in the discussion so far. Two of Doxiadis' statements circumscribe our theme. He says: "Man's relationship to the whole system must be examined by the phases of his life, as in this respect we do witness similar phenomena all over the world." And he concludes: "We are beginning to see that the city should provide opportunities for a gradual increase of freedom, and challenge for each person as it changes in size, structure, and quality, so that these gradual changes will enable the population to gain the maximum benefit by their gradual exposure to more challenging environments, with the greater freedoms and greater potential dangers that these environments present."

But first it is necessary to overcome a certain fixation which all of us share, namely, the vision of Shakespeare's seven ages of man. I speak with feeling, because not so long ago, an inaugural lecturer in an English University managed to make fun of my own "seven stages" without having noticed that in my book there are eight. Doxiadis fits my eight stages into his twelve without doing violence to them; he merely subdivides some of his to be host to mine. (I

First published in *Ekistics,* 35, 209 (April 1973), 216–20. Reprinted in *Anthropopolis* (Athens, 1974).

object only to his calling 40–60 "real" adulthood. In the world of the future, 20–40 had better be "real" too.) But in the middle of Doxiadis' discourse on the city it is somewhat surprising for the reader to encounter such references as: "This is the phase when 'basic trust versus basic mistrust' develops," or: "This is the phase, Erikson says, of 'autonomy versus shame, doubt.' " To those not acquainted with my stages of life the sudden introduction of emotional and partly unconscious matters may seem somewhat forced.

These stages were originally so named to derive, from the psychoanalytic knowledge of the lasting vulnerabilities inherent in each stage, some indication of the lasting strength potentially provided by each. Applied to our theme, this means to demonstrate the vulnerabilities which the spatial arrangement in which people live (the use they make of space, and the meaning they give to it) can aggravate in persons of a given age group and the strengths which the right environment may help to foster. We must visualize, then, not only how each individual passes through his life cycles, but also how a succession of generations unfolds within the confines of a city.

If the infant's relation to his maternal caretakers must establish a certain ratio of trust over mistrust, then a mother's mistrust of her own environment and her disgust with her own placement within the spatial scheme obviously will curtail her capacity to convey trust. Where this is the rule in a whole neighborhood or type of city not only individuals but also communities will suffer some lasting consequences. Correspondingly, if, in the "initiative versus guilt" stage, a child is habitually made to feel that he is a *bad* child because he uses space in a playful and exploratory way and ignores warnings he has not understood, this represents a particular environmental reinforcement of the way in which parents establish inhibitory guilt in the child, instead of making the world—as far as they can—both safe and explainable. Thus, with each stage, some aspect of the architectural environment is "built into" the next generation, becomes part of its tensions and conflicts, and contributes to the disturbances to which individuals and groups are prone. All this can lead to a fatal combination of "forbidding" circumstances and oppressive "bad" conscience, which, perversely, may appear in the form of carelessness or criminality. On the other hand, it must be said that such dichotomies in our inner nature as my formulations reflect are part of our evolutionary heritage. Nobody should assume that we could build such a foolproof environment that man, once and for all, would be free of mistrust, shame or guilt.

What excites me about this whole discussion is the possibility of planning for man, instead of a "forbidding" urban environment, a facilitating one; that is, one which supports man's developmental and creative potentials, and permits him to feel central rather than shunted to the periphery, active rather than inactivated, challenged to participation rather than isolated, enhanced in awareness rather than manipulated by blind forces, etc. For to feel central, active and aware is necessary for the ethical affirmation which induces man to participate in the creation of his environment instead of being caught in the vicious circle of paralysis and excess, of self-hate and the suspicious mistrust of his neighbors. It, therefore, makes sense to me if Doxiadis translates such a vast predicament into the immediacy of architectural space, as when he exclaims: "When we advise that the mother should not always say 'NO,' why do we allow the city to tell us 'NO' in two-thirds of the cases when we reach intersections? (Red and orange lights take two-thirds of our adult walking time.) Are we sure that this is not one cause of the nervous strains that we create?"

Such an attitude would have to be supported, throughout the life-cycle, by a rethinking of the way by which an individual, at a given stage, can govern himself, be given choices he can understand, and not be treated (beyond a reasonable point) as being dangerous to himself or others. By the same token, city planning must somehow make it possible for older children to support and guard younger ones. It is only with such considerations in mind that a *dynapolis* can also reflect the productive side of man's "inner dynamics."

Doxiadis' four principles, then, can be translated into the terms of each stage of life. There should be: (1) A maximum availability of human contacts that can be utilized and of objects that can be "grasped"; (2) A certain parsimony of learnable techniques, and a minimization of repetitive failures; (3) An optimum of needed protection built into the spatial arrangements without restricting playful effort; (4) An optimization of inter-relationships which I would call "mutual actualization."

This brings us to the human bubble. In the developmental sense, each person at each stage lives in an overall bubble, which consists of a variety of subbubbles, marking the extent of his mobility, the horizon of his perceptions, the field of his choices, and the arena of his interactions. But a bubble really is not a convenient metaphor since it does not have that active center which makes a person; nor does a bubble permit interactions with other bubbles without undue consequences.

I have therefore introduced the German word *Spielraum*, literally play space, but meaning a sphere of active leeway and of scope for interaction. Of course, when I use the word here, I do not mean the pretense and the unreality often associated with the word, but rather a maximum of freedom within an optimum of limits, which man needs at all ages. Such leeway, I should add, includes a knowledge of the *factual*; that is, the sum of countable, measurable, and nameable facts which must be respected and, if necessary, avoided. Such a body of known facts, at any given stage, feels varyingly real to the person; that is, they are more or less meaningfully experienced and interacted with. I would then speak of the *actual* as the sphere of interaction with others, whom one actualizes and by whom one is actualized. A child feels active when he is both acted upon and invited to interplay; and what we, in psychoanalysis, call ego is an ordering process by which the person not only organizes his inner world, but, together with others, restores that shared sense of centrality and activation without which we wilt.

Where such a sense of awareness, of centrality and mutuality is denied to man at any stage, a sense of deadness and depression is apt to ensue; and people who habitually suffer such denial in a society in which some others do have a certain freedom of choice and scope within the major social and economic forces must come to hate others and do violence—to somebody. This has vast consequences, aggravated by the fact that in some parts of our world, wars may cease to serve the cathartic purpose they may once have had.

Dr. René Dubos' remark about the city as a stage makes additional sense if one considers the importance of vision as an early integrator of all sensory and social experiences—that is, what man's visual experience can help him see in the factual sense: what he can visualize as vivid reality, and what he envisages as the horizon of a new or renewed order. For this he has always employed, as Johann Huizinga has pointed out in *Homo Ludens: A Study of the Play Element in Culture*, not only the sphere of play in childhood, but also the arenas in which games take place, as well as those courts and holy places on which various realities and actualities fuse ceremonially. In this sense, no doubt, a city is not only an area to exist in, but also (as in the City with a capital C) a stage on which man sees himself build the proper setting for a new cast of men. So you will not mind (knowing of my intensive studies of human play) if I see an important connection between what children visualize when they build with blocks in a given play space, and Doxiadis' proud claim of being a bricklayer who plans and executes a *dynapolis* for the new man.

Now, all of us (I assume) enthusiastically approve of some of Doxiadis' detailed suggestions; from the pedestrian homestreet (rows of homes of distinct identity) to the dwelling group system; from the playing squares and shopping streets to the machine streets underground; from the system of transparent gates (which permit the visual anticipation of space to be mastered later) to the network of youth stations in and way beyond the city. But some of us non-architects, when looking at an architect's drawings, always come to wonder what kind of men are visualized as living in the completed buildings. One wonders what kind of historical coincidence of political and architectural vision (in the widest sense) produced the classical cities of the past?

Does not all city planning visualize a *homo novus*, and is not every *homo novus* to some extent the reintegration of some traditional man? This may be the reason that in Doxiadis' drawings of the future, one detects the latent presence of ancient images: atrium, agora, and Athens—all, of course, adapted to modern materials and needs. By now, there must be a wealth of data on the motivation of different people in different ages concerning the cities they want to live in or will tolerate living in. Maybe wherever something creative is done in building, if first appeals to a new type, maybe a new elite of some kind, who finds reciprocity between their personality type and the new vistas. At any rate, a new sense of perfectability, new tangible techniques of living and new education goals are always implicit in a system of planned dwellings. One has to know (or study), then, what factual aspects of life a given population wants to materialize, what declining reality they want to hold on to, and what joint vision they want to actualize; and then, what they (for whatever reason) do *not* want.

There is a Jewish story, according to which a man who was wrecked on a lonely island was found after many years. He had built himself a very nice little house. A few feet away was a more imposing shell. He explained that it was the synagogue where he prayed. But over the hill there was another shell and they asked him what he built that for. His answer was: "That's the other synagogue which I wouldn't be caught dead in." What I mean to illustrate is that whatever one's vision of a simple or ideal city is, people bring with them dependencies on old forms, ambivalent feelings toward new ones, and (overt or covert) superstitions in regard to what a city must or must not include in order to make life "safe" and "happy"—whatever *their* connotations of these two little words are. Here, incidentally, I would like to know what *were* Aristotle's exact terms for "happy" and "safe," and what were their meanings?

Every one of us, of course, has some kind of a vision that will give different connotations to the two words "safe" and "happy." To me, as I said, happiness has a lot to do with scope and leeway, whatever the techniques by which we make use of that scope. As for safety, I don't think anybody can feel safe who doesn't feel that the world he lives in gives him a kind of inner coherence. I would in fact, relate those two things to what Dr. Dubos said yesterday about the inner shelter and the horizon. We need not only to have an inner shelter around and within ourselves but also to recapture the horizons that we have visualized. Architecture must help us in this.

Yet, as we look at the terrible city districts in the United States, we realize that they, too, were originally built and populated by people with a new vision, for the sake of which they were ready to adapt to the nearly unbearable, to accept hardships and challenges so that their children could become self-made men. In fact, as a friend of mine, Richard Sennett, has suggested, there originally was something of a creative disorder which many productive people would hate to do without. An all too obvious order allows for few idiosyncrasies and no hiding places.

As I enjoy Doxiadis' sketches, the artist in me argues with the Montessori teacher in me, and they banter with each other (and with Doxiadis) on some details. Especially charming is the breast dependent baby in Figure 1. Far from critically viewing his room, he is rightly depicted as looking straight at the architect, wondering what *he* is wondering about. And, indeed, soon he will be hungry and sleepy; that is, interested primarily in the bubble formed by the warm arms that are holding him; by the meeting of his eyes with those of the mother; and his facial contact with the breast; then in the bubble provided by the covers of his crib and his closed eyes, and in his sense of being withdrawn to some inner world. If the question is: "How do we stimulate the infant at this stage?" this can only mean that we must surround him with items which he can grasp in every sense of the word, exercising what is ready in him, and when. In the meantime, the varying limits of his readiness also protect him against over-exposure; and we should discuss carefully whether, and to what extent, he needs a special room (shell) in which he (and his mother) can be encapsulated, but may soon feel imprisoned. Here I only wish Signora Dottora Montessori were still with us. But surely, there are any number of women and men, parents and teachers, alive and ready to help us define such fundamental spatial problems!

Does Figure 2 really show "the room as the infant sees it"? I think that the room as seen by an actual infant in it would take many different forms depending on his selective attention to things and people that suit his always changing mood and quest for expansion at one time, and contraction at another—for plenty of company at one moment and solitary play at another—etc. What one should strive for, then, are built-in choices, not static prescriptions as architectural expressions of his "stage." It seems important, in addition to showing the optimum private world for each stage, to indicate the maximum interplay between (say) toddlers, striders, and players. For each stage must be seen in all its interdependencies, and this is true for all stages. But it clear that we will not be able to discuss the details step for step through the whole life-cycle to the very end.

Figure 3 for example suggests an arrangement for old people which, to the taste of some, may represent more an anticipated mausoleum than a place to keep one's waning senses alert. Maybe, some old people would prefer a safe niche, close to a doorway from which the changing world of children, of youth, and (yes) of motorcars could be watched.

Finally, I will "stick my neck out," and say that my vision of the future city could include in selected areas an imaginative use of (moderately) high-rise buildings. Obviously, for what Aristotle called "partnership," the differing "identities" of circumscribed towns within the megalopolis are as essential as are the identities of neighborhoods. If one asks what gave the "romantic" cities of the past their outspoken identities, one remembers not only cathedrals and castles, but also hills and valleys. A well integrated block of multi-story buildings of different heights, where the roofs of the lower buildings serve as outdoors for the higher ones and are connected with them not only with elevators—manageable for older children—but also with sweeps of ramps and stairs) could be a rather exciting environment. Playgrounds as well as small parks for the aged; small sport fields; communal swimming pools and selected stores could serve not only the spatial expansion but also the visual enhancement of upper stories. Such city blocks, furthermore, could serve the different needs of single and married persons, of childless households and groups of families with children. They could have their own communal and ceremonial centers: kindergartens and pediatric clinics, communal centers for improvised as well as planned contacts between the young, and places for meditation and arts and crafts. Such planning may also help to rephrase and reconsider the community of men and women, for surely Doxiadis' frequent references to women's need for "gossip" must give way to a consideration of the communal function gossip served in the cities and villages of the past, and the technological means which can now serve the purposes of rapid and farflung intercom-

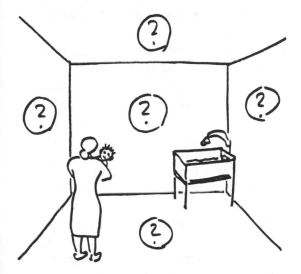

Figure 1: *Breast dependence phase*

Figure 2: *The room as the infant sees it*

Figure 3: *The courtyard as the old man needs it*

munications. In fact, women so far, seem to be underpresented in Doxiadis' city.

And so is worship! For the future community not only needs a minimization of the spatial pressures which would aggravate timidity and guilt as inner guardians of safety but also needs esthetic and ceremonial assurances which represent a sensory affirmation of communal values. This, in the end, is what makes a City. If Doxiadis concludes that at age 100: "God, in several forms, may need to enter by now," he must mean that such (old and new) forms must have entered at every step of life, not only as a kind of death insurance at the end. (In this sense I certainly agree with the suggestion that burying places somehow be made a part of city planning so that they may not be experienced by the young as some kind of pious garbage disposal on the outskirts.)

Come to think of it, work (as well as women and worship) is under-represented in the discussion so far. I assume this consideration is reserved for the question where all those underground cars are going in the morning, and where they come back from at night— although it may well be considered right now that day and night will not be as differentiated in the well-lit future as they are now. But no doubt, also small factories will remain in, or move back into, neighborhoods. The neighorhoods, such as I have described here, will employ a workforce close to the homes in activities visible and comprehensible to children. All this will make a rapprochement of work and home life possible, creating new roles for women and men and thus a new communal spirit.

To conclude with the beginning, this whole consideration of the intermeshing of the city and the life-cycle somehow implies an assumption that the rounding out of the full cycle of life becomes itself a focus of future visions, and a matter of universal interest.

Reflections on Activity,
Recovery, and Growth
(1976)

The psychoanalyst learns above all to listen—and then to speak. So he is somewhat habituated to having the last word. Here, I have the unique mandate of adding some thoughts to a document written by my wife and her co-workers about a project designed by her. But these thoughts are not meant to interpret or to explain what she has done and said. Rather, I will attempt to clarify for clinical and conceptual workers why we need this book. For I was a participant observer of the Activities Program and, as a member of the medical staff, of the whole Riggs experience—an experience as intense in its clinical research and in its conceptual search as it was and is in the communal developments described here. Let me, then, underscore some of what is reported here by recounting my own initial reactions and theoretical surprises, and then comment on the wider implications suggested in this work.

Just because of the special quality of the Riggs experience, however, it may be well to face first the most general objection arising, no doubt, in the minds of some readers, namely, that the Austen Riggs Center is and was an institution so special that few general applications can be made from it to the stark reality of other communities.

First published as a postscript for Joan Erikson's book, *Activity, Recovery, Growth: The Communal Role of Planned Activities* (New York: W. W. Norton, Inc., 1976), 251–66.

And, indeed, when the Activities Program was first presented to a national meeting of private psychiatric hospitals (in San Diego in 1971), we had to acknowledge that even among such special and expensive therapeutic institutions, Riggs occupied an extreme place as far as length and depth of treatment are concerned. In other private hospitals about 70 percent of all patients stayed less than half and 20 percent less than a quarter of a year, while the Riggs average was 400 days. That means that the therapeutic philosophy of most of these hospitals, not to speak of their budgets, was devoted to a rapid undoing of a patient's acute regression and an attempt to relocate him in the community as quickly as possible: with what lasting success or with what "revolving door" readmissions is another matter. And this trend has continued. Hospitals of the Riggs type, on the other hand, seem to invite a patient to settle down to patienthood as a communal norm. And the Activities Program described here did depend, at least for its first experimental stage, on that somewhat paradoxical phenomenon of a patient population "stable" enough to help establish a communal tradition. But then, the patients at Riggs stayed for the very purpose of a treatment procedure which was psychoanalytically oriented—that is, took time; while the Riggs staff was becoming quite aware of the consequences which the mere habituation to an institutional existence may have for patients, and especially for those in the process of identity formation. I can point here to my own work on the dangers of the wrong "confirmation" at a critical age, and to Kai Erikson's sociological discussion with the telling title "Patient Role and Social Uncertainty: The Dilemma of the Mentally Ill," which was written on the basis of some observations made at Riggs. At any rate, such systematic self-appraisal provided an unusual opportunity to observe the effects of an Activities Program on some patients' development.

As a member of the therapy staff, I well remember my own initial conflict between the conviction that the Activities Program initiated by Joan Erikson was vitally needed and my occasional fear that it might impose on the hallowed hospital structure imaginative methods which in this often tense setting could lead to rather catastrophic occurrences. And, of course, there were episodes of self-destructive or destructive behavior on the part of some patients which could be seen to be related to the activities. But the point is, they did not occur *in* the activities setting. There, we observed such surprising developments as are recorded in this book. Among these, incidents in the public sphere of drama production seemed most impressive, simply because they exposed both individuals and the institution to open embarrassment as well as private upset. And so I mention once again the small group of patients who as "Riggs Players" entered a play entirely cast and directed by themselves in a contest in a neighboring city of (mostly academic) New England drama groups. After they had won first prize, the organizers asked us: "How come? These Riggs Players look much too young to be doctors." There was the evening in the darkened theater when I first heard a patient given to mute periods impersonate an oratorical figure before a hushed audience, many of whom were, of course, quite unaware of our tenseness—and our appreciation. There was the occasion when I was told that a patient-actor given to hallucinations, when once committed to his part in making the play go on, had hallucinations during the intermission only. It stands to reason that such occurrences become part of a mythology which is apt to neglect their more complex meaning within the individual case history. But they did throw a new light on patienthood in general.

Only whole case histories, of course, could illustrate one aspect of the matter naturally neglected in this book, namely, the place of *planned* activities between the *spontaneous* activities initiated by some patients in daily hospital life, and the *work jobs* available in the larger community—and it is a special feature of a place like Riggs that a sequence of quite disparate occupations can be an essential part of the therapeutic experience. Here is what one patient of mine "did" while at Riggs. Of the young patient I need only say that he had brought with him from his childhood an intense conflict which was aggravating his identity crisis dangerously: he had been, on the one hand, a vigorous, gifted, and willful boy given to tough and loud behavior that worried his father and seemed to hurt his mother to the point of tears, while, on the other hand, he tried to restrain himself with a pious self-restriction that led to depressive states. I remember a time when I was worried about his depressiveness. Passing the Inn on an evening walk, I heard from the open basement window a trumpet blaring in a way that seemed somewhat incongruous for a hospital at such an hour. I looked down into the window, and there was my patient lustily blowing a big trumpet with the enthusiastic encouragement of other "inhibited" patients. It was somewhat embarrassing to have to admit later to the head nurse, valiant and calm Edith Breed, that I did not know my patient played the trumpet any more. She had, in fact, quietly assigned a specified hour and place for this passionately needed and applauded activity which, I am sure, did not sound very pleasing to her. But such a mixture of hidden competence and mischievousness was just what this patient (and apparently some other patients) needed at that moment, and, in principle, the Patients' Activities Planning Group, of course, encouraged such private initiative.

As to planned activities proper, the patient, on arrival, had dutifully attempted to use the carpentry shop and, indeed, made some excellent furniture. But in that first period he could not quite tolerate success: "I am becoming," he commented, "the slave of wood." In other words, the play had gone out of this activity; he felt coerced by its very success. This kind of difficulty is not atypical for the kind of patient who, far from being ungifted or untrained, tends to be, as Joan Erikson put it, "overcompetent and compulsive in limited and limiting areas." For such patients, to regain a sense of playfulness must precede any work commitment; and here a choice of a variety of activities becomes essential. My patient, in fact, chose for a while to escape the Activities Program and to try out "real" work opportunities. He had a summer job as a bartender and in winter worked in a paper mill. There, he parked blocks away so that his flashy car would not be noted and traced to Riggs. But it was; and to his surprise, his co-workers beleaguered him with questions at lunchtime—not so much about his hospitalization, but about their own families' emotional problems. That he had sought treatment and could afford it made him somewhat of an enviable authority. Finally, the patient role, his work roles, and some of his personality problems were all put to the test when the drama director spotted him as "just right" for a particular stage role. In this, he could abandon himself to a kind of self-caricature and yet transcend it by doing a competent job. It so happened that two of his occasional employers were in the audience, and at the end of the performance he shook hands with them and—as it were—with his own various roles. He seemed very much himself. He later became an outstanding worker in his chosen field.

It must be obvious that the examples given here could (and should) make a therapeutic staff uncomfortable. After all, patients are patients because they cannot help it. Do they have a choice as to when they wish to have symptoms, and if so, do they only "pretend" to "be had by" them when they do have them? In that case, is the patient role and, indeed, are their transitory recovery roles only role play? And how is it possible that the role weighs nevertheless so heavily on them that we can seriously consider them to be in some severe jeopardy just when, in fact, they come through with a reliable performance? And there can be no doubt that the Activities Program exposed patients (as has been described) to dangers which we really could sanction only because the institution as a whole was alerted and yet ready to take a chance.

And this, we learned, is the crux of the matter: the patients could play different roles by taking chances with otherwise neglected or repressed potentials because a planned activities program combines elements which are important in all learning experience—elements of playfulness as well as of work accuracy and task commitment—*and* because it gives to all three the necessary communal sanction.

Nor could we therapists continue to consider all this a mere adjunct to the main vehicle of psychotherapy—the daily one-to-one verbal encounter. It was interesting to observe that the patients themselves at times felt the need for that communal confirmation so strongly that they kept details of their activities from their therapists—partially, no doubt, so that they would not seem to be renouncing their other, their patient, identity, on which their stay at Riggs depended, but also because they did not wish to have them spoiled by too much analysis. "Resistance"?—maybe; but this represented, for some patients, a split which also characterized the community as a whole. Margaret Brenman notes the hesitations of the medical staff: and, indeed, because of their special learning, their responsibilities, and their status, clinical therapists would freely assign to "occupational specialists" a role of adjunct therapists which was by then traditional; but to let writers, artists, and craftsmen become fully engaged with patients often seemed to introduce "unbalanced" as well as untrained personalities into a therapeutic process. The fact is, I believe, that artists can have a profitable influence on patients just because they are apt to experience creative cycles with unhidden mood swings and because their failures and successes are a demonstrable function of the work process which the students are about to learn. In comparison, what the patients observe of their therapists' personalities in their sedentary and verbal work habits—while often idolized, or sympathetically admired—sometimes can do little for their need for tangible identification.

One could speculate, in fact, on how the different sections of the staff, while fulfilling the practical and legal requirements of such an institution, must yet also learn to respond differentially to the emotional needs of its clients—people all of whom by necessity have regressed to a stage of dependency and must now recapitulate the stages of autonomy and initiative, of industry and identity, as outlined earlier. One may, indeed, assume that all patients in the state of hospitalization relive some very basic mistrust and first must learn to believe in the possibility of trust. But even the regaining of such trust in the individual encounter with the personal therapist will lead to new tests of will which are played out against the nurses, present day and night, and can collide with the needs of others to the point of communal crises. That committees of nurses and patients can make such confrontations educational is indicated in this book; and so also a discussion in planning groups of the often antagonistic impulses, fantasies, and ideas which seek a field for irrational or conflicting initiatives. How the Activities staff and the patients' organization into work teams and classes of instruction serve the renewal of competencies in play and work has been discussed here. But patients must also have a chance to be adults, and this on the level previously reached and on future levels to be anticipated. This book abounds with examples of how the permission to plan as well as to take care of others—and of things and plants—can mobilize what is most adult in patients.

These observations suggested a rethinking of a number of conceptual problems. There was the matter of diagnosis, which so often seemed to limit what could be expected of a patient and became puzzling to the clinical observer as he saw these patients shift back and forth between psychotic withdrawal and hysterical histrionics, between delinquent behavior and work commitment. We then learned to look at a patient's present and past case history as a map of regressions and progressions. There was the later stage of sudden *arrest* when the person became a patient and was assigned a particular diagnostic status of deviation from some norm, the depth of deviation being determined by the range of his regression to an early phase of *fixation* which had left some permanent liability in his growth. The earlier that fixation had occurred, the sicker was the patient and the more irreversible his sickness was considered to be. But we came to feel that the more strategic diagnostic criteria were the *range* and the *interplay* between the stages of arrest and of fixation and the potentialities suggested by that interplay, especially in young patients. If often seemed, in fact, that their regression from the stage reached had a kind of semi-deliberate quality, as if an unconscious urge made them return to the earlier stage in order to release a once elastic band now stretched unbearably, and as if they now needed help to complete this mission.

A patient, by definition, is in a given stage of life, but remains partially tied to a previous one; and while he semi-deliberately regresses in the service of recapitulation and recovery, he is in danger of being, instead, confirmed in his regression by debilitating confinement.

As to young patients in particular, we are familiar with the often only too obvious and yet mysterious attempt of adolescents on the verge of mastering the steps into adulthood to insist on a period of seeming inadaptability in the very service of adaptation—a psychosocial "moratorium," as I have called it. Here, our afterhtoughts tell us that all institutionalized individuals to some extent live in an enforced moratorium in which the daily processes of adult adaptation are inactivated and must be relearned. But this means that young mental patients who are dropouts even from the process of normal adolescent dropping out will be in double jeopardy, because institutional life is apt to formalize the very process that caused the illness in the first place. Thus, the negative aspects of each stage of development are tested before the positive ones are dared: mistrust in existence itself, before even the possibility of inner wholeness is hoped for; a total loss of will or, indeed, a random willfulness is tried out before the patient can invest in a will of his own without feeling either possessed or coerced; and so on. Of special interest for theory and practice is, in our time, the shift from the hysterical repression of initiatives, sexual and otherwise, to the reckless experimentation with them.

It is essential, then, not to "confirm" the patient's lowest score on the scale of development by diagnostic name calling. Rather, the institution must be prepared to give special recognition and support to the patient's developmental potentials; in which case, as we saw, a wider range of behaviors can unfold—a range often not anticipated in the diagnosis. And here the variety of planned activities, as guided by a staff quite uninterested in diagnostic classification, can offer remarkable insights.

If the brunt of all this must be borne by the hospital "family," it is the function of planned activities to provide a world of self-verification, to which I will return presently in the wider communal context to which this book points the way. But first we must consider the questions of why such a "natural" approach to both recovery and growth has emerged so slowly, and against what age-old resistances.

Inactivation and Repression

This book begins with a historical sketch of some previous systems of patient care and, in fact, of confinement practices in general. In contrasting them with the emerging philosophy of the central role of activity in all recovery and rehabilitation, it highlights the extreme inactivation (except for some more or less enforced labor) which had come to characterize internment practices. But here, so the review indicates, we must go beyond a historical condescension which would suggest that our ancestors simply did not know any better. Instead, we may try to recognize certain irrational trends in the way deviants are apt to be classified and treated in *all* ages. Whether a historical period considers those who deviate from the norm as possessed by evil forces or obsessed by wayward impulses, as deservedly indigent or as willfully deviant, as congenitally inferior or, in fact, as sufferers with superior sensitivities, the nomenclature which defines them also confines them in special categories and demarcates their place beside or outside the active and interactive life of the community. And it assigns to the guarding and guiding, diagnosing and curative agents a particular role which when seen from within the prevalent world view somehow seems right and rational and yet, to the critic of another period (or the dissident of the same one), can reveal collective rationalizations quite at odds with the professed ends. One begins to suspect, then, that all extremes of special treatment, whether they employ physical torture, public ridicule or banishment, incarceration and inactivation, serve unconscious needs of the society as a whole.

Now, it is rightly considered fallacious to compare the structure of collectives with that of individuals. Yet, Freud refers to the divisions in man's inner structure as our "inner institutions," and it stands to reason that our "outer" institutions are, at least in principle, designed not only to serve major practical ends but also to keep the inner life of a majority of citizens in some vital—or, at any rate, bearable—tension. Thus, it seems that collectives employ institutional rationales corresponding to the defenses active in individuals. It would appear, then, that an emphasis on the confinement and inactivation of deviant minorities has a corollary in one of our basic inner defenses, namely, that of the inner repression of illicit urges which splits off from the "best" and the most conscious part of a person a "bad" part which is thus isolated, inhibited, and forgotten.

Repression is, up to a point, a normal human mechanism—the point being reached when the personality under its domination becomes too deeply inactivated in its negotiation between inner needs and opportunities for realization and actualization in social life. A well-adapted person is one who can repress optimally—that is, without excesive self-inactivation—while joining in a communality with those who, oriented within the same world image, bolster their joint repressions with institutional safeguards and help each other to sublimate unused energies. A deviant person, on the other hand, may be one who represses too much, becomes inactivated by inner conflict, and uses up otherwise aimless energy in the production of symptoms—symptoms which, in spite of the suffering they testify to, can also be seen to protest and even mock the excessive demands of society. Or a deviant may refuse to be even normally inactivated and act out, to the point of illegality, illicit urges only dreamt of by most. For the most intransigent deviants in these and other categories, society has tended to create special places of confinement and inactivation so that they may have time to recover and change.

Now, it is clear that internment is one logical procedure for isolating potential disturbers of the peace—inner or outer. But it also seems that such arrangements are apt to become elaborate systems serving unconscious needs of the community, such as to keep out of sight those who by their deviancy—sick, delinquent, or dissenting—tend to endanger not only the outer but also the inner security provided by norms, rules, and laws. Put in categories as well as special places, the deviants serve, in fact, the projection on them of repressed or barely suppressed asocial urges. As society appoints special guardians for the excluded members, it is apt to permit these wardens, beyond their rational duties, to act toward those confined as conscience does toward illicit wishes—that is, with more or less irrational and outright cruel means.

Let me point here to one example of a collective reaction to deviancy as described in the first chapter, namely, the expression of an eliminative mode in honored judicial and even medical procedures. Human conscience, and with it our sense of righteousness, are formed in childhood. Its earliest expression, namely, a sense of shame—that is, a sudden burning sense of having stepped outside the boundaries of acceptablé appearances—is formed during the period in life when the child must learn to master the avoidance and the elimination of "unclean" matter in the form demanded by the culture. Thus, the self-elimination of the offensive aspects of one's inner life becomes an important, if mostly unconscious, aspect of all repression. Correspondingly, eliminative impulses can become dominant in the treatment of deviancies deemed impure. Not only are their "carriers" eliminated from social life, but all kinds of procedures are employed which are said to help the ill to eliminate their badness or sickness: from blood or bowel purges to electrically or chemically induced spastic states or a treatment philosophy emphasizing "catharsis" or "abreaction." And we may recognize even in the overstrict use of even the best-meant diagnostic categories a tendency to mark classes of individuals as permanently out of bounds.

My purpose in pointing to such parallels is the suggestion that even as Freud has made us see the irrational lengths to which inner repression will lead—and I have described his approach to this destructive aspect of conscience as a method of nonviolence toward the self—he has also pointed to a potentially destructive trend inherent not only in ancient institutions but also in the more verifiable methods of a technological period. Now, many methods can prove beneficial in the treatment of some patients when carried out plausibly and in accord with a communal value system consistent with them; and every society obviously needs its own definitions of deviancy and convincing methods of dealing with it. But the widespread inactivation of deviant individuals under the pretense that they are not ready for or, indeed, do not deserve the freedom to be active and must first earn it by a display of compliance can only further weaken what is left of their active adaptiveness and thus, in the long run, weaken society. For there can be little doubt that traditional forms of prolonged confinement force the inmate, who usually is already at odds with what true communality (if any) he has experienced on the outside, to relinquish any basic wish to find a new beginning in himself, and thus any hope for a new communal beginning. Once forced, however, for lack of any active alternatives, to accept the inmate identity as the only "confirmation" available to him, he can only attempt to put his trust in a common mistrust shared by all fellow inmates; to seek an exertion of his will in smaller or bigger acts of perverted willfulness; to find purpose and competence in playing the devious game of inmateship; and to invest his fidelity in tasks as self-destructive as they are destructive for the community.

What we have to work for, then, are not only methods which will undo what has been overdone (and much remarkable reorientation is taking place in our time) but also a certain insight into the universal reasons for which methods dealing with deviances are apt to be overdone in the first place. For it seems only too obvious that an abrupt "turning into the opposite" of a method previously employed (another well-known defense mechanism) can only result in some additional confusion—as does, for example, the widespread release of confined patients back into their communities before either they or the communities are ready with a new orientation and with new facilities. And all action without insight is apt to result in another "deal" between a seeming practicality that is all too easily rationalized and unconscious remedial impulses which in both origin and effect are apt to prove irrational.

It is the merit of the authors' work in a therapeutic community that, as artists, craftsmen, and educators, they took hold of one of the prime problems of confinement, namely, the problem of inactivation. But as we can see, this emphasis points beyond recovery and rehabilitation. Conceptually, it touches on the relation of the developing ego, the ordering core in the individual, both to activity and to communality. And, indeed, at the time when the Activities Program was created at Riggs, these matters were receiving much attention in the work of Riggs theorists under the leadership of the late David Rapaport, who did his well-known best to make place for them in psychoanalytic theory. At stake here is the nature of the various conditions for an inspired active state: from the ego's activated adaptability and heightened sense of reality, to the mobilized condition of the whole person-in-action, and, finally, to the mutual actualization of individuals on which all communality depends.

On Communality

Having chosen to introduce their account with a brief review of the most constricted habitations reserved for deviants, the authors envision in conclusion the role of planned activities in the community at large. And, indeed, once we perceive what an activities program in a favorable communal setting can help to do for patients, we may well ask what it might have done for them and many others before they ever became patients in search of a communality. But the aspirations given form here go much further. The kind of community center proposed is meant to serve as a medium and a symbol for the realization of islands of active communality serving truly "collective" ends in the midst of that diffused centrifugality imposed on us all by mere quantitatve "growth"—and diffusion.

To be sure, at this very moment, mankind faces quantitative triumphs and disasters which seem to demand that our attention be focused on issues of the largest scale, accessible only to specialists in corporate statistics, and seemingly calling for a relentless specialization of future generations so that they may learn to manage a technological civilization. Who would have the courage, then, to speak of community centers taking up old warehouses and providing centers for neighborhoods where so far there are often only formless aggregates of families, many on the move, living in unrelated rows of dwellings?

But our developmental point of view reminds us that new generations are born every day and that neither social evolution nor planetary technology has changed the laws by which mind organisms grow and are motivated. Thus the motivation as well as the capacity to master the quantitative dangers of the future must be rooted in the quality of daily life. Every single individual develops by physical, cognitive, and emotional steps which begin with a playful acquaintance with the body's instinctual, sensory, and cognitive modes of experience in interplay with the maternal environment; proceed in childhood with the mastery of the toy microcosm and with self-abandonment to the playing out of imaginary roles in games; and lead in school age to the acquisition of some competence in dealing with the rules intrinsic in all materials and techniques. In adolescence and youth, such competencies are gradually combined in a work identity within the technology and ideology of the times. But the law of epigenesis insists that none of the earlier stages are ever abandoned; they may, in adulthood, become part of a style of maturity, but they must continue to be cultivated for the sake of individual integration, and they surely must persist into old age, and this especially where longevity outlasts the life style of specialized commitment.

This means that the playfulness of childhood, which depends on choice and improvisation and yet is filled with curiosity to see how things work, must be neither abandoned nor shunted into the category of mere "recreation." For on its rests the experimentation with the methods and the completion of tasks characteristic of continuous learning. Thus, the work competence which finds both an identity and a communality in the production of commodities not only rests on previous developments, but must continue to refine them. It is in this sense that I find plausible the claim that what is here called planned activities can be shared in communal centers by persons of all ages and backgrounds, and can include a wide variety of tasks and projects, individual and cooperative—if they are only guided by the principles of inspired choice.

It is, then, by no means romantic or reactionary to insist that communal acquaintance with planned activities keep alive those most basic affirmations in the material and the natural world which have guided mankind through most of its social evolution and also remain basic for the comprehension of mechanical laws. Planned activities, with their simple properties, are ready to reward efforts which at the same time form a most natural basis for the kind of communication that makes neighbors of strangers of all ages. For they bypass some of the ambiguities and the ambivalences of verbal communication and thus of language barriers. Materials wordlessly speak for themselves and say the same to everybody. If you prove responsive to them, they will respond to you without argument, apology, or blame. They offer a range of cognitive discoveries and confirmations—from the simplest to the complex. Similarly, things that grow are without ambivalence, without triumph or complaint in their clear indication of what will help them unfold or what will make them wilt, and only demand that you apply to them the simplest wish to foster growth and prevent decay.

It has taken psychiatry a long time to acknowledge the role of communality and activity in the recovery and the growth of the individual. In the meantime, however, a whole array of spontaneous social trends has emerged which indicate a widespread awareness of the fact that the core of the community, in turn, is in the participant individuals. Many modern developments suggest a search for *polarities* (rather than the reciprocal exclusion) of, say, individuality and communality, of neighborliness and worldwide empathy, of erotic and physical experience and spiritual and ideological search, and of a sharpened sense of significant origins as well as the search for an ill-human identity. The list of references attached to this book points to an as yet diverse and dispersed literature on new patterns of communal experience, whether they concern a new attention to the body's indwelling potentials, to the mind's capacity for self-awareness, or to the promises of greater communal honesty in daily life. In all this, there is a search for a training of consciousness which, far from superfluous, may be a necessary counterpart and balance to the as yet so bewildering comprehension of unconscious forces. I am not unaware of the faddish dangers and the exploitability of all such diverse trends. My point is that they have in common a new vision which will find its institutional forms. And here, activities centers may well play a vital role.

If I may, in conclusion, come back once more to our professional experience, Joan Erikson and I had the privilege of participating in some conferences organized by the late architect Constantinos Doxiadis. There, an international and interdisciplinary group of experts periodically discussed the future of cities,* and I was encouraged to enlarge on how the planned city of tomorrow might reflect the spatial needs of a newborn, a growing, a grown, and an aging human being: not a return to the village, to be sure (not even to such "villages" as stubbornly survive in our urban agglomerations), but a planning for

* *Anthropopolis: City for Human Development* (New York: W.W. Norton, 1975).

dwelling places responsive to the needs of individual lives and generational interplay. Fully linked with the best of communication, transportation, and trade, they would yet be literally centered in order to meet the vital needs of individuals of all ages—including their needs for each other. In such new neighborhoods, we could certainly see a truly central function for the kind of activities centers envisioned in this book: they could offer to the most ancient of all arts as well as to their modern proliferations a concrete home.

V.
THOUGHTS ON
THE LIFE CYCLE

Problems of Infancy and Early Childhood (1940)

INTRODUCTION—The present accepted division of labor in the care of the child places him alternately in the hands of the training and punishing, the curing, or the teaching adult. Consequently, the child's problems are variously interpreted: He "just does not know better," is "bad," "physically sick," or "mentally sick." However, under the influence of psychiatric enlightenment, the importance of the *combinations and fluctuations in well-being, well-behaving, and well-learning* are being increasingly understood: It is conceded that a child's scholastic level may decline because of an undiscovered disease; that a naughty child may be hounded by fears or be the victim of environmental shortcomings; that a sickly and irritable one may be "craving for attention" at any price.

What is known scientifically of human behavior problems has its source in *psychopathology* (especially psychoanalysis) and in *psychology*. These branches of science tell how an individual behaves or what he says about himself and his life only (1) if he feels sick enough to *surrender himself* to the guidance (hypnosis, suggestion,

First published in *Cyclopedia of Medicine* (Philadelphia: Davis Co., 1940), 714–30. Reprinted in *Outline of Abnormal Psychology*, eds. Gardner Murphy and Arthur J. Bachrach (New York: Modern Library, 1954), 3–36. This article is Erikson's first paper on human development and the life stages.

psychoanalysis, etc.) of a therapist; (2) if he, for one reason or another, is ready and capable of *lending easily isolated* parts of his mind or body (vision, audition, memory, learning, etc.) to a tester or experimenter. In either case he is not the person met with in the give and take of a family situation.

There are indications that even regarding its most disturbing subject, man's emotions, science is arriving at methods comparable to the use of x-rays in the investigation of the organism, which allow for the study of vital mechanisms under circumstances not constricting or disturbing the integrity of the personality. But today the practitioner, turning to established psychologies to learn what a child is, mentally and emotionally, still finds himself confronted with strange pictures—which depict either psychological mechanisms in the state of pathological insurrection or synthetic robots reconstructed from single isolated reflexes, instincts, growth patterns, or other mechanisms. Each robot functions only in terms of its own terminology, and without a complete knowledge of this terminology (which often excludes the understanding of all the others), the way back to the problems of the living child is a lengthy and a hard one.

What is a virtue in science, namely scepticism as to what can be known, unfortunately in practice often turns into inhibitory fatalism in regard to what may be done. The individual child is rarely as good or as bad as the tests show him to be; there is a large field of balance and chance provided by human contact, which makes practice, inspired and corrected by research as it is, an art in its own right, developing in and by its own experiences.

In this sense the present chapter can only attempt to offer a few guiding concepts which the writer found basic to much that is being done in practice as well as in research, and to problems of the misbehaving as well as the untrained or mentally sick child.

I. Fetal Development

Beginning with an analogy taken from a time of life when the human being cannot possibly be thought bad or stupid, and when a differentiation between physical and mental sickness really does not make sense, namely the fetal stage, what can the consequences of an interference with fetal development teach the investigator about the hazards of all growth?

Embryology has developed from the concept of the homunculus, a minute, but completely preformed man waiting *in utero* to be

awakened, to expand and to jump into life, to the present understanding of what is called *epigenetic development*, the step by step
growth of the fetal organs.

In this development each organ has its time of origin and this time
factor is as important as the place of origin. If the eye, for example,
does not arise at the appointed time "it will never be able to express
itself fully, since the moment for the rapid outgrowth of some other
part will have arrived, and this will tend to dominate the less active
region, and suppress the belated tendency for eye expression."[1]

After the organ has begun to arise at the right time, still another
time factor determines the most critical stage of its development:
"A given organ must be interrupted during the early stage of its
development in order to be completely suppressed or grossly modified. . . . After an organ has arisen successfully from the anlage, it
may be lamed or runted, but its nature and actual existence can
no longer be destroyed by interrupting the growth."

The organ which misses its time of ascendency not only is doomed
as an individual but endangers at the same time the whole hierarchy
of organs. "Not only does the arrest of a rapidly budding part,
therefore, tend to suppress its development temporarily, but the premature loss of supremacy to some other organ renders it impossible
for the suppressed part to come again into dominance, so that it is
permanently modified. . . ." The result of normal development is
proper relationship of size and function among the body organs: The
liver adjusted in size to the stomach and intestine, the heart and lungs
properly balanced, and the capacity of the vascular system accurately
proportioned to the body as a whole. Through developmental arrest
one or more organs may become disproportionately small; this upsets
functional harmony and produces a defective person.

If *"proper rate"* and *"normal sequence"* are disturbed, the outcome may be a *monstrum in excessu* or a *monstrum in defectu*: "The
fact that the normal individual stands between these two arbitrary
classes of abnormalities has no significance other than that the abnormal *deviations* are simply modifications of the normal condition
resulting from unusual reductions in the rate of development during
certain critical stages."

II. Developmental Behavior

The most critical time in terms of possible organic monstrosities are
the months before birth; once born, the body has "successfully arisen

from its anlage," or can soon be diagnosed as being too defective for integrated maturation. The normative steps (and the possible defects) of this extrauterine maturation (in so far as they are more or less independent of the cultural differences in the environment) are being described in child development literature. They build the basis for the individual's search for contact with the stimulating environment and thus for the unfolding of his social potentialities: "Proper rate" and "normal sequence" are the critical factors in the successive manifestations of "personality" as well as in that of intrauterine growth. Naturally, slight individual variations forming an "epigenetic personality" must be assumed to characterize both the physical and mental growth processes before and after birth; the difference between prenatal and postnatal life is further minimized by the fact that a first unfolding of extrauterine behavior can take place only in a balanced maternal surrounding, almost an extrauterine womb, which protects the newborn infant against untimely irritations, slowly training him for the acceptance of the physical and cultural reality into which he has been born.

Animals with a long, protected childhood play most. Least prepared for rapid adaptation, and protected longer than any other being, man begins to learn by means of play, experiment, and speculation. The changing aspects of his bodily growth and the constant increases in his ability to perceive, to touch, to grasp, to master, to make social contacts cause him to "invent" new forms of playful activity involving smaller systems (mouth, hands, speech organs, genitals, feces, etc.) or larger systems of his body (kicking, creeping, climbing, etc.), small or big objects (grasping, throwing, tearing, banging, smearing, filling, pushing, arranging, etc.), imaginary or real persons (playing with nipples or face, smiling, holding, pulling, pushing, etc.). These activities are characterized by periods of exclusive fascination and endless repetition; they shall be called here *developmental habits*. Whether they are the child's official habits, for which tests have been found because they are obvious steps to certain skills; or his unofficial habits, which, as doubtful contributors to the developing personality, are the personal concern of mothers and teachers, *it is first of all important to realize that in the sequence of these habits the child merely obeys, and on the whole can be trusted to obey inner laws of development, namely those laws which in his prenatal period had formed one organ after another, and now (as these organs search out reality) create one behavior item after another.*

III. First Social Problems of Extrauterine Behavior

A survey of the first sequence of developmental problems, *i.e.*, the conflicts of searching impulses with the cultural realities of the very maternal environment under the protection of which they unfold, shows them to be problems of *incorporation, retention-elimination,* and *intrusion*. They develop as the organ systems expressing them first become capable of co-ordinated activity; and as this activity (centered as it is on certain sensitive body zones) is in the process of being modified by the environment, they become the first cultural problems of a new personality. Thus the urge to incorporate parts of the outer world is expressed first in the inborn readiness of *mouth* and *senses*, including the whole *tactual* surface of the body; the discrimination between what portions of this world are to be held on to (retained) and what pushed away (eliminated) is a matter of the more mature *muscle* system including the *sphincter* muscles; while intrusion into the sphere of other beings becomes a major issue when the *locomotor* system is more mature and some *genital sensitivity* established. These systems in which the growing periphery of action and the acculturation of the vital orifices of the body become integrated require detailed attention.

(*a*) INCORPORATION—From the moment the first breath of air is inhaled the baby is dependent on the delivery of environmental "materia" (air, food, sensory stimuli, emotional stimuli, etc.) right to the doors of his organism, so that he can incorporate them and—in constant assimilation—mature. The baby's first vital and pleasurable experiences are feeding (including his olfactory, tactual, and gustatory implications) and sensations such as touching, stroking, rocking, if they are below the threshold at which joyful acceptance changes so abruptly into diffused muscle defense. According to the cephalo-caudal growth tendencies already effective *in utero*, the mouth is the first organ ready to act co-ordinately when stimulated by tactual sensations; the eyes and then the hands follow in the co-ordinated search for objects. Whatever the organism thus learns to grasp goes into the mouth, or if there is nothing to reach, the fingers and later the toes become ready objects for the baby's oral and visual curiosity. Thus the radius of and the initiative in incorporation are increased; incorporation being satisfactorily accomplished, the baby returns for a while to an exclusion of all outer world stimuli, namely, sleep.

(*b*) RETENTION-ELIMINATION—In learning actively to incorporate, the child gradually develops the ability to express individual discrimination for incoming objects more co-ordinately. If the environment's way of delivering or withholding desired objects has not already irritated him during the oral phase (*i.e.*, if the thumb has regularly been removed from the mouth or food forced into it), his discrimination in regard to the outer world becomes now the normal issue of the educational battle. The zone of the body most apt to dramatize retention and elimination, especially if interfered with too abruptly, is the anal zone, which at this time in many children has become the seat of sensual and cathartic experiences (probably initiated also by more formed stools). The general impulses dominating this period can express themselves rather violently. Unlike the previous stages, when incorporation at any cost seemed the rule of behavior, now strong, sometimes "unreasonable," discrimination takes place; sensations are in rapid succession accepted, rejected; objects are clung to stubbornly or thrown away violently; persons are obstinately demanded or pushed away angrily—tendencies which under the influence of educational factors easily develop into temporary or lasting extremes of self-insistent behavior.

It is at this stage that the undisturbed infant, after having experienced delusions of omnipotence and panics of impotence, comprehends "power." Also, after having clung to and disposed of things not belonging to him (and this includes the food which he considers his divine right and the feces which his own inside has manufactured) he experiences what "property" means. The previous stage has taught him: "You may not find pleasure in incorporation except under certain conditions." Now he learns "You may find pleasure in keeping or throwing away, in retaining or eliminating, only under certain conditions."

(*c*) INTRUSION—New problems arise out of the increasing mobility of the child's body and growing curiosity. Suddenly feeling himself in the possession of what must appear to him to be an unbounded mastery over space, the child follows new ideas of attacking and conquering; he wants to be everywhere, to enter everything, and to know all secrets.

It is in this period of violent activity that a divination of what it means to overwhelm and to be overwhelmed (in acts which are felt to be cruel or sexual or both) takes possession of the child. This is the time of increased gential masturbation, since the genital zone, destined later on to search for a partner, together with the locomotor system, has taken over some of the cathartic function for all otherwise frustrated impulses, which before were concentrated on incorporative and eliminative organ systems. For children who have been or are denied too many aspects of self-satisfaction and self-expression, and who are therefore hounded by too many unpacified developmental fears, the genitals are the last zone to hold on to—and that literally. To the girl this latter stage offers special problems, since it is during this period of stronger intrusive tendencies (tomboyishness) and increased curiosity that the girl senses her role as the inceptive object of male intrusive tendencies.

Every new class of spontaneous activity in the healthy child heralds a configuration of new, vital maturation factors such as:

1. An *impulse* emerging from the reservoir of inherited human instincts (first, as was seen, the impulse to incorporate).

2. A specific *sensual* (*libidinal*) *experience* (*i.e.*, tactual and muscular pleasure of lips, gums, etc.) of singularly pleasurable character.

3. A channel for the *release* (catharsis) of *surplus tension* from various sources (*i.e.*, thumb-sucking or other mannerisms as normal developmental habits in connection with feeding, but also when the child is tired, dissatisfied, or scared).

4. Specific trial and error *experiments* of a physical or social nature (*i.e.*, "Can I take my toe in my mouth? . . . Does the toe taste like the finger or like the rubber nipple? . . . Can I get people excited again if I put my thumb into my mouth?")

5. A complex of omnipotence and impotence fantasies depicting the child in the unlimited possession or the complete deprivation of the desired object (breast [?] mother, food).

6. A new focus for the expectation of danger, *i.e.*, an intolerance toward all interferences which may bring frustration to 1, 2, and 3. If increased by constitutional or environmental factors, this intolerance may lead to an abnormal intensity or prolongation of the developmental habit (*i.e.*, excessive thumb-sucking) and severe anxiety and rage in the face of attempts to break it.

7. *Reaction formations* (oral loathing) and other changes in the personality which can be understood as permanent, defensive reactions against the impulse in so far as in the course of maturation it can [be neither] satisfied nor outgrown nor used in socially approved action patterns.

8. *Sublimations*, the utilization of the fate of the impulse for the development and the enrichment of the personality (*i.e.*, oral satisfaction may strengthen confidence and the optimistic anticipation of new experiences *per se*: oral reaction formations may augment caution, restraint, and taste in the acceptance of new experience).

9. A potential *developmental fixation*, building the basis for a

future potential *developmental regression* (*i.e.,* return to oral mannerisms in connection with certain general attributes of suckling behavior when later impulses meet with frustration). The *incompatibility of fixation and progression* is the most common kernel of infantile neuroses.

An effort has been made here to give a rough framework for the innumerable habits of the child as they consecutively dominate his social experiences as well as the *maturation* of his organism. Incorporation, assimilation, retention, elimination, and instrusion are some of the basic problems of organismic existence on all biological levels. In every world contact, be it physical, emotional, or intellectual, some part or stimulus of the outer world will pass through the individual, and his attitude toward this (wished for or imposed) foreign body entering his personal sphere is the main expression of what is called his individual personality. The Arapesh, a tribe in New Guinea, offer this characterology in regard to an individual's ratio of listening and speaking: "There are those whose ears and throats are open; those whose ears are open and whose throats are shut; those whose ears are shut and whose throats are open; and those whose ears and throats are both shut."[2] Physical as well as emotional and intellectual self-preservation demands that one accept, keep, digest, and eliminate; give and receive; take and be taken *in fair ratio*. Whether the under or overdevelopment of one impulse is based on constitutional inclinations or excessive modification by the environment, it decisively and systematically changes the organization of all the others and creates more or less pathological *monstra in excessu* and *monstra in defectu*. There are "suckers," "biters," "retainers," "expellers," and "intruders" in all fields of human life, and there are types of personality which suffer from impotence in or or more of these impulses.

The clinican must be especially interested in the question as to what the range of an individual's tolerance of impulse modification is—and the social scientist must ask how long such modification serves the cultural unit of which the individual is a member.

IV. Latency

If, after infancy, the bodily functions and impulses have successfully arisen in all their importance as intermediaries between inside and outside, the *procreative organs* are the only ones to be arrested by the so-called latency period until adolescence (the last epigenetic crisis), and to unfold only then their full physiological and experiential patterns. In latent genital sexuality are also latent all the associations with the critical impulses, habits, frustrations, and fears of his earlier development. Unresolved developmental problems of the earlier stages, therefore, continue to express themselves often in neurotic sex habits (exceeding normal developmental sex habits) and *in a final association of all the developmental fears into a system of neurotic fears which focus on the danger to the still developing procreative organs ("castration complex")*. In future sex life, there is no part of the body surface which cannot play a role in healthy (preliminary) sex play or make itself an independent subject for exclusive (final) gratification in perversions. It is here, as Freud has concluded from his psychopathological material, that the individual, hunting for the sensual experiences and the self-assertion missed in the sequence of childhood pleasures, is most apt to be driven to seek—and at the same time to be blocked in seeking—fulfillments, the mere idea of which in the vast majority of individuals has to be suppressed before it ever entered full consciousness (repression).[3]

Infancy (the reality vacuum protecting the child's first experimentation in mere existence) and latency (the epigenetic vacuum allowing for instructive experience in the classified world of a culture before any participation in its procreation) are both specifically human and intimately connected with man's creation of cultures. On the other hand, his initial helplessness, his retarded sexual maturation, and the tendency to repress all ideas which are associated with sexuality— and thus, as was seen, many of his most intensive childhood memories—are the strongest factors in man's mental suffering.

In the latency period the child enters school and the foundation is laid for the understanding of those rationalizations and classifications of culture in the frame of which human impulses are trusted to make the world safer.

V. Developmental Fears

Experimenting in physical safety, the infant expands (step by step) the limits which are his protective womb and his prison—until these limits coincide with the adult world in which he finds other members of his society sharing his newly found securities and fears. Until then he is often hounded in a most lonely, individual manner by fears which are never verbalized though he may later find them to be taken care of by religious cults and historical, political, or scientific myths.

Anxiety is for the personality what pain is for the body: a sign that coherence and integration are endangered by what is happening to one part or function. Since the child, in the changing worlds of his growth, has the continuous task of re-establishing coherence, integration, and mastery while threatened with physical perils and psychological frustrations, he is apt to experience moments of anxiety which must be considered normal.

Thus many of the child's first fears are the subjective aspects of growth, *i.e.,* they express the *anxious expectation that in a moment of realignment of forces he may be overwhelmed by a power without or within himself*, that functions of the self or the body may either *not be allowed to manifest themselves fully* or, if unchecked, *overwhelm the whole child.*

Best understood are those based on the infant's helplessness and slowness in co-ordinated defense; anything too loud, too bright, too sudden or quick, etc., seems to cut through his senses right into the heart of his existence. Dependent on being fed, he often seems to be overcome by a panicky rage if nourishment is not forthcoming, and it may be concluded from psychopathological observations that there is an anxiety that he will be left empty and helpless in the face of overwhelming impulses demands. Having filled his stomach all too eagerly, he appears to be bothered by a desperate feeling that he cannot assimilate or eliminate the foreign body quickly and sufficiently enough (an overanxious mother seems to the child to share these fears); later, forced to empty his bowels at appointed times, he may feel deprived of vital possessions. He is, of course, afraid of being dropped, or of falling; on the other hand, he soon hates to be held too tightly, or to be held back, and this ambiguity is basic for the quandary of his extrauterine existence in general.

The continuous change in time and space perspective often makes for insecurity in the mind of the child as to what part of development is predestined, what dependent on human will. Will he grow too much or too little? Will parts of him grow monstrously or shrink again and disappear altogether? Who tells the baby when to be born? Who makes girls out of boys? When does a baby begin; when does a dead person stop living? Already a small child seriously though unsuccessfully theorizes about sex and death, the two incomprehensible dangers which seem to wait at the end of every road of feeling and reasoning.

Except in play, the child rarely verbalizes his world. Only he who enters the child's world as a polite guest and studies play as a most serious occupation learns what a child thinks when he is not forced to adapt himself to the verbalized and classified world. It is the great function of fairy tales that they make play, in safety, of what is too big to be mastered in the child's own play. In *Alice in Wonderland*, most probably, the child finds most of his developmental fantasies verbalized—and played with.

Children, in an unverbalized form, know more about adults (in so far as they are children without suspecting it) than adults know of them. But because of verbal and mechanical virtuosity, they also assume adults to know more than they do. They expect adults, especially those against whom they have aggressive fantasies, to know or feel their thoughts and, furthermore, to have the right and the means to do to a child what the child can only dream of doing to others. Thus the smaller child's only protection against the constantly changing perspectives of dangers arising within or without himself is the experience of meeting on each of his various levels adults who deal firmly and *consistently* with him; only thus can the gradual incorporation of adult standards and characteristics lead to the formation of a stable person consistent in himself.

A child is especially terrified of sudden changes in adults if he lives in an overprotected atmosphere, which means usually one hostile to impulsive expression, so that he has never learned to size up how far the adult actually may go in a really fought-out issue. His confusion is increased if impulsive acts on the part of the parents are denied or rationalized (such as parental ill temper explained as being indulged in only "for the child's good"). He is overwhelmed by the sudden experience of an adult flaring into an impotent tantrum, or giving in to panicky moods. He is appalled to observe sexual activities in which the parents seem overwhelmed by what he has been taught are dirty impulses. "Who then is the really big adult who defends order against chaos?"

It goes without saying that for a child who is frightened by his own impulses and fantasies nothing is "accidental." If he has been threateningly warned against a certain act, any accident or sickness or any kind of traumatic impression experienced in connection with this act is more than accidental; it is Nemesis. Furthermore, if a slight injury is suffered, an accident observed, or a new dangerous fact is discovered (for example, the difference between boys and girls) which has a specific association with the impulses and fears of the period in question, it may take on overwhelming dimensions. Anything can be felt as personal guilt; the mother, having given birth to another child, has "bought another baby because the first one is not good enough for her any more"; the (dead) grandmother or the (dismissed) nurse "went away because one was not nice to her"— and so on *ad infinitum.*

It must be obvious that these fears, if fed by unwise and inconsistent restrictions, lead to an increase of habits as *pacifying activities in moments of extreme subjective danger.* Developmental habits, such as sucking and biting mannerisms, fingerplay involving hair, nose, etc., body-rocking, head-banging, wetting and soiling, spitting, smearing, motor restlessness, tic-like mannerisms, genital or anal masturbation, speech mannerisms, lying, etc., become fixed under the influence of unresolved anxiety, *i.e.,* become fixed under the influence of unresolved anxiety, *i.e.,* become compulsive habits. If they then are "broken," only neurosis or character deformation through excessive inhibition can result; in the paragraph on LATENCY, the author has indicated why the form of interference with genital habits is of special pathogenic importance for later life.

No form of temporary play, habit, or fear is the origin of a neurosis, or is dangerous to the child who is not already neurotic; and for the neuroses, it is always the totality of the child's life situation that should be blamed, or better, should be investigated. It is only known that if anything traumatic does happen to a child, be it an accidental, peripheral happening, or a specific threat to body or self, *the tendencies just "budding up" are the most severely hit, excessive or defective abnormalities in the child's personality are created, and the developmental fears corresponding to his stage of growth and maturation are associated to build a nucleus of the spreading system of anxiety.* Whether and when this will lead to the outbreak of a neurosis depend on many other factors, which will be referred to on the following pages.

VI. Social Relativity of Psychological Status

The child's body is his first vocabulary; and this far into the time when he has been provided with words for a certain selection of experiences. For this reason the psychological aspects of mere growth have been dealt with first.

However, it is obvious that the small individual's psychological status can only be defined in terms of how individuals change in relation to what is moving around them; this fact may be conceptualized as the *social relativity of the individual's psychological status.* Even an organic concept of human behavior, as has been seen, leads unfailingly to social concepts if not to social ideologies. This, it seems, separates, once and for all, human psychology from natural science.

Personality disturbances only in rare cases appear to have been created by any one single factor in body or mind, in heredity, constitution, or environment. Human beings, and especially children, are seen to defend their psychic integrity most successfully in the face of one or more great handicaps. Only where several of these factors unite in crushing the psychological defense system of a personality are real emotional crises created. The most dangerous combination of such factors implies the coincidence in time and the mutual aggravation of the following groups: (1) Changes in the *body* brought about by growth, maturation, or some other disbalancing factor, such as sickness, resulting in new or stronger impulses or fears; (2) changes in the constellation or emotional temperature in the *environment* (*i.e.*, birth, death, sickness, moving, trips, visitors, change of nurses; estrangement between parents and/or grandparents; financial worries; religious scruples); (3) changes in the person's *conception of his psychological status in the world, i.e.*, a tightening of the rules of conscience (guilt feelings) or a change in the conception of psychological causality (inferiority feelings, projective misunderstandings, etc.) because of the irrational association between one's bad deeds, wishes, or fears with extrapersonal changes, such as the above mentioned.

It has been pointed out that nothing appears to be accidental to the anxious child. It is also important to understand that the child's conscience (later on an important part of his unconscious) does not preserve what the parents actually said or meant to say, but what the child, with the selective perception of his particular stage and state of mind, understood them to say.

(Thus a boy with strong aggressive characteristics, during an especially disquieting period of muscular growth, may be fascinated and terrified by mystifying tales of crime and police; if during such a phase something happens to a relative or friend against whom he has recently shown or felt violent aggression, he may take this so much to heart that he will try to inhibit himself beyond his constitutional capacity for self-control. His disturbed psychobiological economy may then react with the formation of a symptom, the potentiality for which has been latent in it.)

VII. The Parents

In the center of the epigenetic description stood the growing body; in the center of the consideration of social relativity naturally is placed the figure of the protecting and training mother. Whatever developmental, whatever accidental factor may have delighted or disturbed the child, he is sure to have experienced it in relation to his mother. Especially if anxious, he is always in flight to her or away from her— a characteristic remaining with neurotics for life (with a transference of the mother-image on other persons or on institutions). The mother stands between the baby and the world; she is the first to gratify and to frustrate, to be loved and to be hated, to be idealized and to create disillusionment. To secure the mother's affection by remaining or *appearing helpless* like the small siblings; to secure her undivided attention and some form of physical contact with her, even by *provoking* corporal punishment; to secure her admiration by doing *"big" deeds* like the older siblings and the father; *to be like her* to the extent of feeling and suffering with her, or *to be liked by her* physically and mentally at any price, even that of turning against otherwise loved rivals (especially the father, who thus may become an object of fear); these are the changing aims for the attainment of which a child often goes far out of his natural way. Only a motherly combination of friendliness and firmness in the face of constantly changing provocation can prevent him from getting stuck in any of his roles, and can help him—always changing, experimenting, pretending, and playing—to become himself. As these tendencies appear and disappear on the surface of behavior, they may result in not so easily observable *lasting identifications* with father, mother, or other important members of the household. If a person of the other sex is chosen as leading image, special conflicts arise.

In the first few years the child is very susceptible to physical and emotional change in the mother, gradually also to that in the father. Often his problem is only a part of a disturbance in the mother (for example, her anxiety over food or dislike of dirt), as his body was once a part of hers; in this case their common anxiety may bind them together to such an extent that interference from outside is impossible; or a queer estrangement may push them apart. A mother and a child are never alone; through the mother's conscience, generations are looking on, integrating the relationship with their approval or dividing it with their disapproval into countless disturbing details. It is always useful to know in what educational constellation the mother and father grew up: whether in a family dominated by the grandfather or by the grandmother; whether the grandparents lived for their children or made the children live for them; whether the parent was the only child or there were many children; whether among them there were one or many brothers, one or many sisters, etc. Often mother and father are fighting educational battles with their children which have remained undecided in their own childhood; families, generations, races, classes, cultures may be found to be represented in small differences which are jealousy guarded. Physicians have no right to belittle them; they once were, are, or are going to be the safeguard and symbol of virtues which helped a group to maintain itself in its historical setting. They are thus comparable to the developmental habits of the child, which, if they become compulsive, deserve serious consideration.

VIII. Habits and Culture

The various experiences described in the previous chapters are not fixated on any one zone or function for a long time unless there are arresting constitutional or environmental factors. A sensible valuation of habits and fears, one would think, would be based solely on the time and duration of their existence. Different habits should be expected from the baby whose mouth is the zone of the body, most urgently demanding experiences by cutaneous contact, than from the infant whose muscles, developing quickly, make him enjoy contraction and relaxation and allow him the first successful acts of self-willed muscle aggression. Different habits should be expected in the child who is just able to move toward fascinating objects (property or not property), and in the child who, still rightfully mistrusting the ambiguity of language, has to experiment with truth and reality by asking and telling more or less humorous nonsense or lies. Habits of an earlier stage should even be expected to return now and again when a later stage passes through a crisis, or a child is tired, frightened, or sick. However, possessed as he is by sensitive zones, developing functions, an increasing social awareness, the child inadvertently reaches into the sphere of adult concern by his intolerance of being interrupted and the stubborn expansion of his activity into what is called naughtiness or diagnosed as a symptom. An anxious quandary arises: "When is it known for sure that he is temporarily misbehaving, and how is it known when he is definitely disturbed?"

The easiest answer to this question is given by the voice of tradition; if this voice fails, great anxiety rises. It is as if everybody felt that tradition (as long as it is a part of a living culture) establishes channels of mutual self-regulation between body and mind, adult and child, individual and culture—poles of existence which are hard to comprehend rationally.

It is no mere accident then that the branches of science most concerned with what seems to be irrational manifestations of the human mind, *i.e.*, psychopathology and recently also anthropology, began to focus their attention on the early training problems of the child in their relation to his total individual and cultural potentialities. To the psychopathologist, and especially the psychoanalyst, the dangers of interrupting the child's behavior development unwisely seem to resemble those in all epigenetic development: If anything is *suppressed at the beginning*, then characterological and mental potentialities may be destroyed and characterological monstra created. The matter is complicated, however, by the fact that spoiling in any single respect, by which is meant active help in overindulgence rather than mere patience with one habit or a group of habits, has the same total effect, because it makes it impossible for the experience involved to find its proper status among other experiences.

Since the forms of neurosis appear to be the price paid in psychological currency for membership in civilization, it seems worth while to compare the present training and education with that of primitives.

Primitive people, though they are relatively freer from the educational guerrilla warfare of the nurseries, and frequently abhor present-day methods of education, nevertheless experience certain very early as well as very cruel educational restrictions. But students of their societies increasingly realize that, far from being arbitrarily lenient or cruel, these educational systems are logical in the sense that they tried to create the anthropological "monstrum" which is, or once was, the *optimum* under the natural and historic conditions of the tribe. Thus, in simple cultures, training of the individual and preservation of the race appear to regulate one another automatically. Primitive societies cannot be used as an argument for hostility to training as such. On the whole, however, they seem successfully to avoid both *the early deep estrangement between body and self in the individual and between children and adults of a generation*—the commonest background of anxiety in individuals (young and old).[4] The secret of their highly successful educational methods, regardless of the type of frustration imposed, seems to be the unquestioned promise of a participation in the (early comprehensible) prestige possibilities of the community.

Present-day education, in comparison, increasingly tends not only to suppress single acts of infantile habits, but also to devaluate in the small child the subjective potentialities of epigenetic development, namely, *pleasure and will as such*. It need only be remembered that the child's personal integrity is violated by calling *bodily expression as such "bad" or "sinful"*; that the security of the child-parent relationship is jeopardized by the threat (to the very small child) of *physical harm or psychological isolation coming from the parents themselves*.

In view of the critical importance of the time element in development, it is furthermore a grave question whether too much of the individual's biological endowment is not risked if it is tried to *mechanize out impulse life* along with the surroundings in resorting to the plausible and comforting assumption that educational conflicts can be avoided by very early training. This, it is supposed, leads to automatic, so to speak, impersonal compliance and maximum efficiency. It is argued that the method works with dogs. Dogs, however, are trained to serve and to die; they will not be forced to represent to their young what their masters represented to them. Children will train their children, and any impoverishment of their impulse life will have to be considered not only in its value for a functioning without too much friction during one lifetime; generations will depend on every procreating individual's ability to face his children with the feeling that he was able to save some vital enthusiasm from the conflicts of his childhood.

There is a tendency in the medical world to help young mothers who are in conflict with the tasks of their maternal functions to rationalize the deprivations which they impose on their babies (*i.e.*, withholding of nursing or caressing), by giving precedence to considerations of personal desires. This meets the tendency of many pediatricians to help an increasingly weakening parenthood to sidetrack the issue of authority and discipline in shifting training to that earlier time of the baby's life when it seems more an automatic than a human issue. Both procedures should be carefully revised; however, it may be that the medical world in many areas is faced here with a cultural process stronger than itself.

It is to be regretted that beyond the suspicions of the psychopathologists and the theories of the experimentalists, no scientific material exists on which a clear-cut answer to the totality of these problems can be based.

What is needed is a comparative science of child training, replacing the traditions which sooner or later will break down in all races now brought nearer to one another by the equalizing systems of inter-national communication and the goals of the machine age. For this task, strict research is needed as much as cultural awareness on the part of the physician practicing in a period which, like a child between 2 epigenetic steps, mistrusts itself and its ancestors. A reformulation of training methods will have to include, above all, developmental time factors: *at what stage of childhood to put most educational pressure; at what stage of a developing behavior item to attempt modification; and what amount of pressure to use in prohibition in general.*

IX. The Physician's Role

A physician, constantly called by complaining parents to a sickly or naughty child, may ask himself whether he has not been given a role in a drama, the plot of which is unknown to him. If he knows the family background, he may be able to reconstruct it and—more than anybody else—to influence the outcome.

The understanding of the 2 principles of *epigenesis* and of *social relativity* forms a basis for child care firm and flexible enough to allow for amendments and interpretations in specific cultural or in-dividual circumstances. These very concepts forbid the formulation of advice for specific situations; their application grows out of clinical experience. Small issues will often show what aspect of training is compulsively overemphasized in a child's milieu: "First of all he must *eat*"; "First of all he must *obey*"; "First of all he must have his *fun*"; "First of all no food should be *wasted*"; "First of all he must be *clean*"; "First of all he must *learn* to eat this or that way," etc. In these cases it is well to look at the child and to determine what he needs most at his developmental stage and in his state of health. The child may appear to be spoiled and a period of firmer training more advisable than any consideration of his physical health or his I.Q. In another child it may be the relationship to the mother which has to be built anew to the exclusion of other factors. A child who has been sick might need nourishment even if he has to be spoiled in regard to the choice and delivery of his food, while another child may appear so restricted in all his expression or so backward in his abilities that new experiences and play adventures must be planned for him.

But the work is only half done when the advice is given. Deep-seated difficulties in the parents may lead any advice *ad absurdum* by the exaggeration of one aspect of it, or the neglect of another; the child or parents may go to extremes and follow advice too literally, considering it law for the entire future of the child or of all children. Thus the therapist has to observe the development of his suggestion when put into actual practice.

In trying to guide, the physician cannot avoid making certain parents dependent on him, while estranging others. This and other aspects of his profession may at the moment make it impossible in most cases to do true guidance work; his may not be the psychological experience or the cultural role of the "family doctor"; but physicians will find it difficult to avoid for long the role thrust on them by questioning parenthood.

While sometimes a state of anxiety in a smaller child can be traced to known and observable changes in body, mind, or environment, an older child often cannot be understood without a psychoanalytic inquiry into the extent and depth of *regression* to earlier stages in which his personality feels safer from inner and outer dangers. Processes of this kind are rarely verbalized even, so it seems, in the child's own mind; they are an unconscious retreat along early established (often preverbal) developmental routes, and direct questioning is fruitless. The physician can only try to study the child's total situation in order to provide him with the stimuli which will encourage him to advance again.

Two promising developments may be mentioned here: (1) The cooperation in clinics which keep the records of the whole family for reference even when various specialists have entered the case, or the family has changed residence; (2) nursery schools. As present-day conclusions in regard to the psychological importance of early childhood are tested, and diagnostic and therapeutic methods improve, not only preventive work and early treatment in the home by the family doctor can be provided, but also an early diagnosis by attending specialists of problem children in nursery schools. Proper treatment in all degrees, ranging from slight changes in routine or play activities to child psychoanalysis (if available in the form authorized by one of the psychoanalytic training institutes), may then be advised and much imbalance kept from becoming chronic.

In the treatment of unwelcome or dangerous habits it is first of all necessary that the physician form a conviction in regard to their danger; only then can we give parents (prejudiced for or against their own upbringing) authoritative security that temporary habits in themselves, *i.e.*, without environmental overemphasis, are not dangerous, and that in general an individualistic approach to matters of early child training does not necessarily imply a leniency that is apt to "spoil" the child. (See Gesell and Ilg.[5])

Neurotic habits differ from developmental habits mainly in quantitative factors, *i.e.*, they may occupy most of the time and attention of a child who should be getting ready for other habits; interference with them may create deeper desperation or tighter closing up or further regression in the child, etc. They require careful investigation of the total lifetime and life space of the individual child. While various forms of not too sudden and not too rigid interference are known to pediatricians (the dangers of calling body functions sinful, threatening physical harm or psychological isolation have already been pointed out), these interferences should be adjusted to the biological and cultural peculiarities of the case; it is never wise to apply them without considering at the same time where in the total picture undue pressure is exerted on the child in terms of the stage of his development and the vulnerability of his personality. Of special and natural help are the new interests which are always ready to be awakened in a child and can draw his fearful attention away from the habit in question. The impulse to be modified can be guided into physiologically or socially less dangerous channels. (If, for example, the habits are characterized by destructiveness, paper and breakable objects of little value can be given to the child; in general, a corner in home or garden should be assigned to him and a period in his day provided where he has to be neither too careful nor too clean.) It is especially important to remember that neurotic habits of long standing are seldom abandoned without the creation of transitory substitute habits which, in terms of the child's development, are less severe, but often more of a concern to the environment than was the old habit. (It may be found, for example, that a child who has given up bed-wetting may masturbate for a while, but in many respects appears more alert and more active.) A violent interruption of this new habit can only throw him back to the old one, or, if the way back is definitely closed, to worse habits or a general personality deformation. New habits should be expected and parents prepared for them. The important thing is not that a child become "faultless" overnight, but that he move forward.

Parents often need to be reminded that play is the greatest balancing factor in a child's life; it is his most serious occupation. Disturbances (acute anxiety, restless shifting, lack of concentration, etc.) in his play are the clearest indicators of deeper disturbances.

The adult dealing with a child helps him most by being playful while playing with him, but realistic when representing future reality. Therefore, as the child grows older, play has to be balanced by regular talks in which the adult says what he knows and what he does not know, but first of all the child should be encouraged to verbalize his changing ideas and fears. Misconceptions of growth, sex, and death cannot be corrected by a didactic attitude on the adult's part; they must correct themselves in repeated discussion in which the adult answers what he is asked—not more and not less.

If respect for children's play and their vivid interests is based on the understanding of their function, certain rules will be kept intuitively, which will allow the child to cross the border between his world and the adult's without too great difficulty. It is wise, for example, to give playing children some warning in advance if an eating or sleeping period if nearing. After they have been given time "to wind up their business," compliance may be urged firmly. Other rules, pleasantly formulated and ready to be handed to mothers (as, for example, "Don't take the child for a walk, go with him," or "Don't laugh at the child, laugh with him") can be found in Susan Isaacs' *The Nursery Years.*[6]

The essence of all these rules is of importance for the physician's relationship to the child: Things which *are done to the child* must be balanced by situations in which he is *actively leading or understanding.* Thus even in his direct contact with the child, it will be rewarding for the physician to take the time to make a game out of what he has to do to the smaller child; or the unavoidably painful session may be closed with some game such as the playful repetition of the medical procedure with, this time, the doctor, parent, or doll the patient. The older child's confidence and consent can often be gained by truthful explanation and an appeal for his intelligent help rather than by assurances later belied.

To be overwhelmed—from within or without—is the growing being's most serious fear. When aroused, it stimulates the impulse to overwhelm, which, in the helpless human infant, can lead only to impotent, frustrating rage.

Physicians can hardly help concluding that man's irrational outbursts, just as much as the rational structure of his culture, which they endanger, are rooted in his prolonged childhood, a fact which science, because often allied with rationalizing rather than with balancing forces, has not yet taken into acount. If the physician learns to lead small children gradually but firmly into reality, and helps them to keep always open the stream of spontaneous activity, it may be that the most reliable characteristics with which to meet the problems of later childhood and adolescence will be developed.

Notes

[1] C. H. Stockard, *The Physical Basis of Personality* (New York: W. W. Norton and Co., Inc., 1931). All quotations in Section I are from this source.

[2] A. Gesell, and C. S. Armatruda, *Developmental Diagnosis: Normal and Abnormal Child Development* (New York: Hoeber, 1941).

[3] Margaret A. Ribble, "Infantile Experience," and Lois B. Murphy, "Childhood Experience," in *Personality and the Behavior Disorders*, ed. McV. Hunt, (New York: Ronald Press Company, 1944).

[4] S. Freud, "Three Contributions to the Theory of Sexuality," in *The Basic Writings of Sigmund Freud* (New York: Modern Library, 1938).

[5] "Proceedings of the Conference on the Psychosomatic Status of the Infant at Birth," Psychosomatic Medicine, 6 (April 1944), 151.

[6] Susan Isaacs, *The Nursery Years* (London: George Routledge and Sons Ltd., 1932).

The Power of the Newborn (1953)

WITH JOAN M. ERIKSON

The helpless newborn presents an all but dictatorial challenge to his family. Babies control and bring up their families as much as they are controlled by them. In fact, we might say that the family brings up a baby by being brought up by him.

Certainly a baby is weak. A shift in temperature or a mistake in formula, a minute accident or an unseen germ can bring mortal danger to him. New life is close to death and new beings are vulnerable in the most lasting way. But to keep new life alive is something that can be learned, and early damage can be recognized, prevented, corrected. The decrease of infant mortality and of the diseases of infancy is now a mere matter of spreading technical progress. And we are beginning to understand—although we are still far from effecting them—the important safeguards of emotional health in babyhood.

Yet beyond questions of death and damage, the baby's genuine weakness exerts a spiritual power over those around him: his arrival precipitates a real and most personal crisis in every single member of his family.

From the earliest and most primitive days down to our own, religion has taken account of the emotional impact of a new arrival

First published in *Mademoiselle*, 62(1953), 100–02.

by encouraging the family to partake in rites and observances that reflect significantly what each participant feels deeply. Ours is a time of emotional enlightenment, the advent of "psychological man." While the mystery of life retains its creative core for each of us to interpret in the light of what is most significant to us, we may, can and must understand some of our important crises more thoroughly and even ruthlessly so that we may gain greater conscious choice in matters not so long ago entirely shrouded in blind superstition and vague suffering.

Wherein, then, lies the baby's power? You know the story of the flustered young husband who, as he helped his very pregnant wife up the steps of a maternity hospital, exclaimed: "Are you sure, darling, you want to go through with this?" We think he expressed very ably the first and basic fact of the unborn baby's power: that he is there to stay and that he must be "gone through with." Let us not deny the quiet despair (and, yes, anger) that this elemental fact can evoke in a newly pregnant woman, even if she has wanted a child with all her heart. For she now has within her a second will, which she has no choice but to voice as her own. If it is her first pregnancy, then this as yet unseen, undefined and unnamed creature within her forces her inexorably to be all woman; it reclassifies her as a "mother." It will change her whole feeling about her body and space and gravity itself. It will give time a different meaning, superseding that of night and day, work and leisure. Time will now be counted in months of pregnancy and in weeks of recovery, in days of crisis and in changing hours of care.

Yet there soon comes the realization that this new being is all hers in an unequaled way. Her life propels another, which in turn brings a more complete life to every part of her body and, in fact, to its total design. She may feel sick at times but in all probability she never felt "wholer." There is a sensuality in pregnancy and in baby care (and some say in some aspects of delivery) that adds new dimensions to the self-awareness of the body. Sexuality, which has come to mean so many different things in human life—love and domination, passion and "outlet," duty and obsession—now fulfills the predestined cycle latent in every sexual act; and, in a good marriage, intimacy promises to prove more secure, more knowing *because* of the child.

There is something consolidating and invigorating about an undebatable responsibility that some of us, unfortunately, learn only in mortal emergencies. If there is one quite undebatable responsibility, it is a mother's response to her baby's needs. Modern psychiatry, in studying what the deepest and earliest calamities in human life are, has also reaffirmed one of the mainsprings of emotional vitality: continuity of loving maternal care. This makes of the young mother a most strategic being, and this entirely on her and her baby's terms, for no other woman's charm, vigor or intelligence can be for her baby what she can be. She is his first day and night, his first sky and earth, his first love—and also his deepest, most desperate anger. His insatiable demandingness, of course, intensifies her postnatal crisis, which she often enters with a sense of empty exhaustion and a need for care, help and advice.

This need, today, is a critical one, for to whom should she, a self-made modern woman, turn for guidance? Her mother? Not invariably by any means. Generations differ and cultural circumstances do not favor the perfection of the role of grandmother or the simple transfer of tradition from one generation to the next. The expert? To some definite and limited extent. He can delineate the dangers that must be avoided, the dangers of carelessness and of overcare, of overleniency and of rigidity. He can outline all those tricks, manipulations and routines that streamline what is technical about baby care. If he is a real expert, however, his delineation and his advice will leave open an area of choice within which the mother will learn to look and listen for the cues and signals that the baby gives her and those that are already in herself.

The responsibility for this most wordless communication, this mutuality of sending and receiving, can never be shed, although it can and should be shared. Husbands (we have not forgotten them) can be quite perceptive if half-encouraged to be—and so can brothers and sisters. And in some communities young mothers are beginning to abandon those restraints of the each-family-for-itself culture (which made a fortified castle out of every apartment and bungalow). The near future will bring more and more study groups where mothers can communicate with one another about what is old and universal and about what is new in this baby business.

But let no experts, ever again, talk mothers out of this most universal fact, which men with their theories and machines are apt to ignore: the miracle, born of crisis, that permits a mother to respond to the needs and demands of the baby's body and mind in such a way that he learns once for all to trust her, to trust himself and to trust the world. Here, we believe, is the cradle of faith.

If the saying "two is company, three is a crowd" ever had meaning, it applies to the expectant father, who, of course, wants children but can never quite understand why this must be so complicated—and so crowded. He is at moments quite emotional about the blessed goings on and he has every intention of being a good father to a child he can see. But pregnancy with its concreteness and mystery arouses mixed feelings in him.

Primitive magic can tell us much about what is involved, as can psychoanalysis; but it is hard to state the father's situation in terms that neither understate nor overdo his crisis. For once (don't tell him) he is a little scared. Since nobody can quite understand anything except by thinking himself into it, he just cannot quite grasp the idea that an "abnormality" such as pregnancy can end well for anybody involved. He also is jealous and—worse—does not quite know it. His wife may look (and feel) lovelier and more mysterious than ever, but he soon realizes it's not he who's in the center of that halo.

This whole situation, somehow, shows up the limitation of the father's own role, which, while clearly indispensable, proves to be less than half *this* story. Let us also not forget that every man, quite secretly, is something of a frustrated mother; for every man was once part of a mother and at one time wanted to be like her. Self-assured men (as some of our young warriors demonstrated at the end of the last war) can be quite maternal in a firm and cautious way if permitted by changing mores. Chances are that our culture will permit them more and more part in baby care and that men will be better men for it.

All of this and more (such as impressions left over from his mother's pregnancies) adds up to the young father's crisis—which can express itself in strange moods and even in passing physical complaints. yet the power of that unborn baby is such that the father not only can stand inner turmoil and outer discomfort (as well as some bantering ridicule) but will in the end achieve an immeasurably more knowing intimacy in his marriage and meaning in his daily pursuits and struggles. And by getting along well without him (at least for a while) the baby forces him into a kind of isolation that calls for new companionship. This he may well find in his already existing child or children, for as never before they need him and he needs them—all temporary exiles.

Much has been learned and described in recent years about the jealousy of children and of the deep impact on them of a new arrival. Brotherhood must be grown—only its roots are given. It must be cultivated, not taken for granted, and it must not be falsified with artificialities. What we described as the father's often more unconscious reactions holds true for much of the young child's more conscious and yet of course often unspoken and quite unspeakable responses to the new member of the family. After all, the child lived not so long ago in that Garden of Eden where he could pluck with ease the rewards of his mother's presence and (friendly or angry) attentiveness. His gradual expulsion from this paradise led him into the joys and the fears of greater independence. It was good to be free as long as he knew that the way back was clear in times of discouragement. The knowledge that Eden has a new occupant brings him closer in spirit to Cain the Killer—and he sometimes looks it.

His bewilderment is heightened by his ignorance of what it is all about—an ignorance of what it is all about—an ignorance that some parents turn into mistrust by telling stupid stories obviously belying even what he can see with his own eyes and conclude with his common sense. The parents—true descendants of that first couple who "saw that they were naked"—(often feel strangely ashamed and flustered when they must explain their own baby to their own child. Yet this new human being is a good argument for simple honesty: it enforces clarification or increases bewilderment. Let your child ask as fast as he can and answer as fast as you can—for here is the cradle of much of man's attitude toward knowledge and truth.

The origin of brotherliness is a vast subject now widely discussed. We would like to add here only one thought. According to more recent custom, mothers and fathers try to help a child overcome his jealousy by telling him that the baby is "ours" to be mothered and cared for jointly. This is good as far as it goes, but it obviously cannot go far because it is not really true and furthermore the baby does not stand for it. Having in the past overestimated the pure naturalness of brotherhood, we now seem to underestimate the power of the baby (and of small children in general) to evoke patience and protectiveness in older children.

Observations during the war indicate that left to themselves children can show an amazing (if sometimes premature) resourcefulness in caring for each other. In daily life too one can observe instances where after a crisis in the older one the power and appeal of the younger one is victorious—with little help from the audience. After all, some babies seem to say a brother's or a sister's name as their very first word—if only the parents are not too intent on annexing that first m-m-m or p-p-p for their own names. At least it would appear that quite a number of nicknames (silly but treasured) have their origin in a baby's first gurgling effort to produce a sound like an older brother or sister's name.

Could it be that in this present state of our family life the necessity for the parents' all-wise manipulation of the love between their children has been somewhat overestimated? Children who are not fooled too often and who are sure of their parents' firm but flexible justice in the checks and balances of the nursery can make more basic and more lasting adjustments to the act of coexistence. Just give the baby a chance to use his native powers of seduction and don't try too hard to help him with the isn't-he-cute strategy.

We knew of a couple who were made somewhat reflective by the following incident. On returning home one day they found their two small boys wrapped all around one another in rare and boisterous affection. When asked what had come over them, they said: "We're pretending we're brothers—you know brothers love one another." Yet playing at pretense is halfway to truth.

Crises are good for people if they force people to enlarge and improve their ways and means of communication with others. Mothers, obviously, must be ready to help quite a number of different people to find one another in such crises. This necessity, one suspects, is the meaning of woman's superior ability to respond to cry and smile and touch and to understand intuitively many of the less obvious ways of saying important things.

Come to think of it, in this world controlled by mortal boasts and infernal machines it is attraactive to consider for once the fact that our newborns, the weakest and most dependent beings on earth, are able to move us with mere whimpers and ever so faint smiles and even to cause crises among the strongest of us, forcing us all to be for a little while more helpfully human. Is there perhaps in this daily occurrence a quiet power and a stubborn pattern that are in line with the dictum that the meek shall inherit the earth?

The Ontogeny
of Ritualization
in Man (1966)

In this zoological setting, I may consider it a sign of hospitality that the ontogeny of ritualization in man is to be discussed before that in animals. This permits me to give full consideration to man's complexity, and to dispense with the attempt to *derive* the human kind of ritualization from what has come to be called ritualization in animals. Rather, I will try to show what in human life may be the *equivalent* of the ethologist's ritualization, and to present a developmental schedule for its ontogeny. To do so, I must first set aside a number of now dominant connotations of the term. The oldest of these is the *anthropological* one which ties it to rites and rituals conducted by communities of adults (and sometimes witnessed by children or participated in by youths) for the purpose of marking such recurring events as the phases of the year or the stages of life. I will attempt to trace some of the ontogenetic roots of all ritual-making but I will not deal explicitly with ritual as such. A more

Presented at a symposium of the Royal Society of London, under the leadership of Sir Julian Huxley. First published in *Philosophical Transactions of the Royal Society of London* (Series B, 251, 772)—(1966), 337–49, also includes concluding remarks to the conference, 523–524. Revised in *Psychoanalysis—A General Psychology, Essays in Honor of Heinz Hartmann*, eds. Rudolph M. Lowenstein, et al. (New York: International Universities Press, 1966). Revised and expanded for *Toys and Reasons: Stages in the Ritualization of Experience* (New York: W. W. Norton, 1977).

recent connotation of "ritualization" is the *clinical* one. Here the term "private ritual" is used to conceptualize obsessional behaviour consisting of repetitive solitary acts with highly idiosyncratic meanings. Such behaviour is vaguely analogous to the aimless behaviour of caged animals, and thus seems to provide a "natural" link with a possible phylogenetic origin of ritualization in its more stereotyped and driven forms. But it seems important to set aside this clinical connotation in order to take account of newer insights both in ethology and in psychoanalysis. There is now a trend in the ethological literature (recently summarized in Konrad Lorenz's *Das Sogenannte Boese* [Lorenz 1964]*) which follows the original suggestion of Sir Julian Huxley to use the word ritualization (and this explicitly without quotation marks) for certain phylogenetically preformed ceremonial acts in the so-called social animals. The study of these acts clearly points away from pathology, in that it reveals the bond created by a reciprocal message of supreme adaptive importance. We should, therefore, begin by postulating that behaviour to be called ritualization in man must consist of an agreed-upon interplay between at least two persons who repeat it at meaningful intervals and in recurring contexts; and that this interplay should have adaptive value for both participants. And, I would submit, these conditions are already fully met by the way in which a human mother and her baby greet each other in the morning.

Beginnings, however, are apt to be both dim in contour and lasting in consequences. Ritualization in man seems to be grounded in the preverbal experience of infants while reaching its full elaboration in grand public ceremonies. No one field could encompass such a range of phenomena with solid observation. Rather, the theme of ritualization (as I have found in preparing this paper) can help us to see new connexions between seemingly distant phenomena, such as human infancy and man's institutions, individual adaptation and the function of ritual. Here, I will not be able to avoid extensive speculation.

I. Infancy and the Numinous

Let me begin with the "greeting ceremonial" marking the beginning of an infant's day: for ritualization is to be treated here first as a special form of everyday behaviour. In such matters it is best not to think at first of our own homes but of those of some neighbours, or

---

* References in parenthesis may be found at the end of this article.

of a tribe studied or a faraway country visited, while comparing it all—how could some of us do otherwise—with analogous phenomena among our favourite birds.

The awakening infant conveys to his mother the fact that he is awake and (as if with the signal of an alarm clock) awakens in her a whole repertoire of emotive, verbal, and manipulative behaviour. She approaches him with smiling or worried concern, brightly or anxiously rendering a name, and goes into action: looking, feeling, sniffing, she ascertains possible sources of discomfort and initiates services to be rendered by rearranging the infant's condition, by picking him up, etc. If it is observed for several days it becomes clear that this daily event is highly ritualized, in that the mother seems to feel obliged, and not a little pleased, to repeat a performance which arouses in the infant predictable responses, encouraging her, in turn, to proceed. Such ritualization, however, is hard to describe. It is at the same time highly *individual* ("typical for the mother" and also tuned to the particular infant) and yet also *stereotyped* along traditional lines. The whole procedure is superimposed on the periodicity of physical needs close to the requirements of survival; but it is an *emotional* as well as a *practical* necessity for both mother and infant. And, as we will see, this enhanced routine can be properly evaluated only as a small but tough link in the whole formidable sequence of generations.

Let us take the fact that the mother called the infant by a name. This may have been carefully selected and perhaps certified in some name-giving ritual, held to be indispensable by the parents and the community. Yet, whatever procedures have given meaning to the name, that meaning now exerts a certain effect on the way in which the name is repeated during the morning procedure—together with other emphases of caring attention which have a very special meaning for the mother and eventually for the child. Daily observations (confirmed by the special aura of Madonna-and-Child images) suggest that this mutual assignment of very special meaning is the ontogenetic source of one pervasive element in human ritualization, which is based on a *mutuality of recognition*.

There is much to suggest that man is born with the need for such regular and mutual affirmation and certification: we know, at any rate, that its absence can harm an infant radically, by diminishing or extinguishing his search for impressions which will verify his senses. But, once aroused, this need will reassert itself in every stage of life as a hunger for ever new, ever more formalized and more widely shared ritualizations and rituals which repeat such face-to-face "recognition" of the hoped-for. Such ritualizations range from the regular exchange of greetings affirming a strong emotional bond to singular encounters of mutual fusion in love or inspiration, or in a leader's "charisma." I would suggest, therefore, that this first and dimmest affirmation, this sense of a *hallowed presence*, contributes to man's ritual-making a pervasive element which we will call the "Numinous." This designation betrays my intention to follow the earliest into the last; and, indeed, we vaguely recognize the numinous as an indispensable aspect of periodical *religious observances*, where the believer, by appropriate gestures, confesses his dependence and his childlike faith and seeks, by appropriate offerings, to secure a sense of being lifted up to the very bosom of the supernatural which in the visible form of an image may graciously respond, with the faint smile of an inclined face. The result is a sense of *separateness transcended*, and yet also of *distinctiveness confirmed*.

I have now offered two sets of phenomena, namely, ritualization in the nursery (as an enhancement by playful formalization of the routine procedures which assure mere survival) and religious rituals (which provide a periodical reaffirmation for a multitude of men), as the first examples of an affinity of themes, which seem to "belong" to entirely different "fields" but are necessarily brought together as subject-matter for this symposium. By suggesting such a far-reaching connexion, however, I do not mean to reduce formalized ritual to infantile elements; rather, I intend to sketch, for a number of such elements of ritualization, an ontogenetic beginning and a reintegration on ever higher levels of development. In adult ritual, to be sure, these infantile elements are both emotively and symbolically re-evoked; but both infantile ritualization and adult ritual are parts of a functional whole, namely, of a cultural version of human existence.

I will now try to list those elements of ritualization which we can already recognize in the first, the numinous instance—emphasizing throughout the opposites which appear to be reconciled. Its mutuality is based on the *reciprocal needs* of two quite *unequal* organisms and minds. We have spoken of the *periodicity of developing needs* to which ritualization gives a *symbolic actuality*. We have recognized it as a highly *personal* matter, and yet as *group-bound*, providing a sense both of *oneness* and of *distinctiveness*. It is *playful*, and yet *formalized*, and this in *details* as well as in the *whole* procedure. Becoming *familiar* through repetition, it yet brings the *surprise* of recognition. And while the ethologists will tell us that ritualizations in the animal world must, above all, be *un-ambiguous* as sets of signals, we suspect that in man the *overcoming of ambivalence* as well as of ambiguity is one of the prime functions of ritualization. For as we love our children, we also find them unbearably demanding, even as they will soon find us arbitrary and possessive. What we love or admire is also threatening, awe becomes awfulness, and benevolence seems in danger of being consumed by wrath. Therefore, ritualized affirmation, once instituted, becomes *indispensable* as a periodical experience and must find new forms in the context of new developmental actualities.

This is a large order with which to burden an infant's daily awakening, and, indeed only the whole sequence of stages of ritualization can make this list of opposites plausible. Yet, even at the beginning, psychopathology confirms this burdening. Of all psychological disturbances which we have learnt to connect ontogenetically with the early stages of life, the deepest and most devastating are those in which the light of mutual recognition and of hope are forfeited in psychotic withdrawal and regression, and this, as Spitz and Bowlby have shown, can develop at the very beginning of life. For, the earliest affirmation is already re-affirmation in the face of the fact that the very experiences by which man derives a measure of security also expose him to a *series of estrangements* which we must try to specify as we deal with each developmental stage. In the first stage, I submit, it is a sense of *separation by abandonment* which must be prevented by the persistent, periodical reassurance of familiarity and mutuality. Such reassurance remains the function of the numinous and thus primarily of the religious ritual or of the numinous element in any ritual. Its perversion or absence, on the other hand, leaves a sense of dread, estrangement, or impoverishment.

In another context (Erikson 1964) I have suggested that the most basic quality of human life, *hope*, is the inner strength which emerges unbroken from early familiarity and mutuality and which provides for man a sense (or a promise) of a personal and universal continuum. It is grounded and fortified in the first stage of life, and subsequently nourished, as it were, by all those ritualizations and rituals which combat a sense of abandonment and hopelessness and promise instead a mutuality of recognition, face to face, all through life—until "we shall know even as also we are known."

II. The Pseudo-species

In order to deal with the total setting which seems to give meaning to and to receive meaning from human ritualization, I must introduce three theoretical considerations of an incomplete and controversial nature.

Since ritualization in animals is for the most part an intra-specific phenomenon, it must be emphasized throughout that man has evolved (by whatever kind of evolution and for whatever adaptive reasons) in *pseudo-species*, i.e. tribes, clans, etc., which behave as if they were separate species created at the beginning of time by supernatural will, and each superimposing on the geographic and economic facts of its existence a cosmogeny, as well as a theocracy and an image of man, all its own. Thus each develops a *distinct sense of identity*, held to be *the* human identity and fortified against other pseudo-species by prejudices which mark them as extra-specific and, in fact, inimical to the only "genuine" human endeavour. Paradoxically, however, newly born man can fit into any number of such pseudo-species and must, therefore, become specialized during a prolonged childhood—certainly a basic fact in the ontogeny of *familiarization by ritualization*.

To speak of pseudo-species may be controversial enough. But I must now face a second conceptual dilemma in the form of Sigmund Freud's instinct theory. Whenever the noun "instinct" appears in psychoanalytic formulations, it is helpful to ask whether the corresponding adjective would be "instinctive" or "instinctual," i.e. whether the emphasis is on an *instinctive pattern* of behaviour, or an *instinctual drive or energy* more or less indifferent and divorced from prepared patterns of adaptiveness.* It will appear, then, that psychoanalysts usually mean instinctual drives, and this with the connotation of a quantitative excess devoid of instinctive quality in the sense of specific patterns of "fittedness" (Hartmann 1938). The evolutionary rationale for this free-floating quantity of instinctual energy lies, of course, in the very fact that man is, in Ernst Mayr's words, the "generalist animal," born to invest relatively non-specific drives in such learning experiences and such social encounters as will assure, during a long childhood, a strengthening and widening of mutuality, competence, and identity—all, as I am endeavouring to show, supported most affirmatively by appropriate ritualizations.

I say "most affirmatively" because man's *moral prohibitions* and *inner inhibitions* are apt to be as excessive and maladaptive as the drives which they are meant to contain; in psychoanalysis we therefore speak of a "return of the repressed." Could it be, then, that true

---

* As Freud put it in his New Introductory Letters: "From the Pleasure Principle to the instinct of self-preservation is a long way; and the two tendencies are far from coinciding from the first."

ritualization represents, in fact, a *creative formalization* which avoids both impulsive excess and overly compulsive self-restriction, both social anomic and moralistic coercion? If so, we could see at least four vital functions served by the simplest ritualization worthy of that designation:

(1) It binds instinctual energy into a pattern of mutuality, which bestows convincing simplicity on dangerously complex matters. As mother and infant meet in the first ritualization described so far, the infant brings to the constellation his vital needs, among them, oral, sensory, and tactile drives (subsumed as "orality" in Freud's libido theory) and the necessity to have disparate experiences made coherent by mothering. The mother in her post-partum state is also needful in a complex manner, for whatever instinctive mothering she may be endowed with, and whatever instinctual gratification she may seek in being a mother, she needs to be a *mother of a special kind* and *in a special way*. This she becomes by no means without an anxious avoidance (sometimes outright phobic, often deeply superstitious) of "other" kinds and ways typical for persons or groups whom she (sometimes unconsciously) dislikes, or despises, hates, or fears as godless or evil, unhygienic or immoral.

(2) In permitting the mother to "be herself" and to be at the same time an obedient representative of a group ethos, ritualization protects her against the danger of instinctual excess and arbitrariness and against the burden of having to systematize a thousand small decisions.

(3) In establishing mutuality in the immediacy of early needs, ritualization also does the groundwork for lasting mutual identifications between adult and child from generation to generation. For the mother is reaffirmed in her identification with those who mothered her well; while her own motherhood is reaffirmed as benevolent by the increasing responsiveness of the infant. The infant, in turn, develops a benevolent self-image (a certified narcissism, we may say) grounded in the recognition of an all-powerful and mostly benevolent (if sometimes strangely malevolent) "Other."

(4) Thus ritualization also provides the psychosocial foundation for that inner equilibrium which in psychoanalysis is attributed to a "strong ego"; and thus also a first step for the gradual development (to be sealed only in adolescence) of an independent identity (Erikson 1965) which—guided by various rituals of "confirmation" representing a "second birth"—will integrate all childhood identifications, while subordinating those wishes and images which have become undesirable and evil.

III. Early Childhood and the Judicious

Any ontological discourse suffers from the fact that it must begin to enumerate its guiding principles at the beginning, while only an account of their progression and differentiation as a whole can reveal their plausibility. The dimensions of ritualization suggested so far must now reappear on higher levels: mutuality between the child and that increasing number of adults with whom he is ready to interact, physically, mentally and socially; the affirmation of such new mutuality by ritualization and this in the face of a new kind of estrangement; and the emergence of a new element of ritual.

A second basic element in human ritualization is one of which the best term would seem to be *judicial*, because it combines *jus* and *dicere*, "the law" and "the word." At any rate, the term should encompass methods by which the *discrimination* between right and wrong is ontologically established. Eventually, this becomes an important aspect in all human ritual; for there is no ritual which does not imply a discrimination between the sanctioned and the out-of-bounds—up to the Last Judgement.

The ontological source of this second element is the second stage of life, that is, early childhood, which is characterized by a growing psychosocial autonomy and by rapid advances in development. As *locomotion* serves increased autonomy, it also leads to the boundaries of the permissible; as *discrimination* sharpens, it also serves the perception of conduct which "looks right" or "does not look right" in the eye of others; while *language development* (obviously one of the strongest bonds of a pseudo-species) distinguishes with finite emphasis what is conceptually integrated in the verbalized world, and what remains outside, nameless, unmeaningful, strange, *wrong*. All of this is given strong connotations by what Freud called "anality." It brings with it a new sense of estrangement: standing upright, the child realizes that he can lose face and suffer shame; giving himself away by blushing, he feels furiously isolated, not knowing whether to *doubt himself* or *his judges*. His elders, in turn, feel compelled to utilize and thus to aggravate this trend; and yet, is it not again in the ritualization of approval and disapproval (in recurring situations of high symbolic meaning) that the adult speaks as a mouthpiece of a supra-individual righteousness, damning the deed but not necessarily the doer?

I will never forget an experience which I am sure I share with all anthropologists (professional and amateur): I mean the astonishment with which we "in the field" encounter for the first time old people who will describe what is appropriate in their culture with a sense of moral and aesthetic rightness unquestionably sanctioned by the universe. Here is an example of what I was told among the Yurok Indians in Northern California, who depended on the salmon and its elusive ways (long hidden to science) of propagating and migrating:

"Once upon a time, a Yurok meal was a veritable ceremony of self-restraint. A strict order of placement was maintained and the child was taught to eat in prescribed ways, for example, to put only a little food on the spoon, to take the spoon up to his mouth slowly, to put the spoon down while chewing the food—and above all, to think of becoming rich during the whole process. There was silence during meals, so that everybody could keep his thoughts concentrated on money and salmon. This ritualization served to lift to the level of a kind of hallucination nostalgic oral needs which may have been evoked by very early weaning from the breast (quite extraordinary among American Indians). Later, in the "sweat house" the boy would learn the dual feat of thinking of money and *not* thinking of women; and the adult Yurok could make himself see money hanging from trees and salmon swimming in the river during the off season in the belief that this self-induced "hallucinatory" thought would bring action from the Providers."

This ceremonial style which undoubtedly impressed the small child and had precursors in less formal daily occasions invested similar ritualizations along the whole course of life, for cultures (so we may remind ourselves in passing) attempt to give *coherence* and *continuity* to the whole schedule of minute ritualizations.

This second element of ritualization is differentiated from the first primarily by an emphasis on the *child's free will.* In the ritualizations of infancy avoidances were the mother's responsibility; now the child himself is trained to "watch himself." To this end parents and other elders compare him (to his face) with what he *might* become if he and they did not watch out. Here, then, is the ontogenetic source of the *"negative identity"* which is so essential for the maintenance of a pseudo-species, for it embodies everything one is not supposed to be or show—and what one yet potentially is. The negative identity furnishes explicit images of pseudo-species which one must *not* resemble in order to have a chance of acceptance in one's own. Behind the dreaded traits are often images of what the parents themselves are trying not to be and therefore doubly fear the child might become, and are thus *potential* traits which he must learn to imagine in order to be able to avoid them. The self-doubt and the hidden shame attached to the necessity of "eliminating" part of himself as well as the suppression of urges create in man a certain *righteous rage* which can turn parent against parent, parent against child—and the child against himself. I paint this matter darkly because here we meet the ontological origin of the divided species. Moral self-discrimination is sharpened by an indoctrination against evil others, on whom the small child can project what he must negate in himself, and against whom he can later turn that moralistic and sadistic prejudice which has become the greatest danger of the species man. His "prejudice against himself," on the other hand, is at the bottom of man's proclivity for compulsive, obsessive, and depressive disorders; while irrational prejudice against others, if joined with mass prejudice and armed with modern weapons, may yet mark the premature end of a species just on the verge of becoming one (Erikson 1965). All of this, however, also underlines the importance of true ritualization as a supra-individual formalization transmitting rules of conduct in words and sounds which the child can comprehend, and in situations which he can manage.

In its full elaboration in a *judiciary ritual*, however, this judicious element is reaffirmed on a grand scale, making all-visible on the public stage what occurs in each individual as an inner process: the Law is untiringly watchful as is, alas, our conscience. It locates a suitable culprit who, once in the dock, serves as "an example," on which a multitude can project their inner shame. The unceasing inner rumination with which we watch ourselves is matched by the conflicting evidence which parades past the parental judge, the fraternal jury, and the chorus of the public. Judgement, finally, is pronounced as based on sanctified agreement rather than on passing outrage or personal revenge; and where repentance does not accept punishment, the verdict will impose it.

Both the ritualized establishment of boundaries of good and bad in childhood and the judiciary ritual in the adult world fulfil the criteria for ritualized procedures as suggested earlier: meaningful regularity; ceremonial attention to detail and to the total procedure; a sense of symbolic actuality surpassing the reality of each participant and of the deed itself; a mutual activation of all concerned (including, or so it is hoped, the confessing culprit); and a sense of indispensability so absolute that the need for the ritualization in question seems to be "instinctive" with man. And, indeed, the judicial element has become an indispensable part of man's phylogenetic adaptation as well as his ontogenetic development.

In seeing the judicial element at work, however, in public and in private, we can also perceive where this form of ritualization fails in its adaptive function, and this means in the convincing transmission of boundaries from generation to generation. Failure is indicated where fearful compulsion to conform replaces free assent to what feels right; where thus the obsessively formalistic becomes dominant over the convincingly ceremonial or where considered judgement is swamped by instinctual excess and becomes moralistic sadism or sensational voyeurism. All of this increases the hopeless isolation of the culprit and aggravates an impotent rage which can only make him more "shameless." Thus, the decay or perversion of ritual does not create an indifferent emptiness, but a void with explosive possibilities—to which fact this Symposium should pay careful attention. For it explains why "nice" people who have lost the gift of imparting values by meaningful ritualization can have children who become (or behave like) juvenile delinquents; and why nice "church-going" nations can so act as to arouse the impression of harbouring pervasive murderous intent.

Here, again, the psychopathology attending individual misfunctioning and the social pathology characterizing the breakdown of institutions are closely related. They meet in the alternation of impulsivity and compulsivity, excess and self-restriction, anarchy and autocracy.

IV. Childhood: The Dramatic and the Formal

I have now attempted to isolate two elements in human rituals which seem clearly grounded in ontogenetic stages of development. In view of the "originology" which is apt to replace defunct teleology, it seems important to reiterate that I am not suggesting a simple causal relationship between the infantile stage and the adult institution, in the sense that adult rituals above all serve persisting infantile needs in disguise. The image of the Ancestor or of the God sought on a more mature level is (as we shall see) by no means "only" a replica of the mother's inclined face, nor the idea of Justice "only" an externalization of a childish bad conscience. Rather, man's epigenetic development in separate and protracted childhood stages assures that each of the major elements which constitute human institutions is rooted in a distinct childhood stage, but, once evolved, must be progressively re-integrated on each higher level. Thus the numinous element reappears in the judicial ritualizations as the aura adhering to all "authority" and later to a personified or highly abstract image of Justice, or to the concrete persons who as justices are invested with the symbolism and the power of that image. But this also means that neither the numinous nor the judicial elements, although they can dominate a particular stage or a particular institution, can "make up" a ritual all by themselves: other elements must join them. Of these, I will discuss, in the following, the elements of *dramatic elaboration*, of *competence of performance*, and of *ideological commitment*. (See Table 1, p. 591.)

First, then, the *dramatic* element. This, I believe, is grounded in the maturational advances of the *play age* which permits the child to create with available objects (and then in games with cooperative adults and peers) a *coherent plot with dramatic turns* and some form of *climactic conclusion*.

While the second, the "judicial" stage was characterized by the internalization of the parental voice, this age offers the child a micro-reality in which he can escape adult ritualization and prepare his own, reliving, correcting and recreating past experiences, and anticipating future roles and events with the spontaneity and repetitiveness which characterize all ritualization. His themes, however, are often dominated by usurpation and impersonation of adult roles; and I would nominate for the principal *inner estrangement* which finds expression, aggravation or resolution in play, the *sense of guilt*. One might think that this sense should be subsumed under the judicial sphere; yet, guilt is an inescapable sense of self-condemnation which does not even wait for the phantasied deed to be actually committed; or, if committed, to be known to others; or if known to others, to be punished by them.

This theme dominates the great tragedies for the *Theatre* is adult man's "play." The play on the toy-stage and the plays acted out in official drama and magic ceremonial have certain themes in common which may, in fact, have helped to induce Freud to give to the dominant "complex" of this stage the name of a tragic hero: Oedipus. That common theme is the conflict between hubris and guilt, between the usurpation of father-likeness and punishment, between freedom and sin. The appropriate institution for the aweful expression of the dramatic is the stage, which, however, cannot do without the numinous and the judicial, even as they, in any given ritual, rite or ceremony, cannot dispense with the dramatic.

What is the form of psychopathology characterizing the play age and the neurotic trends emanating from it? It is the weight of excessive guilt which leads to repression in thought and to inhibition in action. It is no coincidence that this pathology is most dramatically expressed in *Hamlet*, the tragedy of the *actor* in every sense of the word, who tries to solve his inhibitive scruples by the invention of a *play within a play* and prepares his perdition in and by it. And yet, this perdition almost seems a salvation from something worse: that pervasive boredom in the midst of affluence and power, that malaise and inability to gain pleasure "from either man or woman" which characterizes the absence of the dramatic and the denial of the tragic.

The *school-age* adds another element to ritualization: that of the *perfection of performance*. The elements mentioned so far would be without a binding discipline which holds them to a minute sequence and arrangement of performance. The mental and emotional capacity for such accuracy arises only in the school-age; or rather, because it *can* arise then, children are sent to "schools." There, with varying abruptness, play is transformed into work, game into cooperation, and the freedom of imagination into the duty to perform with full attention to all the minute details which are necessary to complete a task and do it "right." Ritualization becomes truly cooperative in the whole arrangement called "school," that is, in the interplay between "teacher," "class," and individual child, and in the prescribed series of minute tasks which are structured according to the verbal, the mathematical and the physical nature of the cultural universe. This, I submit, is the ontogenetic source of that *formal aspect* of rituals, provided by an order in space and time which is convincing to the sense as it becomes *order perceived* and yet also *participated in*. Adding this sense of detail, seriously attended to within a meaningful context, to the numinous, judicial and dramatic elements, we feel closer to an understanding of the dimensions of any true ritual. But we also perceive the danger of over-formalization, perfectionism, and empty ceremonialism, not to speak of the neurotic "ritual" marked by total isolation (and all too often considered the model of ritualization by my psychiatric colleagues).

V. Adolescence and Beyond: the Ideological and the Generational

I have now concentrated on the ontogenetic and, as it were, unofficial sources of ritualizations in childhood. From here, one could continue in two directions: that is, one could discuss the always surprising and sometimes shocking spontaneous "rites" by which adolescents ritualize their relations to each other and demarcate their generation as (slightly or decidedly) different both from the adult haves and the infantile have-nots; or one could now turn to formal rites and rituals, for it is in the formal rites of confirmation, induction, etc., that adolescing man is enjoined for the first time to become a full member of his pseudo-species, and often of a special *élite* within it. For all the elements developed in the ontogenetic sequence already discussed now become part of formal rites which tie the infantile inventory into an ideological world-image, provide a convincing coherence of ideas and ideals, and give youth the feeling of active participation in the preservation or renewal of society. Only now can man be said to be adult in the sense that he can devote himself to ritual purposes and can visualize a future in which he will become the everyday ritualizer in his children's lives.

Our ontogenetic sketch has to include this stage because the reciprocal mechanisms by which adult and young animals complete the interplay of their respective inborn patterns can be said to be paralleled in man by no less than the *whole period of childhood and youth*. To be fully grown in the human sense means the readiness to join not only the *technology* but also certain *irreversible commitments* to one's pseudo-species; which also means to *exclude* (by moral repudiation, fanatic rebellion, or warfare) inimical identities and outworn or foreign ideologies. Elsewhere (Erikson 1965) I have undertaken to delineate the identity crisis which precedes the emergence in youth of a sense of *psycho-social identity* and the readiness for the ideological style pervading the ritualizations of his culture. Only an integration of these two processes prepares youth for the alignment of its new strength with the technological and historical trends of the day. I have called the corresponding estrangement *identity-confusion*. Clinically (i.e. in those so pre-disposed), this expresses itself in withdrawal or in lone-wolf delinquency; while it is often a matter of psychiatric, political, and legal definition whether and where borderline psychosis, criminality, dangerous delinquency or unwholesome fanaticism may be said to exist. Much of youthful "demonstration" in private is just that: a dramatization (sometimes mocking, sometimes riotous) of the estrangement of youth from the impersonality of mass-production, the vagueness of confessed values, and the intangibility of the prospects for either an individualized or truly communal existence; but, above all, by the necessity to find entirely new forms of ritualization in a technology changing so rapidly that change becomes one of its main attributes. There are historical identity vacua when the identity crisis is aggravated on a large scale and met only by an ideological renewal which "catches up" with economic and technological changes (Erikson 1959).

We have also witnessed in our time totalitarian attempts at involving new generations ideologically in staged mass rituals combining the numinous and the judicial, the dramatic and the precise in performance on the largest scale, which provide for masses of young individuals an ideological commitment encompassing perpetual change and, in fact, making all traditional (in the sense of pre-revolutionary) values part of a decidedly negative identity.

I point to all this in the present context primarily because of problems concerning the ontogeny of ritualization. For what is in question is (1) the necessary coherence and continuity between early ritualization and overall technological and political trends, and (2) the role of youth in the rejuvenation of society and the integration of our humanist past with the technological age now emerging world-wide.

But before we come to the question of ritualization in the modern world we must mention a *dominant function of ritual in the life of the adult*. Parents are the earliest ritualizers in their children's lives; at the same time, they are participants of the instituted rituals in which the ritualizations of their childhoods find an echo and a reaffirmation. What, then, is the prime contribution of adult ritual to the ontogenesis of ritualization? I think ritual reaffirms the sanction needed by adults to be convincing ritualizers.

After the *rituals of graduation* from the apprenticeship of youth, *marriage ceremonies* provide for the young adult the "licence" to enter those new associations which will transmit tradition to the coming generation. I am reminded here of a wedding ceremony which took place in a small town in the French Alps. The young Americans to be married faced the mayor; the tricolor was wound round his middle (which was soon to be regaled with ceremonial champagne). Above and behind him, *le Général* looked most distantly out of a framed picture into new greatness; and above him a bust of *l'Empéreur* stared white and vacant into the future, the brow wrapped in laurel, while even higher up, the afternoon sun streamed through a window, all the way down to the book out of which the mayor read phrases from a Code, to which a young bride from America could have agreed only with some reservations, had she fully understood them. Yet we few, in a foreign land, felt well taken care of, for the Western world shares many ceremonial values and procedures; and the couple accepted from the mayor a little booklet which provided for the entry of the names of the next generation.

Whether the ceremonies of the adult years call on personal ances-tors in the beyond or on culture heroes, on spirits or gods, on kings or leaders, they sanction the adult, for his mature needs include the *need to be periodically reinforced in his role of ritualizer*, which means not more and not less than to be ready to become a numinous model in his children's minds, and to act as a judge and the transmitter of traditional ideals. This last element in the ontogenetic series I would call the *generational* which includes *parental* and *instructive*, *productive*, *creative*, and *curative* endeavours.

VI. Conclusion

In the "freer" adult of the Western world we often observe an op-pressive sense of responsibility in isolation, and this under the impact of two parallel developments, namely, the decrease of ritual reas-surance from the ceremonial resources of a passing age, and the increase of a self-conscious awareness of the role of the individual, and especially of the parent and the teacher in the sequence of gen-erations. Adults thus oppressed, however, are of little use to youth which prefers to gather around those who create new patterns of ritualization worthy (or seemingly worthy) of the energies of a new generation. The Symposium, having established the evolutionary sig-nificance of ritualization in man, may thus not be able to shirk the question whether or not fading rituals may not at this time be giving way to ritualizations of a new kind, dictated above all by new meth-ods of communication and not always recognizable to the overtrained eye.

I hope, therefore, that this Symposium will come to discuss not only the question of the weakening of traditional ritual and of "our" traditional sense of ritualization, but also the agencies which provide a reinforcement of ritualization in line with a new world-image.

This new cosmos is held together by the scientific ethos, the methods of mass communication, and the replacement of "ordained" au-thorities by an indefinite sequence of experts correcting and complementing each other. Pediatric advice, for example, offers knowledge and prudence as guides to parental conduct; modern tech-nology attaches new ritualizations to technical necessities and op-portunities in homes and at work; and world-wide communication creates new and more universal parliaments. We must review the

TABLE 1. ONTOGENY OF RITUALIZATION

	NUMINOUS	JUDICIAL	DRAMATIC	FORMAL	IDEOLOGICAL	GENERATIONAL SANCTION
infancy	mutality of recognition					
early childhood	↓	discrimination of good and bad				
play age	↓	↓	dramatic elaboration			
school age	↓	↓	↓	rules of performance		
adolescence	↓ ↓	↓	↓ ↓	↓	solidarity of conviction	
elements in adult rituals	NUMINOUS	JUDICIAL	DRAMATIC	FORMAL	IDEOLOGICAL	GENERATIONAL SANCTION

accreditation of those who rush in to occupy places left vacant by vanishing ritualization, and who offer new "rituals" of mechanistic or autocratic, self-conscious, totally thoughtless or all too intellectual kinds.

However, new sources of numinous and judicial affirmation as well as of dramatic and aesthetic representation can obviously come only from a new spirit embodying an identification of the whole human species with itself. The transition will compound our estrangements, for could it not be that much of the ritualization discussed here owes its inescapability to a period in mankind's evolution when the pseudo-species was dominant? Will a more inclusive human identity do away with the necessity of reinforcing the identities and the prejudices of many pseudo-species—even as a new and more universal ethics may make old moralisms obsolete? If so, there seems to be a strong link between Sir Julian's Romanes lecture (Huxley 1943) and today's proceedings.

I am by no means certain that the elements of ritualization enumerated in this paper and charted with premature finality in table 1 represent a complete inventory. I have outlined what I was able to discern, and what I believe the principles of further inquiry to be. At any rate, there can be no prescription for ritualization, for, far from being merely repetitive or familiar in the sense of habituation, any true ritualization is ontogenetically grounded and yet pervaded with the spontaneity of surprise: it is an unexpected renewal of a recognizable order in potential chaos. Ritualization thus depends on that blending of surprise and recognition which is the soul of creativity, reborn out of the abyss of instinctual disorder, confusion of identity and social anomie.*

We have come to the conclusion of an abundance of papers and of a fascinating series of films. At the end, Dr. Edward B. Shils dropped in to point to the naïve investment of rituals with the hope of salvation. I can not estimate the predictive value of sociology when it comes to salvation. Watching the rituals on the screen, however, one is impressed with the spirit of these occasioins. I recognized what I have called the *numinous* element in a number of examples, even in that of the precarious tower of strength (to which we looked up with audible awe) and certainly in the native queen who became radiant under the eyes of her subjects. I also could point to the presence of the second, the *judicious* element, according to which a ritual elects an *élite* of some kind. But I remind you of my earlier list of criteria only in order to emphasize once more that of all the forms of behaviour which we could call "ritualizations" we probably should limit the term to relatively few which *combine* a number of essential elements, and exclude all those which we could simply characterize as habitual, repetitive, stereotyped, compulsive, or obligatory; or as acts of displaying, posturing, gesturing, or signalizing; or as methods of formalizing, routinizing, conventualizing, etc. Most of these are present in all ritualization, but only a combination of them (as yet to be specified) defines the whole phenomenon.

Coming from psychiatry, I feel that one should also exclude from ritualization proper certain stereotyped formalizations of symbolic behaviour, obviously dictated by "magic" fear and characterized by isolation and compulsion which have been called rituals by analogy: the frightened child repeating a traumatic event in play or the neurotic engaged in solitary or symptomatic acts. Dr. Desmond Morris has added to this list (with diagnostic skill) people speaking in public. Caught in conflicting desires and ambiguous conventions, we seem to resemble the caged animal. But Dr. Morris avoided the term ritualization for such behaviour.

What has come to be called ritualization in free animals actually points away from pathology, in that it reveals the *bond* created by communicative behaviour carrying a highly formalized, unambigu-

* One major example of creative ritualization in the modern era, namely, Gandhi's technique of nonviolent conflict (Satyagraha) has striking analogies to the pacific ritualization of animals as recently summarized by Lorenz (1964). For a preliminary report, see E. H. Erikson, 'Psychoanalysis and ongoing history: problems of identity, hatred and non-violence', *Amer. J. Psychiatry* 122, 241–250, 1965.

ous, and reciprocal message. To match this in the human world we must, I think, postulate a few minimum requirements for calling behaviour ritualized. The discussion of human ritualization pointed first to the bond between mother and child; and, indeed, the ontogeny of ritualization must begin with the mutuality of at least two human beings (with all of evolution and some tradition behind them), and must then gradually include a widening range of individuals and groups with whom the growing human being becomes able to interact in a ritualized fashion. If we should be inclined to ask, "but does not the artist ritualize in solitude?" we must remember that his circumstantial solitude only serves to enhance his freedom of communicating with memories and phantasies, traditions and rules, aspirations and prophesies in the creation of which many have participated. And the result of his solitary work is destined to reach many, even if his audience may at first be small and select. "A hundred years from now," Kierkegaard wrote in his solitude, "all the world will read this diary." The artistic or literary creation, then, shares with other ritualizations a second inherent attribute, namely, *symbolic actuality*, that is an activating, bond-creating quality transcending the rationally real. Thirdly, I would postulate an *instinctual involvement* of all who partake in a ritualization. This was discussed in my paper. But I would like to emphasize once more that ritualization in man must also help to overcome *affective ambivalence*. Both ambiguity and ambivalence, of course, relate to *contradictory affects* which need to be reconciled in favour of survival. In the animal, however, "instinctive" forms of spectacular greeting have absorbed elements of defensive threatening. In man, ambivalence survives along with "bonding" behaviour (such phrases as "I could eat you up" are sometimes not lost on the child who is the recipient of ravenous affection). Then, there is *catharsis*, the "discharge" of affect: and here I regret that time did not permit a discussion of Francis Huxley's paper which pointed to the relaxation of muscle tension (here a somatization of suppressed aggression) in dance rituals. In the end, however, we always return to the importance of the singular *social bond* created in people who have come to activate and thus to verify each other in ritualized and ritual ways; and the simultaneous deepening of the psychosocial identity of each participant. The final question, it would seem, is not whether any of this will "save them" but whether the social animal and, indeed, man would have survived without ritualization or will survive without full and genuine equivalents emerging on a new technological and historical level.

References

Erikson 1950. E. H. Erikson *Childhood and Society* (New York: W. W. Norton [2d ed. 1963]; London: Penguin Books Ltd. 1965).

Erikson 1959. E. H. Erikson, *Young Man Luther* (London: Faber and Faber).

Erikson 1964. E. H. Erikson *Insight and Responsibility* (New York: W. W. Norton; London: Faber & Faber, 1966).

Erikson 1965. E. H. Erikson, "The Concept of Identity in Race Relations." *Daedalus* 95, 145–70.

Hartmann 1938. H. Hartmann, *Ego psychology and the Problem of Adaptation* (New York: International Universities Press, 1958.

Huxley 1966. Sir Julian Huxley, *Evolutionary ethics*. (Oxford: 1966) Oxford University Press.

Lorenz 1964. K. Lorenz, *Das Sogenannte Boese* (Vienna: Dr G. Borotha-Schoeler Verlag).

The Human Life Cycle
(1968)

Introductory Notes*

My psycho-social conception of the life cycle was originally based on Freud's clinical breakthrough into the early stages of life, in which he found the origin of neurotic disturbance. I developed some of what I learned, asking: if we know what can go wrong in each stage, can we say what should have gone and can go right? I then found opportunities to check my assumptions not only in a great number of case histories but also in a "longitudinal" study of a "normal" sample of growing children; in studies of the child-training systems of some "primitive" cultures; and in my own and my students' studies of biographies. I emphasize this as a cross-disciplinary method of ascertaining the value of concepts not immediately conducive to simple measurement. I see no scientific merit in insisting on measuring what by its nature cannot be measured; which does not mean that I consider it impossible in principle, under clearly defined conditions to translate some aspects of the GESTALTEN (configurations) men-

First published in the *International Encyclopedia of the Social Sciences* (New York: Crowell-Collier, 1968), 286–92.
* This introductory section and Table 1 have been excerpted from "Notes on the Life Cycle." In *Ekistics*, (October 1971), 260–265.

tioned here into measurable units. Maybe, ekistics can provide such conditions.

The main emphasis of this conception, then, is on the development of human potentials, and more specifically on the SPIELRAUM, the expanding radius of interplay necessary for them. But it also emphasizes the conflicts inherent in each stage of development, and, therefore, the crises constituted by each new stage of development. Such *crises* (in the sense of turning points or crucial moments) do not only decide possible individual maldevelopment but—more important in this context—what (in groups of individuals seemed "normal" in the sense of "adjusted") may lead to the establishment of what I call a forbidding inner shell, which prevents people from being aware of their potentials and demanding in regard to their environmental needs.

I, therefore, offer such terms as (for example) *Autonomy versus Shame and Doubt* with the assumption that no human being can exist among others without learning to be ashamed or to doubt, but that the ratio of development should be in favor of a sense of autonomy; which also means that the student of ekistics should consider those forbidding aspects of the outer space created for a child which would reinforce the inner development of doubt by the continuous necessity to consider the space necessary for muscular and locomotor development or interplay as an unduly dangerous and suspicious space.

In this sense, ekistics may care to study the development of sensory, muscular and locomotor; cognitive, psychosocial and productive; ideological and ethical development, with the question in mind whether the space planned for the interplay of generations facilitates the inner freedom which, in turn, is needed for the comprehension of ekistic goals both by future builders and future inhabitants. Here, it must be considered, that to limit the developmental space of children, is also an injustice to parents, who are forced to impose on their children restrictions not of their own making.

Such a study would, at the same time keep track of the early experience of space as already internalized by the older child and adult (INNER SPACE); and thus of a generation to be re-educated; of the social space, the space and all the significant individuals and institutions with whom an individual and age group can and must interact at a given time (SOCIAL SPACE); and thus also the economic and political arena which has become forbidding. Finally the architectural space which facilitates or forbids the freedom needed not only for human development but for the creative comprehension of

Table 1 ELEMENTARY MODALITIES

STAGE 1: To receive To give in return	STAGE 5: To be oneself To share being oneself
STAGE 2: To hold on To let go	STAGE 6: To lose and find oneself in others
STGE 3: To make = go after To make like = playing	STAGE 7: To make be To take care of
STAGE 4: To make things (completing) To make things together	STAGE 8: To be through having been and having made to be To face not being

the potentials of the space as created by man (SHELLS).

Table I offers a worksheet on some basic social modalities connected with the stages of life and their spatial needs.

Life Cycle

The observer of life is always immersed in it and thus unable to transcend the limited perspectives of his stage and condition. Religious world views usually evolve pervasive configurations of the course of life: one religion may envisage it as a continuous spiral of rebirths, another as a crossroads to damnation or salvation. Various "ways of life" harbor more or less explicit images of life's course: a leisurely one may see it as ascending and descending steps with a comfortable platform of maturity in between; a competitive one may envision it as a race for spectacular success—and sudden oblivion. The scientist, on the other hand, looks at the organism as it moves from birth to death and, in the larger sense, at the individual in a genetic chain; or he looks at the cultural design of life's course as marked by rites of transition at selected turning points.*

The very choice of the configuration "cycle of life," then, necessitates a statement of the writer's conceptual ancestry—clinical psychoanalysis. The clinical worker cannot escape combining knowledge, experience, and conviction in a conception of the course of life and of the sequence of generations—for how, otherwise, could he offer interpretation and guidance? The very existence of a variety of psychiatric "schools" is probably due to the fact that clinical practice and theory are called upon to provide a total orientation beyond possible verification.

Freud confessed only to a scientific world view, but he could not avoid the attitudes (often in contradiction to his personal values) that

---

* For full citation of references see listing at the conclusion of the paper.

were part of his times. The original data of psychoanalysis, for example, were minute reconstructions of "pathogenic" events in early childhood. They supported an orientation which—in analogy to teleology—could be called *originology*, i.e., a systematic attempt to derive complex meanings from vague beginnings and obscure causes. The result was often an implicit fatalism, although counteracted by strenuously "positive" orientations. Any theory embracing both life history and case history, however, must find a balance between the "backward" view of the genetic reconstruction and the "forward" formulation of progressive differentiation in growth and development; between the "downward" view into the depth of the unconscious and the "upward" awareness of compelling social experience; and between the "inward" exploration of inner reality and the "outward" attention to historical actuality.

This article will attempt to make explicit those psychosocial insights that often remain implicit in clinical practice and theory. These concern the individual, who in principle develops according to predetermined steps of readiness that enable him to participate in ever more differentiated ways along a widening social radius, and the social organization, which in principle tends to invite such developmental potentialities and to support the proper rate and the proper sequence of their unfolding.

"Cycle" is intended to convey the double tendency of individual life to "round itself out" as a coherent experience and at the same time to form a link in the chain of generations from which it receives and to which it contributes both strength and weakness.

Strategic in this interplay are developmental crises—"crisis" here connoting not a threat of catastrophe but a turning point, a crucial period of increased vulnerability and heightened potential, and, therefore, the ontogenetic source of generational strength and maladjustment.

The Eight Stages of Life

Man's protracted childhood must be provided with the psychosocial protection and stimulation which, like a second womb, permits the child to develop in distinct steps as he unifies his separate capacities. In each stage, we assume a new drive-and-need constellation, an expanded radius of potential social interaction, and social institutions created to receive the growing individual within traditional patterns. To provide an evolutionary rationale for this (for prolonged child-

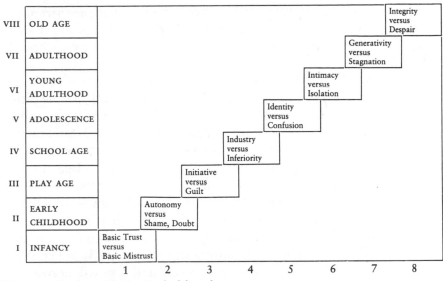

Figure 1— Psychosocial crises in the life cycle

SOURCE: Adapted from Childhood and Society, by Erik H. Erikson, Copyright 1950, © 1963 by W. W. Norton & Company. Reproduced with permission of W. W. Norton & Company, Inc. and Hogarth Press, Ltd.

hood and social institutions must have evolved together), two basic differences between animal and man must be considered.

We are, in Ernst Mayr's terms (1964), the "generalist" animal, prepared to adapt to and to develop cultures in the most varied environments. A long childhood must prepare the newborn of the species to become specialized as a member of a pseudo species (Erikson 1965), i.e., in tribes, cultures, castes, etc., each of which behaves as if it were the only genuine realization of man as the heavens planned and created him. Furthermore, man's drives are characterized by instinctual energies, which are, in contrast to other animals, much less bound to instinctive patterns (or inborn release mechanisms). A maximum of free instinctual energy thus remains ready to be invested in basic psychosocial encounters which tend to fix developing energies into cultural patterns of mutuality, reliability, and competence. Freud has shown the extent to which maladaptive anxiety and rage accompany man's instinctuality, while postulating the strength of the ego in its defensive and in its adaptive aspects (see Freud 1936; Hartmann 1939). We can attempt to show a systematic relationship between man's maladjustments and those basic strengths which must emerge in each life cycle and reemerge from generation to generation (Erikson 1964).

In Figure 1, above, the various psychosocial crises and thus the ontogenetic sources of adaptation and of maladjustment are arranged according to the epigenetic principle. The diagonal signifies a successive development and a hierarchic differentiation of psychosocial strengths.

If a favorable ratio of basic trust over basic mistrust is the first step in psychosocial adaptation, and the second step a favorable ratio of autonomy over shame and doubt, the diagram indicates a number of fundamental facts. Each basic psychosocial trend (1, 2, etc.) meets a crisis (I, 1; II, 2; etc.) during a corresponding stage (I, II, etc.), while *all* must exist from the beginning in some form (broken line) and in later stages (solid lines) must continue to be differentiated and reintegrated with newly dominant trends. An infant will show something like autonomy from the time of birth (I, 2), but it is not until the second year (II, 2) that he is ready to experience and to manage the critical conflict of becoming an autonomous creature while continuing to be dependent. At this time those around him will convey to him a cultural and personal version of the ratio of autonomy and dependence. The diagonal thus indicates a necessary sequence of such encounters but leaves room for variations in tempo and intensity.

The epigenetic pattern will have to be kept in mind as we now state for each stage: (*a*) the psychosocial crisis evoked by social interaction, which is in turn facilitated and necessitated by newly developing drives and capacities, and the specific psychosocial strength emanating from the solution of the crisis: (*b*) the specific sense of estrangement awakened at each stage and its connection with some major form of psychopathology; (*c*) the special relationship between all of these factors and certain basic social institutions (Erikson 1950).

Infancy (basic trust versus mistrust—hope). The resolution of the first psychosocial crisis is performed primarily by maternal care. The newborn infant's more or less coordinated readiness to incorporate by mouth and through the senses meets the mother's and the society's more or less coordinated readiness to feed him and to stimulate his awareness. The mother must represent to the child an almost somatic conviction that she (his first "world") is trustworthy enough to satisfy and to regulate his needs. But the infant's demeanor also inspires hope in adults and makes them wish to give hope; it awakens in them a strength which they, in turn, are ready and needful to have confirmed in the experience of care. This is the onto-genetic basis of hope, that first and basic strength which gives man a semblance of instinctive certainty in his social ecology.

Unavoidable pain and delay of satisfaction, however, and inex-

A Psychosocial Crises		B Radius of Significant Relations
I	Trust vs. Mistrust 　　　　HOPE	Maternal Person
II	Autonomy vs. Shame, Doubt 　　　　WILL	Parental Persons
III	Initiative vs. Guilt 　　　PURPOSE	Basic Family
IV	Industry vs. Inferiority 　　COMPETENCE	Neighborhood, School
V	Identity and Repudiation vs. Identity Diffusion 　　　FIDELITY	Peer Groups and Outgroups; Models of Leadership
VI	Intimacy and Solidarity vs. Isolation 　　　LOVE	Partners in Friendship, Sex, Competition, Cooperation
VII	Generativity vs. Self-Absorption 　　　CARE	Divided Labor and Shared Household
VIII	Integrity vs. Despair 　　WISDOM	"Mankind" "My Kind"

Figure 2*

* In Figure 2 (Erikson 1971), the importance of social interaction is highlighted by the notion of a radius of significant relations.

orable weaning make this stage also prototypical for a sense of abandonment and helpless rage. This is the first of the human estrangements against which hope must maintain itself throughout life.

In psychopathology, a defect in basic trust can be evident in early malignant disturbances or can become apparent later in severe addiction or in habitual or sudden withdrawal into psychotic states.

Biological motherhood needs at least three links with social experience—the mother's past experience of being mothered, a method of care in trustworthy surroundings, and some convincing image of providence. The infant's hope, in turn, is one cornerstone of the adult's faith, which throughout history has sought an institutional safeguard in organized religion. However, where religious institutions fail to give ritual actuality to their formulas they may become irrelevant to psychosocial strength.

Hope, then, is the first psychosocial strength. It is the enduring belief in the attainability of primal wishes in spite of the anarchic urges and rages of dependency.

Early childhood (autonomy versus shame, doubt—will power). Early childhood sets the stage for psychosocial autonomy by rapid gains in muscular maturation, locomotion, verbalization, and discrimination. All of these, however, create limits in the form of spatial restrictions and of categorical divisions between "yes and no," "good and bad," "right and wrong," and "yours and mine." Muscular maturation sets the stage for an ambivalent set of social modalities—holding on and letting go. To hold on can become a destructive retaining or restraining, or a pattern of care—to have and to hold. To let go, too, can turn into an inimical letting loose, or a relaxed "letting pass" and "letting be." Freud calls this the anal stage of libido development because of the pleasure experienced in and the conflict evoked over excretory retention and elimination.

This stage, therefore, becomes decisive for the ratio of good will and willfulness. A sense of self-control without loss of self-esteem is the ontogenetic source of confidence in free will; a sense of overcontrol and loss of self-control can give rise to a lasting propensity for doubt and shame. The matter is complicated by the different needs and capacities of siblings of different ages—and by their rivalry.

Shame is the estrangement of being exposed and conscious of being looked at disapprovingly, of wishing to "bury one's face" or "sink into the ground." This potentiality is exploited in the "shaming" used throughout life by some cultures and causing, on occasion, suicide. While shame is related to the consciousness of being upright and exposed, doubt has much to do with the consciousness of having a front and a back (and of the vulnerability of being seen and influenced from behind). It is the estrangement of being unsure of one's will and of those who would dominate it.

From this stage emerges the propensity for compulsive overcompliance or impulsive defiance. If denied a gradual increase in autonomy of choice the individual may become obsessed by repetitiveness and develop an overly cruel conscience. Early self-doubt and doubt of others may later find their most malignant expression in compulsion neuroses or in paranoiac apprehension of hidden critics and secret persecutors threatening from behind.

We have related basic trust to the institutions of religion. The enduring need of the individual to have an area of free choice reaffirmed and delineated by formulated privileges and limitations, obligations and rights has an institutional safeguard in the principles of law and order and of justice. Where this is impaired, however, the law itself is in danger of becoming arbitrary or formalistic, i.e., "impulsive" or "compulsive" itself.

Will power is the unbroken determination to exercise free choice as well as self-restraint in spite of the unavoidable experience of shame, doubt, and a certain rage over being controlled by others. Good will is rooted in the judiciousness of parents guided by their respect for the spirit of the law.

Play age (initiative versus guilt—purpose). Able to move independently and vigorously, the child, now in his third or fourth year, begins to comprehend his expected role in the adult world and to play out roles worth imitating. He develops a sense of initiative. He associates with age-mates and older children as he watches and enters into games in the barnyard, on the street corner, or in the nursery. His learning now is intrusive; it leads him into ever-new facts and activities, and he becomes acutely aware of differences between the sexes. But if it seems that the child spends on his play a purposefulness out of proportion to "real" purposes, we must recognize the human necessity to simultaneously bind together infantile wish and limited skill, symbol and fact, inner and outer world, a selectively remembered past and a vaguely anticipated future—all before adult "reality" takes over in sanctioned roles and adjusted purposes.

The fate of infantile genitality remains determined by the sex roles cultivated and integrated in the family. In the boy, the sexual orientation is dominated by phallic-intrusive initiative; in the girl, by inclusive modes of attractiveness and "motherliness."

Conscience, however, forever divides the child within himself by establishing an inner voice of self-observation, self-guidance, and self-punishment. The estrangement of this stage, therefore, is a sense of guilt over goals contemplated and acts done, initiated, or merely fantasied. For initiative includes competition with those of superior equipment. In a final contest for favored position with the mother, "oedipal" feelings are aroused in the boy, and there appears to be an intensified fear of finding the genitals harmed as punishment for the fantasies attached to their excitability.

Infantile guilt leads to the conflict between unbounded initiative and repression or inhibition. In adult pathology this residual conflict is expressed in hysterical denial, general inhibition, and sexual impotence, or in overcompensatory exhibitionism and psychopathic acting-out.

The word "initiative" has for many a specifically American, or "entrepreneur," connotation. Yet man needs this sense of initiative for whatever he learns and does, from fruit gathering to commercial enterprise—or the study of books.

The play age relies on the existence of some form of basic family, which also teaches the child by patient example where play ends and irreversible purpose begins. Only thus are guilt feelings integrated in a strong (not severe) conscience; only thus is language verified as a shared actuality. The "oedipal" stage thus not only results in a moral sense restricting the horizon of the permissible, but also directs the way to the possible and the tangible, which attract infantile dreams to the goals of technology and culture. Social institutions, in turn, offer an ethos of action, in the form of ideal adults fascinating enough to replace the heroes of the picture book and fairy tale.

That the adult begins as a playing child means that there is a residue of play acting and role playing even in what he considers his highest purposes. These he projects on a larger and more perfect historical future; these he dramatizes in the ceremonial present with uniformed players in ritual arrangements; thus men sanction aggressive initiative, even as they assuage guilt by submission to a higher authority.

Purpose, then, is the courage to envisage and pursue valued and tangible goals guided by conscience but not paralyzed by guilt and by the fear of punishment.

School age (industry versus inferiority—competence). Before the child, psychologically a rudimentary parent, can become a biological parent, he must begin to be a worker and potential provider. Genital maturation is postponed (the period of latency). The child develops a sense of industriousness, i.e., he begins to comprehend the tool world of his culture, and he can become an eager and absorbed member of that productive situation called "school," which gradually supersedes the whims of play. In all cultures, at this stage, children receive systematic instruction of some kind and learn eagerly from older children.

The danger of this stage lies in the development of a sense of inadequacy. If the child despairs of his skill or his status among his tool partners, he may be discouraged from further learning. He may regress to the hopeless rivalry of the oedipal situation. It is at this point that the larger society becomes significant to the child by admitting him to roles preparatory to the actuality of technology and economy. Where he finds, however, that the color of his skin or the background of his parents rather than his wish and his will to learn will decide his worth as an apprentice, the human propensity for feeling unworthy (inferior) may be fatefully aggravated as a determinant of character development.

But there is another danger: If the overly conforming child accepts work as the only criterion of worthwhileness, sacrificing too readily his imagination and playfulness, he may become ready to submit to what Marx called a "craft-idiocy," i.e., become a slave of his technology and of its established role typology.

This is socially a most decisive stage, preparing the child for a hierarchy of learning experiences which he will undergo with the help of cooperative peers and instructive adults. Since industriousness involves doing things beside and with others, a first sense of the division of labor and of differential opportunity—that is, a sense of the technological ethos of a culture—develops at this time. Therefore, the configurations of cultural thought and the manipulations basic to the prevailing technology must reach meaningfully into school life.

Competence, then, is the free exercise (unimpaired by an infantile sense of inferiority) of dexterity and intelligence in the completion of serious tasks. It is the basis for cooperative participation in some segment of the culture.

Adolescence (identity versus identity confusion—fidelity). With a good initial relationship to skills and tools, and with the advent of puberty, childhood proper comes to an end. The rapidly growing youths, faced with the inner revolution of puberty and with as yet intangible adult tasks, are now primarily concerned with their psychosocial identity and with fitting their rudimentary gifts and skills to the occupational prototypes of the culture.

The integration of an identity is more than the sum of childhood identifications. It is the accrued confidence that the inner sameness and continuity gathered over the past years of development are matched by the sameness and continuity in one's meaning for others, as evidenced in the tangible promise of careers and life-styles.

The adolescent's regressive and yet powerful impulsiveness alternating with compulsive restraint is well known. In all of this, however, an ideological seeking after an inner coherence and a durable set of values can be detected. The particular strength sought is fidelity—that is, the opportunity to fulfill personal potentialities (including erotic vitality or its sublimation) in a context which permits the young person to be true to himself and true to significant others.

"Falling in love" also can be an attempt to arrive at a self-definition by seeing oneself reflected anew in an idealized as well as eroticized other.

From this stage on, acute maladjustments caused by social anomie may lead to psychopathological regressions. Where role confusion joins a hopelessness of long standing, borderline psychotic episodes are not uncommon.

Adolescents, on the other hand, help one another temporarily through much regressive insecurity by forming cliques and by stereotyping themselves, their ideals, and their "enemies." In this they can be clannish and cruel in their exclusion of all those who are "different." Where they turn this repudiation totally against the society, delinquency may be a temporary or lasting result.

As social systems enter into the fiber of each succeeding generation, they also absorb into their lifeblood the rejuvenative power of youth. Adolescence is thus a vital regenerator in the process of social evolution, for youth can offer its loyalties and energies to the conservation of that which it feels is valid as well as to the revolutionary correction of that which has lost its regenerative significance.

Adolescence is least "stormy" among those youths who are gifted and well trained in the pursuit of productive technological trends. In times of unrest, the adolescent mind becomes an ideological mind in search of an inspiring unification of ideas. Youth needs to be affirmed by peers and confirmed by teachings, creeds, and ideologies which express the promise that the best people will come to rule and that rule will develop the best in people. A society's ideological weakness, in turn, expresses itself in weak utopianism and in widespread identity confusion.

Fidelity, then, is the ability to sustain loyalties freely pledged in spite of the inevitable contradictions of value systems. It is the cornerstone of identity and receives inspiration from confirming ideologies and "ways of life."

Young adulthood (intimacy versus isolation—love). Consolidated identity permits the self-abandonment demanded by intimate affiliations, by passionate sexual unions, or by inspiring encounters. The young adult is ready for intimacy and solidarity—that is, he can commit himself to affiliations and partnerships even though they may call for significant sacrifices and compromises. Ethical strength emerges as a further differentiation of ideological conviction (adolescence) and a sense of moral obligation (childhood).

True genital maturity is first reached at this stage; much of the individual's previous sex life is of the identity-confirming kind. Freud, when asked for the criteria of a mature person, is reported to have answered: *"Lieben und Arbeiten"* ("love and work"). All three words deserve equal emphasis.

It is only at this stage that the biological differences between the sexes result in a full polarization within a joint life style. Previously established strengths have helped the two sexes to converge in capacities and values which enhance communication and cooperation, while divergence is now of the essence in love life and in procreation. Thus the sexes first become similar in consciousness, language, and ethics in order then to be maturely different. But this, by necessity, causes ambivalences.

The danger of this stage is possible psychosocial isolation—that is, the avoidance of contacts which commit to intimacy. In psychopathology isolation can lead to severe character problems of the kind which interfere with "love and work," and this often on the basis of infantile fixations and lasting immaturities.

Man, in addition to erotic attraction, has developed a selectivity of mutual love that serves the need for a new and shared identity in the procession of generations. Love is the guardian of that elusive and yet all-pervasive power of cultural and personal style which binds into a "way of life" the affiliations of competition and cooperation, procreation and production. The problem is one of transferring the experience of being cared for in a parental setting to an adult affiliation actively chosen and cultivated as a mutual concern within a new generation.

The counterpart of such intimacy, and the danger, are man's readiness to fortify his territory of intimacy and solidarity by exaggerating small differences and prejudging or excluding foreign influences and people. Insularity thus aggravated can lead to that irrational fear which is easily exploited by demagogic leaders seeking aggrandizement in war and in political conflict.

Love, then, is a mutuality of devotion greater than the antagonisms inherent in divided function.

Maturity (generativity versus stagnation—care). Evolution has made man the teaching and instituting as well as the learning animal. For dependency and maturity are reciprocal: mature man needs to be needed, and maturity is guided by the nature of that which must be cared for.

Generativity, then, is primarily the concern with establishing and guiding the next generation. In addition to procreativity, it includes productivity and creativity; thus it is psychosocial in nature. From the crisis of generativity emerges the strength of care.

Where such enrichment fails, a sense of stagnation and boredom ensues, the pathological symptoms of which depend on variations in mental epidemiology: certainly where the hypocrisy of the frigid mother was once regarded as a most significant malignant influence, today, when sexual "adjustment" is in order, an obsessive pseudo intimacy and adult self-indulgence are nonetheless damaging to the generational process. The very nature of generativity suggests that the most circumscribed symptoms of its weakness are to be found in the next generation in the form of those aggravated estrangements which we have listed for childhood and youth.

Generativity is itself a driving power in human organization. For the intermeshing stages of childhood and adulthood are in themselves a system of generation and regeneration given continuity by institutions such as extended households and divided labor.

Thus, in combination, the basic strengths enumerated here and the structure of an organized human community provide a set of proven methods and a fund of traditional reassurance with which each generation meets the needs of the next. Various traditions transcend divisive personal differences and confusing conditions. But they also contribute to a danger to the species as a whole, namely, the defensive territoriality of the pseudo species, which on seemingly ethical grounds must discredit and destroy threateningly alien systems and may itself be destroyed in the process.

Care is the broadening concern for what has been generated by love, necessity, or accident—a concern which must consistently overcome the ambivalence adhering to irreversible obligation and the narrowness of self-concern.

Old age (integrity versus despair—wisdom). Strength in the aging and sometimes in the old takes the form of wisdom in its many connotations—ripened "wits," accumulated knowledge, inclusive understanding, and mature judgment. Wisdom maintains and conveys the integrity of experience, in spite of the decline of bodily and mental functions. Responding to the oncoming generation's need for an integrated heritage, the wisdom of old age remains aware of the relativity of all knowledge acquired in one lifetime in one historical period. Integrity, therefore, implies an emotional integration faithful to the image bearers of the past and ready to take (and eventually to renounce) leadership in the present.

The lack or loss of this accrued integration is signified by a hidden fear of death: fate is not accepted as the frame of life, death not as its finite boundary. Despair indicates that time is too short for alternate roads to integrity: this is why the old try to "doctor" their memories. Bitterness and disgust mask such despair, which in severe psychopathology aggravates senile depression, hypochondria, and paranoiac hate.

A meaningful old age (preceding terminal invalidism) provides that integrated heritage which gives indispensible perspective to those growing up, "adolescing," and aging. But the end of the cycle also evokes "ultimate concerns," the paradoxes of which we must leave to philosophical and religious interpreters. Whatever chance man has to transcend the limitations of his self seems to depend on his full (if often tragic) engagement in the one and only life cycle permitted him in the sequence of generations. Great philosophical and religious systems dealing with ultimate individuation seem to have remained (even in their monastic establishments) responsibly related to the cultures and civilizations of their times. Seeking transcendence by renunciation, they remain ethically concerned with the maintainance of the world. By the same token, a civilization can be measured by the meaning which it gives to the full cycle of life, for such meaning (or the lack of it) cannot fail to reach into the beginnings of the next generation and thus enhance the potentiality that others may meet ultimate questions with some clarity and strength.

Wisdom, then, is a detached and yet active concern with life in the face of death.

Conclusion

From the cycle of life such dispositions as faith, will power, pur posefulness, efficiency, devotion, affection, responsibility, and sagacity (all of which are also criteria of ego strength) flow into the life of institutions. Without them, institutions wilt; but without the spirit of institutions pervading the patterns of care and love, instruction and training, no enduring strength could emerge from the sequence of generations.

We have attempted, in a psychosocial frame, to account for the ontogenesis not of lofty ideals but of an inescapable and intrinsic order of strivings, which, by weakening or strengthening man, dictates the minimum goals of informed and responsible participation.

Psychosocial strength, we conclude, depends on a total process which regulates individual life cycles, the sequence of generations, and the structure of society simultaneously, for all three have evolved together.

Each person must translate this order into his own terms so as to make it amenable to whatever kind of trait inventory, normative scale, measurement, or educational goal is his main concern. Science and technology are, no doubt, changing essential aspects of the course of life, wherefore some increased awareness of the functional wholeness of the cycle may be mandatory. Interdisciplinary work will define in practical and applicable terms what evolved order is common to all men and what true equality of opportunity must mean in planning for future generations.

The study of the human life cycle has immediate applications in a number of fields. Paramount is the science of human development within social institutions. In psychiatry (and in its applications to law), the diagnostic and prognostic assessment of disturbances common to life stages should help to outweigh fatalistic diagnoses. Whatever will prove tangibly lawful about the cycle of life will also be an important focus for anthropology insofar as it assesses universal functions in the variety of institutional forms. Finally, as the study of the life history emerges from that of case histories, it will throw new light on biography and thus on history itself.

Bibliography

Bühler, Charlotte. (1933) 1959. *Der menschliche Lebenslauf als psychologisches Problem*, 2d ed., rev. Leipzig: Hirzel.
———. 1962. *Values in Psychotherapy*. New York: Free Press.
Erikson, Erik H. (1950) 1964 *Childhood and Society*. 2d ed., rev. & enl. New York: W. W. Norton & Co.
———. 1958. *Young Man Luther*. New York: W. W. Norton & Co.
———. 1964. *Insight and Responsibilty*. New York: W. W. Norton & Co.
———. 1965. *The Ontogeny of Ritualization in Man*. Unpublished manuscript.
Freud, Anna. (1936) 1957. *The Ego and the Mechanisms of Defense*. New York: International Universities Press. First published as *Das Ich und die Abwehrmechanismen*.
———. 1965. *Normality and Pathology in Childhood: Assessment of Development*. New York: International Universities Press.
Hartmann, Heinz. (1939) 1958. *Ego Psychology and the Problem of Adaptation*, transl. by David Rapaport. New York: International Universities Press. First published as *Ich-Psychologie und Anpassungsproblem*.
Mayr, Ernst. 1964. "The Evolution of Living Systems." *National Academy of Sciences Proceedings* 51, 934–41.
Werner, Heinz. (1926) 1965. *Comparative Psychology of Mental Development*, rev. ed. New York: International Universities Press. First published as *Einführung in die Entwicklungspsychologie*.

VI.
REFLECTIONS
ON IDENTITY,
YOUTH, AND
YOUNG
ADULTHOOD

Plans for the Returning Veteran with Symptoms of Instability (1945)

The Veterans' Clinic in the Mount Zion Hospital in San Francisco*
is a nonsectarian clinic open to any discharged veteran with nervous
instability. On the basis of my experience in this clinic, I will discuss
the problems of veterans discharged before the end of hostilities with
the diagnosis "psychoncurosis," and of discharged veterans in general.

The diagnosis of a mental rather than a somatic disturbance at
the time of discharge does not permit any conclusions regarding the
soldier's sanity, character, or abilities. Conditions of modern warfare
cause a considerable number of soldiers at one time or another (often
after discharge) to develop more or less transient symptoms of nervous instability of varying degrees.

"Psychoneurotic" casualties include every variety of personality
with every variety of military experience: men who had never done
well in anything; others who had done well but could not take military life, even behind the front; men who did well in army life but

A report to the 1945 Stanford University Workshop on Community Leadership, based on
Erikson's work at the Veterans Rehabilitation Clinic of the Mount Zion Hospital in San
Francisco. First published in *Community Planning for Peacetime Living*, eds. Louis Wirth,
Ernest R. Hilgard and I. James Quillen, Stanford University Press 1945, 116–21. This article
is Erikson's first published paper on the problems of ego identity diffusion in young adults.
* Directed by Dr. J. Kasanin and Dr. E. Windholz.

were either unprepared or too little motivated to stand the stress of danger; and also a great number of experienced, highly-trained, "natural" soldiers exposed to combat situations which would tax any man's resistance. Combat situations which at times have caused a high percentage of crack troops to develop symptoms of instability usually combine the following:

a) Physical exhaustion, especially lack of sleep.

b) Enforced immobility while exposed to a superior or better-located enemy.

c) Momentary doubt of the wisdom or honesty of military leaders.

d) Excessive sense of responsibility.

e) Basic or momentary lack of conviction regarding "what it's all about."

f) Traumatic factors of a highly individual nature, violating the individual's intolerance (caused by past experience or background) of monotony, sudden changes, violence, separation from home, increased responsibility, life among men, sexual abstinence, and other often minute and unpredictable circumstances.

On occasion the breakdown is delayed and occurs if and when some of these conditions are later added to the others. For example, hospitalization may bring about forced immobility; the separation from the combat unit or the observation of home-front indifference may cause a feeling of unreality of the war and its aims.

Policies concerning the withdrawal of "fatigued" soldiers from combat areas and concerning their diagnosis, treatment, and discharge have been carefully revised during the war so that many men, who otherwise are in no way "different" from those discharged early in the war, have been spared some of the agony acompanying the diagnosis, psychoneurosis. This diagnosis is medically vague; it often signifies the absence of a more clearly defined pathology. It often is a matter of administrative convenience, and its purpose often is the protection of the taxpayer, on whom the burden of caring for the potentially disabled later might fall, rather than the protection of the individual casualty, who might have a good chance for rapid recovery. Nevertheless, this diagnosis in many cases has caused in the patients inferiority feelings, doubts regarding their sanity, and guilt feelings toward their buddies who stayed to finish the job. For some individuals and groups of the community it has led to an economic stigma—unreasonably, since innumerable undiagnosed neurotics do acceptable peacetime work.

During the war it has been found that treatment right behind the lines is effective in many cases and that men thus treated could be delegated to help others at the front. Such observations have provided individual psychiatrists with entirely new experiences which undoubtedly will change the course of psychiatric history. In the meantime, what should our attitude be?

The unfortunate publicity given to neurotic instability in returning veterans has fluctuated from optimistic to pessimistic extremes. The veteran should be treated neither as if he were essentially different from anybody else nor as if nothing had happened. Lots has happened, in everybody's life, and it takes all the resourcefulness of a nation to overcome the dislocation of a global war. In the nation's resourcefulness we must put our prime trust. Community leaders, however, should be aware of certain facts and be prepared to meet their implications. These are:

1. The draft boards had to reject and the armed forces had to discharge such a large number of unstable individuals that the problem approaches that of a social disease. It will not do to meet it with the silence of abhorrence with which other large-scale problems, such as syphilis, have been treated in the past. To take cognizance of diseases of the social body does not mean to "pamper" their victims.

2. There is a whispering campaign which suspects all psychoneurotic dischargees as weaklings. In wartime, there is some sense in a general inclination to condemn all weakness in the prosecution of the war as a danger to morale. In any army there must be a high premium on the determination to "finish the job." However, even among the soldiers who stuck to it, much of the most venomous and heated condemnation of "weak sisters" or "cowards" has come from those who have been closest to a breakdown themselves and do not want to admit it. This condemnation, too, served a purpose. However, now that the war is over, condemnation or suspicion becomes senseless. The conscience of the strong who broke is already overburdened—and the weak will not learn from condemnation. To rehabilitate these men all communities should learn to understand that war under modern conditions is in itself a social disease, dangerous to the best and the strongest—and that pampered weaklings and cynics are the results of irresponsibility in community life.

3. Many soldiers not diagnosed as psychoneurotics will develop anxiety symptoms when they return; a considerable number of men who thrived under military discipline will feel upset when faced with the demands of initiative and competitiveness in free enterprise.

American family life and American economic resiliency will gradually reabsorb the vast majority of those who have suffered dislocation. However, geographic dislocation and the interruption of careers are dangerous things in a competitive system. The American who was called to arms wanted above all to finish the job (as long as he was convinced that there was a job), and he wanted to avoid letting his buddy down (as long as he was convinced his buddy felt the same). But he hated to be a sucker. Only a relatively small number of men have been able to avoid serious doubts in this war. Not every veteran who now, to forget his doubts, only wants to "get home" or only wants his "old job back" will be able at first to make the best of either.

Among the common symptoms of the veterans' unrest are:

1. A mildly confused feeling of unreality, lapses of memory, indecision, inefficiency in regard to simple tasks well mastered before the war. These symptoms often last into the first job, even if this happens to be the prewar job.

2. Restlessness. In addition to a widespread search for new jobs now, it can be expected that future widespread changes of jobs will take place for some time after the war. Undue sensitiveness to noises (metallic noises, approaching motors, shrill or angry human voices) may be one cause.

3. Sleeplessness, in spite of all the dreams of feather beds.

4. Sexual anaesthesia or even temporary impotence, in spite of (or is it because of?) all dreams of pin-up girls.

5. Unusual outbursts of anger at seemingly irrelevant occasions.

6. Puzzling contradictions and ambivalences. Some men will be excessively active, aggressive, talkative; others will be silent, moody, and passive; still others will oscillate between these extremes. At one moment they will pour out their experiences and at the next will resent a simple little question. Some will hate the army, yet resent disparaging remarks, especially against their particular outfit; some will not know what to do with themselves, yet will be provoked by any suggestion as to what they should do; some in many little ways will become quite dependent, especially upon their wives, yet will be angry at any recognition of this dependency; some will want to find things as they left them, yet will complain that nothing has been done while they were away; some will be intolerant of all authority, yet will behave intolerantly and authoritatively themselves; some will act young, yet appear old; some will crave continuity, yet be shiftless; some will be very jealous, yet indicate that faithlessness has not been beyond them.

There will be certain age differences in these manifestations; boys who had not yet been independent before the war and men who had already enjoyed the security of an established eonomic existence before the war in all probability will be least hit. The more severe forms of dislocation will probably be more frequent in the group of interrupted beginners and habitual beginners who were unstable in their economic existence before the war or were just about to make the grade.

The best antidote for all of these phenomena is not publicity but action and observation. Community leaders should be prepared to meet these phenomena in various degrees and combinations in their communities and to give reassurance as to their transitory and nonmalignant nature—but not without keeping an eye on those few men whose instability is more malignant or more tenacious and threatens to endanger themselves, their families, or the morale of the community. One group that in a short while will be most in need of personal advice are the wives of returning men, for the intimacy of the home will often be the only place where symptoms are manifested. With some understanding a wave of divorces and of alcoholic excesses can be prevented and much damage to the coming generation forestalled.

The following suggestions arise from experience with those discharged before the end of hostilities: Wherever economic or personal advice or help are needed, they should be *nationally decentralized*, that is, come from communal rather than from state or federal resources. The men have been dependent upon "Washington" for too long; they want to feel the resourcefulness of the home town. The administration of the help given should be *locally centralized* so that the veteran will not feel "pushed around" and "up against red tape" when asking for a little assistance. This assistance should be handled, not by the impersonal representatives of organizations, but by specially selected people who have a direct, informed, and resourceful approach and preferably are themselves veterans of this war or the first World War.

Statement to the Committee on Privilege and Tenure of the University of California Concerning the California Loyalty Oath (1951)

Dear Sirs: I deeply appreciate the privilege of a free hearing before a committee of colleagues. With you I shall not play hide-and-seek regarding a question which must be implicit in what you wish to ask me and which must be explicit in what I shall have to say: I am not and have never been a Communist, inside "the party" or outside, in this country or abroad.

· Because of my sincere appreciation of the position which I now hold, I shall state (as freely and as briefly as I can) what considerations and feelings have made it impossible for me in good conscience to acquiesce in the latest form of "alternative affirmation" which has been demanded.

I shall not go into matters which carry over from the issue of the special oath. But I may say that the constitutional oath still seems to

While *Childhood and Society* was in press, Erikson, then a member of the University of California faculty, became involved in a struggle with the California Board of Regents. The struggle was over the board's requirement that every faculty member sign a special "loyalty oath" and a declaration that the individual was not a member of The Communist Party, nor did he or she support any party or organization which advocated the violent overthrow of the government. Erikson courageously refused to sign the oath. Instead, he resigned his university position and wrote an explanatory statement which eventually was read to the members of the American Psychoanalytic Association at a midwinter meeting and later published in *Psychiatry*.

First published in *Psychiatry*, 14, 243–45. 1951.

me to cover admirably and fully my obligations to country, state, and job. I still resent being asked to affirm that I meant what I said when I signed the constitutional oath. One could accept such an additional affirmation wherever and whenever it might seem effective in a special emergency. To me, this contract is an empty gesture toward meeting the danger of infiltration into academic life of indoctrinators, conspirators, and spies. For a subversive person need not have a party card; a conspirator is not bound by declarations; a party member may be unknown to any but a few; a would-be commissar would not ask you for a hearing; and a fanatic indoctrinator may not feel that he lies when he says that he represents objective truth.

One may say, then, Why not acquiesce in an empty gesture, if it saves the faces of very important personages, helps to allay public hysteria, and hurts nobody? My answer is that of a psychologist. I do believe that this gesture which now saves face for some important people will, in the long run, hurt people who are much more important: the students. Too much has been said of academic freedom for the faculty; I am concerned about certain dangers to the spirit of the student body, dangers which may emanate from such "compromises" as we have been asked to accept.

For many students, their years of study represent their only contact with thought and theory, their only contact with men who teach them how to see two sides of a question and yet to be decisive in their conclusions, how to understand and yet to act with conviction. Young people are rightfully suspicious and embarrassingly discerning. I do not believe they can remain unimpressed by the fact that the men who are to teach them to think and to act judiciously and spontaneously must undergo a political test; must sign a statement which implicitly questions the validity of their own oath of office; must abrogate "commitments" so undefined that they must forever suspect themselves and one another; and must confess to an "objective truth" which they know only too well is elusive. Older people like ourselves can laugh this off; in younger people, however—and especially in these most important students who are motivated to go into teaching—a dangerous rift may well occur between the "official truth" and those deep and often radical doubts which are the necessary condition for the development of thought.

By the same token, the gesture of the contract will not allay public hysteria. I know that the general public at the moment indulges (as it always does when it is confronted with change) in a "bunching together" of all that seems undefinably dangerous: spies, bums, Communists, liberals, and "professors." A few politicians always thrive on such oversimplification, some out of simplicity, some out of shrewdness. But who, if the universities do not, will lead the countermove of enlightenment? Who will represent, in quiet work and in forceful words, the absolute necessity of meeting the future (now full of worse than dynamite) with a conviction born of judiciousness? If the universities themselves become the puppets of public hysteria, if their own regents are expressly suspicious of their faculties, if the professors themselves tactily admit that they need to deny perjury, year after year—will that allay public hysteria?

If the Regents and the President had asked the faculty to join in a study of what Communism is—abroad, in this country, and on this campus—a study of what we need and can do about it, and what we need and can do against it, we all would have participated to the limit of our competency. Instead, the faculty was taken by surprise and hopelessly put on the defensive, in this most vital matter. This is a thoughtless and, if stubbornly pursued, a ruthless waste of human resources.

I realize that the University of California is a big place, with many purposes. In many departments the danger which I have outlined will not interfere with the finding and teaching of facts. Mine is a highly specialized place in an area of knowledge still considered rather marginal to true science. My field includes the study of "hysteria," private and public, in "personality" and "culture." It includes the study of the tremendous waste in human energy which proceeds from irrational fear and from the irrational gestures which are part of what we call "history." I would find it difficult to ask my subject of investigation (people) and my students to work with me, if I were to participate without protest in a vague, fearful, and somewhat vindictive gesture devised to ban an evil in some magic way—an evil which must be met with much more searching and concerted effort.

In this sense, I may say that my conscience did not permit me to sign the contract after having sworn that I would do my job to the best of my ability.

The Confirmation of the Delinquent (1957)

WITH KAI T. ERIKSON

JUDGE IMPOSES ROAD GANG TERM FOR BACK TALK
Wilmington, N.D. (UP)—A "smart alecky" youth who wore pegged trousers and a flattop haircut began six months on a road gang today for talking back to the wrong judge.

Charles N. Cagle, 20, of Wilmington, was fined $25 and costs in Judge Henry Lee Stevens Jr.'s superior court for reckless operation of an automobile. But he just didn't leave well enough alone.

"I understand how it was, with your pegged trousers and flattop haircut," Stevens said in assessing the fine. "You go on like this and I predict in five years you'll be in prison."

When Cagle walked over to pay his fine, he overheard Probation Officer Gordon Blake tell the judge how much trouble the "smart alecky" young offender had been.

"I just want you to know I'm not a thief," interrupted Cagle to the judge.

The judge's voice boomed to the court clerk: "Change that judgment to six months on the roads."

The news item is quoted here not in order to judge the judge or defend the defendant—for we do not know the facts beyond those which the wires found fit to report and the editor fit to print. Rather,

First published in *Chicago Review*, 10 (Winter 1957), 15–23.

we are concerned with the readers who apparently are the willing recipients of such news. Do they think, we wonder, that the judge is right in his sentiments; and if so, that he is also right in his verdict? How bad, do they think, is the defendant—and how much better will he be after six months in the road gang?

It is not too uncommon that judges indulge in the public abuse of young offenders who act without deference or fail to demonstrate the kind of remorse which, so it seems, would make the predicament of juvenile delinquency more acceptable to the older generation. Other reactions of adults to young offenders, "letters to the editor," and the statements of parents quoted in the more sensational news, all reveal a general mood of petulant condemnation, as if the delinquencies committed by youngsters were acts of deliberate unfairness to the world of adults. Experts, too, by publicly proclaiming contradictory "causes" of delinquency, betray the fact that they feel uncomfortably challenged by an unexpected phenomenon.

In this article a psychoanalyst and a sociologist propose that the reactions cited, far from being side effects of delinquency, may be part of a widespread adult attitude which inadvertently (and in spite of all that public agencies and individuals are doing to *prevent* delinquency) *confirms* a considerable number of faltering young people in the ways of criminality.

The fact is that delinquents are made, not born—and they are made slowly and gradually. *Potentialities* for goodness and badness are inborn in all; they grow to *probabilities* during childhood. But the *certainty* of a man's or a woman's measure is not established before the end of his or her adolescence, and not without some kind of confirmation by the adult world. As Faulkner puts it starkly, "it ain't none of us pure crazy and ain't none of us pure sane until the balance of us talks him that-a-way."

Every one of us has seen his own or other people's youngsters suddenly "grow together" in body and mind and give the convincing impression that they know where they are going. We have seen others temporarily grow apart within themselves or grow apart from us. It often takes considerable time—well into the early twenties—before an adolescent can make a workable whole out of all that became distinctive of him in the years of childhood. For what once was play and pretense, in adolescence becomes rehearsal with different ways of living until the main life performance, namely the individual's lasting identity in the adult world, is established.

Many adolescents seem to find their identity with ease, as their way of life appears to be cut out for them in their parents' expectations and preparations. The roles offered in schools and first jobs come easily to them. Yet, some of these "lucky" people may later come to feel that things, maybe, were too easy too early. For others the right way emerges only after much experimentation and after much wearing effort to find recognition as a new person, i.e., as somebody who takes unexpected turns—and yet makes sense. Here, often, only the outcome can tell what was "right." In the meantime we adults are rarely aware of our essential function in conveying to young people—deliberately or inadvertently—that they do (or do not) make sense. Without knowing it, or, indeed, appreciating it, we may find ourselves in a strategic role as uncles or family friends, as teachers or physicians, as neighbors or significant strangers. Now and again a quotation comes back to us of something which, for all we remember, we may or may not have said, and which nevertheless remained a memorable judgment—for good or for bad—in a young person's life.

Much can go wrong here. For in the adolescent's supreme effort to make sense to himself and to others at the same time, the complexity of the adolescent state and the confusion of the times meet head-on. Young people undergo stages in which they seem stubbornly self-assured, and yet make anything but sense to themselves; while others feel out of place, and yet are on their way. Some adolescents temporarily take a perverse kind of pride in making no sense to anyone—least of all to those immediately concerned with them. Always, however, they secretly strive to make sense to *some* people of their own choice, even if these persons are somewhere on the "undesirable" periphery of their family, their class, or their neighborhood. This is often misunderstood as aimless rebellion or mere egotism, while in many ways it is a search for new loyalties and for new techniques of living. Societies, to remain young, need such search. What would this country have become without those who would not be fenced-in, who courted change, who sought *their* chance in economic expansion, and who insisted on *their* life style? But political and economic developments can come to contradict what children have been led to expect, and adolescence can become a period of confused chances and uncertain choices, a time when much good energy, essential to society as well as to the individual, can go fatally astray.

To prevent what has been called a "diffusion of identity," societies, old and new, design a variety of official confirmations. In primitive tribes the confirmers "initiate" the young into society and with impressive, often frightening, rituals impose clear obligations and privileges. In organized religion the functionaries of a faith offer ceremonial confirmations, linking the individual's small new life with a universal life of fatherhood and brotherhood. Political leaders offer slogans and uniforms, eager to confirm youth as part of a movement, a nation, a class. In traditional institutions of learning, masters of crafts, arts, and sciences offer apprenticeships in which old techniques are reverently reviewed, new ones envisaged. Fraternities and groups of alumni offer identities often all too persistent. In each instance the young person finds himself part of a universal framework which reaches back into an established tradition, and promises a definable future.

Yet the meaning of confirmations changes with the times. Some ceremonies and graduations, while ancient and profound, are no longer vital; others, while sensible and modern, somehow are not profound enough to provide meaning. Many young people, eager for an image of the future, find the confirmations and ceremonies designed by their parents' churches, clubs, or orders too formalized to "speak to their condition." Others go along with the make-believe identities taught in many occupational and professional schools, but find that streamlined adaptiveness can prove brittle when life brings new crises. Thus what official institutions teach and preach often has little to do with the immediate inner needs and outer prospects of young people.

It is here that leaderless and unguided youth often attempts to confirm itself in groups of pals and in organized gangs which offer to those who have lost (or who never had) any meaningful confirmation in the approved ways of their fathers an identity based on a defiant testing out of what is most marginal to the adult world. Among these alliances we are here concerned primarily with gangs: the mocking grandiosity of their names ("Black Barons" or "Junior Bishops," "Saints" or "Navahoes"), their insignia (sometimes tattooed into the skin), and their defiant behavior clearly mark them as independent "tribes" or "sects." As has often been pointed out, these gangs are by no means necessarily malicious or dangerous. True, on occasion they suddenly follow impulses of cold annihilation, such as adults display only in race riots. Usually they only intend to look that way. Yet, given some isolated excesses which make the adults expect that they *are all* that way, they may well be driven in the anticipated direction.

It should be said here that such gang formation is by no means restricted to this country. A South African doctor described bands of young negroes who are called "Zootsies." Their description coincided in many ways with that of Californian Zoot-suiters, of whose existence and name the doctor had been unaware. It is particularly significant that analogous phenomena have been reported from Moscow.

What is, then, the universal urgency, the cruel energy which, to be contained, needs some kind of shared identity at all price? To this psychoanalysis and sociology give different but converging answers.

The psychoanalyst will point to the adolescent's increased physical power, sexual drive, and abundance of fantasy. He will say that the adolescent must make contact with the honest worth of his cultural heritage and of the world-in-progress, because otherwise he will fall victim to his biological heritage. Here we must hasten to add that man's biological heritage, or what are often called his sexual and aggressive "instincts," have long lost the naturalness of animal drives and the adaptiveness of the animal's instincts. Longer than the young of any animal, the children of man remain wards of parents and teachers, and must *learn* to be human—each in his own way. This learning begins with being mothered in the days of utter helplessness and being loved and guided in the years of gradual growth. But it does not end until the struggle for identity and adolescent experimentation ends. If it happens that the young person's preparation in childhood does not add up to the promise of a recognized place in some desirable segment of his society, then the thrill of experimentation with "different" ways of life may well become acutely perverted. He may, then, with the impulsive absolutism of youth, prefer to be nobody when he cannot quite be somebody. Where his imagination cannot be productive, he may experiment with acts and feelings on the very borderline of mental disease. Or he may accept the challenge of sexual dares and cruel pranks. A youth without identity is like a powder keg left unguarded. A seemingly insignificant source of combustion, having remained unobserved, can turn prank and dare into disaster and crime. A mild "lone wolf" of a young man, having playfully threatened a baby sitter and her ward with a big knife, murdered her with wild stabs when she started to scream. Maybe (who knows) her screams, "recognizing" him as a potential murderer, made him one. Afterwards he could only say "it was a prank that backfired." Yet that was neither a psychiatric nor a legal formulation; he was sentenced to die. But many young criminals who (at first) commit minor acts, alone or in the mutual contamination of gang life, could say that it all started with a prank or dare which at the time seemed at worst to be unclean fun.

When that happens, we receive the young individual into our jails and courts. More often than not we admit him into the company of criminals. We deal with him in terms of complicated and outdated laws. For the law of property, say, provides no legal definition for the impulsive appropriation of a motor car for the sake of speeding around a few blocks or for the sake of impressing a girl. We say that a youth stole; we want him to admit theft and say that he is sorry. We want him to accept punishment in the name of the law, even as we find ourselves caught in legal tangles. We appeal to him in outrage or hurt, only to be met with an evasive glance or with a defiant stare. We try to understand this glance and this stare, but in vain. For it merely means that we have not succeeded in making any real, any compelling sense to him. Maybe we should recognize in this glance and stare the universal fact that the technology which we more or less good-naturedly create, the laws which we more or less logically uphold, and the morality which we more or less sincerely confess, do not necessarily add up to a world which makes more sense to a delinquent than delinquency does. And he cannot afford *not* to be a delinquent, until we can convince him that in our scheme there is a safer identity for him.

To understand, then, why a relatively (if not absolutely) large number of youths find themselves in this position, *psychoanalysis* would emphasize the precariousness of the adolescent struggle against vastly intensified sexual and aggressive drives, and thus the individual's *inner* need for an identity and a consistent morality. *Sociology*, on the other hand, would begin with man in the orderly aggregate, with society. The social order, to remain safe and strong, must harness the energies of its young individuals and must try to direct them to productive styles of living. To the young person in search of identity society offers a variety of roles. Whether his identity is clothed in the occupational roles of "doctor, lawyer, merchant, chief" or of "rich man, poor man, beggar man, thief," social usage provides for each a standardized manner and bearing, and a particular kind of recognition and status, and sociology will go along with the children's rhyme in giving the recognition of an occupational role to the confirmed thief and to the beggar as well as to the professional man. As the young person rehearses his roles, society is eager to impress him with the available alternatives by attaching labels to him, often hastily, and often, no doubt, in order to know how to deal with him and with his changeable ways. The press of recent years has clearly reflected the desperate need of policemen and judges, educators, psychiatrists, and clergymen so to label and to diagnose delinquency and delinquents that each profession may retain the comfortable conviction that, if given total power, it alone would have the total method to master the disturbance. To be sure, each of them has something essential to offer, and is most urgently called upon to offer it fast. But it is imperative to pause long enough to consider that some "professional" approaches by insisting on one single interpretation (they are "just" kids from broken homes, or bad chips from bad old blocks, "just" souls in need of salvation or minds in need of treatment) offer conflicting kinds of confirmation while all of them taken together amount to one confirmation, namely, that of a section of youth which makes no sense to its parent-society.

The most widespread criminal violation called car theft may illustrate the limited competency of any one group of experts. More than half of all car thefts are committed by individuals (in the vast majority, boys) under twenty-one years of age—and they by no means all come from lower class families. Psychology can elaborate on the fact that adolescence is a stage of great locomotor urge. Young men "chase after" things, young girls "run around"; this they do differently in different cultures. Given our world of mechanical automotion (in which for adults, too, motor cars are flashy toys as well as useful tools) youth easily falls prey to what may be called automotive intoxication. In order to indulge in it youths appropriate cars; or they enhance what cars they have with hot-rodding and with alcoholic and sexual dares. All of this, while potentially dangerous to life and property, has in its motivation little to do with theft in the sense of appropriation for economic gain or with other established legal categories for motivation and crime. Yet this widespread phenomenon of delinquency, most typical of youth and most representative of our times, is legally ruled by criminal laws designed in the days of a different technology. While, then, neither jurist nor psychologist nor sociologist could alone define this phenomenon, young people get caught in judicial procedures which in their bewildering local varieties cannot possibly be understood by them. And yet it depends on these procedures whether or not the infraction will prove to have been a transitory prank or a fateful first step in the confirmation of a criminal career.

The sociologist would look at such confirmation as the final step in the gradual acquisition of a compelling role. He, too, could go back to the play of children and show the way in which quite early different roles appear. Children are both cops and robbers, cowboys and horse thieves—alternately but passionately. They observe many roles in their elders; and, of course, they soon become acquainted with the particular variety of roles, presented to them ever more impressively by the entertainment industry. As spectators they experience at least some of these roles at some fleeting moments almost as if they had lived them. Any young individual has been *introduced* to a great variety of imaginary roles some of which will become completely dormant, while others, sooner or later, may become a decisive bridge to social reality. The delinquent role may have been only fleetingly envisaged by him as a fascinating or distrubing possiblity; or it may have been presented to him as a compelling example in a delinquent environment. Given a number of circumstances, this role can acquire exclusive importance in the young individual's attempt to make sense to himself and to others. Foremost among such circumstances may be the sudden devaluation of a precious but precarious role such as, for example, Prew's as a bugler in *From Here to Eternity*, a role so convincingly depicted as a possible salvation for a potentially murderous young man. Often, a young person with diminished sources of identity and with a heightened impulsivity develops a temporary low immunity to social infection and falls prey to the inducements, paired with threats, of older and already confirmed delinquents. To this, then, is added the second stage, based on the tendency on the part of society to *attribute* to a young individual as an inborn and permanent part of his personality or of his background what as yet may be only a temporary experimental role. All of us will recognize such "attribution" in the way we look with alarm at individual youngsters when in their dress and posture they dare us to type them, and we know it from the way we "recognize" peacefully loitering gangs as dangerous juvenile delinquents. They, in turn, while seemingly uninterested in our very existence, are sure to perceive our furtive evaluation. And they, more or less inadvertently, provoke policemen into action. A policeman's impression "I don't like his looks" here often becomes a first fateful step in a procedure which from the detection of small irregularities leads to big consequences in the apprehended child's life.

In a similarly accidental way, of course, many a young person gets his chance in life when somebody *does* like his looks. But we are here concerned with that chain of negative evaluations, that chain of persistent attributions which finally commits both society and the young person to the incontrovertible fact that he is somebody "with a record"—or looks like somebody who will have one. This, then, is the third stage: the *commitment* to the criminal role. Again, we are deliberately playing with the double meaning of a word here. For it can happen that a youngster, when *committed* as an official offender to a corrective procedure, decides in defiant despair to *commit himself* to the role of an incorrigible. One third of all delinquents are "caught" again—often having made only the flimsiest attempts to conceal their criminal intentions. The autobiographies of professional criminals of undoubted skill in their craft clearly reveal the clumsiness of their first delinquent steps—a clumsiness inviting detection and, maybe, the corrective influence of somebody who cares. Where such help is not forthcoming, there is only the world of professional crime and of law enforcement to confirm the young deviant in the role of loyal and expert criminal.

Laws cannot, must not, change easily. The executors of the law must try to represent the spirit in which it was created. Yet when sanctioned categories of violation appear to be flagrantly incongruous in a world changed by undreamed-of techniques, then surely a redefinition of the law in line with an emerging science of man must be envisaged. We begin to know that the difference between delinquency and crime is often as great as the difference between childhood and adulthood. Furthermore, we begin to recognize decisive stages within the juvenile age, and gradations and steps in the confirmation of delinquency which must be taken into account. Until these facts are understood to the point where they find reflection in laws, the law itself has no choice but to confirm many a delinquent in the way of crime.

There are, of course, communities, courts, and police departments with civic hearts and practical heads. They establish co-operative plans of prevention (as for example Passaic, New Jersey, has done); they entertain a kind of collaboration with endangered sections of youth (i.e., by organizing hot-rod races and other events); and through the work of parole officers and social workers they offer some young people a kind of personal confirmation of potential worthiness. In doing this, however, communities and individuals must take isolated chances, often against overwhelming odds. Their successes do not make the headlines while unavoidable failures are sure to be laid to a sentimental or unintelligent wish to "coddle." They need universal support from an enlightened public, willing to accept some bitter facts.

Juvenile delinquency deserves to be faced by (any) society as a phenomenon which points to the most glaring discrepancies between technological change, the letter of the law, prevalent morality, and scientific insight. Here it must be remembered in passing that juvenile delinquency, while the noisiest, is not the only unrest in the youth of this country. Doctors in our armed forces and institutions of learning are aware of the inner, the mental unrest which is delinquency's unspectacular counterpart but at least an equal drain on human resources.

The inescapable fact is that we adults, in changing the world with more or less well-intentioned inventions, create disbalances of value which appear as moral and psychological deficits in some (and by no means always necessarily the weakest) segments of youth. This, of course, is a matter of so many implications that only a combination of experts in collaboration with a combination of citizens can even begin to discuss it. The emphasis here is on the beginning and the continuing, not on the concluding: for in most conferences of experts and citizens the necessity to come, in a few hours or days, to "practical" conclusions, hangs like a cloud over the meeting of minds.

Like a wave of hurricanes, juvenile delinquency does not only call for emergency measures. It calls for acceptance of the possibility that the threat may be here to stay for the foreseeable future; and that only long-range planning, based on persistent joint study, may gradually overcome the waste attending each single emergency.

Late Adolescence (1959)

I have been asked to comment this morning on young adulthood, with particular reference to the concept of Ego-Identity. Since my paper "The Problem of Ego-Identity" has been distributed before the conference, I have to overcome something of a sense of deja vu. One must give good reasons—if only to oneself—for ever again restating a subject which one has already submitted to print—knowing that the restatement will be printed as well.

The written word is not what it used to be. We are all deluged with printed and even mimeographed material, and the chance that we have all read the same portions of the same paper with the same attention is very slim indeed. Therefore, meetings like this depend on what we state and restate face to face. Our first mandate, then, is to expose what we may have said elsewhere to the modifications and, above all, the illustrations which only a highly selected group like this can provide.

There is another mandate which makes me feel like repeating myself here. In a group as varied in its experience and as high-minded

Presented to the First International Conference on Student Mental Health, in Princeton, New Jersey, September 1956. The conference was sponsored by the World Federation for Mental Health and the International Association of Universities and later published by them in *The Student and Mental Health*, ed. Daniel H. Funkenstein (Cambridge: Riverside Press, 1959), 66–88.

in its intentions, somebody must try to establish some theoretical coordinates for the central problem to be discussed. Otherwise, general opinions and isolated practical needs will run away with the discussion. The theory of ego-identity is safely anchored in systematic clinical investigation and in psychoanalytic methodology. We can use it as a platform for going in either or both of these directions when the need arises.

But then, some of you will feel from the outset that the psychoanalytic theory is based too exclusively on psychopathology and therefore may have only a limited application to the wider problems of college life. I will be glad to yield to any equally inclusive, consistent, and dynamic theory, based on the observation of the "normal" college population. In the meantime, I must start from a point of view which to a degree minimizes the differences between abnormal states and normal crises. I refer to individual malignant episodes in college life, such as come to the attention of your psychiatric clinics; less malignant but sometimes not less spectacular symptoms of unrest in your college population; such particular crises in individuals and groups as are indicative of the strains experienced by young adults under the conditions of college life; and, finally, the crisis of young adulthood, under any and all cultural conditions.

I may remind you here that there is a good methodological reason why psychopathological observations become one prime source of theoretical insights into the disturbances of lesser malignancy. It is only when Man is motivated to introspect that certain inner mechanisms can be studied (to use conference participant Professor Aríe Querido's phrase) "en detail." And ordinarily Man is probably best so motivated when he needs help. When he seeks help as a result of intense suffering, he has a vital investment in the truth, or at any rate permits himself to be led to the recognition of the half-truth. I will state then what suggests itself from work with severely disturbed students. From there on I will need you and your discussion to see how much of my theory you find relevant. My third and final reason for repeating myself, then, is that we need each other.

I used the term "young adulthood" to locate our joint problem. Yet, in many ways "late adolescence," the subject of this presentation, is a better term because it has the proper double meaning: the later stages of adolescence and belated adolescence. In this latter sense it is most relevant to our consideration here.

The great task of late adolescence has been characterized by me in a series of publications as the establishment of a sense of identity. As long as the establishment of identity is incomplete a crisis exists which, in its conscious and overt aspects, amounts to an identity-confusion. Deeper down, however, there exist certain dynamic dangers which I lump together in the term Identity-Diffusion.

Now, the adolescent crisis during which the dominance of a safe Identity over the threatening Identity-Diffusion is established, is only one of a series of crises. For beginning with birth, each stage of development has its characteristic conflicts and, following adolescence, further stages of development will bring crises, each to be solved at its own stage. For the White House Conference of 1950, I undertook to state systematically what everybody in one way or another knows already.

The Identity crisis, however, is a "prima inter pares," for it marks the conclusion of childhood, in the sense of all preadulthood. It is characterized by an enormous spurt of new needs, new energies and new faculties, and therefore receives special treatment by societies and cultures, for before the young person enters adulthood, he must be sure to put his new needs, energies, and faculties at the disposal of his society's values.

Among the special institutions designed for this stage, college education is probably the greatest organized artificial postponement of adulthood, emotionally speaking, that could be imagined. There were always periods of apprenticeship, in any cultural system, in any culture, which would lead at a reasonable date to the individual entering the life of his people as a worker, earner and homemaker, and thus emancipating himself from his parents' home. College education is one among many of those long apprenticeships of our time, which are getting longer and more specialized, and constitutes a most radical postponement of some emotional satisfactions and a replacement of them by others. It fosters particular forms of extended childishness even as it cultivates certain forms of one-sided precocity. This is so whether or not college education is more a means to an end, such as a trade or profession, or whether it is more an end in itself, as it becomes in some of our alumni who acquire a kind of college identity for life. In some cultures the pursuit of knowledge is the only decent way to escape from one's childhood home and yet to postpone establishing one's own. It offers, as I will discuss later, a "psychosocial moratorium." But since the period between childhood and maturity is what we call adolescence, "late adolescence" becomes for us an important term, not to be taken as a personal disability or fault, but a cultural institution, and this whether it is paid for by the parents or by the state.

In the sense in which going to college prolongs late adolescence, it also postpones the establishment of identity, even while it puts at the disposal of the young individual the knowledge and the techniques which help him define his identity. I sometimes speak more specifically of *ego-identity*, which is meant to connect the theory of identity with the psychoanalytic theory of the ego. Briefly the ego may be defined as an inner agency which integrates the various crises through which Man passes. It is the guard of Man's inner continuity in the face of sudden spurts of drives, alternating pressures of conscience and unexpected changes in natural and social conditions. Incidentally, most of you, especially those from other countries, will be aware of psychoanalytic theory mainly as one which emphasizes drive—which speaks of an ego primarily as the manipulator of defenses (Anna Freud) against drives. In this country, through the work of Hartmann, Kris, Rapaport and others, other functions of the ego have been defined. Among these, I have concerned myself especially with the ego's adaptive function on the psychosocial front.

How can we define *Ego-Identity*, then? Here we must learn to change from simple cause-and-effect thinking to thinking in terms of social relativity.

Ego-Identity can be said to be established when the individual comes to be and feel most himself, and this in pursuits and roles in which he also means most to some others—that is, to those others who have come to mean most to him. This is a "relative" matter involving delicate interplay. For the individual can be said to choose and to create his environment of others, even as he is chosen and created by them.

In a similar way the individual chooses a future, even as he is determined by his past. In this sense *Ego Identity* also rests on the inner continuity between what one was as a child and what one is going to be as an adult. Such inner continuity and sameness are supported by cultural processes so long as they function, with great sagacity. Rites, rituals, and traditions seek to give the individual a sense that, on each stage of his long childhood and apprenticeship, everything occurred in pre-ordained steps, so that he who looks into his future and tests his opportunities will perceive his past stages as adding up to something. It is making a meaningful synthesis of the past, the present and the future.

Let us now discuss a few facets of the "sense" of identity. Is it conscious? And can it be observed? When the sense of identity develops, it is perceived by the individual (pre-consciously, as we would say in psychoanalysis) and observed by others. This is often stated in the terms: "He knows where he's going," or "He's at home with himself," or "He's found himself." Young people at certain times suddenly seem to "grow together." In some dark way this is closely related to health, to those mental mechanisms which help to maintain the vitality of the organism. Every endocrinologist knows that changes in and metabolic activity during adolescence strongly influence and also seem to be influenced by changes in self-feeling and thus by changes in the individual's meaning to others. It is when the various parts of an individual "gel" into a meaningful whole.

Not that the process of identity formation *begins* in adolescence. All through childhood, an individual develops images of himself, evokes images in others, and experiences continuities, and dis-continuities in these images. A boy may be called a "sweet little boy" at one stage, a "tough big boy" at a later one. But he also has to learn to treat his little brother, who is now a "sweet little boy," as something worthwhile. At the same time, he has to be able to "take" it from his older brother, who is supposed to be a tougher, bigger, and wiser boy. All these versions of boyhood are finally blended together when the big boy becomes a young man.

In order to establish an ongoing sense of identity then, an individual must learn to manage a lasting hierarchy of all these various images of himself. What lasting sense of identity has thus developed has to be *maintained* against the adolescent changes and shifts, such as vastly increased sexual drives, greater muscular and locomotive power, greater intellectual power, greater awareness of social values, and thus a deeper concern over one's shortcomings. It is at the conclusion of this life task that the young person leaves home and comes to live in a new institution, which only in sentimental allegory can be called a "home," or a "family," even though it is symbolically situated under the wings of an Alma Mater.

College life is a stage of semi-final experimentation, as was so aptly stated by conference participant Jeré A. Reppert yesterday in terms reflecting the contemporary American scene: "We are testing a personality which we must use for the rest of our lives." This would probably be put differently in other languages and countries; Miss Reppert's remark was all the more enlightening. She also stated convincingly how much one is aware of one's reflection in others at that time, and how one constantly works on creating the right reflection. (She had not read my paper before she formulated that and, therefore, said it better.) Out of a complicated "feedback" which involves individual self-scrutiny as well as the chosen group's self-appraisal do we gradually derive some sense of what we are and what we are supposed to do in this world. Miss Reppert's talk also pointed to the *dilemma of choice*—a particular problem in a culture in which there seems to be a great deal of choice. These are, however, all very relative matters and we need to examine in our study groups the specific relationship of choice to conformity in various cultures. Inner Identity, at any rate, is a combination of the two; for I cannot feel identical with myself if I do not feel identical with something that has been created and distilled in my culture over a long period. To be firmly told by tradition who one is can be experienced as freedom; while the permission to make an original choice can feel like enslavement to some dark fate. In America the image of a free choice often becomes a dilemma because there are rather definite social and economic mechanisms by which the individual is forced into certain choices— and forced to choose them with the gestures of spontaneity. The increasing commitment with each choice can become a burden; your peers are apt to type you at first playfully and yet not apt to let go easily of nicknames and characteristic stories; these you must live down, or learn to live with. Discussions or, indeed, parties can suddenly prove to have led to encounters decisive for identity development. But all in all, the very fact that there is a social machinery, with rules that can be learned, gives most young persons the reassuring feeling that a relevant reception is prepared. On the other hand, as some of the speakers from the various countries indicated yesterday, historical and cultural changes can produce an acute sense that the reception committee is bluffing. If, for example, college education becomes a major value in the Philippines, and the law suggests itself as a desirable professional training, then the fact that economy has place for only a limited number of lawyers could be expected to interfere with law becoming an identity-supporting career. In the United States, many women are in the position of cherishing a college education without being able to expect either the public machinery or the private consent for a later use of their college-identity.

Our study groups will gather and evaluate similar examples. In the meantime, I will turn to the other side of the model, i.e., that inner condition which results from the circumstance that a young person finds himself temporarily or lastingly unable to secure an identity development which takes into sufficient account the nature of his drives and needs, of his interests and capacities, of his ideals and opportunities. Such a person is then exposed to identity-diffusion.

"Identity-Diffusion" should be discussed a great deal by this conference, not because we want to emphasize the pathological, but because we should be aware of the fact even healthy and functioning young people function only through the (often costly) struggle with identity-confusion. While the cost of this struggle is not always mental disorder by any means, it can lead to a vastly limited use of inner resources and outer opportunities. But we must understand that confusion can also presage a new order, a fact which should prevent us from rushing with psychiatric terms into crises which are not only necessary, but maybe desirable.

Although there is insufficient time for a detailed discussion of the main symptoms of identity-diffusion, I will briefly enumerate them. They are briefly treated in my paper; they will be illustrated in detail in a forthcoming monograph. First, a disturbance in the sense of time. This means that a young person feels everything to be mortally urgent—career, immortality, love—or that nothing matters enough to be in a hurry about it. Alternately, then, there is an over-awareness of the constant loss of time—or, there is a complete loss of consideration of time. There is often a decided disbelief in the possibility that time may bring change, and yet also a vivid fear that it might.

Then, there is an exacerbation of what we call "self-consciousness," now more specifically identity-consciousness. This is manifested by a constant preoccupation with one's "types": physical appearance, sexual character, anticipated occupational role, etc. With this goes a sense of bi-sexual confusion—a gnawing doubt as to whether one is quite a man or quite a woman—and what kind of man or woman. The most apparent symptom naturally is a paralysis of workmanship in the form of an inability to concentrate on required or suggested tasks; or a self-destructive preoccupation with some one-sided activity, i.e., excessive reading, listening to music, exercising to exhaustion, etc.

Most important, from the psychiatric standpoint, is the experimentation with what I call the *negative* identity. This can be expressed in a scornful and snobbish hostility toward the roles offered as proper and desirable in one's family or immediate community. Any particular aspect of the required role, or all parts, be it a particular kind of masculinity or femininity, nationality, class membership, or occupational role, can become the main focus of the young person's acid disdain. Such an individual often becomes a little criminal, a little psychopathic, a little eccentric, etc.—and as Kai Erikson and I have pointed out in a joint paper,* much will depend on whether or not society chooses to "confirm" this identity.

For when a young person thus confused shows symptoms of a severe identity diffusion, he is apt to be diagnosed as schizophrenic

* "The Confirmation of the Delinquent," *Chicago Review* (Winter 1956).

or paranoid, as constitutionally psychopathic or as hopelessly criminal—for which indeed, he may have the makings. But we should
understand that a young person thus labelled and treated on the basis
of such diagnosis, often is forced, and on occasion is even eager, to
accept the diagnosis as his identity. In fact, to accept the role of a
patient (or a delinquent for that matter) can be the choice of a negative
identity, i.e. an identity which is perceived as having a negative valence in the wider environment, but had a positive one in a significant
sub-section, and thus ends confusion, forestalling further diffusion.
In this case, treatment becomes difficult indeed. If we can look at
these situations as acute identity confusions taking different social
forms (eccentric, delinquent, neurotic, borderline-psychotic), we may
be able to secure the young individual another chance without burdening him with a malignant diagnosis and lifelong negative identity.
One of the greatest tasks in psychiatry today, you will agree, is to
establish new and specific diagnostic criteria for young people.

In case you are worried, I assume in all this that the identity-
diffusion peculiar to the nature of genius will not become the
professional concern of the psychiatric workers among us. Strong
individuals create their own "psychosocial moratorium." In the paper
which is under discussion here, I quoted Bernard Shaw's views on
that early stage in his life when he was a remarkable mixture of
disagreeableness and withdrawnness. For five years he kept away
from occupational life and from people of his own age. I must urge
you to read his description of how he managed the transitions from
clerk to fiction writer to music critic to playwright. It illustrates the
sleepwalker-like surefootedness which really gifted people have in
negotiating rather dangerous turns. Another outstanding example is
Darwin's voyage on the *Beagle*.*

It is very important for some young people at a certain time to do
"something else" for a while. Of course, for many people to go away
to college is just that "doing something else." In early American
history, to go West was a perfectly acceptable postponement of one's
main career; today still, a period of manual labor is considered an
acceptable moratorium. In England, I assume, the outposts of the
empire provided similar chances. This, then, I would consider part
of the moratorium, for it is a means of postponement of one's commitment to a final career in society. One can experiment without
committing oneself. In rare but to us important instances, when ed-

---

* For a comparison of the moratorium in Darwin's and Freud's life, see E. H. Erikson, "The
First Psychoanalyst," *Yale Review* (Autumn 1956).

ucation becomes more standardized and achievement more and more stratified, a young person with neglected gifts and a history of perverse guidance can find no other moratorium but a "breakdown"—and this especially where the role of a patient is offered as an acceptable one. Needless to say, it is not our job to cultivate this choice in colleges; it is more important that we understand its dynamics. But we may at least see to it that mental consultations will not be considered as stigmatizing the client as a life-long ex-patient.

A grim historical example of the establishment of a negative identity and its later disguise in a mythical role is provided in the fate of Adolf Hitler. In a biography which appeared in England, the only friend of his late teens describes what kind of young man he was. During those years, he was preoccupied with one idea: to rebuild his home town of Linz. He spent his whole time sketching his replacements for the existing buildings. Obviously, that implied the imaginary destruction of these buildings, but the emphasis was as yet on "renaissance." The breaking point came when he sent his plans for rebuilding the opera house in Linz to the city's building committee. It did not honor him with a reply. Defeated as an architect, and later refused admission to the art school, he broke with society. He disappeared completely. It is assumed that he lived in hostels for the migratory unemployed, until the First World War made him one of those corporals who will become dictators. This was the beginning. As to the end, another English book claims that Hitler, during his last days in the bunker in Berlin (probably after he had decided to destroy himself) finished the plans for the opera house in Linz. He had wanted to be a builder. . . .

This is an eerie example, much beyond our means of psychologizing. But it is well for us to consider the desperate need for a "recognition" of their positive side of some young people, who totter on the brink between genius and criminality. By such recognition I mean the process by which society identifies the individual. When we speak of the individual's identifying with others, we usually say little about how these others identified him; and where we speak of a person's inability to identify with others, we fail to consider how significantly—others may have recognized his negative side more than the positive one.

Those of you who have read *From Here to Eternity*, an American best-seller of a few years ago, will recall the central figure, a young bugler in the Army, whose bugle was taken away from him: the story sensitively reveals how important this instrument was to the young man in helping him to overcome murderous identifications which, at the end, dominated and led to his destruction.

Certainly then, many young criminals, leaving sociological considerations aside, represent the fateful dominance of a negative identity as do many young eccentrics, if less fatefully so. Certainly also, some flamboyant young radicals are experimenting with a negative political identity: [Conference participant Dr. Henry B. M.] Murphy tells of the temporary defection of young people from Singapore over the border to Communist China. In Latin countries, the political rioting of students probably permits a noisy moratorium of a mixed idealistic and delinquent character. Our "panty raids" are less idealistic and less serious; but they can be accompanied by truly destructive behavior. I have here deliberately listed a number of very different situations, all on that fringe of the unsafe, the untried and the amoral, which young people are apt to experiment with, provoking one another and the representatives of society. For we must not underestimate the "spontaneous recovery" aspects of many forms of irrational behavior in young individuals and in youth groups. Even the delinquent, in joining his gang, loses the personal syndrome of identity confusion: gang formation takes care of his problems.*

One can think of other marginal groups. Our colleague from Paris yesterday spoke of the pseudo-intellectual, pseudo-philosophical eccentricity in young people. Certain philosophies provide the confused young person with a whole world image in which his confusion appears to be exceptional clear-mindedness; it permits him, in a snobbish way, to feel superior to the uninitiated and to gain; on the basis of such membership, a collective cure of identity-diffusion.

At this point, you will surely accuse me of paying exclusive attention to the "fringe" of things. The fringe can teach us what kinds of forces are held at bay and are successfully utilized by strong orders and by strong ideologies.

Let us now come back to the position of identity in the whole life cycle.

In an ongoing culture, with a well defined family life, an individual can somehow chart a course for himself very early, by perceiving what the situations of other (younger, older; weaker, stronger; poorer, richer) people are. In cultures where to become old makes sense, there is a definite perspective on the whole of life. In our country, for most young people, the idea of becoming old and unable to advance further represents a very questionable future. Grandparents

* See a parallel restatement: E. H. Erikson, *Delinquency and Identity Diffusion, New Perspectives for Research on Delinquency* (Washington, D.C.: Children's Bureau, 1956).

are not experienced as part of the home any more, in wide areas. In other countries they do live at home—but the differences in generations, formerly ameliorated by unquestioned traditions, are that much more obvious. In assessing identity elements we should consider the hierarchy of images offered for the whole course of human life, so that one can grow old in comparison with them. We should thus remember that although the identity crisis occurs during adolescence, identity problems begin early in life and do not end until one dies; for "displaced" old people may argue with themselves and with others about what they *have* been, or should, or could have been. Today, it must suffice briefly to consider the two crises which occur before and after the identity crisis.

There is the earlier crisis of workmanship vs. a sense of inferiority. In school one learns how to work, whatever "school" means in one's culture. At a given stage, when organism and intellect are ready, one learns to know the tools of one's technology and the rules of cooperation and competition in society. But we must consider here the special case, our case and soon the universal case, that, in literate societies, one does not learn to use the tools of technology but of literacy—that intensified and isolated preoccupation with learning, which means not only to read and to write but also to think in terms of history, to learn that there is a formulated tradition and a written past—all of which, for a good while, in some strange way isolates workmanship from occupational identity. Children in many circles do not know what their parents are actually "doing" occupationally. This often results in the substitution of someone else as a parental work ideal. Certain liberal arts colleges extend that isolated preoccupation with refined literacy almost indefinitely—a matter which has recently been underlined by the sudden awareness of reforms of long standing in Soviet Russia, with its emphasis on industrial reality and on the ABC of science, without a complete sacrifice of the humanities.

The Identity Crisis is *followed* by the crisis of Intimacy vs. Isolation. The young people with whom we are concerned here usually are trying to establish an intimate relationship with the other sex or the same sex, and this before their identity is reasonably well established. But one cannot easily "lose oneself" in an intimate or sexual relation before one has "found oneself"—or, before one is ready to find oneself by losing oneself. In this sense, the great gap in some individuals and cultures between sexual potency (attested to by Kinsey), psychosexual potency (which is hard to appraise zoologically), and psychosocial readiness for intimacy becomes a major problem.

I would suggest, in general, that the whole question of the management of sexual drive be reviewed with consideration of identity development, for I suspect that a sound identity development, for I suspect that a sound identity development supports a bearable abstinence as well as enjoyable potency. When young people have heterosexual relationships before the identity crisis is solved, either with simple social sanction or by early marriage as is now more usual in this country, difficulties may result, and divorces may ensue in considerable numbers.

Although derivatives of all the previous stages of development are seen in the psychiatric difficulties of this age group, it is the close interrelationship of these three overlapping crises which is our chief concern. We thus see the crisis of work vs. inferiority, identity vs. identity-diffusion and intimacy vs. isolation telescoped into each other.

As I set out to do, I have spoken here primarily as a clinician. I hope to have made suggestions, however, for the discussion of universal themes which extend from the clinical to the cultural problems of our times. As I did in my paper, I can only conclude by referring to the problems of ideology. For ideology, in its very widest sense, is the cultural support of individual identity. The militant and explicit ideological movements of our time concentrate strongly on youth, and this consciously and deliberately, because they know that the industrial revolution finds youth all over the world with tensions and symptoms of identity confusion. The makers of totalitarian history know that first they must fabricate identities.

In the thought reform procedures of Communist China, one finds an uncanny cleverness in utilizing the identity crises in young people for replacing the agrarian patriarchal identity with an industrial-collective one. Among the procedures used by these "thought-analysts" in their "thought-clinics" is a young man's graduation by way of the public accusation of his own father as a reactionary, while this seems to flaunt one set of Chinese traditions, it is achieved in ways which continues deeper patterns of adaptation to the course of history and to fate. We may wonder how long and how far such totalitarian and "scientific" use of identity-fabrication will work. But we have no right to ignore the powers at work, and the needs and the energies with which they work.

Even in our ideologically less militant cultures, we must think of the ideological counterpart to the identity problem. And we may want to discuss, as very serious and very relevant, the role played by the college in this: played in the past, and to be played in the future. For college education stands for an ideology of its own: the ideology of enlightenment. The large influx of students, the changing value given to education, the necessity for specialization, the radically changed relationship of the arts to the sciences, of scholarship to technical "know-how"—all of these are ideological changes, as well, and have the most direct bearing on the problem of identity.

It is important, then, to realize the ideological significance of the structure of college life. For we are called upon to advance an orientation with a specific circumspection, i.e. with an enlightened consideration for these values (even though they may seem strange and clannish and weird to us) which have in the past supported or are about to support in the present strong identities and great accomplishments.

A Memorandum on Identity and Negro Youth (1964)

Introduction

A lack of familiarity with the problem of Negro youth and with the actions by which Negro youth hopes to solve these problems is a marked deficiency in my life and work which cannot be compensated for with theoretical speculation; and this least of all at a time when Negro writers are finding superb new ways of stating their and our predicament and when Negro youth finds itself involved in action which would have seemed unimaginable only a very few years ago. But since it is felt that some of my concepts might be helpful in further discussion, I will in the following recapitulate the pertinent ideas on identity contained in my writings.* This I do only in the hope that what is clear may prove helpful and what is not will become clearer in joint studies.

First published in The *Journal of Social Issues*, 20, 4 (1964) 29–42.
* See: *Childhood and Society,* New York: W. W. Norton and Co., 1950.
"Wholeness and Totality," In *Totalitarianism*, Proceedings of a Conference held at the American Academy of Arts and Sciences, ed. C. J. Friedrich, (Cambridge: Harvard University Press, 1954).
"Identity and the Life Cycle," Monograph, *Psychological Issues*, I, 1, (New York: International Universities Press, 1959), with an introduction by D. Rapaport.
"Youth: Fidelity and Diversity," *Daedalus*, 91 (1962), 5–27.

The fact that problems of Negro youth span the whole phenomenology of aggravated identity confusion and rapid new identity formation—cutting across phenomena judged antisocial and prosocial, violent and heroic, fanatic and ethically advanced—makes it advisable to include remarks concerning the origin of the concept of ego-identity in clinical observation in this review. However, the concept has come a long way since we first used it to define a syndrome in war—neurotics in World War II: I recently heard in India that Nehru had used the term "identity" to describe a new quality which, he felt, Gandhi had given India after offering her the equivalent of a "psychoanalysis of her past."

1. Childhood and Identity

a. The growing child must derive a vitalizing sense of reality from the awareness that his individual way of mastering experience is a successful variant of a group identity and is in accord with its space-time and life plan. Minute displays of emotion, such as affection, pride, anger, guilt, anxiety, sexual arousal (rather than the words used, the meanings intended, or the philosophy implied), transmit to the human child the outlines of what really counts in his world, i.e., the variables of his group's space-time and the perspectives of its life plan.

Here is the first observation I made (a decade and a half ago) on Negro children. I will quote it to characterize the point-of-view with which I started. The babies of our colored countrymen, I said, often receive sensual satisfactions which provide them with enough oral and sensory surplus for a lifetime, as clearly betrayed in the way they move, laugh, talk, sing. Their forced symbiosis with the feudal South capitalized on this oral sensory treasure and helped to build a slave's identity: mild, submissive, dependent, somewhat querulous, but always ready to serve, with occasional empathy and childlike wisdom. But underneath a dangerous split occurred. The Negro's unavoidable identification with the dominant race, and the need of the master race to protect its own identity against the very sensual and oral temptations emanting from the race held to be inferior (whence came their mammies), established in both groups an association: light—clean—clever—white, and dark—dirty—dumb—nigger. The result, especially in those Negroes who left the poor haven of their Southern homes, was often a violently sudden and cruel cleanliness training, as attested to in the autobiographies of Negro writers. It is as if by cleansing, a whiter identity could be achieved. The attending disillusionment transmits itself to the phallic-locomotor stage, when restrictions as to what shade of girl one may dream of interfere with the free transfer of the original narcissistic sensuality to the genital sphere. Three identities are formed: (1) mammy's oral-sensual "honeychild"—tender, expressive, rhythmical; (2) the evil identity of the dirty, anal-sadistic, phallic-rapist "nigger"; and (3) the clean, anal-compulsive, restrained, friendly, but always sad "white man's Negro."

So-called opportunities offered the migrating Negro often only turn out to be a more subtly restricted prison which endangers his only historically "successful" identity (that of the slave) and fails to provide a reintegration of the other identity fragments mentioned. These fragments, then, become dominant in the form of racial caricatures which are underscored and stereotyped by the entertainment industry. Tired of his own caricature, the colored individual often retires into hypochondriac invalidism as a condition which represents an analogy to the dependence and the relative safety of defined restriction in the South: a neurotic regression to the ego identity of the slave.

Mixed-blood Sioux Indians in areas where they hardly ever see Negroes refer to their full-blood brothers as "niggers," thus indicating the power of the dominant national imagery which serves to counterpoint the ideal and the evil images in the inventory of available prototypes. No individual can escape this opposition of images, which is all-pervasive in the men and in the women, in the majorities and in the minorities, and in all the classes of a given national or cultural unit. Psychoanalysis shows that the unconscious evil identity (the composite of everything which arouses negative identificiation—i.e., the wish not to resemble it) consists of the images of the violated (castrated) body, the "marked" outgroup, and the exploited minority. Thus a pronounced he-man may, in his dreams and prejudices, prove to be mortally afraid of ever displaying a woman's sentiments, a Negro's submissiveness, or a Jew's intellectuality. For the ego, in the course of its synthesizing efforts, attempts to subsume the most powerful evil and ideal prototypes (the final contestants, as it were) and with them the whole existing imagery of superior and inferior, good and bad, masculine and feminine, free and slave, potent and impotent, beautiful and ugly, fast and slow, tall and small, in a simple alternative, in order to make one battle and one strategy out of a bewildering number of skirmishes.

I knew a colored boy who, like our boys, listened every night to

Red Rider. Then he sat up in bed, imagining that he was Red Rider. But the moment came when he saw himself galloping after some masked offender and suddenly noticed that in his fancy Red Rider was a colored man. He stopped his fantasy. While a small child, this boy was extremely expressive, both in his pleasures and in his sorrows. Today he is calm and always smiles; his language is soft and blurred; nobody can hurry him or worry him—or please him. White people like him.

As such boys and girls look around now, what other ideal (and evil) images are at their disposal? And how do they connect with the past? (Does non-violence connect totalistically or holistically with traditional patience and tolerance of pain?)

b. When children enter the stage of the adolescent Identity Crisis, a factor enters which characterizes the real kind of *crisis*, namely, a moment of decision between strong contending forces. "A moment" means that here something can happen very rapidly; "decision," that divergence becomes permanent; "strong and contending," that these are intense matters.

Developmentally speaking the sense of ego identity is the accrued confidence that one's ability to maintain inner sameness and continuity (one's ego in the psychoanalytic sense) is matched by the sameness and continuity of one's meaning for others. The growing child must, at every step, derive a vitalizing sense of reality from the awareness that his individual way of mastering experience is a successful variant of the way other people around him master experience and recognize such mastery.

In this, children cannot be fooled by empty praise and condescending encouragement. They may have to accept artificial bolstering of their self-esteem in lieu of something better, but what I call their accruing ego identity gains real strength only from wholehearted and consistent recognition of real accomplishment, that is, achievement that has meaning in their culture. On the other hand, should a child feel that the environment tries to deprive him too radically of all the forms of expression which permit him to develop and to integrate the next step in his ego identity, he will resist with the astonishing strength encountered in animals who are suddenly forced to defend their lives. Indeed, in the social jungle of human existence, there is no feeling of being alive without a sense of ego identity. Or else, there may be total self-abnegation (in more or less malignant forms) as illustrated in this observation. And here is an example of total denial of identity:

A four-year-old Negro girl in the Arsenal Nursery School in Pittsburgh used to stand in front of a mirror and scrub her skin with soap. When gently diverted from this she began to scrub the mirror. Finally, when induced to paint instead, she first angrily filled sheets of paper with the colors brown and black. But then she brought to the teacher what she called "a really *good* picture." The teacher first could see only a white sheet, until she looked closer and saw that the little girl had covered every inch of the white sheet with white paint. This playful episode of total self-eradication occurred and could only occur in a "desegregated" school; it illustrates the extent to which infantile drive control (cleanliness) and social self-esteem (color) are associated in childhood. But it also points to the extent of the crime which is perpetrated wherever, in the service of seemingly civilized values, groups of people are made to feel so inexorably "different" that legal desegregation can only be the beginning of a long and painful inner reidentification.

Such crises come when their parents and teachers, losing trust in themselves and using sudden correctives in order to approach the vague but pervasive Anglo-Saxon ideal, create violent discontinuities; or where, indeed, the children themselves learn to disavow their sensual and overprotective mothers as temptations and a hindrance to the formation of a more "American" personality.

If we, then, speak of the community's response to the young individual's need to be "recognized" by those around him, we mean something beyond a mere recognition of achievement; for it is of great relevance to the young individual's identity formation that he be responded to, and be given function and status, as a person whose gradual growth and transformation make sense to those who begin to make sense to him. Identity formation goes beyond the process of *identifying oneself* with ideal others in a one-way fashion; it is a process based on a heightened cognitive and emotional capacity to *let oneself be identified* by concrete persons as a circumscribed individual in relation to a predictable universe which transcends the family. Identity thus is not the sum of childhood identifications, but rather a new combination of old and new identification fragments. For this very reason societies *confirm* an individual at this time in all kinds of ideological frameworks and assign roles and tasks to him in which he can *recognize himself* and *feel recognized*. Ritual confirmations, initiations, and indoctrinations only sharpen an indispensable process of self-verification by which healthy societies bestow and receive the distilled strength of generations. By this process, societies, in turn, are themselves historically verified.

The danger of this stage is *identity diffusion*; as Biff puts it in

Arthur Miller's *Death of a Salesman*, "I just can't take hold, Mom, I can't take hold of some kind of a life." Where such a dilemma is based on a strong previous doubt of one's ethnic and sexual identity, delinquent and outright psychotic incidents are not uncommon. Youth after youth, bewildered by some assumed role, a role forced on him by the inexorable standardization of American adolescence, runs away in one form or another, leaving schools and jobs, staying out all night, or withdrawing into bizarre and inaccessible moods. Once [a young person is] "delinquent," his greatest need and often his only salvation, are the refusal on the part of older friends, advisers, and judiciary personnel to type him further by pat diagnoses and social judgments which ignore the special dynamic conditions of adolescence. For if diagnosed and treated correctly, seemingly psychotic and criminal incidents do not in adolescence have the same fatal significance which they have at other ages. Yet many a youth, finding the authorities expect him to be "a nigger," "a bum," or "a queer," perversely obliges by becoming just that.

To keep themselves together, individuals and groups treated in this fashion temporarily overidentify, to the point of apparent complete loss of individual identity, with the heroes of cliques and crowds. On the other hand, they become remarkably clannish, intolerant, and cruel in their exclusion of others who are "different," in skin color or cultural background, in tastes and gifts, and often in entirely petty aspects of dress and gesture arbitrarily selected as *the* signs of an in-grouper or out-grouper. It is important to understand (which does not mean condone or participate in) such intolerance as the necessary *defense against a sense of identity diffusion,* which is unavoidable at a time of life when the body changes its proportions radically, when genital maturity floods body and imagination with all manners of drives, when intimacy with the other sex offers intense complications, and when life lies before one with a variety of conflicting possibilities and choices. Adolescents help one another temporarily through such discomfort by forming cliques and by stereotyping themselves, their ideals, and their enemies.

In general, one may say that we are apt to view the social play of adolescents as we once judged the play of children. We alternatively consider such behavior irrelevant, unnecessary, or irrational, and ascribe to it purely delinquent or neurotic meanings. As in the past the study of children's spontaneous games was neglected in favor of that of solitary play, so now the mutual "joinedness" of adolescent clique behavior fails to be properly assessed in our concern for the individual adolescents. Children and adolescents in their presocieties provide for one another a sanctioned moratorium and joint support for free experimentation with inner and outer dangers (including those emanating from the adult world). Whether or not a given adolescent's newly acquired capacities are drawn back into infantile conflict depends to a significant extent on the quality of the opportunities and rewards available to him in his peer clique, as well as on the more formal ways in which society at large invites a transition from social play to work experimentation, and from rituals of transit to final commitments: all of which must be based on an implicit mutual contract between the individual and society.

2. Totalism and Negative Identity

If such contact is deficient, youth may seek perverse restoration in a negative identity, "totalistically" enforced. Here we must reconsider the proposition that the need for identity is experienced as a need for a certain wholeness in the experience of oneself within the community (and community here is as wide as one's social vision); and that, where such wholeness is impossible, such need turns to "totalism."

To be a bit didactic: *Wholeness* connotes an assembly of parts, even quite diversified parts, that enter into fruitful association and organization. This concept is most strikingly expressed in such terms as wholeheartedness, wholemindedness, and wholesomeness. In human development as well as in history, then, wholeness emphasizes a progressive coherence of diversified functions and parts. *Totality*, on the contrary, evokes a Gestalt in which an absolute boundary is emphasized: given a certain arbitrary delineation, nothing that belongs inside must be left outside; nothing that must be outside should be tolerated inside. A totality must be absolutely inclusive as it is absolutely exclusive. The word "utter" conveys the element of force, which overrides the question whether the category-to-be-made-absolute is an organic and a logical one, and whether the parts, so to speak, really have a natural affinity to one another.

To say it in one sentence: Where the human being despairs of an essential wholeness of experience, he restructures himself and the world by taking refuge in a totalistic world view. Thus there appears both in individuals and in groups a periodical need for a totality without further choice or alternation, even if it implies the abandonment of a much-needed wholeness. This can consist of a lone-wolf's negativism; of a delinquent group's seeming nihilism; or in the case of national or racial groups, in a defiant glorification of one's own caricature.

Thus, patients (and I think it is in this respect that patients can help us understand analogous group processes) choose a *negative identity*, i.e., an identity perversely based on all those identifications and roles which, at critical stages of development, had been presented to them as most undesirable or dangerous, and yet also as most real. For example, a mother having lost her first-born son may (because of complicated guilt feelings) be unable to attach to her later surviving children the same amount of religious devotion that she bestows on the memory of her dead child and may well arouse in one of her sons the conviction that to be sick or dead is a better assurance of being "recognized" than to be healthy and about. A mother who is filled with unconscious ambivalence toward a brother who disintegrated into alcoholism may again and again respond selectively only to those traits in her son which seem to point to a repetition of her brother's fate, in which case this "negative" identity may take on more reality for the son than all his natural attempts at being good: he may work hard on becoming a drunkard and, lacking the necessary ingredients, may end up in a state of stubborn paralysis of choice. The daughter of a man of brilliant showmanship may run away from college and be arrested as a prostitute in the Negro quarter of a Southern city; while the daughter of an influential Southern Negro preacher may be found among narcotic addicts in Chicago. In such cases it is of utmost importance to recognize the mockery and the vindictive pretense in such role playing; for the white girl may not have really prostituted herself, and the colored girl may not really become an addict—yet. Needless to say, however, each of them could have placed herself in a marginal social area, leaving it to law-enforcement officers and to psychiatric agencies to decide what stamp to put on such behavior. A corresponding case is that of a boy presented to a psychiatric clinic as "the village homosexual" of a small town. On investigation, it appeared that the boy had succeeded in assuming this fame without any actual acts of homosexuality, except that much earlier in his life he had been raped by some older boys.

Such vindictive choices of a negative identity represent, of course, a desperate attempt to regain some mastery in a situation in which the available positive identity elements cancel each other out. The history of such choice reveals a set of conditions in which it is easier to derive a sense of identity out of a *total* identification with that which one is *least* supposed to be than to struggle for a feeling of reality in acceptable roles which are unattainable with the patient's inner means.

There is a "lower lower" snobbism too, which is based on the pride of having achieved a semblance of nothingness. At any rate, many a late adolescent, if faced with continuing diffusion, would rather *be a total nobody, somebody totally bad, or indeed, dead—and all of this by free choice—than be not-quite-somebody.*

Thus, individuals, when caught up in the necessity to regroup an old identity or to gain a new and inescapable one, are subject to influences which offer them a way to wholeness. Obviously, revolutions do the first to gain the second. At any rate, the problem of totalism vs. wholeness seems to be represented in its organized form in the Black Muslims who insist on a totally "black" solution reinforced by historical and religious mysticism on the one hand; and the movement of non-violent and legal insistence on civil rights, on the other. Once such a polarization is established, it seems imperative to investigate what powerful self-images (traditional, revolutionary, and, as it were, evolutionary) have entered the picture, in mutually exclusive or mutually inclusive form, and what the corresponding symptoms are, in individuals and in the masses.

3. "Conversion" and More Inclusive Identity

In a little-known passage, Bernard Shaw relates the story of his "conversion": "I was *drawn into* the Socialist *revival* of the early eighties, among Englishmen *intensely serious* and *burning with indignation* at very *real* and *very fundamental evils* that affected *all the world.*" The words here italicized convey to me the following implications. "Drawn into": an ideology has a compelling power. "Revival": it consists of a traditional force in a state of rejuvenation. "Intensely serious": it permits even the cynical to make an investment of sincerity. "Burning with indignation": it gives to the need for repudiation the sanction of righteousness. "Real": it projects a vague inner evil onto a circumscribed horror in reality. "Fundamental": it promises participation in an effort at basic reconstruction of society. "All the world": it gives structure to a totally defined world image. Here, then, are the elements by which a group identity harnesses the young individual's aggressive and discriminative energies, and encompasses, as it completes it, the individual's identity in the service of its ideology. Thus, identity and ideology are two aspects of the same process. Both provide the necessary condition for further individual maturation and, with it, for the next higher form of identification, namely, the *solidarity linking common identities*. For the need to bind irrational self-hate and irrational repudiation makes young people, on occasion, mortally compulsive and conservative even where and when they seem most anarchic and radical; the same need makes them potentially "ideological," i.e., more or less explicitly in search of a world image held together by what Shaw called "a clear comprehension of life in the light of an intelligible theory."

What are, then, the available ideological ingredients of the new Negro and the new American identity? For (such is the nature of a revolutionary movement) the new Negro cannot afford any longer just to become "equal" to the old White. As he becomes something new, he also forces the white man as well as the advanced Negro to become newer than they are.

4. Weakness and Strength

a. In my clinical writings I have suggested that delinquent joining stands in the same dynamic relationship to schizoid isolation, as (according to Freud) perversion does to neurosis: negative *group* identities (gangs, cliques, rings, mobs) "save" the individual from the symptoms of a negative identity neurosis, to wit: a distintegration of the sense of time; morbid identity consciousness; work paralysis; bisexual confusion, and authority diffusion.

Unnecessary to say, however, a *transitory* "negative identity" is often the necessary pre-condition for a truly positive and truly new one. In this respect, I would think that American Negro writers may turn out to be as important for American literature as Irish expatriates were in the Europe of an earlier period.

On the other hand, there are certain strengths in the Negro which have evolved out of or at least along with his very submission. Such a statement will, I trust, not be misunderstood as an argument for continued submission. What I have in mind are strengths which one would hope for the sake of all of us, could remain part of a future Negro identity. Here I have in mind such a traditional phenomenon as the power of the Negro mother. As pointed out, I must glean examples from experience accessible to me; the following observation on Caribbean motherhood will, I hope, be put into its proper perspective by experts on the whole life-space of the Negro on the American continent.

b. Churchmen have had reason to deplore, and anthropologists to explore, the pattern of Caribbean family life, obviously an outgrowth of the slavery days of Plantation America, which extended from the Northeast Coast of Brazil in a half-circle into the Southeast of the United States. Plantations, of course, were agricultural factories, owned and operated by gentlemen, whose cultural and economic identity had its roots in a supra-regional upper class. They were worked by slaves, that is, men who, being mere equipment put to use when and where necessary, had to relinquish all chance of being the masters of their families and communities. Thus, the women were left with the offspring of a variety of men who could give no protection as they could provide no identity, except that of a subordinate species. The family system which ensued can be described in scientific terms only by circumscriptions dignifying what is not there: the rendering of "sexual services" between persons who cannot be called anything more definite than "lovers"; "maximum instability" in the sexual lives of young girls, whose pattern it is to relinquish the care of their offspring to their mothers; and mothers and grandmothers who determine that "standardized mode of coactivity" which is the minimum requirement for calling a group of individuals a family. They are, then, mostly called "household groups"—single dwellings, occupied by people sharing a common food supply. These households are "matrifocal," a word understating the grandiose role of the all powerful mother-figure who will encourage her daughters to leave their infants with her, or, at any rate, to stay with her as long as they continue to bear children. Motherhood thus becomes community life; and where churchmen could find little or no morality, and casual observers, little or no order at all, the mothers and grandmothers in fact also became father and grandfathers,* in the sense that they exerted that authoritative influence which resulted in an ever newly improvised set of rules for the economic obligations of the men who had fathered the children, and upheld the rules of incestuous avoidance. Above all, they provided the only super-identity which was left open after the enslavement of the men, namely, that of the mother who will nurture a human infant irrespective of his parentage. It is well known how many poor little rich and white gentlemen benefited from the extended fervor of the Negro women who nursed them as Southern mammies, as creole das, or as Brazilian babas. This cultural fact is, of course, being played down by the racists as mere servitude while the predominance of maternal warmth in Caribbean women is characterized as African sensualism, and vicariously enjoyed by

* See the title "My Mother Who Fathered Me."

refugees from "Continental" womanhood. One may, however, see at the root of this maternalism a grandiose gesture of human adaptation which has given the area of the Caribbean (now searching for a political and economic pattern to do justice to its cultural unity) both the promise of a positive (female) identity and the threat of a negative (male) one, for here, the fact that identity depended on the procreative worth of being born has undoubtedly weakened the striving for becoming somebody by individual effort.

(This is an ancient pattern taking many forms in the modern Negro world. But—parenthetically speaking—it may give us one more access to a better understanding of the magnificently bearded group of men and boys who have taken over one of the islands and insist on proving that the Caribbean male can earn his worth in production as well as in procreation.)

My question is whether such maternal strength has survived not only in parts of our South but also in family patterns of Negro migrants; whether it is viewed as undesirable and treated as delinquent by Negroes as well as whites; and whether America can afford to lose it all at a time when women must help men more planfully to preserve not only the naked life of the human race but also some "inalienable" values.

c. This brings me, finally, to the issue of Fidelity, that virtue and quality of adolescent ego strength which belong to man's evolutionary heritage, but which—like all the basic virtues—can arise only in the interplay of a stage of life with the social forces of a true community.

To be a *special kind* has been an important element in the human need for personal and collective identities. They have found a transitory fulfillment in man's greatest moments of cultural identity and civilized perfection, and each such tradition of identity and perfection has highlighted what man could be, could he fulfill all his potentials at one time. The utopia of our own era predicts that man will be one species in one world, with a universal identity to replace the illusory super-identities which have divided him, and with an international ethic replacing all moral systems of superstition, repression, and suppression. Whatever the political arrangement that will further this utopia, we can only point to the human strengths which potentially emerge with the stages of life and indicate their dependence on communal life. In youth, ego strength emerges from the mutual confirmation of individual and community, in the sense that society recognizes the young individual as a bearer of fresh energy and that the individual so confirmed recognizes society as a living process which inspires loyalty as it receives it, maintains allegiance as it attracts it, honors confidence as it demands it. All this I subsume under the term Fidelity.

Diversity and fidelity are polarized; they make each other significant and keep each other alive. Fidelity without a sense of diversity can become an obsession and a bore; diversity without a sense of fidelity, an empty relativism.

But Fidelity also stands in a certain polarity to adolescent sexuality; both sexual fulfillment and "sublimation" depend on this polarity.

The various hindrances to a full consummation of adolescent genital maturation have many deep consequences for man which pose an important problem for future planning. Best studies is the regressive revival of that earlier stage of psychosexuality which preceded even the emotionally quiet first school years, that is, the infantile genital and locomotor stage, with its tendency toward auto-erotic manipulation, grandiose phantasy, and vigorous play. But in youth, auto-erotism, grandiosity, and playfulness are all immensely amplified by genital potency and locomotor maturation, and are vastly complicated by what we will presently describe as the youthful mind's historical perspective.

The most widespread expression of the discontented search of youth is the craving for locomotion, whether expressed in a general "being on the go," "tearing after something," or "running around"; or in locomotion proper, as in vigorous work, in absorbing sports, in rapt dancing, in shiftless *Wanderschaft*, and in the employment and misuse of speedy animals and machines. But it also finds expression through participation in the movements of the day (whether the riots of a local commotion or the parades and campaigns of major ideological forces); if they only appeal to the need for feeling "moved" and for feeling essential in moving something along toward an open future. It is clear that societies offer any number of ritual combinations of ideological perspective and vigorous movement (dance, sports, parades, demonstrations, riots) to harness youth in the service of their historical aims; and that where societies fail to do so, these patterns will seek their own combinations, in small groups occupied with serious games, good-natured foolishness, cruel prankishness, and delinquent warfare. In no other stage of the life cycle, then, are the promise of finding oneself and the threat of losing oneself so closely allied.

To summarize: Fidelity, when fully matured, is the strength of disciplined devotion. It is gained in the involvement of youth in such experiences as reveal the essence of the era they are to join—as the beneficiaries of its tradition, as the practitioners and innovators of its technology, as renewers of its ethical strength, as rebels bent on the destruction of the outlived, and as deviants with deviant commitments. This, at least, is the potential of youth in psychosocial evolution; and while this may sound like a rationalization endorsing any high sounding self-delusion in youth, any self-indulgence masquerading as devotion, or any righteous excuse for blind destruction, it makes intelligible the tremendous waste attending this as any other mechanism of human adaptation, especially if its excesses meet with more moral condemnation than ethical guidance. On the other hand, our understanding of these processes is not furthered by the "clinical" reduction of adolescent phenomena to their infantile antecedents and to an underlying dichotomy of drive and conscience. Adolescent development comprises a new set of identification processes, both with significant persons and with ideological forces, which give importance to individual life by relating it to a living community and to ongoing history, and by counterpointing the newly won individual identity with some communal solidarity.

In youth, then, the life history intersects with history: here individuals are confirmed in their identities, societies regenerated in their life style. This process also implies a fateful survival of adolescent modes of thinking in man's historical and ideological perspectives.

Historical processes, of course, have already entered the individual's core in childhood. Both ideal and evil images and the moral prototypes guiding parental administrations originate in the past struggles of contending cultural and national "species," which also color fairytale and family lore, superstition and gossip, and the simple lessons of early verbal training. Historians on the whole make little of this; they describe the visible emergence and the contest of autonomous historical ideas, unconcerned with the fact that these ideas reach down into the everyday lives of generations and re-emerge through the daily awakening and training of historical consciousness in young individuals.

It is youth which begins to develop that sense of historical irreversibility which can lead to what we may call acute historical estrangement. This lies behind the fervent quest for a sure meaning in individual life history and in collective history, and behind the questioning of the laws of relevancy which bind datum and principles, event and movement. But it is also, alas, behind the bland carelessness of what youth which denies its own vital need to develop and cultivate a historical consciousness—and conscience.

To enter history, each generation of young persons must find an identity consonant with its own childhood and consonant with an ideological promise in the perceptible historical process. But in youth the tables of childhood dependence begin slowly to turn: it is no longer exclusively for the old to teach the young the meaning of life, whether individual or collective. It is the young who, by their responses and actions, tell the old whether life as represented by their elders and as presented to the young has meaning; and it is the young who carry in them the power to confirm those who confirm them and, joining the issues, to renew and to regenerate, or to reform and to rebel.

I will not at this point review the institutions which participate in creating the retrospective and the prospective mythology offering historical orientation to youth. Obviously, the mythmakers of religion and politics, the arts and the sciences, the stage and fiction—all contribute to the historical logic presented to youth more or less consciously, more or less responsibly. And today we must add, at least in the United States, psychiatry; and all over the world, the press, which forces leaders to make history in the open and to accept reportorial distortion as a major historical factor.

Moralities sooner or later outlive themselves, ethics never; this is what the need for identity and for fidelity, reborn with each generation, seems to point to. Morality in the moralistic sense can be shown by modern means of inquiry to be predicated on superstitions and irrational inner mechanisms which ever again undermine the ethical fiber of generations; but morality is expendable only where ethics prevail. This is the wisdom that the words of many languages have tried to tell man. He has tenaciously clung to the words, even though he has understood them only vaguely, and in his actions has disregarded or perverted them completely. But there is much in ancient wisdom which can now become knowledge.

What, then, are the soruces of a new ethical orientation which may have roots in Negro tradition and yet also reach into the heroic striving for a new identity within the universal ethics emanating from world-wide technology and communication? This question may sound strenuously inspirational or academic; yet, I have in mind the study of concrete sources of morale and strength, lying within the vitality of bodily experience, the identity of individual experience, and the fidelity developed in methods of work and cooperation, methods of solidarity and political action, and methods permitting a simple and direct manifestation of human values such as have survived centuries of suppression. As a clinican, I am probably more competent to judge the conditions which continue to *suppress* and attempt to *crush* such strengths; and yet I have also found that diagnosis and anamnesis can turn out to be of little help where one ignores sources of recovery often found in surprising and surprisingly powerful constellations.

On the Potential
of Women (1965)

It is a great honor to follow Dr. Lillian Gilbreth [MIT] on this rostrum—even in the absolute certainty that thereby one is going to be an anticlimax. I shall not even try to match her address with another one. I can only conclude the proceedings with a few critical remarks (in the sense of critique rather than of criticism) that reflect on what we have heard in the last two days, and yet also look forward to future meetings of this kind.

In doing so, I hope not to appear unmindful of the labor of others—like the relieved young husband who on viewing their newborn in the hospital said to his wife, "That was easy, why not have another one soon?" Rather, in full awareness of the magnificent job done by the organizers of this meeting, I hope to gain some perspective by speaking of future possibilities.

For one thing I would like to have heard more from you, the delegates. Have you not listened a bit too much and said much too little, at least in open meeting? What you have heard came from many backgrounds and many points of view, and this, to be sure,

Presented to the MIT symposium on American Women in Science and Engineering, sponsored by the Association of Women Students at MIT, on October 24, 1964. First published as "Concluding Remarks" in Women and the Scientific Professions, eds. Jacquelyn A. Mattfeld and Carol G. Van Aken (Cambridge, Mass.: MIT Press, 1965), 232–45.

was a refreshing and enlightening start. But I think that the speakers who participated in this symposium did not mean to ask you to believe at first hearing every thesis they advanced. They meant to stimulate you to think about the alternative conclusions one could draw from all this material, in the hope that you would, surely but slowly, come around to their point of view. We must follow up these leads.

Further reasons for visualizing another meeting bring me back to the first session of this one. Dr. Bruno Bettelheim [Chicago] the first speaker, with the modesty that befits the first (and most exposed) speaker, expressed the hope that on another occasion the first speaker would be a woman. I did wonder, as you may have, why the preparatory committee selected Bruno Bettelheim and me to be the first and the last speakers. Not only two men, but two men with psychiatric backgrounds "made in Europe."

There was a time, of course, when meetings of this and similar kinds were introduced or concluded by members of an entirely different profession, whose sense of continuity and purpose was closer to metaphysics than to metapsychology, to the source of all destiny rather than to the dynamics of individual adjustment. Today, however, much of the daily concern with the continuity of individual lives and of the sequence of generations has (as Mrs. Gilbreth also pointed out) shifted to the clinical field, and I assume that Dr. Bettelheim and I were asked to speak in order to reflect your own concern over the often endangered continuity in the professional life of a modern woman.

President Mary I. Bunting [Radcliffe] also spoke of the necessity to "maximize continuities" under rapidly changing conditions. I remember a little boy who put this dilemma into classic form. He had asked his mother: "What is going to happen to me when I die?" and she had answered, with the finality born of uncertainty, "Well, your body is going to be buried in the ground and your soul is going to go up to heaven." But he was not satisfied. "Mommy," he said, "I'd rather keep my stuff together." This is the challenging task, even in life on this earth: how in changing conditions to keep your stuff together—to be women and workers, wives and colleagues, mothers and creative beings, and have a sense of continuity. But such a sense has always depended on blueprints that anticipated change, whether they were religious or scientific, fatalistic or forward looking. Today, when planning has become our evolutionary heritage, this means to learn to change *actively*, to help *plan* inescapable change, and also to become *aware*, and probably even self-conscious at times, in regard to what one is doing to oneself and to others. For you are pioneers of a new kind. You are pioneers not only on a new frontier of activity and association, but also on an inner frontier, which includes new responsibilities for changes in yourselves and in others: your men, your children—and, yes, mankind. A certain self-consciousness, then, may not be avoidable; it can, in fact, be creatively used if it is not shirked. Here I would think that in any future symposium you might want to include Dr. Benson Snyder and draw on his experience. He is (as most of you know) the chief psychiatrist here at M.I.T., or what our *Harvard Crimson* would call "the top shrink." He has concerned himself with the personalities of the budding engineer and scientist and with the particular tensions that go with that kind of work; and Dean Mattfeld and he have no doubt collected insights and suggestions concerning the role of women in these fields. I missed hearing from them and from you concerning the tensions of your work *as perceived by you.*

I must add to the other characteristics that I share with Dr. Bettelheim that of age. Our conceptual ancestry goes back to the days of Freud, who studied the psychological tensions of his era, which is, in turn, the past of ours: an era of unlimited human progress based on unrestrained commercial expansion, and an all-powerful middle class. While revolutionizing the science and treatment of severe mental suffering, he also recognized conditions that were part and parcel of the changing history and technology, and the scruples and tensions often befalling the sensitive, the advanced, and some of the successful of his time. Maybe, then, our mandate is to help you keep watch over the changes in our society and the tensions that could befall those aspiring to success in the era to come. But instead of basing our assessments on a passing age, on theories of human nature that we now know undergo change at least to some extent as conditions and eras change, we would rather hope that we will hear more from you. For we need to know better where exactly you need our insights.

A second set of reasons for my wish for further meetings concerns you more exclusively, you the young women delegates. What will you do with all the things that you have heard here? Of course, you will report to your colleagues. And, if I may make a guess, you wonder—but why offer you a prophetic interpretation when I can tell you of an experience? Not long ago, I talked about womanhood at one of our technical institutes. Afterwards I had a discussion with a number of alert and attractive young women who seemed strangely pensive. I asked them to tell me what they really felt about what I had said in my lecture. They discussed it for a moment among themselves and agreed on this reply: "What you said makes sense—but *how do we tell our boyfriends?*" This problem is so important that a future meeting might well be named "Women *and Men* in Engineering and Science" with an emphasis on what nowadays is called a dialogue of men and women. I have not checked this with your committee, but maybe each delegate should have the privilege and the duty of bringing one man of intimate acquaintance, if necessary with some assistance from the Marines. For it was clear in this two-day meeting that underlying many of the difficulties of women in the fields discussed (whether discrimination in industry or government, in the home or in society) there is always that most basic discrimination and prejudice against themselves that still exists in the minds of women themselves; and that this (now as in all history) is related to the question of how the men will react if women dare to change. Women, in turn, deeply sympathize with the apprehensions on the part of men as to what might happen if women really did take part in all of those activities that men have considered their privilege and their preserve and *from* which most men seek refuge by returning to women. And it is hard to look refuge in a would-be competitor. In some discussions men otherwise not of a sentimental bent insist so strenuously that children need their mothers at home that one cannot help wondering if it is not the husband himself who is the needy person—the tired husband who wants a ravishing companion free of all connotations of the office and the lab.

But there is a more pertinent explanation for his resistance to a change in the image of the woman: a clear elaboration of sexual types is always essential for the polarization of the sexes in sexual life and in their respective identity formation. For this and many other reasons, there is even a possibility that as the number of competitive women in these fields increases, there may well be something of a male "backlash." I have found among the most educated, the most attractive, the most decent husbands (as you probably have found in more intimate conversation) a certain more or less rationalized stupidity when it comes to the question of women's role in science and government—a fanatic refusal to try to understand, which can only be explained as an expression of an underlying panic. In comparison, the fathers of ambitious women are not such a problem, or so we heard yesterday.

If, as has often been said, the lack of available women in some areas constitutes more of a problem than the lack of available jobs, I think that one reason is to be found in whatever the prejudices of men are against an expansion of women's role in these fields, prejudices, as I have said, that only reinforce what the women themselves feel. The fact is that there is always a historical lag between any emancipation and the inner adjustment of the emancipated. It takes a much longer time to emancipate what goes on deep down inside us—that is, whatever prejudices and inequalities have managed to become part of our impulse life and our identity formation—than the time it takes to redefine professed values and to change legalities. And any part of mankind that has had to accept its self-definition from a more dominant group is apt to define itself by what it is *not* supposed to be. Thus, it is easy to impress on the working women of some classes and pursuits the proposition that they should not be unfeminine, or unmaternal, or unladylike, all of which may well come in conflict with that identity element in many successfully intellectual women whose background decreed that, above all, they should not be unintelligent. It is, then, not enough, as has been said, to be "changing with the changing forces." One must become part of a force that guides change, and this with a reasonably good conscience.

The first step toward this may well be a consideration of whether the working world, where it has been exclusively shaped by men for men, and especially where it has succumbed to the stereotypy of competition, is *really* so conducive to the male sense of continuity in work, home, and citizenship. This cannot be separated from the other, here more basic, consideration, that of the continuity between what woman has always been and always will be; what she is not and never will be; and what she yet can and will become. Permit me to continue in a somewhat personal vein and not to become involved at this point in more than one or two theoretical questions. Since my article on womanhood and in fact the whole special issue of *Daedalus* on "Women in America Today" has been recommended to you, I shall restrict myself to a few further remarks concerning prevalent emotional and intellectual attitudes toward questions of a psychological nature.

I have not made a secret of the fact that it is not easy for a man to discuss sexual differences. My article gives some reasons for this. Prejudice blind us most of all to the fact that prejudice and blindness exist. Nor do women make it easy for men: whenever we come to consider some difference as vital and essential, we are suspected of inventing new rationalizations for the age-old claim that the proper places for women are the bedroom, the nursery, and the kitchen— in whatever order. Any mention of the lasting function and importance of sexual differences is quickly taken to mean a renewed emphasis on inequality or a reactionary insistence that women should keep their place as defined by men. But if I insist on talking about certain differences, it is because I feel strongly that it is no longer the self-preservation of either sex that is at stake but the preservation of the race. Technological and political developments make it necessary that women should take their place firmly in the sciences as well as in the politics of the future.

But here the question arises: how can we agree, or productively disagree, about women's potentials—we as men and women, and we as workers in different disciplines? Let me illustrate this problem by returning to my article in *Daedalus*. The article consists of some reflections on womanhood, which were presented at the American Academy of Arts and Sciences as part of an interdisciplinary symposium. In my paper, I presented some old observations concerning the different ways in which boys and girls use the spatial dimension in imaginative productions, and discussed the conclusion that, in boys, exterior space and its traversion with speed and energy have a certain pervasive importance, whereas girls emphasize arrangements in which people and animals are contained in enclosures. I related these basic tendencies to the anatomical "inner space," the space in which each human being is "born," and which he progressively exchanges for the extended inner spaces of the mother's arms and watchful presence, and of the home's protective milieu. Nothing in human life is purely biological, however, and it is clear that the basic fact and configuration of the inner space and its extensions have been variously elaborated by cultures and religions, which, in fact, under the guise of protecting that sanctum, used it to justify a series of more-or-less strict "confinements," out of which modern woman is only slowly being released. It is, therefore, more than understandable that anything a man says that seems to give new reasons for new confinements is at first resented, and that even rather far-fetched conclusions, quite foreign to the observer, are drawn, in order to test where behavioral generalizations may lead. There was, for example, a brilliant paper that raised some otherwise valid methodological objections to my work. "Are we to conclude," it was asked, "that women might be set to work on the interior of the atom but not on a frontier subject like emission of radioactivity?" Undoubtedly we men, in turn, are too easily offended by this kind of humor. My main point had been that, where the confinements are broken, women may yet be expected to cultivate the implications of what is biologically and anatomically given. She may, in new areas of activity, balance man's indiscriminate endeavor to perfect his dominion over the outer spaces of national and technological expansion (at the cost of hazarding the annihilation of the species) with the determination to emphasize such varieties of caring and caretaking as would take responsibility for each individual child born in a planned humanity.

I mention this in order to point to a universal difficulty in discussions both intersexual and interdisciplinary. We humans are such moral creatures that we invariably react to any generalization regarding *human* behavior, not with questions of method alone but with questions of immediate applicability to conduct. Natural science escapes this dilemma because it has clear rules of verification confirming what *is*, rather than what should or should not be. You (speaking of you now as natural scientists) would not permit behavioral scientists to say in a discussion of relativity, "Are we to conclude, then, that we should act as if all conduct were relative?" Now, no doubt, the discovery of relativity is part of an emerging world view in which human conduct, too, will be re-evaluated; but this was no part of Einstein's intention. Statements concerning human behavior, however, always seem to be saying something that is equally accessible to the untrained eye and to ordinary commonsense, and that is therefore open to immediate translation into pat rules of conduct. Yet, in our so-called behavioral fields, too, the relation of epistemology to conduct is highly complex, and can be discussed only in searching interdisciplinary work—not in addresses. You can see again why I would hope for further meetings.

In conclusion, however, let me offer you a kind of formula for a review of sex differences. If you happen to read my paper, you will see that it strives (within the methodology of my field) to restore as the most positive anatomical specificity of womanhood what is (all too cursorily, of course) referred to as the "inner space," and to establish as more peripheral those "exterior" anatomical differences that have been utilized through the ages as a criterion of female inferiority. But even if, by doing so, I seem to reaffirm woman's central role in the bearing and upbringing of children and the central role of this task in every woman's experience (whether or not she chooses to become a mother), I must add that everybody, besides being a *body*, is *somebody*: a *person* and a *social being* occupying certain roles as worker and citizen. These three categories constitute "the stuff" that is to be "kept together."

Most verifiable sex differences (beyond those intrinsic to sexuality and procreation) establish for each sex only a range of attitudes and attributes which to most of its members "comes naturally," that is, are dispositions, predilections, and inclinations. Many of these could, of course, be unlearned or relearned with more or less effort and special talent. This is not to be denied; with ever-increasing choices given her by the grace of technology and enlightenment, the question is only how much and which parts of her inborn inclinations the woman of tomorrow will feel it most natural to preserve and to cultivate—with "natural" defined in human terms as what can be integrated and made continuous in the three basic aspects mentioned.

As a body, then, woman passes through stages of life that are interlinked with the lives of those whose bodily existence is (increasingly so according to her *own choice*) interdependent with hers. But as a worker, say, in a field structured by mathematical laws, woman is as responsible as any man for criteria of evidence that are intersexual or, better, suprasexual. As an individual person, finally, she utilizes her (biologically given) inclinations and her (technologically and politically given) opportunities to make the decisions that would seem to render her life most continuous and meaningful, without failing the chosen tasks of motherhood and citizenship. The question is how these three areas of life reach into each other—certainly not without conflict and tension and yet with some continuity of purpose.

What I would have to say, then, is not at variance with the assertion that the core of engineering and science is well removed from the workers' sex differences, even as also scientific training is more-or-less peripheral to the intimate tasks of womanhood and motherhood. With you, I am reasonably sure that computers built by women would not betray a female logic (although I do not know how reasonable this reasonableness is, since women did not care to invent them in the first place). The logic of the computers is, for better or for worse, of a suprasexual kind. But what to ask and what not to ask the monsters, and when to trust or not to trust them with vital decisions—there, for example, I would think well-trained women might well contribute to a new kind of vision, in the differential application of scientific thinking to humanitarian tasks.

But I would go further. Do we and can we really know what will happen to science if and when women are truly represented in it—not by a few glorious exceptions, but in the rank and file of the scientific elite? Is scientific inspiration really so impersonal and method-bound that personality plays no role in scientific creativity? And if we grant that a woman is never not a woman, even if and especially when she has become an excellent scientist and co-worker beyond all special apologies or claims, then why deny so strenuously that there may be in science also (on the scientific periphery of some tasks, and maybe in the very core of others) areas where the addition, to the male kind of creative vision, of women's vision and creativity may yet lead, not to new laws of verification, but to new areas of inquiry and to new applications? Such a possibility, I suggest, can be tested only if and when women are sufficiently represented in the sciences so that woman's mind may relax about the task and the role and apply itself to the unknown. Is this really so utopian? If I were a scientist I would at any rate not be dissuaded from such a possibility by the statistical facts that have been presented to us regarding the still very small number of women in science and technology.

As I say this I realize, of course, that our hope lies in a future in which the differential contributions of one sex or another will not be specifiable at all. Here as elsewhere, then, in reaffirming the differences between the sexes I am only trying to disclaim an assumed *sameness* which should not be needed as an argument for *equality* in the first place; and to assert instead an *equivalence* which in many areas of activity has not had a chance to assert itself. In recognizing and developing shared logic and method, we shall be able to reassess with less defensiveness those areas in which sexual differences not only should not be denied but should be affirmed and cultivated.

Whatever economic facts may support the claim that in some areas there is not enough work for either sex as things now are—and whatever practical reasons seem to stand in the way of a contemporaneous development of motherhood and advanced workmanship in those women who choose both—one thing is certain: one reneges on freedoms that one has already grasped only at the risk of becoming illogical or unjust. Circumstances may call on all our inventiveness in new joint adjustments to changing conditions, but they do not excuse prejudices which keep half of mankind from participating in planning and decision-making and this at a time when the other half, by its competitive escalation and acceleration of technological progress, has brought us all to the gigantic brink on which we live with all our affluence.

I have said more about old resistances and prejudices than about the hope that lies in a new era. Yet new strength of adaptation develops in those historical eras in which there is a confluence of emancipated individual resources with the potentials of a new technical and social order. Whether there is any true progress in this world, or only a periodical reintegration of human forces following social conflagrations and technical breakthroughs, may be debatable. But I think I know that new generations gain the full measure of their vitality in the continuity of new freedoms with a developing technology and a historical vision. There, also, personal synthesis is strengthened and with it an increased sense of humanity, which, when it occurs in a woman, even her husband or boyfriend will understand and her children will feel, even if new adjustments are demanded of them too. Social inventiveness and new knowledge can help plan such adjustments in a society that is sure of its values. But without these values, behavioral science has little to offer.

So my conclusion would be that, only when you women come into your own, so will the men, and so will your children.

Memorandum for the
Conference on the Draft
(1968)

Having read the material sent to me on the University of Chicago Conference of the Draft and having had a series of conversations with young people in recent weeks, I have come to a few conclusions which I offer here as illustration of a psychological point of view, and without detailed discussion.

Most of the arguments for compulsory military and other national service seem to be bogged down in the imagery of past national emergencies (as is to be expected if and when a deadline for decision is to be met): "past" in regard to *type of warfare*, "past" in regard to the *technology of armament*, "past" in regard to *manpower needs*, and (most relevant for the social psychologist) "past" in regard to what Kenneth Boulding calls *a sense of legitimacy*. Without committing myself to his statement in its entirety, I find this concept of a *sense of legitimacy* very fruitful, especially in its individual manifestation, that is, a high sense of identity as a member and defender of what is accepted as a legitimate social system, and the resulting increase of energy in the service of what is felt to be a legitimate organizational demand. This has always been the essence of a good

Presented to the University of Chicago Conference on the Draft and first published in *The Draft: Facts and Alternatives*, ed. Sol P. Tax (Chicago: University of Chicago Press, 1968), 280–83.

morale. It cannot be manufactured or enforced, however, and rather than ask ourselves how much we can get out of our young people by a coercion legitimized with the values of the past, we may ask ourselves what we can see developing in them spontaneously at this point in history so we may help to maximize their potentials, as we lead, guide, and teach them.

I would see three legitimate areas in which youth can feel its energies activated or at least not misspent in organized service at this time.

1) An emergency in national security convincingly calling for an all-out mobilization. This is the pattern of the world wars which called for large expeditionary forces. Considering the safety of American borders and the distance of the fighting fronts, this has been the American pattern of warfare. It is important to specify this because Swedish, Swiss, or Israeli conditions are not applicable to it; there the single citizen is so aware of the all-around exposed borders of a society which maximizes his sense of democratic legitimacy, individuality, and welfare that the defense (and I emphasize *defense*) of his security and of national security coincide psychologically.

At this moment in our history, under the conditions of nuclear threat and counter-threat, the semblance of national emergency must be avoided, wars must remain undeclared, and warlike enthusiasms restrained even while the individuals are to be prepared to be *selected* for faraway service in middle-sized wars.

In a selective draft under such conditions, the government wants it both ways: it wants the right to draft all and maintain a sense of universal urgency, but it also wants to select only a few, and leave the others at home. But the draft of a few is no draft at all; and it is experienced by many as a selective sentencing, if as yet more or less legitimate.

The limited emergencies now typical for undeclared war, however, are really police actions secretly sanctioned by large powers who want to avoid attacking each other with nuclear weapons while attacking each other with propaganda. That, I assume, is progress under nuclear conditions. But it is not the kind of legitimacy which will, *in the long run*, arouse a sufficient sense of participation in a sufficent number of young individuals to expect them to be more than passively and fatalistically compliant to any draft or coercion. Such compliance may do for a while as a minimum of necessary morale—that is, as long as the military ideals and identifications of previous wars survive. Otherwise, with the shrewd prolongation by our adversaries of fighting conditions which rarely promise decisive small victories and forever postpone any hope of final victory (not to speak of that total surrender which, according to George Kennan, has so far been the questionable trophy of foreign wars), the military morale on a national scale necessary for an inspired "citizens' army" will, I am forced to predict, sooner or later suffer.

I see no other way, therefore, than a voluntary army composed of men who by ideological choice, by personality, by fortune, or by misfortune find some meaning or some advantage, and preferably both, in military life. To a large extent, this is already the case in our military forces in Vietnam: the sooner the enlisted and reenlisted volunteers are given sufficient status in the national imagery and sufficient reward during their service and especially also at the time of their rejoining the employment at home, the sooner will we have a legitimate expertly trained military force. This will be also available for international ventures, such as actions for the United Nations, which seem already more legitimate to many Americans than does the Vietnam war. Whatever disadvantages are feared in such an army (such as its totalitarian potential, its mercenary character, or the proportion of volunteers from the less privileged classes) are really matters of national education and civil rights which must be discussed in a much larger context.

It is possible, of course, that a *volunteer expert army*, as I would prefer to call it (because it really answers the training requirements of a modern army in a way in which a short-term recruitment of "citizens" cannot possibly answer it), will not provide sufficent reserves for wider emergencies. I think that these reserves, also, should be established on the basis of voluntary enlistments, maybe partially in auxiliary training, such as in the ROTC.

I am opposed to the lottery system for psychological reasons: I do not believe that an abdication to Fate, administered by men, or by man-made machines, is a modern way of utilizing the potentials of a youth trained to think, to predict, and to choose. It can only lead to a more helpless sense of unfairness in those who are thus tapped, because there is nobody on whom they could vent legitimate gripes. By the same token, the guilty discomfort of those who escaped must not be underestimated. And again, if middle-sized wars are to have the legitimacy of national and international police action, then, surely, education as well as tradition should permit a large number of dedicated or adventurous young men to find such service worthwhile.

2) The second legitimacy felt strongly by our youth is humanitarian service. This, however, is more and more internationally or, rather, supranationally oriented. I like the spirit of Margaret Mead's pro-

posal for national service because she makes it clear that it is not enough to be not military. But I would have liked to hear her discuss the question of how the nation, confronted with a sudden oversupply of compulsory services, would find the informed, equipped, and dedicated army of teachers and leaders, without whom such service could be a constant source of nationwide malcontent and disappointment. I could well also see that "elite" organizations (i.e., organizations dependent on a special spirit) like the Peace Corps would shudder to think of being supplied with volunteers by organizational and bureaucratic means. Just because ideological commitment to hardship under accustomed and extreme conditions is the only legitimate counterpart to the rigors and dangers of Army service, a volunteer army of young men and women ready for clearly necessary national as well as international service would, I think, be more desirable. The question of inculcating in our youth the wish to serve in this manner (without being intolerant of those who must develop their own individualized type of "service") is again a matter of education, and of a nationwide awareness that many values once linked to the military posture (discipline, service, and duty) must survive their demilitarization.

3) There is a third legitimacy which I will mention only in passing because it may as yet seem remote to the middle-aged middle class which we represent. I mean service in movements of civil disobedience, on a large and different scale from that of Thoreau's, to be sure, and under very different conditions from Gandhi's. I believe that there is an enormous potential for such action in many of our young people, and especially in our students, a potential which we must not belittle because it is as yet largely leaderless and devoid of a unitary discipline and philosophy. We have, in fact, no right to belittle it, for what is sometimes ridiculous and obnoxious in it is really the result of our ethical hypocrisies as parents and as teachers, which go with the attempt to make youth adjust to outmoded values. We must not overlook the fact that many of the youths now finding some kind of legitimatization in what to us looks like sensory, sexual, and behavioral excesses of all kinds, will be wiser, but I would hope, not altogether subdued adults, parents, and teachers in the not too distant future. I can only indicate, then, that any aggravated and seemingly corrupt alliance of government (and especially the military) with advancing technology will necessarily lead to a new kind of rebellion which, in fighting "super machines" of all kinds, can only fight by refusing services. What once was loudly voiced dissent must, where there is no way of being heard, become non-cooperation. I

know that such a consideration is far from the immediate realities of the draft situation, not to speak of a deadline for a draft law. Yet, if we are really interested in educating, rather than bypassing or resisting, the best potentials of youth, we must, I think, seriously attend to a trend which may provide a high sense of legitimacy, even where it touches on the illegal. How much we can (or should) legalize non-cooperation not sanctioned by past C.O. standards I do not know. But we cannot bypass the problem as one of transient freaks.

This brings me, finally, to the matter of education. I am appalled at the alarmist undertones of many of the reports which try to bolster any particular plan with sinister threats of totalitarianism here and the lack of volunteer spirit there, not to speak of the necessity to advance literacy, discipline, health, love of country, and decent haircuts by governmental regimentation. This, I feel is the payoff in the whole abdication of the older generation which can face the future squarely only by interposing a mirror reflecting the past, always a prime sign of a weakening sense of legitimacy. All in all, I think that what is over-publicized as the dispirited, or merely conformist, or sometimes riotously obnoxious youth of our day is, rather, the potentially most dedicated, because most informed, or better *informable*, youth in history. The draft law calls for immediate action, but between the lines of all the reports submitted there are questions which call for a clearer formulation of traditional and emerging values—those which give our generation the right to recruit youth, and those which would permit youth to insist on alternatives.

Psychosocial Identity
(1968)

When we wish to establish a person's *identity*, we ask what his name is and what station he occupies in his community. *Personal identity* means more; it includes a subjective sense of continuous existence and a coherent memory. *Psychosocial identity* has even more elusive characteristics, at once subjective and objective, individual and social.

A subjective sense of identity is a sense of sameness and continuity as an individual—but with a special quality probably best described by William James. A man's character, he wrote in a letter, is discernible in the "mental or moral attitude in which, when it came upon him, he felt himself most deeply and intensely active and alive. At such moments there is a voice inside which speaks and says: '*This is the real me!*' " Such experience always includes "an element of active tension, of holding my own, as it were, and trusting outward things to perform their part so as to take it a full harmony, but without any guaranty that they will" (1920, vol. 1, p. 199).* Thus may a mature person come to the astonished or exuberant awareness of his identity.

What underlies such a subjective sense, however, can be recognized

First published in *International Encyclopedia of the Social Sciences* (New York: Crowell-Collier, 1968), 61–65.
* References in parenthesis appear at the end of this article.

by others, even when it is not especially conscious or, indeed, self-conscious: thus, one can observe a youngster "become himself" at the very moment when he can be said to be "losing himself" in work, play, or company. He suddenly seems to be "at home in his body," to "know where he is going," and so on.

The social aspects of identity formation were touched upon by Freud when in an address he spoke of an "inner identity" that he shared with the tradition of Jewry and which still was at the core of his personality, namely, the capacity to live and think in isolation from the "compact majority" ([1926] 1959, p. 273). The gradual development of a mature psychosocial identity, then, presupposes a community of people whose traditional values become significant to the growing person even as his growth assumes relevance for them. Mere "roles" that can be "played" interchangeably are obviously not sufficient for the social aspect of the equation. Only a hierarchial integration of roles that foster the vitality of individual growth as they represent a vital trend in the existing or developing social order can support identities. Psychosocial identity thus depends on a complementarity of an inner (ego) synthesis in the individual and of role integration in his group.

In individual development, psychosocial identity is not feasible before and is indispensable after the end of adolescence, when the grown-up body grows together, when matured sexuality seeks partners, and when the fully developed mind begins to envisage a historical perspective and seeks new loyalties—all developments which must fuse with each other in a new sense of sameness and continuity. Here, persistent (but sometimes mutually contradictory) infantile identifications are brought in line with urgent (and yet often tentative) new self-definitions and irreversible (and yet often unclear) role choices. There ensues what we call the *identity crisis*.

Historical processes in turn seem vitally related to the demand for identity in each new generation; for to remain vital, societies must have at their disposal the energies and loyalties that emerge from the adolescent process: as positive identities are "confirmed," societies are regenerated. Where this process fails in too many individuals, a *historical crisis* becomes apparent. Psychosocial identity, therefore, can also be studied from the point of view of a complementarity of life history and history (Erikson 1958; 1964, chapter 5).

In its individual and collective aspects, psychosocial identity strives for ideological unity; but it is also always defined by that past which is to be lived down and by that potential future which is to be prevented. Identity formation thus involves a continuous conflict with powerful negative identity elements. In times of aggravated crises these come to the fore to arouse in man a murderous hate of "otherness," which he judges as evil in strangers—and in himself. The study of psychosocial identity thus calls also for an assessment of the hierarchy of positive and negative identity elements present in an individual's stage of life and in his historical era.

These are dimensions which will prove indispensable to the study of identity in the variety of disciplines now to be listed. In the meantime, I hope to have disposed of the faddish contemporary "definition" of identity as the question "Who am I?"

Interests and Approaches

PSYCHIATRY AND SOCIAL PSYCHIATRY. Intricate life processes often reveal themselves first in epidemiological states of dysfunction. Thus, in our time the significance of the identity process first became apparent to psychopathologists, who recognized pychosocial factors in severe disturbances of the individual sense of identity (alienation, identity confusion, depersonalization) and to diagnosticians of social upheavals, who found psychosocial phenomena at work (role conflict, anomie).

As the theoretical focus of psychoanalysis shifted from "instincts" to "ego," from defensive to adaptive mechanisms, and from infantile conflict to later stages of life, states of acute ego impairment were recognized and treated. A syndrome called *identity confusion* ("identity diffusion" proved a somewhat ambiguous term) was recognized as characterizing neurotic disturbances resulting from traumatic events, such as war, internment, and migration (Erikson [1950] 1964, pp. 38–45). But it also proved to be a dominant feature in developmental disturbances in adolescence (Erikson 1959), pp. 122–146). Identity crises aggravated by social and maturational changes can evoke neurotic or psychotic syndromes but are found to be diagnosable and treatable as transitory disturbances (Blaine and McArthur 1961). Identity confusion, furthermore, can also be recognized in pervert-delinquent and bizarre-extremist behavior, which can assume epidemiological proportions as a result of technological changes and population shifts (Witmer & Kotinsky 1956). Thus theory, therapy, and prevention are seen to lack the proper leverage if the need for psychosocial identity is not understood, and especially if instead the young deviant or patient is "confirmed" as a born criminal or a lifelong patient by correctional or therapeutic agencies (Erikson and Erikson 1957; K. T. Erikson 1957).

CHILD DEVELOPMENT AND ANTHROPOLOGY. The study of a variety of dysfunctions thus threw light on identity formation as the very criterion of psychosocial functioning at, and after, the conclusion of one critical stage of development: adolescence. Identity, to be sure, does not originate (and does not end) in adolescence: from birth onward the child learns what counts in his culture's space time and life plan by the community's differential responses to his maturing behavior. He learns to identify with ideal prototypes and to develop away from evil ones. But identity formation comes to a decisive crisis in youth—a crisis met, alleviated, or aggravated by different societies in different ways (Lichenstein 1961; Erikson 1950).

HISTORY AND SOCIOLOGY. Historical considerations lead back into man's prehistory and evolution. Only gradually emerging as one mankind conscious of itself and responsible to and for itself, man has been divided into pseudospecies (tribes and nations, castes and classes), each with its own overdefined identity and each reinforced by mortal prejudice against its images of other pseudospecies.

In history, identifications and identities are bound to shift with changing technologies, cultures, and political systems. Existing or changing roles thus must be reassimilated in the psychosocial identity of the most dominant and most numerous members of an organization. Large-scale irreconcilabilities in this ongoing assimilation result in *identity panic* that, in turn, aggravates irrational aversions and prejudices and can lead to erratic violence on a large scale or to widespread self-damaging malaise (Stein et al. 1960; Wheelis 1958).

The fact that the remnants of "tribalism" in an armed and industrialized species can contribute to conditions of utmost danger to the survival of the species itself is leading to a new consciousness of man's position in his own ongoing history.

RELIGION AND PHILOSOPHY. While projecting evil otherness on enemies and devils, man has habitually assigned a supreme "identity" to deities who guarantee, under revealed conditions, his chances for individual immortality or rebirth. This tendency is a proper subject for psychoanalytic and psychosocial investigation only insofar as it reveals the psychological and cultural variations of man's projection of his own striving for omnipotent identity on the "Beyond" (Erikson 1958).

Finally, man's psychosocial identity has been related philosophically to his striving to attain and to transcend *the pure "I"* that remains each individual's existential enigma. Old and new wisdom would suggest that man can transcend only what he has affirmed in a lifetime and a generation. Here, clinical and social science will concern themselves with the demonstrable, and philosophy with the thinkable (Lichtenstein 1963).

Out of this multiplicity of approaches we will now select a few converging themes for more coherent presentation.

A Theory of Psychosocial Identity

THE IDENTITY CRISIS. In some young people, in some classes, at some periods in history, the identity crisis will be noiseless; in other people, classes, and periods, the crisis will be clearly marked off as a critical period, a kind of "second birth," either deliberately intensified by collective ritual and indoctrination or spontaneously aggravated by individual conflict.

In this day of psychiatric overconcern, it must be emphasized that crisis here does not mean a fatal turn but rather (as it does in drama and in medicine) a crucial time or an inescapable turning point for better *or* for worse. "Better" here means a confluence of the con- structive energies of individual and society, as witnessed by physical grace, mental alertness, emotional directness, and social "actual- ness." "Worse" means prolonged identity confusion in the young individual as well as in the society which is forfeiting the devoted application of the energies of youth. But worse can ultimately lead to better: extraordinary individuals, in repeated crises, create the identity elements of the future (Erikson 1958).

IDENTITY CLOSURE AND "IDEOLOGY." In the individual, the nor- mative identity crisis is brought about by contemporaneous and in- divisible developments that have received uneven attention in various fields of inquiry. The "growing together" of late adolescence results in increasingly irreversible configurations of physical and sexual type, of cognitive and emotional style, and of social role. Sexual maturation drives the individual toward more or less regressive, furtive, or in- discriminate contact; yet the fatefulness of a narrowing choice of more permanent partners becomes inescapable. All of this is strongly related to maturing patterns of cognition and judgment. Inhelder's and Piaget's studies (1955) suggest that only in adolescence can man "reverse" in his mind a sequence of events in such a way that it becomes clear why what *did* happen *had* to happen. Thus, the ir- reversibility of consequences (more or less intended, more or less "deserved") becomes painfully apparent. With such cognitive orientation, then, the young person must make or "make his own" a series of personal, occupational, and ideological choices.

At the same time, an unconscious integration of all earlier identifications must take place. Children have the nucleus of a separate identity early in life; often they are seen to defend it with precocious self-determination against pressures which would make them overidentify with one or both of their parents. In fact, what clinical literature describes as identification is usually neurotic overidentification. The postadolescent identity must rely, to be sure, on all those earlier identifications that have contributed to a gradual alignment of the individual's instinctual make-up with his developing endowment and the tangible promise of future opportunities. But the wholeness of identity is more than the sum of all earlier identifications and must be supported by a communal orientation which we will call ideological. A living ideology is a systematized set of ideas and ideals which unifies the striving for psychosocial identity in the coming generation, and it remains a stratum in every man's imagery, whether it remains a "way of life" or becomes a militant "official" ideology. An ideological world view may be transmitted in dogmatic form by special rites, inductions, or confirmations; or society may allow youth to experiment for specified periods (I have called them *psychosocial moratoria*) under special conditions (*Wanderschaft*, frontier, colonies, service, college, etc.).

FIDELITY. Sooner or later, the young individual and the functioning society must join forces in that combination of loyalty and competence which may best be termed *fidelity* (Erikson 1963). This may be realized by the involvement of youth as beneficiaries and renewers of tradition, workers and innovators in technology, critics and rejuvenators of style and logic, and rebels bent on the destruction of hollow form in such experience as reveals the essence of the era. For contemporaries, it is often difficult to discern the vital promise of a new and more inclusive identity or to assess the specific alienation inherent in a historical period: there are prophetic voices in all eras which make a profession of ascribing man's existential self-estrangement to the sins of the time.

Obviously, an era's identity crisis is least severe in that segment of youth which is able to invest its fidelity in an expanding technology and thus evolves new and competent types and roles. Today, this includes the young people in all countries who can fit into and take active charge of technical and scientific development, learning thereby to identify with a life-style of invention and production. Youth which is eager for such experience but unable to find access to it will feel estranged from society until technology and nontechnical intelligence have come to a certain convergence.

MALE AND FEMALE IDENTITY. Do male and female identities differ? The "mechanisms" of identity formation are, of course, the same. But since identity is always anchored both in physiological "givens" and in social roles, the sex endowed with an "inner-bodily space" capable of bearing offspring lives in a different total configuration of identity elements from the fathering sex (Erikson 1965). Obviously also, the childhood identifications to be integrated differ in the two sexes. But the realization of woman's optimal psychosocial identity (which in our day would include individuality, workmanship, and citizenship, as well as motherhood) is beset with ancient problems. The "depth," both concretely physical and emotional, of woman's involvement in the cycle of sexual attraction, conception, gestation, lactation, and child care has been exploited by the builders of ideologies and societies to relegate women to all manner of lifelong "confinements" and confining roles. Psychoanalysis has shown feminine identity formation to be prejudiced by what a woman cannot be and cannot have rather than by what she is, has been, and may yet become. Thus the struggle for legal and political equality is apt to be accompanied by strenuous attempts to base woman's identity on the proof that she is (almost) as good as man in activities and schedules fashioned by and for men. However, the flamboyant brinkmanship of technological and political men in matters now of vital concern to the whole species has revived the vision of a new identity of womanhood, one in which the maternal orientation is not at odds with work and citizenship but gives new meaning to both. But here as elsewhere new inventions will not suffice as long as deep-seated negative identities prevail.

NEGATIVE IDENTITY AND TOTALISM. As pointed out, a negative identity remains an unruly part of the total identity. In addition, man tends to "make his own" the negative image of himself imposed on him by superiors and exploiters (Erikson 1959, pp. 31–38). To cite a contemporary issue, a colored child's identity may have gained strength from his parent's melodious speech, and yet he may come to suspect this speech as the mark of submission and begin to aspire to the harsh traits of a superiority from which the "master race" tries by every means to exclude him. A fanatical segregationist, in turn, may have learned to reinforce regional identity with the repudiation of everything colored and yet may have experienced early associations with colored people for which he remains nostalgic. He will, therefore, protect his superiority with a narrow-mindedness so defensive that it fails to provide a reliable identity in an enlightened society.

Two phenomena further complicate these inner rifts. For one, negative images become tightly associated with one another in the individual's imagery. The reinforced defense against a negative identity may make a pronounced he-man despise in himself and others everything reminiscent of female sentimentality, colored passivity, or Jewish braininess and at the same time make him fear that what is thus held in contempt may take over his world. This kind of reaction is the source of much human hate. In the event of aggravated crises, furthermore, an individual (or a group) may despair of his or its ability to contain these negative elements in a positive identity. This can lead to a sudden surrender to total doctrines and dogmas (Lifton 1961) in which the negative identity becomes the dominant one. Many a young German, once sensitive to foreign criticism, became a ruthless Nazi on the rebound from the love for a *Kultur* which in post-Versailles Germany seemed at odds with a German identity. His new identity, however, was based on a totalism marked by the radical exclusion of dangerous otherness and on the failure to integrate historically given identity elements also alive in every German. What differentiates such totalism from conversions promising a more inclusive wholeness is the specific rage that is aroused wherever identity development loses the promise of a traditionally assured wholeness. This latent rage is easily exploited by fanatic and psychopathic leaders. It can explode in the arbitrary destructiveness of mobs, and it can serve the efficient violence of organized machines of destruction.

Historical Considerations

As predicted, developmental considerations have led us to examine historical processes, for identity and ideology seem to be two aspects of the same psychosocial process. But identity and ideology are only way stations on the route to further individual and collective maturation; new crises work toward those higher forms of social identification in which identities are joined, fused, renewed, and transcended.

There are, however, periods in history which are relative identity vacuums and in which three forms of human apprehension aggravate each other: fears aroused by discoveries and inventions (including weapons) which radically expand and change the whole world image, anxieties aggravated by the decay of institutions which had been the historical anchor of an existing ideology, and the dread of an existential vacuum devoid of spiritual meaning. In the past, ideological innovators evolved vital new identity ingredients out of their own prolonged and repeated adolescent conflicts (Erikson 1958; 1964, pp. 201–208). Today, however, the ideology of progress has made unpredictable and unlimited change itself the "wave of the future." In all parts of the world, therefore, the struggle now is for anticipatory and more inclusive identities. Revolutionary doctrines promise the new identity of "peasant-and-worker" to the youth of countries which must overcome their tribal, feudal, or colonial orientation. At the same time, new nations attempt to absorb regions, and new markets attempt to absorb nations; the world space is extended to include outer space as the proper locale for a universal technological identity.

Functioning societies can reconfirm their principles, and true leaders can create significant new solidarities only by supporting the development of more inclusive identities; for only a new and enlightened ethics can successfully replace dying moralisms. Nehru said that Gandhi had given India an identity; and, indeed, by perfecting an active mode of nonviolence, Gandhi had transformed a divisive and negative identity (the "passive" Indian) into an inclusive and militant claim on unified nationhood. In other parts of the world, youth itself has shown that when trusted to do so, it can provide patterns for new elites. One thinks here of Israel's "kibbutzniks," the U.S. Peace Corps, and the American students committed to the dislodgment of racial prejudice. In such developments, young men and women can be seen to develop new forms of solidarity and new ethics.

In conclusion, however, we must remind ourselves that the complementarity and relativity of individual identity and collective ideology (which no doubt has emerged as part of man's sociogenetic evolution) also bestow on man a most dangerous potential, namely, a lastingly immature perspective on history. Ideologies and identities, it is true, strive to overcome the tyranny of old moralisms and dogmatisms; yet, they often revert to these, seduced by the righteousness by which otherness is repudiated when the conditions supporting a sense of identity seem in danger. Old ideologists equipped with modern weaponry could well become mankind's executioners. But a trend toward an all-inclusive human identity, and with it a universal ethics, is equally discernible in the development of man, and it may not be too utopian to assume that new and world-wide systems of technology and communication may serve to make this universality more manifest.

References

BLAINE GRAHAM B., and McARTHUR, CHARLES, (eds.) 1961. *Emotional Problems of the Student*. New York: Appleton.

ERIKSON, ERIK H. (1950) 1964. *Childhood and Society*. 2d ed., rev. & enl. New York: Norton.

———. (1958) 1962 *Young Man Luther*. New York: Norton.

———. 1959. "Identity and the Life Cycle." *Psychological Issues*, 1, 1.

———. ed. 1963. *Youth: Change and Challenge*. New York: Basic Books.

———. 1964. *Insight and Responsibility*. New York: Norton.

———. 1965. "Inner and Outer Space: Reflections on Womanhood." In Robert Lifton, *The Woman in America*. New York: Houghton Mifflin.

———. 1966 "The Concept of Identity in Race Relations: Notes and Queries," *Dædalus 95*, 145–171.

———. and ERIKSON, KAI T. 1957. The Confirmation of the Delinquent." *Chicago Review* 10, 15–23.

ERIKSON, KAI T. 1957. "Patient Role and Social Uncertainty." *Psychiatry*, 20, 263–74.

FREUD, SIGMUND. (1926) 1959. Address to the Society of B'nai B'rith. In Sigmund Freud, *The Standard Edition of the Complete Psychological Works*. London: Hogarth, Vol. 20, 272–74.

INHELDER, BÄRBEL, AND PIAGET, JEAN (1955) 1958. *The Growth of Logical Thinking from Childhood to Adolescence*. New York: Basic Books. First published as *De la logique de l'enfant à la logique de l'adolescent*.

JAMES, WILLIAM. 1920. *Letters*, vol. 1. Boston: Atlantic Monthly Press.

LICHTENSTEIN, HEINZ. 1961. "Identity and Sexuality: A Study of Their Interrelationship in Man." *Journal of the American Psychoanalytic Association*, 9, 179–260.

———. 1963. "The Dilemma of Human Identity." *Journal, of the American Psychoanalytic Association*, 11, 173–223.

LIFTON, ROBERT J. 1961. *Thought Reform and the Psychology of Totalism: A Study of "Brainwashing" in China*. New York: Norton.

STEIN, MAURICE R., VIDICH, ARTHUR; and WHITE, DAVID M., eds. 1960. *Identity and Anxiety*. New York: Free Press.

WHEELIS, ALLEN. 1958. *The Quest for Identity*. New York: Norton.

WHITMER, HELEN L., and KOTINSKY, RUTH, eds. 1956. *New Perspectives for Research on Juvenile Delinquency*. Washington: U.S. Children's Bureau.

On Student Unrest:
Remarks on Receiving
the Foneme Prize (1969)

The immediate causes and local circumstances of student unrest differ so widely on the international scene that it is not easy to find a proper leverage for the discussion of what may be the *inner* motivations common to rebellious youth in our time. Youth, at any rate, is a rather wide conception, including as it does both late teenage students involved in "indiscipline" in India and, for example, German almost *ewige Studenten* in their late twenties. The overt manifestations of youthful unrest are equally wide-ranging, from traditional and periodical rioting to the violent actions of youths never before involved in rebellion, and from the display of genuine ethical concern to that of marked amoral behavior. Such contrasting behavior, furthermore, can occur not only in the same individuals at different stages of their lives but also in otherwise distinct groups which during crises unexpectedly coalesce for purposes of demonstration. Can any one conceptual scheme give at least some initial order to all of these phenomena?

Presented to an international group of college administrators at the Villa Serbelloni in Bellagio, November 1968. Paper included in the brochure concerning the second FONEME International Convention on Human Formation from Adolescence to Maturity, Milan, May 10–11, 1969. Published here for the first time.

Morality and Ethics in Developmental Perspective

Let me begin with a somewhat didactic statement concerning one dominant characteristic of youth. In the life cycle of the individual, adolescence is the period when the *moral* precepts absorbed in childhood must be superseded by an *ideological* orientation on which a future commitment to *ethical* behavior can be based. "Must" is meant to convey that the adolescent is now psychologically ready—cognitively, emotionally, and socially—to envisage himself as part of a world image in which he, as an individual, has irreversible reponsibilities and that the "confirmation" of such an orientation in some form is a vital necessity for him.

Ethics (to begin with the end product) is marked by the capacity and eagerness to assent wholeheartedly to a system of values which one can understand logically, agree to ideologically, and visualize pragmatically. Along the way, however, young people need to absorb an *ideology* which provides a unified world image or universe of ideas. The perceived unity may be both utopian and simplistic and therefore all the more suited to youthful thinking.

All this the child cannot perceive; he is rather forced to absorb a system of *moral values* which he first learns to obey because of the rewards and punishments to be expected and then gradually also because conscience permits of no alternative. Obedience becomes internalized, but there can be little considered assent to the dicta obeyed, wherefore the response to moral pressure, from without and from within, is accompanied by all kinds of ambivalence and often by a sense of vindictiveness. This must be emphasized, for an aggravated sense of inner guilt thus implanted into children can later seek release by moralistic indignation against others.

In childhood, the burden of morality is balanced by *play* and *fantasy* which permit to a varying degree, a free expression of wishes and aspirations not subject to adult supervision and hidden even from conscience. Later, school learning offers the acquisition of techniques which promise to support (as they also narrow down) the child's expectations of future *mastery* and of *power* over others. Only in adolescence, however, can the individual truly envisage his own future or, at any rate, possible futures; it is then that his playfulness (now in possession of powerful new drives and capacities of both a destructive and a constructive nature) begins to experiment with social conditions, testing them cognitively, emotionally, and ideologically. Such playfulness both in sexual matters and on the stage of history can make youth both exhilarating and dangerous; and totalitarian leaders and movements know how to make the most of the enthusiasm *and* the danger. Isolated groups, cliques, and bands, too, can provide at least transitory solidarity in a joint assent to a utopian world image. While ideological world images, however, may be approached with prankishness as well as with *playacting* on the political stage, they are (as we must never forget) endowed with genuine emotion and a deep *commitment* to what is felt to be a necessary rejuvenation of ethical values. This youthful sense of historical necessity has, of course, its counterpart in the needs of society, for societies depend for their rejuvenation on the ideological experiments and commitments of youth. This can take the form of ceremonial *confirmations* of the young in the tradition of the old; of *innovations* in style and manner well in line with the existing order and yet perhaps shocking at the time; or of *radical change* as brought about by conquest, reformation, or revolution.

Thus, charismatic leaders of many kinds can attract among the young those potential *heroes* who are willing to die in the endeavor to kill men or to destroy institutions judged to be inimical to the dominant utopia. Other leaders can arouse an early ethical sense, which wins potential *martyrs*, who will court prison, injury, or death in response to an all-demanding sense of irreversible truth. In some extreme situations, youth is torn between heroism and martyrdom; and in both directions the step from romanticism to deadly involvement is often a short and sometimes an accidental one.

Historical Actuality

Taken together, the developmental and the social necessities sketched here can provide a sense of a *historical actuality* which makes history acutely relevant to youth and youth to history. Once thus engaged, youth and history cannot let go of each other until institutional renewal or change, catastrophe or exhaustion (and perhaps all of these) have taken over. It must be remembered, however, that the young person of yesterday literally is the young adult of today, although it is in the very nature of youth to act as if (and to be perceived as if!) it had permanence and immortality; this illusory sense of a self-fulfilling and eternal stage I have called a *psychosocial moratorium.* Yet the more mature young person of today feels that he will and must be the ethical young adult of tomorrow, an insight which induces in him a deep wish to be led and to be taught by truly ethical adults. Where such leadership fails, group regression can follow—and this is the challenge on which our discussion must focus.

Youth, then, experiences and acts out *the struggle between child-hood morality, youthful ideology, and adult ethics* in a great variety of seemingly contradictory roles and beliefs, ranging from the totally positive to the totally negative. Different young people and the same young people at different times can appear to be advancing to a kind of hyperethical adulthood or to be regressing to amoral or antimoral juvenility or infantility. They can be oblivious of all order to the point of nihilistic vandalism and yet also be willing to perceive and to die for the highest values of some hazy new order; they can be thoughtless to the point of deliberate stupidity and yet also be sharply aware of hidden contradictions, such as the hypocrisies of their elders.

Youth in Our Time

All of the foregoing, if true, could be so universal as to be nonspecific for the phenomena of our time. To be specific, it would have to explain why and how small subgroups, such as activist elites in the academic youth of today, seem to have the power and the capacity to establish the historical actuality of certain concerns and demands on a worldwide basis. This actuality can be measured by three facts: First, these subgroups *have* succeeded in creating convincing slogans, ideals, and images that have appeal or at least interest far beyond their various localities; second, they have been able to impose their slogans and ideals on masses of other students whether according to the local student culture, these masses had been previously engaged in some form of activism or not; and third, where these subgroups were not able to achieve their original demands, they have never-theless succeeded in arousing adult responses of such depth and am-bivalence that teachers and administrators have become personally upset to the point of acute traumatization and have become unsure of their obligations to their profession and to society. Obviously, then, any explanation of the dynamics of such youthful action alone would not be comprehensive enough; the evidence rather seems to indicate that youthful action would be impossible in both conception and execution were it not for specific adult reactions which are an intrinsic part of the historical actuality, for often such actuality is confirmed only by the actions of those who are challenged by youth.

The present situation, then, can be understood only on the assumption that large-scale developments in our time are giving universal relevance to the struggle of (mainly academic) youth for a new ethics. Such developments have been discussed by others; I am not competent to do so. But I must mention a few:

a. New concepts of heroism and martyrdom, such as the guerrilla warfare of unarmed or poorly armed bands against hyperarmed hyperorganizations.

b. A worldwide mistrust on the part of preindustrial and postindustrial youth in the competency of its parent generation that with all its righteousness and "know-how" really finds itself caught in changes and conditions both unpredictable and unsolvable.

c. A shift in the meaning of the life stages in a fast-changing world of specialization and expertise. Where an "adolescentulus," in the past, was a creature in a moratorium, he now becomes more and more the participant in an autonomous stage of life. This autonomy is vastly increased by the fact that sexual life is becoming even more independent of procreation, with a resulting disappearance of the sexual double standard; both women and men can now in principle freely choose their sexual style as well as the time of their commitment to progeny. On the other hand, this newly won autonomy is counteracted by the necessity to make an early commitment to an occupational or professional identity. And where apprenticeship and specialization once promised a distinct identity within a defined ethics, it now often seems to demand an early standardization of experience, with a blunting of both ideological awareness and ethical decision.

d. The resulting danger of masses of young people being drawn into early compromises with specialization, conformity, and premature success and thus losing that capacity for a renewal of humanist values without which, they feel, universal technocracy could become a new serfdom, malignant precisely because of the affluence it promises.

e. The special elaboration and prolongation of the stage of youth in a worldwide new academic subculture which gives masses of young people new forms of autonomous, if transitory, power.

f. Last, but by no means least, loss of authenticity of war as an institution on a large scale, with the result that images of heroism and martyrdom are transferred to internal issues.

All of these developments permit and force well-to-do academic youth to engage in a more concerted exercise of the age-old prerogative to take the side of the dispossessed and thus to give to their own rebellion the (often sincere) cloak of radical altruism. Only that today we see in this same youth, depending on local conditions, an almost desperate search for such masses of dispossessed as might welcome "liberation" from, rather than cohesion with, the "establishment." In this predicament, activist youth often regresses, historically speaking, in the name of "the people," although modern life has united former classes into a classlessness of consumership very different from the dream of joint producership for which millions have died. On the other hand, standardization with the help of the media of communication is so much part of our time that even the most individualistic young person can be submerged (like a modern Narcissus) in his own standardized image, whether the standardization is based on historical models (i.e., Edwardians or revolutionaries) or on relatively new phenomena (i.e., psychedelics). Here, especially, the "types" of dissent vary from place to place.

Much of the present conflict in academic life seems to be based on a late and yet powerful awareness that literacy in its widest sense has made educated man a recorder and professor of traditional meanings while robbing him of the capacity to mean what he says and to say what he "really" means—that is, to profess, "Here I stand." The difference between old-time morality and new ethics is best expressed by the juxtaposition of the statements "It is written, that" and "But I say unto you." The Reformation thus has run full cycle; the printed and durable pamphlet is being replaced by the painted placard dedicated to the moment. For where change was once a transitional stage to a regained equilibrium in line with ancient tradition, change is now self-sustaining, and no generation can predict what the world will look like to the next, although strenuous attempts abound to visualize at least the year 2000. But this also means that youth feels in need of an ethical flexibility, a capacity for "being with it," and for the inspiration of fleeting happenings which convey the depth and often the illusion of fellowship here and now, and, invite a variety of group regressions.

A Typology of Group Regression

I will now attempt to classify certain basic positions discernible in groups of youthful dissenters along a continuum that reaches from a *negative preoccupation with infantile morality* to a *positive affirmation of ethical principles*.

It is as though all these youths were attempting to reach, by way of ideological efforts, a ledge of ethical certainty, and when that remains out of reach or when helping hands prove elusive, they slip back to earlier footholds which they struggle to get away from with all manner of premoral, amoral, and antimoral behavior. If I speak here of retrogressions, however, I will try to resist the clinical habit of thinking primarily of the neurotic, psychotic, and addictive symptomatology which can befall individuals in all the categories to be mentioned. That each individual young person is in danger of falling back into the despair of alienation and isolation is only too obvious, yet adolescent alternatives which a decade or so ago were still matters of mute inner protest, only indirectly expressed in idiosyncratic personal symptoms, now, it seems, are externalized on a large scale, shared with the like-minded and joined with acute historical problems. For this reason it is vitally important that we, as educators and as clinicians, try to understand the singular importance of ideological movements endowed with historical actuality, for they not only seem to save alienated youth from the perdition of the meaninglessness and isolation of neurosis but also challenge us to understand what correctives are needed in our own professions. These, obviously, go beyond (or should go beyond) anything youth is "demanding." While we are on the defensive, or remain at best adaptive, we cannot hope to be convincing.

I will take the motto best describing the *ethical position* from an impressive new ritual. The following excerpt is from the sermon, "A Time to Say No" that Michael K. Ferber delivered at the antidraft service in Boston's Arlington Street Church on October 16, 1967. This speech is one of the counts in the government's indictment against him for conspiracy:

> But what I wish to speak about now is what goes *beyond our saying No*, for no matter how loudly we all say it, no matter what ceremony we perform around our saying it, we will not become a community among ourselves nor effective agents for changing our country *if a negative is all we share*. Albert Camus said that the rebel, who says No, is also one who says Yes, and that when he draws a line beyond which he will refuse to cooperate he is affirming the values on the other side of that line. For us who come here today, what is it that we affirm, *what is it to which we can say Yes?*

I have italicized those simple affirmative phrases which make this statement prototypical for the ethical position which I am convinced almost all young people involved in unrest are striving for. But it must be pointed out that Ferber, while he was speaking for the young who were acting like himself, offered his declaration not in a setting exclusively populated by young people. Next to him were (to mention only the academic figures) a university chaplain, who was reaffirming his Christianity, and a famous baby doctor, who had made more people say yes to more babies with more practical awareness than had any doctor in history before him; whatever we think of his concrete action, the outrage of his No was fully matched by the lifelong affirmation of his Yes.

I believe the ethical Yes to be present in many forms of unrest, even where group retrogressions to destructive negation are more obvious. And here we should remember that a certain retrogressiveness is part of all ideological group formation; if much of ethical youth, before our eyes, seems to indulge in illogical and amoral patterns, so are we, in their eyes, far regressed from the lofty ethical position which we held when we entered into a career of "professing."

I have begun with the Boston Resisters because of my conviction that wherever a disciplined civil resistance to a circumscribed nationwide grievance dominates the orientation, a group retrogression is the least likely to occur. But, of course, there are many kinds of resisters, and any one person or act may be dominated by a number of orientations at the same time. Most obvious, in the context of resistance, is the danger of an arbitrary choice of an exhibitionistic act from a variety of motives which do not add up to a sustaining Yes, with methods uncoordinated with the actions of others and without sufficient awareness of the lifelong consequences for either oneself or others.

For mere contrast, let me now choose as an example of the *premoral* position an orientation which is exposed to the deepest personal and group regression: the hippie orientation. Again I emphasize that I am not speaking here of a type of person or of one communal group; obviously some aspects of a hippie orientation, particulary in unison with modern music and *Wanderschaft*, are permeating youth anywhere. The hippies as a community, however, have attempted to retreat from traditional morality to a kind of premoral subculture which bases a new ethics on naturalness, spontaneity, and mutual closeness: *love*, in one word. In the face of widespread mechanical and logical specialization they cultivate the senses and the sensory and sensual aspects of sexuality, enacting (both mockingly and in utmost sincerity) a utopia which relieves man from any sense of having been driven out of paradise; he (and she) need not be ashamed of being naked and may ignore the *Sündenfall*—the fall from grace. No wonder that the rest of the world is fascinated, for no doubt, in this era of mechanization, the hippies have found a way of speaking to a latent part of man's consciousness, a part often secretly felt to be better and simpler than the visible results of success and conformity.

On the other hand, the premoral orientation sketched here brings with it a partial regression not only to a dominance of the sensory and sensual life but also to that of an infantile kind of dependency. In its proper developmental place (that is, in infancy) this mode was helpful in providing the right food, the proper care, and an unlimited amount of mother love. All of this the hippie orientation attempts to replace with the motherly warmth of communal love and with the nourishment of fantasy by drugs. Mistaking men for flowers, this orientation takes the illustration of the lilies in the field so literally that its adherents forget to feed themselves properly and become even more dependent on being babied by drugs. And when the dream of paradise becomes dependent on the drug trade and suffers the depravity characterizing the borderlines of ill-defined legal issues, a vicious combination is apt to destroy what health the movement prophesied. Nevertheless, I do not believe that the message of the hippies (any more than the messages of the German *Wandervögel*, of the European "artists," and of certain revivalist groups of the past) has been lost on our time.

If it were not for their equal distance from pragmatic morality, there could be no sharper contrast between the *premoral* orientation just sketched and the *amoral* one to be considered next. Yet, as pointed out, we find these orientations alternating in the same individuals and, insofar as they are personified by groups, often joined in demonstrations. Thus, the hippies and the motorcycle gangs have been seen to dwell together like the lambs and the lions; this they do in the common hope that any group which can successfully negate the morality of centuries must be destined to be a new species, whether of flower children or of mechanized supermen. If the amoral orientation, however, has more obviously sinister trends, it is because it is more deliberately destructive than implicitly self-destructive; it includes a sincere belief in the goodness both of physical violence and of defiant defamation. Insofar as the morality of childhood is rooted in shame and self-doubt reinforced by contemptuous and punitive adults, this orientation attempts to effect a complete turning of the tables: Instead of shame, it sports shamelessness; instead of obedience, defiance; instead of respect, contempt. This deliberate display of the worst arouses, of course, the worst in others, wherefore any confrontation with "society" turns into a match of two orientations which confirm each other, for the deliberate amoralist finds himself, sooner or later, confronted not by the moral people whom he would like to expose, but by those who are paid to do the "dirty work" for moral people—namely, the police; and the police, of course, oblige the amoral fantasy life because they behave like the externalized version of a brutal conscience. In this, they often react to the delberate use by the amoral group not only of "obscene" words but on occasion also of fecal matter as weapons of contempt. That once "dirty" children should throw the epithet of "pigs" at the police is a simple enough reversal, especially if interpersed with "motherfucker."

I hope that I will not be misunderstood. I am not calling all those who act out an amoral orientation personally amoral or devoid of an ethical orientation. On the contrary, the very decision to behave in an amoral fashion, and systematically so, can be in part an ethical one, especially where the conviction prevails that the exposure of the hypocrisies of law enforcement as well as of moral orderliness is a first step to national or racial rejuvenation. Often such a conviction is at least explainable as a reaction to a childhood milieu which was totally overshadowed (as is that of most black people in my country) by the illegal violence of righteous people, including the violence of uniformed men employed by "nice" people for the specific purpose of using the law for the protection of privileged corruption. Thus, the amoral position naturally impresses many youths as more heroic or even ethical than the stance of many conformists, who enjoy a freedom and a safety they have never had to fight for.

I would call a fourth orientation, with intended paradoxicality, the *antimoralist moralist* one. Its adherents, far from behaving amoralistically, behave in fact hypermoralistically, but always in a campaign against the assumed moralism of older and established people. In a recent number of the *Harvard Crimson*, one member of the academic community took another to task for what he considered an illogical and unethical point of view. He wrote him: "What truly bothers me is the quality and logic of your justification . . ."; "I find thoroughly naïve your attempt to distinguish between . . .", "Still more ludicrous is the characterization in your letter . . .", "Even if I were to grant you this point for the sake of argument . . .", "What most . . . experts lack is a discernible sense of responsibility. . . ." If I add that this is a *student* writing to one of the most distinguished *professors*, it must be obvious that it is not equality of discourse which is sought here but a total turning against the "authority" of phrases habitually employed by an overweening schoolmaster. This, in turn, seems typical for the stance employed by many self-appointed revolutionaries who, especially in the absence of clear issues to act upon, appoint a given man or group as "guilty." Now, among the antimoralists and the hypermoralists, too, there are many ethical individuals who use these methods without being absorbed by them, but even the most appealing young people with the clearest intelligence and the most ethical intentions are in perpetual danger of becoming involved in the kind of group retrogression which eventually leads to the "liquidation" of friends by friends.

Lastly, I must reach outside the ranks of those acutely involved in student unrest and speak of that vast majority of students who, at this point, may be only latently "upset." Most of them, of course, come to the university in order to acquire methodologies and techniques and do not feel acutely alienated from an industrial world or even a military-industrial complex as long as their studies promise them active participation and advancement in it. Whether or not an industrial society as such harbors more alienation than did other technologies, is probably a moot question. It is quite possible (if a comparison *could*, indeed, be made) that man as a hunter, fisherman, or peasant suffered no less estrangement, in his own way, than man the trader or worker. That man the intellectual, however, both experiences and detects more estrangement than other men accept as their human lot—that, in fact, may be one of the reasons why increased contact with intellectuality on a larger scale supports unrest and revolt. At any rate, since it is my purpose to classify such revolt on a continuum from hyperethical to premoral orientations, we may well find in the middle a technological orientation which I would call *moral pragmatism*.

It exists in those who are preoccupied with the acquisition of one of the occupational specialties which attempt to come to grips with the concrete complexities of modern life, be it production or distribution, transportation or communication, medicine or law, for them (as in all stages of technology from primitive to industrial) what "works" is good, and to make things work, to improve techniques, and to correct what does not work are all a man can do. Morality, ideology, and ethics, too, must be fitted into the cycle of work activity, problems of sin or salvation being delegated to a religiosity which is never in conflict with habit and reason and which rewards him who helps himself (in both meanings of the phrase). In an era of progress, goodness resides in being in motion and in setting things in motion whether behind a wheel or at a job which makes wheels go 'round. Thus, science and technology reward many with a sense of being at one with an energetic cosmos in motion and thus in league with a divine engineering power which has replaced what once was "divine nature." Above all, it is hard and joint work which justifies man's sense of progress and of the eventual manageability of modern complexities, including the all-present and all-denied nuclear threat. A large part of academic youth, especially in the professional schools, lives by this view; and where "upset" youth insists on the necessity to upset the workings of production, pragmatic majorities may sooner or later insist on the maintenance of "law and order," if necessary by reactionary regimentation. If there is any retrogression in the pragmatic position, it may well be that the majority of those given to moral pragmatism in the context of advancing technology are apt to perpetuate the virtues of the schoolchild which they extend into adolescence and apprenticeship; but they probably escape, more than others, that adolescent estrangement which I have called identity-confusion.

It is against this general background that one must review, then, the concerns and the antics of those who would want to change modern man very drastically, while either *dropping out* temporarily from the work assigned to them or demanding vociferously that academic teaching and learning be alerted to a general sense of malaise and meaninglessness and be, in fact, in the forefront of humanist ideals.

And the Professors

Which brings us to us, the professors. If my diagnosis of prevalent retrogressions is correct, then they must be assumed to have their counterparts in us. These appear partially as reverberations of our own half-fulfilled youth which make us idealize the motives of the young; and partially they appear in the form of an angry rejection of the young people before us. As we perceive that much of youth deeply mistrusts us, we are shocked to note that we mistrust ourselves, whether we are overcome by a new sense of awe before eternal youth or by a redoubled fatigue which reminds us that nothing ever really comes of youthful utopias.

The mixture of feelings exposes us to a dangerous doubt as to when to be "permissive" and where to "draw the line." And this is exactly where youth, at its worst, wants us. For if, indeed, a more or less unconvinced and unconvincing permissiveness or grudging moral inaction on the part of the parent generation has anything to do with the unrest of youth, then I would believe that this unrest tests the limits of our permissiveness for the exact point where and when we are going to turn into angry authoritarians anyway or, for that matter, call the police. What is at stake, then, is the *genuineness* of our strictness as well as of our permissiveness.

Given the obvious fact that we are a generation of parents and teachers not guided by ideology, we are asked to prove that our strictness is based on our own ethical commitments and on insights commensurate with our knowledge; that our indignation is more than a retrogression to unreconstructed moralism; and that our permissiveness is really more than a forced suspension of our indignation. And, indeed, parents who themselves were treated punitively cannot in one generation (or in two) overcome the need to relieve their punitive conscience in outbursts against their children—outbursts for which the parent often feels guiltier than the child. This conflict of inner authority, I believe, is now built into the younger generations; their very consciences are alternately too permissive and too punitive, and in order to clarify their own wavering, they must challenge ours. This, of course, calls for firmness, but we must also understand that what is at stake is not our professional esteem (even their own parents' "success" in the world has become less than relevant to some of the young) but our inner authority as adults.

It is, therefore, of great importance that we should gain what insight we can muster into our relationship to our own youth. Do we not feel that we have, indeed, abandoned some of our ethical concerns for the sake of our advancement? In enjoying academic and professional freedom under the protection of the "establishment," what deals have we made unknowingly or quite knowingly, and with what questionable profit? And most of all, what mockery have we made of our student days in trying to remain young in some superficial and ritualized ways, forgetting maybe what universities truly stand for? Are we still "professing" in addition to learning and teaching facts and methods? Are we preserving "universities" as autonomous communities which stand *between* the parents and the state, as guardians and guides of the continued need for ethical reorientation? Have we, maybe, given in too much both to parents *and* to the state, letting the middle ground erode in both directions?

I am not saying that the students are necessarily "right" in the sense that they know what they are doing or indeed would know better how to do what we have done—far from it. But their challenge and our doubts are two sides of the same universal question: the role of education in a technocratic world. If so, should we not, instead of spending our energies defending ourselves against youth that challenges, make it our business to anticipate and to *teach* the relation of our various professional competencies to the ethical tasks of our day? Academic life now seems to depend on a communality of older students and younger faculty in which the social implications of all specialties must be spelled out continuously through newly created permanent bodies of discourse and planning.

To all the obvious factors pointing to this necessity I have undertaken to add a psychological rationale which, I fear, will appear to some of you to be too much determined both by my field and by the situation in my country. But I trust that these thoughts will bear translation into the specific professional and national concerns of my readers in other countries.

On Protest and
Affirmation (1972)

When I was told the other day that members of this graduating class had requested that (in this year of all years) I give the customary address which precedes the joint affirmation called Hippocratic, I was not sure what I was expected to do: to talk around this occasion or to the point of it. It so happened that just about then I heard Dr. Oswei Tempkin of Johns Hopkins University give a lecture right here on the history of the Hippocratic Oath. After the lecture, the more professorial types in the audience converged on the speaker to engage him, no doubt, in erudite questions. A few younger men, however, cornered me. Dr. Tempkin had told us that the Hippocratic Oath was introduced into this country at the request of medical students. They asked me, "Why does one want to take an oath?" Bless you, I thought, here is a theme for my address. Why, indeed, do we, and when? And why and when (I would now add) do we not want to take an oath? Thus extended, I hope, the question concerns the members of the class present today with their families, and also those who are absent—some, no doubt, in sincere avoidance of this ceremonial occasion.

To take an oath obviously means to testify to a joint tradition.

Presented as a class day address to the Harvard Medical School in 1972. First published in the *Harvard Medical Alumni Bulletin*, 46, 6 (July–August 1972), 30–32.

On certain occasions, elders like to demand such an oath (and the Hippocratic elders were refreshingly frank about this) and younger people are not at all averse to taking them. But any formula of what is worth testifying for also delineates what one detests and what is worth protesting. What, then, is the psychological connection between that which is to be reaffirmed today and that which was said in protest this morning?

But let me declare first why I indeed, *wanted* to come today. I am the son of a physician, as I understand are quite a number of the members of this class. But I happen to be one of those sons who resisted the overt identification with the father, and who thought he wanted to be everything *but* a physician. Yet, by a circuitous road, I settled in Vienna, where there lived one of the greatest doctors of all time, Sigmund Freud. He was the center of a widening circle of practitioners, most of them medical men and women, who shared a common fidelity of a revolutionary kind. As I know now, they had something of that original Hippocratic determination about them. For the Hippocratic Oath originally stated certain commitments that doctors of one "sect" felt they had to formulate over and beyond the legal and traditional constraints governing the medical practices of their day.

This morning, one of the speakers, chosen from among you, spoke of a "lost dignity." Young Freud as a medical researcher had been devoted to an "oath," attesting to a "dignity" that some of his teachers had agreed upon. Energy being one of the dominant concepts of the day, they had sworn "to put in power this truth: No other forces than the common physical chemical ones are active within the organism. . . . One has either to find the specific way or form of their action by means of the physical mathematical method, or to assume new forces equal in dignity to the chemical physical forces inherent in matter." And this, believe it or not, was the conceptual model for that sexual energy which Freud called libido, the unperturbed study of which earned him fame, abuse, and misuse as a pansexualist. Undaunted, he always hoped that someday the particular chemical basis of libido would be found. At the same time, however, he invented a revolutionary clinical method. I have described this as a kind of nonviolent attitude toward the healer's as well as the patient's inner life, a recognition of the unconscious (instinctual and repressive) forces in the observer as well as the observed. Thus, a new clinical vision is always based on a new combination of scientific and technological ideology and therapeutic philosophy. This every period has to recover—or discover anew: for aging visions, before long, become pseudo-realities and new ones must emerge from the reaffirmation of a common dignity. As Freud concluded, "Men are strong as long as they represent a strong idea. They become impotent when they turn against it." This was said not by a moralist, but a medical psychologist.

When I came to this country 40 years ago, not a doctor, but a practitioner of Freud's method as applied to work with children, it was the Harvard Medical School that gave me my first appointment. Thus, to be asked to testify here today rounds things out for me. In the meantime, however, I have also had, during the McCarthy era, the experience of having to refuse to take an oath. A prescribed oath, as pointed out, is at its best an occasion for the free and joint reaffirmation of a strong idea which has become part of a shared identity. But, obviously, an oath can also be used to maintain what has become trite, overused or corrupt and therefore must be resisted, even at a risk. In view of these two faces of an oath, it is all the more astonishing that the Hippocratic Oath over so many centuries has served to affirm a shared philosophy which, it seems, only today is undergoing a certain "crisis of identity." Come to think of it, this may be *your* reason for inviting me here.

An oath taken at a graduation, of course, only confirms a fact. You have had your medical school experience, you *are* doctors. The title is only an outer confirmation of an inner conversion. None of you will ever *not* be a doctor. Wherever you are when, figuratively or really, the question sounds, "Is there a doctor in the house?" something in you will respond. From here on you are answerable, because what you have learned to do and to be has become part of your identity.

Let me say a few words, then, about the developmental and historical aspects of a shared identity crisis. You must permit me to do so in my own terms, exploiting this opportunity to use you as a captive audience for a lecture on the life-cycle. It will be brief, almost instant. The period of identity development, and that means also the overcoming of identity confusion, is vitally connected with the emergence of a capacity for fidelity. One develops fidelity as—in young years—one finds people and ideas, methods and practices to be faithful to or, indeed, when one refuses to believe and reaffirm what seems to have become trite and corrupt. Because of its developmental importance, I called fidelity a *virtue*, explaining that what I really meant was the ancient word virtu—which means strength, inner force. One could once say that a bottle of brandy, left open, was losing its virtue. It means inner strength, then, rather than the mere display of shining goodness. (Parenthetically, I am somewhat less proud of this word today, because I typically overlooked the fact that it goes back to the word vir, and once meant *masculine* strength.) Fidelity, then, is a strength and a necessary one, to be firmly established before the next two stages which, "in my book," see the ascendance of the inner strengths of Love and Care. Love includes all that you love to do, and do to awaken love whether it is in your erotic life or in the intimacies of work and play. Care includes what you care for, what you care to do, and have learned to take care of. I will not now go into all the inner conflicts that make these strengths truly dynamic in each stage, and from one to the other. I will only point out, why Identity and Fidelity must precede Love and Care. It is because only a combination of identity, fidelity, and competence makes us able to be *ethical*. Now, I know, every graduation speech praises ethics; this one, in attempting to say what an oath is, must attempt to explain it. In all brevity, then: Our *moral* principles go back into childhood, and are largely unconscious and automatic guides to a not altogether healthy sense of good and evil. We also gradually learn what is *legal* and what is illegal. In youth, furthermore, we absorb much that is *ideological* in religion and politics. But only in early adulthood can we develop values which seem to be confirmed in daily practices and in concrete competency. To be ethical means to know *why* one affirms a set of values. And there are good historical reasons for young adults today to shoulder the burden of a rigorous critique which will confirm living principles, both for their elders and for the rising generation.

What does it mean, then, to confirm ethically that one is a doctor? Let me ask first, what is a patient, and answer by telling you one of my favorite stories, undoubtedly known to most of you. An old patient comes to the office and says, "Doctor, my feet hurt, I have headaches, my bowels are sluggish, my heart pounds. And you know, Doctor, I myself don't feel so good either." As always, there is a Jewish version which throws additional light on the matter. Here the patient says, "Das Ganze von mir"—"the whole of me"—doesn't feel so good either. In both versions, the patient complains that he has lost the connection between the various parts of him. Tell me, he seems to plead, what is wrong with all of my parts—but tell me in such a way that I myself, the whole of me, the middle of me, can feel "Yes, I understand, and I will help you help me to handle it." This, in fact, is the true meaning of the term "ego"; it is the middle that holds us together.

This story, I submit, tells us a lot about what a doctor is, and what "medical" really means. As you have noticed, I feel a bit linguistic today. Medical seems to be related to medialis, middle. It is also related to meditation, because he who meditates, thinks about the center of things. And, of course, it has to do with mediation, for one mediates by stepping in between; and with remedy as that which is to restore balance. (Somehow it also has to do with meddling and mediocrity, but let's not go into that.)

If I now attempt to put together what a patient and a doctor must be for each other, I cannot find a better word than the one I saw used in the last *Harvard Alumni Bulletin*. It is: "identifiable." Only if the patient feels he is dealing with an identifiable, coherent person-and-method does he become (again) identifiable to himself; and only in being such a person-and-method can the doctor remain identifiable to himself.

Seen in this light, the present identity crisis in medicine becomes painfully obvious. But you must know that you are not alone in this. Some time ago the Pope found it necessary to preach against the very term "identity crisis" as taken too seriously by young priests. He implied that true faith does not permit such a crisis. Priests, doctors, and—yes—military men, all deal with ultimate matters of life and death, and therefore depend on certain oaths for superior sanction and mutual loyalty, for delineation and for discipline. And all undergo, at this point in history, the conflict between declining and emerging ethical forces. But you, of course, daily face, with such lofty obligations, the squalor of poverty, the corruptibility of wealth and of power, the senselessness of accident, the cold tyranny of pain, the rage of inactivation, and the finite impersonality of death.

The very "role" of the doctor, however, is in jeopardy today because the doctor's image and self-image is linked with the conflicting images of various pursuits. There is, for example, the self-made man and the medical entrepreneur, the private practitioner who, as a pointed complaint has it, "makes a killing." And there is the devoted teamworker. There is the gadgeteer and computerizer, and there is the depth psychologist. There is the medical elitist in accustomed tweed and the new health populist and activist in "natural" attire. There is the specialist who must play the parts against the middle, and there is what is now called the primary physician, who in a new era insists on being as identifable as the general practitioner of old. And there is the promising new specialty of family doctor.

Are you suffering from a professional identity crisis, then? Not being the Pope, I cannot give categorical answers. I can answer only with a question with which I used to confront students who claimed that they were undergoing a personal identity crisis: "Are you boasting or complaining?" For let me tell you, that much of a real crisis is semi-deliberate. You can go only that far in accusing your elders of not having delivered the goods, of not having fulfilled their promises. You must feel it in your bones that in the middle of a seemingly undeserved crisis, there is no better remedy than to make it more critical, by forcing things to come to a head and to reveal their—and your—true nature. In the critical center today is the doctor's continuing mediation not only between the patient and his wayward body parts, but also the medicines that upset "himself" while relieving his symptoms; between the patient, his family, and his community; the patient and numerous specialists and their distant data banks; the patient and an increasing number of health workers and health services. The new doctor thus must translate an old person-to-person commitment into modern methods of communication.

While the identifiable doctor and his method and philosophy remain the center of all things medical, a new generation must give concerted attention to the question of what makes the various new medical techniques and politics identifiable for the patient, so that an active sense of health is fostered rather than a confusing image of fragmented processes. There is no reason why a medical team should not be as identifiable to a patient as a single doctor can be if the team has only agreed on an identifiable style. Nor should the frequent change of domicile expose a patient to medical homelessness, if such a style is made communicable in the transfer of data to various settings. I know that such "advice" sounds utterly gratuitous; but the fact is that the establishment of intimate intercommunication in an expending world of massive interaction is a universal problem today, a problem at once scientific and political.

Two final remarks on the Hippocratic Oath, truncated and pruned as it now stands. I suggest a historical attitude which remains aware of the continuity of tradition in the flux of historical change. If time would permit, one could take each sentence and interpret the principle hidden in it in the light of the historicity of its origins. And one could then translate every detail into modern conditions and see what formulas would reveal the old principle in the new details. A recourse to tradition always means to acknowledge how much some ancient people knew in their own way of what we only slowly learn to know in ours.

Secondly, and finally, let me tell you that the mere possession of an oath, if ever so debatable in detail, makes you enviable. As the problem of maintaining rather than maiming life becomes a matter of conscience for a mankind gradually recognizing its unity, there are many social as well as natural scientists, engineers, historians, and others who increasingly realize that their every technique has to be reconsidered from the point of view of a joint social responsibility toward man's physical and moral health. In all these and other fields, the experts are becoming aware of the fact that they are working with seemingly innocent forces and insights that cannot only be used for a new way of life but also for many new ways of death, and they are yearning for an oathlike formulation both manageable and understandable, that would make them again identifiable to themselves. The problem is the same anywhere, beginning with the very architecture of our immediate surroundings and reaching into all the networks of communication: how to create islands of identifiable wholeness in a sea of spreading, anonymous bigness. As mankind is spanned by joint awareness, it is more and more essential that its wholeness be reasserted in every here and now.

As physicians, you already have such a tradition, you are in the possession of new concrete, interpersonal competencies without which any affirmation and any protest are empty. Whether you wish to *take* one or the other form of the oath, you *have* it in you. We congratulate you.

VII.
PORTRAIT
SKETCHES

Peter Blos: Reminiscences
(1974)

Peter Blos and I have been friends since our early youth—but not in our most ambivalent dreams did we ever foresee that one of us would talk about the other at the opening of a new lecture series named after him, and here in The New York Academy of Medicine. If this had to come to pass, however, I think I am glad that *I* am the one to speak about *him*. I will never know what he would have said about me, but that may well be all to the good.

On this occasion, then, I will speak briefly as a lifelong friend. I leave it to others to speak of Peter's professional stature, which, after all, is attested to by this very august occasion. So let me briefly describe how our paths brought us together here tonight with Fritz Redl.

Peter and I were friends in three countries—in Southern Germany, in Italy, and in Vienna (by us, that was a country). We grew up in the city of Karlsruhe, the gateway to the Black Forest. We both come from families with mixed regional and religious backgrounds and we are both sons of bearded physicians, a fact which, I believe, gave us a similar professional imprint. His father was a physician of an extraordinary kind, and with an extraordinary beard and—what is

Presented as the First Peter Blos Biennial Lecture, sponsored by the New York Academy of Medicine. First published in *Psychosocial Process*, 3, 2 (Fall 1974), 4–7.

more—with eyes that dominated that beard. His wide interests were never constricted by professional custom or tradition.

It was in Peter's home that one learned something for which I would not have had quite the right word had Peter not telephoned me just the other day about matters concerning the Association for Child Psychoanalysis of which he is now president. After some conversation in the best presidential jargon, Peter suddenly said, in German: *"Und wie geht's mit der Geistigkeit?"* ("And how goes it with the *Geistigkeit?"*) Then I knew that the old Peter is still here! Virtually untranslatable, *Geistigkeit* means an intrinsically German preoccupation with matters on the borderline between the spirit and the mind. At its best, it combines some of both; at its romantic worst, it serves neither. It implies a lofty identification with great humanists, above all, the Olympian Goethe, and yet also the arrogant claim for a German superiority of spirit and mind which made it, during our school years, appear as if the Greeks and Shakespeare were really outlying provinces of the German *Geist*. In fact, the high school we attended was called *Das Humanistische Gymnasium*, The Humanistic Gymnasium.

What was pretentious and loftily apolitical about all of this came apart with a vengeance in the Hitler holocaust. But to the young, at one time, *Geistigkeit* could mean a very special relationship to philosophy, to art, and, above all, to nature. When we walked for hours and days, it was not for "exercise." We walked *in* nature, and somehow nature seemed to know about it. In fact, if Piaget claims that children, when asked what the sun is doing as they walk or run along, firmly respond that the sun is trailing them, I believe that at the age of 20 we were convinced that on our nightly walks our favorite constellation Orion was doing just that! But we were not as far gone as that famous Viennese aristocrat who one starry night, walking with a friend by the Danube, exclaimed: "Look at all those stars, and to think that these are just the ones over the second district of Vienna!"

Our *Geistigkeit*, however, did not preclude our taking a systematic look at nature. I sketched; Peter studied and earned a doctorate in biology. But his studies always were a twofold search for great ideas and for service to humanity. I have mentioned the period when we were friends in Florence, which was then not yet an inner city race course for motor scooters and Fiats. Peter was a "writer" and I was an "artist." Our third friend was the architect Oscar Stonorov, who was then a sculptor; he recently perished with Walter Reuther in the crash of his plane. In putting "writer" and "artist" in quotation marks, I mean to indicate that we went through what some faddish people may call a psychosocial moratorium; we were waiting for a profession to commit ourselves to. In the meantime, in that city of Florence one could absorb principles of artistic form and of the human measure. Fascism we took in our stride; it could only be a passing aberration from the classical spirit.

After a period when we went our separate ways, Peter invited me to Vienna, where he directed a small private school, a school which had, in fact, been founded along his plans by Dorothy Burlingham, Anna Freud, and Eva Rosenfeld. I hope that some day Peter will write about that school.

To make a teacher of me, however, the highly disciplined Peter first had to teach me to keep regular work hours, a task which was initiated every morning, no matter what time of year, by a cold shower, then the preferred shock treatment for identity confusion. It was by teaching school that we found our vocation in the area of child psychoanalysis and education, while a regular and intimate contact with the great August Aichhorn first opened our eyes to the problems of youth. As you now see, Peter and I came to psycho-analysis not merely as non-physicians (or what our other much ad-mired teacher, Siegfried Bernfeldt, in his early lectures in this country innocently used to refer to as "lays"), but we came to it as doctors' sons who found in Freud a Hippocratic spirit beyond medical profes-sionalism and a *Geistigkeit* unafraid of looking at itself with critical precision.

In Vienna, too, we found our wives, a Swede and a Canadian, respectively. We solemnly approved of each other's choices and, what is more, we still do, knowing full well that our wives have saved us from our wandering selves and from *too much Geistigkeit*. (Merta, I salute you.)

Well, we finally came with our families to this great country which can be so hospitable to some newcomers, and which was then so receptive to psychoanalysis. As psychoanalysts we have worked along parallel lines rather than together. The parallel direction is marked by our orientation toward the crucible of youth, while the distance between the parallels is shown by the fact that Peter's interests have remained clinical and psychodynamic, while mine have tended to become psychosocial and historical. Where he speaks of individua-tion, I speak of identity. We read each other respectfully, but with equal respect rarely quote each other.

If you should ask me, however—and I do feel asked—what over all these years I have come to admire most in Peter, and to thoroughly envy, I would say, and here I do have the proper English word, his *workmanship* or, what in German is called more inclusively his *Werk-haftigkeit*. Whether he practices psychoanalysis as his hourly work, whether he plays his beloved cello in the evening in a circle of friends, whether he writes at his desk, or whether he does carpentry work in his barn in New Hampshire, he does it all with an unfailing sense for the nature of the material at hand. This is *spirit made concrete* in that the spirit responds to the material and makes the material respond, in turn. This workmanship is, I am sure, at least one important quality to be transmitted to the future generations by the special Blos lecture series inaugurated tonight upon Peter's retirement from his work in the JBG [Jewish Board of Guardians]. But lest the characterization I have given should sound like the premature summation of a life already lived, let me add that these two traits, *workmanship* and *Geistigkeit*, are among those which old age tends to conserve and to deepen—"to a hundred years" anyway.

I cannot conclude without saying a word about the First Peter Blos Lecturer, another very old friend of both Peter's and mine, Fritz Redl. His professional stature, too, will be delineated here by others. But in anticipation of his festive rendition let me just tell you of one encounter with him. Some years ago, in Norway, he and I were invited to address mental health teams from five Scandinavian countries (and in case you are counting on your fingers, the fifth one is Iceland). Sibylle Escalona was presiding and Fritz spoke, as usual, out of his deep empathy with young delinquents. But when he was carried away and began to use their language, intoning such phrases as "the kids didn't like the smell of the joint," Sibylle interrupted him and cautioned him to be a bit considerate of the Scandinavians. "Oh pardon," he said. "I meant to say, of course, that the young people did not *appreciate* the *atmosphere* of the *establishment*."

Well, here we are, Peter, Fritz, and I right in the Establishment. Fritz will, I am sure, speak tonight in his own best English or, as we used to say in Vienna, *"wie ihm der Schnabel gewachsen ist."* ("How his beak happened to grow.") Oh pardon! I meant to say, of course, that he will speak according to his most natural stylistic and linguistic proclivities.

Thank you for letting me testify for two such friends.

For Joseph Wheelwright—
My Jungian Friend (1982)

Neither my friend Joseph Wheelwright nor his book need a "preface."
He is an acknowledged leader in the Jungian establishment and a
beloved teacher and practitioner in psychiatry. I am writing only as
a spokesman for his friends and students who are convinced that one
has to have seen Jo Wheelwright to believe him and that one has to
have heard him to read him. For he writes as he speaks; and it is his
editor's merit that she preserves his way of crowning the discussion
of exalted concepts and of intimate clinical experience with pungent
personal remarks.

As to his appearance, you cannot avoid looking up to the man if
you want to come face to face with him. For he is very tall and lean;
and in conversation, he persuasively lowers himself toward you. His
accent has strong Bostonian and British overtones which, however,
pass the test of serving with equal naturalness both thoughtful discourse and exquisite vulgarity. And his aristocratic height does not
interfere with his suddenly leaning into any available piano and hammering away in the best worst barroom style.

In fact, to overdo this aspect of the man a little, one of my earlier

First published as a Preface in Joseph Wheelwright, *St. George and the Dandelion. Forty years
of Practice as a Jungian Analyst*, (San Francisco: C. G. Jung Institute of San Francisco, Inc.
1982).

713

Joseph Wheelwright

memories of him is a scene at a party where he joined a rather short Freudian, our late friend Donald (Mac) Macfarlane, at a piano for an especially lowbrow duet. Jo, too, remembers this event because in the stunned silence that followed their performance he heard me murmur, "A Freudian and a Jungian meeting on the lowest common denominator." He appreciated my ecumenical spirit. And, unnecessary to say, we Freudians have over the years met with this Jungian on high common denominators, indeed. But I am glad to report this event because in this instance I for once recognize myself in a quotation ascribed to me by Jo. . . .

Of our joint professional activities, two stand out. During the Second World War we participated in the Mt. Zion Veterans Rehabilitation Clinic. There, we (and others representing an assortment of psychiatric denominations) found that in dealing with the problems of returned combat soldiers we could quietly amalgamate our various views and personalities in a communal common sense. And (to return to the present) when the Freud-Jung correspondence appeared, Jo and I enjoyed offering a public dialogue on this eventually tragic subject and conveying to our colleagues some of that subsequent history which we, in our younger years, had been privileged to witness.

This said, I can leave to the reader the experience of finding out that Jo Wheelwright (whatever his Jungian "type") always conveys the experiential power of living and thinking and thus invites a direct and sturdy understanding of clinical and theoretical issues vital to our work and our time.

Ruth Benedict:
A Memorial (1949)

I am very grateful for the privilege of joining you in this testimony of Ruth Benedict's living and unique image. Each of us, who knew her, knows that it will be with him as long as any vision remains. But what can we say to one another to share our common possession of that image?

Shall I speak of the relation Ruth Benedict had to my field, psychoanalysis? She accepted psychoanalysis as a major humanistic critique of the discontinuities which our civilization forces upon its children. She accepted it concretely, and worked assiduously in her cultural studies to uncover data the relevance of which had become clear through Freud's work. Her acceptance was intuitive, not systematic and argumentative. Of systems and creeds, Ruth Benedict was merely tolerant. As a humanist, she warned against the biologizing of human behavior, be it in the crude form of racism or the refined projection of "human nature." She showed how every step in the unfolding of physiological potentialities in the human child carries with it the experience of a cultural continuity or discontinuity;

Presented at a memorial meeting at the Viking Fund, in remembrance of Ruth Benedict, New York City, November 4, 1948. Other speakers were Cora DuBois, Clyde Kluckhohn, Robert Lynd, Margaret Mead, and Alfred Kroeber. First published in *Ruth Fulton Benedict: A Memorial*, ed. Alfred L. Kroeber, (New York: Viking Fund, Inc., 1949), 14–17.

a sense of being at home, or a sense of being one's own worst enemy. She said: "Insofar as we invoke a physiological scheme to account for neurotic adjustments, we are led to overlook the possibility of developing social institutions which would lessen the social cost we now pay." Here we found common ground for debate and for further search.

But it is not along these lines that I can express what to me is most important about Ruth Benedict. Permit me, for a few minutes, to tell you of more personal things. When I saw Ruth last June, in California, I asked her to sit for a sketch. She was the fourth person in a year or so who had evoked in me—a dealer in words—this irresistible urge to document a face by drawing it. As I sketched Ruth, I thought of the others.

The first had been an old Jewish woman from Mt. Carmel in the State of Israel. Visiting California, she had impressed us all with the new sense of dignity and identity which her work had given her: the work of tending her grandchildren, freeborn Jews in their own State.

The second was a grand old woman of the pueblo community of San Ildefonso in the American Southwest. In perfecting her black pottery she has given new life to one of the oldest arts.

The third was an old skier in the Sierras who as a youth had come from his native Finland to the then lonely country around Lake Tahoe, to range the snowbound trails between the early power stations.*

Before Ruth came I had asked myself why I had wanted to sketch these people. Was it easier to draw old people because of the depth and finality of their facial lines? Or was I getting old, and looking for people who seemed to make aging worthwhile? Ladies and gentlemen, I would not steal this time to discuss autobiographic items with you, were it not for the fact that I found an answer to my question when I sketched Ruth Benedict; and what more can we say of any human being than that, by his mere being, he becomes to us not a question, not an argument, but an answer?

I wish the sketch itself could, as it should, convey what I mean. Let me try to say it.

Here was a person who was not vitally healthy any more. Yet she was not sick. She seemed so calm that to ask whether she was happy in any conversational sense would have seemed incongruous.

Here was a friend, who was deeply alone, who had, in fact, stopped

---

* A sketch of the skier was not available. Here we add, instead, a sketch of an old man friend of Berkeley, California, Alexander Meiklejohn.

Ruth Benedict

Karla Homburger

Maria Martinez

Alexander Mieklejohn

fighting loneliness. She had begun to befriend death, without in any way inviting it or being demanding of it.

Here then, was a consciously aging woman, who looked as much like a young girl, as she looked like a man, without being in the least juvenile or mannish.

Here was a woman who had been denied motherhood, but who had encompassed with motherly care her experiences, her observations, and her thoughts. She did not argue. But when she wrote she dealt with thoughts as a mother deals with impatient children, reconciling content and form until they befriended one another.

Here was an American who had learned to live beside and beyond boast and achievement. In her poetry she had struggled to find words for that other pole, which seems to signify the inner crisis of the observant American. She had gone so far as to call it "faith in failure." For to her victory was to be only a means to a mature end. She warned:

> Strength is good, but not among the victors.
> They march in step on roads they have not chosen,
> They handle weapons not theirs, and carve an idol
> For fools. But their dream is frozen.

In her book on Japan she fulfilled her function in this nation by adding thoughtful understanding to the very vigor of victory, adding the chrysanthemum to the sword.

Above all, here was a scientist, who had focused her analytic gifts on the differences between people and people, not in order to forge weapons of discrimination or even of "scientific" manipulation, but in order to understand the crowning purpose of being individual and of being different: a particular style of simplicity and serenity.

In doing so, she herself acquired what I now saw was the common good of these four old people, Ruth's as well as the Palestinian's, the Finn's, and the Indian's: some of the beauty and simplicity, some of the faith and serenity, announcing clearly and indestructibly the near fulfillment of a life cycle which has found accord with the moral and esthetic realization of its community.

There is tragedy here, we know. Ruth was too young to be completed and detached. What the personal, or, if you wish, clinical, reasons for this were, I did not make it my business to know. Let us not forget that she lived in the thick of an intellectual battle, which puts living on the defensive; and that it literally takes strength to fight and to feel, all the time.

What I have said I have not said in Ruth's praise. I have said it because we owe it to ourselves to think it and to remember it, for the sake of our personal fortunes as well as for the focus of our further work. Beyond that, we respect her choice; she wrote:

> It shall be ended, and no victory
> Bind laurel in your hair. Wherefore to you
> Should they come bannered with the red and blue
> Your eyes are mazed with always? Let it be
> Enough for you that never anyone
> Unblinded sees the glory that you see,
> Enough that you have looked upon the sun.

For Larry Frank's Anniversary— the Couple Who Came to Dinner (1965)

WITH JOAN M. ERIKSON

Once upon a time there was a wide-eyed young immigrant who regularly got cinders in his eyes when visiting New York. In that very condition he attended a meeting one day and sat down beside a rosy, alert, and amused-looking older man. The man, as if he had been waiting to be of help to somebody, guided him to a corner and deftly removed the cinder. Once he had done this, it seemed natural to him that he should also invite the stranger to drop in on him when in New Hampshire. His name sounded like Frank.

A few weeks later the young man and his wife were, indeed, driving through New Hampshire. Noticing a sign "Ashland," they looked up Mr. Frank's telephone number and were promptly invited to dinner. After that it seemed quite natural to Mr. Frank to ask the couple to stay for the night—so natural, in fact, that they stayed for a week. Larry even sent for their children. After that it was not surprising that the host found it natural also to arrange for a research position for the young man, so he could develop some notions he had.

Presented in Boston in December, 1965. Published here for the first time. Appreciation is expressed to Mrs. William G. Perry, Jr., formerly Mrs. Larry Frank, for her permission to print this sketch. Larry Frank was one of the founders and major catalysts of the child development movement. He was instrumental in financing and promoting projects, particularly major child study research programs.

Thus started a friendship typical for Larry: a complete blend of the personal and the professional, of the intellectual and what can only be called the joyful—a combination which has nurtured the work of the many who were likewise understood and encouraged by this rare man.

Larry and Mary, we salute you!

Words for Paul Tillich (1966)

Paulus Tillich's relation to the study of personality has found its most exquisite expression in some autobiographical notes written with care and charity at about his fiftieth year. Simultaneously looking back on the powers that formed him, and ahead to what he yet intended to make of himself, he defined as the *Grundthema*, the basic theme of his life, *Auf der Grenze sein*, Being on the Boundary. "On" here literally means being "upon" a borderline, to straddle it, as it were, never being altogether at home on this side and never deciding altogether against the other. The first boundary of his life he called *Auf der Grenze zwischen den Temperamenten*: on the boundary between two temperaments, namely his father's (a man from the dutiful East-German Mark) and his mother's (a woman from the more sensual Rhineland). The twelfth and last he called *Auf der Grenze von Heimat und Fremde*: on the boundary between homeland and foreign country—*this* country, in which he had then settled. Other boundaries marked geographic alternatives, such as living inland or by the sea; or cultural diversity, such as love of the small town and lifelong nostalgia for the metropolis; or ideological divisions and decisions, as between Lutheranism or Socialism.

Presented as a memorial for Paul Tillich at Harvard University on November 4, 1965. First published in the *Harvard Divinity Bulletin*, 30, 2 (1966), 13–15.

Tillich did not enlarge on the national significance of this choice of phenomenological metaphor: it was, I think, a deeply German one. For the very name of his region of origin, *die Mark*, means "the territory of the boundary" between the West and the slavic East. As such, it was only one of the many demarcations which have delineated and divided the Germans, this people of the geographic center of a continent. Throughout her history national and religious boundaries have cut through Germany (and many a German) and there were concretely forbidding walls such as the Roman Limes and today's Russian Wall.

This dividedness, both geographic and psychological, Adolf Hitler tried to undo forever by the total conquest of all potential invaders on Germany's borders and the total annihilation of all inner dividers. Paul Tillich, however, accepted the boundary as an existential design—and transcended it. This, I think, is and was one of the prime sources of his personal and charismatic strength. Tillich also fused the design of the boundary with his Protestantism; it became, in fact, his own variations of "Here I stand." Referring to the boundary of autonomy and heteronomy he declares: "Ich bin entschlossen auf dieser Grenze zu bleiben," "I am determined to remain on this borderline."

But Paulus Tillich also made the sign of the boundary his message to personology and psychotherapy. For he acknowledged man's existential contradictions, not as conflicts to be "cured" by adjustments and conformity, but as opposites to be bridged and thus transformed into creative polarities. And did not the whole man, when he stood before you in the Harvard Yard, personify a powerful bridge, both feet planted firmly on the ground, like a figure in a relief of Barlach? But with his greeting, the sun broke through all angularity.

When we first met at Paul Lee's house, he reiterated his concern about the faddish aspects of psychoanalysis. Instead of restricting itself to removing neurotic self-contradictions so as to free in man what he called "the moral self-realization of the centered self," did it not attempt to remove man's existential dread along with his neurotic anxiety? And what was man without the awareness of his finitude, what without the realization of his guilt in regard "to acts for which," as he put it elsewhere, "responsibility cannot be denied, in spite of the element of destiny in them"? He did not know (I almost felt that he did not care to know) that Freud would have profoundly agreed with him, although he would have grimly denied the solace offered by any specific faith. Nevertheless, Paulus acknowledged Freud's basic discoveries as having shown up "the ambiguity of goodness as well as of evil," and thus the flabbiness of what he called "men of good will . . . so rampant in . . . Protestantism."

When he was among us, Paul Tillich combined his opposites—and his occasional extremes—in what he called his *glaeubiger Realismus*, his blend of realism and faith, his utter sensual and spiritual Hereness. He has now gone beyond the borderline—unspeakable and inexorable—of all borderlines. From our side of it, we who knew him can say with assurance that as long as we are here, Paulus Tillich will be here.

For Marian C. Putnam (1971)

WITH JOAN M. ERIKSON

There comes a time in life when the death of an old friend causes only a brief spasm of grief and only a passing regret over the last and missed opportunity to see her just once more. What prevails, rather, is the joy over the unbelievable fact that among the multitudes of human beings and in all the vicissitudes of fate we found her and she found us at the right time and in the right place. And we realize once more, that the time and the place are made right only by a certain simplicity with which we can greet the here in the now, in friendship. Few people command this simplicity the way Molly did because few people are able to grow up without abandoning the child in themselves. Molly refused to do so, and so she could look at everybody and everything and especially at growing children, flowering plants, and budding ideas with unceasing surprise and with the gay laughter of recognition. To Joan, the memory of joining Molly in picking Japanese beetles off blossoming rose bushes in Little Compton on a dewy summer morning remains unforgettable; to Erik, the memory of finding with Molly dark and yet enlightening meanings

Presented at a memorial for Marian C. Putnam at the Appleton Chapel of Harvard University in December, 1971. Published here for the first time. Marian C. Putnam, physician-psychiatrist, daughter of James J. Putnam, was known to the Eriksons as a friend and professional co-worker.

in her records of a child patient's sequences of play.

There was, of course, also something of a priestess in Molly, of a responsible warden of the almost holy heritage of being the daughter of a father-doctor, who with quiet courage introduced that formidable man Freud to these Puritan shores: how good, we all feel, that she could see completed that volume which attests, and attests with the help of her own forceful words, to that historical event.*

We are proud and glad that during some important years in our lives Molly was a family friend as well as a co-worker, a sponsor of our ideas as well as godmother to our daughter. That this daughter's middle name is Marian adds one more and most significant image to those which will keep Molly's memory alive as long as we live.

* In 1971 Nathan G. Hale, Jr., edited a book entitled *James Jackson Putnam and Psychoanalysis: Letters Between Putnam and Sigmund Freud, Ernest Jones, William James, Sandor Ferenczi and Morton Prince, 1877–1917.* Dr. Putnam played an important role in the completion of this volume of her father's letters and wrote the Foreward for the book.

Mary Sarvis—a Few Words of Testimony (1972)

In this setting I may be forgiven—and I know Mary Sarvis would forgive me—for just adding a few words of testimony to what her friends have said or will say. I seem to be the oldest speaker and feel doubly the tragic paradox of speaking in memory of a young person who had still so much to give. So may I be the one who expresses our deepest sympathy to her mother.

I knew this singular young woman in a singular way. I cannot help remembering on this occasion how much her early memories concerned death in justice and separation: the death to which new-born Chinese girls were abandoned as too great an economic burden, and her own separation from her Chinese nurse—these are matters which, whatever the facts, we in our work learn to know as the determinants of psychological life and death. And Mary Sarvis made life out of them as vigorously as she could; she translated her melancholy into the passionate wish to help others and to make deprived and homeless people feel close and at home. I have known few individuals who have been so decisive in their yes *and* in their no. When Mary Sarvis said yes, it was with a laughter that shook her and us,

Presented at a memorial for Mary Sarvis at the United Church of Berkeley, in Oakland, California, in 1972. Published here for the first time. Mary Sarvis, social worker and clinician, was a close friend of Erikson's.

731

and when she said no, it was not infrequently with four-letter words which shocked some. But even they felt that here was a person who said no affirmatively. And if and when she said no to herself, we know it was when she felt that the powers of affirmation were failing her or, for that matter, *us*. Now we can only hope that a power greater than she and we will give her peace in the company of the most humorous of angels—and that He will let her help Him with the melancholy ones.

Robert P. Knight:
By Way of a Memoir (1972)

Robert Knight had what in German one might call a *beseelte Sachlichkeit*, "a lively pragmatism which went to the soul of a matter." If it seems strange that a German phrase comes to mind in regard to one of the most American of all psychoanalysts, one should remember that Knight became a leader in the field of psychiatry through his work at the Menninger Foundation and at the Austen Riggs Center, two psychiatric laboratories in which European thought and American group spirit were wedded to each other. This was evident in the composition of their staffs, in their dominant methodology and terminology, and in their management of the communal life of doctors and patients. This European/American union also pervades the papers collected in this volume. However, it is exactly the cool pragmatism present in these papers (sometimes deceptive in its understatements) that makes me wish to describe to the reader the very rare man and colleague who wrote them.

Some might characterize Robert Knight as a man's man; I would qualify this to read a colleague's man, which incidentally will give me license to quote the most telling remarks made about him by both men and women colleagues soon after he died. Karl Menninger summed

First published in *Clinician and Therapist: Selected Papers of Robert P. Knight*, ed. Stuart C. Miller, (New York: Basic Books, 1972), vii–xii.

up the masculine theme in his relationship to Robert Knight: "Too old to be my son and too young to be my brother," he wrote, "he was both: he was my partner. . . . With my own brother—the three of us—we built a clinic, a hospital, a school, and an institute."

Let me begin my account by telling the story of how I became Robert Knight's colleague (I might add that he is the only real boss I have ever had). He had then risen to the position of Chief-of-Staff at Menninger's. In the forties, I had flown from the West Coast to Topeka for regular consultants' visits. Knight and other friends had urged me to move to Topeka. On one occasion he seemed to be particularly determined to have me say that I would join his staff. He detailed some good terms and spoke most warmly of his wish to have me come. I refused on the grounds that I liked my work on the West Coast. Suddenly he said with surprising bluntness, "Is this your final word?" When I nodded, he closed the folder before him, looked me straight in the eye, and said, "In that case, will you come to Stockbridge?" In other words, unbeknownst to me, he had already resigned his position at Menninger's and had accepted the directorship at the Austen Riggs Center; he had felt, however, that he owed it to his friends William and Karl Menninger to see our negotiations through before offering me a job at Stockbridge. Later, when my professorship at Berkeley was terminated in its very first year by the Loyalty Oath controversy, and when we nonsigners found ourselves unsupported by the students and abandoned by most of our colleagues, he was the first to phone and to repeat his invitation. I accepted.

To fully grasp the mixture of decisiveness and warmth and business-mindedness and loyalty in this man, one must visualize him. The Gibsons have described him as "a giant in physical stature, unhurried of movement, calm-spoken, and dryly humorous." I would add to this the image of a strong face, which always dominated his elevated stature: his clear, thoughtful, and sometimes twinkling blue eyes; his long, straight nose; and his firm, yet sensuous mouth. It is true, however, that it was always his enormous height to which each individual reacted in his own particular way.

It so happens that I have a number of very tall friends, which means, in my definition, men taller than myself. Robert Knight was probably the tallest, and he had grown up, it must be remembered, in a generation less used to tall boys than we are now. Bob's height was a problem for him not only when he stood erect and had to stoop down in an attempt to look at others straight in the eye, but also when he sat down because not even the largest chair could permit him to lean back and yet stay aboard with his rump.

Bob's friends and students also remember that he was always in need of a soft drink, and, for many years, a cigarette. After his death, Henry Wexler would imagine him in paradise "in celestial comfort with a king-sized ambrosial cola in hand, the front legs of his chair elevated by two wooden blocks."

Bob's size, no doubt, had caused him embarrassment in his younger years, and indeed the young native of Urbana, Ohio, is said to have been shy and self-conscious, although his height was fully matched by superior muscular development. What posture such a man develops must, of course, remain consonant with a happy constellation of character traits. As I think about this, I realize that at least in my small sample of tall men a common trait is a certain maternal tenderness amounting to a kind of patient permissiveness with the varying opinions and styles of smaller folk, unless, of course, some very high principle is at stake, in which case such men can pull themselves up to their full stature and stand up to be counted. When such men meet men of equal height, it can happen that they will walk and talk around each other with a more or less subtle growl like St. Bernards; and there can be no doubt that big men involved in power struggles can be most determinedly, and I think deceptively, untender; otherwise they will deal with smaller creatures rather gently, reacting to a built-in expectation in all average-sized men that higher-ups will sooner or later use their superior power unfairly. I have, of course, also seen colleagues of smaller stature (like David Rapaport and Margaret Brenman) "face-up" to Robert Knight magnificently. He learned, in fact, to count on this as a most essential corrective.

Robert Knight's former student Cyrus Friedman put into words the sentiments of colleagues-in-the-making. He declared that he had never heard the deceased "act rudely or unkindly toward a student" or, indeed, "pontificate." This remark indicates, of course, that one is inclined somehow to expect such behavior from a tall man; but it also shows, as Friedman concluded, that "the style and the man were one." In other words, his generosity and tenderness were much more than "overcompensation." And, indeed, he combined with his permissiveness the most active kind of encouraging leadership. He created, say the Gibsons, "a center of moral trust in any group he headed, and permitted the most divergent personalities to work in harmony around him."

Here we must record the *width* of activities which Robert Knight was able to pervade with his style, reconciling not only divergent personalities, but such warring methods and theories as have characterized the history of psychoanalysis. In the American Psychoanalytic Association, he rose "naturally" from secretary to president and, in the academic world, from a lectureship at Kansas University to a clinical professorship at Yale. In the psychiatric community, he served for years as examiner in psychiatry on the National Board, while in the federal domain he became a member of the Training Committee for Psychiatry at the Institute for Mental Health. And, of course, he was for decades a training psychoanalyst in Topeka and New York, and finally in the Western New England Psychoanalytic Institute which we used to call, in short, Winnepesaukee. This included analysts and candidates both from Yale and from Riggs, and since our meetings were alternately held in New Haven and in Stockbridge, I enjoyed the comradely pleasure of frequently joining Robert Knight on rides in all kinds of weather through the New England countryside. (That we and the candidates called Route 63 Sigmund Freud Highway has as yet not been registered on the official maps.)

In Stockbridge, we worked together in a strange psychiatric community situated on one of the broadest and most venerable tree-lined Main Streets of America. Robert Knight had taken on the medical directorship in 1947, accompanied and followed by a proud contingent from Menninger which included Margaret Brenman, Merton Gill, Stuart Miller, David Rapaport, Roy Schafer, and Allen Wheelis. They all sought and found an opportunity for intense and interrelated clinical and theoretical exploration. Joan Erikson and I joined them in 1951, she as director of patients' activities, I as therapist, researcher, and training psychoanalyst. In speaking for us, I know that I speak for those who preceded and who followed us. And again, I would contrast, as contained in one style, Bob's extreme permissiveness and his executive firmness. He "protected others' ideals," as Roy Schafer put it, "and whose ideals can't use a little protection?"

Thus, Robert Knight let develop what is probably the most flexible "activities program," often improvised with a trust in the curative value of creative work that, in the case of patients, could only impress some doctors as hazardous. Joan Erikson instituted a patients' drama group, which performed for the sophisticated audience of Berkshire County, without the widely expected failures or breakdowns on the part of sicker patients. She also established a nursery school where the patients could put to work what had remained undeveloped in them and what they had learned from their treatment. The children came from the previously so mistrustful community—and they are still coming. Similarly, Bob permitted other staff members to institute work programs and patient-staff committees at a time when such participatory democracy had not yet become a matter of educational slogans. As Edgerton Howard (the man who, with medical and personal wisdom, maintained a link between the institutional regimes of Austen Riggs and Robert Knight) has put it: "The loss of group unity and control and the resulting chaos was frightening at times. Any weaker leader would have retreated to authoritative methods of bringing order out of confusion. We know how frequently Bob was tempted to do so." Ed Howard concludes: "He created an atmosphere of work, industry, and high scholarliness. He expected the best from everyone—even perfection—but gave each complete freedom to carry on his own endeavors, and to be responsible for his own work. He had a complete, almost naïve, trust in others' ability to do this." And this included me. Without his sanction and support I (like others) would never have been able to do what is almost impossible to arrange in private practice, namely, to continue intensive clinical observation and discussion while following wide ranging interests and to free large blocks of time for travel, studying, and writing.

I might also add that under Robert Knight's leadership the staff meetings at Riggs came to be the best I have known, governed by the principle that young and old staff members alike were sharing in a procedure of joint learning. A certain authoritative propensity on Bob's part came through only in two kinds of situations: he could not tolerate patients with a strong psychopathic propensity, giving them a rough time in what, surprisingly, could turn into an interrogation; and he abhorred any "dangling participle" in the young doctors' case abstracts. This mild obsession apparently went back to the days when the Oberlin graduate had taught English in Ohio, before he had gone to medical school.

Among all his colleagues, the most extraordinary one was undoubtedly David Rapaport. In contrast to Bob's tallness, David was small. To see Bob and David come down Main Street together was an experience. In order to keep up with Bob's long steps, David had to hurry along as if on small, built-in wheels. Where Bob was calm, David was excitable; where Bob spoke softly and evenly, David alternately shouted and whispered. Bob was the doctor and the director; David was the theorist, the encyclopedist, and the conceptual conscience of all of us. He, in fact, assigned us our place in the history of psychoanalytic thought and practice. I think it was Henry Wexler who called Bob the embodiment of the Reality Principle; so was David that of the Superego. This, to be sure, could have been a deadly combination, but the two shared a great sense of humor which made David laugh over Bob's American jokes, and Bob laugh, in turn, over examples from David's inexhaustible Jewish collection, brought over from Hungary—and nothing can reconcile reality and conscience better than humor.

David died before Bob did. He was not yet fifty. I remember hearing about his death while having dinner in Worcester with venerable Heinz Werner, dean of developmental psychology. "Not yet fifty," Werner whispered, "and he acted like my father." I could only add to this that to me he always spoke as if he were my conceptual grandfather. Bob needed and wanted David's brand of wisdom.

Robert Knight's image, however, would not be complete without mention of an extra professional area in which he was (as the Gibsons put it) "a grim competitor." Unlike other people who seek in sports and games a recovery from confining work, Bob, whose work was so many-sided and often hazardous, sought in golf and bridge a world of predictable order and sanctioned competitiveness.

In conclusion, let me characterize Bob's favorite kind of humor with a story Karl Menninger tells, namely, how Bob, for some weeks, repeated with much mirth what he had heard a man say in a gathering: "Now is the time to rise above principle and do the right thing." No statement could better exemplify Robert Knight's greatness, his tallness, and his lack of sham.

In later years, Bob's ever-ready chuckle and occasional explosive laughter were often followed by a deep fit of coughing which worried us increasingly. A few days before Robert Knight, at sixty-three, died of lung cancer he asked me to come up from Harvard and visit with him. When I saw him I was, at first, deeply shocked. The whole big frame of this man was now doubled up in a heap of skinny limbs and his eyes were deeply sunk in his emaciated head. But he put me at ease with a no-nonsense acceptance of his impending death, and with the warm wish to see me (and others) for what was unmistakably the last time. He spoke of his adult sons—all three tall men. The reader may suspect that to be the son of such a man is a much more complex matter than to be his colleague, and I daresay there are sons of other great doctors who would agree with this. This Robert Knight knew. However, he was proud that they, too, had turned to healing professions and had become his colleagues. At the end, we shook hands as simply as we do when we say, "I'll be seeing you."

These, then, are some of the dimensions of the man who wrote the papers reprinted here.

VIII.
CONFIGURATIONS
OF HUMAN
POTENTIAL

Acceptance of the National Book Award for Gandhi's Truth (1970)

You do not make it easy for your prizewinning authors. I was notified of the selection of my book on Monday, invited to produce this note of acceptance by Tuesday, and asked to present myself here this evening. For some of us, who live in the Berkshire hills—Thoreaulike, on the western frontier of Massachusetts—it is not easy to know on Monday what we might want to say, from the heart, in Philharmonic Hall on Wednesday.

I want to thank you, of course. But most of all, I want to congratulate you on your choice. Not that my book is *really* a *good* book. Some of it was hard to write, almost by necessity. It must be hard to read, and I am grateful to those who persevered. But my readers and my judges, I well know, have borne with me because of my choice, at this juncture of history, of just the right man of peace to write about, and this with the method of another just right man of insight, Freud. I congratulate you, then, for sharing my conviction that we must do what we can to transmit the heritage of these two men of the first part of the century as a trust to its remainder.

In our time, revolutionary insights and innovating methods are quickly assimilated, quickly stereotyped, and put into widespread use

Presented at Philharmonic Hall in New York City, upon the acceptance of the National Book Award for *Gandhi's Truth*, on March 4, 1970. Published here for the first time.

in acts and words, whereupon they are quickly declared dead, like the Almighty. In the face of this, we must refuse to abdicate those insights which reveal the poisonous pollution of man's inner motivations and the abysmal self-deceit and destructiveness which he brings to all of his utopian exploits, preferring the license to kill to the knowledge that he himself must die. That there can be no real freedom without such insight, *that* some leaders emerging from the next generation may know without fearing to lose their capacity for "unselfconscious" action.

To trace for the young the balance of living insight in the life of a man probably more honest and therefore more devious, more humorous, and therefore more tragic, more deeply defeated and yet, perhaps, more lastingly influential than his colleagues in charisma—that I must admit, was at times a joy. Thank you for sharing it with me.

Thank you also for the check. The first thing I will do with it is try and take my publisher out for dinner, together with my editor: my wife, without whom—indeed; indeed! When I get home, I will see to it that some of the money reaches men and women who are working and suffering for causes that Gandhi would have considered his own.

In the meantime, my thanks: to you, to Norton, and to Joan.

Words at Delos (1971)

As night falls, the presence of Apollo throughout this theater seems pervasive. I wish I knew how to pray to him, for the god of justice and balance was never more needed in human life. Few of man's potentials ever reach what would seem to be an optimum—or balance with what was neglected and forgotten. Usually some of man's potentials are developed to the point of excess, leading to sin, to hubris, to suicide and to genocide—all symptoms of cancerous overdevelopment. We have discussed under-developed, developing and developed countries, but only Doxiadis admitted to the "crime" of overdevelopment. We have discussed maladjustment and adjustment but not overadjustment. This, I assume, is the hardest to become aware of before it is too late. Yet, between the depths of the inner world that we have learnt to enter and the technological triumphs of walks on the moon—between the sacred centrality of Delphi and the total recklessness of nuclear explosion—we have never been more in need of measure and balance. But I see Apollo at work in our youth. They have indulged in and explored dangerous excess, but some of them seem to have regained a love of the Here and Now as

Presented in a Greek temple on the island of Delos, at sundown, as a prayer to Apollo. First published in *Ekistics*, 32, 191 (October 1971), 259–60.

a measure which they will not sacrifice again to overdevelopment. May Apollo be with them.

But besides the great god of light. I am also reminded here of Oedipus, a man of utter darkness who killed his father and has become a symbol of the ambivalences lurking in our unconscious: the symbol of our wayward human drives. This we have analyzed and overanalyzed. But we have forgotten to ask what made Laius believe the oracle and act upon it. We know much more about the fear of the son and his hate of authority than we do about the mistrust of the father and his propensity for sacrificing his son for his beliefs. Here too we must pray for balance: may the sons (who can now learn so much) come to forgive their fathers (for they knew not what they were doing) and may they strive for a balance between the generations, on which—in the end—the success of all worldwide planning must depend.

Landing on the Moon (1969)

This morning I would like to speak about the landing on the moon, for there is something I must get off my chest. You see, I was asked by a prominent newspaper to state my anticipatory reaction to the expected moment when the first man would set his foot on the moon. This statement was to be published after a man had, indeed, succeeded in landing and, of course, in taking off again. I, like others, did have some thoughts on the subject, but I could not get myself to send them off. The chances our men were taking were too great to permit anticipatory triumph or clever reflection. Furthermore, the well-known names on the list I was asked to join all belonged to individuals over sixty-five. There was no woman among them. What, I wondered, could we old men say about this event, whether it succeeded or whether it failed disastrously? Our language has served to celebrate other kinds of adventures and to mourn other horrors. And indeed, when the event finally did come off, in view of five hundred millions of people, the viewed fact had a simple grandeur so altogether new that one could only react with a mixture of neighborly pleasure and religious awe, and this in spite of the fact that the highest-ranking commentator flatly stated within the hearing of all

Presented at the Appleton Chapel of Harvard University, on September 24, 1969. Published here for the first time.

these millions that the week of the moon trip had been the greatest since creation. This is not at all what I felt. On the contrary, this statement makes it necessary for me to express myself after all. So please permit me to use this occasion to say what I would have said.

The triumph we witnessed belonged to the test pilots. What when we were young seemed a matter of pure imagination because it was, in fact, unthinkable these disciplined men actually did with a friendliness and a sureness that almost amounted to a trained lack of individual imagination. And indeed, they had learned to trust an army of programmers who had made certain exactly what was to be expected from moment to moment between the earth and the moon and back. One can only salute this teamwork with deep respect because the discipline thus learned is absolutely necessary to keep a future technological world within safe and thinkable bounds. Only a hijacker could wish to weaken such discipline at this moment.

But these men can test only the extent to which men can become the superbrains of machines invented by brains. They cannot test the extent and the limits of the motivations which will decide whether the lethal design which all human conquest has helped to spread— in the name of salvation, of liberation, of progress, and, yes, even of evolution—will be extended to what once was known as the heavens. As long as any nation can live affluently in the safe knowledge of a comfortable margin of overkill, there can be little trust in any nation's expansion, spectacular as may be the deed or admirable as may be the men who test its mechanics and are tested by it.

Around the time of the moon landing we held a newborn grandson in our arms. I could not help thinking that every time a child is born, *there* is potentially the greatest week since creation, and the seven seas and the outer spaces pale before its message. Science and insight now make our progeny a matter of considered choice and also of the promise that each child deliberately planned to be born will be brought up to feel at home in his body, mind, and senses so that he may be terrified never by men but only by what in truth is terrible in and about human existence. Without that priority on earth, all landings elsewhere remain footless.

But in the end, what we are learning and teaching will help create truly relevant priorities only by being gathered into a new kind of religiosity. And here, I think, the conquest of the outer space may yet help in a paradoxical way: That men now invade the boundaries of the heavens as concrete goals of science could force man at last to center heaven down on earth, which has, in fact, so patiently and tormentedly waited for it. For the kingdom, as I read Christ's words, has always been within each of us, if we can only learn to face it— and to share it.

Bibliography:
the Complete Writings of
Erik H. Erikson
(1930–1985)

1.   1930   Zukunft der Aufklärung und die Psychoanalyse. *Zeitschrift für psychoanalytische Pädagogik*, 4, 201–16.
   In English: Psychoanalysis and the Future of Education. *Psychoanalytic Quarterly*, 4 (1935), 50–68.

2.   1931   Bilderbücher. *Zeitschrift psychoanalytische für Pädagogik*, 5, 13–19.
   In English: Children's Picture Books. (1986).

3.   1931   Triebschicksale im Schulaufsatz. *Zeitschrift psychoanalytische für Pädagogik*, 5, 417–45.
   In English: The Fate of the Drives in School Compositions (1986).

4.   1936   Book Review: *Psychoanalysis for Teachers and Parents*, by Anna Freud. In *Psychoanalytic Quarterly*, 5, 291–93.

5.   1937   Configurations in Play—Clinical Notes. *Psychoanalytic Quarterly*, 6, 139–214.
   In Spanish: Configuraciones en el Juego. *Revistade Psicoanalisis*, VI, 2 (1948).
   In German: Traumatische Konfigurationen im Spiel: Aufzeichnungen. *Imago*, 23 (1937), 447–516.
   Short version: Traumatische Konfigurationen im Spiel. *Zeitschrift psychoanalytische für Pädagogik*, 11 (1937), 262–92.

6.   1938   Dramatic Productions Test. In *Explorations in Personality*, eds. Henry A. Murray and others, 552–82. New York: Oxford University Press. (Reported in No. 5 above.)

7.   1938   On Play Therapy: A Panel Discussion with Maxwell Gitelson and Others. *American Journal of Orthopsychiatry*, 8, 507–10.

   * Revised in *Insight and Responsibility* (61)
  ** Revised in *Identity: Youth and Crisis* (76)
 *** Revised in *Life History and the Historical Moment* (97)
**** Revised in *Gandhi's Truth* (80)
Note: The first seven items were published under the name of Erik Homburger.

8.   1939   Observations on Sioux Education. *Journal of Psychology*, 7, 101–56.

9.   1940   Problems of Infancy and Early Childhood. In *Cyclopedia of Medicine*. Philadelphia: Davis & Co., 714–30. Also in in *Outline of Abnormal Psychology*, eds. Gardner Murphy and Arthur J. Bachrach, 3–36. New York: Modern Library, 1954.

10.   1940   Studies in the Interpretation of Play: 1. Clinical Observation of Play Disruption in Young Children. *Genetic Psychology Monographs*, 22, 557–671. Revised in *Child Behavior and Development* eds. Roger C. Barker, Jacob S. Kouninand, and Herbert F. Wright. ("Clinical Studies in Childhood Play") New York: McGraw-Hill, 1943, 411–28. Revised in *Child Psychotherapy*, ed. Mary R. Haworth. New York: Basic Books, 1964, 3–11 and 106–10.

11.   1940   On Submarine Psychology. Committee on National Morale (for the Coordinator of Information). Unpublished.

12.   1940   On the Feasibility of Making Psychological Observations in Canadian Internment Camps. Committee on National Morale (for the Coordinator of Information). Unpublished.

13.   1940   On Nazi Mentality. Committee on National Morale (for the Coordinator of Information). Unpublished.

14.   1941   Further Explorations in Play Construction. *Psychological Bulletin*, 38, 748. Abstract.

15.   1942   Comments on Hitler's Speech of September 30, 1942. Committee on National Morale (for the Council of Intercultural Relations). Unpublished.

16.   1942   Hitler's Imagery and German Youth. *Psychiatry*, 5, 475–93.
                Revised in: *Personality in Nature, Society and Culture*, eds. Clyde Kluckholn and Henry A. Murray, 485–510. New York: Alfred A. Knopf, 1948.

17.   1943   A Memorandum Concerning the Interrogation of German Prisoners of War. Committee on National Morale (for the Council on Intercultural Relations). Unpublished.

18.   1943   *Observations on the Yurok: Childhood and World Image.* Monograph. University of California Publications in American Archeological Ethnology, (Berkeley: University of California Press), 35, 10, iii + 257–302.

19.   1945   A Memorandum to the Joint Committee on Postwar Planning. Committee on National Morale (written for the Conference on Germany After the War). Unpublished.

20.   1945   Comments on Anti-Nazi Propaganda. Committee on National Morale (for the Council on Intercultural Relations). Unpublished.

21.   1945   Plans for the Returning Veteran with Symptoms of Instability. In *Community Planning for Peacetime Living*, eds. Louis Wirth, Ernest R. Hilgard, and I. James Quillen. 116–21. Stanford University Press.

22.   1945   Childhood and Tradition in Two American Indian Tribes. In *The Psychoanalytic Study of the Child*, vol. I, 316–50. New York: International Universities Press.
                Revised in *Personality in Nature, Soceity and Culture* (see No. 16), 176–203.

23.   **1946   Ego Development and Historical Change: Clinical Notes. In *The Psychoanalytic Study of the Child*, vol. II, 359–96. New York: International Universities Press.

24.   1949   Ruth Benedict. In *Ruth Fulton Benedict: A Memorial*, ed. Alfred L. Kroeber, 14–17. New York: Viking Fund, Inc. (Includes a portrait sketch of Ruth Benedict as Frontispiece.)

25.   1950   *Childhood and Society.* New York: W. W. Norton. 2nd, enlarged ed. 1963.

26.   **1950   Growth and Crisis in the "Healthy Personality." (With Joan M. Erikson). In *Symposium on the Healthy Personality*, ed. Milton J. E. Senn. 91–146.

New York: Josiah Macy, Jr. Foundation. (Prepared for the White House Conference, 1950.)

Revised in: *Personality in Nature, Society, and Culture* (see No. 16), 185–225.

In German: *Wachstum un Krisen der gesunden Personalichkeit.* Monograph, 63. Stuttgartterlay: Ernst Klett, 1953. Also in *Psyche*, Heidelberg, 7 (1953), 1–31 and 112–39.

27.   1951   Statement to the Committee on Privilege and Tenure of the University of California Concerning the California Loyalty Oath. *Psychiatry*, 14, 243–45.

28.   1951   Sex Differences in the Play Configurations of Preadolescents. *American Journal Orthopsychiatry*, 21, 667–692.

Revised in: *Childhood in Contemporary Cultures*, eds. Margaret Mead and Martha Wolfenstein, 324–41. Chicago: University of Chicago Press.

29.   1952   Book Review: Children Who Hate, by Fritz Redl and David Wineman. In *Basic Book News and Bibliography*, 1–3.

30.   1952   Cross-Cultural Patterns in the Adjustment and Maladjustment of Children: I. Deviations from Normal Child Development with Reference to Cross-Cultural Patterns; II. Etiology of Maladjustment in the Environment of the Child. *Scandinavian Seminar on Child Psychiatry and Child Guidance*, 19–23, 26–8. Geneva: World Health Organization. Abstract.

31.   1952   Remarks Made at an Interagency Conference at Princeton, New Jersey, September 21–25, 1951. In *Healthy Personality Development in Children: As Related to Programs of the Federal Government*. New York: Josiah Macy, Jr., Foundation.

32.   1953   The Power of the Newborn (with Joan M. Erikson). *Mademoiselle*, 62, 100–02.

33.   **1953   On the Sense of Inner Identity. In *Health and Human Relations*. Report of a Conference Held at Hiddensen, Germany, August 2–7, 1951, 124–43. New York: The Balkiston Company.

In German: Uber den Sinn der Inneren Identität. In *Gesundheit und Mitmenschliche Beziehungen*, eds. M. von Eckhardt and W. Villinger, 137–52. München: Ernst Reinhardt.

34.   **1954   Wholeness and Totality—a Psychiatric Contribution. In *Totalitarianism, Proceedings of a Conference Held at the American Academy of Arts and Sciences*, March 1953, ed. Carl J. Friedrich, 156–71. Cambridge: Harvard University Press.

35.   **1954   The Dream Specimen of Psychoanalysis. *Journal of the American Psychoanalytic Association*, 2, 5–56. Also in *Psychoanalytic Psychiatry and Psychology. Clinical and Theoretical Papers, Austen Riggs Center*, vol. I, eds. Robert P. Knight and Cyrus R. Friedman, 131–70. New York: International Universities Press.

In German: Das Traummuster der Psychoanalyse. *Psyche*, 8, 1954–55, 561–604.

36.   1954   Identity and Totality: Psychoanalytic Observations on the Problems of Youth. *Human Development Bulletin*, 5th Annual Symposium, 50–82. Chicago: The Human Development Student Organization.

37.   ***1955   Freud's "The Origins of Psychoanalysis." *International Journal of Psychoanalysis*, 36, 1–15.

In German: Zu Sigmund Freud "The Origins of Psychoanalysis." *Psyche*, 9 (1955), 90–116. 1955.

38.   **1956   The Problem of Ego Identity. *Journal of the American Psychoanalytic Association*, 4, 56–121.

In German: Das Problem der Identität. *Psyche*, 10 1956–57, 114–76.

Also in: *Entfaltung der Psychoanalyse*, ed. Alexander Mitscherlich, Stuttgart: Ernst Klett Verlag, 1956.

39. *1956 The First Psychoanalyst. *Yale Review*, 46, 40–62.
Also in *Freud and the Twentieth Century*, ed. Benjamin Nelson, 79–101. London: George Allen and Unwin, Ltd., 1957.
In German: Sigmund Freud's Psychoanalytische Krise. Festvortrag zu Freud's 100 Geburtstag. In *Freud in der Gegenwart, ein Vortragzyklus der Universitäten Frankfurt un Heidelberg*. Frankfurt, Europäische Verlagsanstalt, 1957.

40. *1956 Ego Identity and the Psychosocial Moratorium. In *New Perspectives for Research on Juvenile Delinquency*, 1–23. Washington, D.C.: Children's Bureau, U.S. Department of Health, Education and Welfare.

41. **1957 The Confirmation of the Delinquent (with Kai T. Erikson). *Chicago Review*, 10 (Winter) 15–23.

42. 1957 Trieb und Umwelt in der Kindheit. In *Freud in der Gegenwart* (see No. 39). ("Instinct and Surroundings on Childhood") ("Instinct and External Reality").

43. 1958 The Syndrome of Identity Diffusion in Adolescents and Young Adults and the Psychosocial Development of Children. In *Discussions on Child Development*, 1955, eds. J. M. Tanner and Barbel Inhelder. Proceedings of the Third Meeting of the Child Study Group, World Health Organization, vol. 3. New York: International Universities Press.

44. 1958 *Young Man Luther: a Study in Psychoanalysis and History*. New York: W. W. Norton & Co. Austen Riggs Center, Monograph No. 4.

45. *1958 On the Nature of Clinical Evidence. In *Daedalus*, Journal of the American Academy of Arts and Sciences, LXXXVII, 4, 65–87. Also in *Evidence and Inference, The First Hayden Colloquim*. Cambridge: The Technology Press of MIT, 1958, 73–95.

46. *1958 Identity and Uprootedness in Our Time. Address, Eleventh Annual Conference. In *Uprooting and Resettlement*, Bulletin of the World Federation for Mental Health. Vienna.
In German: Identität und Entwerzelung in unserer Zeit. Address, Eleventh Annual Congress, World Federation for Mental Health. *Psyche*, XIII (1) (1959).

47. **1959 Identity and the Life Cycle: Selected Papers. In *Psychological Issues*, 1,1. New York: International Universities Press.

48. 1959 Late Adolescence. In *The Student and Mental Health*, ed. Daniel H. Funkenstein, 66–88. The World Federation for Mental Health and the International Association of Universities.

49. 1960 Youth and the Life Cycle, an Interview. In *Children*. Washington, D.C.; U.S. Department of Health, Education and Welfare. 7, 2, 43–49.

50. 1960 Psychosexual Stages in Child Development. In *Discussions on Child Development*, 1956 World Health Organization Child Study Group, eds. J. M. Tanner and Barbara Inhelder, vol. 4, 137–54. New York: International Universities Press.

51. *1961 The Roots of Virtue. In *The Humanist Frame*, ed. Sir Julian Huxley, 145–65. London: George Allen and Unwin, Ltd. New York: Harper & Brothers.

52. 1961 Childhood and Society. In *Children of the Caribbean* 18–29. San Juan: The Commonwealth of Puerto Rico, Printing Division. Also, Postscript to the Conference, 151–54.

53. **1961 Introduction. In *Emotional Problems of the Student*, eds. Graham B. and Charles C. McArthur. xvii–xxx. New York: Appleton-Century-Crofts.

54. **1962 Youth: Fidelity and Diversity. *Daedalus*, XCI, 1, 5–27. (Reported in No. 58.)

55. *1962 Reality and Actuality. *Journal of the American Psychoanalytic Association*, 10, 451–73.
56. 1962 Memorandum for a Seminar on the Life Cycle: Thoughts on Tagore's Childhood. Ahmedabad, India, November 28, 1962. Unpublished.
57. *1963 The Golden Rule and the Cycle of Life (The George W. Gay Lecture on Medical Ethics, 1963). *Harvard Medical Alumni Bulletin*, XXXVII, 2. Also in *The Study of Lives*, ed. R. W. White. 412–28. New York: Appleton-Century-Crofts, 1963.
58. 1963 Editor, *Youth: Change and Challenge*. New York: Basic Books. Also in paperback. *The Challenge of Youth*, a Doubleday Anchor Book, 1965.
59. **1964 The Inner and the Outer Space: Reflections on Womanhood. *Daedalus*, XCII, 2, 582–606.
60. 1964 A Memorandum on Identity and Negro Youth. *Journal of Social Issues*, 20, 429–42.
61. 1965 *Insight and Responsibility*. New York: W. W. Norton.
62. 1965 Psychoanalysis and Ongoing History: Problems of Identity, Hatred and Nonviolence. *American Journal of Psychiatry*, 122, 241–50.
63. 1965 On the Potential of Women (Concluding Remarks). In *Women and the Scientific Professions*. The M.I.T. Symposium on American Women in Science and Engineering. eds. Jacquelyn A. Mattfeld and Carol G. VanAken. Cambridge, Mass., and London: MIT Press 232–45.
64. 1965 For Larry Frank's Anniversary—the Couple Who Came for Dinner (with Joan M. Erikson). Presented in Boston, Massachusetts, December. Unpublished.
65. **1966 The Concept of Identity in Race Relations: Notes and Queries. *Daedalus*, XCV, 1, 145–70.
66. 1966 The Ontogeny of Ritualization in Man. In *Philosophical Transactions of the Royal Society of London*, Series B, 251, 772, 337–49.
Revised in *Psychoanalysis—a General Psychology: Essays in Honor of Heinz Hartmann*, ed. Rudoph M. Lowenstein, et al., 601–22. New York: International Universities Press, 1966.
In German: Ontogenese der Ritualisievung, *Psyche*, XXII, 7 (1968).
67. 1966 Concluding Remarks on Ritualization of Behavior in Animals and Man. In *Philosophical Transactions of the Royal Society of London*, Series B., 251, 772: 523–24.
68. 1966 Words for Paul Tillich. *Harvard Divinity Bulletin*, 30, 2, 13–15.
69. ****1966 Gandhi's Autobiography: The Leader as a Child. *The American Scholar* (Autumn); 632–46.
70. 1966 Remarks on the "Wider Identity." Presented to the Catholic Worker (Tivoli, New York) and remarks made at a senatorial dinner (Washington, D.C.) 1966. Unpublished.
71. ***1967 Book Review, *Thomas Woodrow Wilson*, by Sigmund Freud and William C. Bullitt. *The New York Review of Books*, VIII, 2.
72. **1967 Memorandum on Youth: For the Committee on the Year 2000, American Academy of Arts and Sciences. *Daedalus*, 96, 3 (Summer), 860–70.
73. 1968 Memorandum for the Conference on the Draft. In *The Draft: Facts and Alternatives*, ed. Sol Tax. 280–83. Chicago: University of Chicago Press.
74. 1968 The Human Life Cycle. In *International Encyclopedia of the Social Sciences*. 286–92. New York: Crowell-Collier.
75. 1968 Psychosocial Identity. In *International Encyclopedia of the Social Sciences*, 61–65. New York: Crowell-Collier.
76. 1968 *Identity: Youth and Crisis*. New York: W. W. Norton.
77. ***1968 On the Nature of Psycho-Historical Evidence: In Search of Gandhi. *Daedalus*, 97, 3 (Summer), 695–730.

78.   ***1968   *Insight and Freedom.* The T. B. Davie Memorial Lecture on Academic Freedom, University of Capetown, South Africa.

79.   1969   On Student Unrest: Remarks on Receiving the Foneme Prize. Second International Convention on Human Formation from Adolescence to Maturity. Foneme Institute, Milan. Unpublished.

80.   1969   *Gandhi's Truth.* New York: W. W. Norton.

81.   1969   Landing on the Moon. Appleton Chapel, Harvard University, Cambridge, Massachusetts, September 24. Unpublished.

82.   ***1970   Reflections on the Dissent of Contemporary Youth. *Daedalus,* 97, 1 (Winter); 154–76. Also in *International Journal of Psychoanalysis,* 51, 1, (1970), 11–21.

83.   1970   Acceptance of the National Book Award: for *Gandhi's Truth.* Philharmonic Hall, New York City, March 4. Unpublished.

84.   1971   For Marian C. Putnam (with Joan M. Erikson). Appleton Chapel, Harvard University, Cambridge, Massachusetts, December. Unpublished.

85.   ***1970   Autobiographic Notes on the Identity Crisis. *Daedalus,* 99, 4 (Fall), 730–59. Also in *The Twentieth Century Sciences,* ed. Gerald Holton, 3–32. New York: W. W. Norton, 1972.

86.   1971   Words at Delos. *Ekistics,* 32, 191, (October), 259–60.

87.   1971   Notes on the Life Cycle. In: *Ekistics,* 32, 191, (October), 260–65.

88.   1972   Play and Actuality. In: *Play and Development,* ed. Maria Piers, 127–60. New York: W. W. Norton.

89.   1972   Environment and Virtues. In *Arts of the Environment,* ed. Gyorgy Kepes, 60–77. New York: Braziller.

90.   1972   On Protest and Affirmation. Class Day Address, Harvard Medical School. *Harvard Medical Alumni Bulletin,* July–August, 46, 6, 30–32.

91.   1972   Robert P. Knight: By Way of a Memoir. In *Clinician and Therapist: Selected Papers of Robert P. Knight,* ed. Stuart C. Miller, vii–xii. New York: Basic Books.

92.   1972   Mary Sarvis—A Few Words of Testimony. Presented at the United Church of Berkeley, Oakland, California. Unpublished.

93.   1973   Thoughts on the City for Human Development. In *Ekistics,* 35, 209 (April), 216–20. Also in *Anthropopolis.* Athens, 1974.

94.   ***1974   Once More the Inner Space. In *Women and Analysis,* ed. Jean Strouse. New York: Grossman Publishers.

95.   1974   *Dimensions of a New Identity:* The 1975 Jefferson Lectures. New York: W. W. Norton.

96.   1974   Peter Blos: Reminiscences. Introducing the First Peter Blos Biennial Lecture. *Psychosocial Process,* 3, 2, (Fall), 4–7.

97.   1975   *Life History and the Historical Moment. New York: W. W. Norton.*

98.   1975   *Conversations with Erik H. Erikson and Huey P. Newton.* In *In Search of Common Ground,* ed. Kai T. Erikson. New York: W. W. Norton.

99.   1976   Reflections on Dr. Borg's Life Cycle. *Daedalus,* 105, 2 (Spring), 1–31. Also in No. 105 and in *Aging, Death, and the Completion of Being,* ed. David D. Van Tassel. Philadelphia: University of Pennsylvania Press.

100.   ***1976   Psychoanalysis and Ethics—Avowed or Unavowed. *International Review of Psychoanalysis,* 3, 409–15.

101.   1976   Reflections on Activity, Recovery, and Growth. Written as a postscript in *Activity, Recovery, Growth: The Communal Role of Planned Activities,* J. Erikson, 251–66. New York: W. W. Norton.

102.   1977   *Toys and Reasons: Stages in the Ritualization of Experience.* New York: W. W. Norton.

103.   1978   Reflections on Aging, an Introduction (with Joan Erikson). In *Aging and the Elderly, Humanistic Perspectives in Gerontology,* eds. S. Spicker, K.

		Woodward, and D. Van Tassel, 1–8. Atlantic Highlands, N.J.: Humanities Press.
104.	1978	Reflections on Historical Change: A Foreword. In *Children and Parents in a Changing World*, vol. 5 of *The Child and His Family: Yearbook of the International Association for Child Psychiatry and Allied Professions*, eds. James Anthony and Colette Chiland, xi–xxi. New York: John Wiley & Sons.
105.	1978	Editor, *Adulthood: Collected Essays*. New York: W. W. Norton. (See also No. 99.)
106.	1979	Report to Vikram: Further Perspectives on the Life Cycle. In *Identity and Adulthood*, ed. Sudhir Kakar, 13–34. Bombay: Oxford University Press.
107.	1980	Themes of Adulthood in the Freud-Jung Correspondence. In *Themes of Work and Love in Adulthood*, eds. Neil Smelser and Erik H. Erikson, 43–74. Cambridge: Harvard University Press.
108.	1980	Elements of a Psychoanalytic Theory of Psychosocial Development. In *The Course of Life*. Psychoanalytic Contributions Toward Understanding Personality Development, vol. 1, 11–61, eds. Stanley Greenspan, M.D. and George Pollock, M.D. Washington, D.C.: U. S. Government Printing Office.
109.	1980	Psychoanalytic Reflections on Einstein's Centenary. In *Albert Einstein—Historical and Cultural Perspectives*. (The Jerusalem Einstein Symposium), eds. Gerald Holton and Yehuda Elkana. Princeton, N.J.: Princeton University Press, 151–73. Also in: *Einstein and Humanism, Selected Papers from the Jerusalem Einstein Centennial Symposium*. 1980 Aspen Institute for Humanistic Studies, 151–73. New York.
110.	1980	*Identity and the Life Cycle* (A Reissue). New York: W. W. Norton. (See No. 47).
111.	1980	On the Generational Cycle: An Address. *International Journal of Psycho-Analysis*, 61, 2, 213–23.
112.	1980	(with Joan M. Erikson) Dorothy Burlingham's School in Vienna. In *The Bulletin of the Hampstead Clinic*, 3, 2, 91–94.
113.	1981	The Galilean Saying and the Sense of "I." *The Yale Review*, (April), 321–62.
114.	1981	(with Joan M. Erikson) on Generativity and Identity (from a conversation with the editors). *Harvard Educational Review*, 51, 2, (May), 249–69.
115.	1982	*The Life Cycle Completed*. New York: W. W. Norton
116.	1982	For Joseph Wheelright—My Jungian Friend. In *Joseph Wheelright, St. George and the Dandelion. Forty Years of Practice as a Jungian Analyst*. San Francisco: C. G. Jung Institute of San Francisco.
117.	1983	Anna Freud—Reflections. *Bulletin of the Hampstead Clinic*, 6, 51–54.
118.	1983	Infancy and the Rest of Life: Concluding Remarks. In *Frontiers of Infant Psychiatry*, eds. J. D. Call, E. Galenson and R. L. Tyson, 425–28. New York: Basic Books.
119.	1983	Reflections: On the Relationship of Adolescence and Parenthood. In *Adolescent Psychiatry*, vol. II, 9–13.
120.	1985	Reflections on the Last Stage—and the First. In: *The Psychoanalytic Study of the Child*, vol. 39. New York: International Universities Press.

Index

abandonment, ritualization and, 579
Abraham, Karl, 429, 436, 470
Absalom, 44
accidents, developmental fears and, 557–59
activities:
  communality and, 542–43
  in therapeutic experience, 533–35
actuality:
  play and, 311–37
    in adulthood, 331–37
    in children, 311–16
    interplay of, 316–20
    pseudospeciation in, 327–31
    in revolutionary activity, 325–27
    ritualization in, 320–22
    in young adulthood, 322–25
  reality vs., 336–37
acute dream stimulus, 264
acute life conflicts, dreams and, 264
Adamson, 31, 36
adolescence (adolescents). *See also* delinquency; youth
  essays of, 39–69
  identity and, 622–26
  late, 631–43

in life cycle, 262, 605–6
ritualization and, 587–90
in Yurok culture, 428, 429, 439
adulthood:
  as historical process, 335–36
  in life cycle, 262
  play in, 331–37. *See also* ritualization
adults. *See also* fathers; mothers; parents; therapists
  adolescents' relationship to, 623, 626–30
  children's interaction with, 33, 34, 38, 557
affect (or attitude) criterion, of zonal sensations and frustrations, 437
affective behavior, morphoanalytic description of, 163
affects:
  in dreams, 250–51
  of dreams, 256
affirmation, oath as, 699–701
aggression. *See also* rage, child's perception of, 59
  children and, 26–27
  gap between prevention and, 488

aggression (*continued*)
   in nature, 485–88
   oral, 50–51. *See also* biting; orality
aging:
   in child's fantasies, 67
   identity and, 640–41
   in life cycle, 262, 608–9
Aichhorn, August, xx, 5, 711
Alexander, Franz, 366
Alice in Wonderland (Carroll), 557
all-human identity. *See* wider identity
Allport, Gordon, 341*n*
ambition:
   in Irma Dream, 277–78
   testing of, in boys' training, 266–68
   urinary experience and, 267
America (Americans):
   anti-Nazi propaganda and, 364–65
   ego weakness in, 477–80
   identity of, 499–502
   Indian tribes as minorities in, 447,
      450–52, 504–7
   in Nazi propaganda, 355, 357–59
   postwar Germany and, 368–69,
      373–74
   racial struggle in, 490
   soldiers in World War II
      prisoners of war, 350
      reeducation of, 373–74
      after World War II, 613–17
American Psychoanalytic Association,
      736
Amundsen, Roald, 27
anality (anal stage), 111–12, 582, 602
   fixation, case history of, 97–102
   in infancy, 552
   sexual enlightenment of child and,
      22–24
   in Yurok culture, 436–38, 470–71
   zones of body and, 437
analyst. *See also* psychoanalysis
   dream interpretation and training of,
      238–39
   teacher vs., 14–15
anger. *See also* rage
   in Sioux character, 430, 455, 509
Anglo-Saxons, in Nazi propaganda,
      354–57, 359, 360

animal behavior, 485–88
anthropology, psychosocial identity
      and, 678
Anti-Nazi propaganda, 360, 362–65,
      373–74
Anti-Semitism, in Nazi propaganda,
      352, 356, 358
anxiety:
   castration, 60–61, 555
      case study of, 16–21
      hair symbolism and, 47
      Nazi propaganda theme of, 359,
         360
   developmental fears and, 555–58
   in infancy and childhood, 565
Apollo, 743–44
Arapesh, 113, 554
architecture. *See also* city planning of
      ideal city, 527, 528, 530
Aristotle, 526, 528
arrest, fixation vs., 211–12
artists:
   as adjunct therapists, 535
   identity-diffusion and, 638
   narcissism of, 42–44
Austen Riggs Center (Stockbridge,
      Mass.), xvii, xxiv, 531–44, 733,
      734, 736, 737
   communality of treatment at, 541–
      44
   earlier confinement practices and,
      537–41
   program of, 531–37
authority:
   fear of, 45–46
   inner, 33–35
autobiographical elements, in Freud's
      work, 239–42, 264–69
autocosmic play, 102, 104, 155
autonomy, sense of, 262
   discrimination and, 582
   shame and doubt vs., 602–3
autosphere, 155, 158–59

baby. *See also* infancy; newborns, girls'
      desire for, 112–13, 183
balance, prayer for, 743–44
barbed wire disease, 349, 350

bartlos, 254
Bateson, Gregory, 341*n*
beating, fantasy of, 55–56
beauty, talent and, 43–45
bed-wetting, 58, 61
behavior:
 affective, 163
 animal, 485–88
 in childhood. *See* children
 developmental, 549–50
 in infancy. *See* infancy
 instinct and, 580, 581
 meaning in, 246–47
 ritualized, 592–93. *See also* ritualization
behavior items, 162–64
Benedict, Ruth, 716–17, 722–23
Berdache, 458
Bernfeldt, Siegfried, 711
Bettelheim, Bruno, 661
Bibring, Edward, xx
biological orientation, in psychoanalytic theory, 485–88
biting:
 in play configurations, 106, 109–10
 problems revealed in play, 93–94
 as second oral stage, 211, 212
 Sioux child training and, 430, 433,
  455, 509
 Yurok child training and, 434, 435,
  465
 in Yurok culture, 469
Black Panther Party, 325–27
Black youth. *See* Negro youth
Blaine, Graham B., 677
blocks, building, in play configurations, 290–95
Blos, Peter, xix, 3, 4, 709–12
body. *See also* zones of body
 cars and, 99
 house-form and, 80–85
bonding, 320–21
books, children's, 31–38
Boring, Edwin, 341*n*
Boulding, Kenneth, 493, 670
bowel training. *See also* toilet training
 in Yurok culture, 421–22
bowl, in play configurations, 96–97

Bowlby, John, 579
boxes, in play configurations, 95–96
boys. *See also* childhood; sex differences
 fathers and, 266–68
 in Sioux culture, 454, 509
breast-feeding (nursing):
 sexual enlightenment of child and,
  23
 in Sioux culture, 454, 508–9
 in Yurok culture, 420, 432, 433,
  465, 514–16
breasts, in play configurations, 82
Breed, Edith, 533
Brenman, Margaret, 535, 735, 736
British people, in Nazi propaganda,
  354–57, 359, 360
brotherhood, newborn sibling and
  sense of, 572–74
brothers and sisters, in Sioux culture,
  456, 457
buffalo, in Sioux culture, 447–49, 504,
  505
buildings, in play configurations, 291–
  95
bull, in child's fantasies, 57–59
Bunting, Mary I., 661
Burlingham, Dorothy, xix–xxi, 3–5,
  12–13, 39, 711

cages, in play configurations, 78–80,
  87–88
California, loyalty oath in, 618–20
California, University of, 618–20
capture, as traumatic situation, 348–49
care:
 developmental crisis of maturity and,
  607–8
 life cycle and, 702
Caribbean family life, 653–55
cars, in play configurations, 99
car theft, 626, 627
case studies. *See also* Irma Dream
 A (boy of four), 78–80
 the adolescent (boy of fourteen), 47–
  51
 Asper (male college student), 122–24
 B (girl of twelve), 80–82

case studies (*continued*)
Berry (male college student), 119–22, 124
the bright-eyed one (girl of eleven), 40–47
C (schizophrenic man), 83–84
D (boy of five), 84–85
Deborah (girl of eleven), 284–87
Dick (boy of four), 188–214, 229–31
E (boy of eight), 85–88
F (boy of five), 88–89
Fred (boy of four), 214–28, 229, 231
G (girl of two-and-one-half), 89–94
H (boy of two-and-one-half), 95–97
the inaccessible boy, 56–61
J (boy of eight), 97–102
John (boy of six), 164–71, 228–31
K (girl of eight), 102–5
Krumb (male college student), 132–35
Lisa, 288–89
Margaret (girl of twelve), 51–56
Mary (girl of three), 171–88, 228–31
Mauve (male college student), 128–32
Oriol (male college student), 124–28, 134
Richard (boy of seven), 15–24
the son (adolescent), 64–68
the son (fourteen-year-old), 61–63
the son (ten-year-old), 63–64
Victoria (girl of eleven), 287–88
Vulner (male college student), 135
Zeeno (male college student), 116–19, 121, 122, 124
castration anxiety (or complex), 60–61, 555
hair symbolism and, 47
Nazi propaganda theme of, 359, 360
Richard (case study) and, 16–21
catharsis:
in intrusive stage, 182
play as, 141
cathexis, 146
Catholicism (Catholics), 498, 499, 501
Freud and, 264–66
Catholic Worker, 497
centripetal laws, in Yurok culture, 403–9
change:
developmental fears and, 555
student unrest and, 689–90
women's roles and, 660–69
channelizing, in play configurations, 291, 295
children's picture books, 31–38
child analysis, 564–68
case studies:
A (boy of four), 78–80
the adolescent (boy of fourteen), 47–51
B (girl of twelve), 80–82
the bright-eyed one (girl of eleven), 40–47
D (boy of five), 84–85
Deborah (girl of eleven), 284–87
Dick (boy of four), 188–214, 229–31
E (boy of eight), 85–88
F (boy of five), 88–89
Fred (boy of four), 214–28, 229–231
G (girl of two-and-one-half), 89–94
H (boy of two-and-one-half), 95–97
the inaccessible boy, 56–61
J (boy of eight), 97–102
John (boy of six), 164–71, 228–31
K (girl of eight), 102–5
Lisa, 288–89
Margaret (girl of twelve), 51–56
Mary (girl of three), 171–88, 228–31
Richard (boy of seven), 15–24
the son (adolescent), 64–68
the son (fourteen-year-old), 61–63
the son (ten-year-old), 63–64
Victoria (girl of eleven), 287–88
development and, 149–50
the initial situation and its alternatives, 150–62

insights and, 232–34
interpretation in, 143–44
childhood (children). *See also* boys;
    child analysis; child training;
    girls; infancy; newborns
  adult distortion of, 32–34
  aggression and, 26–27
  black, 645–50
  "creditor," 58–60
  development in. *See* development
  early, problems of, 547–68
    developmental behavior, 549–50
    developmental fears, 555–58
    habits and culture and, 561–64
    latency, 554–55
    parents and, 560–61
    physician's role and, 564–68
    social relativity of psychological
      status, 558–59
  ego development in, 33–38
  interactions with adults of, 33, 34,
    38, 557
  in life cycle, 262, 602–3
  maturation task and, 142
  neurotic episodes in, 183
  newborn sibling and, 572–74
  play in, 311–16. *See also* play
  psychoanalysis and, 40, 475–80. *See
    also* child analysis; psychoanaly-
    sis
  ritualization and, 582–87
    dramatic and formal, 585–87
    judicious, 582–85
  sexual enlightenment and, 15–29
    anxieties, fantasies, and theories
      of, 21–23
    child's ability to accept, 25–26
    Richard (case study), 15–22
    stork fairy tale, 23–24
    teacher's role, 24–25
  symbolism of, in dreams, 131
  in traditional societies. *See* Sioux;
    Yurok
  training of. *See* child training
Childhood and Society (Erikson), xvii,
  xxii
"Child Is Beaten, A" (Freud), 55–56
child training. *See also* education

behavioral development and, 562–64
culture and, 473–80
definition of, 378–80
inner conflict and, 268
personality potentialities and, 430–
  32
physician's role and, 564–68
in "primitive" vs. "civilized" cultures, 473–75
in Sioux culture, 429–30, 432, 433,
  450–51, 454–59
in technological societies, 517–19
Yurok, 384–85, 417–43, 464–73,
  514–16
  adolescence, 428–29
  anal character, 436–38
  education of, 422–26
  fables for, 423–26
  first oral stage, 432–34
  genital attitudes, 439–41
  in infancy, 420–22, 432
  object relations, 434–36
  play of, 426–28
  prenatal, 419, 432
  summary, 441–43
China, Communist, 642
choice, free, 603. *See also* will power,
  dilemma of, 636
Christ Child, medieval depictions of,
  32–33
Churchill, Winston, 352, 354–55
city planning, 543
  life cycle and, 522–30
civil disobedience, 673–74. *See also*
  nonviolence
civilization, guilt and, 27–29, 36–37
Civilization and Its Discontents
  (Freud), 26, 45–46
"claustrum" fantasies, 103
Cleaver, Eldridge, 325*n*
clinical observation. *See also* case studies; child analysis; psychoanalysis
  factors influencing, 140
  importance of, 144–48
  insights and, 232–34
  method of representation of, 162–64
  of prisoners of war, 347–50

clinical observation (*continued*)
among Yurok, 382–83
closed boxes, in play configurations,
95–96
closing up, in play configurations, 106,
111, 112
cognition, play and, 314–15
Colby, Kenneth, 258
Coles, Robert, xxi, xxii
college education, 633–36, 642–43
college students, play constructions of,
114–36
combat situations, 614
Committee for National Morale, xxi-
xxii, 341, 342, 362*n*, 366*n*
communality, 541–44
communication:
with newborns, 571
ritualization and, 592–93
Communist party (U.S.), 618*n*
community, identity formation and,
648–50
comparative trait configurations, 431
competence, developmental crisis of
school age and, 604–5
complex, defined, 180–81
concentration, identity-diffusion and,
637
conception, idea germination and, 255
configurations:
cultural trait, 431
dream, 250–63
interpersonal, 255–63
inventory of, 250–51
manifest, 251, 256–57
verbal, 252–55
dynamic, 164
personality trait, 431
play. *See* play configurations
spatial. *See also* city planning
bowl and, 96–97
boxes and, 95–96
cages and, 78–80, 87–88
in college students' play, 114–36
defined, 78
ekistics and, 596–97
houses and, 78–89
morphoanalytic description of,
163

organ-modes and, 106–12
tube, 420, 422, 460, 461, 513
confinement practices, 537–41
confirmation, Irma Dream as, 260–61
conflict:
capture in war as, 348–49
inner:
dreams and, 240, 263–69, 273
therapeutic situation and, 152
conscience. *See also* superego
developmental crisis of play age and,
603–4
formation of, 33–35, 45–46
constructions, in play configurations,
291–95
contacts, 162
conversion, Irma Dream as, 260–61
Cooper, Alfred Duff, 354, 355
countermode criterion, of zonal sensations and frustrations, 437
cradleboard, 430, 455
craftsmen, as adjunct therapists, 535
creation of the world, Yurok view of,
398–409, 415–17
creativity:
identity-diffusion and, 638
play and, 332–33
symbolized in infancy, 272–73
"creditor" children, 58–60
creeping, 421, 465, 515
criminality, delinquency vs., 625–26
crises, developmental, 262, 595–610
autonomy vs. shame and doubt—
will power, 602–3
basic trust vs. mistrust—hope, 600–
602
generativity vs. stagnation—care,
607–8
identity vs. identity confusion—fidelity, 605–6, 631–43, 676, 679
industry vs. inferiority—competence,
604–5
initiative vs. guilt—purpose, 603–4
integrity vs. despair—wisdom, 608–9
intimacy vs. isolation, 641–42
intimacy vs. isolation—love, 606–7
cruelty:
to oneself vs. to others, 32, 35
in Sioux character, 455, 509

crying, in Yurok culture, 415–17
cultural personality, 419
  factors influencing, 429–30
  potentialities and, 430–32
  Sioux, 429–30, 455–56
  Yurok, 429–43, 468–69
    anal character, 436–38
    first oral stage, 432–34
    genital attitudes, 439–41
    object relations, 434–36
    summary, 441–43
cultural trait configurations, 431
culture:
  child training and, 473–80
  clinical observation and, 140
  development and, 453–54
  ego identity vs., 431–32
  guilt and development of, 27–29,
    36–37
  homogeneous, 517
    mental hygiene in, 473–75
  infancy and, 458–59
  infant and childhood development
    and, 561–64
  inner conflict and, 268
  neurosis and, 468–71
  primitive. *See* primitive culture
  pseudospeciation and, 516. *See also*
    pseudospeciation
  value system and, 508

dam building, in Yurok culture, 462–
  63, 514
Damstags, 486, 487
Darwin, Charles, 520, 638
David, 44
day residue, 264
death, developmental crisis of old age
  and, 608–9
Death of a Salesman (Miller), 648–49
deer, Yurok and, 433
defecation problems revealed in play,
  90–94
defense, national, 671–72
defense mechanisms, 477
defiance, developmental crisis of early
  childhood and, 602
delinquency, 621–30
  black youth and, 649

criminality vs., 625–26
  law and, 626, 627, 629
  Nazism compared to, 342–45, 351–
    52, 355–57, 362, 363
  negative identity and, 639–40
  origins of, 622–26
  psychoanalytic view of, 625–26
  as social role, 626–29
  sociological view of, 626–28
Delos, 743–44
democracy, in Nazi propaganda, 358–
  59
deprivation, development and, 316–20
desire, instinctual, 54
despair, sense of, 274
  integrity vs., 608–9
destruction, restitution and (case
  study), 214–28
Deutsche, Helene, xx
development. *See also specific stages*;
    life cycle
  Anna Freud's contribution to studies
    of, 72–73
  child analysis and, 149–50
  communality and, 542
  deprivation and, 316–20
  discrimination and, 582
  of ego, stages in, 261–63
  fetal, 548–49
  first social problems of, 551–54
  morality and ethics in, 686–87
  neurotic episodes in, 183
  oral phase of, 50–51
  play and, 311–16
  psychosocial identity and, 678
  self-love and, 33–35
  stages of, 114
developmental behavior, 549–50
developmental crises, 262, 595–610
  autonomy vs. shame and doubt—
    will power, 602–3
  basic trust vs. mistrust—hope, 600–
    602
  generativity vs. stagnation—care,
    607–8
  identity vs. identity confusion—fidel-
    ity, 605–6, 631–43, 676, 679
  industry vs. inferiority—competence,
    604–5

developmental crises (*continued*)
  initiative vs. guilt—purpose, 603–4
  integrity vs. despair—wisdom, 608–9
  intimacy vs. isolation, 641–42
  intimacy vs. isolation—love, 606–7
developmental habits, 550
deviancy, societal reaction to, 539–40
Dewey, John, 4
diagnosis:
  of American World War II veterans,
    613–17
  Austen Riggs Center criteria, 536,
    537
discrimination, 114, 490–91. *See also*
    pseudospecies
  origin of, 584
  ritualization and, 582
  against women in professions, 663–
    65
disease, in Yurok culture, 386–95
disgust, sense of, 262, 274
displacement, 94–97, 160
  defined, 94
display, ritualization and, 329
diversity, fidelity and, 656
doctoring, in Yurok culture, 386–95,
    467
doctors, 699–705
dolls, in phallic period, 103
Dostoyevsky, Fyodor, 355
double-vector theme, in Yurok culture,
    461, 462, 513–14
doubt, sense of, 262
  autonomy vs., 602–3
Doxiadis, Constantinos, 519, 522–30,
    543, 743
draft, military, 670–74
drama:
  play compared to, 315–16, 333–34
  ritualization and, 585–87
  as therapy, at Austen Riggs Center,
    532–34
dramatic moments, trauma and, 136
dramatization, spheres of:
  autocosmic, 102, 104, 155
  extensions of autosphere, 158–59
  macrocosmic, 102, 104–5, 154–55
  microcosmic, 102, 104, 154–55, 158
dreams:

acute stimulus of, 264
fusions of a dreamer with dream
    population in, 259–60
hysteria and, 240
interpretation of, 131, 237–78
  acute, repetitive, and infantile con-
    flicts in, 263–69
  conversion or confirmation in,
    260–61
  dimensions of manifest dream,
    246–52
  ego identity in, 276–78
  fixation and arrest in, 275–76
  interpersonal configurations in the
    dream population, 255–63
  Irma Dream, manifest and latent,
    240–246
  life cycle in, 274–75
  orientation, 237–40
  outline of, 251–52
  reflection vs. projection in, 258–
    59
  transference in the Irma Dream,
    269–73
  verbal configurations, 252–55
manifest, 246–56
  chart of, 256–57
  dimensions of, 246–52
  report of, 247–48
  sex differences in, 258
drugs, 693
du, use of, in Irma Dream, 253
Dubos, René, 525, 527
dynamic configuration, 164

eating, in Yurok culture, 420–23, 434,
    465–66, 515
Eden, Anthony, 354, 355
education. *See also* child training
  Anna Freud's contribution to, 71–74
  behavioral development and, 562–64
  at Dorothy Burlingham's school, 3–
    5, 12–13
  college, 633–36, 642–43
  development and, 453
  enlightenment and, 29
  Montessori, 37
  resistance to, 58–61
  superego formation and, 37–38

of Yurok children, 422–26
ego, 475
  Anna Freud's study of, 73
  definition of, 634
  development of, 33–35, 261–63
  humor and, 35–36
ego identity. *See also* identity
  culture vs., 431–32
  identity vs., 634
  interplay and, 316–20
  Irma Dream and, 276–78
  in late adolescence, 631–43
  ritualization and, 581
  weakness of, in Americans, 477–80
  in young adulthood, 322–25
Einstein, Albert, 318*n*, 483, 666
Eiseley, Loren, 501, 520
ekistics, 596–97
elevators, in play configurations, 99
elimination-retention, 551–52
emancipation, superego and, 37
Empedocles, 146
engineering, women in, 660–69
England (English people), in Nazi
    propaganda, 354–57, 359,
    360
enlightenment:
  education and, 29
  sexual, children and, 15–29
    anxieties, fantasies, and theories
      of, 21–23
    child's ability to accept, 25–26
    Richard (case study), 15–22
    stork fairy tale, 23–24
    teacher's role, 24–25
environmental factors. *See also* city
    planning:
  development and, 453
epigenetic development, 548–49
epigenetic personality, 550
epilepsy, case study of, 214–28
erecting, in play configurations, 291–
    95
*Erik H. Erikson: The Growth of His
    Work* (Coles), xxi*n*, xxii
Erikson, Erik H.:
  Committee for National Morale and,
    xxi–xxii
  early career in art of, xxii–xxiii

early psychoanalytic training of, xix–
    xx
Gandhi's Truth, National Book
    Award for, 741
  training psychoanalysis with Anna
    Freud, 70–71
Young Man Luther, 482
Erikson, Joan M., 311, 312, 531, 532,
    534, 543, 736
  "Dorothy Burlingham's School in
    Vienna" (coauthor), 3–5, 12–13
  early psychoanalytic training of, xx
  "Eye to Eye," 316
  "For Larry Frank's Anniversary . . ."
    (coauthor), 724–25
  "The Power of the Newborn" (coau-
    thor), 569–74
  "For Marian C. Putnam" (coauthor),
    729–30
Erikson, Kai T., 5, 491, 637, 678
  "The Confirmation of the Delin-
    quent" (coauthor), 621–30
  "Patient Role and Social Uncer-
    tainty: The Dilemma of the
    Mentally Ill," 532
Escalona, Sibylle, 712
eskimos, 4, 13, 27
estrangement:
  dramatic stage of ritualization and,
    586–87
  identity-confusion as, 588–89
ethics, 502
  morality vs., 658, 686–87, 702
  student unrest and, 689
ethos. *See also* value systems
  Yurok, 382–417, 459–64
    creation, 398–409
    double-vector theme in, 389–95,
      401
    house forms, 395–98
    menstruation, 393–95
    pain and illness, 386–95
    salmon run customs, 409–17
    sex differences, 397–98
    taboos, 392–93
Europe, postwar Germany and, 370–
    74
expelling, in play configurations, 106,
    112–13

experimentation, in intrusive stage, 182
extinction, fear of, 451, 507
"Eye to Eye" (Joan Erikson), 316

fables, Yurok, 423–26, 466
fairy tales:
    developmental fears and, 557
    pedagogy and, 37–38
    of stork (birth), 23–24
faith, adult, 601–2
Fall von Ebstörung, Ein [A Case of an
        Eating Disorder] (Sterba), 94
family (family system):
    Caribbean, 653–55
    Nazism and, 345, 360, 364
    Sioux, 450
family counseling, 565
fantasy:
    in intrusive stage, 182
    masochistic, 55–56
    repetitive, 54
    of sexual violence, 296
father:
    boys and, 266–68
    in child's fantasies, 58–59, 61–68
    cultural milieu and, 268
    infant and child development and,
        560–61
    newborns and, 571–72
    pregnancy and, 572
    primal. *See also* Oedipus complex
        Yurok culture and, 407–9, 463
Faulkner, William, 622
fear:
    in American Indian–white relations,
        451–53, 507–8
    of authority, 45–46
    of conscience, 46
    developmental, 555–58
    in intrusive stage, 182
fecundity, 46–47
Federn, Paul, xx
female image, in Irma Dream, 272–73
female masochism, 183–84
femininity (female sexuality). *See also*
        sex differences; sex roles; sexual
        enlightenment; women
    expressions in play of, 295–99

hair symbolism and, 47
psychosocial identity and, 681
Ferber, Michael K., 691–92
fetal development, 548–49
Fichtl, Paula, 71, 73
fidelity, 323, 655–59
    developmental crisis of adolescence
        and, 605–6
    life cycle and, 702
    psychosocial identity and, 680–81
fish dam customs (Yurok), 409–17
fixation:
    arrest vs., 211–12
    developmental, 553–54
    potential for, in intrusive stage, 182–
        83
    progression vs., 183
    psychosexual, 275–76
Fliess, Wilhelm, 239, 244, 266, 271–
        72
food, in Yurok culture, 420–23, 434,
        465–66, 515
Frank, Larry, 724–725
free association, 335
free choice, 603. *See also* will power,
        identity and, 636
freedom, environmental factors and,
        524–25
free will, 146
    behavioral development and, 563
    ritualization and, 583–84
Fremont-Smith, Frank, 226–28
Freud, Anna, 475, 634, 711
    *Ego and the Mechanisms of Defense,
        The,* 476
    Erikson's training with, xix–xxi
    *Introduction to the Technique of
        Child Analysis,* 77, 86, 148
    tribute to, xxi, 70–74
Freud, Sigmund, xix, 429, 436, 470,
        496, 520
    on aggression, 26–27, 487–89
    ambitiousness of, 277–78
    on anality, 582, 602
    on artists, 43
    autobiographical elements in work
        of, 239–42, 264–69
    "A Child Is Beaten," 55–56

Civilization and Its Discontents, 26, 45–46
conceptualizing of psychoanalysis by, 144–48
as doctor, 700–701
on ego psychology, xxii
Erikson's views vs., xxiii
Fliess and, 239, 244, 266, 271–72
free association and, 335
on guilt, 28–29
on hair symbolism, 47
on humor, 36
on identity formation, 676
instinct theory of, 580, 581, 599
The Interpretation of Dreams, 131, 239, 242, 244–46, 264, 266, 268–70
on invulnerability of ego, 36
Irma Dream and. *See* Irma Dream
letter to Albert Einstein, 485
on maturity, 606–07
on nationalism, 276–77
psychoanalysis of the individual of, 475, 476
religion and, 264–66, 276–77
on repression, 538, 540
world view of, 597–98
Friedman, Cyrus, 735
From Here to Eternity (Jones), 628, 639–40
Frost, Robert, 332

Gandhi, Mohandas K. (Mahatma), 481–85, 492–96, 683
Gandhi's Truth (Erikson), National Book Award for, 741
gangs, 624–25, 640, 693–94
Geistigkeit, 710–12
generation gap, 328–31, 336, 337
generativity, sense of, 262, 274
feminine, Anna Freud's, 71–72
stagnation vs., 607–8
Geneva Convention, 347, 349–50
genitality:
developmental crisis of play age and, 603–4
Yurok, 439–41, 471–73

genital organs, dream symbolization of, 131
genius, identity-diffusion and, 638
geography (geographic concepts), Yurok, 399
Germans (Germany), 363–65. *See also* Nazism
postwar reeducation of, 366–74
soldiers:
in Nazi propaganda, 352–61
prisoners of war, 341, 342, 346–50, 367, 373
Gilbreth, Lillian, 660, 661
Gill, Merton, 736
girls. *See also* childhood; sex differences; sex roles
intrusive stage and, 553
phallic stage in, 112–13
Goebbels, Joseph, 351–53, 355, 359
Goethe, Johann Wolfgang von, 45
grandparents:
in American society, 640–41
infant and child development and, 560–61
gratification, sacrifice and, 46
group disintegration, among German prisoners, 349
group identity, 489–90. *See also* pseudospecies
American, 477–80, 499, 502
black children and, 645–50
fear of loss of, 451
inner conflict and, 265
Irma Dream and, 276–77
national, 369–70. *See also* nationalism
negative, 653
group psychology, postwar German reeducation and, 372–73
group regression, typology of, 690–96
guilt, sense of, 262
development of culture and, 27–29, 36–37
dramatic stage of ritualization and, 586–87
German, 370, 371
initiative vs., 603–4
Irma Dream and, 277

guilt, sense of (*continued*)
national, 370
superego and, 36–37

habits, 558, 561–64
developmental, 550
neurotic vs. developmental, 566
treatment of, in children, 565–66
hair, symbolism of, 42–44, 46–47
Hamlet (Shakespeare), 587
Hargreaves, Donald, 323
Hartmann, Heinz, xx, 489, 580, 599, 634
Harvard Psychological Clinic, 114
hatred:
in nature, 485, 486
pseudospeciation and, 489
healing, in Yurok culture, 386–95, 467
Heller, Peter, 4
helplessness:
developmental fears and, 555
in Yurok culture, 468–70
Henderson, Ambassador, 359
Hermann, I., 43–45
Heyoka, 457, 458
Hippies, 692–93
Hippocratic Oath, 699–705
Hiroshima, 501
history:
of nations, 367–71
psychoanalysis and, 483–85
psychosocial identity and, 676, 678, 682–83
youth and, 657–58, 687–88
Hitler, Adolf, 351–61, 364, 493, 639, 727
Holton, Gerald, 318*n*
homogeneous cultures, 517
mental hygiene measures of, 473–75
Homo Ludens: A Study of the Play Element in Culture (Huizinga), 525
hope:
developmental crisis of infancy and, 600–602
ritualization and, 579
houses (house forms):
body and, 80–85
in play configurations, 78–89, 298

posture of patient and, 81–85
in Yurok culture, 395–98, 461, 514
Howard, Edgerton, 737
Howard-Wheeler Act, 381–82, 418
Huizinga, Johann, 525
humanitarian service, draft and, 672–73
humor, 35–36
Hupa, 380
Huxley, Francis, 593
Huxley, Sir Julian, 320, 576, 591
hygiene, in Sioux culture, 450
hysteria:
dreams and, 240
libido and, 146

id, 146, 475, 476
idea germination, conception and, 255
ideational behavior, morphoanalytic description of, 163
identification, ritualization and, 581
identity, sense of. *See also* ego identity
adolescence and, 622–26
American, 477–80, 499–502
black children and, 645–50
confusion vs., 605–6
crises of, 588–89
ego identity vs., 634
fear of loss of, 451
group identity, 489–90. *See also* pseudospecies
inner conflict and, 265
Irma Dream and, 276–77
national, 369–70. *See also* nationalism
negative, 653
ideology and, 652–53
life cycle and, 702
negative, 490–91, 583–84, 650–52
identity-diffusion and, 637–40
psychosocial identity and, 681–82
negro youth and, 644–59
childhood and identity, 645–50
"conversion" and more inclusive identity, 652–53
totalism and negative identity, 650–52
weakness and strength, 653–59

origins of, 318–19
psychosocial, 675–83
  historical considerations, 682–83
  interests and approaches, 677–79
national, 369–70
ritualization and, 580, 581
territoriality of, 491–92
theory of, 679–82
wider, 497–502, 518–20
Identity: Youth and Crisis (Erikson), xvii
identity closure, 679–80
identity crisis, 497–98, 676, 679
  in medical profession, 701–4
identity diffusion (identity confusion), 588–89, 633, 636–38, 648–49, 677
  identity vs., 605–6
  symptoms of, 637
identity formation, 489–90
ideological group formation:
  antimoralist moralist, 694–95
  ethical position, 691–92
  moral pragmatism and, 695–96
  premoral orientation, 693–94
  premoral position, 692–93
ideology:
  identity and, 642–43, 652–53
  psychosocial identity and, 679–80, 682–83
idiopathic epilepsy, case study of, 214–28
id resistances, 479
illness, in Yurok culture, 386–95
imperialism, American, 500–501
impulses:
  in intrusive stage, 182
  maturation and, 142
  pregenital, 105–14. *See also* libido; *and specific impulses*
inactivation, in conventional patient care, 538
inclosures, in play configurations, 292–95
incorporation, 114, 551
  in oral vs. phallic stages, 113
India, 481–83, 492–95
Indians, American, 450–52, 500, 504–7. *See also* Sioux; Yurok

individual trait configurations, 431
industrialism, American, 500
industry, inferiority vs., 604–5
infancy. *See also* children; child training; newborns; *and specific topics*
  architectural environment and, 523, 527–28
  culture and, 458–59
  definition of, 575–76
  ego development in, 33–34
  in life cycle, 262, 600–602
  problems of, 547–68
    developmental behavior, 549–50
    developmental fears, 555–58
    fetal development, 548–49
    first social problems of extrauterine behavior, 551–54
    habits and culture and, 561–64
    latency, 554–55
    parents and, 560–61
    physician's role and, 564–68
    social relativity of psychological status, 558–59
  ritualization and, 576–79, 581
  in Sioux culture, 454, 508–9
  in Yurok culture, 420–22, 432, 514–16
infantile conflicts, dreams and, 265, 273
inferiority, sense of, 262
  industry vs., 604–5
Inhelder, Baerbel, 315, 679
inhibition:
  learning and, 25–26
  ritualization and, 580–81
initiative, sense of, 262
  guilt vs., 603–4
inner authority, 33–35
inner conflicts:
  dreams and, 240, 263–69, 273
  therapeutic situation and, 152
inner space, 596
instinct (instinctual drives), 54, 488–90, 599
  aggressive, 486
  theory of, 580, 581
Institute of Intercultural Studies, xxi–xxii

institutionalization, ritualization and, 333–34
integrity, sense of, 262, 274
    despair vs., 608–9
internment. *See also* confinement practices
    psychology of, 349–50
    rationale for, 538–40
interpersonal configurations, in dreams, 250, 255–63
interplay:
    ego identity and, 316–20
    ritualization and, 320–22
Interpretation, in child analysis, 143–44
Interpretation of Dreams, The (Freud), 131, 239, 242, 244–46, 264, 266, 268–70
interrogation of German prisoners, 346–50
intimacy, sense of, 262
    isolation vs., 606–7, 641–42
Introduction to the Technique of Child Analysis (A. Freud), 77, 86, 148
intrusion, 114, 552–53
    in play configurations, 106, 112–13, 294–95
intrusive stage, 181–84
Irma Dream (Freud's case), 237–78
    background of, 240–42
    ego identity and, 276–78
    fixation and arrest in, 275–76
    Freud's analysis of, 242–46
    interpersonal configurations in, 257–63
    life cycle and, 274–75
    mistranslations in, 252–55
    narrative of, 241–42
    pregenitality in, 275–76
    sexual interpretation of, 254–55
    transference in, 269–73
    women patients represented in, 242–43
Isaacs, Susan, 567
isolation, sense of, 262–63
    intimacy vs., 606–7, 641–42

James, William, 675
jealousy, newborn sibling and, 572–74

Jews (Judaism):
    Freud on, 276–77
    in Nazi propaganda, 352, 356, 358
Joint Committee on Post War Planning, memorandum to, 366–74
judgment, ritualization and, 582–85

Karok, 380
Keitel, Field Marshal Wilhelm, 352
Kennan, George, 672
Kierkegaard, Soren, 593
Kinsey, Alfred, 641
Klein, Melanie: *The Psychoanalysis of Children*, 99, 148
Knight, Robert P., 733–38
Kotinsky, Ruth, 677
Kris, Ernst, xx, 634
Kroeber, A. L., 377, 380, 382, 384, 394, 399, 404, 405, 410, 413, 415, 417, 446, 447, 503, 514

Laius, 744
language development, 582
latency period, 554–55
latent dream material, 245–46
    manifest dream images and, 251–52
law, delinquency and, 626, 627, 629
learning:
    inhibition and, 25–26
    oral nature of, 51
Lewin, Bertram, 318
Lewin, Kurt, 122, 341*n*
libido:
    in anal stage, 111–12
    hysteria and, 146
    in intrusive stage, 182
    in oral stage, 109–10
Lichenstein, Heinz, 678, 679
life and death instincts, 146
life cycle (life tasks), 261–62, 595–610, 701–2. *See also* development; *and specific stages*
    adolescence, 605–6
    children's play and, 314–16
    city planning and, 522–30
    early childhood, 602–3
    infancy, 600–602
    Irma Dream and, 274–75

maturity, 607–8
old age, 608–9
play age, 603–4
school age, 604–5
young adulthood, 606–7
life-data, in play configurations, 284–90
Lifton, Robert J., 682
Light, trauma involving, 91–93
Lincoln, Abraham, 497
Lincoln, T. S., 458
localization, in Yurok culture, 403–9, 459, 512
locomotor-phallic stage. *See* intrusive stage
Loewenstein, 493
Lorenz, Konrad, 311, 320–21, 323, 327–29, 494
    Das Sogenannte Boese, 485–88, 576
love:
    developmental crisis of young adulthood and, 606–7
    inconsistency in, 58
    life cycle and, 702

McArthur, Charles, 677
Macfarlane, Donald (Mac), 715
Macfarlane, Jean Walker, 380
macrocosmic play, 102, 104–5
macrosphere, 154–55
Madonna and child, 316
    medieval depictions of, 32–33
    Michelangelo's, 317
magic, Yurok, 381–82, 460, 513, 514
male image, in Irma Dream, 272–73
male patients, Irma Dream and, 242
manifest dream images, 245–46
    chart of, 256–57
    dimensions of, 246–52
mannerisms, 558. *See also* habits
marriage ceremonies, 589
Marx, Karl, 335, 520, 605
masculinity. *See also* sex differences; sex roles
    expressions in play of, 295–99
    psychosocial identity and, 681
    Sioux, 472, 515
    Yurok, 472, 515–16
masochism:

fantasies of, 55–56
female, 183–84
masturbation, 552–53
    repression of, 58
    in Yurok culture, 439
Mattfield, Jacquelyn, 662
maturation. *See also* development; developmental behavior
    factors in, 553–54
    historical process as crisis of, 335–36
    impulses and, 142
    sexual, expressed in play, 295–99
maturity, 606–8
Max and Moritz, 31, 36
Mayr, Ernst, 489, 580, 599
Mead, Margaret, 299, 341*n*, 429, 672–73
medical profession, 699–705
Meiklejohn, Alexander, 717*n*
Mein Kampf (Hitler), 355
Mekeel, H. Scudder, 367, 446, 447, 450, 503
memory, 33–34
    of dreams, 248
men. *See also* sex differences; sex roles
    attitude of women toward, 296
    attitude toward women of, 129–32, 296
    maternal instinct of, 572
Menninger Karl, 733–34, 738
Menninger, William, 734
Menninger Foundation, 733, 734
menstruation:
    problems revealed in play, 82
    in Yurok culture, 393–95, 468, 516
methodology:
    in anthropology and psychoanalysis, 379–80
    of therapeutic situation, 162–64
Michelango, 316–18
microcosmic play, 102, 104, 158
microcosmic situation, 154–55
microsphere, 154–55, 158, 159
middle age crisis, Irma Dream and, 262–63, 274–75
military draft, 670–74
Miller, Arthur, 649
Miller, Stuart, 736

mistrust, sense of basic, 262
 basic trust vs., 600–602
mode-behavior (or manifestation),
  159–60
mode criterion, of zonal sensations and
  frustrations, 437
mode-fixations, 159–60
money, in Yurok culture, 381–82, 387,
  405–6, 459, 466, 512
Montessori, Maria, 527
Montessori education, 37
moon, landing on, 501, 745–47
moralism, sadism and, 35
morality, 502
 ethics vs., 658, 686–87, 702
 ritualization and, 487–88
moratorium, psychosocial, 638–39,
  687
Morris, Desmond, 592
mother (motherhood):
 Caribbean, 653–55
 as factor in therapeutic situation,
  150–51
 infant and child development and,
  560–61
 infant's trust and, 600–602
 newborns and, 570–71
 ritualization of relationship to infant,
  577, 581
mother image, dream as, 270
motion, in dreams, 250
motivation(s):
 to dream, 270–71
 psychoanalysis of, 246–47
Mount Zion Hospital (San Francisco),
  613, 715
murder, in nature, 485, 486
Murphy, Gardner, 341n
Murphy, Henry B. M., 640
Murray, Henry A., 114n, 341n
mutuality of recognition, 577–79
mythology. *See also* Ethos; World view
 of Yurok, 385
myths, fables distinguished from, 425–
  26

names ritualization and, 577
narcissism, of the artist, 42–44

nation, tribe vs., 369
National Book Award, 741
national emergency, military draft and,
  671–72
nationalism (national identity), Freud
 on, 276–77
nations. *See also* pseudospecies
 history of, 367–71
 regressive syndromes of, 369
nature:
 hatred and murder in, 485, 486
 Yurok and, 382, 409–17, 432–34
Nazism (Nazi identity or mentality),
  682
 delinquent adolescence compared to,
  342–45, 351–52, 355–57, 362,
  363
 Hitler's speech and, 351–61
 postwar German reeducation and,
  370–71
 of prisoners of war, 346–50
 propaganda by, 351–61
 propaganda against, 345, 360, 362–
  65, 373–74
negative identity, 490–91, 583–84,
  650–52
 identity-diffusion and, 637–40
 psychosocial identity and, 681–82
negro youth, 644–59
 childhood and identity, 645–50
 "conversion" and more inclusive
  identity, 652–53
 totalism and negative identity, 650–
  52
 weakness and strength, 653–59
Nehru, Jawaharlal, 492, 683
neurosis. *See also* case studies
 in children, 566
 culture and, 468–71
 intrusive stage and, 183–84
 oral, 470
 origin of, 558
 primitive ideation and, 517
newborns, 569–74. *See also* infancy
 hope and trust in, 600–602
Newton, Huey P., 325–26
Nietzsche, Friedrich, 23, 33, 40, 491
Nobile, Umberto, 27

noise, trauma involving, 93
nonconformity, in Sioux culture, 457–58
nonviolence, 481
　Gandhi's, 493–96
nostalgia, in Yurok culture, 432–34, 465, 515
number symbolism, Yurok, 412, 419, 426
numinous, the, 578, 579, 586
nursery schools, child analysis in, 565
Nursery Years, The (Isaacs), 567
nurses, in child's fantasies, 53–56

oaths, 699–701
　California loyalty, 618–20
　Hippocratic, 699–705
object, definition of, 318–19
object relations:
　in play configurations, 88
　in Yurok culture, 434–36
obsessive-compulsive patients, 55–56
Oedipus, 744
Oedipus complex, 330–31
　developmental crisis of play age and, 603, 604
　Freud's, 267–68
　masochistic fantasy and, 56
　Richard (case study) and, 19, 22
　ritualization and, 586
old age:
　identity and, 640–41
　in life cycle, 262, 608–9
ontogeny of ritualization, 575–93
　adolescence and beyond: the ideological and the generational, 587–90
　the dramatic and the formal in childhood, 585–87
　early childhood and the judicious, 582–85
　infancy and the numinous, 576–79
　pseudospecies and, 579–81
oral complex (or fixation), 470
　case study: Dick, four-year-old boy, 188–214
orality (oral stage), 50–51, 109–10
　in play configurations, 83–84

sexual enlightenment of child and, 22–24
Sioux child training and, 430, 433
in Yurok culture, 437–39, 470
zones and, 437
oral training, in Yurok culture, 432–34, 465–66
organ modes, 106–12
　extrabodily representation of, 159–60
organs, development and, 549
overcompliance, developmental crisis of early childhood and, 602

pacification, ritualized, 486
pacifism. *See* nonviolence
pacifying activities, 558
pain, in Yurok culture, 386–95
Panel on Education, 366
paranoia, German, 371
parents. *See also* fathers; mothers
　infant and child development and, 560–61
　as ritualizers, 589, 590
　student unrest and, 697
　transference and, 234
Parsons, Talcott, 366
paternalism, 330–31
patient care:
　at Austen Riggs Center, 531–37, 541–44
　conventional types of, 537–41
"Patient Role and Social Uncertainty: The Dilemma of the Mentally Ill" (Kai Erikson), 532
Paul, St., 317
penis-wish, 112–13, 183
Penn, Peggy, 311
peripheries, in Yurok culture, 403–9
Perry, Mrs. William G., Jr., 724*n*
personal factors in clinical observation, 140
personality:
　cultural, *See* cultural personality
　epigenetic, 550
　impulses and, 113
personality potentialites, 430–32

phallic stage, 103–5, 112–13, 181.
See also castration anxiety; intrusive
stage
Philia, 146
philosophy, psychosocial identity and,
678–79
physicians, 699–705
role of, in infant and child development, 564–68
Piaget, Jean, 311, 314–15, 679, 710
plantations, family system of, 653–55
platonism, Yurok, 433, 469
play (play configurations, play situations), 155–58
actuality and, 311–37
in adulthood, 331–37
in children, 311–16
interplay of, 316–20
pseudospeciation in, 327–31
in revolutionary activity, 325–27
ritualization in, 320–22
in young adulthood, 322–25
arrangement of, 164
cathartic theory of, 141
of college students, 114–36
communality and, 542
developmental behavior and, 550
developmental fears and, 555–56
interpretation of, 99–100
physician's role and, 566–67
pregenitality and, 94–114
anal fixation, 97–102
types of, 102–5
zone displacement, 94–97
zones, impulses, and organ-modes,
105–14
psychoanalytic value of, 77–78, 136,
139–40
restructuralization in, 155–58
sex differences in, 280–307
block use in constructions, 290–95
case illustrations of, 299–307
experiment outline, 281–84
life-history elements in, 284–90
sexual maturation elements, 295–
99
significance of, 100
spatial configurations in. *See* spatial
configurations

spheres of. *See* spheres of representation
symbols in, 230
of Yurok children, 426–28
play age, in life cycle, 603–4
play disruption, 143, 452–54
play situation vs., 155–58
play interpretation:
case studies, 164–228
effectiveness of, 232–34
method of representation of, 162–64
play therapy, 142–44
pleasure, behavioral development and,
563
plucking, 110. *See also* biting
possessions. *See* property
posture, house-form representation
and, 81–85
power:
infant's concept of, 552
of newborns, 569–74
practical factors in clinical observation,
140
Prayer to Apollo, 743–44
pregenitality:
chart of, 106–12
in Irma Dream, 275–76
stages of, 159–60
pregnancy, 570
father and, 572
in Yurok culture, 419–20, 432
prejudice, 114, 490–91. *See also* pseudospecies
origin of, 584
ritualization and, 582
against women in professions, 663–
65
preparatory expression, play as, 141
priapic, 254
primal father figure. *See also* Oedipus
complex
in Yurok culture, 407–9, 463
primitive cultures. *See also* homogeneous cultures
adolescence in, 623–24
behavioral development and, 562
primitive ideation, neurosis and, 517
prisoners of war:
American, 350

German, 341–42, 367, 373
interrogation of, 346–50
procreative-protective impulse, 113
professions, women in, 660–69
professors, student unrest and, 696–98
progression, fixation vs., 183
prohibitions:
internal vs. external, 34–35
ritualization and, 580–81
projection, in dreams, 258–59
Project Method curriculum, 4, 5
Promised Land, dream as, 271
propaganda:
anti-Nazi, 345, 360, 362–65, 373–74
Nazi, 351–61
property:
infant's concept of, 552
in Sioux culture, 450, 456, 510
in Yurok culture, 381–82, 405–6, 421–23, 434, 459–60, 464
propylon, 254
pseudospecies (pseudospeciation), 327–31, 333–35, 518–20
definition of, 327–28, 498–99
psychosocial identity and, 678
reactionary, 518
ritualization and, 579–81
Sioux culture as, 516
Yurok culture as, 516
psychiatric treatment, at Austen Riggs Center, 531–37, 541–44
psychiatry:
postwar German reeducation and, 372
psychosocial identity and, 677
psychoanalysis. *See also* child analysis; clinical observation
biological orientation of, 485–88
case studies:
A (boy of four), 78–80
the adolescent (boy of fourteen), 47–51
Asper (male college student), 122–24
B (girl of twelve), 80–82
Berry (male college student), 119–22, 124

the bright-eyed one (girl of eleven), 40–47
C (schizophrenic man), 83–84
D (boy of five), 84–85
Deborah (girl of eleven), 284–87
Dick (boy of four), 188–214, 229–31
E (boy of eight), 85–88
F (boy of five), 88–89
Fred (boy of four), 214–28, 229, 231
G (girl of two-and-one-half), 89–94
H (boy of two-and-one-half), 95–97
the inaccessible boy, 56–61
J (boy of eight), 97–102
John (boy of six), 164–71, 228–31
K (girl of eight), 102–5
Krumb (male college student), 132–35
Lisa, 288–89
Margaret (girl of twelve), 51–56
Mary (girl of three), 171–88, 228–31
Mauve (male college student), 128–32
Oriol (male college student), 124–28, 134
Richard (boy of seven), 15–24
the son (adolescent), 64–68
the son (fourteen-year-old), 61–63
the son (ten-year-old), 63–64
Victoria (girl of eleven), 287–88
Vulner (male college student), 135
Zeeno (male college student), 116–19, 121, 122, 124
childhood and children and, 40, 475–80
conceptual bases of, 597–98
on delinquency, 625–26
dream analysis and, 238. *See also* dreams, interpretation of
education and, 5, 12–13
Erikson's versus Freud's view of, xxiii
Anna Freud's contribution to, 71–74
history and, 336–37, 483–85
limitations of, 141
methods and systems in, 144–48

psychoanalysis (*continued*)
  play studies and, 77–78, 136, 139–40. *See also* play; play therapy
  prepsychological concepts used by, 146–47
  preverbal, case history of, 89–94
  social factors and, 477–80
Psychoanalysis of Children, the (Klein), 99, 148
Psychoanalytic Study of the Child (Erikson), xx
psychology:
  group, 372–73. *See also* group identity
  of prisoners of war, 347–50
psychoneurosis, among World War II veterans, 613–17
psychopathology, behavioral development and, 562
psychosexual arrest (or fixation):
  in infancy, 275
  in Irma Dream, 275–76
psychosexual elements, in play configurations, 297–99
psychosocial development. *See* development
psychosocial identity, 675–83. *See also* ego identity; identity
  historical considerations, 682–83
  interests and approaches, 677–79
  theory of, 679–82
psychosocial moratorium, 638–39, 687
puberty rite, Irma Dream as, 277
punishment, desire for, 27–29, 45–46
puritans, 28
purpose (purposefulness), developmental crisis of play age and, 603–4
Putnam, Marian C., 729–30

Querido, Aríe, 632

racial struggle in United States, 490
racism. *See* anti-Semitism; Nazism; prejudice; pseudospecies
radiators, in play configurations, 99
rage:
  acceptance of, 27–28
  in Sioux character, 455, 509
Rapaport, David, 541, 634, 735, 736, 737–38
rape, Nazi propaganda theme of, 359–60
reaction formation, 553
  in intrusive stage, 182
  national, 370
reading, oral nature of, 51
reality, actuality vs., 336–37
rearrangement in fantasy, 155–58
rebellion, youthful, 328–31
recapitulation, play as, 141
recognition:
  identity formation and, 648–50
  mutuality of, 577–79
reconstruction of dreams, 252
Redl, Fritz, 709–712
reeducation:
  of American soldiers, 373–74
  of postwar Germany, 366–74
reflection in dreams, 258–59
regression:
  adolescent, 329
  developmental, 554
  among German prisoners, 349
  in infancy and childhood, 565
  national, 369
  potential for, in intrusive stage, 182–83
rejectivity, 73
relativity, social, 558–59
release ideology, in play therapy, 143
religion:
  faith and, 601–2
  Freud on, 264–66, 276–77
  inner conflicts and, 265
  psychosocial identity and, 678–79
  ritualization and, 578, 579
repetitive conflicts, dreams and, 266–69
reports of dreams, 247–48
Reppert, Jeré A., 635
representability of dreams, 250
representation:
  spheres of:
    autocosmic, 102, 104, 155
    extensions of autospheres, 158–59

macrocosmic, 102, 104–5, 154–55
microcosmic, 102, 104, 154–55,
    158
style of, dreams and, 250
repression:
in child analysis, 149
individual vs. societal, 538–540
ritualization and, 580–81
resistance, 141
in American Indian–white relations,
    451–53, 507–8
in child analysis, 149
Freud on, 147–48
transference vs., 212–14
restitution, destruction and, case study,
    214–28
retention–elimination, 551–52
in play configurations, 106, 111,
    112
Reuther, Walter, 710
revolutionary activity, ritualization in,
    325–27
ritual(s):
ego identity and, 634
function of, 589, 590
ritualization vs., 590–91
Yurok, 409–17
ritualization:
definition of, 320–21
display and, 329
elements of, 578–79
infantile and adult, 578
institutionalization and, 333–34
interplay and, 320–22
morality and, 487–88
in nature, 485–88
ontogeny of, 575–93
    adolescence and beyond: the ideo-
        logical and generational, 587–
        90
    definition of, 575–76
    the dramatic and the formal in
        childhood, 585–87
    early childhood and the judicious,
        582–85
    infancy and the numinous, 576–79
    pseudospecies and, 579–81
in revolutionary activity, 325–27

ritual vs., 590–91
separation by abandonment and,
    579
in young adulthood, 322–25
Yurok and, 583
rivalry, urinary experience and, 267
Roheim, Geza, 458
role diffusion, sense of, 262, 263
roles, social. *See also* sex roles
changes in women's, 660–69
delinquency and, 626–29
of doctors, 703–4
identity-diffusion and, 637
Rommel, Field Marshall Erwin, 352–
    53
Roosevelt, Franklin D., 354, 355, 358
Rosenfeld, Eva, xx, 3, 4, 711
Rudolph, Susanne, 492
Russians, in Nazi propaganda, 354–57

sacrifice, 46–47
sadism:
child's perception of, 59
in children's books, 31–32, 35
moralism and, 35
salmon, Yurok and, 433, 459, 460,
    462, 512–13
salmon run customs (Yurok), 409–17
Santayana, George, 89
Sarvis, Mary, 731–32
Satyagraha, 481, 493–95. *See also*
    nonviolence
Schafer, Roy, 736
school, ritualization and, 587
school age, in life cycle, 262, 604–5
school essays, 39–69
Schopenhauer, Arthur, 146
Schwartz, Daniel, xxiv
science, women in, 660–69
scientific method:
Freud and, 146–47
symbolized in Irma Dream, 272
Seale, Bobby, 325
secrets:
case study of, 164, 171
dreams as, 271
segregationism, 490. *See also* prejudice;
    pseudospecies

self-analysis, dream analysis and, 238–39

self-doubt, developmental crisis of early childhood and, 602

self-image, ritualization and, 581

self-love:
of artist, 42–44
development and, 33–35
narcissism and, 44

self-realization, as historical process, 335–36

Sennett, Richard, 527

sex differences. *See also* sex roles; sexuality
changes in women's roles and, 664–69
in dreams, 258
inclusive, movements toward, 491–92
in play configurations, 94–114, 280–307
anal fixation, 97–102
block use in constructions, 290–95
case illustrations of, 299–307
experiment outline, 281–84
life-history elements in, 284–90
sexual maturation elements, 295–99
types of play, 102–5
zone displacement, 94–97
zones, impulses, and organ-modes, 105–14
in young adulthood, 607
in Yurok culture, 397–98, 420, 427

sex roles. *See also* sex differences; sexuality
identity-diffusion and, 637
in Sioux culture, 456–58, 510–11
in Yurok culture, 439–40, 471

sexual enlightenment. *See also* sex differences
children and, 15–29
anxieties, fantasies, and theories of, 21–23
child's ability to accept, 25–26
Richard (case study), 15–22
stork fairy tale, 23–24
teacher's role, 24–25

sexual intercourse:
child's perception of, 49–50, 54, 59
in Sioux culture, 472
in Yurok culture, 472

sexuality. *See also* libido
adolescent, 637, 641–42, 656
developmental crisis of play age and, 603–4
hair symbolism and, 46–47
pregnancy and, 570
Sioux, 472
Yurok, 426, 428, 471–73, 515–16

sexual meaning, of Irma Dream, 254–55

Shakerism, 418

Shakespeare, William, 522

shamans:
ritualization and, 467–68
Yurok, 384–95

shame, sense of, 262
autonomy vs., 602–3

Shaw, George Bernard, 638, 652

shells, 598–99

Shils, Edward B., 592

siblings:
newborns and, 572–74
in Sioux culture, 456, 457

singing contests, Eskimos', 13, 27

Sioux (Sioux culture), 447–59, 646
child training of, 429–30, 432, 433, 454–59, 508–11
cultural personality of, 455–56
economic life of, 464
history of, 447–49, 505–7
image of, 447, 504, 505
nonconformity among, 457–58
property in, 456, 510
sex roles in, 456–58, 510–11
value system of, 508–11
white Americans and, 450–52, 505–7

Sistine Chapel, 317–18

slavery, family system of, 653–55

slogans, in American life, 477–79

snake, in child's fantasies, 53–54, 58

Snyder, Benson, 662

social institutions (or factors):
inner conflicts and, 265
psychoanalysis and, 477–80

social order, delinquency and, 626–28

social psychiatry, psychosocial identity and, 677
social relativity, 558–59
  ego identity and, 634
social space, 596
society, identity formation and, 648–50
sociology:
  on delinquency, 626–28
  psychosocial identity and, 678
Sogenannte Boese, Das (Lorenz), 485–88, 576
soldiers:
  American:
    prisoners of war, 350
    reeducation of, 373–74
    after World War II, 613–17
  German:
    in Nazi propaganda, 352–61
    prisoners of war, 341, 342, 346–50, 367, 373
somatic sensations, in dreams, 250
Soviet Union, in Nazi propaganda, 354–57
spatial configurations. *See also* city planning
  bowl and, 96–97
  boxes and, 95–96
  cages and, 78–80, 87–88
  in college students' play, 114–36
  defined, 78
  ekistics and, 596–97
  houses and, 78–89
  morphoanalytic description of, 163
  organ-modes and, 106–12
  tube, 420, 422, 460, 461, 513
spatial extension of dreams, 250, 257
spheres of representation (or play):
  autocosmic, 102, 104, 155
  extensions of autosphere, 158–59
  macrocosmic, 102, 104–5, 154–55
  microcosmic, 102, 104, 154–55, 158
Spielraum, 315, 316, 333, 335, 524–25, 596
Spitz, René, 311, 316, 579
Spritze, 255
stag, in child's fantasies, 53–54, 58
stagnation, sense of, 262
  generativity vs., 607–8

Stein, Maurice R., 678
Sterba, Edith: *Ein Fall von Ebstörung*, 94
stimulus, acute dream, 264
Stonorov, Oscar, 710
stork fairy tale (of birth), 23–24
structures, in play configurations, 291–95
Struwelpeter, 31–32, 35
student unrest, 685–98
  historical actuality, 687–88
  morality and ethics, 686–87
  professors and, 696–98
  typology of group regression, 690–96
  youth in our time, 688–90
sublimation, 182, 553
sucking. *See also* biting; orality
  in play configurations, 106, 109
suffering, acceptance of, 494, 495
Sun Dance (Sioux), 456, 457, 469
superego, 475, 476. *See also* conscience
  development of, 33–35, 37–38
  guilt and, 36–37
  humor and, 35–36
superego resistances, 479
surplus energy, play as, 141
swearing, in Yurok culture, 426, 435, 466
symbolic equation, 164
symbolism (symbols):
  number, 412, 419, 426
  in play, 230
syringe, 255

taboos:
  in Sioux culture, 456, 510
  in Yurok culture, 392–93, 420, 421, 426, 427, 435, 465, 469
talent, beauty and, 43–45
talking, limitations of, 141
teachers. *See also* education
  analyst vs., 14–15
  in Montessori education, 37
  sexual enlightenment of child and, 24–25
  in Yurok culture, 427–28
teaching fables, Yurok, 423–26, 466
technology, American, 500

temper tantrums, Sioux child training
and, 430
Tempkin, Oswei, 699
territoriality of identity, 491–92
theater. *See also* drama
as therapy, at Austen Riggs Center,
532–34
theft, car, 626, 627
therapeutic interpretation, 164
therapeutic process (or situation). *See
also* psychoanalysis
at Austen Riggs Center, 531–37,
541–44
child's vs. adult's, 233–34
factors influencing, 150–52
methodology applied to, 162–64
therapists:
at Austen Riggs Center, 535–37
as factor in therapeutic situation,
151
impressions, associations, and reflections of, 163–64
role of, in infant and child development, 564–68
threatening behavior, ritualized, 485–
87
Tillich, Paul, 726–28
time:
in dreams, 250, 257
identity-diffusion and sense of, 637
Tinbergen, N., 487
toilets, in play configurations, 99
toilet training. *See also* bowel training
problems revealed in play, 97–102
totalism, 650–52
psychosocial identity and, 681–82
totalitarianism:
German, 368–70. *See also* Nazism
ritualization and, 589
towers, in play configurations, 291–95
toys, therapeutic situation and, 151–52
tradition:
ego identity and, 634
infant and childhood development
and, 561–64
traditional trait configurations, 431
training, dream analysis and, 238–39,
247–48

transference, 141, 143
in child analysis, 149
child's vs. adult's, 233–34
Fliess as Freud's, 271–72
in the Irma Dream, 269–73
resistance vs., 212–14
women patients and, 242–43
translations, dreams and, 252–55
trauma:
of capture in war, 348–49
children's play and, 314
dramatic moments and, 136
light as, 91–93
noise as, 93
tribes. *See also* pseudospecies
nation vs., 369
trust, sense of basic, 262
mistrust vs., 600–602
tube configurations, 420, 422, 460,
461, 513
Tucker, Robert, 335, 336
twins, in Yurok culture, 427

United States Indian Service, 503
urination:
childhood experiences of, 267
problems revealed in play, 78–79, 83

value systems. *See also* ethos; world
view
in Sioux culture, 508–11
Yurok, 511–12
vectors:
definition of, 389
in Yurok culture, 389–95, 401, 461,
462, 513–14
Veikos, 146
verbal behavior, morphoanalytic
description of, 163
verbal configurations, in Irma Dream,
252–55
verbalization (verbal report)
clinical observation and, 144–45
of dreams, 247–48
veterans of World War II, 613–17
Vienna Psychoanalytic Institute, xix
Vietnam War, 672
violence, fantasies of sexual, 296

Wallace, Henry A., 358
walls, in play configurations, 291–95
war games, in phallic period, 103
Washburn, Ruth, 84
Waterman, T. T., 410, 412, 413, 415, 417
wealth. *See* property
weaning, in Yurok child training, 432–34, 465, 515
Werner, Heinz, 738
Western New England Psychoanalytic Institute, 736
Wexler, Henry, 735, 737
Wheelis, Allen, 678, 736
Wheelwright, Joseph, 713, 715
wholeness, totality distinguished from, 650
wider identity, 497–502, 518–20
will, 146,
  behavioral development and, 563
Willkie, Wendell, 358
will power, developmental crisis of early childhood and, 602–3
Wilson, Woodrow, 344, 345, 359
wisdom, developmental crisis of old age and, 608–9
"wise people" (or *wage*), 385, 467
wish fulfillment, 54
  Irma Dream as, 244–46
wish to dream, 270–71
Witmer, Helen L., 677
Wohl, Helmut, 316–17
Wolff, Peter, 319
wolves, 486
women. *See also* femininity; mother; sex differences; sex roles
  attitude of men toward, 129–32, 296
  attitude toward men of, 296
  changing roles of, 660–69
  masochism of, 183–84
  menstruation and:
    problems revealed in play, 82
    in Yurok culture, 393–95, 468, 516
  as patients, Irma Dream and, 242–43
  postwar reconstruction and, 373

tasks and ideals represented symbolically by, 270
word play in Irma Dream, 254–55
work:
  identity-diffusions and, 637
  in therapeutic experience, 533–35
  women and, 660–69
workmanship, sense of, 262
world view (or image). *See also* value systems
  life cycle as, 597–98
  totalistic, 650–52
  Yurok, 382–417, 459–64
    creation, 398–409
    double-vector theme in, 389–95, 401, 461, 462, 513–14
    house forms, 395–98
    menstruation, 393–95
    pain and illness, 386–95
    salmon run customs, 409–17
    sex differences, 397–98
    taboos, 392–93
World War I, in Nazi propaganda, 352, 360, 361
World War II. *See also* Germans; Nazism,
  American veterans of, 613–17
  planning recommendations following, 366–74
writers, as adjunct therapists, 535

Young Man Luther (Erikson), 482
youth (young adulthood). *See also* adolescence; delinquency
  ego identity in, 631–43
  in life cycle, 262, 606–7
  Negro, 644–59
    childhood and identity, 645–50
    "conversion" and more inclusive identity, 652–53
    totalism and negative identity, 650–52
    weakness and strength, 653–59
  pseudospeciation and, 328–31
  regression and, 519
  ritualization and, 322–25, 587–90
  student unrest and, 685–98
    historical actuality, 687–88

youth (*continued*)
    morality and ethics, 686–87
    professors and, 696–98
    typology of group regression,
      690–96
    youth in our time, 688–90
  wider identity and, 501–2, 519–20
Yurok (Yurok culture), 377–443
  child training of, 417–43, 464–73,
    514–16
    adolescence, 428–29
    anal character, 436–38
    education of, 422–26
    fables for, 423–26
    first oral stage, 432–34
    genital attitudes, 439–41
    in infancy, 420–22, 432
    object relations, 434–36
    play of, 426–28
    prenatal, 419–20, 432
    summary, 441–43
  cultural personality, 468–69
  economic life of, 381–82, 464
  houses in, 461, 514
  ritualization and, 583

territory of, 380–81, 459, 511
value systems, 511–12
world view of, 382–417, 459–64
  creation, 398–409
  double-vector theme in, 389–95,
    401, 461, 462, 513–14
  house forms, 395–98
  menstruation, 393–95
  pain and illness, 386–95
  salmon run customs, 409–17
  sex differences, 397–98
  taboos, 392–93

Zeitschrift für psychoanalytische Päda-
  gogik, xx
zone arrest (or fixation), 159–60, 211–
  12
zones of body:
  defined, 94
  displacement of, 94–97, 160
  in infancy, 552
  oral vs. anal activities and, 437
  in pregenital phase, 105–14
Zulliger, Haus, 24